Jesse James

Jesse James

Last Rebel of the Civil War

T. J. STILES

JONATHAN CAPE
LONDON

Published by Jonathan Cape 2003

2 4 6 8 10 9 7 5 3 1

Copyright © 2002 by T.J. Stiles
Maps © 2002 by Alfred A. Knopf, a division of Random House, Inc.

T.J. Stiles has asserted his right under the Copyright, Designs
and Patents Act 1988 to be identified as the author of this work

First published in the United States of America in 2002 by Alfred A. Knopf

First published in Great Britain in 2003 by
Jonathan Cape
Random House, 20 Vauxhall Bridge Road,
London SW1V 2SA

Random House Australia (Pty) Limited
20 Alfred Street, Milsons Point, Sydney,
New South Wales 2061, Australia

Random House New Zealand Limited
18 Poland Road, Glenfield,
Auckland 10, New Zealand

Random House South Africa (Pty) Limited
Endulini, 5a Jubilee Road, Parktown 2193, South Africa

The Random House Group Limited Reg. No. 954009
www.randomhouse.co.uk

A CIP catalogue record for this book
is available from the British Library

ISBN 0-224-06925-X

Papers used by The Random House Group Limited are natural,
recyclable products made from wood grown in sustainable forests;
the manufacturing processes conform to the environmental
regulations of the country of origin

Printed and bound in Great Britain by
Clays Ltd, St. Ives plc

To Nadine,
for everything

I consider Jesse James the worst man, without any exception, in America. He is utterly devoid of fear, and has no more compunction about cold blooded murder than he has about eating his breakfast.

—Robert A. Pinkerton,
Richmond Democrat
November 20, 1879

[Jesse James] laughed and remarked that he might have to go under eventually, but before he did he would shake up the country.

—Robert Ford,
St. Louis Republican
April 7, 1882

You're going to learn that one of the most brutal things in the world is your average nineteen-year-old American boy.

—Philip Caputo,
A Rumor of War

Contents

PART FOUR: FATE: 1876–1882

Illustrations

Maps

Jesse James

Prologue

The rumor rolled through the town of St. Joseph, Missouri, like floodwaters, reaching the reporter's ears around ten o'clock on the morning of April 3, 1882. He grabbed his notebook and ran onto the street, which was already saturated with the news, the sidewalks alive with disbelieving chatter. Within a few minutes, he joined a river of people flowing uphill to the story's source: a modest house on the corner of Thirteenth and Lafayette Streets, "a frame building, a story and a half high," he wrote, "in a little grove of fruit trees." He pushed his way through the crowd of gawkers and moved inside.[1]

He stepped straight into a strange and dreamlike scene: a little girl—a mere toddler—and a seven-year-old boy, standing silent and afraid in the kitchen; their slender, trembling mother, at once hateful, angry, and grieving, words tumbling out of her mouth in a blend of pleas and screams; and teeming strangers, reporters and onlookers, who crowded into her home. Next to the door in the front room was the center of this vortex: a man, "lying upon the floor cold in death," the reporter wrote, "blood oozing from his wounds."

The wails, the babble of words, the murmuring of the crowd suddenly stopped as two young men appeared. They stepped past the body, approached a town marshal who stood close by, and offered to surrender. They had killed this man, one of them declared, and now they expected their reward. The lawman looked at them in astonishment. "My God," he said, "do you mean to tell us that this is Jesse James?"

"Yes," the pair replied in unison.

"Those who were standing near," the reporter wrote, "drew in their breaths in silence at the thought of being so near Jesse James, even if he was dead."

Here in this little house, in this otherwise commonplace domestic set-ting, one of the great mysteries of the age had appeared incarnate. Every one of the onlookers knew the name *Jesse James*. He was a figure as publi-cized as the president. And yet he was also a shadow, a man who lived underground eternally and was literally a legend—formed of rumors and stories, bearing an unknown relationship to fact. Even his own children did not know his identity; they knew him by another name. As the marshal pressed the widow to confirm that this was indeed Jesse James, her boy wailed in confusion, "God Almighty may strike me down if it is not Pa."

And so the crowd drew in their breaths, stunned at the enormity of this event: the immense, dangerous, mysterious force known by the name of Jesse James was now revealed, though cold and still. So many questions would now go unanswered, so many events unexplained. But the mysteries that lay undiscovered at the feet of that newspaperman and the surround-ing crowd were not all the same as those hidden from us now. We want to know, as they did, the demons that danced in his head; we want to know the details of his loves and hates, his daily life and epic crimes. But as we stand on this side of the historical canyon, we must strain our eyes to glimpse what those people in St. Joseph saw so clearly: the public impact, the over-arching significance, of his outlaw career.

A single fact illustrates the problem. From the end of the Civil War to the hour of James's death, the governors of Missouri proclaimed rewards for the capture of criminals more than three hundred times; perhaps four of these proclamations touched on Jesse and his brother Frank. Those hun-dreds of other outlaws, along with hundreds more who failed to attract gubernatorial attention, committed murders, broke out of jails, robbed stages, banks, and trains, even killed a U.S. marshal and burned a county courthouse—but every one has been forgotten, except for the James broth-ers and their confederates.[2] The obvious question is, Why? Why should one set of criminals be so much more memorable than another?

Every attempt to understand Jesse James has stumbled on this question, because the real key to explaining him is to explain the world he lived in. "The Life and Times" is the classic formulation of the biography, of course, appearing in many a subtitle, but rarely has the interconnection of subject and context been so critical as in this particular case. James lived underground from the age of sixteen, scrupulously avoiding scrutiny, yet his half-hidden life was rife with symbolism. He became an emblem of con-flicts that were as real and raw to his contemporaries as a bad burn. He made old wounds ache again; he reminded the public of precisely where the blows had fallen, where the social fabric had been torn. He not only repre-sented forces larger than himself, he made them concrete, understandable, undeniable.

But *what* forces, *what* conflicts, *what* wounds? Almost all examinations of this famous outlaw by serious historians have been in studies devoted to particular topics—industrialization, the Civil War, the phenomenon of banditry around the globe—leaving us with an incomplete picture, at best. The antiquarian research of the large and dedicated fraternity of Jesse James admirers has turned up many details on the man, his family, and his crimes, but has left the all-important context unaddressed. The one truly scholarly biography, the landmark *Jesse James Was His Name,* by the late William A. Settle, Jr., inevitably suffers from age.[3] (A great deal of historical research has come to light in the more than thirty years since that book's publication.) But it also stumbles on a critical point where our subject and his context meet: To what extent was Jesse James a participant in his rise to legend, in his symbolic role in the public eye?

In these pages, answers will be given to all these questions. Here, the greatness of his image is seen to emerge from the greatness of the issues that flowed through his life. Some of the central questions and conflicts in American history defined his existence: the fight over slavery and abolitionism, the great catastrophe of the Civil War, the revolution of freedom represented by emancipation and Reconstruction, the spread of railroads and industrialization, and the first signs of a corporate economy. The social and political fire fueled by all these things burned at a white heat in Jesse James's homeland of western Missouri—a border state tucked into the Midwest, sharing traits of the industrial Northeast, the family-farm Northwest, and the slave-driving South. Here, every political issue was personal, every conflict real and concrete, every dispute bitter.

Would slavery spread? Would the slave states secede? Would emancipation mean equality for African Americans? Would the South be revolutionized into the model of the North? The James family debated such questions long before Jesse was born, and he threw himself into the storm over them at the tender age of sixteen, when he joined the gangs of Confederate guerrillas that battled Union forces in Missouri. With the coming of peace, he and his fellow "bushwhackers," as they were known, continued their wartime ways, and emerged as central figures in the state's political struggle over Reconstruction. Like the Ku Klux Klan and other groups of rebel veterans in the Deep South, the bushwhackers served as irregular shock troops in the Confederate resurgence after the war—though in border-state Missouri, the bushwhacker bandits usually played a more symbolic role, one cultivated by the influential newspaper editor John Newman Edwards.[4]

Jesse James was not an inarticulate avenger for the poor; his popularity was driven by politics—politics based on wartime allegiances—and was rooted among former Confederates. Even his attacks on unpopular economic targets, the banks and the railroads, turn out on closer inspection to have had political resonances. He was, in fact, a major force in the attempt to create a Confederate identity for Missouri, a cultural and political offensive waged by the defeated rebels to undo the triumph of the Radical Republicans in the Civil War. His robberies, his murders, his letters to the newspapers, and his starring role in Edwards's columns all played a part in the Confederate effort to achieve wartime goals by political means (to use historian Christopher Phillips's neat reversal of Clausewitz's dictum).[5] Had Jesse James existed a century later, he would have been called a terrorist.

Terrorist? The term hardly fits with the traditional image of him as a Wild West outlaw, yippin' and yellin' and shooting it out with the county sheriff. But he saw himself as a Southerner, a Confederate, a vindicator of the rebel cause, and so he must be seen in the context of Southern "outlaws"—particularly the Klan and other highly political paramilitary forces. Even more important, he was not simply a puppet of John Edwards, but an active participant in the creation of his own legend. Edwards's glorification of the bushwhacker bandits only began after the publicity-minded James rose to leadership and began to demand attention on his own. An avid student of current affairs, he sometimes outdid his editor friend in his public attacks on the Radical Republicans (to Edwards's evident alarm). Was he a criminal? Yes. Was he in it for the money? Yes. Did he choose all his targets for political effect? No. He cannot be confused with the Red Brigades, the Tamil Tigers, Osama bin Laden, or other groups that now shape our image of terrorism. But he was a political partisan in a hotly partisan era, and he eagerly offered himself up as a polarizing symbol of the Confederate project for postwar Missouri.[6]

There remains, of course, the straightforward power of his story. His is a tale of ambushes, gun battles, and daring raids, of narrow escapes, betrayals, and revenge. Even his oddly alliterative name seems to have been conjured up by a novelist of overripe adventures. But an accurate understanding of his world can only add to the drama. When we look at his life in its proper setting—if we see it as did that crowd that held its breath around his body on Thirteenth and Lafayette—we see that the life of Jesse James was as significant as it was thrilling.

This is, at bottom, a story of how Americans have hated Americans, how Americans have killed Americans, how both winners and losers refused to forget or forgive. It is a story of the Civil War and what it left unsettled—the open-ended consequences that still shape our lives. It is a story of murder, atrocity, and terrorism, of the hunger for revenge, of struggles for power and freedom and the definition of freedom. The darker angels of our nature beat their wings throughout this book, for they often guided the life of, the hunt for, and the celebration of Jesse Woodson James.

He promoted himself as a Robin Hood; his enemies derided him as a common thug. His sudden death froze those masks in place, leaving later generations to consider him either as myth or anti-myth, unaware that each characterization is equally empty. This book cannot make the dead man speak, but it can take the masks away, pull a syllable or two from his lips, and set them amid the chorus of his contemporaries. In the end, he emerges as neither epic hero nor petty bully, but as something far more complex. In the life of Jesse James, we see the place where politics meets the gun.

PART ONE

Zion

1842–1860

Walk about Zion, and go round about her; tell the towers thereof.
Mark ye well her bulwarks, consider her palaces, that ye may tell
it to the generation following.

—Psalms 48:12–13

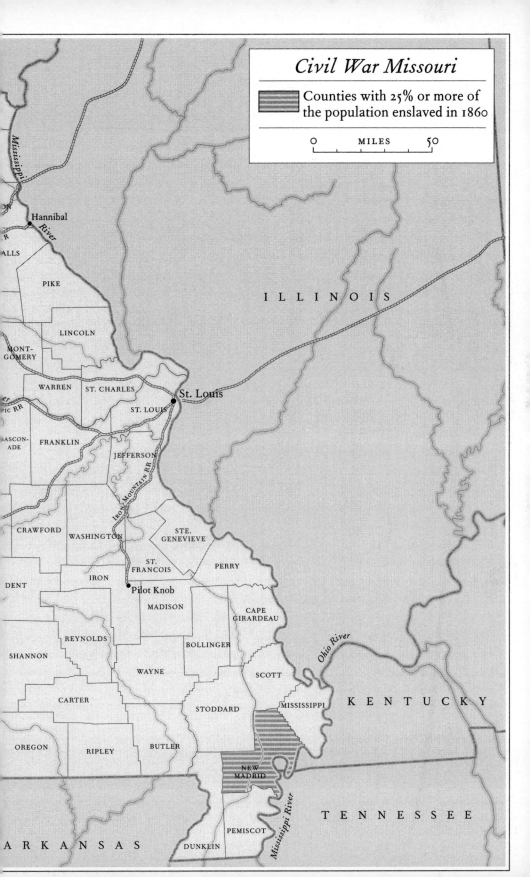

Mississippi

River

Hannibal

ILLINOIS

PIKE

LINCOLN

MONT-
GOMERY

WARREN

ST. CHARLES

St. Louis

ST. LOUIS

GASCON-
ADE

FRANKLIN

JEFFERSON

IRON MOUNTAIN RR

CRAWFORD

WASHINGTON

STE.
GENEVIEVE

DENT

IRON

ST.
FRANCOIS

PERRY

Pilot Knob

MADISON

CAPE
GIRARDEAU

REYNOLDS

BOLLINGER

Ohio River

SHANNON

WAYNE

SCOTT

KENTUCKY

CARTER

STODDARD

MISSISSIPPI

OREGON

RIPLEY

BUTLER

NEW
MADRID

Mississippi River

TENNESSEE

PEMISCOT

ARKANSAS

DUNKLIN

FALLS

ALLS

CHAPTER ONE

The Preacher

IN THE BLIND man's memory, the river ran west. It was in the spring of 1846 when young Francis Parkman had first looked on the Missouri, and he had seen clearly that its wide and silty waters flowed east to the Mississippi. But when he closed his faltering eyes in a clinic on Staten Island in 1847 and began to dictate the story of his adventure of the previous year, he had already begun to think like the great historian he would soon become. As he scanned in his mind the lines of passengers and clots of wagons and piles of goods crowding the St. Louis levee, as he recalled the sound of steamboat paddles slapping and churning against the Missouri's current, he could see the life of the nation pulsing westward up the river like blood cells pouring through an artery. In the most important sense, the river ran west.[1]

Parkman did not record how he arrived in St. Louis from his home in Boston, but he undoubtedly spent most of his trip on the water. It was virtually his only choice. Most roads amounted to little more than muddy ravines—in Missouri, it was said that roads were *worn*, not made—and the first, pioneering railways had yet to cover much territory. So, whenever possible, Americans set out in schooners and square-rigged ships, paddle-wheel steamboats, or mule-drawn canal barges. He might have taken a ship to New Orleans, then a riverboat north; or he could have sailed up the Hudson, been towed down the Erie Canal, then shipped through the Great Lakes before crossing to descend the Mississippi, or taking another canal to reach the mighty Ohio.[2]

North and south, east and west, these flowing highways met at the metropolis of St. Louis. One of Parkman's contemporaries, a farm woman named Elizabeth Carter, wrote that merchants swarmed in and out of the place "like bees." The water off the city's tightly packed levee presented a breathtaking spectacle, as dozens of teetering, wedding-cake paddlewheel-ers pressed in to find a landing. "The steamboats were strung up and down the river for miles as close as they could stand," she wrote to her family in Kentucky.[3]

Some fifty of those vessels regularly plied the Missouri River, hauling passengers and goods between St. Louis and the state's inner river towns. But the twenty-two-year-old Parkman's imagination was captured by the immense throng of settlers and traders bound for Oregon, California, and Santa Fe. "The hotels were crowded," he wrote, "and the gunsmiths and saddlers were kept constantly at work in providing arms and equipments for the different parties of travellers."[4]

On April 28, 1846, Parkman left St. Louis on a Missouri steamer named the *Radnor*. "The boat was loaded until the water broke alternately over the guards," he recalled. "Her upper-deck was covered with large wagons of a peculiar form, for the Santa Fe trade, and her hold was crammed with goods for the same destination. There were also equipments and provisions of a party of Oregon emigrants, a band of mules and horses, piles of saddles and harness."

For the next week, the heavily laden steamboat chugged up the winding river, forcing its way against the swift current. The Missouri ran high in the spring, making the pilot's job simpler—but not simple. The channel con-stantly shifted back and forth across the soft-soiled floodplain; sandbars swelled into islands and then dissolved; snags of drifting dead trees came and went, threatening to spear the hull of a poorly guided boat. Everything rested on the pilot's knowledge and skill. He had to learn and relearn the river, read the water for shoals and snags, know how to time a burst of steam to carry the boat through a shallow chute. It was a dangerous career. Between boiler explosions and the river's own obstacles, an average of three boats each year sank to the Missouri's muddy bottom, often taking dozens of lives at a time. The pilot, Mark Twain later wrote, ruled over his vessel "in glory," trumping even the captain in pay and authority.[5]

During that week, the *Radnor* existed as a floating town, piled high and trailing a cloud of smoke. The average boat was a sidewheeler, some 165 feet long and 28 feet wide—though they often reached 250 feet with a 40-foot beam—and some could hold as many as 400 passengers. "In her cabin were Santa Fe traders, gamblers, speculators, and adventurers of various descriptions," Parkman observed, "and her steerage was crowded with Oregon emigrants, 'mountain men,' negroes, and a party of Kanzas Indi-ans, who had been on a visit to St. Louis." Also on board, unmentioned by the young Bostonian, would have been country lawyers, frontier mer-chants, and farmers returning home, along with dozens of women, chil-dren, and teenagers. "The young people seemed to enjoy themselves very well," Elizabeth Carter noted on a similar trip, "with music and dancing every night."[6]

"In five or six days we began to see signs of the great western movement that was then taking place," Parkman recalled. Tents and wagons began to appear on the bank as the boat drew near Independence. When the *Radnor* steamed in to the landing, he gaped at the wild diversity of the scene: dozens of Mexicans, "gazing stupidly out from beneath their broad hats"; clusters of Native Americans, gathered silently around campfires; a few long-haired, buckskin-clad French hunters, fresh from the mountains; and crowds of Anglo-Saxon pioneers.[7]

There was probably no other place in the country like Missouri's western border. The aptly named town of Westport served as the access point between the settled states and the Great Plains, the Rocky Mountains, and the Pacific coast. Traders came and went, spending the Spanish silver coins they acquired in Santa Fe; Native Americans of countless nations and cultures visited and passed through; and settlers departed by the thousands in their ox-drawn wagons. The first large group of emigrants had departed for Oregon just three years before, starting a steady flow to that distant territory; and now the Mormons were gathering for a long trek west that would end at Great Salt Lake, deep in Mexican territory. Westport's shops were filled with the sounds of English, Spanish, French, along with the occasional German and various Indian languages.

And yet, as wild as the region might have seemed to the eye, it was hardly a raw, untamed frontier. A full decade before Parkman's arrival, one writer thought that many of the towns "would lead the visitor to believe, were he governed by appearances, that he was in the heart of the best settlements of one of the older states." A few years afterward, another visitor made a telling observation: Missouri's western border, he wrote, "is fenced up all on one side with old and well improved farms as far east as we could see, while on the right . . . it is open, wild prairie."[8]

Hard against this boundary—next to the vast plains that President Andrew Jackson had set aside as the "permanent Indian frontier"—sat this long-settled, thriving community, bustling with commerce. Hemp and tobacco fields abounded; river towns rang with noise from carriage workshops, tobacco stemmeries, and leaf-prizing houses, as well as ropewalks, where hemp's rough fibers were turned into twine. Both farmers and merchants prospered by selling supplies to the migrants marching by. Passing wagon trains kept cobblers, saddle makers, and blacksmiths busy; they also provided a major market for locally raised food and livestock. In May 1848, for example, outfitter Edward M. Samuel in the town of Liberty announced that he needed at least two thousand pounds of bacon to keep up with demand.[9]

When Parkman looked over these Missourians, he found them "yellow-visaged," with "lank angular proportions, enveloped in brown homespun, evidently cut and adjusted by the hands of a domestic female tailor." Though his description seems at odds with this general picture of prosperity, it was nonetheless accurate. Almost everything had a handmade look out here, on the far end of the bending limb of the Missouri River. "From all I have seen," Elizabeth Carter wrote from Clay County, "I would judge that the people are very plain." Even residents whose homes dated back to the early 1820s sometimes lived in log cabins, though well-improved ones; many used walnut or butternut oil to die their homespun clothes a distinctive brown, earning these people the nickname "butternuts."[10]

Butternuts could be found all across Missouri, Illinois, Indiana, and Ohio, where they had moved from the upper South—especially from Kentucky, the great fountain of settlers that flooded the Ohio and Mississippi valleys in the early nineteenth century. They went by other nicknames as well, such as crackers, hoosiers, pukes, and rednecks—terms that originated in Ulster, Scotland, and northern England, where this long movement of peoples began a century earlier. Even the wealthiest among them—those who could afford fine wool and cotton clothes, rather than walnut-stained homespun—shared common cultural traits: a willingness to resort to violence, for example, to resolve private disputes or keep public order.[11]

Parkman continued on into the vast expanse of the Great Plains, where he joined a wandering Oglala band of the Lakota people; but when he turned in his saddle to glance over his shoulder, settled Missouri itself looked like an alien land to his Harvard-bred, Bostonian eyes. How different it must have seemed to another passenger who stepped off a steamboat that spring; to him, Missouri's western reaches would have been little less than Zion.

This man had also spent a slow week in early 1846 on a paddlewheeler from St. Louis, as it churned toward the setting sun. If he had been aboard the *Radnor,* Parkman would have noticed him: he was a commanding figure, a tall man with a long, thin face, his hair parted on one side and combed across to leave his high forehead bare. Perhaps he carried a Bible when he appeared in the dining room for his meals; though his name was Robert Sallee James, this twenty-eight-year-old was better known to his Baptist neighbors as *brother* or *Preacher* James.[12]

He probably disembarked at Liberty landing, in Clay County, across the river from Independence. There he would have hired a horse or a wagon for the long ride home along those rutted tracks that Missourians called roads, across a landscape that resembled a rug pushed into a corner: rumpled, wrinkled, rippled with ravines and dusted with timber. His route would have carried him through the town of Liberty, the prosperous but modest county seat, and a dozen miles farther into the northern reaches of Clay. There he would have ridden over a low rise and caught sight of a humble three-room house with a narrow porch stretching across its single story, perched with a barn and a few outbuildings above a deep streambed. It was home.[13]

James had clearly given careful thought to the timing of the extended trip he had just completed. The month of January, though the deepest trough of winter, overflowed with labor for the typical Missouri farmer, but eight to twelve weeks into the year the demands temporarily lightened. The river, too, would finally be free of ice, as the first paddlewheelers puffed into the landings along Clay County's long waterfront. After selling his annual harvest of hemp, he would have had several weeks free before new seed had to go into the ground. So church member Jane W. Gill expressed little surprise when she noted in a letter that "Preacher James" had departed in late March to visit his native Kentucky.[14]

But there was something odd about that journey. He apparently went alone, leaving behind his wife of five years, Zerelda Cole James, and their two-year-old son. Robert looked uncertain and uneasy when he left, a condition that his neighbors kept in mind as they welcomed him home. "Preacher James," Gill wrote on June 15, 1846, "was here with his wife a few days after his return, and seems better contented to live in Mo."[15]

Better contented. These modest words suggest a disquiet not quite dispelled. But the cause of his discontent is unclear. By any measure, he had already come far from his humble beginnings. Born on July 7, 1818, he became an orphan at the age of nine and went to live with his sister Mary Mimms (eighteen years old and already married). In 1838, he enrolled at Georgetown College, Kentucky, a rare distinction at a time when primary education was haphazard, secondary education rare, and illiteracy all too common. There he met Zerelda E. Cole, a strikingly tall girl who attended a Roman Catholic school in town. And she was indeed a *girl*. Born on January 29, 1825, she was only sixteen when she engaged to marry the devout college student.[16]

Zerelda, too, was a native of Kentucky, and she, too, had lost a parent at an early age. Her father had died when she was just two, and she was left by her mother with her grandfather, Robert Cole. After he died, her mother married Robert Thomason—reportedly ignoring Zerelda's disapproval— and moved to distant Clay County, Missouri. Once again, the girl found herself packed off to live with relatives, this time with her uncle James M. Lindsay in Scott County, Kentucky. Though a Protestant, she entered the Catholic school in Georgetown, the community where she met her future husband. On December 20, 1841, they said their vows at Lindsay's home.

The wedding of such a young girl was not an ordinary event in antebellum Kentucky: Lindsay had to give county officials his written permission for the minor to marry. Once Robert James received his diploma, in the spring of 1842, the pair packed their things and traveled to Clay County, where they moved in with Zerelda's mother and Thomason. The child bride soon showed signs of pregnancy. Nineteen days before her eighteenth birthday, on January 10, 1843, she delivered a boy. They named him Alexander Franklin James, or Frank, for short.[17]

All in all, Robert James found himself in a seemingly blissful domestic setting, with a young, attractive wife and a newborn son. But he was a restless, driven man. In short order, he found a forum for his ambition at the New Hope Baptist Church. Founded in 1828, it was a humble affair: a log structure twenty feet square, with a haphazard stone chimney that opened into a gaping fireplace. Even in this cramped space, worshippers had plenty of room during Sunday meetings. Their recently departed preacher had driven away most members with heated doctrinal disputes over communion. When James first arrived, a mere fifteen people gathered for services.[18]

In that dim, gritty church, James discovered his own inner light; and in him, the tiny church found its salvation, in both the spiritual and the worldly sense. Baptist congregations ordained their own preachers from among their membership; nothing more was required than a mutual agreement that a man had received a divine calling to speak the word of God. And the pious, charismatic, well-educated young fellow from Kentucky inspired immediate consensus among these "very plain" people. One neighbor recalled how he had attended the ordination service as a boy. "Your correspondent was present," he later wrote, "a ten-cent straw hat on his head, no coat, no boots or shoes, but had the necessary spur on his heel, and heard his first sermon." For this suffering, divided congregation, James's preaching was a revelation. "His manner of speaking was sublime," the neighbor added, and his "exhortations were inimitable."[19]

In other words, James combined his college education with the emotional passion of the Second Great Awakening, the wave of religious fervor that had swept the country since its beginnings in upstate New York in 1826. Here, within the log walls of this country church, people prayed in shouts and tears to a deity who offered redemption to all those willing to confess their sins and accept forgiveness. Though the cold Calvinist God of predestination was hardly dead in Southern Baptist theology, the preacher's call for repentance and conversion struck a chord of popular Arminianism—a widespread belief in one's own moral agency, a conviction that each person could choose to accept or reject salvation. In Robert James's native state, in fact, evangelical fervor predated the Second Great

Awakening, stretching from Scottish "Holy Fairs" to the Great Revival of 1800–1805.

Standing in the pulpit, James would single out unconverted individuals and call them up to the mourners' bench, where the other congregants could pray for them. "When he went for a sinner he never failed to secure him," wrote that anonymous neighbor—though he did recall one exception. "He noticed a man by the name of Henderson sitting by himself and taking no part in the meeting. He started towards him; the man well knew what was coming, and jumped out of a convenient window and made his escape."[20]

Word spread of James's passionate, eloquent sermons. Like most preachers in Clay County, and in keeping with Baptist custom, he began to ride the local circuit, traveling to other churches in the area that needed a talented voice in the pulpit. In 1844, he organized his growing following into the North Liberty Baptist Association. At New Hope, the original fifteen members soon shared their crowded little sanctuary with dozens of tearful new worshippers. So he raised money to build a new brick church, one worthy of the congregation's size and vigor. By the end of 1845, the new building was ready, thanks in part to a large cash gift from Preacher James himself, along with the generous donation of the labor of two of his slaves.[21]

THE PRESENCE OF those slaves testifies to both James's worldly success and his spiritual judgment. Slaves were common enough in Clay County: one person out of four there was held in bondage, a fact that helped make Clay the westernmost of a string of river counties that would later be known as Little Dixie. James received no income in the pulpit, since Baptists expected their preachers to earn their own living. So if he possessed enough slaves in 1845 to be able to lend out two, he had come very far, very fast.[22]

Unfortunately, the James family had picked a particularly bad time to start in Clay County. In 1842, as the newlywed couple carried their possessions into the Thomason house, Missouri reeled from the smashing blow of the national depression that had started in 1837. This economic crisis produced a condition virtually unthinkable in later centuries: money literally disappeared, driving the local marketplace back to the barter system.[23]

"Times here is very hard," Missourian George F. Terry complained in 1841, "& money scarce." The sort of scarcity Terry wrote about was absolute—a complete absence of the medium of exchange. This drastic cash shortage even forced the state government to accept shelled corn for taxes up to $500 (at 50 cents per bushel). These conditions made it extraordinarily difficult for a new farmer to buy basic equipment—a shovel plow, a scythe, and a wagon—along with draft animals, hogs, and seed. So Robert and Zerelda James struggled along at first, sharing a home with her mother and her stepfather. After the birth of Frank, they finally moved onto the land that would be their home for the rest of their lives: that three-room cabin hard by a creek in the northeastern corner of Clay.[24]

The year of Frank's birth, 1843, revolutionized the fortunes of the western border of Missouri. The first large wagon train to Oregon—a thousand men, women, and children who would soon be dubbed "the Great Migration"—departed that spring, starting the annual movement that would total ten thousand settlers by the end of the decade, and pour tens of thousands of dollars into Missouri's rural economy. Commercial agriculture picked up again, too, part of a web of business ties that connected this western county to Southern markets. In part, this revival was due to Congress: in 1841, it enacted a protective tariff for hemp, the raw material for rope. Robert James, like many Clay farmers, knew about the crop from Kentucky, and he began to raise it as its price outstripped tobacco and other cash crops. He carted his annual harvest to the Missouri river landings, where he sold it to commission merchants who sailed upriver from St. Louis, or to buyers from local ropewalks (as rope factories were called). It eventually made its way down the Mississippi and onto the plantations of the Deep South, where it served as baling twine for cotton.[25]

As a border state, Missouri shared characteristics of both North and South; indeed, many residents considered it part of a third section, the border West. But slaveholding families such as the James clan—born in Kentucky, living in slave-dependent Clay County, shipping their hemp down the Mississippi—felt themselves to be a part of the seamless fabric of the South. In their eyes, Southern people, Southern agriculture, and Southern markets made the Missouri River valley "Little Dixie" indeed. And like most Southern commercial farmers, Robert began to buy slaves as he prospered, probably paying between $200 and $400 for each of the boys and girls who populated his spread by the end of the decade.[26]

Boys and girls? The image is jarring: the pious, beloved man of God, shouting out bids for toddlers at auction. But that is indeed what he did. By 1850, he came to own at least five black children, ranging in age from two to eleven (in addition to a black woman, age thirty).[27] And those child slaves on the James farm were not only evidence of affluence, but an indication of a spiritual choice on the part of the preacher. Despite the omnipresence of slavery in Clay County, some local Baptists began to question its morality. By 1845, two circuit-riding evangelists named Chandler and Love had turned this ambivalence into a crusade. "No slave holder," they declared, "had a right to an office in the church, or a place in the church."

They carried a surprising number of people with them. Jane Gill described Chandler as "an avowed Northern man" who "influenced the most of the preachers under him to go with him," and badly divided the Liberty church membership. "Two local preachers, Huffaker & Garner, got such a tincture of abolitionism last year," she wrote in 1846, "that they lost their usefulness and have been exerting an unhealthy influence ever since."[28]

Clay County's furor played out against a backdrop of turmoil in the national church. In the eighteenth century, evangelical Christians throughout the American colonies-turned-states had raised serious questions about slavery; by the early nineteenth century, however, Southern preachers and congregations had come to accept "the peculiar institution," as it was called, with few, if any, reservations. But the issue flared into public debate once again as Baptists began to organize on a large scale in the 1830s and '40s. This time, the antislavery critique took on a distinctly sectional character, as Northern congregants pressed abolitionist sentiments on their Southern brethren. In 1845, Baptists below the Mason-Dixon line split off to form the Southern Baptist Convention—an explicitly proslavery denomination—which the Missouri Baptist General Association soon joined.

It was a grim omen. For border-state Missouri, this religious dispute was an early challenge to its regional status, forcing individuals to choose between North and South. Back in Clay, the controversy burned with bitter intensity. "Chandler and Love," Tabitha Gill wrote, "almost broke up all the churches." Their goal, Jane Gill believed, was to "have a northern conference in this state," but large numbers of local Baptists opposed them, as did most others in the county; as across the South, the challenge of abolitionism drove slaveholders into a fierce defense of their institution. "The world was enraged against them," Jane observed, referring to the non-Baptist public, "and threatened Love so that he could not preach there."[29]

"The church at New Hope," on the other hand, "seems to get along in peace and harmony." Robert James had made his choice: a slaveowner himself, he rejected the crusade of Chandler and Love. The controversy must have been troubling, even baffling to him. He had profited from the labor of bondservants all his life; slavery was central to the South's social order. But here in Missouri, abolitionist emissaries had almost turned the people against it.[30]

The preacher soon had far more to worry about than this local, spiritual war. By 1846, a far larger battle—a real battle of flesh and blood—darkened the future. It, too, sprang from the issue of slavery. In 1836, American settlers in Texas defeated Mexico in a war of independence. For the next eight years, this new Lone Star republic petitioned its American parent for admission as a slave state. But apathy and Northern opposition kept the Texans out until 1844, when Congress finally acted on its request. "The treaty for the annexation of Texas was this day sent in to the Senate," abolitionist John Quincy Adams noted in his diary, "and with it went the freedom of the human race."[31]

Annexation passed though Congress just five days before James K. Polk took the presidential oath of office, in March 1845. Polk's overriding goal was to extend the nation's borders to those places where its settlers had spontaneously gone—Oregon, Texas, and at least part of California. But the absorption of Texas virtually guaranteed war with Mexico, which had never accepted the independence of its rebellious province. In January 1846, the president ordered General Zachary Taylor to lead American troops to the disputed border, where they were ambushed a month later by Mexican forces. News of the battle arrived in Washington four hours *after* Polk and his cabinet had decided to open hostilities, giving them a convenient excuse for their existing plans. On May 13, Congress declared war.

Military fervor gripped Clay County. Men flocked by the dozens to join the First Regiment of Missouri Mounted Volunteers, under Colonel Alexander Doniphan; in Liberty, more than one hundred recruits signed up for Company C under Doniphan's prominent brother-in-law, thirty-three-year-old Oliver P. Moss (universally known as "O. P. Moss"). On June 6, 1846, the troops departed for war.[32]

AND SO HERE Robert James found himself, as he packed his bag to visit Kentucky in the spring of 1846. He could boast an enthusiastic spiritual following and considerable worldly success, but both had come through ceaseless struggle. Threats of disaster had hovered over him the entire time, droning in his ear like a horsefly: economic depression, abolitionists in the church, and now war. The cruelest blow, however, had come from an invisible, unknowable hand—the sort of blow one might expect from an angry God. On July 19, 1845, Zerelda had endured the harrowing (and life-threatening) agonies of childbirth, bringing into the world a boy the couple named after his father. The infant lived only five days. Such deaths were disturbingly commonplace in the 1840s, but no less heartbreaking for their frequency. Perhaps, in its aftermath, the preacher asked himself what he had done wrong, if there was more he should do to save the souls of mankind.[33]

Robert journeyed to his old home of Kentucky and back again, even as long files of men from neighboring farms and towns marched off for Mexico (running into Francis Parkman on the Great Plains along the way).

When the pastor returned, "better contented," he poured himself into his preaching.

James's religious activity filled the pages of the press after 1846, as he piled up victories for Christ. Couples sought him out to preside over their weddings, including Zerelda's brother Jesse Richard (Dick) Cole and his bride, Louisa G. Maret. The preacher won particular acclaim for his role in bringing a new Baptist college to Liberty. The project began when William Jewell gave an endowment worth $10,000 to the General Baptist Association. In 1849 an intense rivalry arose among different towns that wanted to host the school. Robert stumped the countryside to raise money (personally pledging $196); by the time a convention met, on August 21, 1849, to decide the location, Clay County's subscriptions outstripped all others. William Jewell College opened its doors in Liberty on January 1, 1850, with James serving as one of its trustees.[34]

By then, the distant sounds of war had long since died off—Mexico's capital was captured, and the northern third of that republic was sheared off and stitched onto the burgeoning United States. Here in Clay County, Robert's own little empire burgeoned as well. After his 1846 trip, he purchased his homestead, along with adjoining land belonging to R. G. Gilmer and Alvah Maret, giving him a farm of more than one hundred acres, plus another eighty that he rented out. His hemp crop alone brought him roughly $70 a year, far more than his annual state and county taxes (which totaled $10.58 in 1850). He had hogs and corn to sell, along with the wool from his thirty sheep, and six slaves to tend it all. Robert stuffed a bookcase in his little three-room house with fifty-one volumes. The library testified to his education; it ranged from Charles Dickens to the ancient Jewish historian Josephus, from works on Greek and Latin to books on astronomy and theology. He subscribed not only to the local papers, but also to the *St. Louis Western Watchman*.

Then came a sign of his personal redemption, after his season of discontent—a blessing to counteract the pain of the infant Robert's death. On September 5, 1847, Zerelda gave birth to a healthy boy. They christened him Jesse Woodson James.[35] That day, it would have seemed absurd to suggest that Robert would be remembered primarily as the father of this infant.

The charismatic preacher, as the *Liberty Tribune* reported, was now "well known in this community . . . a man much liked by all." The climax of his career came in the memorable summer of 1849, the season of his greatest coup in his gentle war for God. On the third Saturday in July he began the largest and longest camp meeting Clay County had ever seen. Local Methodist and Presbyterian preachers joined in, filling each lamp-lit night through the end of August with emotional pleas for conversion. Forty people joined the New Hope church before the meeting was half over, "which surprised a good many," Elizabeth Carter observed. Robert's conquests for Christ provided a domestic victory as well. "Dick Cole and his wife has joined," Carter wrote; "he is a brother to Mrs. James."

Called by Robert's compelling voice, the people of Clay County experienced an emotional and spiritual catharsis at the six-week revival. At one point fifty-five trembling sinners simultaneously went up to the mourners' bench. "It looks like the good Lord has began a good work," the preacher declared, saying that he had never seen so many come forward at one time. He baptized some twenty-five that day, as pregnant Zerelda and little Jesse—not yet two years old—looked on.[36]

There was something foreboding, however, in Robert's words of satisfaction, hinting perhaps that he heard the Lord calling him elsewhere—to California. The first rumors of gold in that newly conquered province appeared in the Missouri press as early as September 1848; by the end of November, men were returning to the state with evidence of the abundant precious metal to be found in the far west. The ultimate confirmation came on December 5, 1848. "The accounts of the abundance of gold in that territory," President Polk reported to Congress, "are of such an extraordinary character as would scarcely command belief were they not corroborated by the authentic reports of officers in the public service." Soon every local paper carried tales of the fortune-filled earth on the Pacific coast. Books and pamphlets giving pointers on the trip to California sold as fast as they could be printed. When William Gilpin of Independence wrote a letter describing the route west for his friend Samuel Ralston, it quickly emerged as a printed circular.

In January 1849, the *Liberty Tribune* reported the story of Joseph H. Cutting, who had spent forty days digging in California; the gold he found yielded an average of $37.50 per day. This figure was more than half of the annual proceeds of James's hemp harvest. In April 1849 the *Tribune* printed a remarkable account from Clay Countian Peter H. Burnett. "Men here are nearly crazy with the riches suddenly forced in to their pockets," he wrote. "The accounts you have seen of the gold region are not over colored. *The gold is positively inexhaustible.*"[37]

"I have never heard of as many families being left alone or placed in other's houses in all my life before," Jane Gill wrote from Clay County; a "strange infatuation," she called it. "Well might the Apostle say, the love of money is the root of all evil." Preacher James might have agreed—except that he himself fell victim to the "strange infatuation" (despite the birth of another child, Susan Lavenia, on November 15, 1849).[38]

"Brother Robert James preached his farewell sermon to us at New

Hope two weeks since, and left for California the Wednesday after," Gill wrote on April 14, 1850. "Brother James seemed very much affected at parting from us and said his object was not to get gold but to preach, and numbers think he was justifiable in going." Gill, however, does not seem to have been among them. "Aaron made a golden calf to worship whilst Moses was on the mount," she chided, "and priests and ministers with their members may do the same in this day, and have done it no doubt." But she did reserve judgment on her beloved preacher, adding, "We will miss him very much."

Three decades later, after this contented corner of Missouri had passed through biblical plagues and apocalyptic trials, locals would recall this moment with vivid but unreliable memories. "To this day," a newspaper would report, "the old settlers about the James home say, and it has been a tradition, that the Rev. Robert James was driven from home by his wife." Robert's brother would agree, saying the sharp-tongued Zerelda had bitterly resented her husband's peripatetic preaching.[39]

Perhaps. He was a restless, driven man, and once before he had seemed discontented with life in Missouri. The 1846 trip had made clear that he was comfortable taking long absences from his wife and children. The movement to California, however, was a force far larger than any domestic squabble, and the preacher's sense of calling loomed larger still. The 1850 migration from Clay County dwarfed even that of the previous year; some thirty men made the journey with Robert (including the abolitionist Huffaker).[40]

But a sense of fatalism hovered around him as he departed. Cholera and other diseases plagued the California migrants, and James had spent heavily on medicine. Zerelda later claimed that, in a telling gesture, little Jesse clutched his father's leg before he left and begged him not to go; of course, at two years old, the boy could not have grasped that his father was leaving for a year or more. Robert's brooding echoed throughout his letters, as he wrote Zerelda from the overland trail. "Train up your children in the nurture and admonition of the Lord," he urged on April 14, 1850, "and live a Christian life yourself. . . . Give my love to all inquiring friends, and take a portion of it to yourself and kiss Jesse for me and tell Franklin to be a good boy and learn fast." On May 1, he began to voice explicit fears. Robert commented darkly on the long eighteen months he planned to spend in the mining camps, where dozens at a time succumbed to epidemics. "Pray for me," he wrote to Zerelda, "that if [we] no more meet in this world we can meet in Glory."[41]

A few months later, Robert James was dead.

CHAPTER TWO

The Widow

A DEATH REQUIRES record keeping—a coroner's inquest, a cemetery plot, a probate court proceeding—but no files can be kept of grief. So the moments following the news of Robert James's passing, on his farm in far Missouri, can only be imagined. A succession of neighbors, bearing gifts of food; round after round of relatives, lingering for long afternoons to comfort the baffled three-year-old Jesse, the seven-year-old Frank, and the tall, young widow Zerelda, who cradled Susan, her infant daughter. Local dignitaries might have called to offer condolences; New Hope church would have held a memorial service within its new brick walls; then came the nighttime hours alone.

But there would be no funeral, no burial, and no headstone. Robert had met his end in the California gold fields in September 1850, in a camp tellingly named Rough and Ready. He had lingered in illness for some two weeks, with a Dr. Newman in attendance at his bedside, before he passed away. Then the gold seekers he had come to convert had thrown his body into a hastily dug grave near their hastily built dwellings. Robert had died deeply in debt for room and board and medical care to another Missourian named Daniel H. Wright, who collected most of the bill by selling the dead preacher's mule, valise, and boots, and by emptying his wallet of his last ten dollars and fifty cents.[1]

It was not until October 25, 1850, that a small headline in the *Liberty Tribune* announced, "DEATH OF REV. ROBERT JAMES," as heralded in "our last advices from California." The story offered no hint of the gritty indignity of his bootless demise; instead, the editor warmly eulogized the preacher's prominence, popularity, and piety. "As a Revivalist," he mused, "he had but few equals in this country. . . . More additions have been made to the Baptist Church, in Clay County, under his preaching (length of time considered) than under that of any other person."[2]

The *Tribune* was a weekly paper, so the letter most likely arrived some five to ten days before its news appeared in print; during that interim, someone probably rode to the James farm to give Zerelda the news. Though many wives and children of gold-hungry migrants moved into the houses of friends and relatives, Robert had thoughtfully made other plans. "I think his wife intends living at home with her children and servants," Jane Gill had written to her sisters upon his departure. "A white man is living close by who is to cultivate their ground and give them a certain portion." The man's name was Garland Gentry. He could be seen gathering wood in the timber around the James family's house, or out in the fields cutting, breaking, and hauling away the harvest of weedy hemp. He used Robert's own livestock, equipment, and slaves for the work, and he kept a quarter of the crop for himself. But now that arrangement—everything about Zerelda's life—was plunged into cold, stomach-churning uncertainty.[3]

The death of Zerelda's husband pushed her to the helm of her family, and there she would remain until the end, charting a course for her children and herself through the years to come. She was twenty-five, perhaps six feet tall, with two toddlers and an infant, a three-room house, and six slaves. Little more is known of her at that time. Her temperament and outlook, her likes and dislikes, her sense of humor and sense of honor were only described after tumultuous decades filled with experiences she could scarcely imagine in that grieving winter of 1850.

"She is a remarkable woman!" a reporter would comment thirty years later. "The sentence is well worthy of the exclamation given it," he asserted. "Her eyes a steely blue; her face is a long oval, set off by a firm, determined expression about the mouth. . . . She is shrewd, has dauntless courage," while her devotion to her children "can be likened to nothing else but a tigress's love for her cubs." It was her inner strength that drew the most remarks from those who knew her in those later years. "She is said to be a hard woman to deal with," remarked a neighbor in 1882. "I never heard of her wilting but once," he added, and that would not be until long after Robert's death. "Zerelda," said her grandson's wife, "had always given orders, but she had never taken any. . . . The mother of Frank and Jesse James was strong-willed and had plenty of determination." Her exuberant sense of humor inclined toward practical jokes, particularly as "a way to get even." Perhaps the most telling observation came nearly a quarter century later, when a man came to Liberty intending to arrest Jesse and Frank. Ex-sheriff O. P. Moss advised the man to stay far away from Zerelda's farm. "The old woman would kill you if the boys don't," he warned. The next day, the man turned up dead.[4]

Did these strands dominate the tapestry of her personality when she was just twenty-five? We can never know. But the iron lady of later years seemed a vulnerable, untempered, uncertain young woman in 1850. She waited two full weeks after hearing of Robert's death before she stepped into a local store, on November 11, to buy black calico and gingham to make the family's mourning clothes. A week later she returned to purchase black crepe and ribbon to shroud her home in grief. She also bought a small pair of shoes—perhaps for her little boy Jesse, perhaps so he could join her in her first public appearance as a widow.[5]

That occasion came on November 21, 1850, when her brother Dick Cole and her stepfather, Robert Thomason, accompanied her to Liberty for the initial probate court proceeding. If she was unfamiliar with the common law regarding the estates of men who died without wills, then that day must have been a shock: as widow, she inherited nothing. Her children were Robert's only heirs; since they were so young, the court appointed a local official, James Harris, to administer the estate. Zerelda dutifully signed an agreement accepting this arrangement, but the court required her male relatives, Cole and Thomason, to sign as well.

The months that followed brought a chilling education in the legal limits on women's rights. "For many women, a husband's death brought his creditors down on the estate like vultures," notes historian George C. Rable. "She might have little to say about its disposal."[6] And so it was for Zerelda. Two weeks after she submitted to Harris's control of Robert's property, Harris and three court-appointed assessors rode onto the farm. Memorandum books in hand, they picked their way through the fields, the outbuildings, and finally through the house itself, carefully counting every cup and saucer. Two beds (and steads), two tables, one bookcase with fifty-one books, one set of dinnerware, one kettle, two ovens with lids, one skillet with lid, one grindstone—their inventory missed no detail. Harris reserved the agricultural machinery and draft animals for Gentry's use during the following year; he also temporarily granted to Zerelda ten pigs, two milk cows, one mare, and ten sheep, as well as selected dinnerware, some furniture, one of the beds, two trunks, two carpets, and eighty dollars. The rest would go up for sale to pay her many debts—from the bill for the tablecloth that Zerelda had purchased in October to the personal notes (or IOUs) that her husband had handed out with seeming abandon before his departure.

On the brisk winter day of January 4, 1851, Zerelda stood by with thirteen-month-old Susan, three-year-old Jesse, and Frank (just six days short of his eighth birthday), as a crowd of friends, neighbors, and strangers gathered in her yard and listened to an auctioneer cry out for bids on her possessions. She bought back what she could, including a rocking chair and the dinner table; her mother, her brother, and her brother-in-law William James helped by buying a sow, the grindstone, the other bed, works on the Baptist faith, and John Bunyan's *The Holy War*. Much of the rest was sold—a stove and pipe, Robert's rifle, the unallotted livestock.

In the weeks after that estate sale, hardship crept onto the James farm like the first frosts of winter. On April 19, 1851, the condition of Zerelda and her children moved the congregation of New Hope to take a collection. "He was the humble instrument of God," they wrote in tribute to their late preacher. He helped them "to see the awful condition we were in; and knowing we righted [sic] to aid him in his temporal wants," they added sheepishly, "as we should have done during his pastoral charge of New Hope church for 7 years . . . we hereby agree and bind ourselves to relieve his heirs" of at least part of their debt.[7]

This financial strain was typical for widows in slaveholding society. In 1851, bills continued to accumulate, from county clerk Greenup Bird's fee to the second installment on Robert's $196 pledge to William Jewell College. Garland Gentry sold the year's hemp crop for $66.50, giving the estate $51.84 as its share, but he charged $38.45 for his services.[8] And then there was the cost of school. Free public education scarcely existed in rural Missouri in those years; instead, local parents banded together to hire free-lance teachers for their children, with mixed results. Throughout the 1840s, neighbor Jane Gill complained that the opportunity for educating her daughter in rural Clay County was "so poor that I can't rely on it." But Zerelda found a place to enroll six-year-old Frank, paying cash for the privilege.[9]

The threat of destitution, however, could not compare to the ever-present shadow of death. Annual epidemics scourged Clay County with increasing intensity, including a ruthless cholera outbreak in the summer of 1849. The next year it was smallpox. "It has been in and around Liberty more or less for 3 months," Elizabeth Carter wrote on August 30, 1850, "but now it is within 2 miles of us. . . . It has thrown a general consternation and alarm through the neighborhood and caused the school to be stopped." In the summer of 1851, she wailed that "sickness death disease sorrow & tribulation are abroad in our land. The cholera has been raging in Independence, St. Joseph, Weston, and there has been several cases in Liberty." The people abandoned towns—even farms adjoining those of the plague's victims—leaving them deserted in the heat of midsummer. "I pray that God in mercy may stay the scourge a little longer," Carter wrote, "and give poor sinners time and opportunity to repent of their sins."[10]

In these uncertain times, Zerelda had reason to repent not her sins but her widowhood. On February 27, 1852, she once again bore the pain and humiliation of an estate auction; this time, the crier asked for bids on the agricultural equipment—her only means of making money. Zerelda had to ask Tilman H. West, the husband of one of her closest friends, for $3.40 to buy back a hoe for her garden and Robert's silver watch. West was more than a friend: under the harsh hand of the common law, he—not Zerelda—served as legal guardian for her children.[11]

With her source of income extinguished, and with Frank, Jesse, and Susan under another family's legal protection, Zerelda saw one clear strategy for regaining both her prosperity and progeny: marriage. On September 30, 1852, she wed Benjamin A. Simms, a farmer who lived a few miles away. Everything about the match breathed cold calculation. He was wealthy and almost twice her age; she was widowed, with rapidly dwindling resources. Simms owned extensive lands in both Clay and Clinton Counties, as well as a large "family" of slaves (as one neighbor described them). He also belonged to Zerelda's social circle of Kentucky expatriates; his son Richard had died in California along with Robert James, and notices of both deaths appeared in the same issue of the *Liberty Tribune.*[12]

At the age of about fifty-two, Simms may have been drawn to what the *Kansas City Times* would later dub "the famed beauty in all the country around about." But if he provided her with security, he would not provide fatherhood. Zerelda later said that she had "humored and indulged" Frank, Jesse, and Susan in the aftermath of their father's death; to the elderly Mr. Simms, however, they gave "no end of annoyance." Reportedly at his insistence, she left them in the Wests' care as she settled herself into her new husband's home.

For Jesse, the weeks that followed his fifth birthday brought the latest in a series of blows. In all likelihood, he could not remember his revered father, who had departed when he was two. His earliest memories would have been of strangers taking inventory of his family's possessions; the estate auctions; the threat of poverty; and now, separation from his mother, as she struggled to regain prosperity. The impact of these grim years would remain unknown, but they were unquestionably filled with confusion and pain.

Then Zerelda fell ill. Simms's probate records show that Dr. Absalom Kerns regularly attended her from January 9 through March 15, 1853; the extended visits suggest a troubled pregnancy, with potentially lethal consequences. On March 8, her condition grew so severe that Kerns spent the night at her bedside; and then the crisis passed, possibly with a miscarriage.[13]

Zerelda's calculations in marrying again had gone disastrously wrong. Even as she struggled back to health, she later told a local historian, "her near relatives informed her that if she [did not take her children back] . . . they would never more recognize her, so she separated from Mr. Simms." On June 12, 1853, Elizabeth Carter sent the news to the Simms family back in Kentucky. "Old Ben's young wife has left and gone to live with Mrs. West," she wrote. Then she added cryptically, "They soon got their satisfaction." Six months later, on January 2, 1854, Benjamin Simms died.[14]

Zerelda must have wobbled on a slender rail between losing her children, losing her farm, and losing herself. But in the aftermath of her failed marriage, her illness, and her exile from her first husband's farm, her inner strength began to emerge. In previous months, Zerelda had made her purchases on credit, and let James Harris as administrator pay them off; now, she simply demanded cash from the estate. Her children restored to her, she resumed life on the farm. And she managed to keep hold of all but one of her six slaves. (Harris auctioned off Alexander, at twelve the oldest boy, to pay the last debts.) On February 6, 1854, the administrator made final settlement of the estate, distributing the assets among the heirs—Frank, Jesse, and Susan—"according to their just rights."

But Zerelda had not yet completed her project of recovery—the restoration of her autonomy, her property, and her family. Tilman West remained the legal guardian of her children and her farm (since it legally belonged to Frank, Jesse, and Susan). Despite her recent, bitter failure, she knew only one sure way to resolve that intolerable situation. She had to find a husband. On September 12, 1855, she married Dr. Reuben Samuel. He, too, belonged to Clay County's fraternity of Kentucky natives. Zerelda had probably met him through family connections, for his office was in a store belonging to William James, Robert's brother, in nearby Greenville.[15]

Calculation of a different sort marked Zerelda's third and final marriage. Reuben struck observers as a far less weighty figure than his widow bride. Born in 1828, he was three years younger than Zerelda. While she was giving birth to Susan and enduring the loss of her first husband, he had been in school, studying at the Medical College of Ohio, in Cincinnati. His tall wife overshadowed him physically as well as emotionally; many years later, her granddaughter-in-law Stella James remarked that he was "a small, meek, and quiet man, and I suspected that Zerelda had always 'worn the pants.' " Just nine years after the wedding, Liberty merchant Edward M. Samuel drew similar conclusions. "He is no kinsman of mine, thank God," he wrote, "yet I think he is an easy, good natured, good for nothing fellow who is completely under the control of his wife."[16]

On November 3, 1856, Zerelda's new husband assumed legal guardianship of her children and her farm. But in every respect, Reuben was tethered firmly in her orbit. He moved onto the James farm (known after that as "Mrs. Samuel's place"), and he gave up the practice of medicine to attend to its fields and livestock, in accordance with his wife's wishes. He did everything, in fact, in accordance with Zerelda's wishes. He had even signed a prenuptial agreement to guarantee her ownership of the farm and slaves after his death—an uncommon if not unheard-of step, indicating her unsentimental determination. As a reporter commented decades later, Reuben was "under her dominion, for that is the way her neighbors speak of 'Aunt Zerel's' management of the farm and everybody on it."[17]

This timid, unambitious physician gained more than he lost in his unequal marriage. His willingness to abandon medicine, for example, made perfect sense, since farming was the more respectable occupation in 1855. Doctors could best be described as skilled tradesmen with pretensions. They relied on late-eighteenth-century theories that irritation and excitement caused most illnesses; their cures included bleeding, sweating, and vile emetics. Former president Andrew Jackson had recently died while his doctors plied him with calomel, a compound that included the lethal ingredient mercury. Even when doctors got it right, they looked more like commercial showmen than scientific professionals. Missouri's Dr. John Sappington, for example, discovered that quinine effectively countered malaria—and he made a major business of his patented "Dr. Sappington's Anti-Fever Pills." Small wonder that physicians met skepticism, or that many Missouri doctors spent most of their time running farms or businesses.[18]

So Reuben Samuel laid his hands on the plow, apparently happy to live as a respectable farmer under his wife's dominion. On December 26, 1858, came a kind of confirmation of his satisfaction: a baby girl, whom Zerelda named Sarah. The Samuels were an outwardly mismatched but inwardly contented couple.[19]

It seemed as if Zerelda had finally steered her family out of the storm, back into the quiet haven of Robert James's farm. In the years ahead, its acres would be the center of the universe for her and her two young boys, who now attended school and learned to ride horses and explored the fields and woods around their home.[20] But how different it all would have looked if she could have seen it as it would be: that gate, where Frank would depart when he first went off to war; that tree, where her husband would swing from a rope when the soldiers came; that wagon, in which she would pile her possessions when she and her family were sent into exile; that barn, from which Jesse and his brother would burst on horseback to flee a posse; that window, through which the iron ball would fly, to explode and tear off her arm and kill one of her sons. And how different her little boy Jesse would have seemed, if she could have seen him as the man who would one day defy the world, and die at a traitor's hand.

WITH THE FARM restored, the work began. As mistress of the place, Zerelda was nothing less than the proprietor of a year-round business, one that revolved around the manufacture, preservation, and preparation of food. The cycle began with slaughtering, an activity reserved for the beginning of the year. "This is the season to which the swine look forward with feeling of fear and trembling," wrote the editor of the *Westport Border Star* on New Year's Eve, 1858. "Now, from morn till night, their agonizing shrieks fill the air." In early January, when the cold kept flies and spoilage at bay, groups of neighbors rode from farm to farm to help with the butchering. The men would begin by gathering in the yard to kill the steer or swine. The crew would then lift the pig into the scalding box, where they drenched it with boiling water. (They would skin cattle instead.) They sawed off the hog's head, scraped the hair off its hide, hung it up, slit the body from neck to tail, and gutted it. As they scooped out the internal organs, they carefully preserved the fat, separating the lower-quality variety that stuck to the entrails from the highly prized "leaf fat" that lined the abdominal cavity. (They saved beef and mutton tallow for candles and soap.) After the meat had cooled, the farmers would cut it up.[21]

Now Zerelda would take over—if she were not already managing the entire affair. Most, if not all, of the newly slaughtered flesh had to be preserved. This was one reason why pork was so popular in Missouri; unlike other meats, its flavor improved with curing. It was also the easiest kind of meat to treat, since its oils prevented the absorption of excess salt, and it kept very well. "I hold a family to be in a desperate way," wrote a farmer's wife in the 1840s, "when the mother can see to the bottom of the pork barrel."[22] Zerelda would have brought out the pickling brine—a concoction of salt, brown sugar, saltpeter, pearlash, and water that was poured over the meat as it sat in casks. A heavy, flat stone weighed the pork down, and it would be left to sit. Meanwhile the lard would be rendered in pots over a low fire in the gaping hearth in the Samuel kitchen, ladled into cooling pans, and poured into jars.

During this time, most likely in February, Reuben would replenish the icehouse from a river or pond. Ice would be hauled back to the farm, trimmed, packed into the double wall of the icehouse (really more of a shack), then stuffed with sawdust to fill any air spaces. Now they had their cool storage area, one that would last far into the warmer months of spring and summer.[23]

One, two, or maybe three months would pass after the day of the slaughter before Zerelda would order the curing meat removed from the brine and smoked. If no smokehouse existed on the farm, an upside-down barrel or hogshead would do, once a foot-deep hole had been dug for the coals. After two to four weeks, the meat would be removed, wrapped in muslin, and hung someplace safe from rats.

By now, winter would be passing away. The "six weeks' want" would set in—the time when the stock of vegetables ran low, before new plantings could be gathered. They would have sloshed the wagon through the soft, wet roads of spring to buy spinach or eggplant or parsnip seeds from a merchant, then planted them in Zerelda's garden.[24] Fruit came in abundance with the humid heat of Missouri's summers, and it, too, had to be prepared. The Samuels might have made preserves, cooking the fruit with large amounts of sugar, canning it in the newly patented Mason jar. In the autumn, before the first frost dusted the fields, the vegetables had to be gathered, cleaned, and stored in dry boxes or pickled. And all throughout the warm part of the year, much of the cows' milk would be turned into butter and cheese through the art of separating, churning, salting, and, finally, storing in jars.[25]

No diary tells us what the daily chores entailed, or how the family filled its larder, but if the Samuel clan bore any resemblance to others in Clay County, we can trust that this was how life went by month after month, season by season. By the time the census taker came, in June 1860, to count the family, Jesse was twelve and attending school, together with sixteen-year-old Frank and ten-year-old Susan. In the fall, when Jesse turned thirteen, he enrolled for another year of studies—little realizing that it would be his last.[26]

The children and adults made up only a small part of the teeming population of life on the farm. Aside from the livestock, there were rodents, reptiles, insects, and bacteria that swarmed over the fields and into the buildings. Rats and mice posed a constant hazard to the food supply, as did the buzzing black fleet of flies; mosquitoes, horseflies, and gnats harried human skin; and many a Missouri farm child awoke at night to feel a snake sliding across his or her leg. In this age before aspirin, pain was a familiar companion, from nagging headaches to the agonies of a sprain or a broken bone. Soot and smoke were constantly present, thanks to the open fire in the kitchen and the candles and grease lamps that gave off a dim, flickering light.[27]

If all this seems like frontier life, it most certainly was not. Despite all the effort expended on food, despite the precarious existence, despite the four-month isolation each winter from St. Louis and other cities (when the frozen river kept steamboats downstream), the Samuel family was tied to the outer world with bonds far stronger than the cotton-baling twine made from Clay County's hemp. They were no subsistence farmers: they ran a profit-centered, commercial operation, intricately interwoven with the web of local and national business transactions that lifted long-settled Clay to prosperity. As early as 1837 a farmer from another river county noted, "There is a market for everything from an egg to a [hogshead] of tobacco. . . . The fact is [the] market is at every man's door."[28]

Reuben and Zerelda probably continued the farm's specialization in hemp, a trade that stretched from their fields to St. Louis factories, New Orleans warehouses, and Mississippi plantations. In February or March—after the previous fall's hemp crop had been dried, rotted, broken, and its fibers separated—Reuben would haul it to a warehouse in Liberty to be crushed into bales of up to five hundred pounds each. When the ice broke on the Missouri River and paddlewheelers began to chuff into Clay County's landings, Reuben would cart his bales to the waterfront, if he had not already sold them to a warehouse owner. These late February or March days filled market towns with a frenzy of activity. The levees would be crowded with stacks of crates and barrels; mules and oxen would pull heavily laden wagons down to the river through milling merchants, farmers, tobacco inspectors, and slaves; a cloud of smoke would rise from the forest of smokestacks as steamboats churned in to unload sugar, coffee, iron, plows, reapers, and newspapers. Then hogsheads of tobacco and bales of hemp would be rolled aboard, and muddy herds of hogs and mules would be driven onto the lower decks. Reuben (or the couple together) would spend a day or two in Liberty during these busy weeks, haggling with a commission merchant from St. Louis or a buyer from a local ropewalk. He would come away with a bundle of banknotes or, if all went well, a stack of precious-metal coin—cold, hard cash.[29]

In 1858, *Liberty Tribune* editor Robert Miller took his own census of this prosperous marketplace. Any visitor, he crowed, "will be led to exclaim, 'This is a great town for a new country.' " He counted a wagon, a copper, and a gunsmith shop; two livery stables, two carriage shops, two saddlers, and two tin and stove stores; three cobblers, three blacksmiths, three cabinet shops, and three housepainting and wallpapering businesses; four tailors; five carpenter shops; and no less than five millinery establishments (all owned and operated by women). There were bricklayers, stonemasons, and plasterers, not to mention the Clay Seminary for Young Ladies, and William Jewell College.[30] It might seem strange that only one gunsmith could be found in this western Missouri town, but guns (though common enough) did not define life in Clay County—at least, not yet. Congress grew so worried that California-bound migrants lacked the means to defend themselves, it passed a law that allowed them to buy army revolvers at cost.[31]

Clay County rattled ahead smartly, like a well-built carriage pulled by a well-tended team. Between 1850 and 1860 the white population surged up from 7,585 to 9,568. The town of Centerville sprouted not far from the Samuel farm in 1858. Neighbor Waltus Watkins emerged as a leading businessman and public spirit, building a large brick woolen mill in 1860. Rural stores popped up everywhere; neighbors gathered there to discuss politics or religion, phrenology or spiritualism—often over a little rye whisky, as they browsed through bolts of calico, bowls and plates, and green, unroasted coffee. Glittering (and sometimes gritty) entertainment could be had just down the road: horse races, traveling lecturers, minstrels, debating societies, theater, even an occasional ballet—or one of the sixty-one circuses and menageries that hurdy-gurdied through rural Missouri. And at home, the Samuel clan had abundant books and newspapers to read.[32]

For Jesse, who had witnessed years of turmoil and stress, the world had finally knit itself together again. As he wandered the farm and went to school and rode the wagon to town, he was not repulsed by the heavy odor of livestock, nor oppressed by swarming pests, nor frightened by the threat of epidemics. Restored to the farm where he was born, reunited with his family, he beheld the Zion that his father had seen. And presiding over it all was the towering presence of his mother, determined never to be a victim of circumstance again.

Zerelda called herself "a woman of fortitude and resolution." On that, all agreed. Everyone who ever met her came away impressed with the force of her personality and her lacerating tongue. "She has had the advantages of an early education," judged artist George Caleb Bingham, some years later, "and seems to be endowed with a vigorous intellect and masculine will." These were strong words, given that society's idealization of feminine frailty. Though future events would hone her edge to a lethal glint, even now she undoubtedly could cut the strongest man in a duel of words. One who later made an enemy of Zerelda would put it bluntly: "I regard her as being one of the worst women in this state." Opinionated, assertive, ferocious in social combat, this remarried widow played the proverbial tigress to her cubs, forming a fiercely protective bond with her sons. As the years passed, no matter what charges would be directed against Jesse and Frank, she would repeat a constant refrain: "She was proud of them."[33]

Such was the world that Zerelda lost and found again, a world of agriculture and commerce, of wariness and prosperity. And then there were the slaves, the silent chorus of the South. There were 3,455 of them in the county and seven in the Samuel home as of 1860. They were the source of the family's wealth, and the sign of a coming tribulation.

CHAPTER THREE

The Slaves

THE SILENT WITNESSES may be the most eloquent of all. The seven slaves knew better than anyone else the intimate world of the Samuel farm. They could recount with perfect clarity its fields and trees, each horse and hog, and each emotional quirk of Zerelda, Reuben, Frank, Jesse, and Susan. Indeed, though they were called "hands" or "servants" in the parlance of the times, their lives wound around this clan's existence more intricately than those of nearby cousins and friends.

In many ways, the black residents of the farm shaped the private realm in which Jesse Woodson James grew up, yet they can tell us nothing. In slave-regime Clay County, the written word was only white. Even the carefully completed grids of the census slave schedules offer only single names—Robert James in 1850, Reuben Samuel in 1860—with no names listed for the six and seven slaves, respectively; the enumerator recorded only age, sex, and color (black or mulatto). That very silence speaks volumes about this family and its society. And those slaves, though denied their voices, show us how the crisis of the age penetrated into the heart of the Samuel household.

A visitor to Missouri in 1860 could be forgiven for mistakenly believing that slavery was in decline. In contrast to the Deep South's vast plantations, tended by large gangs of black men and women, Missouri's family farms would reveal only one or two slaves each—and often none at all. In Mississippi and South Carolina, blacks outnumbered whites, as they nearly did in Louisiana, Florida, Georgia, and Alabama. But Missouri—with only 9.8 percent of its population enslaved, down from 12.8 percent in 1850—resembled colonial New York more than Carolina.[1]

Once a traveler stepped off a boat in St. Louis, she might think that she had left the South entirely. Almost 167,000 people teemed through the streets of the great city in 1860. Some 12,000 industrial workers manned its factories and workshops, creating an atmosphere more Yankee than Dixie. A cosmopolitan chorus of foreign languages and accents rose from its side-walks: three out of every five people in St. Louis arrived from overseas, the largest proportion of immigrants of any American city, including New York. The German or Irish populations alone, at 60,000 and 39,000 respec-tively, outnumbered the residents of the next largest city in Missouri. But fewer than one out of a hundred faces on those crowded streets was black. In 1856, the city even elected antislavery men as mayor and congressman (the latter being Frank Blair, Jr., from a famous political family).[2]

To some, St. Louis may have seemed to define Missouri; in fact, there was not one Missouri, but several.[3] There were the hubs of Westport, Kansas City, and St. Joseph on the western border, where Pacific-bound migrants and merchants prepared for the overland crossing, mingling with mountain men and Native Americans. There was the northern fringe, so close to Iowa, so like Iowa, with nearly all-white towns and family farms. There was the white and very poor southern fringe, the Ozark fringe, where scattered farmers scratched a bare subsistence out of the unforgiving hills. And then there was the heart and central artery of the state, the coun-ties arrayed along the Missouri River, the region that would be known as Little Dixie.

A Southerner who took a steamboat west up the river, chugging past Callaway, Boone, Cooper, Howard, Saline, and Lafayette Counties, would have felt at home. Here, one out of four, and sometimes one out of three, faces was black. In this region, the percentage of slaves in the population had remained the same from 1850 to 1860—or even increased in places. True, the number of slaves owned by the average master was half that of the Deep South (6.1 to 12.7); and true, it was even lower in Clay County (with a mean of only 5.3); and true, this agricultural district seemed a far cry from St. Louis's industrial dynamism[4]—but these slaveowning river counties were the great wheel that powered the entire state economy. In St. Louis's factories, Clay County's hemp was turned into rope and bag-ging for sale to Dixie's cotton plantations; Callaway County's hogs were slaughtered and packed to feed the great cities; Lafayette County's tobacco was turned into cigars and snuff. Many of the plows, harnesses, and car-riages produced in St. Louis's workshops were sold in those counties. Missouri remained an agricultural state, its wealth growing out of its soil— and the richest soil was along the Missouri River. Small wonder that the state university and capital had been placed in this region, or that the lead-ers of the ruling Democratic Party—a group known as the "Central Clique"—were all Missouri valley slaveowners.[5]

If a visitor from the Deep South continued on to Liberty landing, she would see scores of wagons rattling to and from the boats, filled with hemp and tobacco. These products brought wealth and commerce; they even fostered manufacturing, as seen in the tobacco stemmeries and ropewalks in every substantial town. The locals argued that only slaves could provide the year-round, backbreaking labor to raise these crops—and even Congressman Frank Blair agreed (Blair himself had owned slaves). Even if white workers were willing, Clay County's gentlemen would snort, they could hardly be had at any price. Slave labor, they claimed, was cheaper and more efficient. When traders from the Deep South came to purchase human beings, Missourians refused to sell, driving prices to record levels.[6]

A ride through the streets of Liberty would show black men and women laboring in every aspect of life: They served as teamsters, personal servants, maids, cooks, and skilled workers. At the courthouse steps or a probate sale, an auctioneer might be heard asking for bids on a man, trumpeting the man's skills as a carpenter, blacksmith, or stonemason. Almost every businessman owned one or more slaves, and they could be found in workshops, warehouses, ropewalks, and sawmills. The Southerners in Clay County were proud to have adapted chattel labor to a highly diversified economy. Owners with excess hands rented out their surplus; such hired slaves provided virtually all of the wage labor in the region (though the wages went to the owners). And despite the doubts of Yankee critics, slavery did nothing to slow the spread of technology. By 1860, local farmers spent just as much on machinery as their counterparts in the North, some $500 each. Slavery, locals believed, had made this region the most advanced, most commercial, most successful part of the great state of Missouri.[7]

So goes the tale of numbers. But a statistical overview strips the slave economy of its humanity—something white Missourians often did when they thought of their society. Farmers, preachers, coopers, and carriage makers viewed their bondservants through a lens that refracted their lives into numerical values, investments, *property*. Not all the slaves' names, however, have been lost. Along with the ovens, skillets, and pots in the inventory of Robert James's possessions made in December 1850, there appear six names, including "one black woman, Charlotte." She was the only adult among the slaves; the census states that she was thirty years old, more than a decade older than the eldest of the five children who complete the list.[8]

Decades later, Stella James reported, "I heard a great deal about Aunt Charlotte," using the classic American term for a senior female slave. Stella's grandmother-in-law Zerelda told her that Charlotte had belonged to her family and moved to Missouri with her and Robert. Of course, in

1842 the twenty-two-year-old Charlotte was no elderly "aunt." But whites fondly used the language of family to depict their ties with their slaves, ignoring the fact that the bonds were utterly involuntary at the other end. "As slavery was an organic part of the Southern household," notes historian Leeann Whites, "it became organic to the slaveholders' very conception of themselves as men and as women, as mothers and fathers." In Zerelda's eyes, Charlotte would have seemed less an aunt than a child—a dependent in her household, incapable of making decisions yet essential to family life.[9]

More than likely, Charlotte spent most of her waking hours in the kitchen. It would have been her, not Zerelda, who rendered the lard on slaughtering day, churned the butter, cooked dinner, washed dishes, boiled and scrubbed clothes. It would have been this tireless, enslaved young woman who bathed, clothed, and fed Frank and Jesse.

Charlotte's life wound intimately around those of this family, but she also belonged to the shadow society of Clay County's slaves. Many bondservants in Little Dixie received a limited freedom of movement during the daylight hours, and they used it to mingle with each other. In 1850, Elizabeth Carter observed both this mobility and the ties of slave society in a letter about a smallpox outbreak in the area near the James farm. One of the first victims, she noted, was a "negro man" on a nearby homestead. "While he had the fever raging upon him and before they knew what was the matter with him," she wrote, "there was a good many blacks to see him." This horrified Carter—not because the slaves socialized with each other so freely, but because they might spread the disease.[10]

Charlotte was a young woman when she arrived in Missouri in 1842, at an age when young women make romantic attachments where they can. She may even have accepted a proposal from a man enslaved on a nearby farm. In "abroad" marriages, as these weddings across property lines were called, the man would ask his master for permission; if granted, the plan would be put to the owner of the bride. Leland Wright in Howard County, for example, wrote to Abiel Leonard to tell him that his servant Flem wanted to wed one of Leonard's slaves. "I expect him to remain in my family," he added soothingly, "as long as he lives."[11]

Such assurances were rare. As property, each partner might be sold away at any given moment. One study of Boone County turned up documentation of thirty-six such weddings between 1830 and 1864; at least twenty-seven broke apart because at least one spouse was sold. Under the law, slave marriages simply did not exist, and owners did not hesitate to sunder them if it suited their finances.[12]

As with married adults, so too with children. As Robert James prospered, he acquired five new slaves, all minors: Nancy, age eleven in 1850;

Alexander, age nine; Maria, age eight; Mason, age six; and Hannah, age two. As to whether any of them were Charlotte's offspring, the minister's probate records offer no clues. The census, however, tells us that they were all black, not mulatto, which disperses any suspicion that the preacher fathered any of them himself.[13]

But most of the children probably passed into Robert's hands with a bill of sale. Most slaves were sold locally in Little Dixie, so he most likely went no farther than Liberty. Perhaps he stood in a crowd and made bids as a dealer held little Nancy or Mason on the auction block, or perhaps he went to an estate or bankruptcy sale. A slave dealer would ask for cash, but Robert could have paid half down for Alexander at an estate sale, settling the balance over the next nine to twelve months. By buying young he was buying cheap: little Hannah would have cost only $200, but her value would double, then triple through puberty. A shrewd investment indeed.[14]

These children had parents, of course, whom they would probably never see again. Even owners who freely purchased boys and girls sometimes acknowledged the agonies they caused. In October 1845, for example, J. Bull of Howard County dispatched a slave to Abiel Leonard to pay a debt. "I send you a little boy named Alick or Alicsander," he wrote. "He is about 3 or 4 years old, and the child of Caroline. I cannot be present [for the transfer]. The negroes will look to me for help and I cannot give it." These words say everything about the trade in children. No matter how many times black Missourians experienced such events, the pain and injustice remained fresh, incomprehensible, and unbearable.[15]

And so the wheels of commerce and Robert James's wagon brought a family of black children onto the farm, where they mingled with Frank, Jesse, and infant Susan. How easy it would be to conjure up a false image of this situation—to picture little Jesse (three years old in 1850) playing with a host of laughing black children close to his own age. Reality, of course, was far crueler. Everything spoke of the assumed, enforced inferiority of these children. Most of them probably slept in an outbuilding with Charlotte, in a simple, dirt-floor cabin, or in the kitchen in winter. They almost certainly ate separately from the white family, their fare quite often beans, potatoes, cornbread, and milk. "All us kids ate on da floor," recalled Louis Hill, another Missouri slave, "and da biggest dog got da mos'."[16]

In the summer, they went barefoot; for the winter, they perhaps received a pair of shoes. Judging from other farms, the boys wore nothing more than long, coarse shirts that hung down to their knees. When they reached the age of twelve or so, Zerelda might have given them heavy brown jeans, a couple of shirts, a hat, and a coat.[17] Studies of probate records suggest that most slaves received about as much medical care as their owners. Sometimes whites even paid tribute to the slaves' knowledge by approaching herb doctors. Here and there these black men and women might be found, hunting up remedy weed near springs, or collecting dogwood buds for use as a laxative, or butternut root for chills. Later they would prepare teas for clients who were suspicious of the mercury handed out by doctors.[18]

The black children on the James farm spent most of their lives at work. Nancy, Alexander, Maria, and Mason would have cut grass along fences, pulled weeds in Zerelda's garden, helped with the hoeing, fed the livestock, and carried water. Indoors they would cook, clean, iron, wash dishes, and scrub the laundry. Alexander would have shouldered the heaviest tasks: chopping wood, plowing, cutting hemp with a cradle scythe, beating the stalks with a flail called a swingletree to shake loose the seed, crushing the stalks on the hemp break with a large stone, then separating out the fibers.[19]

Robert James's demise may have more thoroughly shattered the lives of Charlotte's ad hoc black family than any others in the household. Robert Harris, the estate administrator, sold Alexander in 1851; the next year he rented out Nancy and Maria. It would not be surprising if Charlotte saw these children as her own, even if they were not hers by blood, but she had no control over their allocation.[20]

In 1860, the African majority on the Samuel farm looked very different than it had a decade earlier. Charlotte still presided, now forty years old, but (in addition to Alexander) Nancy, Mason, and Hannah were gone. Perhaps Zerelda and Reuben sold them to J. H. Adams, a dealer who toured the county in September 1856, specifically seeking young slaves without families. Or perhaps they carted these children to one of the permanent slave-trading houses in St. Joseph or Lexington, where R. J. White maintained a three-story pen. But the Samuels acquired more servants than they sent away. By 1860, Charlotte and eighteen-year-old Maria shared their quarters with a sixteen-year-old girl, a thirteen-year-old boy, an eight-year-old girl, and two little boys, ages three and one.[21]

Some of the children Zerelda and Reuben sold may have been Charlotte's (just as the toddlers may have been hers or Maria's). No matter, in Zerelda's eyes: the trade in bondservants was business, not philanthropy. But the relationship between master and slave was complicated, contradictory, and sometimes unsettling. Charlotte most likely shared emotional ties with her white possessors. She had attended Zerelda since they were both girls, and had helped to raise her mistress's children. This family, she knew, depended on her completely, and that knowledge may have fostered a sense of responsibility, satisfaction, and even loyalty.

Zerelda and her children most likely felt some real affection for Charlotte and the others in return. We can never know their true feelings, but fellow Baptist neighbors sometimes spoke of their slaves in the most intimate terms. Jane W. Gill, a devout member of Robert James's church, wrote "my children black and white." Slaveowners entertained a convoluted, paradoxical outlook. On one hand, they believed that blacks were intrinsically inferior; on the other, they implicitly acknowledged their humanity.[22]

Like any set of human relationships, those on the Samuel farm may have warped in surreptitious ways. Slaves often engaged in subtle acts of resistance—working slowly and sullenly, for example (though Missouri masters often assigned tasks with fixed targets, and financial incentives for finishing early). They would sometimes ruin food they were preparing, in the hopes that it might be given to them to eat, or they might steal it outright. And there are all the possible entanglements of two adolescent boys (Frank turned seventeen and Jesse thirteen in 1860) living with two girls, one eighteen and one sixteen.

Even if we imagine that all was happiness on the farm, that the hirings and sales of the children, the racial overlordship, meant little to the black majority—that Zerelda, Reuben, and the boys were all kindness and propriety—even in this blissful state, the humanity of the slaves would assert itself. "Whenever my condition was improved," wrote Frederick Douglass, "instead of it increasing my contentment, it only increased my desire to be free." Later he put it another way: "If a slave has a bad master, his ambition is to get a better; when he gets a better, he aspires to have the best; and when he gets the best, he aspires to be his own master."[23]

"I SEEN PEOPLE turned across barrels and whipped. Dey was whipped 'cause de white people was mean. Sometimes dey tied dem to trees and whipped 'em. Dey didn't have no clothes at all—dey was just like dey come into de world!" The words belonged to Marilda Pethy, a very old woman who was thinking back to when she was enslaved in Missouri. She did not recall being whipped herself; but the memory of seeing someone else beaten and humiliated still burned in her mind.[24]

No evidence exists that Zerelda or Reuben Samuel ever beat their slaves, nor was any whip listed on the probate inventory of Robert's possessions. And yet, as Pethy's memories show, the threat of violence by white masters hovered in the air. Frederick Douglass argued that such violence was essential to keep the slave from thinking of freedom; as the testimony of Pethy shows, its mere proximity proved effective. But the whip was also necessary for white Missourians' peace of mind. "There was a constant state of apprehension and uneasiness among most slave owners," wrote one resident of Clay County, "a fear not alone of an exodus, but of an insurrection on the part of the negroes."[25]

White Missourians' vulnerability began with the knowledge that their state was a slaveholding outpost pressed into the lines of the free states. In 1840, reports spread that the Underground Railroad—the secret network of abolitionists dedicated to helping slaves escape to the North—had formed new lines in Illinois and the Iowa Territory. Suspicions seemed to be confirmed when Missouri authorities captured abolitionists George Thompson, James Burr, and Alanson Work as they tried to smuggle slaves out of the state. Governor Thomas Reynolds declared that antislavery raiding parties were crossing into the state to steal its human property.[26] Fears of abolitionists and rebellious slaves even penetrated the churches. In 1844, the Methodists split into Northern and Southern factions over the issue of slavery; the Baptists followed in 1845 (a division that forced Robert James to stand firmly for slavery). In 1847, the state legislature prohibited slaves from gathering in any kind of assembly, barred any religious services that were led by a black minister (unless a white official was present), flatly outlawed the immigration of free black people into the state, and prohibited anyone from teaching a slave to read or write.

It also refined the rules for a traditional Southern institution, a feature of Missouri life since at least the 1820s: the patrol. The state government codified the power of counties, townships, and municipalities to form squads of civilians with the purpose of searching out and punishing escaped slaves—any black person twenty miles from home without a pass, or simply out after curfew (nine o'clock in most localities). Black Missourians called them "PAT-er-rollers"; how many runaways they actually caught is open to question, but they undoubtedly spread fear wherever they went.[27]

Tensions mounted. In Missouri, unlike the Deep South, slaves received trials for their offenses—but mob action became increasingly common. In 1850, a Clay County slave woman murdered her master with an axe, and implicated a white man in the plot. In May, a mob in Liberty broke into the county jail, hauled out the two suspects, and hanged them both. In October 1853, local slaveowner T. P. Diggs saw a runaway mingling with his field hands; the escapee, realizing that he had been discovered, stabbed Diggs to death. In the same month, the citizens of nearby Fayette held a mass meeting to "suppress insubordination among slaves." In August 1853, planter Eli Bass led a mob in Boone County that interrupted the trial of a bondman named Hiram, who was accused of raping a fifteen-year-old white girl. Prosecutor Odon Guitar announced that he wanted everyone to act "coolly, and do it decently in order." Coolly and decently, the orderly crowd hanged Hiram.[28]

Only 60 out of 87,422 Missouri bondservants ran off in 1850. A decade later, the numbers rose only to 99 out of 114,931. This ratio was higher than the national average of 1 out of every 4,919, though a Missouri slaveowner was still more likely to lose one of his hands to illness.[29] But it was the immense scale of the possibilities, not the minuscule size of probabilities, that dominated the thinking of white Missourians when it came to slave rebellions and escapes. Next to land, slaves represented the single most valuable type of property in the state; demand pushed prices ever upward, leading one historian to call the 1850s the "golden age of slave values." At the same time, whites had to confront the fact that this sort of property was fully conscious, with the entire range of human emotions, reactions, and aspirations. Inwardly, they knew that a slave who could master such skills as carpentry, blacksmithing, and stonemasonry also had the cunning to plot a revenge killing or an escape to free territory. Small wonder that whites wildly overreacted to the handful of runaways, or that they screeched (as the *St. Louis Democrat* did in 1859) that murders of masters were "alarmingly frequent" when in truth they were exceptionally rare.[30]

As the 1850s progressed, these fears increasingly led to action. In Platte County, two slaves landed in jail for preaching; in Chillicothe, a committee of vigilantes ordered minister David White to leave because of his insufficiently proslavery views; in St. Joseph, a college student who gave a vaguely antislavery talk had to flee for his life. There was resistance, of course, but white mobs increasingly enforced a rigid orthodoxy, almost a kind of thought control, in an edgy atmosphere verging on hysteria. Black, white—the enemy was everywhere.[31]

On the Samuel farm, those six or seven silent witnesses stood watch as these years unfolded. Yet their presence tells us that Jesse grew up in a household more black than white (if we count numbers alone); that he was raised as much by a black woman as a white one; that he was reared in a family that counted its wealth in human beings; that he saw children his own age bought and sold by his mother and his stepfather; that he grew up immersed in the implicit and explicit cruelties of slavery; that he learned from infancy that all this was as it should be, that African Americans were inferior, that their subjection was the inescapable basis of Southern society.

They also bear witness to the vitally important fact that Jesse and Frank came of age in an atmosphere of suspicion and anxiety. Slavery's confused cloud of mutual dependence and mutual fear cloaked the Samuel farm. Zerelda and her family relied on their slaves for their prosperity, yet they also had to see them as a potential threat, or at least as a potential loss. This defensive tension might have dissipated with time. But a peculiar confluence of events turned Clay County into center stage in a great national drama over the fate of slavery, and in that drama, Frank and Jesse would find lifelong roles.

On October 5, 1855, a small notice in the *Liberty Tribune* announced the September 25th marriage of Zerelda James Simms and Dr. Reuben Samuel.

The item might have been missed by the average reader, however, for much of the paper was devoted to another matter entirely. With emphatic language, editor Robert Miller urged the people of Clay to attend "a grand mass meeting of the pro-slavery party." At stake was the expansion of slavery into Kansas, the newly opened territory just a few miles west. On the issue of Kansas, Little Dixie's anxiety over its peculiar institution emerged as hard-bitten militancy, and that militancy was about to veer from lynchings and riots into open war.[32]

WAR MADE SLAVERY a matter of politics. Until the day when American troops marched into Mexico, Missouri politicians had generally ignored it, largely because of the Missouri Compromise, the agreement that had brought the state into the Union in 1820. Under its terms, slavery was forever barred in all the territory north of latitude 36°30′ (roughly the line of Missouri's southern border), with the exception of Missouri itself. A balance in the Senate between North and South was maintained in the years that followed as the territories were organized into an even number of free and slave states. The Missouri Compromise allowed the two great parties, the Democrats and the Whigs, to span both North and South by focusing on such national themes as banks, internal improvements, and tariffs (with Whigs in favor, Democrats opposed). Slavery remained an issue for a hard core of abolitionists, but the two parties largely suppressed it.

The Mexican War upset this balance—indeed, it toppled the scale itself. Victory over Mexico expanded the nation by a third, much of this new territory below the Missouri Compromise line. Northerners, accustomed to the idea that slavery had been fenced in, awoke to find that Southerners had their wagons hitched, ready to carry their human property all the way to the Pacific. So in 1846, Representative David Wilmot of Pennsylvania attached an amendment to an appropriations bill prohibiting the expansion of slavery into any territory acquired in the war. Dubbed the Wilmot Proviso, it passed in the House with votes from Northern congressmen of both parties, though the Senate blocked it.

Wilmot's amendment enraged Southerners. On January 19, 1849, Missouri state senator Claiborne F. Jackson sponsored a series of declarations, written by proslavery ideologue William B. Napton but immediately dubbed the "Jackson Resolutions." In ferocious language, these statements denounced abolitionism, proclaimed the right to carry slavery into the territories, and called for cooperation among Southern states against "Northern fanaticism." The legislature passed these startling resolutions by large majorities.[33]

Even the defeat of the Wilmot Proviso did not end the question of slavery in the new territories. The discovery of gold brought a vast number of Yankees to California, where they petitioned for admittance to the Union as a free state. In the convoluted Compromise of 1850, the South agreed, in return for the Fugitive Slave Act. This law guaranteed the cooperation of U.S. marshals in capturing escaped slaves—an unprecedented expansion of federal power at the insistence of self-proclaimed defenders of state sovereignty. Now it was the North's turn to be furious. State legislatures passed "personal liberty" laws in an attempt to nullify the act. In Boston and elsewhere, mobs attacked jails and freed recaptured slaves; in Christiana, Pennsylvania, two dozen armed black men battled a slave-catching party on September 11, 1851, killing the slaveowner who led it.[34]

"Although the loss of property is felt," said Senator James M. Mason of Virginia about such defiance, "the loss of honor is felt still more." Mason belonged to a small group of hard-line proslavery senators known as the F Street Mess (they boarded together on F Street in Washington, D.C.). The Mess's leader was a tall, quick-tempered Missouri Democrat, David Rice Atchison, a rawboned country lawyer given to hard liquor and plain speaking who was about to help change the direction of American history, and the life of young Jesse James of Clay County.[35]

Though Atchison's constituents often asked that the lands just west of Missouri be opened to settlement, the senator resisted because the Missouri Compromise—"that infamous restriction," he later called it—prohibited slavery there. The leaders of the Central Clique, the slaveowning Democrats who dominated Missouri politics, wholeheartedly agreed. "If we can't go there on the same terms, with all our property of every kind," Claiborne Jackson wrote to Atchison, "I say let the Indians have it *forever*. They are better neighbors than the abolitionists. . . . If this is to become 'free-nigger' territory, Missouri must become so too, for we can hardly keep our negroes here now." Jackson and Atchison shared an almost hysterical fear of antislavery designs on poor, exposed Missouri. "All the territories of the United States [are] to be abolitionized," Atchison declared on one occasion; "colonies are to be planted in all places where slavery and slave institutions can be assailed; and Kansas is now a favorite position."[36]

Atchison's use of the word "Kansas" sprang from an important new development in this struggle for the territories. At the end of 1853, Senator Stephen A. Douglas of Illinois became the champion of the plan to organize the territories west of Missouri. He was particularly interested because he wanted to promote a transcontinental railroad that would run through the region. On January 22, 1854, he reached an agreement with Atchison and the F Street Mess. The next day, he offered a bill to create two new territories—Kansas to the west of Missouri and Nebraska to the west of Iowa—and explicitly repeal the prohibition enshrined in the Missouri

Compromise. Instead, settlers would vote on whether they wanted slavery or not, an idea known as "popular sovereignty." On May 30, 1854, President Franklin Pierce signed the Kansas-Nebraska Act.[37]

PERHAPS NOTHING destroys a political system more quickly and efficiently than paranoia. The situation can be grave enough when one party to a quarrel believes the worst of the other, when it pictures its opponents as conspirators. But when both sides see the other as ruthless, treacherous, and unwilling to abide by the rules, then all room for compromise disappears.

The fantasies of scheming hordes of abolitionists conjured up by Atchison and Jackson were standard material in Southern newspapers and political speeches. "Northern resistance to the fugitive slave law," writes historian David Brion Davis, "aroused nightmare images of vast organizations of slave stealers who would drain the South of its wealth." Political argument and agreements would not stop abolitionists, they thought; only facts on the ground, the actual rooting of slavery in the territories, would preserve the peculiar institution.[38]

The North had its own paranoid, conspiratorial image of the South: the Slave Power. The phrase appeared in the 1830s, and abolitionists repeated it endlessly during the Wilmot Proviso controversy.[39] True abolitionists were hard to find in the North, but even racist Yankees feared and resented the Slave Power and its works. "Slavery withers and blights all it touches," asserted an Iowa politician, because it made it impossible for free workers to earn a decent living. Even worse was the ruling planter class. Nowhere on earth, claimed one Yankee, "are the people subjected to a sterner despotism than are the *white* population of our own Southern States." Northerners complained that slaveowners had maintained a persistent grip on the presidency, the Supreme Court, and the congressional leadership.[40]

If the Slave Power was to be stopped, it was in the territories. The question of extending slavery into new lands united Northern public opinion like nothing else. "We are all personally interested in this question, not indirectly and remotely as in a mere political abstraction—but directly, pecuniarily, and selfishly," declared politician Oliver Morton. "If we do not exclude slavery from the Territories, it will exclude us." David Wilmot himself drove home this point. No "morbid sympathy for the slave" moved him to offer his Proviso, he said. "The negro race already occupy enough of this fair continent," he argued. "I would preserve for free white labor a fair country . . . where the sons of toil, of my own race and color, can live without the disgrace which association with negro slavery brings upon free labor."[41]

When the Kansas-Nebraska Act repealed the Missouri Compromise, outrage erupted, instantly remaking the political landscape. The Whig Party virtually dissolved: its Northern members refused to accept the repeal, while its Southern members refused to remain in a party that rejected slaveowners' rights in the territories. Many Whigs fled to the secretive American Party, nicknamed the Know-Nothing Party (since its members refused to say anything about its workings), which rested on two foundations: a nationalistic devotion to the Union, and a fear and hatred of foreigners. Less xenophobic Yankee politicians formed temporary coalitions, identifying themselves simply as "anti-Nebraska." As early as May 9, 1854, thirty congressmen endorsed a new name that finally stuck: they called themselves the Republicans.[42]

Amid all this political fury, a group of abolitionists saw the need for direct action to stop the Slave Power. In Massachusetts—probably the only stronghold of humanitarian abolitionism in the country—legislator Eli Thayer addressed a public meeting in Worcester on March 11, 1854. If popular sovereignty would decide the fate of Kansas, he argued, they should form a company to help antislavery settlers fill up the territory. A month later, a charter was issued to the Massachusetts Emigrant Aid Society (later renamed the New England Emigrant Aid Society). Other companies were organized in Washington, D.C., New York, and Connecticut. The fate of Kansas would be decided by a race between North and South.[43]

JESSE JAMES WAS a mere boy in the 1850s, doing nothing that contemporaries found worth recording, and there is little to be said about him during his childhood. But his world was changing rapidly, preparing a place for him to stand and command attention.

Even before he reached adulthood, his life would become one of ceaseless conflict. And the conflicts that would frame his existence were to be both deep and wide, ranging from a nation-splitting war to invisible lines of enmity that would sunder one farm from another in the fields all around his mother's house. Before he reached the age of ten, the great struggle had already begun. It was during these years of peace and prosperity in this Missouri Zion that the great issues of the age penetrated to the grass roots of Clay County, dividing one family from the next.

As American politics exploded over the Kansas-Nebraska Act, David Atchison departed Washington in the summer of 1854, bound for Missouri. The nation's future, he believed, would be decided on the ground in the Kansas Territory. "We are playing for a mighty stake," he wrote to messmate Robert Hunter. "If we win we carry slavery to the Pacific Ocean, if we fail we lose Missouri, Arkansas, and Texas and all the territories. The game must be played boldly," he added, observing darkly, "I know that the Union as it exists is on the other side."[44]

When Atchison stepped off the steamboat *Australia* in Platte County at the beginning of August, he found that the people had already begun to organize. A full year earlier, a group of men in Liberty had formed a paramilitary company to fight abolitionists. Starting in June 1854, public meetings on Kansas had taken place each week across western Missouri. In Weston, a thousand men joined the new Platte County Self-Defensive Association on July 20, 1854.[45]

The leader of this group was Benjamin F. Stringfellow, one of Atchison's closest allies. A former state attorney general, he and his brother now led the proslavery extremists under Atchison's command. He and Atchison launched a speaking tour to organize secret, armed organizations based on the Platte County model. They called these bodies "Blue Lodges," "Sons of the South," or "Social Bands." With deadly seriousness, the members greeted each other with secret signs and handshakes; they used passwords, saying, "Sound on the goose" and "Alright on the hemp," and wore strands of hemp in their buttonholes. They also drilled for combat in hidden camps, including several in Clay County.[46]

"We will have difficulty with the negro thieves in Kansas," Atchison wrote to Secretary of War Jefferson Davis on September 24, 1854, referring to the abolitionist emigrant-aid societies. "They are resolved, they say, to keep the slave holder out, and our people are resolved to go in and take their '*niggers*' with them." He bluntly planned to win at all costs. "We will before six months rolls around, have the Devil to pay in Kansas and this State," he added. "We are organizing to meet their organization. We will be compelled to shoot, burn & hang, but the thing will soon be over. We intend to '*Mormonize*' the Abolitionists." This last sentence was a dark reference to the mob attacks that had driven the Mormons out of Missouri and later Illinois, at the cost of many lives.[47]

Over the next several months, Atchison organized the systematic theft of Kansas elections. With two Bowie knives and four revolvers thrust under his belt, he roused mass meetings in Liberty and elsewhere, led columns of proslavery Missourians across the border, cast fraudulent ballots, then promptly rode home again. An ever-increasing majority of actual Kansas residents, however, were "free soil," and they were outraged. "What are we? Subjects, slaves of Missouri," roared Charles Robinson at an Independence Day rally in Lawrence (a town created by the New England Emigrant Aid Society). "We must not only see black slavery planted in our midst, and against our wishes, but we must become slaves ourselves."[48]

Both sides prepared for open warfare as 1855 drew to a close. Charles Robinson wrote to allies in New England, appealing for rifles and ammunition. Free-state men with sharper and harder edges—James Lane, James Montgomery, Charles R. "Doc" Jennison, and John Brown ("Old Brown," as everyone called him)—assembled bands of antislavery "jayhawkers" and demanded retaliation. On the other side were proslavery Missourians, derided by the freesoilers as "border ruffians." It was a name they gloried in: merchants renamed their businesses "Border Ruffian Co." or "Border-Ruffian Store." George S. Withers, a proslavery leader in Clay County, even named his son Border Ruffian Withers. Many Missouri notables, including Claiborne F. Jackson and Joseph O. Shelby (owner of a ropewalk in Waverly and one of the wealthiest slaveowners in the state), organized armed squads to fight in Kansas.[49]

Then came the first killing, on November 21, 1855.[50] That death set off a year of warfare in Kansas—a year of complicated maneuvers, small-scale skirmishes, and occasional pitched battles between free-state jayhawkers, proslavery settlers, squads of border ruffians, and a handful of federal troops—that dominated life in Clay County. In the opening days of combat, two hundred men from Clay collected $1,000 from local citizens, purchased arms and equipment, and ferried over the Missouri River to fight. On December 4, 1855, approximately one hundred local men stormed the federal arsenal in Liberty, arresting the major in command and removing rifles, pistols, cannons, and a large store of ammunition, which they conveyed to border ruffian camps in Kansas. In March 1856, a meeting at the Liberty courthouse raised a large amount of money for the cause. In June, the most prominent local politicians organized the Pro-Slavery Aid Association. Meanwhile young men purchased firearms, mounted their horses, and rode to join the skirmishes and raids.[51]

On May 21, 1856, Atchison joined eight hundred border ruffians in the looting of Lawrence.[52] John Brown led his sons on a raid against proslavery settlers and murdered five. Columns under Brown, Atchison, Jim Lane, and others crisscrossed the land.[53] Atchison ordered the Missouri River closed to free-state migrants and goods during the summer of 1856. Armed squads of men stood guard along the waterfront in Platte, Clay, Lafayette, and Jackson Counties; they stomped aboard each steamboat, interrogated the passengers, and hauled out anyone who seemed suspicious. "We give you no mere rumors," Atchison declared to the people of Missouri on August 16, 1856, "but a simple statement of undoubted facts. We say to you that war, organized, matured, is now being waged by the Abolitionists.

And we call on all who are not prepared to see their friends butchered, to be driven themselves from their homes, to rally instantly to the rescue!"

In September, he led perhaps as many as three thousand men into Kansas in an attempt to trap the forces under Jim Lane. Instead, he encountered the new federal governor, John W. Geary (the third in the troubled territory's brief history). Geary told Atchison that he intended to use his now-reinforced U.S. troops to vigorously suppress the militia on both sides. The tall chieftain of the border ruffians agreed to send his men home. Geary kept his word. The fighting slowed, scattered, then finally stopped. After the loss of perhaps two hundred lives, the war in Kansas was over. And the freesoil settlers continued to pour in.[54]

In many ways, the bloodshed in Kansas proved to be both a precipitating factor in the outbreak of the Civil War and a first skirmish in the conflict between North and South. But the Kansas fight played another, largely overlooked role. The proslavery mobilization divided Missourians against each other. It created a hard core of militants who championed the state's Southern identity, battling a prevailing sense that Missouri was more West than South.[55] The border ruffian organizations swiftly marched beyond mainstream opinion, arguing that slavery mattered more than the Union itself. And as they did so, they became increasingly intolerant.

The Platte County Self-Defensive Association, Clay County's Pro-Slavery Aid Association, the Blue Lodges, and all the other proslavery bodies had another purpose besides conquering Kansas: social and political control. From the beginning, they set out to stifle white dissent. Benjamin Stringfellow began by targeting Frederick Starr, a Presbyterian minister in Weston from the quietly abolitionist American Home Missionary Association. On July 29, 1854, the Platte County Self-Defensive Association put Starr on trial in his own church. Southern civilization, Stringfellow declared to the crowd, was superior to that of the North; only in the slave states could a white man truly be free. "Every man who works for his living is a slave," he shouted, "and every poor white working woman a whore."

The proslavery extremists demanded absolute unity in the white community. On August 9, 1854, the Platte association called for a boycott of those who did not agree with them. In the spring of 1855, a committee banged on Starr's door, hauled him out, and bundled him onto a steamboat to St. Louis. On April 14, a crowd stormed into the village of Parkville, Platte County, and attacked the offices of the *Parkville Industrial Luminary*. The paper had earned the hatred of the extremists by taking a freesoil stand on Kansas—and by remarking on Atchison's tendency to give speeches while drunk. A mass meeting gathered in the Liberty courthouse on April 21 to hear Stringfellow speak, and heartily endorsed the destruction of the *Industrial Luminary*. It passed its own ominous resolution: "We will begin at

home, and rid ourselves of the traitors harbored in our midst." To say anything "calculated to render slaves discontented, to irritate them to escape or
rebel," it stated, "is not an exercise of the 'liberty of speech,' but is an act of
positive crime of the highest grade, and should receive summary and exem-
plary punishment."[56]

As Atchison's forces crushed dissent in Missouri, they polished and
hardened their arguments. Stringfellow authored *Negro Slavery; No Evil; or
the North and the South*. Stringfellow's brother edited the *Leavenworth
Squatter Sovereign*, a ferociously proslavery newspaper. Robert Miller, editor of the *Liberty Tribune*, followed their lead. "Where there is no legal
sanction of slavery the *masses*, the laboring portion of the people, are
oppressed and run over," he wrote.

But Miller was not in the same camp with Stringfellow, Atchison, and
the others. He had pitched his tent a little farther off, where most Missourians could be found. At bottom, he defended slavery because it was "indispensible to the preservation of the Union, and to the great principles of
Republican Liberty which are secured by the Federal Constitution."[57]
Miller's Unionism marked a very fine distinction between himself and the
Atchison extremists—but it mattered immensely to those on his side of the
line. He was a Whig, struggling like all Missouri Whigs to cling to his party
even as it disintegrated. The Whigs, wrote party elder James S. Rollins in
February 1855, were "ready to resist illegal Northern aggression and abolitionism on the one hand, and to suppress the Southern fanaticism and nul-
lification on the other." In other words, they supported the extension of
slavery, but they would not destroy the Union in the process. Like most
Missourians, including some Democrats, they saw their state as part of the
border West—a section with strong affinities for the South, but regionally
distinct from it. They placed themselves in the middle, both geographically
and ideologically.[58]

Once the national party came crashing down, Rollins and most Missouri Whigs moved into the American (or Know-Nothing) Party. In the
fall of 1855, Clay County's farmers organized Know-Nothing councils in
most townships; like the Blue Lodges, they adopted secret signs, handshakes, and passwords (a favorite was "Have you seen Sam?," meaning
Uncle Sam). Several prominent slaveowners, including brothers James H.
Moss and O. P. Moss, joined the new party. They formalized their organization with a meeting at the Liberty courthouse on January 1, 1856, where
they passed a resolution firmly condemning Southern secessionism. The
party even carried the county in the presidential election that fall.[59]

The Know-Nothings' success in Clay was only one sign of the widespread dissent against the extremism of Atchison's Southern-rights
Democrats. As early as September 1, 1854, a large group in Weston

denounced the Platte County Self-Defensive Association, which was soon replaced by the secretive Blue Lodges. In Parkville, a body of citizens eventually spoke out against the destruction of the *Industrial Luminary;* the owner even won damages in court for his losses.[60]

In standing for slavery *and* the Union, Missouri's Whig/Americans balanced on a very slender wire. Miller received threats when he mildly suggested in the *Liberty Tribune* that the destruction of the *Industrial Luminary* might have been excessive. On June 2, 1855, a large public meeting in Columbia met to support the spread of slavery into Kansas, but the resolutions offered by Whigs James Rollins and Odon Guitar were not enough for hard-line Democrats, who threatened violence unless the meeting called for armed force against abolitionists. In June 1856, a proslavery mob attacked Darius Sessions, a Know-Nothing leader in Clay County, who was saved from death by the intervention of a few neighbors.[61]

On July 12, 1855, a large proslavery convention gathered at Lexington, across the river in Lafayette County. The 205 delegates included David Atchison, Claiborne Jackson, and Governor Sterling Price. The meeting endorsed a set of resolutions that carefully papered over the split between the extremists and moderates, between standard-bearers of the South and those of the border West. But the division could be seen by all who cared to look for it. "Let us . . . save the Union if possible from the vandal assaults of abolitionist traitors," declared secessionist James Shannon on the second day. "If a dissolution is forced upon us by domestic traitors," he added grimly, "then I, for one, say . . . we will stand to our arms."[62]

Through all this angry rhetoric, Whigs and some of the more moderate Democrats could be seen nervously edging away from the fire-eaters (as secessionists were called). Of course, there was far more to Missouri politics than the tension between revolver-waving border ruffians and their Union-minded neighbors. The public life of the state can be compared to a frozen river, seamed with dozens of cracks—but this was the one that would split open the sheet of ice and send everyone plunging into the torrent below. And once the drowning were submerged in its chilling waters, they would claw each other without pity.

Out of those waters, Jesse James would emerge transformed, baptized in horrors that had their origins in these tumultuous years of his childhood. As time would soon show, his mother held decided opinions about the crisis enveloping the nation and dividing her neighbors. Sharp-tongued, intelligent, outspoken, she sided with the large and active community of proslavery militants in Clay County—the men who drilled and marched and went off to fight the abolitionists, who returned and hounded those who doubted Missouri's sisterhood with the South. The crisis struck close to the hearth of Zerelda's own home: slaves were her most valuable property, and free-state jayhawkers were not very far away. Through both the headline-grabbing Kansas struggle and pure self-interest, a Southern identity rooted itself firmly in her household.

From the age of eight, Jesse lived a life imbued with a cause, immersed in a militant air of defiance that rang from dinner-table conversation to churchyard talk to the tramp of border ruffian squads riding through the countryside. They would be ready, the people assured each other; they would fight for their rights and their property. But even here, in fire-eating Clay County, the population was not unanimous; the harder the proslavery extremists pushed, the greater the determination of some residents to preserve the Union at all costs. Already some could hear the ice cracking beneath their feet.[63]

PART TWO

Fire

1861–1865

How doth the city sit solitary, that was full of people; how is she become a widow! She that was great among nations, a princess among the provinces, how is she become a tributary! . . . The Lord hath accomplished his fury; he hath poured out his fierce anger, and hath kindled a fire in Zion, and it hath devoured its foundations.

—Lamentations 1:1–2, 4:11

Each day I live proves to me the total depravity of man.

—Sarah P. Harlan
Haynesville, Missouri
June 9, 1865

CANADA

MICHIGAN

Detroit

NEW YORK

VT.

N.H.

MASS.

CONN.

PENNSYLVANIA

New York

NEW JERSEY

Philadelphia

ANA

OHIO

Columbus

GETTYSBURG✕

Baltimore

MARYLAND

polis

WEST
VIRGINIA
(1863)

Washington,
D.C.

DELAWARE

Louisville

Richmond

ENTUCKY

VIRGINIA

ville

NESSEE

NORTH
CAROLINA

Raleigh

SOUTH
CAROLINA

Wilmington

Atlanta

Charleston

AMA

GEORGIA

gomery

Savannah

Tallahassee

FLORIDA

The Civil War

Union States and Territories

Confederate States

Border States

Slave states which did not secede
from the Union; West Virginia
seceded from Virginia in 1861 and
joined the Union as a state in 1863

O   MILES   200

CHAPTER FOUR

Rebels

IN EARLY MAY 1861, as the days swelled into the cool fullness of
spring, Frank James slid into a saddle or mounted a wagon seat and set
out on the short ride into the village of Centerville. The slender, long-
faced eighteen-year-old would have ridden with his quiet stepfather and
probably his forceful mother. It would not have been strange if they took
his thirteen-year-old brother Jesse as well, for this was a great and memorable occasion. Frank was going to war.

The people of Missouri traditionally relied on mass meetings to express
their opinions. They gathered in courthouses, churches, and town squares
to speak on matters great and small, from unruly slaves to demands for a
local railroad (like the one planned for Clay County). But as the members
of the Samuel family joined their neighbors at a rally in Centerville, there
was only one issue to be discussed. Days before, on April 12, 1861, rebel
troops in South Carolina had fired on Fort Sumter in Charleston harbor.
On April 14, the bastion's Federal garrison had surrendered. On April 15,
President Abraham Lincoln had called for seventy-five thousand troops to
suppress the Southern insurrection. And on April 20, the conflict had come
to Clay County, when a group of local secessionists seized the U.S. arsenal
in Liberty. Now citizens were gathering in every village and crossroads in
the county to voice their feelings on the war erupting around them.

So Frank and Reuben and perhaps Zerelda and Jesse joined their fellow
farmers and merchants in Centerville, where conversations turned from
hemp prices, tobacco shipments, and the latest marriage to a set of resolutions, prepared by a committee over the previous week.

"WHEREAS," the preamble began, "civil war has been inaugurated
in the United States by the extreme men of the North and the South, and
whereas Missouri occupies a central position between the two extremes,
and has hitherto earnestly opposed all hostile demonstrations . . ."

It was a good beginning, neatly capturing the crowd's mixed emotions in these worrisome days. Some of them, like most Missourians, hoped to stay out of the impending war. They honestly felt themselves to be part of a distinct section of the country, the western border, that was caught in the middle. But Clay County was also home to many of the state's most militant proslavery partisans, who had come to strongly identify with the South during the Kansas conflict. Their influence would soon be seen as the resolutions proceeded.

"*Resolved*," the document continued, "That the true policy at present is to maintain an independent position within the Union, holding her soil and institutions [i.e., slavery] sacred against invasion . . . from any quarter whatever." To the audience, this was a modest statement of border-state neutrality. The proslavery fire-eaters may even have seen it as a concession to the moderates in the crowd. But it was no Unionism. The entire thrust of this assertion was directed against the federal government; certainly the South was not threatening to invade, let alone undo slavery. Indeed, the resolutions grew more militant as they progressed. "*Resolved*," that Missouri should supply no troops for the Federal army. "*Resolved*," that, if forced to fight, they should stand with the South. "*Resolved*," that they should form an independent military company to that end. The crowd gave its unanimous assent. After the briefest nod toward moderation, the people had pledged their sons and husbands to war.

Forty men stood to be sworn into the company, from the newly minted captain down to the twenty-eight privates—including that sober eighteen-year-old, Frank James. Jesse's feelings, as his brother became a soldier, were never recorded. Perhaps he was happy for Frank, but he also might have been a bit jealous. According to conventional wisdom, the war would be over by his fourteenth birthday, and Jesse himself would never have a chance to fight.[1]

ON THE PRINTED page, the Civil War can seem a sudden thing. Bracketed by those tidy dates, 1861 and 1865, it appears as a self-contained story, beginning with a bombardment and ending in surrender. To young Jesse and his family, however, it was a murky experience, lacking the clarity of hindsight. As they had moved forward toward 1861, war loomed ahead, anticipated but not certain. In 1858, Republican William H. Seward called the struggle between North and South the "irrepressible conflict"; but no one could tell if the two sides would actually resort to arms.[2]

As Jesse approached and passed into adolescence, the air was heavy with this paradoxical sense of inevitability and uncertainty. Even though the fighting in Kansas died down after 1857, the territory's fate continued to cloud the public debate. "If Kansas is *driven out of the Union for being a Slave State*," demanded Senator James Hammond of South Carolina, "can any Slave State remain in it with honor?" The tension ran so high that a wild fistfight broke out in Congress, involving some fifty representatives. "All things here," commented Georgia congressman Alexander Stephens, "are tending my mind to the conclusion that the Union cannot and will not last long." In the end, Kansas moved toward becoming a free state in 1861, David Atchison retired to his farm in Missouri, and the white South seethed.[3]

But the lingering ghost of the border war continued to haunt Missouri. In May 1858, a border ruffian band gunned down nine freesoil farmers in Kansas, killing five. On December 20, John Brown led a raid into Vernon County (the eighth such foray into Missouri), freeing eleven slaves and killing one slaveowner. Less than a year later, he struck against the Slave Power for the last time, at Harper's Ferry. In November 1860, Charles "Doc" Jennison led his band of freesoil jayhawkers on another strike from Kansas. More than six hundred militiamen marched from St. Louis to protect the western border, adding to the sense that the state was already—or still—at war.[4]

By then, the hazy mirage of a much bigger war—the long-feared war between North and South—had finally appeared on the horizon. In April 1860, the Democratic Party's national convention had broken apart over the extension of slavery into the territories. After the Republicans, old Whig centrists, and Southern fire-eaters finished their work, a total of four serious candidates ended up on the ballot for president in 1860.[5]

Jesse was just twelve that summer. He may well have worried about the drought that crisped Clay County's fields more than he worried about the presidential election. "Jesse is light-hearted, reckless, devil-may-care," a close friend wrote more than a decade later; Frank, on the other hand, was "sober, sedate." Even at this early age, the distinction between the exuberant younger brother and his studious senior would have been apparent. "Jesse laughs at everything—Frank at nothing at all," the friend observed. But Jesse was also thoughtful, he added; he "discusses the whys and wherefores" of things. Even at age twelve, he would have noticed the splash and rush of the tide of events.[6]

Missouri voters followed the national trend, splitting into secession-ready Democrats, regular (Unionist) Democrats, and Whig/Know-Nothings (now gathered in the Constitutional Union Party). Only St. Louis, with its many antislavery Germans, offered the Republicans a foothold. White Missourians referred to Abraham Lincoln and his supporters as "Black Republicans," a racist twist on the term for Europe's revolutionaries of 1848, the "Red Republicans." Southern fire-eaters made clear that secession would be the consequence of a Lincoln victory. Senator Robert Toombs of Georgia had openly declared that the South could "never permit this Federal government to pass into the traitorous hands of the Black Republican party." South Carolina Congressman Laurence M. Keitt believed that slaves would rebel if Lincoln won. "I see poison in the wells of Texas—and fire for the houses in Alabama," he fretted. *"It is enough to risk disunion on."*[7]

Missourians lined up to cast ballots for governor in August and narrowly elected the regular Democratic candidate, Claiborne F. Jackson. But Democrats felt grim as they looked ahead to the national election in November. "I think the future prospects look gloomy," wrote T. M. Scruggs from Clay County. Indeed, Lincoln swept the North, giving him the presidency despite his loss of every slave state. South Carolina promptly seceded from the Union, on December 20, 1860. The dissolution of the republic, long predicted, long feared, perhaps never quite believed, had finally come true. Mississippi seceded on January 9, 1861, followed by Florida, Alabama, Georgia, Louisiana, and finally Texas, on February 1. On February 4, all these states sent delegates to Montgomery, Alabama, to organize the Confederate States of America.[8]

What to do? If Missouri seceded, it would have no Fugitive Slave Act to help retrieve its runaways. "Howard County is true to the Union," wrote Whig leader Abiel Leonard. "Our slaveholders think it is the sure bulwark of our slave property." Ironically, slavery was leading many in Missouri, especially old Whigs, to cling more tightly to the Union.[9]

The situation was volatile, and opinions in Clay County seemed to shift every day. Because of the mobilization of border ruffians over the Kansas struggle and their campaign of harassment against dissenters within the county, there now existed a hard core of militants on either side who struggled to capture the public mind. Four days after South Carolina seceded, a group of secessionists in Liberty organized an armed company of "minute men." On January 28, 1861, a group of loyalists (or "unconditional Unionists") responded with a rally at the county courthouse. On February 1, a mass meeting for "Southern Rights" gathered at the same place. But Whig politician James H. Moss interrupted the proceedings, spoke eloquently for the Union, and persuaded the crowd to pass resolutions condemning secession. The political crisis brought business to a halt. Starting in December 1860, almost all the banks in Missouri had stopped redeeming their notes in gold.[10]

When the new governor, Claiborne F. Jackson, took the oath of office in Jefferson City, on January 3, he sought to seize control of these chaotic events. In his inaugural address, the former border ruffian and sponsor of the extremist Jackson Resolutions refused to offer "submission to a [federal] government on terms of inequality and subordination." The very morning of Jackson's inaugural, Lieutenant Governor Thomas Caute Reynolds secretly met with Southern congressmen in Washington to plan for Missouri's secession; among other things, Reynolds agreed to seize the large Federal arsenal in St. Louis, which housed some sixty thousand firearms. In Jefferson City, Jackson convinced the General Assembly (as the legislature was called) to take control of the militia and constabulary of St. Louis away from its antislavery citizens and put it in the hands of a police board appointed by the governor. The legislators also set February 18, 1861, as the date for a special election for a statewide convention that would decide the question of secession.[11]

In the Unionist camp, Congressman Frank Blair worked frantically to keep the state in the Union. A personal enemy of David Atchison, Blair had founded the Republican Party in the state, relying heavily on the support of German immigrants. Now he armed Home Guard units of his "Dutch" allies in order to defend St. Louis in the event of a crisis. Calling in favors from the outgoing administration, he arranged for additional troops to protect the arsenal; they arrived under the command of a combative Connecticut Yankee, Captain Nathaniel Lyon.

The state convention on secession met in St. Louis on March 4, the day of Lincoln's inaugural, in a thickening atmosphere of crisis. Secessionist forces in the city were organizing their own companies of minute men. Blair narrowly survived an assassination attempt. Intrigue bubbled on both sides. But there was no doubt about what the convention would decide. The delegates' sentiments could be seen in the decor: oversized U.S. flags and stars-and-stripes bunting. Even Clay County had elected a Unionist slate of delegates, headed by James H. Moss. When a commissioner from the new Confederate States of America made his plea to the convention, he had to raise his voice to be heard above the hisses. Before adjourning on March 22, the assembly voted ninety-eight to one against secession.[12]

Governor Jackson, it seemed, had been checkmated. Then came news of the Confederate attack on Fort Sumter and Lincoln's call for seventy-five thousand soldiers to put down the rebellion. The breathtaking impact of those events can scarcely be imagined. Thousands of Missourians who had hesitated to secede themselves angrily rejected the idea of going to war against the South. In Clay County, crowds cheered for South Carolina and waved rebel flags. On April 20, secessionist Henry L. Routt gathered a company of two hundred men and captured the small Federal arsenal in Liberty. The mayor of St. Joseph, M. Jeff Thompson, drafted a confident letter to Confederate president Jefferson Davis. "I . . . have reasonable expectations now," he wrote on May 6, "that Missouri will soon wheel into line with her Southern sisters."[13]

Both sides prepared for open war. The state militia established Camp Jackson in St. Louis, where 890 men trained for combat. At Governor Jackson's request, Jefferson Davis sent siege artillery for an attack on the federal arsenal in the city. Lyon mustered Frank Blair's Home Guards into the U.S. Army and smuggled the arsenal's weapons to safety in Illinois. Blair, meanwhile, secured a commission for Lyon as a brigadier general of U.S. Volunteers. All across the state, the countryside buzzed with military activity as amateurs on both sides raised homegrown companies. In Clay County, Frank James and his fellow recruits learned the rudiments of military drill under equally inexperienced officers. Paper money was now virtually worthless, hemp markets in the South were closed off, hog and tobacco shipments to St. Louis were thrown into doubt. Neighbors eyed each other suspiciously in the streets of Liberty; outspoken Unionists found themselves shunned by old friends.[14]

Who would strike first? Lyon knew of the plans for an attack on the arsenal, but he had already removed its valuable supply of arms; he also had more than enough troops to stand off any assault. Politically, he had every reason to wait. As long as the secessionist militia chief, Daniel Frost, made no hostile moves, his encampment was entirely legal. Moreover, a first strike by Frost would unleash a Unionist wave of indignation in Missouri.

On May 10, Lyon's combativeness and patriotic indignation got the best of him. Moving swiftly, he surrounded Camp Jackson with his German volunteers and forced the surrender of the militiamen there. Then he marched his prisoners back to the arsenal through the St. Louis streets, which were lined with onlookers. A shot rang out; the inexperienced soldiers fired back; twenty-eight civilians died in the mayhem.[15]

The capture of Frost's camp removed any secessionist threat to St. Louis, but it was little short of a catastrophe for the Federal cause. Lyon was seen as launching an unprovoked attack, and when his troops opened fire on a civilian crowd, he was seen as a ruthless butcher. The shock of it turned borderline Unionists into secessionists, and brought rebellion to the fore. The legislature abruptly reorganized the militia as the Missouri State Guard and gave the governor sweeping emergency powers. The president of the convention on secession, former governor (and Mexican War general) Sterling Price, rushed to Jefferson City, where Jackson made him the guard's commander. In Liberty, a delegation of Clay County women presented secessionist leader Henry L. Routt with a flag of Missouri as he prepared to lead a company to help defend Jefferson City.[16]

Even after all this, however, it still seemed as if war in Missouri would be averted. On May 21, General Price signed a truce with Lyon's military superior, General William S. Harney. Harney wished to avoid further bloodshed, while Price and Jackson wanted more time to prepare their troops.[17] But Frank Blair pulled strings in Washington (including the one attached to his brother Montgomery, the new postmaster general): he had Harney removed, leaving the decisive Lyon in charge. On Monday, June 11, 1861, Lyon confronted Jackson and Price in a tense meeting at the luxurious Planter's House hotel in St. Louis. Missouri, he told them, could not be neutral, let alone Confederate. "Better, sir, far better," he thundered, "that the blood of every man, woman, and child within the limits of the State should flow, than that she should defy the Federal government. This means war." They had one hour to leave the city, he told them. Then he turned and stormed out of the room.[18]

Now Jesse and his family waved good-bye to Frank as he marched off to war in the second week of June. He was an amateur indeed. He and his ragged band from Centerville, like the rest of the army they joined, wore no uniforms. Officers pinned bits of calico to their shirts to designate their rank. Even Price rode about in a dirty white flannel suit, a "stout farmer-looking old gentleman," in the words of one militiaman. Many of the rebel troops Frank met did not have a gun.[19]

After the Clay County recruits crossed the Missouri River on June 13 to rendezvous with Price, the Samuel family waited for news of the war. Word came that Lyon had swept out of St. Louis; that he had seized Jefferson City; that he had routed the State Guard at Boonville. As Jackson and Price hastily retreated toward Arkansas, it became clear that secessionist feeling in the rest of Missouri was not what it was in Clay County. A pitiful six thousand men had responded to the governor's call for fifty thousand volunteers.[20]

But how quickly the fortunes of war can change. One moment, it appeared that Lyon had won control of Missouri with a swift, brilliantly executed campaign; the next moment, Price's victorious army was marching back to the welcoming arms of Clay County. The turnaround began on August 10, when Lyon attacked the camp of Price and Confederate general Ben McCulloch along Wilson's Creek in southwestern Missouri. The secessionists stood firm and soundly thrashed the Union army. The battered Federals retreated to the northeast, less hundreds of casualties, including Lyon, struck down on the field.

In the days following, Price marched north with the State Guard, gathering recruits along the way. With him came Private Frank James, veteran soldier of a conquering army that would soon drive the Union from the soil of Missouri.[21]

IN THE BUOYANT days of early 1861, towns and villages of the North and South united in military fervor. Neighbors and lifelong friends joined regiments together; women strung bunting from houses and storefronts; children and older citizens lined the streets as the young men marched to war. But in Missouri, things were different: neighbors eyed each other with suspicion; lifelong friends joined rival military companies; women divided between those who sewed U.S. flags and those who made state and Confederate banners. It would not take much to transform these differences of opinion into widespread bloodshed.

Treason has long been considered the unforgivable crime. To the secessionists of western Missouri, the traitors were those who refused to rebel—and so they swept the Unionists from their villages and fields as General Price marched north in the blistering days of August and September 1861. In the town of Savannah, nestled against the Kansas border in Andrew County, secessionists organized themselves into regiments after the victory at Wilson's Creek. Swaggering down country roads, they began to intimidate their neighbors, taking what they wanted from the stores in town. "Some of us in Savannah, who were Union men, fought it as long as we could with words," reported John R. Carter. "Some 300 came into town, raised a secesh flag and made a big yell over it." Carter joined a company of local men who pledged to fight the rebels. But the secessionists, he said, "were too strong for us; we retreated towards the Iowa line."[22]

"When the war broke out rebels ruled this town," newspaper editor Charles Monroe Chase later said of St. Joseph. "More than half of her citizens were genuine secesh, and it was only after the severest military discipline that Unionism triumphed." But it took time to recruit, train, and deploy Union soldiers. In the meantime, loyal citizens suffered. "Old man Brinton told me," said another St. Joseph Unionist, "that myself and all men of my principles had got to leave this country in a few days."[23]

All across the state, armed rebels instituted what James H. Moss called a "reign of terror" against their neighbors, driving columns of refugees into St. Louis, Kansas City, and neighboring states. The ruts and roads of Jackson County carried an exodus west as early as July 1861. Wagons filled with loyal families crossed into Kansas; in Independence, four men barely escaped hanging when they tried to enlist in the Federal army. Halfway through the month, fighting erupted. Hundreds of local Unionists, led by Kansas City businessman Robert T. Van Horn (and aided by 45 Kansas militiamen under Charles "Doc" Jennison) battled 350 secessionists in Morristown and Harrisonville.[24]

When General Price besieged the Union garrison in Lexington on the southern bank of the Missouri River on September 13, a tsunami of rebel enthusiasm swept Clay County. "At the start of the rebellion, the people of Clay were a unit for the Union," commented loyalist F. R. Long, with some exaggeration, "but in the fall and winter of 1861 . . . it was quite the other way." By the time Price reached the Missouri, he estimated that "firmly three-quarters of our people were disloyal." Unionist merchant Edward M. Samuel thought the situation was even worse: of 2,000 voters, he could number only 150 to 200 loyal men.[25] Secessionists formed committees in every township to gather supplies for Price's army. Fresh recruits filled the ranks of new companies that crossed the river to join the siege of Lexington. Still others galloped with loaded guns to the homes of those few loyal men still living in the area.

"There were organized bands in the county at that time," recalled O. P. Moss, the brother of Whig leader James H. Moss, "and we received information that the two Mosses, [James M.] Jones, and [Edward M.] Samuel must be got out of the way." And so, "persecuted and driven from our county," these outspoken Unionists fled to Caldwell County; behind them, the secessionists helped themselves to their horses and possessions for the benefit of Price's army.[26]

How could civil society collapse so quickly? Many historians explain it away with a deus ex machina: Outsiders did it. "The most direct factor" leading to violence in the state, wrote Richard S. Brownlee, "lay in the abuses visited upon the civil population of Missouri by the Union military forces." Invading Kansas troops, writes William E. Parrish, "found it impossible to think of Missourians as anything other than . . . natural enemies."[27]

But, in fact, most Missourians had little or no contact with Union forces during the summer and fall of 1861. There were only a few thousand Federal troops in the state at that time, most of them collected into large camps to guard railroads and cities and to fight the main rebel army. Clay County, for example, experienced one brief raid in June, followed by limited incursions in September and December; none lasted more than three or four days. As for the Kansans, they had yet to make their presence felt, nor were they entirely indiscriminate. Jennison's Seventh Kansas Cavalry Regiment did not move to Kansas City in force until November. His previous forays into Jackson County were made in coordination with local Unionists, in pursuit of existing rebel units. Indeed, the classic version of how rebellion rose in Missouri has it backward: most counties swung toward secessionism when the Union seemed weakest, when Union troops were farthest away. Nor was the rebellion largely a reaction to Lyon's hasty attack on the state militia in St. Louis, though it certainly gave Southern partisans a boost.[28]

In truth, the secessionist movement was a force of its own, part of a drama that predated the war, that pitted Missourian against Missourian, with Federal forces appearing on the scene after the action had begun.

"The germ lies in the troubles of 1855, relating to Kansas," said John R. Carter. "The pro-slavery party remained in the ascendancy," he reported, until Union troops moved in. During this period of border ruffian supremacy, "the rabid pro-slavery men" dealt out "oppression" to their opponents. "This feud existed in that region of Missouri before the commencement of the rebellion," concluded a committee of the state legislature. "The original Union men in that region were opposed in the older day [the 1850s] to the raids that were made into Kansas," and so they "engendered a bitter hatred against themselves from the strong pro-slavery men."[29]

The division between Unionists and secessionists emerged out of the prewar split between the old Whigs and Know-Nothings on one side, and the Blue Lodge, border ruffian Democrats on the other. Both factions had favored slavery, but the extremists had championed armed force to get their way. Their movement became a cult of violence and intolerance, and they directed much of their fury at fellow Missourians who dared to dissent. These were the men who threatened a Whig meeting in Boone County in 1855, forcing it to call for the use of arms against abolitionists; these were the men who destroyed the *Parkville Industrial Luminary* that same year; these were the men who nearly lynched Darius Sessions, the Know-Nothing leader in Liberty, in 1856. Their mobilization against their neighbors was the essential ingredient in Missouri's burgeoning internal war.[30]

When war erupted, the proslavery fire-eaters believed that Lincoln was carrying out a secret plot to free the slaves. "The secessionists have charged that the purpose of this war was to free the negroes," reported the *St. Joseph Journal*. In 1872, a leading Missouri Confederate wholeheartedly agreed. The Civil War, declared newspaper editor John N. Edwards, "was fought that slavery might live or die." Frank James and his fellow recruits expressed this idea when they said that they aimed to keep Missouri's "soil and institutions sacred against invasion." They had a personal stake in the question: one study of Confederate fighters from Jackson County shows that their families were almost twice as likely to own slaves as those of other men their age; and the total number they held averaged twice that of typical local slaveowners. In the dense clouds of paranoia wafting up from the fire over Kansas, they struck first—and their first target was the Unionists among them.[31]

Historians have often clouded the fraternal nature of Missouri's internal strife by calling Confederate sympathizers "Southerners." But their opponents were just as Southern, having been born in Missouri, Kentucky, and other slave states. Indeed, some of the men who fought hardest for the

Union, in Clay County and elsewhere, owned slaves. Better is the term "secessionist," or, to use the nickname of the times, "secesh." The rift between the two sides was ideological rather than cultural or geographic. The secesh believed that slavery was under threat, and that it was more important than the nation itself. The loyalists did not see any danger to the peculiar institution, and in any case they cherished the sanctity of the Union above all else. "I am a Union man by nature," wrote one man in Saline County, a slaveholding stronghold, and he spoke for many on his side. But Missouri's Unionists faced a looming contradiction between their acceptance of slavery and their patriotism. As the war progressed, they would eventually divide among themselves between those who embraced emancipation and those who resisted.[32]

In the meantime, a large percentage of the population swung between the poles of Unionism and secession, suspended between their conflicting feelings of patriotism, affinity for the South, and fear of the consequences of taking sides. But this middle segment of the people was not inert. It shifted back and forth as the currents of war carried one side or the other toward victory. In those counties where slavery was insignificant, many people had only a limited notion of themselves as Southerners, and loyalty reigned more or less unchallenged. These areas helped make Missouri overall a predominantly loyal state. But in Clay and other bastions of slave-holding society, the situation was much more volatile.[33] First the people there voted for Unionist James H. Moss to represent them in the convention on secession; later, as Price marched north, they acquiesced as the rebels prodded Moss out of Liberty with their rifle barrels.

And there was one other strand in this tearing social fabric: the slaves. With the chaos of war erupting around them, slaveholders eyed their human property nervously, while slaves themselves watched for opportunities that could lead to freedom.

As General Price ordered trenches to be dug around the Union forces in Lexington on September 14, 1861, those opportunities looked distant indeed. The Federal cause was in chaos. The main U.S. army had been thrashed at Manassas, Virginia. The victorious State Guard had already reconquered almost half of Missouri. The capture of Lexington, just downstream from Clay County, would give Price control of the most important river town between Jefferson City and the western border.[34]

At sunset on September 16, as rain clouds cleared overhead, Jesse James, just fourteen, had his first chance to see the enemy: five hundred sodden recruits of the Third Iowa Infantry Regiment, who tramped into

Centerville and camped for the night. By sunrise they were gone. Later that day, south of Liberty, they clashed briefly with a few State Guard regiments that were ferrying over the river to aid General Price. On September 21, they marched away, leaving Clay County to its own devices once again.[35]

Jesse's family awaited information about the battle taking shape at Lexington. If Price succeeded, the entire state of Missouri might fall into the hands of the Confederacy. For all anyone knew, it would force Lincoln to accept the South's independence, in light of earlier rebel victories. After all, no one expected the war to last much longer. Then came the ecstatic news: Lexington had fallen on September 20, the day before the Union troops evacuated Liberty.

But, without a single battle, the momentum suddenly shifted. On September 26, Federal commander General John C. Frémont moved west from St. Louis with thirty-eight thousand troops. He soon arrived at Sedalia, southeast of Lexington, threatening to trap the rebels against the river. Price had no choice but to abandon his prize, setting out on September 29 for the southwestern corner of the state. The days of great marches and battles in Missouri came to an end, and they would not return for three years, when Price would once again look down from the bluffs of Lexington. (When that moment finally came, Jesse would be there to welcome him back, sitting astride a horse with a half-dozen revolvers in his belt.)[36]

As the hopes of the Samuel family rose and plunged with Price's fortunes, their lives changed in profound ways. With the South's cotton fields fenced off by war, the hemp market collapsed; if Reuben and Zerelda had not already shifted their fields to tobacco before Fort Sumter, they certainly did so afterward. An adult male slave tended the farm. He would have been a bargain: after reaching an all-time high in 1860, prices for human beings plummeted once war broke out.[37]

The news from St. Louis that arrived each week in the *Liberty Tribune* also reflected change. With Governor Jackson in exile and the legislature dissolved, the only elected body still in existence was the convention on secession. It had reconvened in July 1861 and duly assumed power as a provisional government, electing its presiding officer, Hamilton R. Gamble, as governor. A firm Unionist, an old Whig, and the only member of the state supreme court to have voted to free Dred Scott, Gamble had the stature necessary to win public confidence under these strange and trying conditions. Though a strong minority of state residents still gave their allegiance to Jackson, most (perhaps two-thirds) accepted the self-appointed provisional government and its distinguished head. Lincoln quickly recognized Gamble and his regime, happy to have a loyal government in the state.[38]

As a conservative man grappling with a revolutionary situation, however, Gamble had to struggle to moderate the growing anger of loyal Missourians against their secessionist neighbors. "To bargain, temporize," or "talk soft to traitors," argued Unionists in the town of Mexico, "is like using the same on water to persuade it to run uphill."[39]

Even more troubling for Gamble were the steps now taken by the military command. On August 30, Frémont declared martial law in Missouri. He warned that civilians who aided the rebellion would be shot—and he announced the emancipation of all slaves of active rebels in the state. (Lincoln soon forced the general to rescind the lines relating to slavery.) It was an earth-shattering step. Never before had a state been placed under the control of the armed forces; the idea was so new that Lincoln himself mistakenly referred to "military law" instead of "martial law." Missouri was a complicated case, the scene of both outright rebellion and Unionist fervor, with a functioning, but ad hoc, loyal government. But the president merely insisted that no civilians be shot without a White House review of each case, and he cautioned against capital punishment lest the rebels retaliate in kind.[40]

For the first time in American history, military commissions began to prosecute U.S. civilians. The inaugural trial took place on September 5, when Joseph Aubuchon was found guilty of having "an attitude of open rebellion." A network of provost marshals, headquartered in St. Louis, began gradually to spread across the state, taking responsibility for ferreting out rebellion in the civilian population. By the end of the war, Missouri would see 46.2 percent of all the recorded military trials of civilians—almost 45 percent more than the army conducted in all eleven Confederate states combined.[41]

Amateurism exacerbated the inherent brutality of martial law. The Union army consisted largely of men who had been civilians until April 1861, and most were new to all things military. With each month, more and more arrested civilians arrived from the country in St. Louis and other cities, often with little paperwork to define their crimes or the evidence against them. "Washington," comments one historian, "never exercised much control over Missouri."[42]

This last point is essential to understanding what was happening to this beleaguered state. The phrase "martial law" conjures up misleading images of invading outsiders, of a military bureaucracy that paid little attention to the sensitivities of residents. But the provost marshal system and the "occupying" regiments were largely staffed by Missourians themselves, thanks both to the self-organization of the Unionist population and the diligent efforts of Governor Gamble and his administration. In November 1861, with the cooperation of Frémont's replacement, Major General Henry W.

Halleck, the provisional government created a local force that would bear the primary responsibility for pacifying the state: the Missouri State Militia (MSM). When recruiting came to a halt on April 15, 1862, the MSM boasted fourteen regiments of cavalry, along with another regiment of infantry (more than ten thousand men in all). Outfitted with the same arms, equipment, and uniforms as the U.S. Volunteers, these state troops emerged as full-time, professional fighting men; though they fell under Federal command, they could only be used within Missouri's borders.[43]

Missouri-based or not, the military rapidly began to supplant civil government in many areas of life. The army enforced a loyalty oath that Gamble's administration required of all officeholders, jurors, and, finally, voters.[44] It put the press under strict censorship. It required passes for much travel, and military baggage inspectors made the rounds of hotels. Military officers regulated commerce and imposed fines and assessments on secessionists. The provost marshals constructed secret networks of detectives.

These drastic steps were fueled by pity, fury, and the need for control. Starting in July 1861, secessionist bands struck across the state, destroying railroad tracks, tearing down telegraph wires, burning bridges, sniping at Federal sentries, and terrorizing loyal families. Army officers—far from seeing all Missourians as disloyal—submitted report after report bemoaning the suffering of Unionist refugees. General Ulysses S. Grant vividly remembered Jefferson City in the summer of 1861, a town "filled with Union fugitives who had been driven by guerrilla bands to take refuge with the National troops. They were in a deplorable condition. . . . They had generally made their escape with a team or two, sometimes a yoke of oxen with a mule or a horse in the lead. A little bedding besides their clothing and some food had been thrown into the wagon. All else of their worldly goods were abandoned and appropriated by their former neighbors."[45] In the fall, Brigadier General William T. Sherman found the countryside around nearby Sedalia "full of returned secessionists who are driving out all Union men."[46]

Bridge burners struck all along the Missouri Pacific and Hannibal and St. Joseph Railroads. On September 3, twenty civilians died when a train tumbled off a wrecked span. Halleck estimated that fifteen thousand men were in a state of "insurrection" north of the Missouri River. On December 22, he issued General Order No. 32, one of many directives that were aimed at Missouri's civilians. "Any one caught in the act [of sabotage]," he wrote, "will be immediately shot." At the end of 1861, he put his regiments on the march to destroy or disperse the guerrilla squads. "Scour the country and arrest all enemies," he ordered. One column tramped from St. Joseph into Liberty, tore down the Confederate flag, arrested veterans of Price's army, and forced them to take the loyalty oath. After a few days the column moved on.[47]

One thing can be said for all this marching, this fighting, these harsh measures: to a limited extent, they worked. Towns—such as Liberty— where the stars and bars had floated over county courthouses became somewhat safe again for loyal citizens, who started to trickle back as Federal troops and the MSM established garrisons. The Clay County Court, the county government, assembled again in January 1862 and took the loyalty oath. One of the justices was Alvah Maret, the man who had sold land to Robert James and would soon reappear in the life of James's widow.[48]

The very success of Union efforts, however, merely weeded out the weak and disorganized insurrectionists. The smarter, tougher, angrier rebels survived, and grew more skilled in the ways of partisan warfare. From the Mississippi River to the Kansas border, small bands continued a deadlier, if less pervasive, guerrilla struggle. They were not a new phenomenon. They, too, emerged from the slaveholding counties' secessionist fervor, which had grown out of the border ruffian mobilization. Under the pressure of the Union counteroffensive, these secessionist guerrillas broke into small cells that fought without central direction or official Confederate sanction, passing under the nickname of "bushwhackers."[49]

Nowhere would the bushwhackers be smarter, tougher, and angrier than in Jackson County, just across the river from Clay. There the rebel forces regrouped as guerrillas amid the most furious Union campaigning in the state. In November 1861, "Doc" Jennison returned to Kansas City as leader of the Seventh Kansas Cavalry Regiment. Jackson County, wrote the regiment's chaplain on November 15, "has been represented as conquered by the Union troops 5 times, but no sooner are the forces withdrawn from their midst than they rise up and commence anew their depredations and persecutions of the Union men, confiscating their property, shooting, hanging, or driving them from the country." The Kansans sought to protect loyal citizens, and often used them as guides to hunt down secessionists. And that hunting was harsh. "I am fully convinced," continued the chaplain, "that the only way to subdue them is to take from them all means of subsistence and execute their leaders as fast as they fall into our hands."[50]

The jayhawkers focused their fury on the secessionists, but they aroused widespread discontent with their destructive methods. "Westport was once a thriving town, with large stores, elegant private dwellings, and a fine large hotel," wrote a Union officer on December 31, 1861. "Now soldiers are quartered in the dwellings and horses occupy the storerooms. The hotel was burned down three days ago. The houses are torn to pieces . . . the mantles used to build fires, and doors unhinged. I presume the place will be burned as soon as the troops leave." In the countryside, he saw "crops ungathered, houses deserted, barns and stables falling to pieces, fences torn down, and stock running loose and uncared for." Jennison started to call his unit the "self-sustaining regiment," and "jayhawking" became a synonym for plundering (by Union forces in particular). And wherever they went, they invited slaves to join them—which the slaves happily did.[51]

Jennison's men were not the worst Kansans striking Missouri. Senator (and General) Jim Lane liked to tell his men to clean out "everything disloyal, from a Shanghai rooster to a Durham cow." Captain Marshall Cleveland resigned from the Seventh Kansas in November 1861 and set up shop as a straightforward bandit. Once the Missouri River froze over, Cleveland raided the border counties for loot. In January 1862, General Halleck ordered his troops to drive the Kansans out. "They are no better than a band of robbers," he fumed. "They cross the line, rob, steal, plunder, and burn whatever they can lay their hands upon." As a general description of their actions, Halleck exaggerated. As harsh as they were, most Kansas troops came to fight existing secessionist forces, and they cooperated with local Unionists more often than they despoiled them. Their methods, however, became a rallying cry for the rebels in the winter of 1861–62.[52]

In the meantime, Price and his men lingered in southwestern Missouri, a refugee army guarding a refugee government. In the border town of Neosho, Governor Jackson called the General Assembly into session; a mere handful of legislators answered the roll and voted to join the Confederacy. The measure—carried out by a rump of an assembly—ran counter to the earlier actions of the special state convention on secession, but it gave a legal gloss to Jackson's stand. On November 28, 1861, the Confederate Congress formally accepted Missouri, adding its star to the stars and bars. Missouri now had two governments: a loyal one that had the support of most of the population but virtually no constitutional basis, and an exiled one headed by the elected governor but in open rebellion against the Union.[53]

On February 12, 1862, advancing Federals forced Price's dwindling army to abandon Missouri entirely. Less than a month later, on March 7 and 8, the Union troops thrashed the combined forces of the State Guard and the Confederate army at Pea Ridge, Arkansas, locking Price and his men out of their state. On April 8, the general resigned from the militia and accepted a Confederate commission; most of his four thousand troops followed his example. The State Guard was no more.

Frank James, however, remained behind in Missouri. When Price retreated from Springfield, the young soldier lay sick with the measles, a potentially fatal illness in the mid-nineteenth century. The advancing

Union troops took him prisoner, then paroled him, releasing him on the promise that he would not fight again—a common expedient, especially at this stage of the war. It appeared that Frank's war—the family's war—was over.[54]

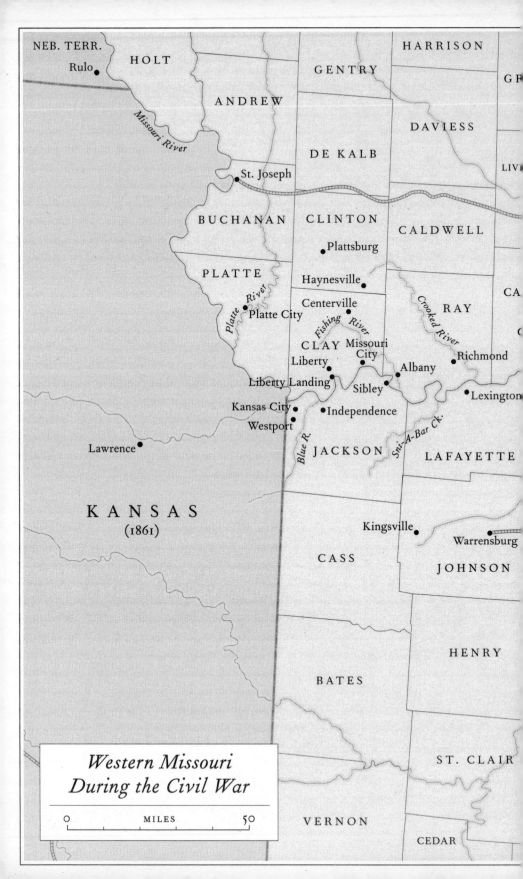

NEB. TERR.

Rulo

HOLT

Missouri River

ANDREW

GENTRY

HARRISON

GR

DAVIESS

LIV

DE KALB

St. Joseph

BUCHANAN

CLINTON

CALDWELL

Plattsburg

PLATTE

Haynesville

Platte River

Centerville

Platte City

Fishing River

Crooked River

RAY

CA

C

CLAY

Missouri
City

Liberty

Richmond

Liberty Landing

Albany

Kansas City

Sibley

Westport

Independence

Blue R.

Lexington

Lawrence

JACKSON

Sni-A-Bar Ck.

LAFAYETTE

KANSAS
(1861)

Kingsville

Warrensburg

CASS

JOHNSON

HENRY

BATES

ST. CLAIR

*Western Missouri
During the Civil War*

0   MILES   50

VERNON

CEDAR

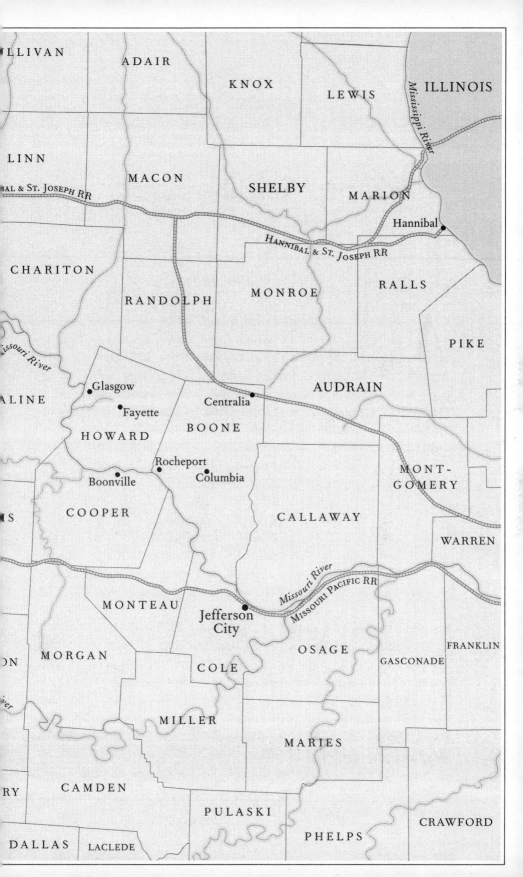

CHAPTER FIVE

Neighbors

As Jesse welcomed Frank back to the farm in the cold, dry spring of 1862, the brothers faced a most distressing fact: The Union stood triumphant. General Price had been chased to Arkansas, and Missouri had fallen under the heavy cords of military control—strands that were woven, day by day, into an enveloping blanket. On February 16, General Grant had completed the capture of Forts Henry and Donelson in Tennessee, taking some twelve thousand Southern prisoners; then, on March 7 and 8, came the bitter Confederate defeat at Pea Ridge. In Clay County, schools were shut down and businesses disrupted.[1]

"You asked me to tell you about the state of affairs in Mo., that you had awful accounts," wrote Kate Watkins, neighbor to the Samuel family, on June 9, 1862. "Well, you have never heard the half of the outrages that have been committed, and you never will, for it all could not be told. All the western border counties have been almost ruined by the Kansas jayhawkers. . . . The newspapers give accounts of a great many misdeeds which they say the rebels have done," she said, though she personally believed the Kansans were the worst by far. "The jayhawkers have stolen all the stock, run off all the negroes, and burnt a great many dwellings."

Kate exaggerated. Few armed Kansans had visited Clay County. There and elsewhere, most of the livestock and slaves remained, as farmers continued to plant and cultivate their crops. And, she admitted, "there has not been much of this done lately," for most of the jayhawkers had been ordered—or chased—out of the state by the Union army. But tales of their very real depredations had spread far and wide, and they infuriated her, as they did so many other Missourians.

And then there was the occupation—or the legitimate Union effort to maintain peace and order, depending on one's point of view. To Kate, it was definitely an occupation. The first permanent military presence in Clay

County began on March 15, 1862, in response to a raid on Liberty by three dozen bushwhackers from Jackson County; in April, the Fifth Cavalry Regiment of the Missouri State Militia, under Colonel William R. Penick, assumed control. Penick, like most Missourians, was Southern-born, and a slaveholder as well, but he took a grim view of secessionists. He soon had his men scouring the countryside, looking for guerrillas and stores of arms.

"The Feds condescended to pay us a visit," Watkins wrote, "though they were uninvited and unwelcome. They got in and were over half of the house before we knew they were on the place. They turned beds upside down, searched drawers and trunks, and jawed and disputed around considerably." The "Feds," of course, were all fellow Missourians, members of Penick's command. They found only a few small items that could be considered contraband. Frustrated, powerless, embittered, Watkins closed her letter by warning that the authorities might open it, "and if the writer is found out it may not be so well." She signed, "Your affectionate niece, Secesh."[2]

What seemed like oppression to Watkins looked like half-measures to Missouri loyalists. "We Union people are very low up here," wrote Anna Slayback from St. Joseph on May 9, 1862. "The laws are becoming more stringent on the rebels in Mo. & they must be put down. They are impudent & rejoice over our defeat. This must not be." But in another letter, she paused to contemplate the true horror of the war. "I think every victory is maiming our nation," she wrote. "Were the rebels a foreign foe or a stronger people, then subduing them might be called victories. But this is a family quarrel, brother against brother, & we bite & devour one another that other nations may mock & laugh at our folly."[3]

Such honest reflections, it seems, rarely shadowed the minds of most Missourians as they killed each other. They wanted not saints but heroes. For secessionists, one had already appeared in Jackson County. "There is a man by the name of Quantrill," Kate Watkins observed, "who is fighting the Feds on his own hook." This Quantrill, she wrote, "is giving the Feds some trouble."[4] And so he was.

William Clarke Quantrill was Ohio-born but had drifted west to serve as a freelance fighter on both sides of the struggle over Kansas. Just before the war erupted, he had shifted his field of operations to Missouri. Starting with just fifteen men, he began to fight Union forces at the end of 1861. He was hardly the only guerrilla leader in Missouri—perhaps not even the best—but he came to be remembered, revered, and reviled as was no one else. As early as February 3, 1862, Union captain W. S. Oliver wrote of him as "the notorious Quantrill." Reporting from the town of Independence, Oliver growled, "I have seen this infamous scoundrel rob mails, steal the coaches and horses, and commit other similar outrages upon society even within sight of this city. Mounted on the best horses of the country, he has defied pursuit." Even as Quantrill struck government posts and ambushed Federal patrols, he remained focused on the internal war against Missouri's Unionist civilians, and continued the political cleansing of the countryside. "I hear of him tonight fifteen miles from here," Oliver added, "with new recruits, committing outrages on Union men, a large body of whom have come in tonight, driven out by him."[5]

What lifted Quantrill above the scores of bushwhackers operating in Missouri was less his talent or personal magnetism than his ambition. On February 22, he had the audacity to ride through the streets of Independence (though he and his men were quickly chased away by Union cavalry). On March 7, he raided into Aubry, Kansas. On March 22, after learning that General Halleck had decreed the execution of captured guerrillas, he personally shot one of his prisoners, declaring, "Halleck issued the order, but we draw the first blood!" In April, he issued a proclamation, telling Jackson County Unionists that there was no point in planting their crops, because they would be dead or driven out before they could harvest them. On April 18, the *Kansas City Journal of Commerce* reported that the guerrillas had stopped all mail into the town for three weeks.[6]

Across the river in Clay County, news of such exploits lifted the spirits of the beleaguered Samuel family. After Frank learned of one bushwhacker raid, he reportedly ran about in frenzied joy, blasting his pistol in the air and cheering for Jefferson Davis. But guerrilla successes inevitably led to a Union backlash. In early April 1862, Lieutenant Colonel Bernard G. Farrar, provost marshal general for Missouri, advised his subordinates to arrest "disloyal persons," then make them take a loyalty oath and post a bond for good behavior. Before the end of the month, a squad from Colonel Penick's regiment hauled Frank to Liberty. There, on April 26, he duly swore his allegiance to the United States, posted a bond, and returned home. By the end of the year, 612 men in the Liberty district alone underwent the same process.[7]

In peacetime, Clay County had had a traditional society, built on shared values and personal relationships. The same handful of men had led civic organizations and held public office; elections had been held in the open, with no secret ballot; citizens had voiced their opinions through mass meetings at churches, taverns, and the courthouse in Liberty. At the same time, much of life there passed beneath an awning of privacy. Farm families lived in isolation down eroding dirt lanes; men eagerly joined secret organizations, the Masons and the Oddfellows; and slaves furtively pursued their own social relations.

Unionists no less than secessionists quailed as Colonel Penick tried to hack his way into this now-decaying structure. On August 14, 1862, for example, Penick fought a group of bushwhackers on the Platte County border. "Previous to attacking their camp I had found three men at the [nearby] house, who denied having any knowledge of any camp or gathering of armed men," he wrote the next day. "After the skirmish was over I sent two of these men out . . . and had them shot." His superiors once rebuked the overzealous colonel for calling the venerable Masonic Order a disloyal organization (an unfortunate bit of paranoia, since his commander was a Mason). Even Unionist leader Edward M. Samuel thought Penick was "very rigid," and often went to MSM headquarters to plead for the release of arrested neighbors.[8]

On July 22, 1862, the new commander in Missouri, Major General John M. Schofield, issued General Order No. 19, instructing all men of military age to enlist in a new force, the Enrolled Missouri Militia (EMM), intended to relieve the full-time MSM and U.S. Volunteers of garrison duty, mail escort, and other simple work.[9] "Disloyal persons or sympathizers with the rebellion," on the other hand, "are required to report at the nearest military post or other enrolling station, be enrolled, surrender their arms, and return to their homes or ordinary places of business." In September 1862, Reuben Samuel rode to Colonel Penick's office in Liberty, where he had to take a loyalty oath and pay a $10 commutation tax to avoid service. Frank James, on the other hand, had to mark himself down as disloyal because of his service in the State Guard, despite his earlier surrender.[10]

Clay County's Unionists rapidly filled four EMM companies; across Missouri, more than fifty-two thousand men enlisted. They joined an admittedly ad hoc force. They served only as needed, received little or no training, wore their own clothes on duty, and elected their own officers. In Clay, each of the first companies was led by a former Whig/Know-Nothing politician; James H. Moss was named colonel of their regiment, the Forty-eighth. Colonel Penick relocated to Independence in September, leaving Clay and Platte Counties to their homegrown militia.[11]

The Clay County EMM consisted of local, conservative men, but that hardly mattered to secessionists. Even though Anthony Harsel owned at least sixteen slaves, Confederate sympathizers derided him as an "abolitionist." The day after he was elected captain of his company, the rebels burned down his house. They began to call EMM soldiers "radicals," even though many were slaveowners.[12] But as some of these conservative Whigs faced the abuse of their secessionist neighbors, admitted E. M. Samuel, "they were becoming more radically Union." The hostility of rebel sympathizers infuriated the Unionists as they chased after guerrillas who ambushed militia patrols and burned out loyal families. "I have been on some thirty scouts with the militia," testified Lieutenant Robert W. Fleming, "and could never obtain any information from the citizens relative to bushwhackers." He often disguised his men as guerrillas when he sent them to farmhouses; they always received a warm welcome and a hot meal before they identified themselves and arrested the occupants.

"Many [of the local women] have told me that they, the bushwhackers, had as much right there as I, with my company," reported Captain William Garth. On one occasion, he captured a pair of guerrillas at a farmhouse that was ruled, like so many during the war, by a lone woman. "One of the bushwhackers was the lady's son; she is a strong rebel, and gave me thunder that night. She said she had always understood I was a Southern man, and I ought to be hunting red-legs [Kansas bandits] instead of Southern boys."[13]

The militiamen had plenty of opportunities for retaliation. The EMM received no pay or equipment; instead, as Colonel Penick related, they were "authorized from headquarters to subsist on the rebels, and their aiders and abettors." These untrained and often undisciplined men went to the homes of their neighbors and took what they liked, from horses to hogs to furniture.[14]

The EMM was created for a straightforward military reason: to provide manpower as regiments of U.S. Volunteers were withdrawn from Missouri for service in the campaign against Corinth, Mississippi.[15] It was imagined as an ad hoc shelter for Unionists. Instead, it completed the architecture of enmity among the civil population. Under General Order No. 19, there could be no neutrality; every adult male became a Union soldier (however part-time) or was marked down as disloyal. The only escape was the commutation tax, and those who paid it were usually regarded as secret secessionists by the men who chose to fight the rebels. The division of the countryside into armed camps was complete.

This was a decisive moment. By pitting local Unionists against their neighbors, the EMM planted the seeds of a grassroots political movement that was unimaginable only a year or two earlier—a Radical Party, increasingly convinced of the necessity of abolishing slavery and imposing merciless measures against rebels. The new force also had lasting repercussions in the life of Jesse James. In later years, skeptics would scoff at the notion that the Civil War shaped his thinking in his career as an outlaw, noting that most of his victims were Missouri Southerners. But in the burgeoning war of bushwhackers against Unionist civilians, of Unionist militia against secessionist civilians, he learned that his enemies were not invading Yankees, but the men who lived next door.[16]

"I LONG TO be free from this world with all its turmoil and deceit," Sue Carter wrote from Clay County on March 22, 1863. "I think every day of my life that I surely was created to see trouble." In the very midst of scratching out this letter, she was interrupted by a militia raid. Afterward neighbors began to drop by. "The women kept gathering in," she chuckled, "until we had a room full of the most ranting, torn-down secesh you ever saw. . . . Hurrah for Price but Devil take the abolitionists I say." But then she went on to relate an interesting anecdote. Uncle Philip, she wrote, had been threatened by a slave—so he called in the militia to help. And they did, chasing the slave for half an hour through the woods, administering thirty-six lashes to his bleeding, ravaged back. "It is a common report here," wrote a militia officer from St. Joseph on February 14, 1863, "that Col. Moss of Clay County uses the Enrolled Militia of said county to prevent the escape of negroes."[17]

But the time was quickly passing when the militia would simultaneously fight bushwhackers and chase slaves. The war was steadily polarizing everyone. In the state legislature elections in 1862, old parties disappeared. Candidates were categorized instead by their attitude toward secessionists and emancipation (ranging from the Charcoals, soon renamed the Radicals, to the Claybanks and the Snowflakes, who became the Conservatives). The actions of Colonel Moss's slave-catching militiamen shows this split at the grass roots. Moss and other conservative soldiers were appalled at the radical turn the war was taking. On January 1, 1863, for example, the Emancipation Proclamation went into effect. Though it freed no slaves in Missouri, Kate Watkins reported that it aroused "a great deal of excitement" in Clay County. It was a sign that the conflict was going to the roots of Southern society, including the Southern society of officially loyal Missouri.[18]

On February 3, 1863, the state government radicalized the war still further by creating yet another military force: the Provisional Enrolled Missouri Militia, staffed by men handpicked from the EMM. Designed as a more durable and professional organization than the EMM, it marginalized conservative soldiers such as Colonel Moss; his Forty-eighth Regiment essentially dissolved as its most effective soldiers were detailed to the new Fourth Provisional Regiment. By early April, the only Clay County men still serving were organized into Company L, led by Captain William Garth; they were joined by units from Ray, Mercer, Andrew, and Clinton Counties. There were "some bad men" among the new arrivals, Edward M. Samuel thought. They were "strangers to the people," groused the now-displaced Moss. "They were from the northern counties."[19]

Those northern counties were not very far away from Clay, but they were home to far fewer slaveholders, and far more bitterness toward rebels. Many now saw slavery itself as the source of the rebellion. Once they raided a local farm, recalled Sheriff F. R. Long, and one of the slaves there "went off with them." Long's deputy tried to retrieve the runaway, but was driven out of the Provisionals' camp. "I then, a couple of hours afterwards, arrested the negro and took him from the government wagon which he was driving, and instantly fifteen bayonets were pointed against me."[20]

Perhaps it was the Emancipation Proclamation that proved too much for the Samuel family. Perhaps it was the invasion of the hard militiamen from Andrew, Mercer, and Clinton, or the hopes raised by Lee's stunning victory over the Union army at Chancellorsville, May 2–6, 1863. Perhaps it was simply the reappearance of the guerrillas with the coming of spring, after many had gone to Arkansas for the winter (when the lack of leaves and abundant snow made it hard to evade detection by Union troops). Or perhaps a persistent story is true, that the Provisionals rode onto the farm that spring, tied up Frank, and hauled him off to jail in Liberty, where he escaped with help from the outside. Whatever other factors were at play, the James brothers had inherited their mother's ideological commitment to the South's cause, and her determination never to be under anyone's control again. In the war so far, one outside force after another had driven this family's fate, but the time had come for the family to become their own protagonists and take control for themselves. At the beginning of May 1863, Frank loaded his pistols, saddled his horse, and stole into the woods.[21]

AS THE SUN seeped between the houses of Missouri City,[22] Clay County, on Tuesday morning, May 19, 1863, Lieutenant Louis Gravenstein looked ahead to a day of hard work and nervous anticipation. He commanded sixteen men posted in the village, soldiers of the Twenty-fifth Missouri Infantry, a regiment of U.S. Volunteers that had been pulled from the main front in Mississippi to fight the elusive guerrillas. Today Gravenstein expected no combat; instead, he would hector his troops to get ready for a major operation—what a later generation of American soldiers would call a "hammer and anvil" sweep. The next morning, two companies were to drive up the rugged bottom of the Fishing River, one company on each bank. This was prime bushwhacker country; Gravenstein hoped the two-company hammer would drive the rebels out into the open, straight into the anvil of his squad, which would lie hidden on either side of a bridge upstream.

Greeting the dawn with Gravenstein was his guide, Captain Darius Sessions of the EMM. If Gravenstein knew this local man's background, he would have found it ironic that they should be fighting side by side. In the 1850s, Sessions had helped lead the anti-immigrant Know-Nothing Party in Clay County, and Gravenstein was a German from St. Joseph, like many men in the Twenty-fifth. But Sessions had felt the wrath of proslavery extremists, and he shared the German's fierce Unionism. And so the Know-Nothing and the foreigner prepared for battle together.

As the sun passed its peak, one of the town's citizens ran up with some unexpected news: two bushwhackers had just come to his house, obviously drunk, boasting of being Quantrill's men. Quickly Gravenstein and Sessions picked three soldiers and set out in pursuit. The lieutenant probably looked forward to an easy capture of two intoxicated bushwhackers, and perhaps some intelligence that might make the next day's operation a complete success. Instead, as the party approached a bridge, he saw the dense green leaves alongside the road erupt in flame and smoke, dissolving in the crackling roar of an ambush. As Sessions and another man collapsed to the ground, Gravenstein tried to surrender. The guerrillas responded by shooting him dead. Another bushwhacker walked over to the fallen Sessions and blasted three more rounds into his skull.

Whoever squeezed off those shots knew the captain's name, for there were a number of Clay County men in the rebel squad: Fernando Scott, for example, the former saddler who led this gang, and a young recruit from Centerville named Frank James.[23] For Frank, the Fishing River skirmish was a fantasy of warfare come true. He had seen combat before, of course, most notably at Wilson's Creek. But he had been a private in an army then, subjected to endless hours of marching and camp duty and drill, punctuated by a single day of battle. Now he belonged to a small squad that initiated combat at will, deceiving and defeating the enemy in ecstatic bursts of fighting.[24]

It was also an exercise in brutality. After the murder of the prisoners, Frank joined his comrades in a dash into Missouri City, where they spent the night pillaging local Unionists. Then they raced north into Clinton County on a plundering raid, before burning a path back into Clay. On Sunday, May 24, Frank was recognized by neighbor David M. Bivens when the guerrillas rode onto Bivens's farm and demanded dinner. With stunning courage—or stubborn idiocy—Bivens refused, and plainly told them he would report them immediately. The next day, Frank stopped his fellows from robbing an old friend; the would-be victim, like Bivens, informed the authorities.[25]

As the guerrillas raided through Clay County, they moved carefully, often taking over a farm, holding the family prisoner, and posting pickets (military watchmen) to stand guard during the night. These were wise precautions: the embarrassment at Missouri City had startled the Union command into action. The two Provisional militia companies currently in Clay (the Clinton men in Company F, under Captain John W. Turney, and the local unit, under Captain Garth) began to scour the countryside. In Liberty, the atmosphere was tense; with all the troops in the field, O. P. Moss organized an impromptu squad to protect the county seat.[26]

On May 25, Scott and his men made their way back to a refuge where they were certain of a warm welcome: Zerelda's farm, outside of Centerville. Frank led his fellow guerrillas to a spot in the woods not too far from the farmhouse; meanwhile, his mother undoubtedly told Charlotte to prepare a meal. And Jesse, now a slender fifteen-year-old, would have watched in envy as the fighting men rode by with revolvers, shotguns, and carbines clanking at their sides.

Even though Frank had been in the saddle for only a few weeks, his family already knew Scott and his crew, having supplied them with food, information, and Zerelda's outspoken support. Reportedly, and credibly, Jesse had tried desperately to join them, only to be turned away for being too young—though they put him to work loading revolvers. It was a vital if tedious task. The most common pistol in use in Missouri was Colt's 1851 Navy model, a .36 caliber revolver, which had not yet been adapted to take the new all-in-one metal cartridge. Instead, each of the six chambers in the revolving cylinder had to be filled with gunpowder and a lead ball, which was then rammed home and sealed with a bit of grease. A percussion cap, containing fulminate of mercury, had to be fitted on a nipple outside each chamber; when struck by the hammer, the cap would set off the charge inside. Loading was such time-consuming work that each guerrilla carried four or even six revolvers into combat, simply drawing a new pistol when one was emptied or jammed. Loading was also dangerous. According to one account, Jesse blew off the tip of the middle finger of his left hand while loading a Navy revolver sometime in 1863.[27]

Frank and his friends settled into their camp in the woods, where they threw down a blanket, dealt out cards, and began to play poker. Jesse went back to work in the fields, along with the adult male slave. By now, the year's crop of tobacco plants had sprouted and grown quarter-sized leaves, and had to be transplanted from the seedbeds into the fields. After that, Jesse and the hands had to cultivate them with a shovel plow, and hoe continually to destroy cutworms near the roots. The work could not wait, even with the bushwhackers on the farm.[28]

As he manned the shovel plow, Jesse probably never heard the militiamen until they caught him round the throat. They dragged him—and whipped him, or beat him, or choked him, or pricked him with sabers, depending on the account—his feet sinking into the soft, upturned dirt, scraping through the fragile green tobacco plants all the way to the house. He saw militiamen everywhere, carbines and pistols in their hands, the unknown faces of Clinton County Provisionals interweaving with those he recognized—the despised Clay County Unionists of Captain Garth's Company L (apparently led by Lieutenant John W. Younger).

In the front yard, in the center of a circle of troops, was Reuben, timid and terrified, aged beyond his years. Lieutenant Henry C. Culver of the Clinton company hammered him with questions about the bushwhackers. Reuben pleaded ignorance, but Culver had information enough to damn him. Frank James had been identified as one of Scott's men. Fresh reports put the band close by. "The militia judged him to be speaking falsely," Lieutenant James H. Rogers reported, "and at once procured a rope, placed it about his neck, and gave him one good swing."

At that moment, as the rope was tied around Reuben's neck and tossed over the limb of a sturdy tree, Jesse's uncle, William James, appeared. A Baptist minister like his late brother Robert, he, too, had heard of Frank's role in the guerrilla mayhem and decided to ride out to see the family. Jesse's mother, the pastor recalled, was "making such an outcry and giving them such a tongue-lashing as only she could give." William urged Zerelda to be quiet, whereupon she wheeled in his direction. "How can I be still," she howled, "when they are hanging my husband?"

And so they were, for now the militiamen—not occupying Yankees or rampaging jayhawkers, but neighbors and fellow Missourians—gripped the rope and pulled, making the tree groan as the frail doctor rose in the air by the twine around his throat. And then he came down in more senses than one. Breaking completely in his fear and pain, he surrendered his wife's child to save himself. After that "one good swing," Rogers declared, "his memory brightened up, and he concluded to reveal the hiding place of the rebels. He led the boys into the woods a short distance, and there, squatted upon the ground in a dense thicket, was discovered the whole band."

Then it was a mad dash through the trees, the sharp crack of gunfire echoing back to Jesse and his mother, the startled scrambling of guerrillas and horses through the brush. The militiamen shot two of Frank's companions. When the bushwhackers gathered themselves together a short distance off, the Union troops found them again, gunning down three more and wounding others. Then the survivors made a relentless dash for miles through the country with the Provisionals and the Twenty-fifth Missouri after them on every road, every streambed, every ford, until they finally slipped over the Missouri River in skiffs, rowing through the scattered bullets from Union troops on the bluffs above.[29]

Back at the house, the militiamen hauled away the shattered Reuben, carrying him off to the district headquarters in St. Joseph. They soon returned for Zerelda. A week before, on May 18, district commander Colonel Chester Harding, Jr., had ordered Assistant Provost Marshal Rhea to "arrest the most prominent and influential rebels and sympathizers. . . . Women who are violent and dangerous secessionists must be arrested as well as men." Zerelda clearly qualified. So she was taken into military custody as well, leaving the teenage Jesse in charge of her fields.[30]

That day in May, when the militia descended on the farm, has been described as the moment when Jesse James set out on his quest for revenge. But it was, in fact, the culmination of a process that stretched back to the day when Frank had joined the State Guard, back to the attack on Darius Sessions by a proslavery mob, back to the destruction of the *Parkville Industrial Luminary,* back to the battle Robert James had waged against abolitionists in the Baptist Church. For Jesse and his family, the dream of returning to life in a peaceful, tight-knit society had now ended, never to recur; from this day forward, they would count every neighbor as either an ally or an enemy.

On June 5, after perhaps a week in custody, Zerelda returned to her family. She signed a loyalty oath that day, and Major J. M. Bassett, provost marshal for the northwest district, granted her a parole. She had lied in signing the oath, of course, but what of it? She and her children saw themselves adrift in a sea of enemies, and they would lie to survive. Reuben, on the other hand, did not return for another two weeks. Bassett waited until June 24, 1863, to issue him a parole, with the condition that he report to the provost marshal's office in St. Joseph every twenty days. It was ironic that he should be held so long and placed under such restrictions: it was Zerelda, not her husband, who railed against the Union, who fed and spied for the bushwhackers. In 1863, however, the authorities inevitably saw the man of the house as the moving force.

Jesse's thoughts as his bedraggled stepfather shuffled back into the house can only be guessed at. Were they surges of concern, pangs of embarrassment, or flashes of anger at how he had broken so quickly? The doctor himself was clearly uncomfortable. Within a week of his return, he approached Alvah Maret (the county court judge who had sold land to Robert James) and asked for his help in loosening the terms of his parole. Maret could do little; the military had assumed most governmental powers, making him almost as much a bystander as anyone else. But together with two other neighbors, A. C. Courtney and L. J. Larkin, Maret composed a letter to Major Bassett, urging him to release Samuel from his requirements. "We regard him as a peaceable, quiet, inoffensive man, who would harm no one," they wrote. "He is, we hesitate not to state, under the control of his wife & stepson, and is really afraid to act contrary to their wishes in anything. This fear, we believe, caused him to make a false statement he would not otherwise have done. We know no man who is more peacefully inclined and who is more inoffensive."[31]

For Reuben Samuel, to be "peacefully inclined" was to be an outsider in his own home. When his wife and his stepsons slammed the gate on the Union authorities and their Unionist neighbors, he found himself caught in the doorway, unwilling to seal himself behind their wall of lies, deceit, and distrust—yet unable, or afraid, to abandon them. His stepson Frank belonged to a gang that murdered its prisoners and robbed civilians; the Union militia, on the other hand, had nearly tortured him to death; and the provost marshal simply ignored his terrified supplications. There was no place in this war for an inoffensive man.

Zerelda, on the other hand, gloried in her offensiveness. When she gave birth to a girl that year, she named her Fannie Quantrell Samuel (using a common spelling of the famous bushwhacker's name), "just to have a Quantrell in the family," as she later put it. Imprisonment had only further hardened this hard woman. As for Jesse, he tended his trampled tobacco field with the remaining slaves and looked south to the Missouri River for signs that Frank had survived.[32]

CHAPTER SIX

Terror

T HE ONSET of summer brought fear and triumph in equal measure. In May 1863, Lee and the Army of Northern Virginia turned back yet another Union offensive against the Confederate capital with a stunning victory at Chancellorsville—a masterpiece of tactics, deception, and courage. In the same month, Grant delivered his own stroke of genius at Vicksburg, Mississippi, trapping a rebel army of thirty thousand men in a campaign every bit as daring as Lee's. All through June, Grant besieged the Mississippi river town, one of the last two links between the Confederacy's eastern half and its western states; meanwhile, Lee embarked on a bold invasion of Pennsylvania.

Then an overconfident Lee finally overreached himself at Gettysburg, as he smashed his regiments against Union lines on heights named Little Round Top, Culp's Hill, Cemetery Hill, and Cemetery Ridge. On July 4, he led his shattered army south in retreat. That same day, the laconic Grant accepted the surrender of Vicksburg and its garrison. When news of its fall reached the besieged Confederates at Port Hudson, the final rebel stronghold on the Mississippi, they too surrendered. "Yesterday we rode on the pinnacle of success," wrote Josiah Gorgas, chief of Confederate ordnance, in his diary on July 28, "today absolute ruin seems to be our portion. The Confederacy totters to its destruction."[1]

The Confederacy's cast-off children in Missouri despaired at the disastrous turn of summer. But the changing tide of war made no difference within the state, where the fighting continued on more savagely than before.

"We are getting quite hardened to this kind of thing," wrote Union lieutenant Sardius Smith in his diary, "and I can go into a house with a pistol in my hand, with a smile on my face, speak politely to the ladies, ask where their men are in order that I may shoot them or take them prisoner

with as much grace as though I was making a call for friendship sake."
That was in 1862. In January 1863, Colonel Penick reported that the bushwhackers were now mutilating their victims. On March 29, Brigadier General Ben Loan angrily forwarded a report to headquarters that the
guerrillas had murdered twenty escaping slaves. "The contest for the
supremacy in this State," he fumed, "must be made a war of extermination."[2] During the tense summer of 1863, Loan's idea spread to the public.
"The whole population of the country," reported a depressed Edward M.
Samuel from Liberty, "may be said to have been . . . demoralized by this
war." By *demoralized* he meant that their ethics and decency had evaporated in the heat of the killing.[3]

General Schofield worried most about the strife in Jackson County, the
most "demoralized" area of all. As the new commander of the Department
of the Missouri, on June 9 he created the District of the Border, which
included both the two western tiers of Missouri counties and those parts of
Kansas that were north of the thirty-eighth parallel and south of the Missouri River. He put Brigadier General Thomas Ewing, Jr., in charge of this
vital district. Politically connected and shrewdly intelligent, Ewing
grasped the essential problem in crushing the insurrection. "About two-
thirds of the families on the occupied farms of that region are of kin to the
guerrillas, and are actively and heartily engaged in feeding, clothing, and
sustaining them," he wrote to Schofield on August 3, 1863. "I can see no
prospect of an early and complete end to the war on the border, without a
great increase of troops, so long as those families remain there."[4]

In strictly military terms, Ewing had hit upon the classic answer to partisan warfare. Throughout the nineteenth century, the U.S. Army coped
with Native American insurrections by relocating entire populations.
Almost forty years later, the British would subdue the intractable Boer
insurrection in South Africa by placing all civilian Afrikaners in concentration camps. The people, as Mao Zedong famously wrote, were the sea in
which the guerrilla swims; Ewing wanted to drain the ocean dry.[5]

In many ways, Ewing's plans to move against civilians simply extended
existing policies. In late July, his provost marshal used a three-story building at 1425 Grand Avenue in Kansas City to imprison ten female relatives of
bushwhackers William Anderson, John McCorkle, Cole Younger, and others. On August 13, the building collapsed, killing five of the women and
badly injuring others. Rumors spread that the building had been sabotaged
by the army. Unmoved, Ewing pressed ahead with his program. On
August 18, he issued General Orders Nos. 9 (freeing slaves of rebels) and
10 (banishing bushwhackers' families). Neither order affected Jesse James
and his family, but within Ewing's district, the long-suffering civilians
would suffer as never before.[6]

. . .

FRANK HAD SURVIVED. In the first week of August, Jesse saw him at the farm, where he had arrived with two companions. He had stories to tell. After his harrowing escape across the Missouri River (losing his horse in the process), he had made his way to the main guerrilla encampment. There, deep in the Sni-A-Bar wilderness on the border of Jackson and Lafayette Counties, Frank had met the greatest bushwhacker of all. "I will never forget the first time I saw Quantrill," he recalled years afterward. "He was nearly six feet in height, rather thin, his hair and moustache was sandy and he was full of life and a jolly fellow." Frank was awed by how natural he was. "He had none of the air of the bravado or the desperado about him," he later said, but "he was a demon in battle."[7]

In Jackson County, Frank had met most of Quantrill's followers and allies, men such as the hulking Cole Younger, who had gained notoriety by ambushing and killing most of the militiamen who had murdered his father, and John McCorkle, whose sisters would soon die in the Kansas City prison collapse. They fought together under Quantrill and such guerrilla leaders as George Todd and David Pool—raiding, skirmishing, burning Unionist farms and killing informers. On June 17, Fernando Scott was killed in fighting near Westport.[8]

Frank and his two friends soon went back across the Missouri, stopping only to rob a traveler on the way. The longer Frank stayed in Clay County, the more dangerous he made it for his mother and his stepfather. But he had a pressing reason to return to Jackson County: Quantrill had called. A rendezvous of his followers and fellow bushwhackers had been set for August 10, near Blue Springs.[9]

What happened there and in the days that followed, Jesse only learned secondhand. But at that Blue Springs meeting, the ambitious Quantrill presented his grandest scheme to date. He wanted to attack Lawrence, the abolitionist capital of Kansas and home to Senator Jim Lane. The guerrillas had plenty of resentments that cried out for retaliation: the Emancipation Proclamation and the Union victories at Vicksburg and Gettysburg. Lawrence, meanwhile, had long been a center for the recruitment of black troops.[10] Quantrill's followers and allies swiftly agreed to his plan.

For all its symbolic importance, Lawrence was in many ways a typical American town, resembling those in Ohio and New York and the more peaceful parts of Missouri. Its children played and went to school; its women labored at sewing, laundry, butter-churning, and domestic manufacturing; its men unloaded sacks of grain from wagons, hammered horseshoes into shape, and haggled over prices. Its families went to church on Sunday, attended dances and parties, wrote letters to sons serving in the

Union army in a dozen different units. It was no den of evil, nor even a military target; at the moment, only a handful of raw recruits slept in tents on the edge of town.

But that is precisely why Quantrill wanted to go, and why his allies and adherents agreed. He spoke to his men of getting "revenge," and to Quantrill, revenge meant *terror*. The bushwhackers went to Lawrence not to score a victory; they went to inflict pain—not because of who their victims were, but because of who they, the guerrillas, had become.

On the night of August 18, the Missourians began to collect for the strike into Kansas. Estimates of the force range up to 450 men, though McCorkle later put the figure at 150, and the first Union report counted only 200. On the morning of August 21, after an all-night ride from Missouri, they arrived at Lawrence. Quantrill led them on a thundering gallop into the center of the town. "Kill!" he ordered. "Kill and you will make no mistake! Lawrence should be thoroughly cleansed, and the only way to cleanse it is to kill! Kill!"

They killed. They shot every man and boy they saw. They pulled them out of cellars and attics, knocked them off horses, and executed them in front of their families. They clubbed them, knifed them, stole their money and valuables, burned their homes and businesses. Black and white, ministers, farmers, merchants, schoolboys, recruits: at least two hundred died in terror, while others lingered wounded in the ashes of the town. Jim Lane, the man they most wanted to kill, narrowly escaped by dashing through a cornfield in his nightshirt. Did Frank James stand in the parlors, front yards, and side streets of Lawrence, firing his revolver at helpless civilians? That is what he came to do, though no specific act has been attributed to him.[11]

The slaughter of innocents was hardly unknown to Americans. But massacres had almost always occurred—and almost always would occur—on the frontiers of race. A year before Lawrence, an even bloodier butchery took place in Minnesota, as frustrated, starving Dakota warriors broke out of their reservation and murdered homesteaders southwest of St. Paul. A year after Lawrence, an atrocity almost as costly would be inflicted on the Southern Cheyenne by Colorado settlers at Sand Creek. In the decade to come, hundreds if not thousands of African Americans would die in mass murders across the South. What made Lawrence particularly shocking to Unionist contemporaries was the common identity of the killers and most of the killed: white Protestant men of old American families. And what made Lawrence so acceptable to secessionists was the notion that the people of that town had deracinated themselves, since they consorted with blacks, treated slaves as equals, even gave them arms and put them in uniform. "One of them damned nigger-thieving abolitionists ain't dead yet," one of the guerrillas exclaimed to a companion during the raid. "Go and kill him."[12]

Retribution and countermeasures came in one package. On August 25, 1863, as Frank and the other raiders raced back to the refuge of the Sni-A-Bar ravines, General Ewing issued General Order No. 11: Everyone living in the counties in his district that bordered Kansas (Jackson, Cass, Bates, and the northern half of Vernon) was ordered to leave within fifteen days. Only those who lived near Kansas City or within one mile of four designated towns were spared. General Schofield approved. "The measure which has been adopted seems a very harsh one," he explained; "but . . . I am satisfied it is wise and humane. It was not adopted hastily, as a consequence of the Lawrence massacre. The subject had long been discussed between General Ewing and myself." The slaughter at Lawrence simply made it unavoidable.[13]

And brutal. "There is hundreds of people leaving their homes from this country and God knows what is to become of them," wrote Lieutenant Colonel Bazel F. Lazear of the First Cavalry Regiment, MSM. He observed the desperate evacuation from his post in Lexington, and poured out his reaction in a letter to his wife at their home in Louisiana, Missouri. "It is heart sickening to see what I have seen since I have been back here. A desolate country and women & children some of them almost naked. Some on foot and some in old wagons. Oh God what a sight to see in this once happy and peaceable country."[14]

The area depopulated by General Order No. 11 became known as the Burnt District. Columns of Union troops marched through, killing abandoned livestock, seizing harvested crops, starting blazes in empty barns and houses. In Cass County, only 600 people were allowed to remain, out of the 9,794 counted in the 1860 census. When the refugees crossed to Clay and other neighboring counties, the military ordered them to move on, forcing them to resettle far from their homes.[15]

General Order No. 11 aroused pity in the minds of Union soldiers, but not guilt. After Lazear described the horrors of the civilian evacuation to his wife, he placed the blame firmly on the bushwhackers. "There is no punishment on earth great enough for the villains who have brought this Rebellion about," he fumed. "I yesterday had one publicly shot. . . . He was in the Lawrence raid. He is the second prisoner I have had shot and I will have every one of them shot I can get hold of, as such inhuman wretches deserve no mercy and should be shot down like dogs wherever found."[16]

Lazear's Missouri militia struck at Quantrill's stronghold along the Sni-A-Bar Creek from the east as the Eleventh Kansas Cavalry moved in from the west. It was grim work. On October 1, for example, Sergeant Sherman

Bodwell and a detachment of Kansas troopers captured a bushwhacker, and the major in command began to interrogate the wounded Missourian. He "was talking, claiming to be a prisoner, etc.," Bodwell scribbled in his diary. "Lt. asked Maj., Are you through with him? Maj. nodded assent. Lt. said to men standing about 'mount your horses' & as they drew off aimed & fired the revolver, ball striking just back of the eye." Over the next few days, contacts with the enemy grew scarce. On October 4, they found an ominous abandoned camp, occupied only by a dog and the hanging corpse of a Union soldier. "Quantrill has evidently gathered his bands and left," Bodwell concluded, "maybe for Kan., maybe for the South."[17]

IN NORTHEASTERN Clay County, the slaves were whispering among themselves. In the first weeks of August 1863, messages flew from farm to farm—rumors of free black men, heavily armed, crossing over from Kansas to free their comrades. The moment has come, they whispered; wait for the designated night, when all would go in one general escape across the Missouri.

On the morning of August 14, they were gone. "Seven of the negroes left," reported Kate Watkins, just over the hill from Zerelda's farm. "They left on the night of the 13th of August, taking 6 horses, and a quantity of stolen clothes. . . . There was a general stampede the night they left. There is very few negroes left in the country." No one knows how many of Zerelda's slaves joined the "general stampede," but Charlotte remained, along with at least one of the two teenage girls.[18]

All of this enraged Colonel James H. Moss. Like Governor Hamilton R. Gamble, he was a conservative Whig to the core. But unlike his longtime friend Edward M. Samuel, he would never declare that he was "an Unconditional Union man, even *radically so,* if necessary to put down this rebellion." Quite the contrary: Moss saw no point in destroying the old slaveowning society in order to save it. And when he returned to Clay County from St. Louis in September 1863, that society was in chaos: respectable old citizens in military jails or under bond, the civil authorities ignored, bandits loose, and slaves running off en masse. "When I reached home," he wrote to Alexander Doniphan, "I found that the entire military force in Clay and Platte was nothing more or less than an armed mob."

Moss came ready to do something about it. Gamble had given him the authority to reorganize the militia in the two counties to protect them against the expected retaliation from Kansas for the Lawrence massacre. With Gamble's letter in his pocket, Moss planned to do far more: he was going to clear away the radicalism wrought by the Provisional EMM. "My arrival," he boasted, "was like the falling of a thunder bolt in their midst."

He immediately called a mass meeting in Liberty of all able-bodied men. It didn't matter if they were under bond, had enrolled as disloyal, or even if they had fought in General Price's army, he told them; they had to protect Clay County from Kansas bandits, the Red Legs. He armed two new companies of militia under John S. Thomason and George S. Story; within ten days, he claimed, they wiped out the bandits and stamped out anarchy. And he made a point of turning his prisoners over to the civil authorities, not the military provost marshal. "We have had perfect quiet in Clay & Platte for five days and nights past," he wrote on October 3, 1863, "and the people look refreshed after enjoying a few nights of quiet sleep."[19]

Not everyone was so enthusiastic about his enlistment of secessionists and former rebel soldiers. His own brother, O. P. Moss, pulled him aside to voice his concerns. "I remarked to my brother that we were running considerable risk in putting arms into the hands of such men indiscriminately," he said—but the colonel cut him off. "The war was far down South," he replied; besides, these "disloyal" men were old friends, and the most substantial citizens in the county.[20]

Colonel Moss's troops, however, soon lived up to his brother's fears. Organized into the Eighty-first and Eighty-second Regiments of the EMM, they won the nickname "Paw Paws," after the river-bottom bushes where the guerrillas made their camps. Though they vigorously pursued bandits from Kansas, they ignored—even aided—bushwhacker activity (with the notable exception of Captain John S. Thomason's faithful company). During the month of October, Confederate colonel Joseph O. Shelby mounted an epic raid into Missouri from his base in Arkansas; the celebrated cavalry leader dashed as far north as the Missouri River before retreating. The Paw Paws responded to the crisis by cheering Quantrill and Jefferson Davis in the streets.

A political hue darkened the issue. Colonel Moss bitterly denounced the Radical Party in a public speech. He deployed his troops to catch runaway slaves. When a Union officer came to Liberty to recruit black troops, the Paw Paws chased him out of town. And Moss dismissed the local Provisional EMM from service. All this terrified many loyal citizens. On December 26, the civil and (former) military officials in Clay—Edward M. Samuel, James M. Jones, William Garth, William Rhea, W. T. Reynolds, and Greenup Bird—petitioned army headquarters for a unit of "loyal men."

As complaints about the Paw Paws mounted, President Lincoln himself ordered General Schofield to look into it. But Colonel Moss survived, in part because old Whigs in uniform rallied to his defense. Even a full-scale investigation by the state legislature went nowhere. Indeed, Moss's experience underscores the growing division of the Unionist population into radical and conservative camps, a split that would have lasting political repercussions.

And so Clay and Platte Counties continued under the control of admitted rebels, armed by the state government. In one of the most ironic results of the massacre at Lawrence, the woods around Jesse James's home became safer for the guerrillas than at any time since early 1862. But where were the the guerrillas themselves?[21]

"YOU CANNOT IMAGINE what pleasure it gave to hear from an absent and beloved husband," wrote Amanda Savery to her spouse, Phineas, on January 27, 1864. "It has been one year since I received a letter or heard one word from you." Phineas Savery, once a respectable lawyer in peaceful Liberty, now served with the Confederate army in Mississippi. Even after a year, he had been lucky to find a messenger to slip through Union lines and carry a note to his home in Clay County. Meanwhile, his wife had waited, and fretted.

"You cannot imagine my dear what anxiety—so long a silence I thought a thousand things," she scrawled, virtually weeping ink onto the page. "I thought you was wounded or lying sick and suffering for the want of attention or perhaps you were killed and laying on the ground." She moved on to the news, all of it bitter. "Your brother Cyrus died of consumption over two years ago, [in] Illinois, in a land of strangers," Amanda wrote. "Your brother Abram died in camp near Brandy Station [Virginia] on the 16th [of January]. . . . He was a soldier of the United States service."[22] Savery's was indeed a family divided and destroyed by the war, like so many others.

In a few words, she summed up the miseries of a family cut off from its military men, and the terrors of war in Clay County.[23] For Jesse James and his family, the terrors subsided during the winter of 1863–64. The Paw Paws mostly left secessionists alone during the snowbound months. Meanwhile, two colonels from General Price's army, John H. Winston and John C. Calhoun Thornton (Colonel Moss's brother-in-law), remained in the county, gathering recruits for an uprising in the spring. From farm to farm, they whispered the rumors: Jo Shelby, now a brigadier general, would lead an invasion of Missouri, and a secret rebel organization, the Knights of the Golden Circle, was preparing to rise. Despite all their setbacks, secessionists renewed their faith in the cause. "The South is stronger now than ever before," they assured each other; "she will certainly gain her independence." Missouri, they nodded, would surely go with her.[24]

We can only imagine that Jesse, Zerelda, and her other children feared for Frank as Amanda Savery feared for her husband. Not until April, perhaps as late as May 1864, did they see again his long nose and lanky frame, uninjured after adventures and barbarities beyond description. It seems that he remained with Quantrill when the guerrillas pulled out of Jackson County for a march to Texas on October 1, 1863. Union troops were swarming then, and an early chill began to take leaves off the trees and lay frost on the ground, making trackers' work far simpler. Frank was with Quantrill at Baxter Springs, Kansas, where the bushwhackers annihilated the one-hundred-man guard of General James G. Blunt (though the general himself managed to escape). Frank passed the winter in Sherman, Texas, where the Missouri guerrillas disintegrated into quarreling gangs of bored, murderous bandits, feuding with the Confederate command as well as each other. By the time the bushwhackers set out in early spring for the long ride north, Bill Anderson and others had split off on their own. Quantrill went back to Missouri with sixty-four followers, only to lose command of this remnant to George Todd in a face-off over a poker game.[25]

It was a savage set of men who returned with Frank that April. Already hardened by war, they had been blistered by butchery at Lawrence and debauchery in Texas. And Charles Fletcher Taylor, the man who led the small squad that crossed over to Clay County, was one of the hardest. Short, broad-shouldered, sporting a neatly trimmed mustache and beard, "Fletch" had fought with Quantrill from the beginning, scouting out Lawrence before the raid, murdering the innocent in its streets, then riding to Texas. But there he turned against his master, murdering a Confederate officer and resisting Quantrill's attempt to arrest him. Now he fought (in the phrase of the times) "on his own hook." Cantering beside him was an even smaller, even more vicious killer: "Little Archie" Clement, a gray-eyed eighteen-year-old from Johnson County. Barely five feet tall, he looked more like a jockey than a guerrilla. But he was already an experienced gunman, and he would soon win the lasting admiration of Frank's little brother.[26]

These were the men who brought sixteen-year-old Jesse James to manhood. A year after being dragged through the tobacco field by the Provisional militia, three years after Frank first enlisted in the State Guard, Jesse rode to war. Guided by Frank or another Clay County recruit in late May, he would have crept out at night and sneaked down hog trails to the rugged Fishing River, where Taylor and Clement lay hidden. "There seems to be something of the deathlike brooding over these camps," wrote Sergeant Bodwell in his diary, after finding an abandoned bushwhacker bivouac. "Always hidden where hardly more than a horse track points the way, in heavy timber and creek bottoms, offal lying about, cooking utensils, cast-off clothing."

Jesse would have seen a cluster of men gathered around the fire under an awning of low leaves and branches, cooking a meal, drying out socks, cleaning and loading weapons. A strong smell of horses, sweat, and waste (human and animal) would have struck him, followed by the dense smoke of burning green wood with undertones of oiled leather and wet flannel. They were all young—some astonishingly young, like Jesse himself. "If you ever want to pick a company to do desperate work," Frank later mused, "select young men from 17 to 21 years old. . . . Take our company and there has never been a more reckless lot of men. Only one or two were over 25. Most of them were under 21. Scarcely a dozen boasted a moustache." Or, as another grizzled veteran put it, almost exactly a century after Jesse crept into that camp, "You're going to learn that one of the most brutal things in the world is your average nineteen-year-old American boy."[27]

Now the ritual began. First was the matter of equipment. Either Zerelda or Charlotte sewed a guerrilla shirt for Jesse—a loose pullover with two deep breast pockets for percussion caps, powder charges, and .36 caliber lead balls. Then he needed pistols, a horse, and a saddle. The revolver was the primary weapon, its rapid rate of fire well suited to guerrilla ambushes. Before the war, Colt's revolvers had been somewhat uncommon, even in Missouri, and they were hard to get legitimately after the conflict began. But the bushwhackers equipped themselves through smuggling, theft, and plundering of the Union dead; so if Jesse did not have a set, one was given to him. As for horses, he would have been told to steal them.[28]

This last lesson was the start of a much deeper, more lasting education. They were guerrillas. They were not engaged in a war that a colonel of the Army of the Potomac or a general of the Army of Northern Virginia could recognize. They had no lines, no objectives, no strategy, no command structure. Theirs was a purely tactical war, a war to inflict pain, to punish, to kill and destroy. Every barn and brook was a battlefield; every civilian, either an ally or a target. By stepping into that brooding, deathlike camp, Jesse James entered a race to find and kill as many enemies as he could.[29]

ON APRIL 29, 1864, Major General William S. Rosecrans telegraphed an alert to Colonel Moss in Liberty. The guerrillas were returning, he warned, "to reinaugurate the scenes of murder and robbery which have desolated your country during the past three years." Rosecrans, humiliated by defeat at the battle of Chickamauga, had been shifted in January to command the Department of the Missouri, a strategic eddy far from the main channels of the war. The state might have been a backwater, but Rosecrans learned that its currents were swift and unpredictable. Accustomed to wielding brigades, divisions, and corps as he marched toward objectives, he now had to weave a net out of slender companies, battalions, and regiments as he waded into guerrilla waters. And no units threatened to unravel more quickly than Colonel Moss's troublesome Paw Paws. "I expect from you and the Enrolled Militia under your command," he wrote, "such a reception . . . as will amply vindicate you from all the charges of disloyalty which have been urged against you." Moss assured Rosecrans that all would be well.[30]

Brigadier General Clinton B. Fisk was not so certain. After a military reorganization in January, this stern and voluble officer had assumed command of the District of North Missouri, after serving in the southeastern corner of the state. Fisk had received his rank, in part, through connections in the northern branch of the Methodist Church, an avowedly abolitionist denomination; the savagery of the guerrilla war, however, had negated whatever Christian charity remained within him.[31] Rather than rely on Moss, he shifted Captain William B. Kemper and part of Company K, Ninth Cavalry Regiment, MSM, to Liberty in early May 1864. "Clean out and kill every marauding, thieving villain you find," he wrote to Kemper on May 15, adding, "Keep your eyes on the Paw Paws."

The captain needed no instructions on that point: he intended to avoid Moss's men at all costs as he pursued the bushwhackers. And the guerrillas *were* back—he could feel it. But every time he sent squads to scout the countryside, they came back emptyhanded. On May 24, Kemper changed tactics. After nightfall, he ordered fifteen men to draw rations, mount their horses, and follow him into the country, where he deployed in ambush. After spending a day waiting for the enemy, he gathered his troopers out of hiding and moved on to another spot. Meanwhile, he sent out two spies; each night he rendezvoused with them to better plan his trap for the following day.[32]

Across the Missouri River, the Second Colorado Cavalry employed the same tactics with devastating effect. Kemper, however, had fewer men and experienced opponents. Fletch Taylor and Archie Clement easily slipped past his ambushes to deliver a sharp reminder that there was no line between combatants and civilians. On June 1, they led their Clay County recruits (dressed in captured Union uniforms) to the farm of Bradley Bond. Gathering outside the front door, they asked to see the man of the house. When Bond stepped outside they shot him to death. The next day, they murdered Alvis Dagley in a field not far from the Samuel place, then trotted to his house and coldly told his widow.

Over the next few weeks, the gang killed at least eight Unionist civilians. "Men were slain before the eyes of their wives and children," one resident wrote, "or else shot down without mercy by the roadside and their bodies left to fester and corrupt in the sun. Property was taken and destroyed on every hand, business of all kinds prostrated, values were unsettled, everything was disturbed." They killed one slave "for fun," and they looted as freely as the worst jayhawkers or militia.

Jesse James never attempted to distance himself from this slaughter; in later years, one of his closest friends boasted of how Jesse and Frank went alone to the home of a local Unionist, just after the death of Dagley, and murdered him outside his house. This, then, was his introduction to warfare: not as a gladiator in battle against a tyrannous foe, but as a member of a death squad, picking off neighbors one by one.[33]

OF ALL THE departures in Jesse James's dramatic life, none would ever be so momentous—or portentous—as this one. More than a hundred years after Jesse first fired a revolver at another human being, sociologist Lonnie Athens laid out a process he calls "violentization," which may best describe what the young Missourian passed through. It is how dangerous violent criminals come into being.

In violentization, Athens writes, an individual passes through four stages. First is brutalization, which consists of violent subjugation by an authority figure, witnessing the subjugation of a close friend or family member, and violent coaching by an intimate—who may ridicule the subject, repeatedly urge him to hurt others, or glorify violence through storytelling. Brutalization leads the subject to reject religious and cultural norms of civil behavior. The next stage is belligerency, as the subject resolves to respond to provocations with force. Then comes the third and most difficult stage, violent performances. The subject pushes through a psychological barrier, and actually inflicts pain on another person. That leads to the final step in the process: virulency. The subject feels his social status change after his violent performance; he sees that others now fear him, while some of his intimates congratulate and reward him. He feels enormously powerful—in sharp contrast to the helplessness he had endured at the brutalization stage—and decides to respond with overwhelming force to the smallest slight.[34]

This narrative seems to echo Jesse's life. As a boy, he was turned out of his home and sent away from his mother by his first stepfather; he probably witnessed the beating of slaves, perhaps even hangings; and, most important, he and his family were brutalized by the Provisional militia that stormed onto the farm in May 1863. He had violence coaches on every side, from Zerelda (who explicitly praised the worst rebel atrocities) to his brother Frank. After he took to the brush, Taylor and Clement took over as his mentors; they mocked him for his boyish diffidence, nicknaming him "Dingus" after a euphemistic curse he once uttered. But once he joined in the killing, they gave him their respect. "Not to have any beard," one of the deadliest guerrillas supposedly said of him, "he is the keenest and cleanest fighter in the command." Jesse abandoned all civil norms, even the blunt-instrument morality of a slaveowning culture. He now belonged to a group that believed a man must murder for respect.[35]

Jesse, like other products of violentization, did not act on impulse. He reflected on what had happened to him, and how he should respond. He reportedly blamed those first two victims, Bond and Dagley, for his beating on the day the militia raided the farm, and for hanging his stepfather. Popular tradition describes Jesse's trip to the brush as a quest for revenge against such men—a simplified (and sanitized) version of the violentization process. Indeed, there was nothing military about the decision to kill either Bond or Dagley; they had long since left the militia, and had been tending their fields and livestock in peace.[36]

These facts compellingly fit Athens's model—though of course Missouri was at war. The guerrilla conflict may have been an intensely personal struggle, but it was still part of a much larger clash of ideologies. Hatred of abolitionism ran deep in Jesse's family; Rev. Robert James had battled antislavery Baptists as far back as 1845. The Kansas conflict had sharpened the proslavery argument to a lethal edge, and Zerelda had led her children to the Confederate side at the very beginning of the war, long before the Union authorities inflicted any suffering upon them.

By the time Jesse put on his guerrilla shirt, a full year had passed since the brutal raid by the Provisional militia. After a quiet Paw Paw winter, with the conservative Colonel Moss and former Confederates in control of the county, Jesse and his family faced the smallest threat of danger and harassment since the arrival of Union forces. Once he joined the bushwhackers, the process of violentization sped rapidly ahead—but it cannot fully account for his decision to enlist in the first place. In perhaps the most hotly ideological era in American history, Jesse was a true believer. He fought not as a victim, but as a warrior in a cause.[37]

In one of George Orwell's earliest and best essays, "Shooting an Elephant," he describes how, as a colonial policeman in Burma, he shot to death an elephant that had gone on a rampage. Orwell was troubled by the fact that the animal had ceased to be a danger by the time he confronted it. But as a crowd of native Burmese gathered around and watched him stand there with his rifle, he felt compelled to fire. "I perceived in this moment that when the white man turns tyrant it is his own freedom that he destroys," he wrote. "He wears a mask, and his face grows to fit it. . . . A sahib has got to act like a sahib."[38]

Outwardly, there was nothing unethical about his shooting of that elephant: Who could say the animal would not go berserk again? Indeed, the author acted as everyone expected him to act. But he refused to congratulate himself; instead, with searing honesty, Orwell recognized the small atrocity he had committed, and saw that he had committed it against himself. His words remind us of the power of a civilized mind, of how a humane imagination may defy evil, even the subtlest kind, and penetrate the veils of self-justification. He reminds us that no one is simply a creature of circumstance, even among a hostile people in a restive colony halfway around the globe.

Jesse was no stranger in a foreign land—he was at home among old neighbors and friends. Yet he helped to tear apart his community without reflection or self-doubt. He did far more damage, both outwardly and inwardly, than Orwell ever would, yet he never questioned the justice or effects of his actions. Seized by his hatred and ideological convictions, he could not see himself for what he was. Unlike the Unionist Anna Slayback of St. Joseph, he never moaned, "But this is a family quarrel, brother against brother, & we bite & devour one another that other nations may mock & laugh at our folly."[39]

Instead, he reveled in the power his murders earned him. It may not have been easy at the beginning. Perhaps his legs felt weak as he rode to his first killing; perhaps nausea swept over him in a fit of nervous tension when the gunfire erupted; perhaps his heart pounded when he first squeezed the trigger. But his mind was prepared for the work, honed by his beliefs, his experiences, and his family—and repetition soon made it routine. Jesse James's face did not grow to fit the mask of the bushwhacker; by the time he put it on, in the third year of the war, it was already close to a perfect match.

WITH THE COUNTRYSIDE dissolving into chaos, Colonel Moss dropped out of view; in Clay County, his Paw Paws were largely deactivated. To replace them, Captain Kemper asked three of the best local guerrilla-fighters, John S. Thomason, John W. Younger, and William Garth, to organize new companies of Enrolled Militia. General Fisk kept the telegraph busy with a flurry of orders, sending a fifty-six-man militia company from Ray County on the march west and reinforcing Kemper with the rest of his MSM cavalry company. Meanwhile, Edward M. Samuel and other Unionist leaders pleaded for more troops.[40]

More troops were exactly what Kemper needed. "There is a great number of men of Clay County who had left their homes in the last few days and gone in the brush," he informed Fisk on June 15. He compiled a list of men whom Colonel Thornton had sworn in for regular Confederate service, then went house to house, arresting dozens, including some once thought to be strong Unionists. Taylor's guerrillas were another matter. "I have a scout of thirty men," Kemper wrote to the general, "lying on the road for the purpose of capturing them as they pass. I did not succeed in seeing but one whilst I was out. I shot his horse, but failed to get him."[41]

Stymied, Kemper resorted to old-fashioned detective work. Scouting the heavily timbered Fishing River, he found signs of guerrilla activity on the farm of John Eaton. "I noticed at the yard fence a path made, both by horses and men," he reported. "I was convinced at once that the track must be that of the bushwhackers. . . . I took the track at once, and followed it through a pasture adjoining the yard into a densely brushy pasture, where I came upon this party of bushwhackers." Jesse was probably sitting in that camp when the captain and his troopers burst in, revolvers barking, bullets spitting through leaves and branches. But the rebels scrambled to safety, returning fire as they scattered through the brush, a typically frustrating skirmish for a Union soldier in Missouri.[42]

Fisk dearly wished to exterminate the guerrillas, but he reluctantly agreed to let two local citizens negotiate a cease-fire. In late June, they found their way to Taylor's camp with a message: If he promised to abandon Clay County, the military authorities would leave secessionist families alone. All the residents wanted, they told him, was peace—a return to the status quo, much as Colonel Moss had maintained with the Paw Paws. Taylor accepted their terms.

Then the militia shot a secessionist, and Taylor decided to retaliate. This time they were going to kill Solomon G. Bigelow, one of the first organizers of the EMM in Clay County. In late June, Jesse cleaned and loaded his revolvers, threw a saddle over the back of his horse, and rode with Frank and a dozen other bushwhackers to Bigelow's house. When Taylor asked his victim to step outside, however, he was answered by a blast of gunfire that sparked a grueling siege. Jesse experienced hostile fire for the first time as Bigelow and his brother defended the house to the last, even tearing apart furniture to make clubs when they ran out of ammunition. When the brothers finally fell, Jesse looked down to see his own blood dampening his clothing; by one account, this was when he lost his fingertip.[43]

Tellingly, Jesse's first real fight had not been on a grand field of battle, but at the home of a local farmer who was no longer an active soldier. But neither the petty brutality of it nor the Bigelows' stiff resistance cut short his growing ferocity. In the company of armed, unrestrained, and angry young men, he who was most savage garnered the most respect; he who was the least bit sensitive was accounted a fool. The very next day, the guerrillas murdered a Unionist civilian who had the misfortune to meet them on the road. Meanwhile they gathered up new recruits, swelling their numbers to twenty-five or more.

On the rainy night of July 3, the bushwhackers rode to a new camp on the Fishing River. With battle-tested instincts, Taylor kept an eye on his own trail; after the attack on the Bigelows, he expected a response from Captain Kemper. The next morning, he learned that Kemper was indeed close behind. Taylor ordered the men over a steep bank along a bend in the river, just above a ford. The young James scuffled with the others through the sticky mud to the water's edge, then crouched down and waited.

Soon he heard the heavy tramp of Kemper's horsemen crashing through the brush toward the water, then splashes as they moved into the river. Taylor gave the command. The line of guerrillas rose up and blasted the patrol with a hurricane of bullets. Kemper himself tumbled out of his saddle, his leg torn by a lead ball. The militiamen immediately broke off the disastrous fight, carrying their injured commander back to Liberty.[44]

Jesse could only have been ecstatic. His second pitched battle had been an exhilaratingly one-sided victory, the sort of textbook ambush that Frank had seen a year earlier on the same river. Taylor, on the other hand, was enraged. He sent a letter to Kemper, lacerating him for breaking the terms of the cease-fire. "I am going to stay here," he wrote, "until the Radicals all leave this county." This was a revealing admission, though fully in keeping with his recent attacks: it acknowledged that the guerrillas' primary target was not the detachment of soldiers in Clay, but the *civilian* "Union party." Now, however, Taylor brashly offered to fight the MSM alone, provided the Union captain stopped harassing rebel civilians. "I will carry war on as you carry it on," he declared. "You can't drive me out of this county. . . . If I find that you are warring on the citizens, so be it; *I will retaliate*—if you fight me alone, I will return the compliment."

He signed the letter, published on July 8 in the *Liberty Tribune*, "Chas. F. Taylor, Captain Commanding the Country," and addressed it to "Capt. Kemper, Commanding the Town." The choice of words was clever, an apt summary of the classic situation in a successful guerrilla insurrection. Of course, Taylor had no such rank as "captain"; none of the guerrillas, with the exception of Quantrill, held a formal Confederate commission. They often affected such titles, but all (even Quantrill's) were truly meaningless. Military ranks reflect the subdivision and articulation of a military force, which allows a commander to manipulate the elements under his control. Bushwhacker gangs, however, were spontaneously organized, forming and dissolving almost randomly, men rising to power through personal ability and popularity. Only once during the war would a sizable number of guerrillas within Missouri respond to the Confederate chain of command—a time that was rapidly approaching, bringing with it disaster.[45]

The guerrillas' war on the civilian population had nearly succeeded. "A general terror prevails," wrote one former militiaman on July 12, 1864.

"Today there is not in the county of Clay one unconditional loyal Union man who dares to go into the harvest field to do a day's work. Many of them have left the State; all are now talking of going." On July 20, some fifteen hundred citizens gathered in a mass meeting in Liberty and condemned Taylor's gang in the starkest terms. "Guerrillas—whatever the name they assume—and bushwhackers are the ravenous monsters of society," they declared, "and their speedy and utter extermination should be sought by all brave and honorable men."[46]

The bushwhacker leader had already left, however, taking Jesse, Frank, and the rest of his men west into Platte County, where Colonel Thornton had gone to gather more recruits. On July 6, they attacked the village of Parkville. On July 10, they linked up with Thornton's makeshift regiment for an assault on Platte City. At ten o'clock that morning, their column of three hundred to four hundred men marched into its deserted streets. Within fifteen minutes, the Paw Paw defenders confronted the invaders— in Confederate uniforms. The entire force had defected.

Platte City took on all the appearances of a liberated town. The population poured into the streets and chatted amiably with the rebels, and cheerfully looted a Unionist-owned dry-goods store. Jesse went to a photography studio and posed in his guerrilla shirt, one revolver in hand and two in his belt, his eyes staring hard and cold from his soft sixteen-year-old face. Fletch Taylor, overcome with enthusiasm, delivered a harangue, waving a bloody knife that he claimed to have thrust into the chest of a Radical only moments before. Then the bushwhackers dashed to the county's northern border, where they murdered an abolitionist minister of the Northern Methodist church. With Taylor and Thornton around, the secessionists could congratulate themselves, who needed General Price's army?[47]

Unfortunately for the Confederates, that was precisely the thought that occurred to Thornton. When the civilian crowds turned out to welcome him, when the Paw Paws defected, he began to believe that he could hold Platte County as a liberated zone until Price came to free the state. This sort of thinking rapidly sobered Taylor out of his speech-making megalomania. Now was the time to scatter, he told Thornton, before the enemy could counterattack. Thornton waved him off. After a couple of days, he shifted his little army to Camden Point, where the local ladies presented him with a flag reading, "Protect Missouri." Disgusted, the bushwhackers trotted away, leaving the recruits and rebellious Paw Paws to their fate.

Taylor, of course, was exactly right. On July 12, as Thornton admired his flag, General Fisk spent the day in his telegraph office, coordinating three columns of troops that converged on Camden Point. At dawn on July 14, Colonel James H. Ford led the attack. The result was less a battle than the start of a mad chase. Surprised and outfought, Thornton fled east, trailing stragglers all the way through Clay County. Back in Platte City, Charles Jennison, now in command of the Fifteenth Kansas Cavalry Regiment, sent his men from house to house, methodically burning the town as repayment for its rebellion. When they finished, only fifteen residents remained.[48]

The bushwhackers had long since returned to Clay County. According to one source (an intimate of Jesse James, though an unreliable chronicler), Jesse's close friend Archie Clement accompanied him on the ride home. As the pair arrived there, they surprised two militiamen picking apples from a tree. Yanking their pistols, the pair of teenagers blasted them out of the branches, laughing happily, "and made sport of the fruit that such apple orchards bore." Many historians believe that Clement was elsewhere, but the story may be true. "This moment the news comes in," wrote a Unionist in Liberty on July 12, 1864, "that two young soldiers were bushwhacked today at Centerville."[49]

Home, however, would soon be no place for a guerrilla. Clay County now swarmed with perhaps five hundred Union troops. "I have my whole force since my arrival at Liberty constantly scouting," wrote Colonel Ford on July 18. Many of them haunted the landscape around Zerelda's house. "Look where you will, you see one," wrote a teenage girl from the Watkins farm. "So many of the confounded Feds were here, and doing us so much mischief," she wrote on July 24. Small wonder, then, that the guerrillas broke up into small groups and fled.[50]

The "enemy here seemed to have scattered in every direction," Colonel Ford reported on July 25. "We labored under a great disadvantage," he complained; "the citizens gave the enemy information of any movement I made, stand picket for them, and I can get no information whatever, only as I send out small parties to play bushwhacker."[51]

Ford's words provide a fitting conclusion to the first phase of Jesse's guerrilla education. Missouri's war was no longer a struggle over a line on a map, whether an international boundary would be drawn along Iowa's southern rim. It was now a war to remake society itself. In Clay County, Jesse and the other bushwhackers spent most of their time slaying Unionist civilians, clashing with Kemper's troops only when Kemper tracked them down. In Platte County, Taylor had gone out of his way to kill a Northern Methodist minister—who, as an abolitionist spokesman, was as great a threat to Missouri's Southern identity as an entire company of Federal troops. He abandoned Thornton not only for tactical reasons, but because conventional warfare was a distraction from the bushwhackers' political cleansing of the countryside. The Unionists fought the same kind of war, against each other as well as against secessionists. The controversy over

Colonel Moss's Paw Paws represented a clash between a conservative, proslavery Unionism and the growing abolitionism of the Provisional militia and EMM captains Anthony Harsel and John Younger.

This was the lasting lesson that Jesse learned in his first days as a gunman. It was a lesson that would stay with him until the end of the war, through the tumultuous year that followed, through a decade more of life as an outlaw. Guerrilla warfare was deeply personal, yet also purposeful. It was small-scale and vicious, with none of the standard trophies of conventional victories. Rather, its successes could be measured from farm to farm, in the sentiment of the people, in the flight of frightened foes. "At the start of the rebellion, the people of Clay were a unit for the Union," thought Sheriff F. R. Long. But at the end of 1864, Captain Kemper would write, "I feel today that I am almost as much in 'rebellion' here in this county as I would be in South Carolina." This was the bushwhacker goal, and the bushwhackers triumphed. By attacking the dissenting population, they waged a war of ideology, in which their most effective weapon was pure terror.[52]

Jesse's time with Fletch Taylor had come to an end. After the guerrillas scattered, Taylor crossed the Missouri River, and Jesse and Frank looked for a new leader. Their choice showed how deeply they had absorbed all these lessons. They were going to join the most brutal gang of terrorists in Missouri, whose leader, "Bloody Bill" Anderson, was rapidly becoming the personification of horror.

CHAPTER SEVEN

Horror

WILLIAM T. ANDERSON was a hard man. A handsome twenty-five-year-old, he had grown up tough in Kentucky, Kansas, and Missouri. After his father was killed in the Kansas Territory, he had drifted into simple banditry. Then the Civil War unleashed his full potential. Already an embittered, brooding man, he had filled with bile after one of his sisters died and two others suffered injuries in the Kansas City prison collapse. At Lawrence, he had killed the innocent with a special passion, telling one woman, "I'm here for revenge and I have got it." Afterward in Texas, he began his rise to notoriety by breaking away from Quantrill, leading his own column of guerrillas back to Missouri in the spring of 1864. He brought terror to the Unionists in Jackson and Lafayette Counties. As he operated outside of Lexington in July, he sent a letter to the newspapers that exceeded even Fletch Taylor's megalomania. "I will hunt you down like wolves and murder you," he warned the loyal citizens. "You cannot escape." Small wonder they began to call him "Bloody Bill."[1]

On July 11, 1864, he crossed the Missouri River into Carroll County with twenty-one men. Archie Clement is usually thought to have been among them, riding as Anderson's close companion. (If so, he could not have been on the Platte County raid with Jesse James.) They immediately killed nine civilians—murdering as many noncombatants in four hours as Taylor's band had in four weeks. Then they scorched their way across Chariton, Randolph, Monroe, Howard, and Boone Counties, killing and robbing with impunity. After gunning down one man in Anderson's hometown, Huntsville, the bushwhackers told a sobbing woman, "We would shoot Jesus Christ or God Almighty if he ran from us."

At some point during Anderson's parade of terror north of the Missouri River, Jesse and Frank James rode to join him, along with the other Clay County guerrillas who had followed Taylor. Given the massive influx of

Union troops into their old killing grounds, they may have linked up with him as early as the third week in July. If so, Jesse would have been back with his friend Archie Clement when the rebels ambushed a patrol near Huntsville, killing two. After the fight, Clement scalped the dead—an act that was fast becoming his trademark. "You come to hunt bush whackers," Anderson (or one of his followers) scratched on a piece of paper. "Now you are skelpt. Clemyent skept you. Wm. Anderson." Then he pinned the note to one of the bodies, and the guerrillas rode off.[2]

One way or another, the James brothers joined up with Anderson, who set up camp on or near their mother's farm in the first week of August 1864. The arrival of "Bloody Bill" was a grand occasion for local secessionists, and small bands of local, less notorious bushwhackers rode in. "In evident anticipation of the gathering together," wrote a friend (and embellisher) of Frank and Jesse, "Mrs. Samuels [sic], as much devoted to the cause as her two heroic boys, had prepared a splendid dinner."

The impact of all of this on the sixteen-year-old Jesse can scarcely be exaggerated. As a member of the most dangerous guerrilla organization in Missouri, he was now at the center of the secessionist cause. Indeed, with his mother playing hostess to Anderson's crew, his farm became the cause's physical home. But there must have been something even more personal that thrilled him. He had never known his father, and Reuben Samuel offered a poor substitute; but as he rode with the bushwhackers, he finally found himself in the company of authoritative men. This is not to say that Anderson had instantly become a father figure to him, or that Anderson alone was the definitive influence in his life—but Anderson, Taylor, Clement, and other guerrilla leaders did indeed become Jesse's role models. Far from being repelled by their savagery, Jesse was attracted to it. As his long career would show, he admired the way they inspired fear in their victims. He sought to emulate them and win their respect.

Anderson had much to teach the teenage boy. The education began with a quick plundering raid into Platte County. As Jesse and the others watched, Anderson tortured a prisoner with a knife, slicing off both ears before firing his revolver into the man's head. Then he led the gang back to Clay County. On August 10, they encountered "a harmless, inoffensive Union man" (according to locals) as he was on his way to get a doctor for his sick mother. By now, Jesse would have vied with the others to empty his pistol into the man's body. The victim had married three days before; now he was a naked corpse on the muddy bank of a creek.[3]

All this proved too much for Reuben Samuel. The year before he had been hanged for the sake of one stepson and a relatively obscure guerrilla chieftain. Now he had two stepsons in the brush, and the most notorious bushwhacker in Missouri in his yard. So as his domineering wife laughed with the visiting guerrillas and ordered Charlotte to throw another ham into the pot, he quietly slipped off the farm for the twelve-mile journey to Liberty. There he made his way to Edward M. Samuel, most likely in his office at the Clay County Savings Association. Hat in hand, he begged the influential Unionist to write a letter on his behalf to the provost marshal. Under his parole, he explained, he needed explicit permission to leave the state—and he had decided to go to Indiana.

As E. M. Samuel looked over the broken figure in front of him, he saw "an easy, good natured, good for nothing fellow." This pathetic man, he remarked, was "completely under the control of his wife," a woman with a formidable reputation as a razor-tongued secessionist. A year earlier, the politic banker had spoken up for Reuben; now he had no interest in helping him. "I told him, very bluntly and plainly, that it was his *duty* to help the military authorities in finding out his stepsons," he wrote to the provost marshal in St. Joseph, "and in bringing them to justice." When Reuben saw that he would never get his pass to Indiana, he quietly returned home to the twin dangers of bushwhackers and militia.[4]

The Union authorities had no intention of letting him stay there. By now it was common knowledge that both Jesse and Frank rode with Bill Anderson, and that Zerelda had assisted the bushwhackers at every opportunity. In the second week of August, Colonel Edward C. Catherwood, the new MSM commander in Liberty, ordered the Samuel clan and ten other Clay County families to prepare for evacuation from Union-held Missouri. He gave them just ten days; after that, they would be banished from the state (as General Fisk wrote) for being "the most disloyal of that disloyal locality."

Zerelda and her shattered husband no doubt loaded their things into a wagon and waited for the final order to leave. It never came. A bureaucratic glitch stalled their banishment: Union headquarters in St. Louis sent back Catherwood's list, telling him to annotate it with "the reason why, with evidence," each person should be banished. As the fighting intensified in August and September, the colonel never found time to return to the matter.[5]

If Jesse and Frank's recruitment into Anderson's band made things worse for their mother and stepfather, it magnified their stature among the bushwhacker fraternity. Bloody Bill was, quite simply, the most vicious man in Missouri. "You talk about Quantrill, Todd, and Taylor being reckless raiders and fighters," wrote fellow Clay County bushwhacker Jim Cummins, "but Anderson I thought was worse than any of them when I joined him." He stood a slender five feet ten inches tall in his captured Union officer's coat, "quick and lithe in action as a tiger—whose nature he at times possessed," wrote one observer who spared no tender feelings for the guerrilla leader. "His hair was his greatest ornament," a mass of shoulder-length, brown, wavy strands that surrounded a tanned face with a full beard, topped by a cavalryman's hat. Most striking were his eyes, a blend of blue and gray. "They were cold, unsympathizing and expressionless, never firing in anger or lighting with enthusiasm in battle." And yet, by all accounts, battle is what he hungered for.[6]

Fletch Taylor had since gone across the Missouri River. On August 8, 1864, a shotgun blast forced the amputation of his right arm (which led editor Robert Miller of the *Liberty Tribune* to express his sincere hope that the wound might prove fatal).[7]

By now, the woods and roads echoed with the relentless tramp of Catherwood's Sixth Cavalry Regiment, MSM, and two local EMM companies under Captains Garth and Younger. They interrogated civilians, burned down the houses of sympathizers, occasionally caught a guerrilla or two in the open.[8] On August 11 or 12, Anderson decided to move east into Ray County. After two months in the brush, the ritual would now be familiar to Jesse: currying his mount, cleaning and loading his revolvers, packing his bedroll and clothes. "Anderson always made us keep our horses in good condition," Frank later remarked. "If a man did not keep a good horse and good pistols," he found himself in trouble. As the column of guerrillas trotted out of their creek-bottom or farmyard camp, Jesse may have kept close to his friend Arch Clement, who was feared and admired by all the bushwhackers. If so, he also kept close to Anderson himself, who relied heavily on the ruthless Little Archie—"the real brains of Anderson's command," in Frank's words.[9]

On August 12, just across the Ray County line, Anderson's column of fifty to seventy-five bushwhackers thrashed one EMM patrol, then lured another into a trap.[10] For the men of the Enrolled Missouri Militia, these encounters were harrowing indeed. Most of the men were just farmers, as one general noted, "leaving their homes at a time of the year when their services on their farms was badly needed . . . and without any preparations for the comfort of their families, or without any pay or prospects of being reimbursed for money and time expended in defending their government." Nor did they have any prospects of glory when they died, as they did so often when facing the bushwhackers.

The next day, Anderson drove his men on a rapid march from west-central to southeastern Ray County. The bushwhackers carefully kept clear of the professional, well-equipped Missouri State Militia, now pursuing from the west, but they eagerly fell on the ill-prepared EMM. They came across one man riding in his wagon, and casually shot him out of his seat. They caught two troopers on the road and cut their throats from ear to ear, then scalped them. They tied the bloody scraps to their saddles and bridles, in the increasingly popular style among Anderson's men. Jesse himself, according to one source, put his knife to the skull of one of these victims.[11]

As the James brothers trotted along together, toward the latter part of this swift and deadly ride across Ray County, Jesse caught sight of a fine-looking saddle balanced on a fence rail. His own, he mused, was rather poor by comparison, so he did what any guerrilla would do: he reined in his horse, slipped to the ground, and reached out to take it. Suddenly he heard a pop and felt the searing bite of a bullet tearing through his chest. In the doorway of a nearby house stood a man with a smoking gun, a German immigrant named Heizinger; the man turned and fled out the back, escaping through a cornfield as Frank rushed to help his brother.

At first, Jesse probably felt little pain. With Frank's help, he climbed back into the saddle, then rode on for three more miles, clinging to his brother for support. The shock soon wore off, however, and was replaced by piercing agony as blood soaked his bullet-torn shirt. Finally he could no longer keep his balance. The guerrillas commandeered a wagon, set him inside, and drove to the home of John A. Rudd, a secessionist who lived close by on the Missouri River. As he bounced along in the rattling wagon, Jesse reportedly explained to a friend, he was in such intense pain that he wished the Federals would catch and kill him.[12]

He apparently remained in Rudd's home until a doctor came to see him. The physician's name was I. M. Ridge, and he had known Jesse since he was a boy. Dr. Ridge had been at home in Kansas City when Thomas James, a wealthy uncle of Frank and Jesse, came to ask for his help. "It was a dangerous undertaking," Ridge recalled, "but I agreed to do the best I could." He traveled "by a circuitous route on horseback," to throw off Union scouts. "I hitched my horse out in the thick underbrush and made my way into the house by the back way, the family aware of my coming. I was shown to a room in the second story and then into a clothes closet, from the floor of which a small moveable ladder reached to a trap door opening into the loft. There lay Jesse in great pain and in a very dangerous condition, for he had received no medical attention."

Examining the injured boy, he saw that a large-caliber bullet had struck him outside the right nipple and passed clear through his chest. There was little Ridge could do, given the time that had passed and the limited nature of medicine in 1864. Already scar tissue may have begun to form; perhaps a mild infection had set in, turning the ragged holes red and swollen. The doctor probably cleaned up the entrance and exit wounds, changed the bandages, and perhaps gave Jesse some useless medicine. Then he left, promising to return every week or so.[13]

And so Jesse lay there, hidden away in an attic, staring at the ceiling in the choking August heat. One moment, he had been an invincible bush-whacker; the next, he was on his back with a searing pain in his chest. Instead of catching a bullet in battle, he had been shot while stealing a sad-dle. Worst of all would have been the sense that he was missing out. His brother and friends were suffering, fighting, and winning without him; later he would have to listen to their stories. He must have wondered if he would ever rejoin them.[14]

BILL ANDERSON WAS weeping. "Great tears coursed down his cheeks, his breast heaved, and his body shook," recalled one of his followers. Then the bushwhacker lapsed into silence, "morose, sullen, and gloomy." For half of September he had ruled Boone County from the waterside town of Rocheport—"my capital," as he called it—stopping riverboat traffic and collecting "taxes" from the population. Then things turned sour. Five of his tax collectors died at the hands of the Ninth Cavalry Regiment, MSM, which also had captured their scalp-decorated horses.[15]

All this made Anderson the silent, brooding figure that Jesse saw when he rejoined the band. The wound turned out to be less severe than it looked. The low-velocity bullet had probably skipped along the outside of Jesse's rib cage, missing his internal organs. Four weeks of rest and an active immune system had allowed him to saddle his horse again, probably by September 23, when Anderson ambushed an MSM wagon train, killing twelve troopers and three black teamsters. But the Ninth struck back the same day, catching seven bushwhackers sleeping in a hayloft. The Union troopers killed and scalped six of them, and made a prisoner of the seventh, Cave Wyatt.[16]

Early on September 24, 1864, Bill Anderson mounted his distinctive black horse and led his men north to Fayette, determined to hit the Ninth in its base. Jesse and his brother cantered toward town in the column of bush-whackers, and they caught sight of another body of mounted men, some in blue uniforms, some in civilian dress, carrying a mix of carbines, shotguns, and revolvers. It was typical of an EMM company—or a guerrilla band. After a few tense moments, they learned that it was a bushwhacker gang under George Todd, the other leading heir of Quantrill's command.[17]

Todd's band numbered well over one hundred men, gathered from var-ious squads (including that of a bushwhacker from Lexington named Dave Pool). As Anderson rode forward to meet them, his men caught sight of a slender fellow with sandy hair and a calm, self-assured presence—Quantrill himself. He had put aside the humiliation of the rebellion against him, and rejoined his old followers for a special purpose. General Price, Todd explained, had sent word that the long-awaited liberation of Missouri was about to begin; the guerrillas were to raid the Hannibal and St. Joseph Railroad and draw Federal forces north of the Missouri River.[18]

Anderson may not have trusted what Todd told him. Like Confederate currency, promises of a rebel liberation of Missouri had circulated a little too freely to be worth much. But Bloody Bill was happy to unite with his guerrilla comrades, if they would help him attack Fayette. Todd agreed to the plan, over Quantrill's objections. Their combined force—anywhere from two hundred to four hundred men—would surely overwhelm the garrison, disguised as they were in captured Union uniforms.

At 10:30 on that Saturday morning, Anderson's boys pulled on their blue coats and formed a column. Jesse kept close to his friend and mentor Arch Clement as they trotted into town. They were in luck: much of the Ninth MSM was still on patrol, leaving behind only 150 men. Anderson's force cantered through the streets, arousing no suspicion.[19] Then one of the bushwhackers saw a black man in a Union uniform. It was more than he could stand. Pulling his revolver, he shot him down. The echoing crack of the pistol immediately caught the attention of the garrison. In the center of Fayette, twenty men of the provost guard raced into the courthouse and barred the door. The guerrillas scattered as this small squad cheered loudly and poured fire out of the windows, impervious behind brick walls to all but the luckiest shots. Anderson and Clement waved their men off, beckoning them on a half-mile dash to the edge of town. There they could see the main militia camp, a cluster of tents they could riddle with bullets.

Sitting in that camp was Captain S. S. Eaton, who was tending to his paperwork when an old German appeared at the tent flap and started chattering about how the troops were cheering. Annoyed, Eaton was ready to tie the tent shut when he heard gunfire. Darting outside, he saw the bushwhackers approach. He ran through the camp, ordering his men into some cabins they had built out of logs and railroad ties. They scrambled into the heavy-sided buildings, where they manned windows and knocked out chinking for gun ports. As the troopers cocked revolvers and carbines, Eaton peered out at the charging enemy, now less than seventy-five yards away. Turning to his troops, he shouted, "Let them have it!"

As Jesse charged forward in the mass of galloping guerrillas, a blade of fire erupted from the cabins, cutting through their line like a bandsaw. "Not one of the enemy could be seen, but the muzzles of the muskets protruded from every port hole, belching fire and lead," wrote one guerrilla. "Horses went down as grain before the reaper." A second assault met the same fate. "It was like charging a stone wall," Frank recalled, "only this stone wall belched forth lead."

Jesse and Frank went in again to help rescue the wounded. They surged forward, then dropped down to the ground under the scant cover of a slight rise. "We were in plain view of the Federals and they simply peppered us with bullets," Frank remembered. "I was mightily scared. I knew if we raised up we would expose ourselves to the fire of the Yankees [actually, fellow Missourians] and we couldn't stay still. I tell you, pride makes most of us do many things we wouldn't do otherwise. . . . Well, pride kept us there until we got [the wounded] rolled up in a blanket and then we made tracks." Frank and two others rescued Oliver Johnson, while Jesse helped save Lee McMurtry, who had been blinded by a grazing shot.

The rebels retreated. Thirteen had died, at least eight of whom they left behind on the field, and some thirty had been wounded. In turn, they had killed one, maybe two Union soldiers. As Frank admitted, they were "whipped" by a force less than a third the size of their own.[20]

They rode away from Fayette, their mood bitter and brittle. In the biggest fight since Jesse's return, he had been lucky simply to survive. Anderson and Todd commanded the largest force of guerrillas in Missouri since Quantrill's march to Texas in October 1863—perhaps the largest ever—and they had wasted it, abandoning their accustomed tactics to hurl their men against experienced, prepared defenders in fortifications. It was as if their very numbers had gone to their heads.

But this unusually large gathering of bushwhackers totaled at most 400 men—less than half a full-strength regiment. On the main battlefronts, generals threw regiments about like handfuls of rice. On May 5, 1864, Grant had begun the Wilderness campaign with an army of 115,000 men, facing Lee's 64,000, and both commanders worried about a lack of manpower, as they clashed again and again. That same month, General William T. Sherman led some 98,000 on a campaign to capture Atlanta. Even lesser battles occurred on a comparatively vast scale. At Winchester, in Virginia's Shenandoah Valley, General Philip T. Sheridan led 37,000 men to victory against 15,000 Confederates under General Jubal Early on September 19, 1864. No action in Missouri would ever boast as many combatants as this somewhat peripheral event in the eastern theater. The Confederate army alone at Fisher's Hill (a nearly forgotten battle fought by Sheridan and Early on September 22) may have outnumbered all the men who ever wore the guerrilla shirt or the insignia of the Missouri State Militia.[21]

Missouri's war was small-scale, intensely personal, and intensely vicious. Its signature weapons were the revolver and the scalping knife, close-range arms that required the killer to look his victim in the eyes, even to reach out and tear his flesh apart. The guerrillas' enemies were not alien invaders, but men from their own state. They saw them as traitors and heretics who deserved the worst kind of fate. And in the aftermath of the Fayette defeat, they would soon inflict on their foes the most grisly atrocity ever seen in long-suffering Missouri.

. . .

To Jesse James, the sprawling camp on Young's Creek was a rare sight. Only once before (with Thornton in Platte County) had the seventeen-year-old wandered among so many campfires, so many horses unsaddled, so many boots being shaken out, so many blankets and socks hanging out to dry. Some two hundred to four hundred guerrillas spread out on the property of Colonel M. G. Singleton, a Confederate officer now living at home on parole.

Though Jesse began to forge friendships with many of the bushwhackers gathered there, he probably settled on the grass among the cluster of Clay County guerrillas who now rode with Anderson. Having fought together under Taylor and Clement, they formed a tight-knit group that played a leading role in Bloody Bill's band. "There was one reason that I liked [Anderson]," recalled Jim Cummins, "and that was because he always stood up for the Clay County boys."[22]

On the night of September 26, 1864, Anderson sat in conference with Todd and the other commanders while the men slept, cooked dinner over their flickering fires, or stood guard on the edge of camp. The next morning, Bloody Bill roused his crew. They were going into Centralia, he told them, a mile and a half to the northwest. Anderson had agreed to go there, in part to gather newspapers for more information about the Federal troops concentrating in their area—and especially for reports of General Price's advance into Missouri.[23]

On the morning of September 27, Jesse and Frank—part of a column of about eighty men—formed up behind Anderson and trotted toward Centralia, a mere bump on the horizon. It was scarcely a dozen buildings, almost all one-story structures, but it had blossomed around its new depot for the North Missouri Railroad, which connected St. Louis to the Hannibal and St. Joseph line.

Young Jesse was merely a member of the rank and file, though an especially eager one. In clashes with Union militia, he had shown that he could maintain discipline and follow orders, remaining patiently in ambush or charging headlong against a fortified enemy. But he and his comrades were guerrillas—irregulars, to use another term—and they often degenerated into a barbarian horde, each man following his own whim. This was not necessarily a failing from their point of view: ultimately, theirs was a war against the loyal population, and terror was their greatest weapon. And so Jesse guided his horse the way he wished as the bushwhackers fanned out through the streets of Centralia, eager to spread horror on what would prove to be one of the most important days in his short and violent life.

In a few moments, the sleepy railside village was transformed into a carnival of the absurd. Blue-clad guerrillas burst into house after house, shoving pistols into startled faces, demanding cash, sampling spoonfuls out of pots and plates. Breaking into Centralia's two stores, they plundered for the sake of plundering. Laughing young men ran through the streets trailing rolls of calico and muslin. Suddenly a shout went up from the depot: "It's whisky!"[24] The smell of alcohol and cries of delight attracted the bushwhackers to a busted-in barrel like flies to a corpse.

After an hour of looting and drinking, they saw a stagecoach clatter toward town, pulled by a four-horse team. A squad of guerrillas quickly rode out to meet it. As they robbed the hapless passengers, only one man dared to protest. "We are Southern men and Confederate sympathizers," he said. "You ought not to rob us."

"What do we care?" a bushwhacker replied. "Hell's full of all such Southern men. Why ain't you out fightin'?" Unnoticed in the stage was Congressman James S. Rollins, a former Whig leader and a prominent Unionist. He and most of the other passengers were on their way to the Conservative Party's state convention. They represented an invaluable haul of hostages, but went unrecognized by the drunken rebels.[25]

Then someone heard a steady chuff in the distance and saw the trail of smoke that signaled an approaching locomotive. Yipping and cheering, the bushwhackers abandoned the stage and galloped back to rejoin their comrades at the depot. Anderson, they knew, had been waiting for the train, and had ordered his men to pile heavy wooden ties and other obstructions on the tracks. The bushwhackers rode alongside and opened fire. Bullets ricocheted off the iron-sided engine and smashed through windows. Finally the locomotive screeched to a halt.

Hooting guerrillas immediately surged through the doors. Anderson himself led a cluster of men, including Frank James and other Clay Countians, into the baggage car, where they looted thousands of dollars in crisp new greenbacks.[26] Some of the rebels scrambled into the passenger cars, where they were taken aback by the sight of twenty-three blue uniforms. The guerrillas rapidly sobered up, pointing their revolvers toward the Union troops. "Surrender quietly," one of the bushwhackers said, "and you shall be treated as prisoners of war."

"We can only surrender," a soldier replied, "as we are totally unarmed."[27] Many of them were veterans of Sherman's army, returning on furlough to their homes in Missouri and Iowa after the recent capture of Atlanta. Each of the relieved bushwhackers singled out a man to rob. Then they heard their chief shout for all the passengers to step outside.

As the train emptied, Anderson strolled down the platform beside Clement. As usual, Bill had a cavalry hat on his head, a Union officer's coat on his shoulders, and pistols strapped outside a pair of black pants. He waved the civilians to one side, where his men shoved them into two files; he pointed the soldiers in another direction, ordering them to "fall into line."[28] Two of them hesitated as they came down the steps, whispering to each other. Anderson pulled his pistol and fired two shots, and they tumbled to the ground. The remaining passengers rushed to obey his orders, stutter-stepping out the doors to their assigned positions. Jesse, like the other guerrillas, would have been cursing civilians and military men alike, cocking his pistols and pointing them at the prisoners.

Strip, Anderson told the soldiers. The frightened men—one on crutches and others recuperating from wounds—unbuttoned their uniforms, throwing their shirts and trousers into a pile. "What are you going to do with them fellows?" Clement asked his chief.

"*Parole* them, of course."

The little teenager laughed. "I thought so," he smiled. "You might pick out two or three, though," he suggested, "and exchange them for Cave, if you can." (Cave Wyatt, of course, had been taken prisoner by the Ninth MSM Cavalry.) At this, Jesse might have nodded; it was the kind of foresight he expected from Little Archie, who was always, as Frank put it, the "brains" of the outfit.[29]

"Oh, *one* will be enough for that," Anderson replied. "Arch, you take charge of the firing party, and, when I give the word, pour hell into them."[30] Then he stepped toward the line of nervous soldiers in their underwear. "Boys," he demanded, "have you a sergeant in your ranks?" No one moved. Glowering, the bearded guerrilla repeated his question, louder this time. "If there be one," he added, "let him step aside." Thomas Morton Goodman, a burly six-footer, jerked forward, and he looked like a man who expected to be killed.[31]

The guerrillas pulled Goodman aside as Anderson strode in front of the remaining soldiers. "You Federals," he shouted, "have just killed six of my soldiers, scalped them, and left them on the prairie. I am too honorable a man to permit any man to be scalped, but I will show you that I can kill men with as much rapidity and skill as anybody. From this time forward I ask no quarter, and give none. Every Federal soldier on whom I put my fingers shall die like a dog."

A quiet clatter accompanied his words as the bushwhackers thumbed back the hammers on their revolvers, underscored by the continual sobbing from the crowd of civilians. "If I get into your clutches I expect death," he continued. "You are all to be killed and sent to hell. That is the way every damned soldier shall be served who falls into my hands." As Clement and the others raised their pistols, some of the soldiers frantically protested. They were from Sherman's army, they babbled; they had nothing to do with scalping the guerrillas. "I treat you all as one," Anderson snarled. "You are Federals, and Federals scalped my men, and carry their scalps at their saddle bows." Then he nodded to Clement.[32]

An overwhelming sense of inevitability had hung over this scene from the moment soldiers were discovered on the train. It had built as Anderson shot down the men who hesitated on the cars, as the Union troops were separated from the civilians, as they were stripped while Clement laughed over their impending "parole." Now the inevitable was real. A crackling roar swept over the line of prisoners; they screamed in the mist of blood and smoke—lit by the flames that shot from pistol barrels—then collapsed. One enormous soldier dashed straight at his attackers and knocked down two before he was killed.

Then the guerrillas walked slowly up and down, looking for survivors. Here they clubbed someone's head with the butt of a carbine, there they slit someone's throat with a knife. Now and then the report of a revolver punctuated the weeping of the civilians. One unconscious victim, bleeding from two head wounds, spasmodically jerked his right leg back and forth, over and over. Archie laughed and pointed. "He's marking time," he quipped. Then he or one of the others knelt down to take a pair of scalps.[33]

The guerrillas began to rob the stunned passengers. One prosperous-looking young man, accompanied by his mother, handed over a few dollars. A suspicious bushwhacker told him that he would be searched, and if any more money was found he would be shot. Immediately the man kicked off his boot and pulled out $100 in greenbacks. The rebel pocketed the bills, then shot him dead. Now the guerrillas ordered all the passengers to take off their shoes. When one of them yielded a gold watch, its owner received a bullet in the head.[34]

When the guerrillas remounted their horses, laughing in exultation as they galloped up and down the streets, Anderson ordered the tracks cleared and the train set on fire. He told the engineer to open the throttle and let it run. The engine chuffed away, trailing a line of flames as the cars burned. One of the stranded passengers asked Anderson if they could continue on to Sturgeon. "Go on to hell, for all I care," he replied. Then he and his men rode away, leaving behind a burning depot, a slowly dispersing cloud of gunsmoke, and a lifeless mass of nearly naked men. "At last it was over," reflected Sergeant Goodman, the sole surviving soldier, as his captors led him away, "the carnival of blood ended."[35]

BACK IN CLAY County, September was marked by signs and horrors. "There are so many reports," wrote schoolgirl Kate Watkins, "that I cannot tell the true from the false." George Todd and his men passed through on their way to join Bill Anderson, murdering Unionist farmers on the way. Even the heavens punished the county. Toward the end of the month, the sky erupted with a clattering roar, and a bombardment of gigantic, egg-sized hail battered the earth, snapping off branches, even killing rabbits and chickens. But nothing was so terrible as the news that flooded in from Centralia.[36]

The assistant provost marshal in Liberty, Captain William B. Kemper, heard the tales as well, and he was determined to find out the truth. He had not held the position long, but he knew the county well, having hunted Fletch Taylor back in June, catching a bullet in the leg for his trouble. Now, as he prowled the countryside, he discovered that the names of the men involved in the recent atrocity were common knowledge. Both of the James boys, he reported, "were with Bill Anderson and assisted in the murdering of 22 unarmed Federal soldiers at Centralia."

"I speak not merely from hearsay," he added, "but from my own personal knowledge." Drawing on the expertise he had accumulated in his many months of service in the area, he pursued his investigation personally, secretly visiting the farms of Anderson's men. One day, when he was lurking near Zerelda's home, he observed a neighbor storm up to her.

Angry and indignant, the neighbor confronted Zerelda with the news of her sons' participation in the Centralia slaughter. Aren't you ashamed of them, she (or he) demanded, after what they had done? The dowager reared to her full height. "She rejoined that she was not," Kemper reported, "that she was proud of them, that she prayed to God to protect them in their work." There was no doubt in the captain's mind that both Jesse and Frank had stood beside Clement on September 27, 1864, and had gunned down those men. As for their mother, he wrote, "I regard her as being one of the worst women in this state."[37]

IT HAD COME to this, Sergeant Goodman reflected. After all his comrades had endured, after all the bloody fighting and lethal disease of the campaign through Tennessee and Georgia, they had died, unarmed and naked, just a few hours from home. And it seemed he would soon join them. As he rode back to the camp on Young's Creek, trotting between his two guards, guerrilla after guerrilla cantered up to him to spill a few curses. Occasionally one of them would pull a revolver, cock it, and press it against his head. "I would like to kill the damn Yankee," they snarled. "Hellfire is too good for you, you son of a bitch!" Only the threat of Anderson's wrath, continually repeated by the guards, kept them from squeezing the triggers.

Back at the camp, the bushwhackers spread out to unsaddle their horses and sleep off the whisky and murder. Goodman could see Anderson, Todd, and the other leaders sitting in a small circle on the ground some distance away, Todd sketching a map as Anderson nodded.[38]

"Bill! Our scout!" someone shouted. Goodman and the others looked up to see a rider gallop in. Instantly the sleepy camp came alive again, as the rebels mounted and formed into squads of ten to twenty. Anderson gave a quick command to the scout, sending him galloping back the way he came. Then he spurred his horse over to Goodman and his guards. "Have your prisoner saddle yon gray horse, and mount him quick," he snarled, "and mark me, if he attempts to escape in the battle, kill him instantly!"

The battle, Goodman mused. That meant the scout had brought word of approaching Union forces. "I wondered," he recalled, "if God had sent his Avenging Angel." Bracketed by his guards, the Union soldier trotted behind Anderson's men as they spent most of an hour maneuvering into position. They deployed in a line facing west, at the edge of the brush that lined Young's Creek. They looked out onto a large, rectangular meadow that rose up to a low hill or ridge on the far end; it was bounded on the north and south by overgrown ravines that ran due west from the creek. Into these flanking gullies rode the remaining bushwhackers, where they hid themselves. Now only Anderson's men—the connecting link in a great U-shaped trap—remained visible from the meadow.[39]

The intended victim of this ambush was Major Andrew Vern Emen Johnston—better known as "Ave" Johnston—and a battalion of the Thirty-ninth Missouri Infantry, U.S. Volunteers. The Thirty-ninth was a green regiment, recruited scant weeks before, but Johnston himself was an experienced guerrilla-fighter. When he arrived in Centralia and saw the burning buildings and pile of bodies, he ignored the warnings of the shocked civilians and prepared to track down the marauders. Johnston ordered Captain Adam Theiss to remain in town with 33 men, and Johnston led 115 men on a hunt to the south.[40]

Less than two miles away, Jesse sat in the familiar curve of his worn leather saddle, waiting. By now he had participated in several ambushes, and he knew that they required patience above all else. So he waited and watched. Bill Anderson was at the center of the line. Behind him, the tall Union prisoner loomed comically in his underwear between his guards, his face pale with anxiety.[41]

Then came the sign they had been waiting for: a ripple of pistol shots, then a small cluster of guerrillas galloping toward them across the meadow. It was Dave Pool and his squad, decoys whom Anderson and Todd had sent out to lure the Union troops into their trap. Pool led his men behind Anderson to form a second line, as Johnston's men appeared on the top of the low ridge to the west.

Jesse now experienced the strange pause before a battle, after the enemy has been sighted but combat not yet joined. Anderson shouted for his men to check their saddles and weapons. Like men all along the line, Jesse must have dismounted to tie up clothing and equipment, fix loose percussion caps, and pull tight his saddle girth. At the other end of the meadow, he could see Johnston waving to his troops; they dismounted, every fourth man leading away the horses of the others. They, too, would have checked their weapons—long Minié rifles, the standard infantry arm of the Civil War.[42] They were deadly at a distance, but they were slow-loading: after each shot, a soldier had to tear open a paper cartridge, pour gunpowder and a bullet down the muzzle, and ram it home with an iron rod.

Looking out at the dismounted enemy, one of the guerrillas hooted loudly. "Why, the fools are going to fight us on foot!" he shouted. Then he muttered, "God help 'em." They were accustomed to charging from ambush at close range against small clusters of the enemy, and believed a man on foot was helpless in such situations. But if the bushwhackers had experienced the war outside of Missouri, they would not have laughed. The long-range killing power of modern rifles made horsemen vulnerable targets; now cavalry usually rode to battle but fought on foot. The mounted charge across open ground against a line of infantry—the tactic the guerrillas planned to use against Johnston's men—had become virtually a guarantee of disaster.[43]

As tension filled the air, Anderson pulled out of line and trotted up and down behind his men. "Boys, when we charge, break through the line and keep straight on for the horses," he said quietly. "Keep straight on for the horses! Keep straight on for the horses!" He returned to his place and took a final look at the enemy, where bayonets could be seen glinting on the ends of long rifles. He smiled and leaned over to Archie Clement. "Not a damned revolver in the crowd!" Actually, there was one—carried by Johnston, who stood in front with his horse's reins in one hand and a six-shooter in the other.[44]

Anderson tore off his hat and swung it around three times. Now it began, not with an instant gallop but a steady trot, as the guerrillas saved their horses for the final sprint. Up the slope they rode, as Johnston waved his arm and shouted a command. A rippling crackle of gunfire sounded, heavy black smoke lifting from the Union line—but scarcely a rider went down. The Federal infantry had fallen prey to one of the oldest problems in combat: when firing downhill, inexperienced soldiers often aim too high, as Johnston's men did now.

With wild screams, Jesse and the others spurred their mounts, competing to be the first to reach the enemy. From the right and left, Todd and the other commanders led their squads out of hiding and enveloped the Union troops, who were now desperately tearing open cartridges and ramming home bullets. In the center of Anderson's line, Jesse bounded forward. He aimed right for Johnston, who shouted and snapped off shots. The boy aimed his revolver and fired. The Federal officer pitched to the ground. Then Jesse or another rider pulled up close, reached down with a pistol, and fired another round into his head.

The guerrillas surged into the enemy, sweeping through scattered knots of infantrymen who swung their rifles like clubs, jabbed with bayonets, or desperately tried to surrender. All were gunned down. One Union officer grabbed a bushwhacker's horse by the bridle, explaining, "I always spare prisoners." The guerrilla aimed his pistol and said, "I *never* do." Anderson's men, true to their orders, kicked their mounts straight through, running down the horse-holders who were trying to save themselves.

The chase continued into Centralia itself, where the rebels dispersed to track down hiding Federals. They shot them on the road, in bedrooms, even in an outhouse. One guerrilla rode up to a house and demanded a drink of water. As a woman came out with a cup, the guerrilla saw an infantryman jump over a fence and run. The bushwhacker quickly spurred forward, brought the man down with a quick shot, then trotted back, saying, "I'll take that drink now."[45]

As evening approached, the guerrillas gradually drifted back to the meadow. Jesse was convinced that he had personally shot down Johnston. His older brother, meanwhile, had to wipe his boot clean of the blood of Frank Shepherd, an unusually tall guerrilla who had been one of only a handful of bushwhackers to catch a bullet that day. It was a small cost for having annihilated the Union force; only a few Federals had escaped to the town of Sturgeon, miles away.[46]

The bushwhackers now celebrated, becoming "drunk on blood," Goodman thought. Pool danced across a cluster of bodies, hopping from one to the other. "Counting 'em," he explained. The rebels walked among the dead, crushing faces with rifle butts and shoving bayonets through the bodies, pinning them to the ground. Frank James bent down to loot one of the corpses, pulling free a sturdy leather belt. Others slid knives out of their sheaths and knelt down to work. One by one, they cut seventeen scalps loose, then carefully tied them to their saddles and bridles. At least one guerrilla carved the nose off a victim. Others sliced off ears, or sawed off heads and switched their bodies. Someone pulled the trousers off one corpse, cut off the penis, and shoved it in the dead man's mouth.[47]

In this blood-drunk crew, of course, stood Jesse James. It is impossible to imagine him shying away, let alone disapproving, as the knives slit the bodies. No record exists of what he did on the field of the dead that day, but if he cut the scalp off a victim or two, he would simply have been a typical member of Bloody Bill's gang. In a very real sense, his education was complete.

The dismemberment of enemy dead is hardly unknown in the history of American warfare. Just two months later, U.S. forces would carve up Southern Cheyenne victims at Sand Creek, Colorado; eight decades later, in a very different war, they would do much the same to dead Japanese. Anderson's men were not simply "sadistic fiends," as one historian has dubbed them. They merely proved that the peculiar social conditions of young men in a bitter war can create a culture of atrocity, as they cease to think of their enemies as human beings. What most shocked Americans was that, as at Lawrence, their victims were fellow white men—and at Centralia, they were fellow white Missourians.[48]

Amid the laughter and cutting and celebratory whisky, Todd and Anderson had not forgotten their original purpose that day. Soon they hounded their men back to camp, giving orders for a mere three hours' rest before they resumed their march. "The land will be swarming with blue coats by tomorrow eve," one of Goodman's guards explained. "Our late fight will only waken up a hornet's nest about our ears." More to the point was the news that Anderson had collected in Centralia: after all the rumors and promises, General Price was finally returning with his army. The Confederate liberation of Missouri, it appeared, was about to begin.[49]

CHAPTER EIGHT

Exile

THE MISSOURIANS were intensely loyal to their state. Tens of thousands of them chose to stay and fight at home as both Unionists and rebels—joining the various militia organizations or taking to the brush as guerrillas—rather than enlist in the primary armies across the Mississippi River. Many of those who entered the regular Confederate ranks still lingered just over the border to the south in Arkansas, a refugee army that kept its gaze fixed on the abandoned homeland. Each year, recruiting officers and raiding parties struck north. Each year, Major General Sterling Price pleaded with his superiors not to forget Missouri.

After Price took command of the Confederate District of Arkansas, on March 14, 1864, he begged for a chance to free his home state. In July he reported that the people were ready to rise up against their Federal oppressors; if he personally could lead an invasion, he argued, thousands would flock to his army. On August 4, Price learned from Major General Edmund Kirby Smith, commander of Confederate forces west of the Mississippi, that he would have his chance.[1]

"Make St. Louis the objective point," Smith told him; capturing the great city "will do more toward rallying Missouri to your standard than the possession of any other point."[2] This was a grandiose objective indeed— but then Price's invasion itself was an enormous gamble. "Old Pap" led barely twelve thousand men north through Arkansas in the last days of August, at least four thousand of them carrying no arms at all, hoping to equip themselves with captured Union weapons. Price's three divisions consisted entirely of cavalry, with scant artillery—hardly the force to besiege one of the largest cities in the country. Swift marching, however, might make the plan work. Price's spies told him that Union forces in Missouri were understrength, with only a handful of Federal regiments to back up the militia, and all were spread thinly across the state to cope with the guerrilla insurrection. Most important, the people would rise once they saw the rebel banner floating above a conquering army. Of that, Price was certain.

Besides, what did they have to lose? Everywhere the Confederate situation looked desperate. In Virginia, Grant had pressed on against Richmond all spring, slipping around Lee after each bloody battle. Finally Grant had pinned down Lee in Petersburg, the main rail junction for the Confederate capital, reducing the campaign to the bloody stalemate of trench warfare. Sherman had reached Atlanta in July; in August, he marched around the city in a circle, destroying its rail links with the outside world, forcing the battered Confederates to abandon it on September 1. On the gulf coast, Admiral David Farragut dashed into Mobile Bay on August 5, closing down the most important rebel seaport. If Price managed to seize St. Louis—even if he simply sparked an uprising in Missouri—he might create a large enough diversion to allow the rebels to retake some of the lost ground.[3]

On September 19, Price's Army of Missouri crossed the Arkansas border. At the head of the three divisions rode Major General James Fleming Fagan, Brigadier General John Sappington Marmaduke, and perhaps the most famous Missouri horseman of all, Brigadier General Joseph Orville Shelby. This was the man who had led the epic raid of 1863. His swaggering troopers never failed to rile their fellow soldiers with the boast, "You've heard about Jeb Stuart's ride around McClellan? Hell, brother, Jo Shelby rode around *Missouri!*"[4] A wealthy former hemp planter, rope maker, and border ruffian, Shelby affected the outsized look of a cavalier, with large round eyes, a large goatee, and a long black feather trailing from his hat. "There is about the man," declared his adjutant, Major John Newman Edwards, "a subtle essence of chivalry—a dash of the daring and romantic, which will have him pictured only as leading his troops rapidly amid the wreck and roar of battle; his black plume guiding his men, and his own splendid example nerving them to deeds of immortal endeavor."[5]

But then, Edwards had more than a dash of the romantic in his pen. He had been born in Virginia in 1839, trained as a compositor, came to Lexington, Missouri, around 1854, took a job as a printer for a newspaper, befriended Shelby, and became his hunting and fishing crony. When war broke out, he rode with him as his aide. As the author of Shelby's flowery official reports, he did more than anyone else to burnish the commander's reputation. But Edwards, too, had his admirers. "I cannot speak of John Edwards without emotion," said one wartime companion. "He was the noblest man of the many noble men who took part in the great struggle. . . . He soon became the hero of Shelby's old brigade." That unit—the Iron Brigade—now formed the core of Shelby's division, a wild group of men that fought exceedingly well. "Shelby's command was never in a high state of discipline, but reliable in battle," thought Captain T. J. Mackey. "They were the right arm of the army."[6]

This horde of cavaliers, romantics, and unarmed men clopped toward St. Louis through southeastern Missouri, covering barely eighteen miles a day—an excruciatingly slow pace. The word "cavalry" conjures up images of smartly trotting horsemen riding circles around plodding foot soldiers. This army, however, dragged along some three hundred wagons, including eighteen ponderous pontoon boats for bridge construction. In a symbolic abandonment of speed, General Price traveled in a carriage rather than on a horse. He was accompanied by a political entourage led by Thomas C. Reynolds, who was recognized by Confederates as governor of Missouri after the death of Claiborne F. Jackson. Reynolds hoped to be installed in an official ceremony after Price captured the state capital, Jefferson City.[7]

Unknown to the rebels, their plans had already started to unravel. In St. Louis, Major General Rosecrans first received confirmation of an invasion on September 2. All through the month these reports multiplied with increasing accuracy, convincing him to prepare for the worst. And he had to prepare quickly: at the end of August, he had only eighteen thousand full-time troops in all of Missouri. The telegraph now clattered with a flurry of orders: supply depots were to be fortified, along with Jefferson City and St. Louis; inactive EMM units were mustered back into service; six thousand troops at Cairo under General Andrew Jackson Smith were requested and granted, along with nine regiments of one hundred–day volunteers from Illinois. Major General Samuel R. Curtis in Kansas also promised cooperation.[8]

Rosecrans issued one order in particular that would prove decisive in the coming days. On September 24, he told Brigadier General Thomas Ewing, Jr., to concentrate a body of troops at Pilot Knob in southeastern Missouri. This little village was a strategic treasure: eighty-six miles below St. Louis, it was the southern terminus of the Iron Mountain Railroad and an important supply depot. Ewing—the same man who had issued General Order No. 11 a year earlier—arrived on September 26, taking command of Fort Davidson and its garrison of 1,051 men. When Price learned of the troops (and supplies) at Pilot Knob, he decided to attack; Ewing decided to stay and fight.[9]

On September 27, the same day as the slaughter in Centralia, Price hurled his men against the Federals at Pilot Knob. He launched charge after charge into the curtain of rifle fire and exploding circle of shells erupting from Fort Davidson. One column of attackers finally succeeded in approaching the walls, then pulled up short: the Confederates were stunned to discover in front of them a ditch six feet deep and ten feet wide.

Most turned and ran, and were shot in the back; others tumbled into the dry moat, where they were picked off. That night, as the wounded groaned and screamed, an enormous explosion lit the darkened town. Dawn revealed that Ewing had blown up his own magazine after evacuating his troops under the cover of darkness.

When Shelby and Edwards looked over the torn-up field and abandoned fort, they could only shake their heads at Price's stupidity. Shelby had warned against attacking Pilot Knob, but the commander had insisted, and now he had lost some fifteen hundred men—almost one out of five of his veteran troops. The outnumbered Union forces had suffered only twenty-eight dead, fifty-nine wounded, and perhaps one hundred taken as prisoners—and they had escaped through rebel lines. Even worse was the precious time the Confederates had lost. With every passing hour, Rosecrans further strengthened the defenses of St. Louis. To make matters worse, Price wasted three more days trying to catch Ewing's retreating men. Speed was of the essence, Shelby knew, but now it was too late. The campaign had barely begun, and already it was headed for disaster.[10]

ON OCTOBER 11, Jesse James proudly sat astride his horse, tugging on the reins to keep it neatly in the column led by Bill Anderson. This was a moment to be savored: a victory parade into Boonville, a swaggering trot past the awed faces of civilians and Confederate troops (whose ragged gray uniforms and old muzzle-loading rifles looked rather pathetic next to the bushwhackers' smart guerrilla shirts and multiple revolvers). After Centralia, how could the guerrillas not feel boastful? Let the plodding regular soldiers worry about orders and logistics and the patience-breaking minutia of military life; the bushwhackers had taken matters in their own hands, fought on their own hook, and annihilated the Federals. The column reached the town square, where the stately, rotund figure of General Price stood waiting.[11]

The ceremony was a welcome relief after the past few harrowing days. The double slaughter at Centralia had indeed cracked open a "hornet's nest," as one of the guerrillas put it. The rebels had hardly left the scene when, as they were feeding their horses in a cornfield, they discovered enemy soldiers doing the same thing on the far side. So the guerrillas had moved rapidly, winding through overgrown creek bottoms and thick woods, often traveling at night. At one point, they found themselves on a hill with columns of Federal troops in every direction, but the bushwhackers dispersed, meeting later at a prearranged rendezvous. After days and nights of hard riding and scant rest, they finally arrived at the Missouri River, where they ferried themselves to the southern bank in the darkness.

In the confusion of the crossing, Sergeant Goodman managed to slip away, escaping to a Union outpost.[12]

When Anderson and his men rode into Boonville, the Confederate troops gaped. What astounded them was not simply the fine dark suits worn by the irregulars, or their ease on their powerful horses, or even the rather odd trails of ribbons that many had dangling from their hats. It was the trophies they carried: human scalps, tied by the hair to their saddles and bridles, flaking off dried blood as the horses bounced along. As if to punctuate the impression, the guerrillas suddenly went wild when they saw a line of Union prisoners, captured by Shelby the day before. Wheeling their horses around the frightened bluecoats, they drew their pistols, whooping and screaming, "We had better shoot the sons of bitches!"

Price's face reddened. He rushed forward, shouting at them to get away from the prisoners. The bushwhackers reluctantly backed off. Now Anderson rode up to the general to offer a formal greeting, only to be cut off by the angry Confederate "governor"—Reynolds pointed a shaking finger at the display of scalps and lacerated Anderson for his barbarity. Price agreed and told Anderson to discard them. Bloody Bill could only have been amused at such delicate feelings as he waved to his men to throw away—or hide—the scalps. Then he presented Price with an ornate wooden box. Opening the lid, Price saw a pair of silver-plated pistols. Forgetting his earlier shock, the visibly delighted commander expressed his hearty thanks. "If I had 50,000 such men," he rejoiced to the crowd, "I could hold Missouri forever."[13]

John Edwards nodded enthusiastically at Price's words. He had met the guerrillas before, when they had spent winters with the Confederate forces in Arkansas and Texas, but the arrival of Anderson's conquering legion overwhelmed him. Edwards, of course, could not have been prouder of Shelby's men, but there was something about the bushwhackers that warmed the darker side of his romantic heart. Just twenty-five years old himself, he thrilled to their wildly independent, freebooting ways. "The guerrilla organization of Missouri needs a word in its defense," he wrote three years later, as he reflected on that day in Boonville, "although its warfare was pitiless, its banner the black flag, and its battle-cry the fearsome monosyllable *Death*. Composed of men driven to desperation by the unceasing persecutions of Federals and militia, they had been outlawed and hunted. . . . They accepted the black flag as an emblem, because it suited their ideas of murder—and having no hope themselves, they left none to their victims."[14]

What a sad contrast his own army made, he thought. The foolish, costly assault at Pilot Knob and the pursuit of General Ewing had made the capture of a now-reinforced St. Louis impossible. So Price had veered west, aiming at Jefferson City. But rapidly concentrating Union troops had filled the capital's fortifications, and Pilot Knob had spoiled the rebels' appetite for attacks on entrenched defenders. Slipping around the town, Price had moved into Boonville on October 10. Meanwhile, Confederate sympathizers had rushed to join what they saw as an army of liberation. This vast crowd of fair-weather friends, unarmed and ill-equipped, trailed behind the troops, a "rabble of deadheads, stragglers, and stolen negroes on stolen horses," in Reynolds's words. The soldiers themselves looted as they went, swelling the wagon train with scores of stolen carriages stuffed with booty. The invasion force, Reynolds complained, had begun to look like a barbarian "Calmuck horde." Edwards fully agreed.[15]

Price himself seemed to enjoy the slow march through welcoming towns, the cheering crowds of secessionists who greeted him with gifts, and the speeches he gave in village squares. Perhaps at times he actually imagined that he was liberating the state, as his eager supporters clearly believed. To remind him of his failure, however, he had the angry Reynolds, who was sorely miffed at missing a formal inaugural in Jefferson City. And even though Price smiled and waved to the crowds, he had already begun his retreat. General Kirby Smith had instructed him to come back to Arkansas through Kansas, should he fail to take St. Louis. Unknown to the population, Price was now faithfully following those orders.[16]

As delighted as he was with Anderson's gift, Price preferred to keep the bushwhacker chieftain at arm's length. After the ceremony in Boonville, he scratched out a formal order, instructing "Captain Anderson" to return across the Missouri River and destroy North Missouri Railroad "going as far east as practicable"—the opposite direction from Price's own march.[17]

THE MISSOURI RIVER ran low in the autumn months. Looking out over the water from the Boonville ferry, Jesse would have seen sandbars breaking the current, mudflats left behind and forgotten by the torrents of spring. Earlier that day, he and the other bushwhackers had basked in the admiration of the Confederate Army of Missouri; now they were returning to their work.

For a few days, Anderson and some of his men lingered on the northern banks of the river, watching as Shelby's troops seized the waterside town of Glasgow. There, Anderson raped a black woman and then tortured a local banker to the edge of death. Others galloped east, where they burned a couple of depots, looted the town of Danville, murdered several Unionists, and torched their homes. It was the closest they got to inflicting any damage on the North Missouri Railroad.[18]

The bushwhackers reunited and turned west, moving parallel to Price's march. They faced little resistance: the Federal and MSM cavalry had concentrated south of the river to fight the main rebel army, leaving behind EMM troops of decidedly uneven quality. On October 17, the guerrillas stormed into the center of Carrollton, where the 160 men of the EMM garrison immediately surrendered. The guerrillas marched them toward the Missouri River, picking out a man to shoot down here, another there, until a half-dozen bodies marked the trail of prisoners. Then, with equal caprice, they let the rest go and continued their westward ride. Later they forced a German farmer to guide them west; when his knowledge ran out, Archie Clement shot him, sawed off his head, and placed it on the dead man's chest, with his hands wrapped around it. Then they resumed their march.[19]

On the night of October 19, Jesse slogged with the guerrilla band through the cold, dripping branches of the overgrown Crooked River country in west-central Ray County. With them rode James Crowley, a Ray County militiaman they had captured in a skirmish the day before. Crowley had been spared because of a quirk of geography: he lived close by, and the guerrillas needed a pilot. With a pistol at his back, he led the column upward, guiding the line of scrambling horses up a muddy bluff above the Crooked's Rocky Fork. There familiar routine took over. The riders spread out, pulled saddles off horses, prepared quick meals, and took turns standing guard. For cover in the steady downpour, they threw horse blankets over small shrubs and low-hanging branches to make improvised tents. In short order, most of them were fast asleep.

A shrieking whistle shattered the morning, sending the bushwhackers scrambling. The enemy had found them. Blurry-eyed, sliding around in the mud in stocking feet, the guerrillas hurriedly buckled on their revolvers and tossed saddles over their horses' backs. When the first crackle of gunfire spat through the brush, some of the guerrillas simply abandoned their boots and saddles, riding bareback to freedom. Anderson cocked his pistol on prisoner Crowley. Lead us out of this trap, he told him, or you'll die.

Jesse and Frank plunged down a narrow trail after the panicked guide, bounding down between the steep bluffs of the Crooked River. After running for half a mile, they pulled up in a creekbed at Anderson's command and listened for signs of further pursuit. Then they heard the crackling rush of horses galloping through the brush. Anderson ordered the James brothers and some others to form a rear guard as the rest tried to escape.

Cocking and firing in rapid succession, Jesse blazed away at the men on horseback as they appeared through the trees. He clicked through one cylinder, then pulled another revolver, emptied it, and pulled another, until finally both he and Frank had spent all their loads. They succeeded in holding back the enemy for a few precious minutes, but now they were cut off from the rest of the guerrillas, who were themselves scattered by another squad of militiamen that had caught them in an open field. The brothers wheeled their horses into the brush and spurred east, the unexpected direction.

After a few hours more of running and hiding, the James brothers found their way back to Anderson. The scattered band eventually drifted back together, minus a few men who had fallen in the attack. If they were thoughtful, they would have reflected on their experience: clearly not all the EMM were inexperienced, unskilled, and cowardly. As for their own leader, he was as unpredictable as ever: after Crowley successfully guided the bushwhackers to safety, Bloody Bill let him go.[20]

"IF YOU HAVE got to a place where there is peace you ought to be content, for we still have none here," wrote Sarah Harlan as she sat at a table in her home in Haynesville, Clinton County, a few miles north of the Samuel farm. She struggled to remain clear and calm. "I hardly know where to begin to tell you the news," she wrote to her parents. "The next day after you left home there was about eighty bushwhackers and conscripted men in here. I knew a great many of them." She ran through the list of names her parents would recognize: Will Courtney, Clell Miller, Ol Shepherd (who had joined the State Guard with Frank James in 1861), and the two James brothers.

After recovering from the scare on the Crooked River, Jesse and the rest of Anderson's band had continued their march west, moving into northern Clay County, where Zerelda and other secessionists welcomed them with hot meals and hiding places. Then they dashed to the Clinton County line, where they surprised Harlan as she sat alone in her house. After swarming over her home and farmyard, they mounted up and rode to the village of Haynesville. There they repeated the same scenes and replayed the same themes of this Sisyphean war, all under a brilliant canopy of red, yellow, and orange leaves that signaled the approaching end of the year. They kicked in the door of a general store and looted it; they stole horses where they found them; they searched houses for arms and saddles, overturning beds and pulling out drawers. "They took Mr. Parks off with them," Harlan added, "and they went on from here, robbing as they went."[21]

The guerrillas drifted south toward the muddy Missouri. On the night of October 26, they camped in deep woods near the rugged Fishing River, just west of Albany, Ray County. Anderson, the ruler of all he surveyed, a movable kingdom of terror, was feeling smug again. The morning of

October 27, he and a few of his boys demanded breakfast at a home. As the occupants nervously cooked the meal, they glimpsed the cocky rebel bowing to himself in a mirror. "Good morning, Captain Anderson, how are you this morning?" he grinned. "Damn well, thank you."[22]

He swaggered to the camp, ready to give the orders for the day. Then a ripple of gunfire cracked from the east. Anderson knew there were Union forces in that direction, since some of his men had skirmished with them that very morning. Now, it appeared, they wanted to fight. Leaping into his saddle, Anderson called for his men to mount and follow him. Archie Clement soon wheeled his horse alongside Anderson, followed by a cluster of boys from Clay County, including that new recruit, Clell Miller. With the rest of the band following close behind, this small group galloped after their attackers.[23]

SCARCELY A MILE to the east, Lieutenant Colonel Samuel P. Cox waited patiently for Anderson. A tough thirty-six-year-old, Cox defied the amateur-soldier stereotype of the EMM. As a teenager, he had fought in the Mexican War, then went on to crisscross the Great Plains and Rocky Mountains for a freighting company, to serve as an army scout, even to survive a shipwreck in the Gulf of Mexico. After returning to his hometown of Gallatin in Daviess County, he had fought briefly on the Union side, then returned to service during the harrowing summer of 1864. As an EMM officer, he fought under state, not Federal, authority, but he still followed the orders of U.S. and MSM generals. So when he was told to take command of the forces in Ray County in order to defeat Bill Anderson, he had obeyed.[24]

Marching south from Daviess County, Cox had concentrated the Thirty-third and Fifty-first Regiments of EMM in the town of Richmond, Ray County, on October 26. Several hundred strong, they were numerous enough to give the bushwhackers a good fight—if they could find them. That night a woman came into camp and asked to see the commander. The guerrillas were camped in the timber just west of the village of Albany, she said. As Cox listened, he may have hesitated before trusting her; after all, Confederate sympathizers were known to spread misinformation. But he decided to take her at her word. Early the next morning, he ordered his men to move out.

Long and painful experience had taught Union officers two ways to fight the guerrillas successfully. First, there was the surprise attack on a rebel camp. This required excellent intelligence and even better luck; if the bushwhackers took even halfhearted steps to protect themselves, they usually escaped with only a few casualties. Second, there was the ambush, a tactic used to good effect by the "foot scouts" of the Second Colorado Cavalry early in the summer. Cox decided to go one better: he would adopt Bloody Bill's own favorite method—the decoy. He would lure the wily guerrilla into a carefully prepared trap.

After chasing away some of Anderson's sentinels on the outskirts of Albany on the morning of October 27, Cox marched his men to the western side of the village. There he deployed his force of farmers and part-time soldiers, armed with muzzle-loading rifles and a handful of revolvers, along the edge of some woods that extended on either side of a road running west. He sent their horses and supply wagons to the rear, guarded by a small detachment. Then he dispatched perhaps fifty men on a ride to Anderson's camp. Theirs was the critical part: they would find Bloody Bill, taunt him, and lead him back—hopefully too mad to think clearly.

Lieutenant Thomas Hankins waited in that line of Union militiamen, looking west for some sign of the enemy. "Everything seemed to stand still," he wrote in his diary, "not even a horse appeared to move. 'Bang,' a single shot, then a sharp volley, followed by the 'rebel yell'—once heard, never to be forgotten." Hankins saw the decoy unit "tearing down the road" with screaming bushwhackers close behind. The Union riders dashed through the opening in their line, which waited for the guerrillas "without a break," Cox reported.

Down the lane came twenty to fifty guerrillas, probably including Jesse James, galloping after the militiamen who had dared to fire into their camp. They kicked their spurs into their horses, balancing in the stirrups with revolvers in one hand and reins in the other. Anderson pulled ahead, together with another rider; they could see their prey, almost within range, running toward a line of timber.

Suddenly a crackling wave of fire erupted along the trees, throwing up a dense cloud of smoke. Balls of lead tore through horses and riders. The bushwhackers who survived reined in and turned back for cover, but Bloody Bill and his companion kept on, spurring their horses toward the hole in the Union line. The guerrillas could see more small puffs of smoke as Cox and a few others fired revolvers. Then Anderson pitched forward, his horse still galloping on, until finally he tumbled to earth some fifty yards behind the front.

The other rider yanked his horse around and spurred back to his companions. He escaped unharmed as the Union troops frantically rammed home a second load into their muzzle-loading rifles. But the militia were ready when Anderson's men launched another charge. Once again, the line of muskets erupted, toppling more horses and riders. The shattered bushwhackers retreated, leaving behind a badly wounded Clell Miller. Cox immediately ordered a squad of his best men to follow the bushwhackers. "Our cavalry pursued them some ten miles," he reported, "finding the road strewn with blood for miles."[25]

As the militiamen gathered around Anderson's inert form, they could scarcely believe their accomplishment. The terror of Missouri was dead, his men scattered and defeated. The Unionists gathered up his body and carried it to Richmond, where a photographer snapped some memorable photographs of the long-haired man in his embroidered guerrilla shirt. They caught his horse, too, a fine, powerful animal with two fresh scalps swinging from the bridle.[26]

FOR REBEL CIVILIANS such as the Samuel family, the dream of a Confederate Missouri had never seemed more real than in early October, when Price marched from Boonville to Lexington and on toward Kansas City. Crowds cheered him; recruits rushed in from Clay County and other secessionist strongholds; even the enemy seemed incapable of stopping him. Most Kansas militiamen initially refused to cross the state line to stand in his way; only two thousand troops advanced to Lexington. Then, suddenly, the dream evaporated.

From October 19 through 21, Jo Shelby led the rebel vanguard in a bitter fight that gradually drove the Union detachment back through the streets of Lexington, past Independence, to the banks of the Big Blue just east of Westport and Kansas City. But Price was fighting on two sides: from the east came General Alfred Pleasonton—the former cavalry commander for the Army of the Potomac—with eighty-five hundred troops, followed by many more. Meanwhile General Samuel R. Curtis crossed the Kansas border with some thirteen thousand men. On October 22, Shelby pushed Curtis back into the town of Westport, but to the east, Pleasonton routed Price's rear guard. The Confederate Army of Missouri had shoved itself into a trap.

The fighting that took place on the next day, October 23, is usually dignified with the name "the Battle of Westport." Though it was just one day in more than a week of continuous combat, it deserved the distinction: on that chilly Sunday, the Confederate cause in Missouri permanently collapsed. On the rebel left, Shelby threw his men uselessly against the enemy line outside of Westport; on the right, the Union attack broke through. Before long, the Confederate army crumbled into a panicked mob. Over the next one hundred hours, Price and his shattered divisions raced south, covering as many as fifty-six miles in one day. Only Shelby's tired but resilient men held back the pursuing enemy. After a final skirmish on October 28, the rebel Army of Missouri abandoned its home state forever.[27]

Many explanations would eventually be offered for Price's failure, some of them contradictory: he tried to carry out an invasion when he should have confined himself to a mere cavalry raid; he did not move quickly enough to take St. Louis; he simply wasn't up to the job. Ultimately, however, Price failed because the people of Missouri, on the whole, wanted him to fail. For every family that turned out to welcome him, there were two that sent their men into battle in the ranks of the MSM, the EMM, or the U.S. Volunteers. More ominous for the rebel cause, a number of the faces in the Federal ranks were black—former Missouri slaves, now Union soldiers.

Perversely, the bushwhackers understood this better than Price did. Theirs was a war against the Union population, whether uniformed as militia or working peacefully in the fields. Anderson's band was hardly alone in this respect: as Price moved west through Saline and Lafayette Counties, guerrilla leaders George Todd and Dave Pool burned the homes of Unionist Germans, murdering dozens on October 10 and the days that followed. In one immigrant community, forty-five men—20 percent of the male population—died at the hands of bushwhackers. Ironically, Price indirectly contributed to the destruction of Todd and his band. Unlike Anderson, they fought alongside the Confederate army, and on October 21 Todd was killed by a Union bullet in skirmishing near Independence.[28]

Price's war ended at almost the same moment that Anderson toppled from his horse. But Bloody Bill's war against the Union population continued even after his death. On October 29, Sarah Harlan reported that Ol Shepherd and the James boys were back in northeastern Clay County, which was now, as always, their refuge. But they did not act like refugees. About nine o'clock that night, wearing their captured blue uniforms, they rode to the home of a Unionist named Baynes. They banged on the door until the farmer poked his head out. They were Federal soldiers, they told him, and they had gotten lost. Could he show them the way to the main road? The gentleman agreed—cheerfully, perhaps, now that Price's army had been routed and Anderson and Todd were dead. He walked out into the yard, pointing and explaining, as the bushwhackers followed. Then they pulled their pistols and fired. Baynes collapsed to the ground, dead from five close-range bullet wounds. Then the men rode to the home of an elderly man named Farran and murdered him in the same fashion. Word of the murders led other Unionists to flee the area, but the guerrillas continued their harassment, sending death threats to, among others, the prominent merchant and banker Edward M. Samuel.[29]

Jesse James's five-month war had come full circle. He had returned to where he began—the familiar wooded country around his mother's farm. And he had returned to his original role as a member of a death squad, murdering loyal citizens in their homes. But the changes wrought by Price's defeat and Anderson's demise were inescapable. The old band was breaking up, as small clusters of men drifted off, each taking its own direction, and the James brothers drifted off as well. They may have parted as early as November, when an old acquaintance was surprised to see Frank on the road, riding alone. Or the brothers may have split after meeting with Quantrill south of the Missouri River in December, where the guerrilla leader had called together his old followers. Ultimately Frank headed east to Kentucky with Quantrill, while Jesse rode south to Texas.[30]

Back in Liberty, Captain Kemper was doing his research. After the mayhem surrounding Price's invasion, he had revived Colonel Catherwood's plan to banish the leading rebels in Clay County. On December 2, he finished writing an eight-page report that detailed the evidence against ten families. "It is not through anything personal that is existing between these parties and myself that I speak thus," he wrote. Indeed, his assessments were quite accurate, though his evidence was sometimes thin. He proceeded from one case to the next, saving the most dangerous for last: the family of Reuben and Zerelda Samuel. Their banishment was essential, he wrote. "I feel today that I am almost as much in 'rebellion' here in this county as I would be in South Carolina."

Edward M. Samuel, together with Unionist official James M. Jones, strongly endorsed Kemper's report. On December 9, the document arrived in St. Louis bearing the endorsement of General Fisk, who observed that it should be acted on before spring, when the leaves would return and provide cover for the bushwhackers. On January 9, 1865, the new commander of the Department of the Missouri, Major General Grenville M. Dodge, issued General Order No. 9, requiring the banishment of the ten families on Kemper's list within twenty days. The assistant adjutant general forwarded the order to Fisk with a few words of advice. General Dodge, he wrote, "directs me to state that it embodies the policy intended to be pursued by him in all similar cases. He desires, however, that it should not be made public, any farther than may be necessary."

On January 29, 1865, Kemper summoned Reuben and Zerelda, along with fifteen-year-old Susie James, into his office in Liberty. If anything could have added to Reuben's despair or Zerelda's bitterness, it was the words of General Order No. 9. Then Kemper presented a form, an acknowledgment that they had heard and understood. They signed.[31]

General Order No. 9 required that the family be shipped via Little Rock or Memphis through Union lines to Confederate territory. That movement never took place, perhaps because of the discretion requested by General Dodge, perhaps because there was so little Confederate territory left. Instead, the clan went west to the southeastern tip of Nebraska. In the little town of Rulo, Zerelda and her family began their exile within eyesight of their home state, separated only by the sandbars and muddy current of the Missouri River.[32]

ON THE AFTERNOON of January 15, 1865, Brigadier General Adelbert Ames stood with Major General Alfred Terry on a sandy peninsula on the coast of North Carolina, a spit of land separating the Cape Fear River from the sea. They were looking at the northern wall of Fort Fisher, the massive bastion that guarded the entrance to the river, which made it the gateway to Wilmington, North Carolina, the last seaport left to the Confederacy. If Fort Fisher fell, the rebels would be left without any means of importing arms and supplies. It would be all but the final blow.

But Fort Fisher, Ames knew, would not be easy to take. He had already served on one expedition against it, under Major General Benjamin F. Butler, who had retreated without even attempting an assault. The north wall, running from river to sea, stood twenty feet high, shaped out of tons of sand, with a parapet twenty feet wide. Twenty cannons bristled from its face, with immense mounds, or "traverses," that flanked the gun chambers. Terry gestured to the wall and ran through the plan once more. A force of sailors and marines would attack the seaward bastion, he explained, while Ames would storm the river end with his division of three brigades, some thirty-one hundred men in all.[33]

Shortly before 3:30, as shells from sixty-four Union ships exploded on Fort Fisher's walls, Terry told Ames to send forward his First Brigade under Colonel Newton Curtis. "Before starting to the assault," Ames wrote to his parents a few days later, "I asked General Terry when he wished my 2d and 3d lines moved up. He replied whenever in my judgment I thought best. And so I fought the battle as much as though General Terry was miles away."[34]

Ames could be excused for a bit of boastfulness. Just twenty-eight, the boyish general had marched straight from West Point to the first battle of Bull Run, where his bravery had earned him a promotion (and a future Medal of Honor). He had gone on to fight in dozens of major campaigns and battles—the Seven Days, Antietam, Gettysburg, the siege of Charleston, the bloody assault on Fort Wagner, Cold Harbor, and the siege of Petersburg, to name a few. Among his personal treasures was the smoke-stained battle flag of the Twentieth Maine. It had been his first regimental command; soon after he was promoted to general, it had gone on to save the Union line at Gettysburg under his old protégé, Colonel Joshua Chamberlain. After the battle, the unit had honored him by presenting him its banner.[35]

Now, as the bombardment lifted, Ames watched his first brigade struggle to capture the traverse at the end of the wall. After twenty minutes he ordered his second brigade to advance; turning to his staff, he said, "Gentlemen, we will now go forward." As the cluster of officers walked toward the fort, rebel sharpshooters zeroed in. Two of Ames's assistants staggered and fell, followed by a third, but Ames strolled into the fort unharmed, wearing a brigadier general's full dress coat.[36]

At the far end, Confederate defenders butchered the sailors and marines, but on the river flank, Ames's division swarmed up and into the fort. For five long hours, the young general directed the fighting inside that sand-encased inferno, sending most of his men down the massive north wall while he fortified a position within the interior. All three of his brigade commanders fell dead or wounded, along with countless junior officers. After nightfall, naval shells continued to scream and plunge into the works, as rifle and cannon fire raked the Union position. Terry eventually joined him in the fort and ordered that the battle continue; around nine o'clock, Ames organized a flanking maneuver that finally drove out the remaining defenders. The impregnable Fort Fisher fell.[37]

Elsewhere on that sandy peninsula, Sim Younger helped dig a line that protected the rear of Ames's division. Though Younger did not fight inside the fort, he and the other black troops on the expedition probably appreciated the victory more than anyone else. It brought freedom for African Americans that much closer—even for those still in bondage in far-off Missouri, where Sim's white nephew Cole Younger had fought as a rebel bushwhacker.[38]

TO THE DWINDLING guerrillas and Confederate soldiers wintering in Texas, the fall of Fort Fisher looked like only one domino in a long toppling row. On December 15 and 16, 1864, the Union army under Major General George H. Thomas had annihilated the rebel Army of Tennessee at Nashville. At the end of the same month, Sherman had completed his March to the Sea. "I beg to present you, as a Christmas gift," he had wired to Lincoln, "the city of Savannah." From there Sherman marched into South Carolina, capturing Columbia on February 17 and Charleston the day after. After torching Columbia, Sherman moved into North Carolina, easily throwing back Confederate counterattacks in the middle of March. As April began, Grant forced Lee out of his lines around Petersburg, capturing Richmond soon after; on April 7, Grant finally trapped the Confederate commander. On April 9, 1865, at the home of Wilmer McLean in Appomattox Courthouse, Virginia, Lee surrendered the Army of Northern Virginia. The war was over.[39]

More than any other group of Confederates, the Missourians found it almost impossible to reconcile themselves to defeat. General Shelby and Major Edwards discussed their options, spoke with their men, then made a drastic decision. They would not surrender. Together with 132 die-hard troopers, they broke camp and set out for Mexico.[40]

By then, the guerrillas were already gone. As warm weather crept back in late March or early April, Archie Clement told his friend and follower Jesse James to saddle his horse for the long ride north. They were going to end their exile. They set off for Missouri with perhaps one hundred other bushwhackers, unaware of Lee's surrender. It scarcely mattered. Where they went, the war would continue.

PART THREE

Defiance

1865–1876

O then at last relent: is there no place
Left for repentance, none for pardon left?
None but by submission, and that word
Disdain forbids me, and my dread of shame

—Paradise Lost

It is of no use to shut our eyes to the facts, and to pretend that a lit-
tle thieving is at the bottom of all this. It is a deeper and more seri-
ous evil than that. . . . These guerrillas, in addition to being
thieves and robbers and murderers, are rebels.

—*Kansas City Journal of Commerce*
May 11, 1865

They looked upon it as merely a continuation of the war. Don Car-
los refuses to recognize the Spanish government, and why should
not the Jameses decline to recognize the terms of Appomattox?

—*Kansas City Journal of Commerce*
October 20, 1876

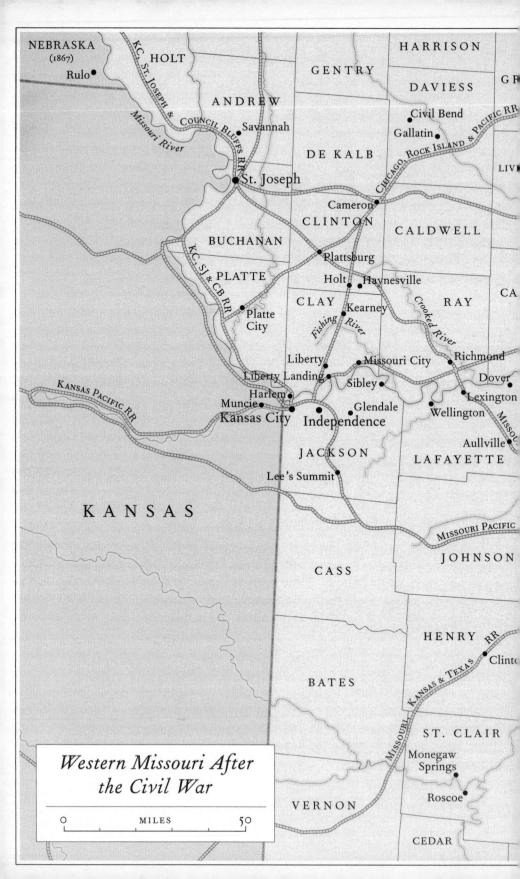

NEBRASKA
(1867)

Rulo

HOLT

HARRISON

GENTRY

DAVIESS

GR

ANDREW

Savannah

Civil Bend

Gallatin

LIV

DE KALB

St. Joseph

Cameron

CLINTON

CALDWELL

CA

BUCHANAN

Plattsburg

PLATTE

Holt

Haynesville

RAY

Platte City

CLAY

Kearney

Fishing River

Crooked River

Richmond

Liberty

Missouri City

Dover

Liberty Landing

Sibley

Lexington

Harlem

Muncie

Glendale

Wellington

Kansas City

Independence

Aullville

JACKSON

LAFAYETTE

KANSAS

Lee's Summit

JOHNSON

CASS

HENRY

Clinto

BATES

ST. CLAIR

Monegaw Springs

Roscoe

VERNON

CEDAR

Missouri River

KC, St. Joseph & COUNCIL BLUFFS RR

KC, SJ & CB RR

CHICAGO, ROCK ISLAND & PACIFIC RR

KANSAS PACIFIC RR

MISSOURI PACIFIC

MISSOURI, KANSAS & TEXAS RR

MISSOU

Western Missouri After the Civil War

0   MILES   50

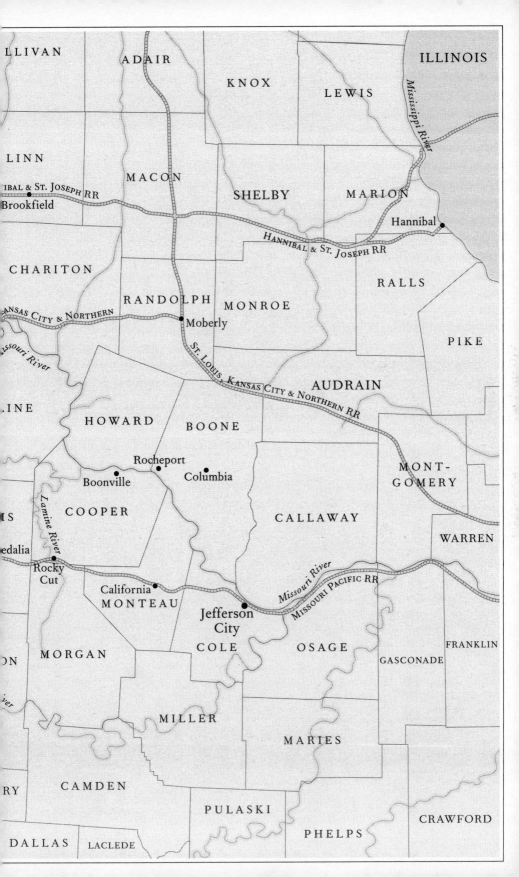

CHAPTER NINE

A Year of Bitterness

FOR NEARLY TWO WEEKS, the killer ran free. Day after day, the nation held its collective breath as soldiers and Federal agents scoured the countryside around Washington. Finally, on April 26, 1865—twelve days after the assassination of President Abraham Lincoln—the searchers trapped John Wilkes Booth in a barn near Bowling Green, Virginia. They set fire to the building to flush him out, and the fugitive soon died from a bullet that he may have fired himself. If he did commit suicide, it would have been a fitting end, for Booth had played Judas Iscariot to Lincoln's Redeemer, even to the extent of killing him on Good Friday.

Back in Washington, Lincoln's body remained in the White House, lying in state until April 19. Not far away, Secretary of State William H. Seward lingered close to death, having been wounded by one of Booth's co-conspirators; rumors of Seward's demise spread across the country. Then Lincoln's funeral train began a slow, winding trip back to Illinois, with some seven million grieving Americans weeping beside the tracks. The president's assassination provided a shocking counterpoint to the triumph at Appomattox. That Good Friday gunshot echoed across the North, warning that peace would not erase the South's bitterness.[1]

Missourians needed no education in bitterness. In their farmyards and creek-bottom brush, far from the famous battlegrounds, no one really believed the war had ended. "We hear great talk of peace," wrote Sarah Harlan, "but the bushwhackers are plenty." Three days after Lee's surrender, she learned that such guerrillas as Ol Shepherd remained in the area, dodging army patrols sent out from Liberty. "I think they are waiting for Captain [Jim] Green to come so that they will have a better show," she mused. Still, she held on to hope. As she looked out her windows at the pouring rain, she wrote eagerly about "the indications of peace."[2]

The next Saturday, Harlan traveled up to the festively decorated town of Plattsburg, where a weekend celebration heralded the end of the war. "But on Sunday morning, the people were cut down very much," she wrote to her sister, "on account of the news coming into town that our President and Seward were killed, which has proved to be a sad truth." Her letter palpitated with despair as she reflected on these events. "We were all so set up to think that peace was so near at hand," she mourned. "I fear that we will have worse times now on account of it."[3]

Nothing, the military authorities believed, could make the times worse in Missouri. Lee's surrender meant that U.S. troops in the state would soon be demobilized; meanwhile, the bushwhackers were sure to return from their winter refuge in Texas. "Organize! Organize!" General Fisk urged a Unionist elder of Platte County on April 26, 1865. "All volunteer troops are being withdrawn from North Missouri; martial law will soon be abrogated; civil law will be supreme. Spencer rifles must aid in the good work."[4]

And the guerrillas did come. Telegraph wires hummed across the state as various posts tracked the bushwhackers' approach from the south. On May 5, the garrison at Fort Scott, Kansas, reported that 150 guerrillas had passed by on their way north. Major General Grenville Dodge, the commander in St. Louis, immediately sent warning to Colonel Chester Harding, Jr., who commanded the Central District, and various other subordinates. "Keep all your cavalry in the saddle," he ordered. Two days later, almost exactly a month after Appomattox, the rebels struck.[5]

SOMETIME IN THE first week of May 1865, Jesse James watched with admiration as Archie Clement flourished his Bowie knife over a struggling militiaman whom Jesse and two other guerrillas held pinned to the ground near the banks of the Osage River. With practiced skill, Little Archie cut through the skin and arteries of his victim's throat, then carved away the scalp, his characteristic trophy.[6] "Clement," Jesse would reflect a decade later, was "one of the noblest boys, and the most promising military boy, of this age."[7]

During the damp weeks of April 1865, Clement had led Jesse and perhaps 70 other bushwhackers on the long ride from Sherman, Texas. Their group formed part of a larger mass of some 150 guerrillas, who coalesced around the strongest personalities among them: Dave Pool, the laughing prankster from Lexington; Jim Anderson, the less-accomplished brother of Bloody Bill; and, of course, Clement himself. After they crossed into Missouri, the bushwhackers told the beleaguered farmers they met that they knew nothing of Lee's surrender, which they dismissed as "a damned Yankee lie." What they did know was that the trees and brush had filled out with leaves again, giving them ample cover to continue their war of ambush and murder.[8]

It was a war they carried steadily north as they rode toward the big river. After the scalping on the Osage, the guerrillas moved up to Johnson County. It was a homecoming for Clement, who had spent most of his life within its boundaries. At two o'clock in the morning on May 7, the teenager celebrated his return by leading a charge through the darkened streets of the village of Holden. Perhaps thirty guerrillas plundered a pair of stores, stopping only to gun down a civilian before they rejoined their comrades.

At the first glow of the approaching dawn, Clement roused his fellows for another strike. Jesse and some one hundred bushwhackers donned Union uniforms in the thinning darkness, mounted up, and spurred toward Kingsville, the town closest to Clement's boyhood farm. Kicking their way into homes and stores, they shot down eight startled men and boys stumbling out of bed, and set fire to five houses. Jesse, a friend later wrote, fired four bullets into the trembling postmaster, Leroy Duncan, who died soon after. Leaving the corpses and smoldering ruins behind, the guerrillas rode north into Lafayette County, where they rapidly murdered fifteen more civilians.[9]

In the hours after the massacre at Kingsville, General Dodge's staff groped for information. Gradually the guerrillas' identities emerged as fresh intelligence blew away the fog of uncertainty. On May 8, reports came in that Pool and Jim Anderson led many of the guerrillas; on May 11, a surrendering Confederate soldier told the authorities that he had seen seventy men led by Clement, "Bill Anderson's scalper and head devil." On the same day, Clement announced himself with a letter to Major Berryman K. Davis, commander of the garrison at Lexington:

SIR: This is to notify you that I will give you until Friday morning, May 12, 1865, to surrender the town of Lexington. If you surrender we will treat you and all taken as prisoners of war. If we have to take it by storm we will burn the town and kill the soldiers. We have the force, and are determined to have it.

I am, sir, your obedient servant,
—A. CLEMENT

This absurdly polite note agitated the army high command. Major General John Pope, commander of the vast Division of the Missouri, demanded full details from Dodge, who scoffed at the rebels' ability to capture Lexington. The town was garrisoned by at least 180 men, including a company of former slaves who were grimly determined to fight to the last man.

Dodge believed that the message was designed to trick the troops into barricading themselves in Lexington while the guerrillas slipped over the Missouri River. He immediately telegraphed orders to seize all boats and keep a careful watch on the most important crossing places.[10]

Clement's message signified many things, none of them explicitly stated in his letter. For one thing, its very formality seemed to reflect his vision of himself as a legitimate Confederate. But Clement certainly knew by now that the Confederacy had ceased to exist. His surrender demand was a ruse, meant to buy the guerrillas more time—but time for what? The guerrillas reportedly debated the question fiercely among themselves. They could see that with each passing day, more and more rebels were giving themselves up and, once they took an oath of allegiance, were being allowed to go free. But pride, hatred, and fear of civil prosecution weighed heavily with these former followers of Quantrill and Bloody Bill. As the debate progressed, Pool seemed to lean toward surrender, but Clement was inclined to cross the Missouri River and continue his depredations on the northern side, where there were fewer Union troops.[11]

The guerrillas investigated both options. On May 12, a group of bushwhackers fired on a detachment that stood guard over the abandoned village of Sibley, west of Lexington. Located just across the Missouri from the mouth of the Fishing River, Sibley was one of the rebels' favorite crossing points. On the same day, Captain Clayton E. Rogers, the provost marshal in Lexington, received word that one hundred guerrillas wanted to surrender. Before long, Pool arranged to give himself up and bring in many of the bushwhackers still lingering in the hills. Even Clement sent a conciliatory note on May 14; this time, Major Davis reported, he "proposed with five men to meet an equal party [on May 17] . . . to learn particulars of terms, &c."

Despite this talk of surrender, Clement, Anderson, and Jesse thought they might still continue the fight, if only they could get across the Missouri River. "I am almost certain that Clement, with five or six men, was on the river yesterday," Davis wrote on May 16, "prospecting for crossing the river. He talked with persons near there, and declared his [intentions] to be such. I am confident he and his party were fired upon yesterday, about six miles out on the Salt Pond road, on his return from the river."[12]

This little skirmish was hugely significant in the life of Jesse James. Before it was over, he would be prostrate with the second serious wound of his brief career, a wound that looked like it would be mortal. Such an injury would be important enough, but in surviving it Jesse was to swell the memory of this fight to epic proportions.

MOST INDIVIDUALS CREATE inner narratives of their lives, reshaping memories in light of subsequent experiences. In the lives of public figures, private events take on mythic meaning, as society comes to see them as representative of its sense of itself. Benjamin Franklin's youthful studying by the light of the fire and Abraham Lincoln's rail-splitting, for example, echoed the American ideal of the self-made man. Such incidents need not be true: George Washington's honesty about the cherry tree was completely fabricated, yet it won acceptance as a symbol of the United States as a republic of virtue. In 1865, at the age of seventeen, Jesse James was far from a public figure, yet already he had started to construct an inner narrative that would one day grow into a symbolic tale for one particular segment of society—the Confederates.

As Jesse bounced along atop his horse on the Salt Pond road on May 15, the lines of his story were already appearing, formed by persecution and revenge. In his inner—soon to be outer—mythology, ordinary events were exaggerated. The raid on his home in May 1863—a perfectly routine, if harrowing, search for a guerrilla gang—turned into an unforgivable act of tyrannical oppression. The massacre and battle at Centralia—a day of shocking brutality, even in this shockingly brutal war—was transformed into a noble duel between Jesse and the Union commander. These were the bricks that built his legend, and now one more was set in place.

In the moments before the skirmish began, Jesse and Clement were returning from the Missouri River, where they had been looking for a safe crossing point, torn between surrendering or continuing to fight. They still had two more days before their proposed meeting with Major Davis. While they were considering their options, they suddenly confronted a squad of cavalrymen from the Third Wisconsin, who promptly yanked out their pistols and opened fire.

In later years, Jesse would claim that he was riding into Lexington to surrender when the gunfire erupted; he even insisted to one neighbor that he was carrying a flag of truce at the time. The soldiers were drunk, he said, and recklessly opened fire. In 1882, a resident of Lexington would assert that Captain Rogers, the provost marshal, had actually dispatched the cavalrymen to escort the rebels into town, "but by some mistake an alarm was given and some of the [bushwhackers] attempted to escape and were fired upon by the Federals." By then, however, the myth had taken hold. The simple truth—that a group of indecisive guerrillas blundered into an army patrol that reacted first—had become a tale of how the vindictive Federals refused to accept an honorable surrender.[13]

For the moments that followed the first crack of gunfire, we have only Jesse's word, filtered through friends, and the evidence offered by his corpse. Almost immediately, a .36 caliber bullet fired from a Navy revolver tore into the right side of his chest, inches from his wound of the year before. Apparently the lead ball passed between his ribs and carved its way though his lung. It would remain lodged in his body for the rest of his life.

In the hailstorm of gunfire, the other guerrillas wheeled their horses and fled, but Jesse's mount staggered and fell under the impact of a bullet. Untangling himself from his animal, Jesse ran into the woods, blood spouting from his wound. Close behind came two Union troopers, the leader spurring on a large black mount. "I turned and killed the big black horse," Jesse reportedly said. "That will stop a man every time. That ended the fight. I was near a creek, and I lay in the water all night—I felt as if I was burning up. The next morning, I crawled up the bank and there was a man plowing nearby who helped me get to my friends."[14]

"I was in a dreadful fix," he recalled. He lay in a nearby farmhouse, utterly incapacitated, and "everybody thought the wound would be mortal." Continued resistance was no longer an option; he was in serious need of medical attention. His fellow guerrillas converged on the farm as his host procured a carriage. His comrades lifted him in and drove him to Lexington, riding alongside toward their inevitable surrender. A local man remembered the bushwhackers as they came in—long lines of men with "bronzed faces, long hair, rough and well worn garments," their horses drooping and exhausted after weeks of hard riding. Once in town, they carried Jesse to a room in a hotel, where, like all surrendering Confederates, he raised his hand and took the oath of allegiance on his sickbed on May 21, 1865.[15]

In later retelling by Jesse and his mother, the months that followed brought pain, helplessness, and misery. Day after day, more bushwhackers rode into Lexington to give themselves up. Not until June 13, Jesse claimed, was he able to make the trip across the Missouri River to the village of Harlem, just north of Kansas City, where his uncle John Mimms (husband of Mary, his father's sister) ran a boardinghouse. For another month, he said, he remained in their care, attended by various doctors. On July 15, his sister Susie came to take him to Rulo, Nebraska, where the family remained in exile, living off Reuben's meager earnings as a physician.

Jesse remained there for eight weeks, Zerelda said later, sinking closer to death. Finally, she claimed, "he drew my face down close to his and whispered, 'Ma, I don't want to be buried here in a Northern state.' " She reassured him that she would never bury him in Nebraska. "But, Ma," he reportedly said, "I don't want to die here." The next day, she claimed (August 26, by Jesse's account), they carried him on a sofa down to the landing, where they put him on a boat back to Clay County.

But Jesse was too ill to accompany his family all the way home, we're told. Instead, he was taken back to his uncle's boardinghouse, where his

cousin Zerelda—named for Jesse's mother, but better known as Zee—
nursed him back to health. Only in October was he supposed to have
improved to the point where he could risk the journey back to the old farm.
He was "emaciated, tottering as he walked, fighting what seemed to everyone a hopeless battle," wrote a loyal defender. "His wound would not heal,
and more ominous still, every now and then there was a hemorrhage. In the
spring of 1866 he was just barely able to mount a horse and ride a little."
The injury to his lung, it was said, would plague him for at least another
two years, until he finally made a miraculous recovery.[16]

It all makes for a compelling story, hallowed by tradition. But this tale
looks on closer inspection like a fact-based narrative greatly exaggerated.
A bullet through the lung was not necessarily as grave an injury as common sense and Jesse's own account would make it seem. A study of lung
injuries conducted at Rama War Hospital in Croatia from 1992 through
1994 concluded that "The wounds inflicted by classic firearms need not be
primarily severe and destructive. A direct wound of the . . . lungs is limited
to the wound canal. . . . If none of the large blood vessels is involved, the
bleeding is limited and diminishing, and ventilation disorders are not very
pronounced." As particularly soft tissue, the lung suffers less from the
shock of a bullet than do bone or dense organs such as the liver. Wounds
inflicted by weapons with low muzzle velocities—comparable to the Navy
revolver fired at Jesse—are particularly survivable, and "can be treated
conservatively."

Still, reliable contemporary accounts by disinterested parties confirm
that Jesse was left prone for many weeks by his injury. Possibly an infection
set in—the most common complication with lung wounds, according to
the Croatian study. This, together with misguided nineteenth-century
medicine, would have been the primary threat to his health, the threat that
left him helpless in bed in his uncle's house. And Zee Mimms did indeed
tend his fever and change his bandages, according to her brother.[17]

But the story of Jesse's extraordinarily long recovery reeks of inven-
tion; no witness outside of the James family and its circle of friends and
defenders ever supported it; other sources described him as active and
apparently healthy by 1866 at the latest.[18] Indeed, his wounding and recovery mark the beginning of the real mystery surrounding his life, when the
inevitable incompleteness of the historical record becomes complicated by
deliberate misinformation, misdirection, and lies. In truth, Jesse James's
multiyear recuperation was a retroactive alibi, manufactured after he had
become famous to hide his activities in the years immediately following the
war's end. In those years of bitterness, there would be much to conceal.

· · ·

WAR HAD UNMADE the world. Four years of bloodshed had paved the
American landscape with gravestones. At least 620,000 soldiers had died
(360,000 Union, 260,000 Confederate), more than the combined total of all
the nation's other wars, before and since. Were the United States to suffer
an equivalent toll at the start of the twenty-first century, almost six million
people would be dead.

The South lay in ruins. Farms and villages along the paths of the major
armies had been wrecked. Cities ranging from Jackson, Mississippi, to
Columbia, South Carolina, from Atlanta to Richmond, were smoldering
ruins. Basic infrastructure such as levees, roads, and bridges had gone
unrepaired or had been destroyed by raiders from both sides. The financial
capital of the rebel states had been annihilated as well, spent on arms and
supplies, or converted into now-worthless Confederate bonds and currency. Across the region land values fell, crops went unplanted, workshops
went unmanned.

As for slavery, the great wheel that drove the South's economy, advancing Union armies and the Emancipation Proclamation had knocked it
loose, and it would soon be smashed to pieces. On January 31, 1865, the
U.S. House of Representatives approved the Thirteenth Amendment to the
Constitution; once ratified by the states, it would abolish slavery completely, without compensation or qualification. An enormous portion of the
South's wealth had once been measured in human bodies, and now it would
disappear.[19]

But the war had scourged Missouri as perhaps nowhere else. Homes had
been torched, horses stolen, fence rails broken up for firewood, livestock
killed by soldiers and bushwhackers. The population of Missouri fell by an
estimated 300,00 people between 1861 and 1865. Roughly one out of every
three citizens had been killed in battle, murdered at home, driven out by
guerrilla threats, banished by the authorities, or simply had fled to a more
hopeful place.[20]

In Clay County, the trend was clear as early as 1864. A local census that
year showed that the white population had fallen to 9,421 (104 fewer than in
1860), while the black population had plummeted by almost 50 percent, to
1,756. Most of the remaining black residents—still largely enslaved—were
women and children, who lacked the option of enlisting in the army. In the
mayhem surrounding Price's raid, the flight, murder, and expulsion of
both whites and blacks had intensified. "Most all of the families that used to
live here moved away," Amanda Savery wrote to her Confederate veteran
husband in 1865. "The Eatons are all banished with many others. . . .
There has been a great many deaths among your friends."[21]

The war had torn apart Missouri's political landscape like a volcanic
eruption. The old parties had vanished, replaced by the Radicals and the

Conservatives. Whigs, Democrats, even Republicans had spilled into one party or the other regardless of prewar affiliations. The defining question had been the conduct of the war.[22]

The Radicals had argued for the iron fist. In their eyes, the Civil War was—as it was officially called in Washington—the War of the Rebellion, a war against treason. And in Missouri, those traitors were a very personal threat. Many of the sternest Radicals lived in the guerrilla-plagued regions and suffered directly, and bitterly, from the fighting. They were the rank and file of the militia, the volunteers in the Federal army, the farmers burned out by bushwhackers and chased into garrison towns. Once casually opposed to abolitionism, they came to see slaveowners as the cause of the war; by the end of 1864, most Radicals believed that opposition to emancipation was as much treason as carrying Confederate arms.

The Conservatives, on the other hand, had struggled to ease the pressure of the military presence and preserve the peculiar institution. No better example can be found than Clay County's Colonel James H. Moss, the former Whig, who had used his intermittent command of the militia to catch runaway slaves and reintegrate returning rebels. Despite the suspicions of Radicals, however, neither Moss nor the Conservative Party in general had been disloyal. Led by such stalwart old Whigs as James Rollins and William F. Switzler, they had specifically rejected the Democratic Party label because it had been tainted by sympathy for secession, thanks to antiwar Democrats in the North, known as Copperheads. Many Conservatives, such as Moss and Odon Guitar, served in the militia. The party had even nominated Lincoln for president in 1864, and had competed with the Radicals to send a delegation to the national Republican convention.

The Radicals had won that fight, and once their delegates had been seated, they had voted *against* Lincoln's renomination. These angry Missourians wanted sterner stuff—and they were prepared to provide it themselves. In 1864, in the midst of Price's invasion, they had swept the legislative elections and voted in a new governor, Thomas C. Fletcher. The Radicals owed their victory to their adamant Unionism. Fletcher had been a brigadier general in the Army of the Tennessee, and actually had participated in the fighting against Price during the political campaign.[23]

The Radicals had wanted to go deeper still. In perhaps their most important victory in the 1864 election, they had won approval for a constitutional convention and gained two-thirds of the slots for delegates. The stated purpose of this body, which assembled in St. Louis on January 7, 1865, was to free Missouri's slaves. This was no mere technicality; tens of thousands still remained in bondage in the state. The convention swiftly enacted an ordinance of immediate emancipation, supplanting an act of 1863 that would have delayed freedom until 1870 at the earliest. On January 14, black Missourians poured into the streets to celebrate, marching in joyous parades through every major city in the state.[24]

In the mind of Charles D. Drake, the convention still had much to do. An energetic, articulate, intemperate Radical from St. Louis, Drake immediately asserted leadership over the politically inexperienced delegates and directed the writing of an entirely new constitution. Blessed with a capacity for endless work and cursed with a bullying, intolerant personality, he drove his fellows forward, completing a final draft in a matter of weeks. On April 8, 1865, the convention voted overwhelmingly to send it to the voters for ratification.

In most respects, the new constitution was a sound, even admirable, work. It barred the state government from lending its credit to private individuals and corporations, which closed off a major source of corruption; it restored some of the balance in the legislature toward urban areas, which had been badly underrepresented under the old constitution; and it extended critical civil rights, including property rights, public schooling, and access to the courts (though not the vote) to the newly freed slaves. Viewed from the 1861 perspective, these measures were astonishing. If there had been one thing that united white Missourians before the war, it was opposition to emancipation. Now the state had stepped out in front of the rest of the Union in extending rights to its black citizens. As historian Eric Foner writes, "Here were men acting as if in the midst of a revolution."[25]

The Conservatives were allergic to revolution, and they found little to like in the new constitution. Hailing largely from the old slave-dependent riverside counties, they did not want to lose power to the cities—and they especially did not want any rights extended to black Missourians. Even in this moment of emancipation, blatant, vicious racism was a basic ingredient of political debate. "Any Democrat who did not manage to hint that the negro is a degenerate gorilla would be considered lacking in enthusiasm," wrote Georges Clemenceau, a future French premier who covered the national election of 1864 as a newspaper correspondent. In the former slave state of Missouri, such feelings were never far from the surface of conservative politics. "In the name of God," protested Samuel A. Gilbert, a convention delegate from Platte County, "if you are going to free negroes, send them from us."[26]

As much as they disliked liberty for all, Conservatives found something else to hate above all else in the proposed constitution: the Oath.* Intended to "preserve in purity the elective franchise to loyal citizens," the Oath required each potential voter to swear that he (women could not cast bal-

---

*I have capitalized "Oath," both to stress its importance and to avoid partisan labels.

lots) had not committed any of eighty-six acts of rebellion, including simply expressing sympathy for the rebels in general or any individual rebel. The convention mandated the Oath not only for electors, but also candidates for office, jurors, lawyers, corporation officers and trustees, and teachers. It was even required of Christian ministers. A comprehensive registration system was to sift through the voters every two years; county supervisors and local boards would have the right to bar anyone from the polls whom they suspected of disloyalty.

The Radicals called it the Iron-Clad Oath; the Conservatives dubbed it the Code of Draco, after the ancient Athenian legislator who made almost all criminal offenses punishable by death. "The Constitution," William F. Switzler argued, was created "in a spirit of malice and revenge . . . unworthy of a victorious and magnanimous people." On a less lofty plane, they feared that it would cost them any hope of winning statewide elections, for the Radicals had a clear majority of the Unionist population. "If the letter of the law is carried out," explained one Missourian, "very many who stayed out of the rebel army, but sympathized with & otherwise aided the Southern cause, will be disfranchised . . . and here is where the shoe pinches." The Oath promised to strip the ballot from perhaps thirty-five thousand to fifty thousand men, all of them likely Conservative voters.[27]

The Radicals, on the other hand, saw the Oath as the constitution's most important element. On one level, it represented the final triumph of free-labor ideology. Slavery, the Republicans had always argued, blighted society in general. The Oath would drive the old rebels and slaveholders out of Missouri and attract Yankee immigrants, remaking it into a Northern state and unlocking growth and prosperity. "Which would you prefer," asked Radical leader B. Gratz Brown in May 1865, "to have Missouri filled with men from Price's and Dick Taylor's armies, or with loyal men from Ohio, New York, and New England?"[28]

On a more emotional level, the Radicals saw the Oath as an explicit rebuke to treason. "The people of the North are not such fools as to fight through such a war as this," declared Senator Jacob Howard of Michigan, "and then turn around and say to the traitors, 'All you have to do is come back into the councils of the nation.'" In Missouri, such feelings were greatly intensified. More than 110,000 Missouri men had fought for the Union; at least 12 percent of them had died. Across the state, families had suffered directly at the hands of the bushwhackers. "I would rather today see a rebel with a musket in his hand than with a ballot," declared the editor of the *Kansas City Journal of Commerce*. "If he outvotes me, I must take my musket and support the law or policy which he may impose. . . . Are the people prepared for this alternative? Is Missouri never to have peace? Is treason to become a virtue and loyalty a crime?"[29]

This was the indignant wrath of righteousness—and who could blame them? But in their anger and their zeal, the Radicals began to see themselves as the only legitimate political party. Joseph Dixon of Independence summarized their case neatly in a letter to Governor Fletcher. "The Radical Union men," he wrote, "are the government." He equated Conservatives with secessionists, warning, "You know that secesh and bushwhackers have the same object, are of the same stock, and are therefore friends." With this uncompromising outlook, the Radicals took every conceivable measure to ensure victory for the new constitution in the election set for June 6, 1865. The convention declared that the Oath would be applied to the ratification vote itself. It had poll books sent to Missouri troops still in the field, who were urged to—in the phrase of the times— vote as they had shot. With all this, plus a patriotic boost from Lincoln's assassination, passage of the constitution seemed a foregone conclusion. Ultimately, though, it succeeded with only 52 percent of the vote.[30]

"It is said the new constitution has a majority," Amanda Savery wrote to her husband on June 18, 1865. "Don't know what the Southern people will do. The country will be depopulated." Her words would have made the Radicals smile.[31]

ON MAY 2, 1866, a newspaper in Lexington, Missouri, published a letter from a man who was visiting the town for the first time since before the war. He was flabbergasted, he wrote, at the changes in "this once beautiful and pleasant, now dilapidated and ruined city." As he walked through the streets, he declared, "I thought I could see much bitterness and opposition expressed, one to the other, in the countenances of citizens. . . . I inquired at the hotel of some stranger, what could have brought about such a change in the town and in her citizens, and the ready reply was, 'The war.' Said he, 'We have here three papers, and three parties:—Democracy [Conservative], Radicalism, and Southern.' "

Such was the triangle of power in the heart of postwar Missouri: two hostile parties of Unionists, locked in a struggle for control of the government, and in the third corner, the former rebels—angry, isolated, alienated from politics. The newspaper that published this letter was the recently founded *Lexington Caucasian*, which claimed the largest circulation in the state outside of St. Louis. It was the "organ of the disfranchised and proscribed citizen," proclaimed the masthead. "We are and have been Southern in our sympathies," the editors declared, "and opposed to a mongrel breed, or a mongrel government." Clearly the spirit of the rebellion survived along the banks of the Missouri River.

Though former Confederates were barred from the political arena, their presence in the countryside was palpable. The same traveler who commented on Lexington went on to the town of Waverly, where he wandered outside his hotel. "I looked over across the street towards the stores," he wrote, "and I saw several good-looking young men ride rapidly to the fence, tie their horses, and make for the stores. Arriving, I noticed they were all doubly armed. Said I to a young lady, 'Who are they?' She laughed, and said they were bushwhackers. The blood seemed to get cold in my veins."[32]

If the traveler had understood the full significance of what he had witnessed, his blood would have frozen solid. A full year had passed since the bushwhackers had surrendered at Lexington—yet here they were, riding in a group, going "doubly armed," even *shopping* together. This persistence of organized rebel bodies speaks to the deeper revolution wrought by the war and the Oath: the creation of an explosive culture of hatred, personal firearms, and political alienation.[33]

The trouble began immediately after the end of the war. Embittered Unionists could scarcely believe that surrendering bushwhackers were being treated identically to regular Confederates. "It looks very strange to me that such robbers and murderers can be turned loose to do as they please after causing so much trouble," Sarah Harlan wrote to her parents on June 8, 1865. The bushwhackers themselves, conscious of their own deeds, understood this anger perfectly. "We must keep our side arms," Ol Shepherd wrote on May 25, 1865, as he was negotiating the surrender of his band, "for you know we have personal enemies that would kill us at the first opportunity."[34]

Retribution hung in the air. "Don't know who to trust [in] these times," wrote Amanda Savery to her husband on June 18, 1865. "Your friends," she told him, "would like to see you, if it was safe for you to come." But it wasn't, she thought. On July 1, she nervously scribbled that returning Southern soldiers "were shot as fast as they came, as civil war is in force."[35]

"Diaries, letters, even military reports, were filled with stories of old neighbors returning home to get even with each other, man to man," comments historian Michael Fellman. On July 21, 1865, for example, a former Union scout named James Butler Hickok—already known as Wild Bill— confronted bushwhacker Dave Tutt in the town square in Springfield, Missouri. Both men fired one round, and Tutt fell dead with a bullet in the heart. Hickok was tried for murder before a jury that consisted entirely of Union men (thanks to the Oath) and a judge who had been the Federal commander in Springfield. Not surprisingly, they swiftly found him innocent on grounds of self-defense.[36]

In other cases it was the loyal men—and the law—who got the worst of it. In Jackson County, bushwhacker Bill Runnells called two Unionists out of their homes and murdered them. When Sheriff James W. Holmes tried to serve him with a warrant on January 8, 1866, Runnells shot him, then killed James Copeland as he came to the sheriff's assistance. Personal feuds smoldered on as late as June 15, when Lass Easton stormed up to bush-whacker Jim Green in a grocery store in Haynesville, just a few miles north of the Samuel farm. "Easton accused Jim of being in the company that burned his father's house," Sarah Harlan wrote. Green shot Easton in the ensuing melee, and fired two more bullets into his fallen form to be sure he was dead. "One of Easton's brothers says he intends to kill Jim if he follows him to the end of the world," Harlan added. "I fear it is not done with yet."[37]

On one level, this outbreak of personal violence represented a general crisis in American society. With the onset of peace, a nationwide crime wave filled prisons with returning soldiers. "The crime cause arises from the demoralization which ever attends on war and armies," concluded the administrators of a Pennsylvania penitentiary in 1866. "Familiarity with deeds of violence and destruction . . . leaves its impression after the one is over and the other disbanded. We find in all parts of the country the most distressing evidence of this fact." In Kansas in 1867, 83 percent of the state prisoners had served full terms in the army before taking to crime. "The mass are willing to tell you with great frankness," officials reported, "that they are not old in crime and confirmed in a state of wrongdoing." The incredible bloodshed of the war had put many soldiers through a social process of violentization, a process that was particularly intense in guerrilla-plagued Missouri.[38]

The war was not the only cause. In Missouri and much of the South, the heritage of mayhem can be traced to long-standing traditions of personal violence. In the upper echelons of society, men sometimes settled matters of honor with duels. Public figures from Senator Thomas Hart Benton of Missouri to Andrew Jackson faced off with rivals. At the bottom there were the "rough-and-tumbles," anything-goes battles between backwoods "gougers." These men were the heirs of the violent culture of the Scots, Protestant Irish, and border-county Englishmen who had settled the Appalachian hills and valleys. Every bit as proud as the upper-crust duelists and far more boastful, they bit off fingers, tore off ears, and gouged out eyes (the height of the rough-and-tumble art), in a surreal ritual of combat.[39]

The war drew out and exaggerated the personal aggressiveness of the South's culture of violence, but the gun shattered its formalized, ritual quality—specifically, the rapid-firing revolver invented by Samuel Colt. The war put weapons in the hands of millions of men, who were allowed to carry them home. The new custom of carrying firearms astonished contemporaries, who had seen nothing like it before the war. A Yankee in Mississippi noticed that "a great majority of the country white people wore [pistols] strapped outside their pants, and many outside their coats." In Richmond, Kentucky, "all wear Navy revolvers strapped around their waist," observed a reporter in 1866. "This habit of wearing firearms is not confined alone to the men, but boys scarcely fifteen years of age."[40]

In Missouri, mandatory militia service, guerrilla warfare, and aggressive postwar marketing by firearms manufacturers had saturated the population with six-shooters. In October 1866, Lieutenant James Burbank went to investigate reports of "an armed pistol company" in St. Clair and neighboring counties. "Nearly every man I saw during my stay in these counties carried army revolvers," Burbank reported, "even men at work in their fields, and boys riding about town." He described it as "a habit which grew out of the unsettled condition of the country since the war." Unsettled indeed. Given the omnipresence of pistols, the persistence of wartime hatreds, and a fresh familiarity with death, confrontations rapidly turned lethal. "Fist and skull fighting has played out here," wrote one Missourian in May 1866. "They now do that business in a more prompt manner."[41]

This new culture of gunslinging—and the personal feuding that went with it—was bad enough, but in Missouri it intersected with a social and political revolution sweeping the countryside at the grass roots, making the situation especially dangerous. All along the Missouri River—in the very stronghold of the old elite—the Radicals overthrew traditional leaders, tearing down the hemp growers and tobacco merchants, the slaveowners and slave traders, from their seats of power. Under the terms of the Ouster Ordinance, passed by the constitutional convention, no less than eight hundred civil offices were declared vacant on May 1, 1865. Conservatives were tossed out of office at every level, from Supreme Court justices to county clerks, to be replaced by Governor Fletcher's appointments. Dozens of letters from Radical committees poured onto his desk, recommending men in terms that would have horrified the old order: one man enlisted black recruits in the army as a provost marshal; another gave "the first emancipation speeches ever heard in this county"; all were "active," "zealous," and "unflinching loyal men." These were the men the governor named.[42]

In Clay County, Alvah Maret—the man who had sold land to Robert James and tried to help ease Reuben Samuel's parole—lost his post on the county court, as did every other official. Their replacements were hard-line Radicals, men who had protested against Colonel Moss and petitioned for sterner measures against their rebel neighbors. Across the river in Lafayette County, Conservative officeholders refused to go. The governor had them dragged out by a company of militia that consisted entirely of black men. With an acute sense of poetic justice, the militiamen threw two of the resisting officials into the old slave jail in Lexington. Rebels and loyal Conservatives alike were shocked.[43]

The Oath scoured the legal system, the schools, and the churches. Lawyers, teachers, and ministers faced a deadline of September 2, 1865, to swear by its eighty-six proscriptions or abandon their professions.[44] For many, the law was not enough. Here and there in the countryside, Radicals turned to extralegal measures to carry out their revolution. As early as March 1865, a Unionist committee in Clinton County issued a stark warning to secessionists: "We advise them not to make their abode with us, and if they do so, they do it at their peril." In July, an organization of "Cass County Union Refugees" declared, "We warn those who . . . have helped in destroying and plundering Union men, that we will hold all such amenable to the laws they have outraged." In the threefold division of Conservatives, Radicals, and rebels, observed a Lexington secessionist, the bile between the latter two was especially bitter. A full year after the war, he claimed, the Radicals "still feel and act like they were in the tented field."[45]

In this moment of turmoil and bloodshed, the bushwhackers were bound to reappear. The most coherent and consistent groups would reemerge in precisely that triangle of counties—Clay, Jackson, and Lafayette—where resistance to the Radicals was fiercest; and (as the *Lexington Caucasian*'s correspondent noted) they moved about with the respect of the secessionist community. All of this suggests that their reappearance was a response to the revolution around them—a response that could hardly be surprising. "Military service has often been a politicizing and radicalizing experience," historian Foner notes. In the North, veterans formed the backbone of the Republican Party, while in the South they fought to restore the old social order. The situation was similar in some ways to Europe after World War I, when reactionary soldiers' groups such as the Italian Fascists and German Freikorps battled socialists in the streets. In the American South, the target was less a political party than the entire race of African Americans. "They govern . . . by the pistol and the rifle," wrote a visitor to Louisiana in 1865. "In some areas," Foner observes, "violence against blacks reached staggering proportions in the immediate aftermath of the war."[46]

In Missouri, the guerrillas had filled the same role during the war. They had often brutalized escaping slaves, sometimes killing them, sometimes recapturing them and selling them in the Confederacy. When black men began to enroll in the Union army, the guerrillas had swept in to terrorize them. After emancipation, bushwhacker Jim Jackson pledged "to hang and shoot every negro he can find absent from the old plantation." He went at it with vigor until he was finally caught, tried, and hanged in June 1865. "Slavery dies hard," mused General Fisk. "I shudder for my race when I discover the wicked barbarity of the late masters and mistresses of the recently freed persons."[47]

But this was not the Deep South. For one thing, it was heavily white; nowhere in Missouri had slaves made up much more than a third of the population. And the white majority was bitterly divided. The shock of the Confederate surrender had left many guerrillas confused and indecisive, unprepared at first to resist the Radical regime. On July 1, 1865, Captain Clayton E. Rogers—the same man who accepted Jesse James's surrender in Lexington—reported that the rebels "seem thoroughly subdued and willing to accept peace on any terms our government might dictate." A few remained at large—notably Archie Clement and Jim Anderson, who never gave themselves up. Under relentless pressure from pursuing militia, they had fled the state about the same time that Jackson swung from a rope, taking refuge in Texas. There the renegade Missourians became "a scourge and terror to the good citizens," according to one Texan. But they did not remain south for long.[48]

In the summer and fall of 1865, it became clear that the Union victory meant a *Radical* victory. Society was changing drastically, and the winners of the war meant to change it still further, until Missouri had truly become a Northern state. In the face of political revolution and private revenge, in the face of former slaves who now carried muskets and asserted their freedom, it was only a matter of time before the bushwhackers resisted in the manner to which they were accustomed.

IN AUGUST 1865, the Samuel clan started to drift back to the old homestead, which had been ravaged by war and left untended through winter, spring, and summer. Susie, Zerelda, Reuben, and the couple's young children came first. Charlotte came too—perhaps out of loyalty, perhaps because, though free in name, she was a forty-five-year-old, illiterate black woman who could realistically imagine no other future than a continued life of labor on this farm. Perhaps she was given no choice. One or two other former slaves returned with her, including a nine-year-old boy named Ambrose and possibly a young woman. They would all work as they did before the war, but their freedom meant the dissolution of much of the family's wealth.[49]

According to Jesse's own account, he rejoined his mother, sister, and stepfather in October, five months after being shot in the chest. By now, any infection would have either killed him or subsided—it was clearly the latter—and his lung would have sealed and reinflated. If he did still suffer, as he later claimed, it would likely have been from the pressure of pneumothorax—an air pocket in the lining of the lung, sometimes the result of a penetrating wound. Such a condition would have been uncomfortable, but far from crippling. Frank, too, returned home late that year. He had been with Quantrill in Kentucky on May 10, 1865, when the old bushwhacker was bushwhacked himself and killed. Frank and the other survivors had surrendered in Nelson County, Kentucky, on July 26, 1865.[50]

In the secessionist corner of Clay County society, the James brothers received a warm welcome home. "Jesse joined the Baptist church in this place after he came out of the army," recalled an old friend of the boys, Dr. W. H. Ridge, sixteen years later. He joined a Southern Baptist congregation, of course, firmly sympathetic to the rebel cause. "I think he was baptized, and for a year or two acted as if he was a sincere and true Christian," Ridge added. "He was quiet, affable, and gentle in his actions. He was liked by everyone who knew him." For a supposedly sick and suffering man, he was surprisingly active. "I have been personally acquainted with Jesse James since 1866," wrote former Confederate soldier John S. Groom in 1870. He often saw the teenager in his store after the war; he was "respectful," Groom added. "I have never known a more honest person in all his business transactions."[51]

Relations among former secessionists were one thing; relations with the Unionists, especially the Radicals, were quite another. In December 1869, merchant Daniel Conway reported local rumors about the James brothers. Jesse, he said, "has been leading a wandering, reckless life . . . and ever since the war has been regarded as a desperate and dangerous character."[52] Even one of Jesse's stalwart defenders later claimed that he "rode armed, watchful, vigilant, haunted." The young guerrilla might be ambushed at any moment by his enemies, he added, "but he would be killed with his eyes open and his pistols about him."

Filaments of truth run through these blankets of rumor and hyperbole. When Jesse's comrade Ol Shepherd surrendered, he voiced a fear of "personal enemies." A year later, the Easton brothers pursued a vendetta against bushwhacker Jim Green, just a few miles north of Zerelda's farm. Clearly Jesse also had reason to fear retribution from them, because he had been seen in the company of Green on their murder spree in October 1864. As the biblical proverb wisely observes, "The wicked flee when no man pursueth."[53]

As the winter of 1865–66 descended, Jesse was deep into his "wandering, reckless life." He and Frank began to gather again with their wartime comrades. Young Clell Miller, Jim Cummins, Ol and George Shepherd, and others lived close by, but the James boys also reunited with Dave Pool and his brother John, now resettled across the river in Lexington. At some point before or soon after the new year, Jim Anderson and Archie Clement returned from Texas, closing the circle of Bloody Bill's inheritors. According to one report, this reunion landed the James brothers, Miller, George White, and one of the Pools in a minor scrape in Liberty.[54]

On January 1, 1866, local Radicals prepared for the year ahead by formally organizing themselves as the Republican Party of Clay County (though the Radical label would continue in use for years to come). The central committee was virtually identical to the roster of officials appointed by Governor Fletcher under the Ouster Ordinance. Former militia officers played a prominent part. In the Samuel family's own township, the Republicans were led by none other than Captain John W. Younger, the man who had likely commanded the squad of Clay County militia that took part in the fateful raid on the farm back in May 1863.

On January 29, the Republicans of Clay County held a mass meeting at the Liberty courthouse. With control of state government, with a lock on the door to the polls, with a thorough township organization, they swelled with confidence. They believed that the tide of the times was with them: they would bring their revolution to fruition, even here in the heart of secessionist Missouri. Their leaders spoke for long hours to a crowd of enthusiastic supporters as bitter rebels and bushwhackers watched. The next day, they went back to their shops and offices, including one business where most of them shared an interest: the Clay County Savings Association.[55]

CHAPTER TEN

The Guerrillas Return

THE CLAY COUNTY Savings Association was more than a bank: it was the physical embodiment of the Radicals' vision of themselves as the party of progress and industry. They were concentrated in the major centers of commerce, from St. Louis to Kansas City to county seats (though that was partly a result of being driven there during the war by bushwhackers). In Liberty, the nascent Republicans* had coalesced around Edward M. Samuel, the town's most enterprising merchant for the past twenty years.[1]

In 1863, Samuel and a group of Radical allies had purchased the assets of the Liberty branch of the Farmer's Bank of Missouri and reopened in the same building, as the Clay County Savings Association. Samuel himself had left in early 1865, driven away by rebel death threats, and he began a new life as a commission merchant in St. Louis (where he would commit suicide in 1869). But the Association continued on as a distinctly Radical institution, staffed by Radical officials, including circuit clerk James Love, the bank's president.[2]

As Clay County's Republicans organized their local bank, the realm of money and banking was passing through a revolution as sweeping as emancipation itself. In the decades before the guns erupted at Fort Sumter, the most important function of a typical bank was to issue notes. Normally it would build a reserve fund of gold coin, then make loans by issuing its own paper money. People paid each other with these privately printed notes, trusting that they could be redeemed at the issuing bank for gold. A well-run institution circulated paper worth no more than two or three times its holdings in coin.

---

*Hereafter the terms "Radical" and "Republican" will be used interchangeably for the party in Missouri. The state party, however, must be distinguished from the Radical faction of Republicans in Congress, a distinct subset of the national party.

That, at least, was the ideal. In reality, many firms—nicknamed "wild-cat" banks—recklessly issued bills far beyond their gold reserves (if they had any at all), leading to frequent crashes. Under the best circumstances, banknotes would be discounted when accepted as payment, based on the issuing bank's reputation and distance, since both affected the likelihood that the bills could be redeemed in precious metal. "A man could not travel from one state to another," complained the *St. Louis Democrat*, "without suffering a shave from five to twenty-five per cent on his money." Counterfeiting was rampant: by 1860, an estimated five thousand varieties of fake notes circulated. With more than a thousand legitimate varieties in the marketplace, detecting the phonies was almost impossible. Herman Melville parodied the situation in his 1857 novel *The Confidence-Man*, in which he depicted a man trying to detect counterfeits with a counterfeit-detector that itself was counterfeit.[3]

This confusing, inconsistent system crashed for the last time in 1861. As war erupted, nervous Americans rushed to return their bills for gold. At the same time, the federal government was draining specie out of banks by borrowing for the war effort. From Manhattan to rural Missouri, banks suddenly stopped redeeming their notes. "There is no such thing as gold and silver coin circulating in the country," observed Senator John Sherman. "It is stowed away." The people were left with nearly worthless banknotes, while the U.S. government could no longer sell bonds to banks to finance the war effort. One way or another, Congress had to step in. As Sherman declared, "We must have money or a fractured Government."[4]

The federal response to the crisis changed the face of the American economy forever. First, Congress created a national paper currency, immediately nicknamed the greenback. Unlike private banknotes, the greenback was legal tender—it had to be accepted as payment in all private and public transactions (except customs duties)—and, unlike almost every other kind of paper money in American history, it could not be redeemed in gold. It was money not because it represented an underlying, intrinsically valuable commodity, but because the law said so. Next, Congress established a system of national banks with federal charters (all existing banks were either private or state-chartered). It took this step partly to stabilize the country's financial structure, partly to guarantee a market for U.S. bonds (each national bank was required to maintain a reserve of federal securities). To drive state-chartered banks into the system, it levied a lethal 10 percent tax on their notes. As a result, only national banks could afford to issue paper money—and this, too, was standardized. The new national banknotes were stamped with the issuing bank's identity, and made redeemable in greenbacks, not gold. By the end of 1865, almost a thousand state banks across the country had converted into national ones.[5]

But, at the same time, the law created a rural niche for state and private institutions, because congressional requirements made it almost impossible to organize a national bank outside of a large city. In towns with fewer than six thousand people, a national bank had to have a minimum capital stock of $50,000—a figure that was doubled for towns of between six thousand and fifty thousand residents. This was an immense sum at the end of the Civil War, especially in war-racked Missouri. The second problem was that national banks were forbidden to make mortgage loans—and, needless to say, land was the primary asset in farm country. On both counts, then, there was plenty of room in Clay County for a private or state-chartered bank, even if it could not issue notes of its own.[6]

What Clay County Savings Association did was buy and sell money. And in postwar Missouri, money was physical, and it was scanty. It was physical because the checking account remained a largely urban phenomenon; only in the great cities, where banks were dense and clearinghouses had been established, could it play a significant role. Rural areas depended on cash—as of October 1, 1865, only $460,844,229 in greenbacks and national banknotes were in circulation. In a nation of roughly 35 million people, that meant that only $13.17 existed per person (plus 43¢ in coin). Even this figure exaggerates the amount of money available, since a significant proportion of physical currency, along with almost all checking deposits, was concentrated in the bank-rich Northeast, especially in New York City.[7]

The result was sometimes a staggering cash drought, as families often went for weeks at a time without any coin or currency on hand. "When I was growing up there was no such thing as money," recalled Clark Griffith, the cofounder of baseball's American League, who grew up in a cash-starved town in post–Civil War Missouri, where "the medium of exchange was apple butter." Things were never quite so grave in Clay County, a center of commercial, market-oriented agriculture. But there as elsewhere improvisation reigned. The most popular form of ad hoc currency was government securities, especially Missouri's Union Military bonds and the federal 5:20 and 7.30 bonds (the first named after its minimum and maximum terms of maturity, the second after its interest rate). But they could not simply be traded at face value due to the complications of accruing interest, paid in gold dollars, which had a much higher value, dollar for dollar, than greenbacks.[8]

In this cash-bare economy, country banks such as the Clay County Savings Association made money available by purchasing bonds, gold, silver, and old banknotes, all at a healthy discount, so they could profit by reselling them in New York through correspondent banks. They also took deposits and made loans against real estate, often for small amounts, frequently as low as $100, and for terms as brief as thirty days. Rural Missourians went to banks not only to finance large purchases of land or equipment, but simply to get ready cash for a short period.[9]

Given the dependence on physical cash, the busy trade in bonds and other financial instruments, and the raw shortage of money, the heart of the bank was the vault. Its master was the cashier. He oversaw discounting on bonds and loans, paid out cash, and kept the keys to the vault and the safe that usually sat inside. His name would appear on the bank's letterhead, across from the president's. In the Clay County Savings Association, this important personage was, as of late 1865, the peculiarly named Greenup Bird. Unlike the owners, Bird was not active in politics, but he had long been a fixture of Clay County's public life. He had signed at least one petition against the Paw Paw militia, for example; he also had served as county clerk in the 1850s, when he had helped to administer the estate of one Robert James.[10]

At two o'clock on February 13, 1866, exactly two weeks after the owners of the Clay County Savings Association led a mass meeting of Radicals in Liberty, Bird sat at his desk in the bank writing a letter. His son William worked at a desk to his left; apart from that, the bank was empty. Suddenly the quiet scratching of nib on paper was interrupted by the creak of the door and a gust of cold air, as two men in blue soldiers' overcoats strode in. They paused in the warm space around the stove, then one of them walked up to the counter and asked to have a ten-dollar bill changed. Young Bird stood up to attend to the task—and saw a revolver in the man's hand.

William backed toward his desk as the gunman scrambled up onto the counter and leaped down. "Also the other man, drawing his revolver, followed over the counter," Greenup Bird reported. "One presenting his revolver at Wm. Bird & the other man presenting his revolver at me, [they] told us if we made any noise they would shoot us down, demanded all the money in the bank, and [said] that they wanted it quick." William stood stunned and speechless. Infuriated, his attacker spun him around and smacked him on the back with his heavy metal revolver, snarling, "Damn you, be quick!"

The first bandit pushed William into the open vault and handed him a cotton sack, telling him to put the money into it. The young clerk knelt down in front of the safe and began to pull out bags of gold and silver coin. These were special deposits (much like modern-day safety deposit boxes). In a quirk of the marketplace created by the new greenback, gold dollars were actually worth much more than the more abundant paper currency, so consumers hoarded rather than spent or invested them. "The other robber had me in tow outside of [the] vault," Greenup Bird recalled, "and demanded the greenbacks. I pointed to a tin box on the table." The man emptied it of paper dollars and bonds, then handed them through the vault entrance to the first robber, telling him to put them in the sack "and to be in a hurry." Then they shoved the cashier and his son in the vault and closed the door.

Greenup Bird listened carefully as the two men rushed back outside. When all was quiet, he shoved the door gently; it was unlocked. He cracked it open, looked and listened, then ran to the front window. "As we were going from the vault door to the window," he wrote a few days later, "I saw several men on horseback pass the window, going east, shooting off pistols." Bird hoisted open the window and shouted out the news of the robbery. At that moment, one of the horses on the street reared on its hind legs as its rider fired, killing nineteen-year-old George Wymore, who was standing opposite the bank. Wymore may have repeated Bird's shouts before he was shot, though the *Liberty Tribune* reported that he "knew nothing of the robbery, like everyone else."

Between the pair who came in the bank and their comrades waiting on the street, perhaps thirteen men galloped down Franklin Street, firing their pistols all the way. After killing Wymore they hurt no one else, thundering east out of town.

Two large posses quickly collected in Liberty and galloped in pursuit. They followed the raiders to Mount Gilead Church near Centerville, where the bandits had stopped to divide up the loot, then tracked them to a spot on the Missouri River just opposite Sibley, the bushwhackers' favorite crossing point. There the posses lost the trail. Back in Liberty, Greenup Bird and his son tallied the losses: $58,072.64 at face value.[11]

The raid on the Clay County Savings Association was a classic bank robbery—except there was no such thing in 1866. Criminals had frequently plundered banks, of course, but almost exclusively through fraud or late-night burglary. Indeed, this event has often been called America's first daylight bank holdup in peacetime; certainly there had never been anything like it in Liberty.[12]

From the moment that Greenup Bird shouted the alarm, it was clear that the robbers were (as bank president James Love declared) "a band of bushwhackers." In the *Liberty Tribune,* editor Robert Miller noted the universal belief that the bandits were guerrillas. "But it makes no difference who they are, or what they claim to be," he wrote, "they should be swung up in the most summary manner."

This was a startling and revealing statement. Simply put, it was an argument against the notion that *being bushwhackers* somehow justified them in their crime, or at least entitled them to sympathy. Miller never would have made this argument if a significant part of the population was not speaking of the bandits in these terms. Miller's sentence illustrates once again the three-way split between Conservatives, rebels, and Radicals, for clearly those whom Miller was trying to convince were the secessionists. After all, the Radicals hardly needed to be persuaded that the robbers should be hanged *even if* they were bushwhackers.

With blood on the streets of Liberty, the Conservatives sided with the Republicans. The pursuit of the bandits was led by William G. Garth and John S. Thomason, former militia officers who now voted the Conservative ticket. (Thomason had been a Paw Paw commander—one who actually chased and fought guerrillas—while Garth was a leading Conservative.) The other bank in town, the Liberty Savings Association, had no Radicals or even prominent Unionists among its officers, but it quickly offered its own $2,000 reward, on top of $5,000 from the victimized bank. Editor Miller, a Conservative, called for "a thorough organization of the people . . . to enable the people at a moment's notice to pursue and kill all violators of the law." On this issue Unionists of every political stripe stood together.[13]

The Radicals, however, saw the Liberty robbery as a sign that the smoldering hatred between themselves and the bushwhackers was flaming into open warfare. With the dawn of the new year, gunfights between angry neighbors had begun to coalesce into violence on a larger scale. Already Governor Fletcher had ordered a company of militia into service in Johnson County to suppress guerrilla activity; the company killed two bushwhackers just days before the Liberty raid.[14]

The Clay County robbery focused Radical attentions on a single rebel organization. When James Love published the bank's offer of a $5,000 reward, he blamed the robbery on "a band of bushwhackers, who reside chiefly in Clay county, and have their rendezvous on or near the Missouri River, above Sibley in Jackson county." At least nine men were named in succeeding days by witnesses to the robbery and pursuit: Ol Shepherd, Bud and Donny Pence, Jim and Bill Wilkerson, Frank Gregg, Joab Perry, and Redman Munkers (though Munkers soon provided an alibi, supported by five witnesses). These men were the surviving core of Bill Anderson's terrorist gang, who had followed Pool, Clement, and Jim Anderson back from Texas in early 1865.[15] Rumors and hard evidence would soon point to Anderson and particularly Clement as the leaders of the raid.

If the James brothers were with their old friends on February 13, few in Liberty would have recognized them, since neither had spent time in Liberty for at least five years, since Jesse was a child. A Captain Minter reportedly identified the brothers as two of the perpetrators, then he retracted his statement after being threatened. In any event, it seems safe to assume that Frank and Jesse were still stalwarts of Clement's crew.[16]

In Jefferson City, Governor Fletcher personally directed the state's response to the bushwhacker threat. The former general gathered intelligence reports, drafted plans, and dispatched orders to various counties. On March 10, he received a man named T. L. Byrne, who carried a letter from Sheriff H. H. Williams of Jackson County. Byrne, the sheriff wrote, had been selected to lead a platoon of militia (about forty men) to track down the Liberty bandits, but he needed specific authorization for the force. More important, however, was the intelligence that Williams had gathered. "I have advices from the sheriff of Lafayette County," he wrote, "that Clements & Anderson are organizing a large band of bushwhackers at Waverly for some purpose and cautions me to be prepared for them."[17]

Clement and Anderson: If they were behind the mayhem in western Missouri, Fletcher realized, then the state faced a serious problem. The governor acted quickly. The same day, he authorized Byrne's platoon of militia. Two days later, on March 12, he signed a proclamation that offered a $300 reward for "the apprehension and delivery" of Archie Clement—or Clements, as he was called in the document—as well as bushwhacker Frank Gregg, another Liberty suspect. On March 14, the governor signed into law a bill that had been rushed through the General Assembly, explicitly empowering him to call out the militia to aid county sheriffs. A general enrollment in the militia was ordered; eventually 117,411 citizens were made eligible for duty. On March 16, he sent a special message to the General Assembly, asking for more money for his efforts "to break up these lawless bands."[18]

A few days later, James Love arrived in Jefferson City to confer with the governor. As a Republican leader and Clay County official, Love was well known to the governor, who called him "a good Union man and a clever gentleman." Fletcher explained to him his strategy for destroying Clement and Anderson's band, then dispatched him on March 19 to coordinate the effort with an unnamed colonel—presumably a Union veteran and Radical public official. "I have requested him [Love] to confer with you, and [learn] if you think well of the plan suggested by me," Fletcher wrote in a letter of introduction. "I hope you will cooperate in the movement. I am told that Jim Anderson & his men are about Franklin, Howard County. If they can be captured or killed it would be the best thing for the state I know of." Fletcher authorized the recipient to raise a platoon of militia, urging him "to take hold of the matter."[19]

The governor's information was accurate. Not long after Love departed on his mission, Jim Anderson and follower Isaac Flannery showed up just across the Howard County border in Rocheport, Boone County. There, in the town that Bloody Bill had called his "capital," the pair tried vainly to persuade local merchants to accept Missouri Union Military bonds extraordinarily reminiscent of those stolen in Liberty. As they rode back into the country, they ran into an ambush. Five men opened fire, killing Flannery. In all likelihood, the gunmen were members of Fletcher's militia platoon.[20]

At best, the governor's counteroffensive merely forced the guerrillas to disperse for a few weeks. Though Anderson now disappeared from view, Clement and his followers soon reassembled in Lafayette County, the band's base of operations. Clement's mother had a house there, while Dave Pool lived in Lexington, home of the *Caucasian* and virtually the secessionist capital of Missouri. Here the bushwhackers found a warm reception; when one observer saw them in Waverly on April 28, he noted that the local citizens seemed to respect them.[21]

The only other success against the bushwhackers came in late spring, when Joab Perry, one of the Liberty suspects, landed in an Independence jail for horse stealing. Even this went awry. On June 14, 1866, a half-dozen men demanded that Marshal Henry Bugler surrender Perry; when he refused, they gunned him down, wounding his seven-year-old son in the process. Outraged Radicals promptly held a mass meeting, where they condemned anyone who incited resistance to state law, and resolved that "every rebel or supposed bushwhacker, having no visible means of support, should be notified to leave the city within twenty-four hours."[22]

That crowd voiced the deeper convictions of the Radicals by explicitly linking the bushwhackers with those who incited resistance to state law. Clement and his followers were not making public speeches attacking the legal code, but the Conservatives were. Starting in the summer of 1866, the Radical battle against the bushwhackers became entangled with the larger political crisis that gripped Missouri and the nation at large. In an increasingly poisonous partisan atmosphere, with gangs of armed men roaming the countryside, the Conservatives, Radicals, and rebels alike convinced themselves that a second civil war was about to begin.

"ANDREW JOHNSON WAS the queerest character that ever occupied the White House," thought Illinois congressman Shelby M. Cullom. One of the moderate Republicans on Capitol Hill, Cullom reflected the broad spectrum of Northern political opinion. Johnson was elected on Lincoln's ticket, he noted, but he never pretended to be a Republican. He was an old-fashioned Jacksonian Democrat from Tennessee whose outspoken Unionism had made him Lincoln's running mate—he had been the only U.S. senator from the eleven Confederate states to denounce secession as treason. And that aspect of his personality was precisely what made him so peculiar. "He sought rather than avoided a fight," Cullom observed. "Headstrong, domineering, having fought his way in a state filled with aristocratic Southerners from the class of so-called 'low whites' to the highest position in the United States, he did not readily yield to the dictates of the domineering forces in Congress."[23]

After struggling with the moderately minded Lincoln, the Radical faction of Republicans in Congress thought they saw a kindred spirit in the sharp-tongued, rebellion-hating, planter-resenting Johnson. But the new president drew a clear distinction between opposing secession and extending civil rights to freed slaves. "Damn the Negroes," he once exclaimed, "I am fighting those traitorous aristocrats, their masters."[24]

He first made Republicans nervous in May 1865, when he began issuing a series of proclamations to reconstruct the former Confederate states. One by one, he appointed provisional governors, ordered new elections, and implicitly barred blacks from voting. Only the congressional Radicals, however, were truly alarmed. "Johnson was, probably in good faith, pursuing the Lincoln policy of reconstruction," thought Cullom. His fellow moderates agreed; they would wait and see.[25] Congress could do little anyway, as it was in a long recess until December 1865.

If Johnson had stopped at his proclamations, moderate Republicans would probably have supported him. But the president quickly overreached. Instead of hanging prominent rebels as he had promised, he handed out mass pardons, until every former Confederate was beyond the reach of the law. He ordered the return of seized lands to the pardoned rebels—halting efforts to provide homesteads to freedmen—and withdrew black troops from the South. At the same time, the Southern states began to pass "black codes," laws that virtually reenslaved African Americans through a combination of contract-labor requirements, vagrancy laws, and apprenticeship arrangements. White violence against blacks proliferated, with the approval of the Southern press. "If one had the power," said the *Memphis Daily Appeal*, "it would be a solemn duty for him to annihilate the race."[26]

All of this upset even those Yankees who snorted at the idea of giving black men the vote. Radical orators and newspapers succeeded in making the issue one of Unionism as much as race. Johnson's policies, they argued, rewarded the rebels while penalizing the freed people—the only truly loyal population in the South.[27] So when the Thirty-Ninth Congress assembled, it tried to take some control over Reconstruction. The majority Republicans began by voting unanimously to exclude the new senators and representatives elected by the former Confederate states. Then they focused their efforts on two bills: a renewal of the Freedman's Bureau (the national bureaucracy established to help freed slaves get education, work, and land) and the groundbreaking Civil Rights Bill. The latter legislation in particular promised a revolutionary change in American law. For the first time, Congress would offer a national definition of citizenship (one that included

African Americans), specify basic rights that went with it (not including the vote), and extend federal protection over those rights. The Republicans thought the bills were quite reasonable, and moderates and Radicals united behind them.

Johnson vetoed both, leaving the Republicans stunned, then outraged. The two bills, declared Senator John Sherman of Ohio, were "clearly right." The protection of freedmen's rights "followed from the suppression of the rebellion," argued a Republican newspaper. "The party is nothing, if it does not do this—the nation is dishonored if it hesitates in this." The president made matters worse by explaining his actions in terms that were notable, as historian Eric Foner writes, for their "explicit racism." The veto of the Freedman's Bureau renewal on February 19 flummoxed Congress, but after the Civil Rights Bill veto a month later it rallied and overrode the president. The time had come, one Republican wrote to Senator Sherman, "to draw our swords for a fight and throw away the scabbards."[28]

The fight proved to be more than a metaphor. On May 1, a three-day race riot erupted in Memphis, as policemen and firemen led white mobs on a rampage through black neighborhoods. Forty-six African Americans and two whites died, seventy-five people were wounded, five black women were raped, and ninety-one houses, twelve schools, and four churches were burned to the ground. A second outbreak occurred on July 20 in New Orleans, when the white police force attacked a meeting of Louisiana's state constitutional convention, which was considering the enfranchisement of black men. General Sheridan called the ensuing events "an absolute massacre." Thirty-four blacks and three white Radicals were killed and 119 were wounded.[29]

The slaughter in Memphis and New Orleans echoed across the country like war drums in the night. Now no one could mistake the gravity of the fight between Congress and the president. This was a battle over the meaning of the Civil War, over the very nature of the American republic, and the casualties were already mounting. The election of 1866 would be far from a typical midterm campaign—it would be a referendum on two versions of Reconstruction, on two visions of the nation. The threat of violence hung in the air; Johnson even ordered measures to protect the capital from "insurgent or other illegal combinations."[30]

The fury of 1866 erupted in Missouri with heat and force unseen almost anywhere else in the Union. In some respects, Missouri was a microcosm of the United States; its people had split in the Civil War, had fought with each other, then had imposed on themselves their own, entirely home-grown Reconstruction. "The condition of Missouri," wrote St. Louis Conservative Edward Bates to President Johnson, was not "*local* and peculiar to us. . . . It is part and parcel of the condition of the nation." National issues immediately colored the state campaign because they spoke directly to Missouri's internal struggle, a struggle of rapidly escalating bitterness. "We unhesitatingly denounce him [President Johnson] as a traitor," resolved a Republican meeting in Putnam County. Conservatives in Vernon County castigated the "fanatical Radical majority in Congress. . . . All attempts to elevate [the black man] to the level of the white man," they declared, "by making him politically and socially his equal, we will resist."[31]

The man who led the Conservative effort in Missouri was Frank Blair—the founder of its Republican Party, the mastermind behind the Federal seizure of the state in 1861, and a successful Union general. Like his friend Andrew Johnson, Blair was an old Jacksonian Democrat, and, also like Johnson, Blair condemned slavery but intensely loathed black people. The two men hated slavery in large part because of the power it gave rich planters; they believed the Southern yeoman farmer was loyal in his heart and had been duped into secession by the slaveowning aristocracy. With slavery dead, Blair's racism became the flagship of his political principles. "No man can advocate an amalgamation of the white and black races and so create a mongrel nation," he wrote to Johnson, in one of his mildest statements. "The policy of the country must therefore be a gradual segregation of the races."[32]

Blair led Conservatives by example. He personally challenged the Oath, daring the officials to bar him from registering to vote; he also served as attorney for Father John A. Cummings, a Roman Catholic priest who refused to take the Oath. The case went before the U.S. Supreme Court in March 1866, and the decision was eagerly awaited as the campaign proceeded. With the return of warm weather in May, Blair traveled across the state, delivering dozens of speeches to rouse his party into action. Meanwhile, in virtually every county, Conservatives organized "Johnson Clubs" to voice their support for the president and do battle with the Radicals.[33]

And a battle it would be. The alarms sounded as early as May, when Missouri Conservative Abner Gilstrap warned President Johnson that the Radicals planned assassinations, even a new civil war. "And secret military organizations are now going on," he wrote, "in many parts of this state." What Conservatives feared most were the militia companies that Governor Fletcher had deployed; they believed that the bushwhackers were simply an excuse for putting troops on the streets to carry the election by force. "I am fully satisfied that the militia in the hands of Governor Fletcher," wrote one captain in a letter of resignation, "will only rob the people of the state of their liberties, to forward the interests of a political party."[34]

On July 24, Conservative Thomas C. Ready wrote to the president

Robert James, the father of Jesse and Frank James, moved from his native Kentucky to Clay County, Missouri, in 1842. There he emerged as a prosperous hemp farmer, slaveholder, and prominent Baptist preacher. He died in California in 1850 during the gold rush, leaving Jesse fatherless at the age of three. (James Farm & Museum, Kearney, Missouri)

Wedded to Robert James at age sixteen, widowed at twenty-five, Jesse's mother Zerelda remarried for the second time at age thirty to Dr. Reuben Samuel. She was a dominating figure, a fierce secessionist with steel nerves, a lacerating tongue, and a vigorous intellect. (State Historical Society of Missouri, Columbia)

The farmhouse where Jesse James was born, as it appeared in 1877. Note the outbuildings, rail fences, and timber surrounding the home, all of which played a role in various raids on the farm by militia, sheriffs' posses, and Pinkerton detectives. (Library of Congress)

Although this small sternwheeler was photographed in the 1870s, its heavily laden decks offer a glimpse of the brisk river traffic that sustained western Missouri in the antebellum era.
(Denver Public Library)

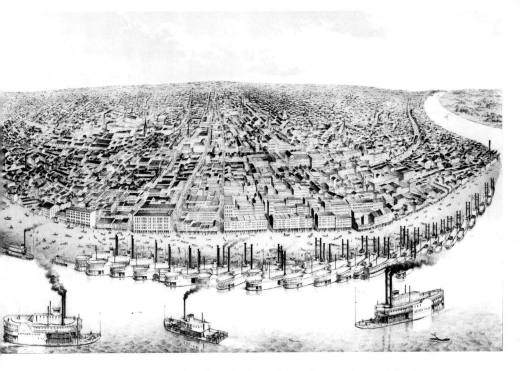

This 1859 engraving captures the urban density and frenetic waterfront activity that made St. Louis the commercial capital of Missouri. Scores of steamboats jostled for a landing on the levee, unloading goods and passengers from the Ohio, Missouri, and Mississippi Rivers, including tens of thousands of German and Irish immigrants. Here, too, hemp and tobacco grown by slaveholders was transshipped to the South, making the city both a Northern-style metropolis and a critical junction in Missouri's links with Dixie. (Library of Congress)

Sterling Price—former Missouri governor, commander of the State Guard, and Confederate major general—led the military struggle to take Missouri out of the Union and into the Confederacy. His unsuccessful campaigns in 1861 and 1864 framed the beginning and end of the guerrilla conflict that defined the state's Civil War experience. (State Historical Society of Missouri, Columbia)

Above: *This 1872 engraving is based on* Order Number Eleven, *a famous painting by George Caleb Bingham, noted Missouri artist. This melodramatic scene captures the secessionists' resentments of the Union military authorities in Missouri that fed the guerrilla movement and animated the former rebels during Reconstruction.* (Library of Congress)

An 1864 photograph of three bush-whackers, as Confederate guerrillas were known. Often hailing from prosperous slaveholding families, they divided their efforts between battling Federal forces and murdering or burning out their Unionist neighbors. Two of these men, Archie Clement (1) and Dave Pool (2), were close friends and allies of Jesse James. (Library of Congress)

osite page: This 1862 photograph shows slaves ...ing to Federal lines in Virginia. Identical ...es became commonplace in Missouri by 1863 as ...ncreasingly radicalized Union militia offered ...ection to fugitive African Americans. (Library of ...ress)

This photograph shows Jesse Woodson James at age sixteen, during his first summer under arms. He is sporting the bushwhacker's customary multiple revolvers and "guerrilla shirt" with breast pockets for percussion caps and lead balls. The distinctive clearness of Jesse's blue eyes is detectable even in this black-and-white image. (Library of Congress)

From left, Fletch Taylor, Frank James, and Jesse James. Frank fought in the Confederate army, under William C. Quantrill, and then with his younger brother Jesse under Taylor. This photograph was taken in 1864, in the first weeks of Jesse's guerrilla career, prior to the amputation of Taylor's right arm. (State Historical Society of Missouri, Columbia)

William "Bloody Bill" Anderson was a guerrilla chieftain who conducted a campaign of terror along the Missouri River in 1864 that is widely regarded as one of the most brutal episodes in American history. Jesse James followed him for most of this period, and spoke proudly in later years of the affiliation. (State Historical Society of Missouri, Columbia)

In Centralia, Missouri, in 1864, Bill Anderson's gang hauled two dozen unarmed Union soldiers off a train and murdered them. Major A. V. E. Johnston, shown here, gave chase with a battalion of mounted infantrymen. He and almost all of his men were killed, and many were then dismembered. Jesse was credited with killing Johnston.
(State Historical Society of Missouri, Columbia)

General Joseph O. Shelby emerged from the Civil War as Missouri's most famous Confederate officer. After the Confederate surrender, he went into exile in Mexico for almost two years. After his return to Missouri he extended personal and political support to the James brothers.
(State Historical Society of Missouri, Columbia)

Major John Newman Edwards served as Jo Shelby's adjutant during the Civil War. Upon his return to Missouri he became an influential newspaper editor and voice of the Confederate wing of the Democratic Party. An unapologetic champion of the Lost Cause and a close friend of Jesse James, he largely shaped the outlaw's public image and political strategy, spearheading the former Confederates' rise to political and cultural preeminence in the 1870s. (State Historical Society

Decoyed, ambushed, and killed by a Union militia detachment, "Bloody Bill" Anderson was photographed in his embroidered guerrilla shirt. His followers regrouped under Archie Clement, giving rise to the James-Younger gang after the war. (State Historical Society of Missouri, Columbia)

from Jackson County, where the state's fight against the bushwhackers raged with particular intensity. Since the arrival of the militia, Ready claimed, the county had become a "theater of anarchy and confusion. Every day brings its fresh outrages and indignities. No man lies his head upon his pillow at night, but dreads to hear the tread of soldiery and the reports of the death-dealing musket ere morn." A week earlier, he wrote, Deputy Sheriff James Meader—also a militia captain—had ambushed a man named Hulse as he returned from working in a neighbor's field; Hulse drew a pistol in self-defense, but was quickly gunned down.[35]

The combative Blair family confirmed Ready's letter. "You do not realize the truth of your own words," Frank's brother Montgomery told Johnson, "that the Radicals are preparing a new war to maintain themselves in power." Fletcher, he claimed, was "openly arming his followers, including large numbers of Negroes." This was more than Johnson could stand. He immediately ordered General Sherman, commander of the Division of the Mississippi, to confer with Fletcher and shut down the militia. At Sherman's request, the governor came to see him in St. Louis on August 9, only to find that the general—himself a most unradical, even racist fellow—had invited Conservative leaders Thomas Gantt and Samuel Glover to attend. The two politicians peppered Fletcher with hostile questions in front of the suspicious Sherman; the enlistment of blacks into the militia particularly enraged them. The governor was flabbergasted at their refusal to believe that the bushwhackers were a real threat. Finally he agreed to disband the militia, if Sherman provided U.S. troops to keep the peace.[36]

It soon turned out that the Conservatives' real problem was less the organized militia than unofficial Radical bands in the countryside. In Gallatin, Daviess County, John W. Sheets, a banker, expressed "little faith" that the governor's action would save Conservatives from Radical "lawlessness and mobs." Anarchy reigned in nearby towns, he wrote. "Armed bands of men are also seen in our county." When an attempt was made to organize a Johnson Club in Gallatin, even Samuel P. Cox, the famed slayer of Bloody Bill Anderson, was "afraid to go in for the present." Sheets summed up the situation with a single word, one that became a Conservative refrain: "Mobocracy."[37]

Sheets's worries were founded in fact. By the middle of August, Union veterans across Missouri had organized Soldiers' Leagues and posts of the Grand Army of the Republic (GAR). Secretive and extremely militant, these groups operated as an underground extension of the Republican Party. In Gentry County, for example, they warned all ministers to take the Oath or stop preaching—or face the consequences. "There has been a great deal of murdering done in this state," wrote Missourian F. R. Sieg on August 26. "This summer a great many ministers of the gospel have been shot at their churches, whilst ministering the gospel, by the Radicals." The state GAR commander even offered to march on Washington with fifty thousand veterans to enforce Congress's will.[38]

"Have we not good reason to apprehend another civil war?" mused one secessionist in Missouri City. "A war, too, in comparison to the atrocity of which the last one was a mere nothing. . . . And I say let the issue speedily come. There is not on the face of the earth a body politic so foully disgraced and so wretchedly misgoverned as ours. Yankee avarice, Yankee intolerance, Yankee oppression, Yankee hypocrisy have so permeated our whole country that it is as rotten as a dead Dutchman."[39]

As the election approached, Conservative appeals piled up in army headquarters in St. Louis. In Daviess County, it was reported, a man named Broomfield stormed an outdoor religious debate and gunned down a political opponent; with a band of more than one hundred men, he began to drive Johnson supporters out of their homes. In Hickory County, an armed company of Radicals prevented a pro-Johnson speaker from addressing a crowd. Another gang interrupted a political rally in Caldwell County; afterward, a half-dozen of them halted a Conservative activist on his way home. "They told him that they had come to kill him—asked him if he was ready to die," wrote an observer. "He replied he was not and had done nothing worthy of death. They then commenced firing." Shortly afterward the man's son and son-in-law were also found dead. "There is a complete reign of terror," the writer continued; its leader, Daniel Proctor, was a Radical state legislator.[40]

Missouri, declared the Conservatives, was "groaning under Radical tyranny and terrorism." Rumors of plots and arms shipments proliferated. The voter registration process in particular became the focus of paranoia on both sides, as Radical officials strictly enforced the stringent Oath. "We have been outrageously disfranchised in the registration," wrote Conservative former governor Austin A. King, "and now we *know* that a Radical mob is intended at the polls, as a means of intimidation."[41]

Paranoia was one thing that Republicans and Conservatives had in common. On September 6, the *Kansas City Daily Journal of Commerce* accused Conservative leaders of urging the assassination of Radical registrars. The Conservative *St. Louis Republican*, it claimed, was advising its readers to "collect arms and ammunition, organize and drill." The Radicals, it warned, were about to have "war . . . forced upon them." The next day, a Republican in Fredericktown wrote to his brother that "there is a great deal said about another war." Like his leaders, he believed "the rebel or Johnson party will resort to arms."[42]

In this poisoned pond of electoral politics, Republicans sometimes ignored the fact that Conservatives and secessionists swam in separate schools. Even Conservatives tended to think of the former rebels as their automatic supporters.[43] In fact, many Missouri secessionists were embittered and unreconstructed. "I am a stronger rebel than I was 5 years ago," wrote L. M. Matz in Pettis County on April 2, 1866. "I don't feel like the war is over." Matz viewed both parties with deep suspicion. "Although A. Johnson seemed to try to do some good, I have always looked up on him with distrust," she wrote at the end of October. "I didn't think he was the clean thing, or he never would have required us to give up our slave property." Rebels such as Matz could never forget that the Conservatives were still Unionists, led by former Federal soldiers, militia officers, and Frank Blair.[44]

But who could speak for the secessionists? Unlike Kentucky or the former Confederate states, Missouri had virtually no rebel leaders left. After Lee's surrender, Confederate governor Reynolds, General Price, and General Shelby, along with Shelby's prolix adjutant, John Edwards, had led an exodus to Mexico, where they had established colonies under the protection of Emperor Maximilian, an Austrian aristocrat placed in power by the French. Missouri secessionists closely followed newspaper stories about their exiled leaders, but at home they had no spokesmen, no representatives, no one to forge a strategy to resist this peculiar Reconstruction-within-a-Reconstruction.[45]

The bushwhackers were the one (relatively) organized group of rebels who remained. Accustomed to violence, angry at the Radicals, alienated from Unionist society in general, they continued to be the most dangerous and unpredictable fish in these political waters—something Governor Fletcher never forgot. Others also grasped the complexities, and danger, of the situation. Kansas City Conservative H. D. Branch, for example, argued that the battle between Radicals and rebels threatened to topple Missouri's three-legged political stool. "If the Sheriff of this county is permitted to ride over the county with a military force and murder a bushwhacker every opportunity," Branch wrote in late August, "it is certain that they will concentrate and the company of militia at Independence will be put to death." The Conservatives, he claimed, wished "to prevent the Radicals and the bushwhackers from involving our county in a state of civil war."

But that was precisely what the rebels themselves expected. "The Radicals have been planning all summer to hold this state," wrote L. M. Matz in October. "We are waiting to see if we are going to have another war."[46]

DAVE POOL WAS not drinking. That alone was enough to capture attention in Lexington. Normally the lunch hour would find the bushwhacker chief in the barroom of the City Hotel or one of the other saloons in town, awash in liquor with his well-armed friends. But at noon on October 30, 1866, Pool and his brother John stood out on the sidewalk, patiently waiting for something.[47]

They were conveniently on hand, then, when four men fled from the nearby private bank of Alexander Mitchell & Company, carrying $2,011.50 in stolen greenbacks and national banknotes. Before the robbers had gone very far, the brothers organized a party of five former bushwhackers and gave chase. Eventually the posse ambled their horses back into town, where they explained that the bandits had driven them back in a brisk gunfight and escaped. According to one newspaper, when some in Lexington wondered aloud if the chase might not have been what it seemed—or, rather, was exactly what it seemed—Dave Pool and his boys began "swearing around the streets that they would shoot any man who dare say they had anything to do with the robbery."[48]

As Alexander Mitchell fretted over his losses, the bushwhackers tucked his money into their pockets and returned to more pressing business: their escalating campaign of harassment against the Republican government. In Saline County, for example, a bushwhacker gang under Woodson Thornton menaced the registration officials when they refused to allow former rebels to sign up to vote; local Radicals, including William Penick, once the militia commander in Liberty, complained to the governor of systematic intimidation at all the registration places.[49]

Saline's troubles could not compare to the mayhem in Jesse James's backyard. Tensions heightened in Clay County with the approach of election day, as the supervisor of registration, Anthony Harsel, denied the right to vote to rebel after rebel in this most rebellious of counties. In September, for example, an unknown party stopped a former Missouri State Militiaman on the road near Centerville and shot him to death. On November 7, Republican officials sent a desperate plea for help to the army commander at Fort Leavenworth. "We deem the lives of Union men in great danger at the present time in this county," they wrote; "several of the most respectable citizens have been ordered to leave and many others have been publicly insulted and their lives threatened. An armed mob consisting of the most dangerous men in the county, numbering more than a hundred men, resisted the sheriff . . . while [he was] attempting to arrest a man for breach of the peace." The appeal ended with an ominous warning: "We believe unless [troops are provided], every Union man will be driven out of the county or murdered."[50]

"Clay county, Lafayette county, and Callaway county are today worse, if possible, than they were five years ago," wrote the Republican *Journal of Commerce*. "Why is this? It is simply because these men [the Conservatives] have been for six months preaching violence from the stump."[51] In reality, the bushwhackers needed no encouragement from Conservatives to rebel against the government; the Radicals (and freed slaves) were their common enemy. In Lafayette County, however, particularly in Lexington, the well-organized population of secessionists vigorously attacked the Republicans in a seemingly coordinated campaign with the Conservatives, making this place the epicenter of Missouri's election crisis.[52]

The rebel rallying cry echoed from the pages of the *Lexington Caucasian*. "Our citizens," it noted proudly, "have no respect for the municipal authorities of this city," deriding them as "worthless scamps." The paper called for a boycott of the Radical businessmen of the town, darkly pointing out that many were Germans (as indeed they were). It regularly blasted the voter registration board as "The Farce," sneering at supervisor Dr. Frank Cooley as "Pontius Pilate Cooley." Secessionists particularly resented the large number of blacks who had moved into town and, though they could not vote, now sided openly with the Republican Party. The Radicals "are understood to have control of the worst of the negroes," the *Caucasian* claimed, and were "endeavoring to form the blacks into companies, and addressing them in such words as 'defend yourselves.' " When gunfire broke out between whites and blacks on a Saturday in November, the paper blamed the fight on the Radicals, who "induced it as a means of drawing out the bushwhackers, to give the negroes a chance to kill them."[53]

The bushwhackers hardly needed Radical plots to bring them into the streets. Lexington was Dave Pool's hometown and the rendezvous of Archie Clement and his followers; it was also the place where James M. Pool, a close relative of Dave, was running as the Conservative candidate for county sheriff. Here, even more than in Clay County, the guerrillas directly confronted Radical rule. A week before the robbery of Alexander Mitchell, Dave Pool disrupted the proceedings of the registration board with angry shouts and gunfire, sending Cooley and his fellow officials scrambling for their weapons; bloodshed was only averted when James Pool convinced Dave to go home. Then came election day, and the real hell began.[54]

A deadly bitterness permeated the air in this bluff-top community as morning dawned on the day for balloting. At the suggestion of Captain James J. Emerson, commander of the U.S. Army company stationed just outside of town, the mayor closed the liquor stores. The captain and his men, however, were called away to other villages, and were unavailable to keep the peace. Then the streets began to echo with the footfalls of scores of horses. "About one hundred bushwhackers came into town the morning of the election," Sheriff Thomas Adamson wired to Governor Fletcher, "and were fully backed by the desperadoes from our town. They rode through the streets defying all law and officers; and if I had attempted to arrest them, we would all have been murdered."

They were almost certainly the same company of one hundred guerrillas who terrorized Clay County that same week. Clay's sheriff called them "the most dangerous men in the county," which points to the many veterans of Bloody Bill's old band, including the James brothers, who haunted both Clay and Lafayette. In light of subsequent events—and the fact that these same men were known to gather in Lexington—it seems the group that stormed in that day was led by Arch Clement and Dave Pool, two of the men behind so much of the trouble plaguing Missouri that year. And this election-day expedition was no lark: it was an organized and highly effective effort at intimidation. "They were placed in houses, ready to fire out of the windows," Adamson wrote. "Over two hundred shots were fired in the streets. . . . For God's sake, send help!"[55]

With Governor Fletcher away from the capital, Adjutant General Samuel Simpson forwarded Adamson's letter to Major General Winfield S. Hancock, the commander of the Department of the Missouri. But Hancock, a conservative Democrat himself, was not about to intervene. "I cannot remedy the state of affairs at Lexington," he sniffed. "The civil authorities must first be legally insufficient." And so the crisis continued for another month. "This county," the Radicals explained to Hancock at the beginning of December, was under "the ignominious rule and control of the most fiendish, brutal wretches, viz. the bushwhacking, murdering, and thieving debris of the rebel army."[56]

When Fletcher returned, he swiftly took matters into his own hands. Now that the bushwhackers had "boldly taken possession of certain localities" (as the newspapers pointed out), it was time to break his agreement with Sherman and deploy the troops. By December 2, Fletcher had a platoon of militia on the march to Lexington. On December 10, he issued a call for volunteers to fill two regiments of cavalry and one of infantry. "A portion of the state of Missouri is infested with murderers and robbers who defy the civil authority and have the sympathy and aid of a number of the people of the counties where they have their haunts," he proclaimed, "and have . . . intimidated or obtained the sympathy of local authorities." Little did he realize that this state of affairs would continue far beyond the election of 1866—until a day in April 1882, in some respects, when a young man from Clay County would turn up dead in a modest house in St. Joseph.[57]

On December 2, a platoon of thirty-seven militiamen galloped into Lexington, which was now strangely quiet, for the bushwhackers had withdrawn upon the soldiers' approach. The soldiers rode straight for the courthouse in the center of town, took up residence in the ground floor, then strolled proudly through the streets in their cavalry overcoats, with pistols on their hips and carbines slung over their shoulders. Their leader, Bacon Montgomery, went about in civilian clothes, with a revolver strapped outside his pants, as he gave orders to his men or conferred with Republican leader Cooley. Despite appearances, he was the most soldierly in his crew. During the war, he had been a major in the U.S. Volunteers, rising to lead the Sixth Missouri Cavalry Regiment as he won a reputation for bravery and initiative in the Vicksburg and Red River campaigns. He was also an outspoken Radical, as the rebels of Lexington would long remember when they recalled his name.[58]

With the bushwhackers in hiding, it was now the Conservatives' turn to complain of armed intimidation. Angry letters poured into army headquarters in St. Louis. "If you do not interpose," former governor Austin A. King wrote, "1,000 men will be rallied to exterminate this rabble." A U.S. Army officer arrived to investigate, and filed a report scornful of the militiamen. The state troops were indeed a rough crowd, swaggering through the streets intimidating the non-Radical citizens. One of them even robbed the hapless Alexander Mitchell, prompting him to flee for his life.[59] But they were also war-hardened veterans who were ready for action when, on the morning of December 13, a column of twenty-six bushwhackers led by Archie Clement galloped into the center of Lexington, with Dave Pool bringing up the rear. J. M. Turley, one of the militia officers, later identified four of the men: Pool, Clement, and Frank and Jesse James. As Montgomery stood in the square, he faced the very men he had come to suppress, especially their leader, Clement. There was still a $300 reward on Clement's head, and Montgomery had a warrant for his arrest. But rather than stage an all-out battle in the middle of town, Montgomery managed the next few moments with self-possession and tact. He had received reports that the guerrillas planned to come to Lexington on the pretext of forming a militia company, according to the terms of the governor's order, in order to reoccupy the town under the cover of the Radicals' own authority. Montgomery allowed them to go through the motions of enlisting, then he ordered them to leave town and disperse. The rebels followed orders and rode out of town—that is, all rebels but one.[60]

In a few minutes, someone ran into the courthouse and reported that Clement had gone to the bar in the City Hotel, where he was drinking with an old friend. This was precisely the moment Montgomery had been waiting for. Clement was now isolated and vulnerable. Montgomery immediately ordered Turley and two other soldiers, George N. Moses and Tom Tebbs, to go to the hotel and arrest him. He kept the rest of his men in place at the windows of the courthouse. Soon, worried that three men might not be enough to capture Clement, he sent the unpredictable Sergeant Joe Wood, the roughest man in his command, to help.

As Turley, Moses, and Tebbs rode over to the City Hotel, Moses recalled, "we discussed the situation, finally determining that we should take them [Clement and his friend] if possible without shooting. Our plan was to get them into conversation and then ask them to take a drink, and while drinking get the drop on them and cause them to surrender." When they arrived, they ordered drinks for themselves, hoping to put Clement at ease.

Suddenly Wood burst in the door, bellowing "Surrender!" Immediately Clement leaped from his chair and drew his revolvers, as his friend hopped over a billiard table and scrambled for the stairs. Moses snapped off a shot that caught Clement's companion in the leg, then chased after Archie as he ran into a side office, where Moses shot him in the right side of his chest, sending him sprawling. Scrambling to his feet, Clement ran outside to his horse; Moses, Tebbs, and Turley sprinted after him. The wounded bush-whacker and his pursuers fired rapidly at each other as they careered down the icy street, past the courthouse where the rest of the militiamen were waiting. A roar sounded from its windows, and Clement tumbled to the ground. He was defiant to the last, trying to cock a pistol with his teeth. "I saw his eyes were glassy," Turley recalled, "and said to him, 'Arch you are dying. What do you want me to do with you?' He said, 'I've done what I always said I'd do—die before I'd surrender.' " As Montgomery later remarked, "I've never met better 'grit' on the face of the earth."[61]

Clement's death did not end Lexington's troubles. Montgomery threatened to burn down the City Hotel unless Clement's companion was turned over. He decreed that all movement in and out of the city would be stopped. When the *Missouri Freeman* in Richmond criticized the militia, Turley took a squad of men over the river, destroyed the presses, and arrested the editor. Finally, on December 20, a detachment of U.S. troops moved into Lexington to restore order. Montgomery soon had to defend himself against a lawsuit filed under—of all things—the Civil Rights Act, though the judge dismissed the case.[62]

Governor Fletcher and Montgomery were unrepentant. Fletcher named Montgomery a brigadier general of the militia and commander of the Second Military District, the portion of the state south of the Missouri River. On February 4, 1867, Montgomery posted his first order in Lexington. "The friends of the conduct of lawless desperadoes, who have terrorized Lafayette county . . . are now at our mercy," he intoned. "I warn those who have, by a defence of Arch Clements, identified themselves with the men of that class, that if there is not protection given to law-abiding citizens, and if the law is not enforced against criminals, that I will return to

Lafayette county with a force, and . . . there will then be no law but the law of the bayonet."[63]

Of all the angry men in bitter, wounded Missouri, perhaps the angriest was the nineteen-year-old bushwhacker named Jesse James. It is likely that he was with Clement for all but the final, bloody moments of those days in Lexington, and it is certain that he retained a deep-seated fury at the fate of his friend. In his mind, Montgomery would always be the commander of "Tom Fletcher's cut-throat militia . . . the scoundrel that murdered Capt. A. J. Clement." A full decade later, he would still seethe. "He had Arch. Clement, one of the noblest boys, and the most promising military boy, of this age, murdered in cold blood," he would write.[64]

The death of Archie Clement never became one of the canonical stories in the myth of Jesse James; it conflicted too directly with his grand alibi, the tale of his three-year recovery from the wound to his lung. But it was as important a moment as almost any other in his postwar life, a deeply personal loss that would nurture his long years of anger and defiance. On December 13, 1866, he lost his mentor, his companion in battle, and perhaps his best friend. At the same time, Clement's death opened the way for Jesse's rise to leadership, to become the man who would shake up the country.

CHAPTER ELEVEN

The Death of Captain Sheets

"I**S THE WAR OVER?**" It was a headline that could have been read anywhere in the early days of 1867. In Boston, Cleveland, or Chicago, it would have referred to outrages against freed slaves in the South; in the press of Charleston, New Orleans, or Memphis, it would have been directed at the Republican Congress and the Federal troops that still patrolled the streets and roads of the old Confederacy.[1] But this particular headline ran in Missouri.

It appeared in the *Lexington Caucasian* on January 9. The editors spoke for the rebels, who counted the late Archie Clement as one of their own, who knew that *they* were the real targets of Governor Fletcher's militia, of secret vigilante squads, of grand juries that issued indictments for wartime crimes and perjury in taking the Oath. To old Confederates, the *Caucasian*'s question answered itself, for the Radicals would never leave them alone.[2]

"I suppose you hear terrible accounts of our oppression by the powers that be," wrote L. M. Matz to a cousin in the South on February 13. "I don't see how we are to have permanent peace," she mused. "Last fall when the Gov. was arming his militia . . . it looked to me like getting up civil war right under our noses." Matz and other secessionists believed they were locked in a battle with the Radicals for the soul of Missouri—a cultural, political, and even military war. She wanted to move her family to friendlier territory, but her son argued that they could not abandon the state now. "My son Franklin says it is too good a country to give up to the Yanks," she wrote, "& he is going to stay here & if it's necessary to fight them will do his part."[3]

The band of men who had terrorized Lexington still lurked in Lafayette County. On December 27, 1866, Montgomery's temporary replacement, Captain W. E. Chester, wired to Governor Fletcher, "I am confident that they are organizing and making their preparations to do some devilment." Even the Conservatives were afraid, Chester wrote, "for they say if they were to assist the sheriff to arrest one of those men that their lives would most certainly pay the forfeit. . . . If you would give us the permission to scout for them, we would be able to kill or drive them out in a short time."[4] How different Missouri's history would have been if Chester had made good on his boast—but he could not, for the bushwhackers did not remain together for long. It was a long-standing guerrilla tactic to disperse when pursued, and Clement's death may also have left them leaderless for the moment, so they scattered to their homes and hiding places.

It has been customary for historians to assume that the Confederate guerrillas made a sudden and complete transformation into common criminals, that the end of the Civil War dropped onto the personal histories of Jesse James and his comrades like a meat cleaver, severing what was from what would be. They have been seen as simple men, acting almost compulsively. "In all probability, boredom and an inability to adjust to the calm of postwar life," writes esteemed James biographer William Settle, "drove them to crime."[5]

But postwar life was anything but calm, and the bushwhacker reaction to it was anything but simple. At first they surrendered and returned home. Then they bridled against angry Unionist neighbors and hostile Radical authorities. Some of this was simply the friction of wartime foes living side by side in a new culture of arms-carrying and personal vengeance. But the guerrillas went further, turning to organized resistance. Their ideological commitment should not be surprising: the veterans of Quantrill and Anderson's bands hailed from some of the wealthiest, best-established families in western Missouri. They had risked their lives for secession, and their families had suffered terrible retribution from the Union authorities.[6] In letters to military commanders, they had demanded recognition as legitimate Confederate warriors.

After the war was over, they had returned to a community inflamed with partisan fury, and their activity increased proportionately with the political crisis. In 1866, they began to rebel against Missouri's homegrown Reconstruction with the same methods they had used during the war, ranging from robbery to intimidation to murder. As November approached, they directly confronted the political process, harassing registration officials, threatening Radical leaders, and even occupying Lexington on election day. To believe that there was no political content in their actions, we would have to believe that they were the only Missouri secessionists who were not enraged by the situation.

The bushwhackers were men with beliefs, men radicalized by war like so many veterans of the North and South. But the great weakness of the guerrillas had always been their lack of a strategic design; they had had no farseeing leader—no George Washington, no Mao Zedong, no General Giap—to guide their insurgency to victory. Theirs had been a spontaneous war, a tactical war, a war of isolated clashes; not even the most significant guerrilla triumphs had changed the strategic situation in Missouri. They knew how to strike back, but they did not know how to win.

Having scattered to their homes as 1867 began, these angry, violent men were utterly unsatisfied with the state of affairs but lacked a clear path of resistance. In Lafayette County, their intimidation may have secured the Conservative victory in the election—as the Radicals angrily claimed—but almost everywhere else their enemies had won. Northern voters had overwhelmingly endorsed the Republicans in their battle with President Johnson over Reconstruction, giving the party a sweeping congressional majority. In Missouri, the Radicals had routed their Conservative foes, thanks both to the restrictive Oath and to fears of a rebel resurgence.[7] The state's electorate had slammed the political door in the secessionists' faces.

Their defeat was seemingly absolute. In the coming months, they would maintain their identity, preserve their organization, and plunder the institutions of Unionist society, but little meaning would be seen in their actions, apart from a general defiance of the Radical authorities. And moving among them, unnoticed as the authorities focused on his older and better-known comrades, would be Jesse James.[8]

IN MAY 1867, newspapers and telegraph wires carried news of continuing political tension. In Lexington, the Radicals disputed the election results. In Jefferson City, Judge Walter King of Clay County's circuit court was undergoing an impeachment trial for throwing out indictments of bushwhackers for wartime crimes. And Liberty Tribune editor Miller was rallying the defeated foes of the Radicals with explosive language. "Organize! Organize!" he wrote. "November next [1868] is to decide whether this country is to be a Republic of white men, or a nigger despotism. . . . Better death than a nigger government."[9]

All along the Missouri River valley, the press reported, "robberies, shooting affairs, and other crimes appear to be frightfully on the increase." On March 3, 1867, there had been yet another bank robbery, this time in Savannah, a town that the Liberty Tribune described as "literally overrun with thieves, burglars, and highway robbers." The half-dozen bandits had botched the attempt, however, and had retreated under heavy fire from their intended victims. Some of the same men were thought to be responsible for a jail break in Buchanan County. On March 28, John Bivens and three Titus brothers broke out of jail in Liberty, where they were awaiting trial for assassinating a Clay County deputy sheriff in 1866.[10]

Little of this turmoil affected Richmond, Ray County. True, the Conservatives fumed at the triumphant Radicals, and several horse thieves had been thrown into jail over the last few days, but on the whole it was a steady community that enjoyed the end of a long and stormy winter. On May 22, the townspeople looked ahead to a typically quiet Thursday, a day when few farmers came into town and merchants expected little bustle.[11] So no one gave much thought to the small clusters of men who guided their horses into Richmond around 3:30 in the afternoon—that is, until a dozen of them had collected in front of the Hughes & Wasson bank. Four of them dismounted; the others rested in their saddles and silently scanned the streets.

As those four men swung the door open and stepped inside, they entered a bastion of Richmond society. Owners Joseph S. Hughes and George I. Wasson had lived in the community for two and a half decades; Wasson had served as a deputy sheriff and town constable, while Hughes had been a merchant in town since 1844. In 1859 the pair had opened a branch of the Union Bank of Missouri, and they had kept it open all through the war. When the parent body had reorganized as a national bank, they had purchased their branch's assets and reopened on January 1, 1866, as a private firm. Hughes & Wasson could not be considered a Republican institution—Hughes, for one, was an influential Conservative—but its owners were solid Unionists.[12]

Outside on the street, someone grew suspicious at the sight of mounted men in front of the bank. A query, a cry of warning, perhaps a gunshot sounded, and the battle erupted. The men on horseback fired as the locals ran for cover or scrambled to get their guns. Lieutenant Frank B. Griffin ran out into the courthouse yard, positioned himself behind a tree, and took aim with a carbine. Mayor John B. Shaw sprinted down the street, pistol in hand, shouting for the people to fight the invaders. The gunmen at the bank held their ground and returned fire with astonishing precision. Shaw collapsed to the ground, shot through the heart, while Griffin fell back with a bullet hole in his forehead. The elderly father of the slain lieutenant, B. G. Griffin, ran toward the bank in grief and rage, and received a slug through his brain as he reached the doorway. As the four robbers inside emerged onto the street, one of them aimed his pistol at the crumpled old man and fired another round into his corpse.

The bandits mounted and spurred their horses west toward Liberty, then galloped northwest into the rugged Crooked River country. They left behind a town in shock, as the community where Bill Anderson's corpse had been posed for souvenir photographs now cradled its own dead. "Heartrending beyond description were the plaintive wails of those near and dear relations—wives, children, mothers and sisters," said a local newspaper. Amid the sobs, a posse of some fifteen men gathered behind Deputy Sheriff Tom Reyburn. After an hour or so of hard riding, Reyburn and his force caught sight of their prey under the rays of the descending sun. A running fight ensued, as the bandits turned in their saddles and fired while they galloped on.

Reyburn lost sight of them. Shortly outside of Elkhorn, he found a fence rail taken down where the raiders had left the road and filed into the woods. He would never be able to track them now; clearly they were bush-whackers, familiar with the hidden trails through the bottomland of the Crooked and Fishing Rivers. The displaced rail was wet with blood; at least one bullet had found its target.[13]

Somewhere in the old guerrilla haunts among the timber and paw-paw bushes, the raiders split the $3,500 they had taken, then scattered. Perhaps ten of them crossed the Missouri River at Sibley; most of the rest probably returned to homesteads in Clay County. But it would be difficult for them to lie low in the coming days. "This horrible affair has created a profound sensation throughout the State," reported the *St. Louis Republican* on May 30, "and the utmost efforts have been made to apprehend the perpetrators." After more than a year of repeated clashes with bushwhackers, the author-ities were ready to strike when old Quantrill and Anderson men appeared on the list of suspects.[14]

On May 26, Marshal P. J. Miserez of Jackson County received a warrant for the arrest of seven men: Dick Burns, Payne Jones, Andy McGuire, John and James White, a man named Flannery, and Allen Parmer. All were bushwhackers.[15] At ten in the evening, Miserez led a posse of ten men on an all-night ride through pelting rain, arriving at the home of Jones's father-in-law at six in the morning. As they gathered outside, Jones burst out the door, fired two rounds from a shotgun that killed a posse member and an eight-year-old neighbor girl, then escaped through a field. In the pursuit, one of the lawmen encountered Burns and other bushwhackers, who took away his guns and, the press reported, "advised him to return to Kansas City at once."[16]

Despite this humiliating setback, the search continued. More guerrillas were added to the list of suspects, including Bill Hulse, member of a noto-rious bushwhacker clan that had fought against the authorities repeatedly since the end of the war. Vigilante squads began to post warnings in Clay County's Washington and Fishing River townships (home to the James brothers and the site of many guerrilla hiding places). In Richmond, rumors spread that horse thief Felix Bradley, currently locked up in the county jail, was linked to the robbery. A few days after the raid, an angry crowd hauled him out of his cell and hanged him. The fury of the community could be seen in the pages of the Conservative *Richmond Conservator,* which encouraged support for the Radical sheriff Adam Reyburn. "No politics is known in this matter," the paper declared. "Our lives and property are at stake."[17]

As he did the year before, Governor Fletcher took personal charge of the government's counterattack. First he offered a $300 reward for each bandit. Then, on May 29, he learned that suspect Tom Little had been seen on the riverboat *W. L. Lewis* as it steamed out of Jefferson City. Immediately he wired instructions to St. Louis chief of police William P. Fenn to have him arrested. Little and a companion were duly seized when the boat landed in the city. They were sent west and lodged in the jail in Warrensburg. A mob stormed the jail, hauled the suspects out, and hanged them from a tree.[18]

Neighbors and acquaintances whispered that Jesse James—"regarded as a desperate and dangerous character," according to one merchant—had joined the robbery. Seven years later, a man who grew up with the brothers and was in Richmond that day said "positively and emphatically that he recognized Jesse and Frank James . . . among the robbers," the press reported. At the time, however, their names remained unspoken by the authorities. Jesse and his older brother were simply not prominent enough among the guerrilla fraternity to draw any attention from the law.[19]

The lynchings in Richmond and Warrensburg marked a grim new turn in the bushwhackers' history, as their casualties mounted. On November 22, 1867, the blanket-wrapped body of Dick Burns turned up in a field three miles south of Independence, his head crushed by a blunt object. Payne Jones turned up dead as well—reportedly at the hands of Jim Chiles, another old bushwhacker and bandit suspect.[20]

At the close of the business day on November 27, the robbers struck again, holding up the First National Bank in Independence with quiet efficiency. One of the men who plundered the vault was James M. Devers, a suspect both in the Richmond affair and in a recent murder.[21] Before the end of the year, the authorities captured Andy McGuire in St. Louis. Like Frank James, he had been with Quantrill when the guerrilla leader was killed in 1865, and he was another suspect in the Richmond robbery. After he was transported to the Ray County jail, he broke down and told Sheriff Reyburn that Devers had also taken part in the bloody raid. In February 1868, one of Reyburn's deputies captured Devers in Kentucky and brought him back. At midnight on March 17, vigilantes removed McGuire and Devers from the Richmond jail and hanged them both from a tree.[22]

For the bushwhackers, war had hardly been more deadly than these days of peace. But as the "old men" disappeared, their younger and lesser known companions would carry on the fight. Out of the slaughter of 1867 and 1868 the twenty-year-old Jesse James was about to emerge.

THE JAMES BROTHERS may have reached Kentucky the same way their father did in 1846, booking passage on a paddlewheeler that rode the high spring waters of the Missouri River, into the wide Mississippi, and up the Ohio. Or perhaps they decided to cut several days from their trip by taking the train, riding the newly completed Missouri Pacific from Kansas City to St. Louis, where they boarded a steamboat for the rest of their journey. In early March 1868 Jesse and Frank James were in a hotel in Chaplin, Kentucky, together with five former guerrillas: Ol Shepherd and his cousin George Shepherd, Arthur McCoy, John Jarrette, and Cole Younger.[23]

They were most likely in Chaplin to finalize a plan conceived some weeks before by George Shepherd, now a resident of Kentucky. According to one report, he had returned to Missouri at the beginning of the year to tell his cousin Ol about a rich and vulnerable bank in the town of Russellville. The pair had gathered McCoy and Jarrette for the robbery; Jarrette, in turn, had recruited Younger. Cole had only recently returned to Missouri after spending the end of the Civil War in California, followed by a prolonged stay in Texas.[24] Not surprisingly, Jesse and Frank appear to have been relegated to peripheral roles; unlike Younger and the two Shepherds, neither had been a leader during the war, and Jesse was still quite young. The other five men, it seems, were to ride to Russellville to visit the Nimrod L. Long & Co. bank.[25]

Great care marked the Missourians' passage through the Kentucky countryside. On March 10 and 18, they scouted the interior of their intended target, the private bank owned by Nimrod L. Long and George W. Norton (brother of Elijah H. Norton, a prominent Unionist politician in western Missouri). An experienced banker, Norton had joined Long to open the firm in 1863, when many of Kentucky's rebels were in exile. But Nimrod L. Long & Co., unlike the Clay County Savings Association, was not a political target.[26]

The reconnaissance aroused Long's suspicions. First one of the bandits—posing as Thomas Colburn* of Louisville—tried to sell him a mature $500 U.S. 7.30 bond at par, even though it would normally fetch a 6 to 7 percent premium. Long declined. The second time "Colburn" showed up, he tried to get change for a $100 bill, which convinced the banker that

---

*Some reports give "Coleman," not Colburn; Cole Younger's full name was Thomas Coleman Younger.

he was dealing with a counterfeiter. He gruffly refused to accept the note, and the man left. Two days later he returned.

At two o'clock in the afternoon of March 20, 1868, Colburn strode into Nimrod L. Long & Co. with a companion glowering over each shoulder. He slapped down a $50 bill with a fierce glare. "Is *that* good, sir?" he snarled. It's a fake, the crusty Long replied. Colburn drew a revolver, pushed the muzzle against the banker's head, and told him to empty his vault. Suddenly Long darted for the back door. Somehow he escaped safely, and townspeople ran to the scene with weapons in hand. But for every bullet they fired, the press reported, they received three in return from the pair of mounted gunmen who stood watch outside, wielding seven-shot Spencer carbines. The two bandits killed one local citizen before their comrades emerged with $9,000 in paper currency and $3,000 in gold coin.[27]

When news of the Russellville robbery appeared in the press, Louisville detectives Delos T. Bligh and John Gallagher took up the hunt, with Bligh in the lead. The raid had originated in Chaplin, Kentucky, Bligh learned; he placed the James brothers there, though he could not identify them as members of the robbery party. On March 28, he and his partner arrested George Shepherd, who was eventually convicted and sentenced to three years in the state penitentiary. Bligh then tracked Ol Shepherd to his father's home near Lee's Summit, Missouri, and sent the information to the Jackson County sheriff. Since Shepherd was also a suspect in the Richmond affair, the sheriff easily procured a warrant. He placed it in the hands of a deputy, dispatching him and a posse to make the arrest in early 1868.

When the lawmen knocked on the door to Shepherd's father's house, they met a blast of gunfire through the weatherboarding. They besieged the house all night. At daybreak, the fugitive burst out the door carrying a shotgun and a brace of revolvers. As Shepherd darted into a nearby field, the posse opened fire. The James brothers' old friend and leader, the man who had once scoured Clay and Clinton Counties with a death squad, was now dead himself.[28]

In the months that followed Clement's death, the old Anderson guerrilla organization had increasingly descended into simple crime. But the bloody hunt for the outlaws led to one more incident with political overtones. In the early summer of 1868, a Ray County deputy sheriff went to Kentucky to capture Bud Pence, a suspect in the Richmond robbery who, with his brother Donny, had served under Anderson and had settled in Kentucky's Nelson County after the war. Pence, the deputy claimed, escaped from custody with the aid of the Nelson County sheriff and Kentucky's lieutenant governor, William Johnson. Missouri's Radical press raised an uproar. Kentucky, the Republicans noted, was governed by former Confederates, who had won control of the state's Democratic Party after restrictions on former rebels there were lifted in December 1865.

Missouri's Democratic newspapers swiftly replied, showing that the bitterness of 1866 still lived. "The present State government is one of force and not of consent," said the *Jefferson City People's Tribune*. "Physical force alone prevents the people from meeting and abolishing the odious form under which we live. . . . If this were attempted, the people would be read the registration law, and if they disregarded that law, the Radical . . . Montgomerys, with their brigands, would be turned loose upon a defenseless people."[29]

IF THE WORLD could be judged by a single corner, then a visitor to Zerelda Samuel's farm in 1868 would imagine that the South had won the Civil War. The family was prospering again, with real estate and personal property that compared favorably to those of the neighbors. The old house rattled with noise from the children whom Zerelda had brought into the world, year after year, all through her late thirties and early forties. Nine-year-old Sarah and seven-year-old John would be scampering about, with four-year-old Fannie Quantrell toddling after. Eighteen-year-old Susie James would be cradling the infant Mary, or perhaps playing with two-year-old Archie—named in honor of Archie Clement, at Jesse's insistence.

The women had help as they cared for Zerelda's many offspring: Charlotte—Charlotte Samuel, now—was still there, nearly fifty. She was illiterate, alone, without relatives, without special skills, and here, at least, was security and perhaps the closest thing she had to a family. But the grim abuse inflicted on women under slavery still haunted her life. In September 1868, someone on the farm—either Charlotte or, more likely, the young woman recorded as an eighteen-year-old slave in the 1860 census—gave birth to a biracial boy, Perry. His white father was never named, though three obvious candidates—Reuben, Frank, and Jesse—lived on the farm. If the mother was the younger woman, then she soon fled and left the child in Charlotte's care.

From the beginning, Perry was reared to serve the Samuel family, alongside Ambrose, another former family slave, who was twelve when Perry was born. The two never went to school, never learned skills or trades; they simply worked for the Samuels all through their childhoods and adult years. When Ambrose turned eighteen, he would still be an illiterate worker living on the farm, and the 1880 census would list Perry as a member of Reuben's household, giving the eleven-year-old's occupation as "servant." One might easily have wondered if the news of emancipation had reached Zerelda's farm.[30]

But just beyond Zerelda's reach, the slow-paced life of hemp and tobacco farming, of muddy roads and chugging steamboats, was dying. In its place rose a new economy, closely resembling that of the North, linked to the rest of the country by a spreading rail network. A mania for rail construction erupted, sparked by the Radicals' devotion to economic progress and kindled by simple self-interest. County governments issued millions of dollars' worth of bonds to finance local railroad extensions, though the constitution of 1865 prohibited state aid. The craze crossed party lines; even the *Lexington Caucasian* called for a local railway link, noting that it "will benefit every man in the county who owns a foot of land, or who raises or makes anything for sale."[31]

Construction boomed in 1867. In Clay County, a line connecting the Hannibal & St. Joseph Railroad junction at Cameron to Kansas City marched steadily south, built by a rowdy crew of Irish laborers; by the end of September, it had reached the neighborhood of Centerville. "I believe the railroad is engaging the attention of a great many people at this time," wrote Sarah Harlan from nearby Haynesville. "There is a great part of the population of this wooded country that had never seen a car," she added. "The ladies go out by the dozen from town to see them and ride. The engineer had nothing better to do with the greater part of his time but to take the ladies on a pleasure ride." A new depot town named Kearney rose on the line in 1867, absorbing the old village of Centerville.[32]

The new rivers of iron, however, were a mere undercurrent in the tsunami unleashed by the Union victory. A flood of people deluged the countryside, as Radical plans to remake Missouri fortuitously met an epic tide of migration. In the first four months of 1866, private individuals acquired almost 250,000 acres of public land in the state, often through the Homestead Act. In 1867, the state Board of Immigration began to advertise for immigrants on a large scale, though the real work was done by county boards, which competed for settlers. Many battered, war-weary residents were only too happy to sell out. The wave crested against the very edge of the Samuel farm, as neighbor and entrepreneur Waltus Watkins purchased six thousand acres of land and resold them to newcomers at low prices. "I can buy first rate improved land here in Missouri from 5 to 10 dollars per acre," wrote A. J. Spease from Lexington in April 1868.[33]

"There are a great many that are thronging the railroad stations, exceedingly anxious to sell lands," wrote Daniel Fogle on August 8, 1867. Like so many others, he came to St. Louis to scout the state for settlement. "We find numbers at the stations on the same errand we are on. We see them from all parts, some from Pennsylvania, Ohio, Tennessee, etc., etc.

The excitement is not overrated." More than three-quarters of these immi-grants came from the North. By 1870, the number of Missourians born in the original free states had increased from 155,000 ten years earlier to 345,000. By contrast, the number born in the old slave states remained vir-tually the same, the immigrants barely replacing those who fled the war. By 1870, Yankee-born residents had become a majority of the non-native pop-ulation, though natives predominated overall.[34]

The Southern character of Missouri was increasingly challenged by land-hungry Union veterans. But as Daniel Fogle wandered across the state on his mission, he learned that this peaceful invasion was stirring the still-burning fire of wartime enmities. Many of the tracts offered to immi-grants had been seized by county governments for nonpayment of taxes; millions of acres went up for auction. "These lands sell for near nothing—but it is considered very hazardous to buy and occupy them," Fogle observed, "as they mostly belong to men who went into the Southern army and dare not return, and there is a large band of them sworn together, and unknown to the authorities, who will and do kill every man who attempts to occupy their former homes."[35]

In many respects, these changes and conflicts reflected a national trans-formation, as the Republican Congress crafted a dramatic program to remake the South. After launching the Fourteenth Amendment to the Con-stitution, Congress had passed the Reconstruction Act of 1867 over the president's veto, dividing the old Confederacy into five districts and plac-ing it under army jurisdiction. Each rebel state except Tennessee was now ruled by a military governor, and would be until it ratified a constitution that gave black men the vote. The Republicans had acted on their vision of a South where slavery's legacy would be crushed and the economy would blossom along Northern lines. "My dream is of a model republic, extend-ing equal protection and rights to all men," declared one. "The wilderness shall vanish, the church and school-house will appear . . . the whole land will revive under the magic touch of free labor."[36]

All of this had leaped away from the past in breathtaking ways. Never before had the federal government intervened at the individual level; never before had black suffrage been an issue, let alone a demand placed on state governments; never before had martial law been established in peacetime. As recently as 1865, the congressional Republicans themselves would never have imagined taking these remarkable steps. But the brutality directed toward the African Americans in the South, and the president's own intran-sigence, radicalized even moderates. In early 1868, Johnson's continuing resistance led to the first impeachment of a chief executive; he escaped con-viction and removal from office by one vote.[37]

Radical Reconstruction set off an explosion of political activity among freed slaves. "By the end of 1867," writes Eric Foner, "it seemed virtually every black voter in the South had enrolled in the Union League or some equivalent local political organization." Necessarily lacking experience in government—and usually lacking literacy as well—they allied themselves with white Northerners who had arrived since the war, already derided by native whites as "carpetbaggers." Union army veteran Albert T. Morgan, for example, was asked by a delegation of black voters in Yazoo County, Mississippi, to run for the state's constitutional convention on a ticket with an African-American blacksmith. He agreed, and went on to become an able and articulate spokesman for his black constituents.[38]

The white South struck back. Squads of heavily armed Confederate veterans terrorized politically active blacks and Northern immigrants. In the first four months of 1868, white terrorist bands across the South rapidly adopted the guise and ritual of the Ku Klux Klan, a hitherto obscure body that had originated in Pulaski, Tennessee, in 1866. Often led by the most prominent local citizens, wearing a vast array of disguises, Klansmen broke up Union League meetings, terrorized teachers of black schoolchildren, and murdered opponents. Even Kentucky, a state unaffected by the Reconstruction Act, became the scene of devastating political violence. As 1868 progressed, the terrorism became "systematic," in the words of one historian. In ill-fated Russellville, five Unionists were killed, along with a U.S. marshal.[39]

As the nation bled, so bled Missouri. Throughout the Mississippi and Missouri River counties, former Confederates adopted the KKK model as they lashed out at black activists. Secessionist newspapers, especially the *St. Joseph Vindicator* and *Lexington Caucasian,* eagerly promoted the bloody campaign. On November 30, 1867, the *Caucasian* published a letter from Thomas G. Graves, who had just learned that a party of African Americans had been holding Union League meetings at a house he had rented out. "Now this won't do," he wrote. "I wish to give you a word of advice, that is, do not rent any of your land to a nigger. . . . Thar is a party of men, I among the rest, who have swarn if you do, not to leave a hat nor board nor rail standing." By mid-1868, the Klan had begun to operate openly in Lafayette County. "It is the Ku Klux Klan that has scared the Radical fraternity into fits," the *Caucasian* noted on May 2. The editors were cheered that the Radical *St. Louis Democrat* was "terribly alarmed" about "the Ku-Klux design to assassinate 'Union' men."[40]

Tensions escalated as the election approached, leading many to fear a repeat of 1866. The Klan began to threaten Union veterans and ordered their organization, the Grand Army of the Republic, to stop meeting, and brawls frequently erupted at campaign rallies. Former secessionists, still firmly locked out of the political process, focused much of their fury on freed slaves. Every issue of the *Caucasian* contained a vicious attack on "niggers." In July, militia general Montgomery threatened to occupy Lexington again, due to reports that white supremacists were arming. "Even sane men, Radical office holders, say they fear the same thing," the *Caucasian* groused; but whites, it noted tersely, had always had the right to arm themselves.[41]

On September 5, 1868, Jesse James turned twenty-one. In an ordinary time, he would now enter upon the civic responsibilities of adulthood, and could look forward to voting in the November election. But in these bitter postwar years, not even the most lenient registration officer would have allowed him to take the Oath and cast his ballot. He led "a wandering, reckless life," according to merchant Daniel Conway, "and ever since the war has been regarded as a desperate and dangerous character."[42]

In any case, the election offered him little to choose from. The Republican ticket was headed by Ulysses S. Grant, now making his first run for the presidency; Joseph W. McClurg, a former Union officer and three-term congressman, was the party's candidate for Missouri's governorship. The state's Conservatives had now remade themselves as the Democratic Party, dominated by Unionist former Whigs. Near the very top sat Frank Blair, Missouri's original Unionist and now the Democratic candidate for vice president on a ticket with Horatio Seymour.

Blair gave full voice to his deep-seated racism. He openly called on the president "to declare these [Reconstruction] acts null and void, compel the army to undo its usurpations at the South, disperse the carpetbag Southern governments, allow the white people to reorganize their own governments." On the campaign stump, he attacked "a semi-barbarous race of blacks who are worshippers of fetishes, and poligamists." If given power, he shouted, they would "subject the white women to their unbridled lust." Republicans condemned such statements as treason.[43]

To some of Missouri's Confederates, on the other hand, his words were sweet honey. Democratic leader James Rollins noted in a letter to Blair that there was "an old rebel element" working within their party, looking forward to the day when they could vote again. But a hard core of secessionists despised Blair. "[In] a little cabin within speaking distance lives two lone widows," wrote one Missouri rebel on October 25, 1868, "whose husbands fell fighting in the Southern army against Blair's commands—and now none [are] so true to the South as Frank Preston Blair, Democratic candidate for Vice President." The South was devastated, he noted bitterly, by "such heaven-forsaken wretches as Blair."[44]

All around Jesse James, the things he had fought for fell to a Radical onslaught that seemed to grow with each passing year. Even the party that best represented his cause was dominated by his enemies. He himself was as loyal as ever, but to a diminishing circle of family, old comrades, and Confederate friends. He had nothing but defiance for the outside world, as he rode about, well dressed and reckless, astride an exceptional bay mare named Kate. But in September 1869, he made a strange request of the Mount Olive Baptist Church, in Kearney. He asked that his name be stricken from the rolls, the congregation recorded, because "he believed himself unworthy."[45]

AT 12:30 IN the afternoon of December 7, 1869, Jesse James swung to the ground from his saddle, arousing no suspicion among the people of Gallatin, Missouri. He had one companion—apparently Frank—who remained mounted beside him. Then he opened the door to the Daviess County Savings Association.

He stepped into a simple, one-story brick structure that was barely twenty feet wide and perhaps twice as deep. In one corner, he saw William A. McDowell, a lawyer who kept his office in the bank building. At the back he saw the cashier, the man the young bandit had come to see, seated in front of a large safe. Looking carefully at the cashier's face, Jesse held out a $100 note—probably a bond or old state banknote, which would not pass at face value. He wanted it changed, he said. The banker turned toward the safe as Frank walked in. "If you will write out a receipt," Frank said, "I will pay you that bill." The man sat at his desk and began to write as the two brothers stared at him intently.

Jesse reached under his coat, pulled out a revolver, and cocked the hammer. Cox, he said with a curse, thinking he was talking to Samuel P. Cox, caused the death of my brother Bill Anderson, and I am bound to have my revenge. He aimed the barrel at the cashier's chest and squeezed the trigger. The ear-splitting crack would have echoed in that small room, flame from the slow-burning black powder leaping out of the muzzle as the bullet tore straight through the man's heart. Before the cashier could topple from his chair, Jesse aimed squarely at his forehead and fired again. A startled McDowell leaped for the door. Jesse wheeled and snapped off two quick shots, one of them tearing through the lawyer's arm as he darted to safety. His shouts reverberated outside as the brothers snatched up a portfolio on the cashier's desk and turned to flee.

Out in front of the bank, the brothers quickly mounted and spurred their horses for the edge of town. Already they could hear the townspeople rallying, as they had in Richmond and Russellville, running into the streets with rifles in hand. The first crack of gunfire sounded. Kate, Jesse's fine bay mare, suddenly reared, throwing Jesse clear out of the saddle, though he still had one foot caught in the stirrup. His horse dragged him thirty or forty feet before he finally cleared his boot. Frank circled back, reached a hand down to his brother, and pulled Jesse up behind him. With the citizens' shots echoing behind them, they rode hard toward the southwest.

Barely a mile outside of Gallatin, the brothers spotted a good-looking saddle horse tied to a fence on the farm of a Captain Woodruff. They aimed their pistols at the head of its owner, Daniel Smoots, who watched helplessly as Jesse untied the reins and mounted his animal. Then they were off again, an impromptu posse close behind. Perhaps three miles from town, they rode into Honey Creek and apparently splashed up the streambed, its running waters masking their trail. They had safely escaped. When they glanced inside the portfolio, however, they saw only some papers and a few county warrants.

Jesse James was exultant nonetheless. As he and his brother trotted out of the stream toward the town of Kidder, they repeatedly ran across strangers; each time, Jesse could not help gloating that he had taken revenge for the death of Bloody Bill Anderson by killing his slayer, Samuel P. Cox.[46]

Perhaps the James brothers went to Gallatin only to assassinate Cox. His residence there was quite well known; the bandits spent little time looting after the murder, in contrast to previous holdups; and Jesse boasted of his deed, heedless of the attention he drew. A more likely scenario, however, is that they came simply to rob, but as Jesse—acutely conscious of Cox's presence in town—stared at the cashier, he saw what he hoped to see, a precious opportunity for revenge. Certainly his reckless bragging along the escape route attests to the sincerity of his belief that he had killed Cox.[47]

But he hadn't. The riddled body on the floor of the bank was that of John W. Sheets, who held a place of prominence in Gallatin. As primary owner and sole operator of the Daviess County Savings Association, he was one of the wealthiest men in the community. He was also a local Democratic leader, and had complained bitterly of Radical "mobocracy" in the tumultuous election of 1866.[48] The people of Gallatin wept bitterly over their loss. "Should the miscreants be overtaken it is not probable that a jury will be required to try them," commented the St. Joseph Gazette. "They will be shot down in their tracks, so great is the excitement among the citizens of Daviess and the adjoining counties."[49] When they traced the bay mare that had run away from the killer back to Jesse James, two heavily armed citizens immediately saddled up and rode south.

When they arrived in Liberty and explained their mission, Sheriff O. P. Moss turned to deputy John S. Thomason. If any Unionist in Clay County was the equal of young James with the horse and revolver, it was Thomason. His exploits as a wartime militia captain had won him renown; when he joined the Paw Paws, even Radical critics of those rebel-ridden regiments singled him out for praise. "Thomason was the most active officer in the EMM in hunting out bushwhackers and thieves," Moss had said in 1864, noting the great risks Thomason had taken in singlehandedly tracking guerrillas. Little wonder that Moss now asked him to arrest Jesse.[50]

"Prompt, fearless, and always ready," as the newspapers described him, Thomason gathered his son Oscar and the two men from Gallatin, loaded his weapons, and set out for Zerelda's farm on December 14. At the edge of the property, he dispatched the Gallatin pair to circle through the woods until they had a clear view of the yard. Then he and his son dismounted at the gate and strode directly to the door of the little three-room house.

They were expected. Just as they were about to knock, the door suddenly swung open. Out came thirteen-year-old Ambrose, the servant and ex-slave, who ran to the stable door and threw it open. The stunned Thomason watched as Jesse and Frank James sprinted out "on splendid horses," as the press reported, "with pistols drawn, and took the lot fence at a swinging gallop." Immediately the two Gallatin men in the woods opened fire, followed by the deputy sheriff and his son. With the brothers rapidly gaining distance, the party ran to their mounts. Thomason jumped his horse over the fence and gave chase, galloping at top speed.

He soon discovered that he was all alone. The others' animals had balked at jumping over the fence, forcing the men to dismount in order to remove the top rail. Jesse and Frank, meanwhile, returned fire as they rode on. Suddenly Thomason reined in, jumped down, and took careful aim. He had only two rounds left. He fired—and missed. Even worse, his horse started at the sound and darted ahead without him. The riderless animal caught up to the James brothers; one of them calmly reached out with his revolver and fired, killing the horse. Thomason trudged back to the Samuel farm, where he commandeered a horse and led his party away.

Less than ten minutes later, the fugitives returned home and found that the posse had left. Immediately they galloped into Kearney.[51] To all appearances, they arrived in a state of rage. For half an hour they terrorized the town as they cantered through the streets, Frank with five revolvers tucked into a belt outside his coat, Jesse with three revolvers and a Colt's revolving rifle. They stopped in front of a store owned by a man who would soon become a major figure in their lives, a former Confederate and future sheriff named John Groom. Jesse aimed a pistol at the door and ordered Groom to come out. He declined. They shouted that they had just killed Thomason and his son, and they told Groom to take some men to bury the corpses. Then the brothers left, saying they had nothing to do with the murder in Gallatin. A mile and a half out of town, they terrified two men who were passing along the road, declaring "that they would never be taken alive, and would kill every man who attempted to follow them." It was the beginning of a long pattern of intimidation of the James brothers' unfortunate neighbors. When Thomason and a large force returned to the Samuel farm the next morning, Frank and Jesse were not there.[52]

For the first time in the bloody history of peacetime bushwhacking, Jesse James's name appeared in the press. But no one who lived near the Samuel farm, it seems, believed that Jesse and his brother were novices in bloodshed. Locally, at least, they "were noted bushwhackers during the war," the *Liberty Tribune* reported, "and are regarded as desperate men." Now they were so noted and so regarded across the entire state. Governor McClurg offered a $500 reward for each of them—$200 more than the customary amount, reflecting the public furor. This came on top of identical rewards posted by Sheets's widow, his bank, and the people of Gallatin, plus $250 from Daviess County. McClurg telegraphed the Jackson and Platte County sheriffs, ordering each of them to organize a platoon of thirty militiamen to go to Thomason's aid, should he locate the James boys. The *Platte City Reveille* made a point of noting that every man in the Platte County unit was a Democrat. "Parenthetically we would observe," the paper added pessimistically, "that there is not much prospect of this valiant company being put on the warpath."[53]

For years, Jesse James had been a follower, known and dreaded only by his immediate neighbors, passing unseen amid the crimes of his bushwhacker fraternity. One by one, his leaders had been killed: Clement, Jones, Burns, Devers, and Shepherd, among others. Their deaths had forced the James brothers to decide whether to give up the guerrilla life, as Dave Pool and the Pence brothers had, or take command for themselves. With the murder in Gallatin, they gave their answer.

Of all the citizens who now discovered the identities of the slayers of Captain Sheets, one swelled with immense satisfaction. He was charmed, delighted, thrilled by their exploits; more than that, he would come to see in them a way to undo a little bit of what the Union army had won four years before. Before long, the life of Jesse James would be inextricably intertwined with that of John Newman Edwards.

CHAPTER TWELVE

The Chivalry of Crime

W HAT BEGAN IN WATER would end in fire. On July 4, 1865, in what must have been the final ceremony of the Civil War, the tattered remnants of the Iron Brigade wrapped their Confederate flag around a stone and hurled it into the Rio Grande. Then General Jo Shelby led his last, loyal horsemen, a few hundred at most, across a makeshift bridge over the gritty current into Mexico. Others rode with him—senators, governors, generals, and soldiers of various regiments who refused to surrender—but the core of these refugees were "Missouri's orphaned children," in the words of Shelby's adjutant, Major John Newman Edwards.[1]

Edwards rode beside his general, as he had at Westport, Lexington, Pilot Knob, and countless hunting excursions before the war. Just twenty-seven years old, he had barely begun his career as a newspaper editor when the war began. Then, as Shelby's ever-present aide-de-camp, he had whisked up frothy, romantic reports of the general's deeds that would make a teenage poet blush. In truth, he worshipped his commander with a thick, Ishmael-for-Queequeg love that raised few eyebrows in the overwrought nineteenth century. Some would later speculate that this entire expedition to Mexico was Edwards's idea, for it was exactly the kind of desperate, quixotic adventure that best suited his sensibility.

Shelby and his men, however, were not the first Confederates to flee the verdict of Appomattox, nor would they be the last. Soon they would be reunited with such Missourians as Sterling Price and Thomas C. Reynolds, along with Generals Jubal Early, Thomas Hindman, and Edmund Kirby Smith, and other rebel notables. They came because no government had been friendlier to the South than that of Mexico, though it was not exactly a government *of* Mexico. In 1863, the beleaguered republic had fallen prey to invading French forces, dispatched by Napoleon III—or Louis Napoleon, as he was also known—a nephew of Napoleon Bonaparte. In 1848, he had won election as president of France, and within four years had installed himself as emperor. The self-made monarch had restlessly asserted his power overseas, launching the Crimean War in 1854, supporting the unification of Italy in 1859, and sending an expedition against China shortly afterward. During the Civil War, he had taken advantage of Washington's distraction to install Archduke Maximilian of Austria and Princess Carlotta of Belgium as "emperor" and "empress" of Mexico. From the beginning, this Napoleonic regime had quietly supported the Confederacy, welcoming Southern settlers and allowing the transshipment of supplies into Texas.[2]

As the ragged rebel column crossed the border, it passed from one civil war into another. An insurrection of Juaristas—supporters of deposed president Benito Juárez—was rapidly gaining strength. On July 28, 1865, these guerrillas ambushed the Confederates, though Shelby's troopers fought their way out. Later the weary Southerners faced off with a body of French troops that viewed them with intense distrust. Finally they reached Mexico City. On August 16, Maximilian and Carlotta gave an audience to the general and his adjutant; the ersatz empress was particularly warm, winning Edwards's lasting affection. The rulers cheerfully offered to create colonies for them between Mexico City and Vera Cruz, seizing large tracts of land from their legitimate Mexican owners for the benefit of the expatriates.

The exiles slowly settled into new lives, establishing large plantations under the protection of French troops. Edwards received "500 acres of magnificent land," as he wrote to his family, and he joined the management of the *Mexican Times,* an English-language newspaper subsidized by the imperial regime. The restless Shelby experimented with various enterprises, from new settlements to a profitable freighting operation that hauled supplies to imperial military posts.[3]

As the Confederates mingled with French officers in the hallways of the royal palace or labored in the fields of Carlota—the colony they named in honor of the empress—they did not forget their native land. "I am here as an exile, defeated by the acts of the Southern people themselves," Shelby wrote angrily on November 1, 1865. "Damn 'em, they were foolish enough to think by laying down their arms they would enjoy all the rights they once had. . . . I am not one of those to ask forgiveness for that which I believe *today* is *right.*"[4] Edwards was even more bitter. "It is . . . only a question of time, I think, before the Radicals triumph and commence their devastating work upon the South," he wrote to his sister on September 18, 1866. The South, he added, "must either submit to the greatest possible degree of social and political degradation, or appeal again to the sword. The latter I fear will never be done no matter what provocation is offered or what insult given."[5]

After four years of war and another of exile, it seems that Edwards still hungered for bloodshed. And bloodshed he would have. As 1866 progressed, the Juaristas steadily gained ground, drawing the Confederates into the battle as they attacked their colonies. Shelby found himself repeatedly under fire; he even took command of the evacuation of French troops from Cesnola late in the year. In November 1866, under pressure from the United States, Napoleon III informed his Mexican puppet that he would do nothing more for him.

In early 1867, French forces withdrew to the coast under constant Juarista attacks. Panicked Southerners raced after them, clogging the seaports in their frantic search for escape. The insurgents captured Maximilian outside the capital and executed him on June 19, 1867. Two days later, Juarista general Porfirio Díaz captured Mexico City. On July 4, exactly two years after the Iron Brigade crossed the Rio Grande, Vera Cruz fell. Their Mexican adventure was over.[6]

About the time of Maximilian's execution, Shelby and Edwards set foot on Missouri soil for the first time in three years. In June 1867, Shelby and his family returned to his old plantation in Aullville, Lafayette County; Edwards settled briefly in St. Louis, where he took a job as a reporter with the *Republican*. There he finished his florid history of the Iron Brigade, *Shelby and His Men*, which he published that year. The young writer had hardly reconciled himself to Radical rule, as his book made clear. He reserved his highest praise for Shelby's ruthless intransigence. "Time has demonstrated the strength of his judgment," he wrote. "The South, despite the sentimental ravings of her delicate generals, will be crushed and ground into powder under the ponderous wheels of a brutal and successful North."

In 1868, Edwards quit the *Republican*, perhaps because of his increasingly virulent alcoholism. Or perhaps he had already learned of an opportunity in the burgeoning railroad metropolis of the western border. That year he and Colonel John C. Moore launched the *Kansas City Times*. As editor of a new daily in a fast-growing town, Edwards rose quickly in fame and notoriety. He serialized his accounts of Shelby's exploits in its columns, winning himself literary acclaim and an enthusiastic audience of ex-Confederates. In his stories and editorials, he continuously stressed the righteousness of the rebel struggle.[7]

Ultimately, he would not be satisfied with a sheet that was merely a groaning requiem for the Lost Cause. The openly partisan newspapers of the era wielded tremendous political influence, but the constitution of 1865 had effectively shut Edwards and his fellow Confederates out of politics. In 1870, he finally glimpsed a path back from political exile.

The Radical front was crumbling. As early as November 1866, a faction, known as the Planter's House group, after a pivotal meeting in the famous hotel, had formed within the party. The group wanted to enfranchise both black men and former secessionists; its slogan, coined by journalist and politician B. Gratz Brown, summed up their cause: "Universal Suffrage and Universal Amnesty." Hard-line leader Charles D. Drake, father of the state's constitution, had balked at the idea. "If it is right to make the Negro a voter," was his reply, "let it be done because it is right, not as a swap with the rebels." The Radicals had followed his lead, presenting to voters a measure to extend the ballot to black Missourians, only to have it decisively defeated in 1868. Then Drake began to lose influence in the party. First, his choice for an open U.S. Senate seat, Benjamin Loan, was resoundingly defeated by Carl Schurz, an ally of the Planter's House group. The final blow for Drake, ironically, was the nation's ratification of the Fifteenth Amendment, which removed racial restrictions on voting; now the Radicals could no longer postpone the reenfranchisement of rebel whites by arguing that loyal blacks should come first. As 1870 began, it appeared that Confederates would soon be back at the ballot box.[8]

At this propitious moment, Edwards heard of how Jesse James had tried to take revenge for Bloody Bill Anderson. The tale would have appealed to his morbid fascination under any circumstance—the cold-blooded nature of the killing, the bold defiance of the authorities, the daring escape from a posse—but Edwards must have taken particular pleasure in the crime's Confederate overtones. Here was one Southerner willing to, as Edwards had written, "appeal again to the sword."

At some point in the spring of 1870 Edwards made contact with the James brothers. Introductions were required, for nothing indicates that Edwards knew them during the war. (He had praised Cole Younger and Dave Pool in *Shelby and His Men* in 1867, but had made no mention of the James boys.)[9] It was the beginning of a lasting friendship that would change the lives of all three men. A few years later, Edwards would write about Jesse with honest affection. "There is always a smile on his lips, and a graceful word or compliment for all with whom he comes in contact. . . . Jesse laughs at everything—Frank at nothing at all. Jesse is light-hearted, reckless, devil-may-care—Frank sober, sedate, a dangerous man always in ambush in the midst of society. Jesse knows there is a price upon his head and discusses the whys and wherefores of it—Frank knows it too, but it chafes him sorely." In the miles and miles of yarn that Edwards would later spin, these words, at least, seem a reasonably direct assessment of the brothers as he saw them. Edwards also introduced them to a wider

Confederate circle, including Shelby, who became their lasting patron and protector.[10]

The first public sign of Jesse's budding relationship with Edwards came in June 1870, when the *Kansas City Times* published a letter from the outlaw, addressed to Governor McClurg. In it, Jesse pleaded his innocence in the Gallatin attack; more than that, he made a call for public sympathy. "Some of the best men in Missouri," he wrote, could prove his alibi, "but I well know if I was to submit to an arrest, that I would be mobbed and hanged without a trial. The past is sufficient to show that bushwhackers have been arrested in Missouri since the war, charged with bank robbery, and they most all have been mobbed without trials." He continued with a thinly veiled appeal to the secessionist public. "It is true that during the war I was a Confederate soldier, and fought under the black flag," he added, "but since then I have lived a peaceable citizen." He admitted that he had fought the posse, even that he personally knew Oscar Thomason, the deputy sheriff's son, but that they had refused to identify themselves, and he could not recognize Oscar with his face muffled against the cold. "As soon as I think I can get a just trial I will surrender myself to the civil authorities of Missouri," he concluded, "and prove to the world that I am innocent of the crime charged against me."[11]

The peculiar timing of the letter—six months after the crime—suggests that it had more to do with Jesse's growing friendship with Edwards than anything else. It has even been suggested that Edwards heavily edited, even authored the note.[12] The latter is almost certainly untrue. As time would show, the former guerrilla was a prolific correspondent, especially when it came to asserting his innocence. Nor did he need the newspaperman to polish his prose. Though Jesse had a limited education, his brother Frank had enjoyed more than ten years of schooling, and both were voracious readers.[13] This letter features few of Edwards's characteristic flourishes—but it does have one. "The black flag" was an expression for bushwhacker warfare that the editor had diligently popularized, starting in 1867 with *Shelby and His Men;* the phrase both veiled and celebrated the cold-blooded murder that marked the guerrillas' methods.[14] The letter as a whole began a similar process for Jesse himself, presenting him as the target of unjustified, vindictive persecution, while hinting at his dangerousness.

In July, the bandit published another brief note to the governor. "I have been influenced by my friends to prove an *alibi*," he wrote, adding that proof would follow.[15] And it came: affidavits from three residents of Kearney, who swore that he had been in town the evening before the Gallatin murder, and visited a Mrs. Fox the day after. One of the statements was from the notably discreet John S. Groom, who swore that young James had made some purchases in his store on December 6. "I further state that I have known Jesse James since 1866, and I have never known him to act otherwise than respectful, and I have never known a more honest person in all his business transactions."

The only individuals to swear to Jesse's whereabouts on the day of the Gallatin raid were from his own family. Susie James claimed that she and her brother had "attended a preaching in Greenville" on the day before, that the bay mare Kate was hers, and that Jesse had sold the horse to some men from Kansas just before the Gallatin raid. The implication was clear: *jayhawkers* had killed Sheets. This would prove to be a characteristic ploy by Jesse, who often would claim that his enemies had committed the crimes he was accused of. Susie and Zerelda both asserted that Jesse was home when Sheets was murdered. Reuben said that he had been gone all day, helping his brother-in-law Jesse Cole kill hogs, though he had seen his stepson at home that morning.[16]

Despite the alibi's obvious hole—the fact that only Jesse's immediate family accounted for his whereabouts the day of the murder—the campaign to exonerate him succeeded to some extent. Suspicions began to thin. At the beginning of August, Jesse and Frank appeared openly, albeit warily, in Kearney. "They were heavily armed, and well mounted," noted a correspondent to the *Liberty Tribune*. "They soon left." But Clay County was still not safe for the now-notorious brothers. True, the local Radicals had been driven from power in 1868, but the resurgent Democrats in the county were all old Unionists. William G. Garth, once a captain in the Provisional EMM, now served in the state legislature; neither Sheriff Moss nor Deputy Thomason had any sympathy for the bushwhackers-turned-bandits.[17]

The Samuel family still fretted for Jesse's life. "I heard Mrs. Samuels, his mother, ask the prayers of the Baptist church in this town in 1870," recalled Dr. W. H. Ridge of Kearney a dozen years later. "I believe it was for her erring boy, Jesse. . . . Susie James made one of the most touching appeals to heaven for him that I ever heard made in any church, in the New Hope Baptist Church in 1870." Under the circumstances, it was hardly strange that Jesse departed for Texas in August 1870 (as he later claimed, in one of his few statements about himself that ring true). He had been there in the winter of 1864–65, when he had gone south with Clement. And the Younger clan was spending much of its time in Dallas County, where Cole's younger brother John killed Deputy Sheriff Charles H. Nichols on January 15, 1871.

A fugitive could easily disappear in Texas, especially one who was comfortable in the saddle. The cattle business was booming, offering no-questions-asked employment on the long drives to the railhead towns in Kansas. In February 1871, the James brothers returned home through the Indian Territory, perhaps to visit Shelby's farm in Lafayette County, where

Edwards was to wed Mary Virginia Plattenburg on March 28. About the same time, Jesse began to furtively court the quiet Zerelda Mimms, who had cared for him when he was bedridden after being shot through his lung. The affair would have been a psychoanalyst's playground: Zee was not only Jesse's first cousin; she had been named for his mother.[18]

Frank began his own surreptitious courtship around this time, of a schoolteacher named Anna, or Annie, Ralston, who lived with her father, Samuel, near Independence. The two apparently met at a racetrack near Kansas City. Horse racing was an intense passion with both of the James brothers, a natural interest for men who lived by the speed of their mounts, and Anna shared it. "I would call on Anna in the late evening and leave before dawn," Frank recalled many years later, "and this arrangement worked well for some time."

A reporter later asked Samuel Ralston if he had had any inkling of Frank's intentions toward his daughter. "Not the least in the world," the father replied. "Frank James, however, was an occasional visitor at my house after the war, and from 1870 [to 1874] . . . was at the house perhaps a half dozen times. The idea that he wanted my daughter for his wife, or that she would accept him never entered my head. I know all about his actions and doings during the war and didn't want such a man for my son-in-law."[19]

AMID THE EARNEST protestations of innocence, the banditry continued. On June 3, 1871, four horsemen rode into the town of Corydon, Iowa. Two of them were the James men; the third was Clell Miller, the fellow veteran of Anderson's band who had been captured in Bloody Bill's final battle in 1864. The fourth was Cole Younger. The men's appearance in Iowa was not entirely a novelty. At least once before, during the war, a bushwhacker crew had raided the state. This time, by accident or design, the bandits arrived on a day when the famous orator Henry Clay Dean had come to speak, and virtually the entire population had jammed into the yard of the Methodist church to hear him.[20]

Dean, wrote Mark Twain, was "a volcano" who "drew farmers to his stump from fifty miles around."[21] With his shouts and jests echoing down Corydon's deserted streets, the four horsemen quietly rode to the bank, where they convinced the cashier, the lone occupant, to hand over the esti-mated $6,000 that sat in the safe. Then they rode to the churchyard. The mass of people sat spellbound as the orator bellowed on, and still no one paid any attention to the outlaws. Finally one of the bandits could stand no more, and interrupted the thundering Dean.

They had just robbed the bank, he announced. "They shook the stolen money at the crowd," reported one newspaper, "defying pursuit."[22] The

disbelieving audience turned back to the famous speaker with great irritation. The bandits "took their departure with the utmost coolness," claimed
one man, "loudly cursing the 'damned Yanks' for cowards as they left."[23]
Not until the frightened cashier was discovered did the people of Corydon
understand what had happened.

The bank officials immediately sent a telegram to Chicago, requesting
the services of Pinkerton's National Detective Agency. The company's
founder, Allan Pinkerton, promptly dispatched his son Robert to the scene.
In the meantime, the county sheriff organized a large posse and set out in
pursuit. The bandits escaped across the state line. Over the next two days,
they rode south, stopping with friends and supporters, as they had when
they were guerrillas.

On June 5, the robbers relaxed around the dinner table in the home of
George Lee, in a part of Daviess County known as Civil Bend, just northwest of Gallatin. Somehow they learned that a few of their pursuers were
approaching the house. Immediately the James brothers and their companions raced out the door for the stable. The posse opened fire, but the bandits found shelter. In their excitement, the attackers quickly emptied their
weapons. As soon as the shooting dropped off, the robbers threw open the
stable doors and galloped outside, firing rapidly as they went. Someone in
the posse let loose with a shotgun blast that sent a bandit reeling in his saddle, forcing him to drop his coat and a revolver as his hat flew off his head.
The robbers escaped, riding toward the heavy timber along the railroad
between the towns of Kidder and Cameron, but a member of the posse
picked up the fallen coat and found it stained with blood.[24]

One of the men who studied that red-spattered garment was Robert
Pinkerton. He had evidently caught the first train from Chicago, and he
and the sheriff had continued on the robbers' trail after the rest of the posse
turned back at the Missouri border. Being a party of only two men, however, they had been unable to stop the bandits from escaping at Civil Bend;
afterward, the sheriff, whose horse had been shot by the outlaws, returned
home (most likely catching the train at Cameron), while Pinkerton continued the search alone. He tracked the crew to the Missouri River, "and spent
several days in the vicinity," his brother William reported a decade later,
"acquainting himself with the history of the men who were engaged in the
expedition. During the progress of his investigation he visited the house of
Mrs. Samuels, the mother of the James brothers, and called on several persons who were intimately connected with the gang." He failed to learn
anything of use, however, and when the bank called off the hunt he
returned empty-handed.[25]

Despite Pinkerton's failure, there seemed to be little doubt that Jesse and Frank James had led the raid. "From a description of the robbers it is believed that the James boys, the Gallatin bank robbers, are of the party," reported a newspaper in Hamilton, just south of Gallatin. "They seemed to know every inch of the ground, and to be familiar with the names of parties along the road." On their way to and from Iowa, they had charted their course along the railroads that cut through the woods and untrafficked backcountry—just as they had in December 1869.[26]

Almost immediately, Jesse and Edwards began a new publicity campaign, beginning with another letter to the *Kansas City Times,* dated June 24, 1871. This time, however, Jesse adopted a markedly different tone from that of the previous year. Now his words were explicitly, even harshly, political. "I have just seen an article in the Lexington *Register,*" he began, "charging myself and my brother Frank with robbing a bank in Iowa." This complaint immediately staked out a partisan approach, since the *Register* was vehemently Republican (its owner later shot the editor of a Democratic paper in a political brawl). Jesse claimed, as before, that he could prove his innocence by the "best citizens in Missouri," but there was no point in doing so. The year before, he wrote, "the degraded Radical party criticised my *alibi* and insinuated that I had bribed my witnesses, and just so it would be in this case if I was to prove an *alibi*. But I don't care what the Radical party thinks about me, I would just as soon they would think that I was a robber as not." He concluded with a veiled appeal for political change that dripped with partisan sarcasm. "If times ever get so in Missouri that I can get an impartial trial, I will voluntarily go to Clay county and stand my trial. But I am satisfied that if I was disarmed at present, that those brave Radical heroes in Missouri would try to mob me."[27]

There can be little doubt that Jesse himself wrote at least part of this letter. His accusation of his accusers was characteristic of later missives that were indisputably his own work. "I have no doubt but the authors of some of those pieces published against Frank and I," he wrote, "are the perpetrators of the crimes charged against us."[28] But seeping from the letter is political calculation that bears the mark of Edwards's budding political strategy for Missouri's ex-Confederates.

In the year since Jesse's previous letter, Missouri's politics had passed through a revolution. Not only had the Radicals lost power, but, even more important, secessionists now had the vote. The change had begun within the Republicans' own councils. Against the weakening opposition of Charles Drake, party elders had agreed to a proposal by the old Planter's House group to put a referendum on the ballot in 1870 to allow former rebels to vote and serve on juries. The strain of the dispute, however, had split the Republicans in two. The Radical stalwarts had put Governor McClurg back up for reelection, but the Planter's House forces had created the new Liberal Republican Party, nominating B. Gratz Brown for chief executive.* The Democrats had shrewdly adopted a "possum policy," declining to post their own gubernatorial candidate. Since the Liberals would reenfranchise tens of thousands of likely Democratic voters, they quietly supported Brown, and let the Republicans destroy themselves.

The Democratic plan succeeded brilliantly. In a desperate play for conservative support, McClurg had let it be known that he would look kindly on a lenient application of the Oath in the voter registration for 1870, but the result was a virtual Democratic sweep in the races for Congress and the state legislature. The removal of restrictions on secessionists had easily passed, and Brown had routed McClurg. "I recognize," Brown had declared on November 14, 1870, "that my obligations are in the largest measure due to the Democratic party."[29]

As a statewide force, the Radicals were dead. Legions of former rebels would return to the ballot box in the next election, 1872, virtually guaranteeing an electoral landslide for the Democrats over the divided Republicans. Ironically, this made it the perfect time for Jesse James's harshly political attack on the virtually powerless Radicals. The next political struggle loomed *within* the Democratic Party, between Unionists and old rebels. "The Missouri populace now created a worldview in which race, region, and above all wartime allegiance defined their sense of identity," writes historian Christopher Phillips. "Out of the anger and betrayal of the wartime experience a Confederate memory was emerging."[30]

In cultural terms, Edwards had been fighting for a rebel resurgence since his return from Mexico, starting with *Shelby and His Men* and continuing with editorials, stories, even poems that exalted Confederates. Now he could open a political front in this campaign. Kentucky had already shown the way. There the Confederates had taken control of the Democratic Party early on, repudiating the values of Reconstruction and turning the state into a model of postwar white supremacy. It was an example that made Missouri's Unionists increasingly nervous and its secessionists increasingly hopeful.[31]

The explicitly political phrasing of Jesse's 1871 letter echoes Edwards's own editorial language. The year before, the bandit had written in generic language: "I never will surrender to be mobbed by a set of bloodthirsty poltroons."[32] Now he paired the word "mob" with "Radical," a reminder of the once ubiquitous term for the armed groups that had harassed secessionists in the 1866 campaign. He condemned the Republicans as "degraded," a white-supremacist code word for those who mixed the races.

---

*Under the constitution of 1865, the governor's term had been reduced to two years.

Most important, he now specifically blamed the Radicals for turning him into a fugitive, for hounding him unjustifiably. And in the midst of these charges, he winked at his audience, saying that he did not care if the Radicals thought he was a robber or not. It was the beginning of a remarkable—and remarkably successful—attempt to foster cognitive dissonance among the secessionist public. He was an innocent martyr, he announced, a victim of Radical vindictiveness; at the same time, he presented himself as a figure of defiance, a dangerous man who would never be taken alive. The old rebels could look at Jesse James and mutter, "You poor, persecuted boy—let those damned Radicals have it."

It was the beginning of Jesse's rise from common criminal to symbolic hero, of a legend that resonated with the lives of Missouri's secessionists. He and Edwards began to project a glorified version of what all the rebels felt they had endured in war and Reconstruction. The mythical Jesse James they created refused to apologize for fighting for a just cause; he refused to lay down his arms and self-respect, and was being persecuted as a result.

As a rising figure in the Democratic Party, Edwards did not want to offend conservatives who had fought for the Federal cause. Instead, he made the Radicals into a proxy for all of Missouri's Unionists, creating an ideologically safe way to arouse rebel fervor. Edwards wanted to mobilize former secessionists within his party to establish a Confederate identity in a state that had divided against itself.

For Missouri's ex-Confederates, the Republican Party was still seen as a force of oppression. Political violence by angry Radical organizations still sputtered here and there in the countryside.[33] Far more important, the Republicans remained firmly in power in the nation's capital. From 1870 on, Congress reacted sharply to racial violence in Dixie. It created the Justice Department, for example, and launched a series of Enforcement Acts; in April 1871, it passed the most potent of these measures, the Ku Klux Klan Act. The Grant administration initiated an aggressive new legal offensive against white paramilitary groups, eventually deploying troops in South Carolina to attack the state's deeply rooted Klan; the same issue of the *Richmond Conservator* that reprinted Jesse James's letter also announced the start of such prosecutions in Tennessee. In Missouri, the state that had waged its war-within-a-war, where every wound went unhealed, all these national issues struck home.[34]

AFTER DEFYING THE crowd in Iowa, the James brothers learned that bravado had its price. Frank had almost certainly caught a blast of heavy buckshot in the gunfight at Civil Bend. He appeared at Jo Shelby's farm in Lafayette County about that time, barely able to stay in the saddle. "He was bleeding from the lungs," Shelby later testified, "and Dr. Orear was attending him. . . . He was at my house some sixty or eighty days."[35] Jesse lived quietly during the succeeding months, as Frank recovered from the wound. While the gang was dispersed, one of them fell into the hands of the law. "Old Mose Miller's son Clell was hung a few days since for robbing a bank in Iowa," wrote a Liberty resident on March 8, 1872. "They caught him and he acknowledged the crime, and they hung him on the spot."[36]

The reports of Miller's death were nonsense. He was lured into a trap by a detective "under pretense of engaging with him in stealing some horses," the *Liberty Tribune* reported, then was captured, dispatched to Iowa, and tried for the Corydon robbery—but a jury acquitted him.[37] It is difficult to know for certain if he was actually guilty. The gang now had even less structure than a wartime band of bushwhackers. Given the long months that separated their raids, the crew took on a somewhat new shape with each robbery, drawing from a small pool of relatives and former guerrillas. And even though the talkative, letter-writing Jesse represented the public face of the bandits, it would be a mistake simply to deem him the leader. When they made a strike, in a group numbering a half-dozen at most, the battle-tested Frank and Jesse and Cole Younger most likely formed a criminal cooperative, with no man issuing orders to the rest.

Not until April 1872 did they gather for their next exploit. Again they selected Kentucky, where they had so many hiding places among family and friends. Their target was a bank in the town of Columbia in Adair County, in precisely the center of the state. With practiced caution, they rode carefully through the countryside, scouting their routes, resting their horses, posing as livestock buyers. The local residents who noticed them remembered five well-dressed men in expensive new saddles, sitting astride unusually fine horses.

On April 27, three of these men spent the night in Russell Springs, leaving the next morning for the vicinity of Columbia. Two others, representing themselves as brothers, spent Saturday night at a boardinghouse belonging to Jack Webb, fifteen miles from the town. Observers described one of this pair as a tall, sandy-haired fellow who was unusually talkative, riding an excellent sorrel horse; his sibling sported dark hair and a goatee, and was "very erect, carries his head up." The next morning, a local resident reported, "one of them . . . was very intently engaged studying a pocket-map, which he carried with him, and which, Mr. Webb says, seemed to have all the roads in the state on it. The other was apparently of a devotional turn of mind, and spent the morning reading *Pilgrim's Progress* and talking about Scripture." With bloodshed only hours away, it appears that the gregarious, outwardly devout Jesse James delved into his father's favorite author, while his studious brother prepared for the consequences of their impending sins by planning their escape route.[38]

That night, the five bandits rendezvoused eight miles from Columbia. One of them reported the results of a reconnaissance he had made that day. He had gone into Page's drugstore, just behind the bank, purchased a few things, and asked to be shown the water closet. From there he had been able to view the rear of the bank building, barely thirty feet away. The next morning, they dressed in their customary finery—the press would describe them as "well-dressed men, in dark frock coats"—saddled their horses, and rode into town. The highway they traveled fed directly into the street where the bank could be found. Jesse and two others reined their horses into an alley adjacent to their target and dismounted. Cole Younger and the remaining outlaw rode on a short distance to the public square and posted themselves on either side of the courthouse, where they had a commanding view.

The trio in the alley tied up their horses, pulled off their saddlebags, and opened the door to the bank. Inside they saw cashier R. A. C. Martin, who leaned against the front of the counter as he conversed with three other men: merchant William H. Hudson, circuit court clerk James T. Page, and state representative James Garnett. "Good evening," the foremost bandit said politely—then he reached under the saddlebags draped over his left arm, pulled out a revolver, and fired at Martin. The muzzle was so close to the cashier's chest that the flame from the erupting gunpowder singed his clothing as the bullet tore through his body just below his left armpit. Martin toppled face first to the floor, and his three companions leaped for the door. The shooter whirled and fired at Hudson, who knocked the barrel aside at the last instant, the blast burning his hand as the round went wide.

Outside, Younger and his comrade fired wildly into the air as they ordered everyone off the street. "By this means," the *Louisville Courier-Journal* reported, "they conveyed the impression that they were a large number of men, as no one dared to look out and see." Only one citizen dared to fire at Younger, but the Kentuckian quickly retreated to safety.

In the bank, meanwhile, the three bandits dragged the mortally wounded cashier into the vault and leaned him against the locked burglar-proof safe. Columbia resident W. W. Morris could hear their muffled demands drifting across the narrow space between the bank and Page's drugstore, where he listened and watched at a window. What Morris could not hear—and what the bandits could not know—was that Martin was keeping a vow he had made years before, when he had heard of the Russellville robbery. If the same thing happened to him, he had told his friends, the robbers would have to cross his dead body to get his bank's money. As conscientious as he was determined, he had carefully kept the safe sealed at all times, with almost all the cash and the most valuable bonds inside. Now, moments away from death, he stood by his words and refused to open the lock.

Looking down the alley, Morris saw Jesse James—"a sandy-haired man," as he called him, "seeming very much excited"—run out to his horse and mount. "For God's sake, hurry," Jesse shouted to his companions. "Come along and leave the thing." The two others, having forced open a small iron box and emptied it, came darting out. In a moment they united with their fellows and galloped away. They were seen heading for Bardstown, home of their old comrades, the Pence brothers.

Behind them, the countryside erupted into a panic, as one innocent man after another fell under suspicion and was arrested. From the descriptions, Detective D. G. Bligh of Louisville was convinced that the bandit in the square, described as a "burly fellow" with a "roman nose," was the same fellow who had led the Russellville raid—Cole Younger. But neither Younger nor any of the other robbers would ever be arrested for what happened that day in Columbia.[39]

IN KANSAS CITY in September 1872, John Edwards's headlines and editorials in the *Times*, like the conversations heard on street corners, in taverns, in barbershops, and on church lawns, revolved around the presidential election less than two months away. For the first time since 1860, Missouri's secessionists would be able to cast ballots, and the die-hard rebel Edwards urged his readers to vote for a once-hated abolitionist, *New York Tribune* editor Horace Greeley, Liberal Republican candidate for president.*

Few bodies have represented the folly of wise men better than the Liberal Republican Party. Born in the Missouri experiment of 1870 that had elected B. Gratz Brown as governor, the party had become a national force in September 1871 after Senator Carl Schurz delivered a pivotal speech in Nashville. The men of the North who flocked to the Liberal standard saw themselves as the "best men." Educated at Harvard, Yale, and similar schools, the party leaders were men who made investments, who traveled abroad, who read *The Nation*, the *North American Review*, and other highbrow journals of public affairs. For the Liberals, elitism was no vice.

"Universal suffrage can only mean in plain English the government of ignorance and vice," wrote Charles Francis Adams, Jr.—grandson of President John Quincy Adams—in the *North American Review* in 1869.[40] Just what, the Liberals asked, had democracy wrought? A political spoils

---

*Missouri governor B. Gratz Brown was the Liberal candidate for vice president.

system that turned public offices into a tool for perpetuating party power, and a federal government that continued to grow at an explosive rate (between 1871 and 1881, the national bureaucracy would double). Federal taxes imposed to fight the Confederacy continued with the peace, and so did attendant graft. The supervisor of internal revenue for upstate New York earned an estimated $500,000 a year in bribes and kickbacks—twenty times the president's salary—and in 1868, the superintendent of internal revenue in St. Louis was indicted on corruption charges. In 1872, the Crédit Mobilier scandal erupted when it was revealed that this dummy construction company had vastly overcharged the federally subsidized transcontinental railroad as it was built across the West; shares had been given to key congressmen to cover the scheme. Though the operation had ceased after the railroad's completion in 1869, the scandal tainted Speaker of the House James G. Blaine and Grant's vice president, Schuyler Colfax.[41]

Grant had done almost nothing to reform the system. His administration had begun with an episode that left him badly singed, though the president himself had done nothing wrong. In 1869, railroad barons Jay Gould and Jim Fisk had lobbied the new chief executive to keep the greenback cheap against gold. Ever since the introduction of legal-tender paper money, a market in New York had existed to exchange greenbacks for gold. Since gold was the only medium of exchange used in foreign trade, driving up the price of gold would devalue American currency; a cheap greenback would mean more exports of American grain, which would mean more business for the Erie Railroad, which was controlled by Gould and Fisk. The pair had also intended to make a killing through old-fashioned speculation. Since the Treasury Department was the biggest player in the gold market, they recruited Abel Corbin, the president's brother-in-law, to persuade Grant to stifle government gold sales; they tried to manipulate the chief Treasury official in New York for inside information; they even set up a gold account for First Lady Julia Dent Grant. The president, however, had refused to be a party to their plans, and he finally ordered a large sale of U.S. gold to stop the wild financial speculation.[42] But Grant seemed to draw few lessons from this bitter incident. He proceeded to dole out public offices to political supporters and his wife's many relations; by the end of 1871, he had named some twenty-three in-laws and relatives to government posts.[43]

Schurz, Brown, Charles F. Adams, Jr., Henry Adams, and other Liberals thought they knew a better way. They launched their new national party on a platform of civil service reform, free trade, and smaller, less intrusive, more economical government. But their elitism led them down a dark road. Distrusting government power and even democracy itself, they pledged an end to Reconstruction. In a state of self-deceit, they had convinced themselves that white-supremacist violence, as Eric Foner writes, "resulted from the exclusion from government of men of intelligence and culture," the former slaveowning planters. The Liberals opposed the Ku Klux Klan Act and spoke of restoring "home rule" in the South. "Home rule" was a favorite phrase at the time, masking the fact that the region had *too much* home rule in the eyes of most whites, because the black population—a majority or near majority in several states—finally had a voice in public affairs.[44]

Idealists, it seems, will often fall prey to cynics. Ex-Confederate Democrats such as John Edwards quickly seized on the Liberal Republican movement as a means of destroying the nation's new commitment to racial fairness. The very idea of running Horace Greeley for president had originated with Peter Donan, the rabidly rebel editor of the *Lexington Caucasian,* who had first suggested it in October 1871. But this pragmatic extension of the "possum policy" ceded nothing in terms of ideology. Donan continued to rail against the "yankonigger bayonet amendments" to the Constitution that had brought freedom and civil rights for African Americans. To undo Reconstruction, he told his readers, he would "stand by the Devil, on a platform of coagulated hell's scum." Edwards, on the other hand, like many Southern Democrats, picked up the themes of extravagance and corruption. When the Liberal Republicans held a large meeting in Sedalia, for example, Edwards stressed how the speech makers had attacked Grant's "corrupt, tyrannical administration" and discussed "the carpet-bag dynasties of the Southern States in all their terrible and tyrannical deformities."[45]

Amid this political tumult, the second annual Industrial Exposition started in Kansas City on September 23. Tens of thousands of people crowded into the city on horses, in carriages, in tightly packed trains. They pushed through the gate, paying fifty cents each to attend the grandest of some forty-four town and county fairs that sprouted each fall in Missouri. Those who braved the gale-force winds that tore off hats and rippled skirts on the first two days could crowd into the Main Hall, or walk appreciatively through the Fine Art Hall, shout over the drone of engines in the Power Hall, bask in the perfume of the Floral Hall, or flock to the track, where horses thudded around the dust-blown course in race after race.[46]

By the fourth day, Thursday, the weather was splendid, and the town virtually shut down by noon. Only businesses serving food remained open as train after train disgorged passengers from St. Louis, Iowa, Illinois, Kansas, even Texas. "Between the crowded sidewalks," reported Edwards's newspaper, "rushed hither and thither saddle horses, carriages, omnibuses, buggies, sulkies, phaetons, drags, and every imaginable variety of vehicle, drawn by every imaginable variety of horseflesh." The publication declared, with only slight exaggeration, that sixty thousand people pushed through the gates that day.

As the sun began to set, three mounted men guided their horses through the dense crowd that surged out of the Twelfth Street gate. They wore masks of checked cloth pulled up under their eyes. The largest of the men dismounted, strode to the ticket window, and seized the cash box as his comrades warned away the startled crowd. The big man crammed the money into his pockets and returned to his horse; then the ticket seller impulsively darted out and grabbed him. One of the mounted bandits leveled his pistol and fired, wounding a little girl in the calf. The man with the cash swung back up into the saddle, and the three men spurred toward the woods east of town. They carried away $978; if they had arrived thirty minutes earlier, before the fair treasurer had collected the booth's funds, they would have garnered some $12,000.[47]

It was a remarkable crime, especially considering the large special police force that guarded the fairgrounds. But the deed itself could not compare with Edwards's front-page story about it in the *Kansas City Times*. The frothing editor devoted most of the article to high-pitched hyperbole. "It was one of those exhibitions of superb daring that chills the blood and transfixes the muscles of the looker-on with a mingling of amazement, admiration, and horror," he wrote. "It was one of those rare instances when it seems as though Death stood in the panoply of the flesh and exhaled a PETRIFYING TERROR from his garments. It was a deed so high-handed, so diabolically daring and so utterly in contempt of fear that we are bound to admire it and revere its perpetrators for the very enormity of their outlawry."[48]

Edwards's enthusiasm was not entirely unique. Most newspapers, even those with little sympathy for the bandits, habitually described their deeds as "daring" crimes, conducted with "cool audacity" that "has never been surpassed," no matter how many had come before.[49] In fact, armed robbery remained quite rare, despite the flood of pistols that clattered across the county after the Civil War. Bankers worried about burglars, not gunmen, and with good reason. The professional safecracker and confidence man dominated both press reports and popular literature about crime. As late as 1876, noted detective Phil Farley declared that violence went against the nature of the American criminal. Most outlaws, it seems, lacked the peculiar training for organized holdups that the Missourians had received in guerrilla warfare.[50]

But only Edwards would have called on the public to "revere" the bandits. His vehemence on the subject strongly suggests that he already knew who had carried out the crime, and that their names were Younger and

James. Indeed, his initial story on the robbery marked the first stage of a multipart effort to depict the outlaws as Confederate heroes, an effort that became increasingly political as the election approached.

The second phase came just two days later, with one of the most famous pieces Edwards would ever write. In an editorial titled "The Chivalry of Crime," Edwards drew a sharp distinction between armed robbery and skulking crimes such as burglary. But where most Americans snapped up books about the professional thief and scorned the gunman, Edwards exalted the holdup man. "There are things done for money and for revenge of which the daring of the act is the picture and the crime is the frame it may be set in," he wrote. "A feat of stupendous nerve and fearlessness that makes one's hair rise to think of it, with a condiment of crime to season it, becomes chivalric; poetic; superb."

His premise established, he now placed a name on these "chivalric" bandits: bushwhackers. "There are men in Jackson, Cass, and Clay—a few there are left—who learned to dare when there was no such word as quarter in the dictionary of the Border," he continued. "Men who have carried their lives in their hands so long that they do not know how to commit them over into the keeping of the laws and regulations that exist now. And these men sometimes rob. But it is always in the glare of day and in the teeth of the multitude." Guerrilla-bandits such as this belonged to another time, he wrote. "The nineteenth century with its Sybaric civilization is not the social soil for men who might have sat with ARTHUR at the Round Table, ridden at tourney with Sir LAUNCELOT or worn the colors of GUINEVERE."[51] The medieval touches reflected Edwards's romantic temperament, of course, but they were also well suited to the canvas of his times. Secessionists often imagined themselves in such courtly colors. After the war, for example, Southern relief societies in Missouri hosted chivalric tournaments as fund-raising events.[52] By painting the outlaws as knights, Edwards presented them as the embodiments of the Confederate ideal.

For two weeks, Edwards tapped out a steady drumbeat of partisan political stories, mixing support for Greeley with calls to old rebels to mobilize come November. The Radicals still plotted to use the registration laws where they could, he warned; Democrats must remain ready.[53] Then, on October 15, he unleashed the third wave in his glorification—and politicization—of the Kansas City fair outlaws. It came in the form of a letter— one strikingly reminiscent of Jesse James's notes—from one of the bandits. It openly adopted Edwards's themes. "Some editors call us thieves. We are not thieves—we are bold robbers," the anonymous author wrote. "I am proud of the name, for Alexander the Great was a bold robber, and Julius Caesar, and Napoleon Bonaparte." He added that he and his crew "rob the rich and give to the poor," and he signed off as Jack Shepherd, Dick Turpin, and Claude Duval—all famous bandits of European folklore, mentioned in Edwards's previous writings.

In later decades, the romantic aspects of the letter would draw the attention of scholars and popular writers. Here one of the outlaws—most likely Jesse James—is casting himself as Robin Hood, a bandit who was a great man, who righted the upended scales of justice. But the attention would be somewhat misplaced. This famous note was, in fact, most remarkable for its vicious ruthlessness and its explicit political content. "We never kill," the author wrote, "only in self-defense. . . . But a man who is a d——d enough fool to refuse to open a safe or a vault when he is covered with a pistol ought to die. There is no use for a man to try to do anything when an experienced robber gets the go on him. If he gives the alarm, or resists, or refuses to unlock, he gets killed." The writer devoted much of his space to a thundering denunciation of the Republican Party and administration: "Just let a party of men commit a bold robbery, and the cry is hang them, but Grant and his party can steal millions, and it is all right. . . . It hurts me very much to be called a thief. It makes me feel like they were trying to put me on a par with Grant and his party." Placed in full context, the Robin Hood passage turns out to be a partisan attack. "Please rank me with [Alexander the Great and Napoleon] and not with the Grantites. Grant's party has no respect for any one. They rob the poor and rich, and we rob the rich and give to the poor. . . . I will close by hoping that Horace Greeley will defeat Grant, and then I can make an honest living, and then I will not have to rob, as taxes will not be so heavy."[54]

In this, the climax of the bandit-glorification campaign, Jesse James (we presume) endorsed Greeley for president. It was a masterful conclusion to a skillfully conducted propaganda effort. First came the dramatic deed, then the steady buildup of the outlaws as noble exemplars of Confederate manhood, and finally an explicit partisan call from the bandit leader to mobilize the rebel vote. He even excused his actions with a line torn straight from Democratic speeches, blaming Republican corruption and government extravagance for his bandit career.* October 15, 1872, marked the maturation of Jesse James into a self-conscious political symbol.

No direct proof exists that Jesse was the author. This letter, however, appeared right in the middle of a series of notes he wrote for publication in Edwards's newspapers, beginning in 1870 and continuing for years to come. Time would show that it was he, of all the outlaws, who was most obsessed with his public image, who sought to push himself into the news.

---

*This was the essence of the "New Departure" criticism of Reconstruction, an approach developed by some Democrats to shift attention away from racial violence in the South; see Eric Foner, *Reconstruction, 1863–1877: America's Unfinished Revolution* (New York: Harper & Row, 1988), 415.

"He read the newspapers constantly," one relative later noted, "and frequently wrote letters. He would dash off a letter without pausing once." And more than one of his confederates would observe that he planned robberies with an eye on the public reaction.[55]

After Jesse's previous crimes and missives to the press, the public quickly connected him to the robbery at the fair. Suspicion grew into general belief when Jim Chiles, a former guerrilla, casually mentioned in Liberty that he had seen Jesse, along with Cole Younger and his brother John, outside Kansas City on the day of the crime. This led to the denouement of Edwards's publicity effort: the creation of cognitive dissonance, so that the outlaws would be admired as skilled and desperate men, yet considered innocent of any specific charge. On October 20, 1872, the *Kansas City Times* published a letter from Jesse, signed in his own name, in which he once again claimed that he could prove his whereabouts at the time of the robbery. He specifically cited Chiles as an accusing witness and warned him to retract his statements. Five days later, Chiles's denial duly appeared in the *Times*. "I should not have appeared in print," he wrote, sounding distinctly nervous. "I am engaged in attending to my own business."[56]

Edwards and the James brothers would take the details of their alliance to their graves. None of them would ever reveal if Edwards wrote any of the lines in Jesse's letters, or if they told him of their robberies in advance, or how specific their goals were when they waged a coordinated publicity campaign like the one in 1872. But they clearly had an alliance, and its politics and importance could not be mistaken. It if were not for Edwards, Jesse James would probably have passed into obscurity with hundreds of other criminals; and were it not for Jesse James, Edwards's burgeoning role as a Confederate spokesman within the Democratic Party would never have loomed so large.

Under the influence of Edwards, age, and notoriety, Jesse James had grown in sophistication and ambition, both criminal and political. In the aftermath of the Kansas City fair, Jesse and his comrades would make a dramatic new departure, and strike at the very arteries of the Union: the railroads.

CHAPTER THIRTEEN

Invisible Empires

N OW FAMOUS BUT FEARED, Jesse James could no longer live like other men. With each headline, he became more and more isolated. Old neighbors thought of him differently now, and it irked him, especially when the neighbors were young, single women. "By the way, what do you think of Jesse's letter? Would like to see me and wants me to write," scribbled Bettie A. Scruggs to her brother on April 3, 1873. "Oughtn't he to be hanged? He says the time is not far off when he can prove to the world that those charges against him are false, and that he is neither a robber or a murderer. What can he have in mind? I guess he can make his *demonstrations* when I write." Clearly Scruggs believed the worst about the local boy, though she was flattered by his attention.[1]

Jesse's little-known correspondence with her reflects his penchant for letter writing—more evidence that John Edwards had not been the sole creator of the bandits' press campaign, and had not authored Jesse's published letters (though he may have edited them). But Jesse's private note reveals something else about him: in the wake of the Kansas City fair robbery, he had internalized his public persona. Ultimately it was the grandiosity of the image he projected that left Scruggs puzzled and amused.

But, in fact, a sense of meaning had crept back into his life, an echo of the purpose he had felt during the war, until the death of Archie Clement. By 1873, it appears that Edwards's editorials rang in Jesse's ears as he plunged deeper into his underground life. He seems to have truly believed that he was "chivalric; poetic; superb," that his crimes were "for money *and* for revenge."* Call it rationalization, call it empty self-justification, but Missouri's former rebels had suffered twelve years of military defeat and political repression, and many craved revenge of any kind.

*Emphasis added.

In the months leading up to the election of 1872, Edwards had pounded the rebel war drums in the *Kansas City Times*. He devoted front-page stories to convicted Ku Klux Klansmen, calling them "Victims of Grant's Bayonet Law."[2] He railed against Republican congressional candidate and editor of the rival *Kansas City Journal of Commerce* Robert T. Van Horn, deriding Horn's followers as "that coterie of militia officers."[3] On election day itself, he howled in an apocalyptic frenzy about the need to unseat President Grant. "Without victory, the cause of humanity is set back for twenty years. The work of imperialism and centralization goes on unchecked," he raged. "Democrats of Jackson county . . . show to the world how you remember tyranny and how you revenge yourselves upon your oppressors. . . . Run up the black flag. Give no quarter. Strike, that the world may know how Democratic vengeance lingers yet in the bosoms of Missourians."[4]

Grant, of course, won, which was a matter of great distress to the white South and Southern-minded Missourians. But the Democrats swept the state elections. Having used the Liberal Republicans to defeat the Radicals two years earlier, they discarded their now-useless allies. Democrat Silas Woodson went to Jefferson City as governor, and his party took firm control of the legislature. It was a moment savored by all the old rebels, who had voted in their first election since 1860. Secessionist newspapers, including the *Lexington Caucasian* and the *Cass County Courier,* demanded that a Confederate veteran be named to the U.S. Senate; they even suggested that secessionist legislators abandon the party caucus and unite with Liberals to defeat the Democrats' dominant Unionist faction. The enthusiasm was so exuberant that it began to make even Edwards worry that the party would fall apart.[5]

On the morning of May 27, 1873, four men held up the Ste. Genevieve Savings Association in southeastern Missouri. The old French town of Ste. Genevieve was located near the most important stronghold of the Missouri Ku Klux Klan.[6] The robbers had rebel politics on their minds that day: as they galloped off, they fired in the air and shouted, "Hurrah for Hildebrand!"—a tribute to Samuel S. Hildebrand, a Confederate guerrilla as notorious in this section of the state as Quantrill was on the western border. On June 3, 1865, Governor Fletcher had proclaimed a $300 reward for his capture, but the old bushwhacker had lived long enough to publish his memoirs in 1870. A few months before the Ste. Genevieve robbery, however, Hildebrand had been shot to death by an Illinois lawman, who duly received the long-standing reward.[7]

The St. Louis police would soon identify the James and Younger brothers as the perpetrators.[8] The evidence would never be publicly known, but the cool professionalism and raw daring of the crime pointed to the increasingly famous bandits. On their way out of town, for example, they stopped a traveler headed in the opposite direction and asked him to pick up a box they had left on the road and return it to the bank.[9] Perhaps most telling, however, was the Confederate sloganeering that marked their departure from town.

Symbolism increasingly infused Jesse James's thinking in the months after "The Chivalry of Crime." He never put appearances above plunder, of course, but he and his fellows thought more and more about ways to use their raids to "shake up the country," as Jesse would later put it.[10] And in the summer of 1873, the bandits found a target that equally suited their tastes for booty and bravado: the railroads.

In terms of cash alone, the decision to strike the railroads was ingenious, revealing a knowledge of how money moved through the economy. The nation's financial structure after the Civil War resembled a vast watershed. In the interior were the catchpools—rural banks that collected the capital of farmers and merchants. Country bankers sent much of this money to larger cities, where they placed a large portion of their funds in interest-bearing accounts with other institutions; despite the low return, they were often seen as safer investments than anything to be found in the country-side. This process was mandatory for national banks, which were required by law to maintain reserve accounts with banks in designated cities. In turn, banks in these reserve cities had to maintain accounts with banks in New York. As the nation's money supply poured into the great financial basin of lower Manhattan, bankers there invested much of it in very-short-term, high-interest call loans to brokers, tying the fortunes of the most remote rural communities to the fate of the stock market. The connection worked both ways. In the late fall, country banks drew down their reserve-city deposits as farmers and rural merchants made withdrawals for the flurry of transactions associated with the harvest and its shipment to cities and sea-ports. This annual drain on the money market in New York inevitably led to a shortage of financing on Wall Street; almost every panic on the stock market in the nineteenth century occurred in autumn, during the "moving of the crops," as the process was called.

Starting in the twentieth century, the Federal Reserve system would enormously simplify the large-scale movement of money across the coun-try. The twelve branches of the nation's central bank would hold the reserve accounts of most financial institutions, which would make the set-tling of accounts between them mostly a matter of bookkeeping. In the 1870s, however, banks depended heavily on cash. With clearinghouses restricted to a few large cities, a primary way to make payments and adjust balances between banks was to ship bundles of currency across the land-scape.[11] All year long, physical stocks of money moved toward New York, to return in the fall to the spawning grounds in the countryside. And it all went by rail.

The railroad corporations themselves did not handle shipments of cash; that was left to the express companies, which signed exclusive contracts with the various railways. The United States and Adams Express companies dominated the northeast, the Southern—a wartime spinoff of the Adams—controlled Dixie, and Wells, Fargo & Co. and American Express nearly monopolized business in the West. From offices in countless cities and towns, they moved packages of all kinds—from currency to corpses—via wagon, steamboat, and rail. On the trains, the express material went into the baggage car under the watchful eye of a messenger who traveled alone with the goods. "Do you know what it means to be a messenger?" groaned one of them. "It is to be the whole company—on wheels!" He would track packages, heft them between trains and stations, record deliveries, and update waybills, while riding alone "in a rumble, tumble-down old car," as another messenger wrote, where "mail, baggage, express matter, dirty oil cans, train boxes and trash of all sorts were mixed up together." There he sat, because there sat the cash and valuables, tucked in an iron safe.[12]

By striking the railroads, the Missouri bandits would slice into the monetary pulse of the country. But there was symbolism to consider as well. In 1872, many Missourians had grown indignant at how railways had been financed. Ironically, the anger was the indirect result of the Radicals' efforts to distance the state government from the railroad corporations. The state had shelled out $31,735,840 to build several trunk lines, starting in the 1850s, but all but one of them were bankrupt and incomplete in 1865. In disgust, the Radicals had sold the government's stake immediately after the war, and had written a ban on further state aid into the 1865 constitution.

Counties, towns, and townships leaped into the funding gap, firmly believing that government subsidies for railroads were essential; private investors lacked both the money and the will to build more lines. Meanwhile, a general belief prevailed that railway links would raise land prices, attract immigrants, and give farmers access to distant, lucrative markets. And to a large extent this idea proved to be correct: the areas where tracks were laid grew the fastest in the decade after the war, in terms of population and land value. Aided by a newly invigorated general incorporation law, more than forty local railroad companies were formed in Missouri between 1866 and 1873, backed by $17,199,950 in local government bonds, as country folk looked forward to high-speed connections to the great railroad network that wrapped the country together.[13]

For many, the trains never came. Corruption, incompetence, and overoptimism about the potential profits left some lines half-finished, others entirely unbuilt. More than $2 million was paid to companies that never laid a single rail. Local taxes rose relentlessly; after less than a decade, Missouri's local-government per capita debt amounted to three times that of its seven neighboring states. In August 1871, Ray County stopped paying the interest on its railroad bonds; a dozen other counties soon did the same.[14]

In April 1872, the railroad-bond resistance movement took a dark turn. In Cass County, a ring consisting of county officials and the construction company hired to build the St. Louis & Santa Fe Railroad plotted to issue $229,000 worth of railway bonds that had been authorized in 1860 but never marketed. In a sweetheart deal, the county court changed the subscription from the original beneficiary, the Missouri Pacific, to the St. Louis & Santa Fe and issued them on March 1, 1871. The infuriated public brought pressure to bear, and the county court judges soon found themselves under indictment. After being released on bail, two of them tried to escape to Kansas City by rail; a large, well-organized group of vigilantes stopped their train at the village of Gunn City. The mob shot them (and an innocent friend) to death, and left them beside the tracks.[15]

The fury continued. On April 21, 1873, the U.S. District Court in Jefferson City began hearings in a lawsuit brought by outside investors against thirteen Missouri counties and five towns that had stopped paying interest on their bonds. But angry bondholders were the least of the state's railroad worries. The local lines built after the war put Missourians face-to-face with the most powerful forces in the nation's economy: the great railway corporations, which absorbed many of the local companies. The mighty Atlantic and Pacific Railroad, for example, leased the Missouri Pacific, the Osage Valley and Southern Kansas, the Lexington and St. Louis, the Missouri River Railroad, and several others. Control of these short lines gave the big corporations a monopoly on the business of rural communities, and they used it mercilessly, keeping local rates high to subsidize their competition on trunk lines for long-distance through traffic. Even local lines that remained independent were at the mercy of the giants for outlets to the national railway network.[16]

The power of the great railroads—the first large-scale corporations to emerge in the United States—stunned Americans of all backgrounds and opinions. "Modern society has created a class of artificial beings who bid fair soon to be the masters of their creator," wrote Charles Francis Adams, Jr., in 1869. "It is but a very few years since the existence of a corporation controlling a few millions of dollars was regarded as a subject of grave apprehension, and now this country already contains single organizations which wield a power represented by hundreds of millions."[17] The Chicago, Rock Island, and Pacific Railroad earned more than $7 million in 1873. That figure equaled 1 percent of all the nation's currency and exceeded the total amount of national banknotes circulating in either Missouri or Iowa.[18] And the Rock Island could not compare to the greatest of the great: the Central Pacific, which sat astride California; the Union Pacific, which controlled the transcontinental route; or the Pennsylvania and the New York Central, which dominated the East. Their might was represented in an apocryphal story told later about railroad tycoon Edward H. Harriman. On one occasion he arrived at the court of Emperor Franz Joseph of Austria-Hungary, only to be told that the monarch was running late. Harriman smiled. "I, of all people," he replied, "know the problems of empire."[19]

This power was no abstraction to Missouri farmers. They suffered directly from a conspiracy among the four companies that controlled traffic between the Union Pacific's terminal at Omaha and the cities of Chicago and St. Louis. In 1870, the Rock Island, Council Bluffs, Burlington, and Hannibal and St. Joseph lines organized the Iowa Pool to prevent competition among themselves. They shared roughly half of their revenue and manipulated rates to control the flow of traffic. They saw to it that the route from Omaha to St. Louis, for example, would be as expensive as the longer passage to Chicago. The details of the pool remained a secret, but the public felt its effects. "Foreign capital comes in," stormed John Edwards in an angry editorial, "resulting in [railroad] consolidation, the establishment of through or trunk lines, with through rates of freight and discriminations against the very cities whose means have contributed to build them."[20]

Over the course of 1873, the *Kansas City Times* heralded a new sign of popular resistance: the emergence of the Patrons of Husbandry, better known as the Grange. "At the present time the farmers and producing classes are very greatly oppressed," Edwards wrote on February 19, 1873, "and it is but meet and proper that they should unite and as a body endeavor to bring about a state of affairs more favorable to themselves." New lodges popped up everywhere in rural Missouri, totaling 1,732 within a year of Edwards's editorial—and they spoke out. On July 16, 1873, the Central Council of the Cass County Grange passed a series of resolutions attacking the railroads. "We hold," the Grangers declared, "that a State cannot create a corporation that it cannot thereafter control."[21]

"There are things done for money and for revenge," Edwards had written in his "Chivalry of Crime" editorial, "of which the daring of the act is the picture and the crime is the frame it may be set in." As the summer of 1873 began, Jesse James and his comrades could not help but see that the railroads offered more money, and sweeter revenge, than any target they had hit since Archie Clement's death. All that remained was the daring.

· · ·

THE CAPTAINS OF industry had made it easier to rob the captains of industry. As Jesse and Frank James, Cole Younger, and three colleagues prepared for their next raid, technological advancement spared them the time-consuming process of loading pistols and the need to carry a half-dozen revolvers at a time. The all-in-one metal cartridge, containing per-cussion cap, gunpowder, and lead ball in a single round, had become standard in most firearms (such as the new model .45 caliber Colt's Peace-maker). With reloading made easy, the crew now needed only two pistols each. They also carried long guns: shotguns or lever-action repeating rifles, such as the older Henry or the Winchester introduced that year.[22] But certain necessities remained: securing good horses, mapping the route, reconnoitering the target.

On Monday, July 21, 1873, the bandits trotted up to their destination, an isolated stretch of the Rock Island Railroad between Council Bluffs and Des Moines, deep in Iowa. The location suited their purpose: the track curved sharply here, which would force an engineer to slow down; it sat only two hundred yards from a bridge, in a shallow cut—a dug-out depres-sion—which would allow them to easily control the occupants from the banks above; and it was far from any house or settlement, the nearest being the Adair signal station, some four miles away. It was there that they had begun their work, breaking into a handcar house to steal a crowbar and a hammer. They bent over the tracks, using the tools to pry out a pair of spikes on the northern side. Then they ran a rope through the holes in the rail and hid themselves some fifty feet away. And waited. Waiting was an art they had each learned in the Sni and Fishing River bottoms, and prac-ticed many times in the years since. No technology would ever eliminate the tedium of their work.[23]

At about 8:30 in the evening they heard the chug of the steam engine in the distance, as the five o'clock express train from Omaha approached the Turkey Creek bridge just to the west. The locomotive dragged a coal-filled tender behind it, along with two baggage cars, a smoking car, two more passenger cars, the ladies' car, and, finally, two Pullman sleepers. In that second baggage car, the bandits expected to find the weekly transcontinen-tal express shipment, sent east each Monday night.

They watched the train slow sharply as it approached the curve, its speed slackening to just twenty miles an hour. As it drew close, they yanked on the cord, displacing the rail. Immediately the axles groaned as the engine went into reverse and the air brakes clamped tight. With the train screeching toward the fatal break in the track, the Missourians opened fire, spattering the locomotive with bullets. Then the locomotive slipped off the rails and toppled over. In a roaring crash, the tender upended, spilling its load of coal; the first baggage car jackknifed, crashing onto its side; the next baggage car and the smoking car popped off the rails. Out of the wreck the fireman appeared, dragging the inert form of the engineer.

The six bandits darted forward to their assigned places. Two stood guard outside, one walking along each bank, shooting and cursing. "Get out of sight, damn you," they bellowed at every face that appeared in a door or window, "or we will shoot you."[24] Two others jumped inside to keep an eye on the passengers, and the last two stepped up into the second baggage car.

Eyewitness accounts are rarely completely accurate, but the descriptions that emerged leave no doubt that the James brothers and Cole Younger walked the cars that night. When the crash occurred, the occupants of the express car—Assistant Superintendent H. F. Royce, register clerk O. P. Killingsworth, and express messenger John Burgess—piled into one another, leaving Royce with a bloody nose. As they distentangled themselves, they saw two masked men in the door, one of whom promptly yanked off his disguise. "The one whose face was uncovered was of sandy complexion, full whiskered, and wore a broad brimmed hat," Burgess said.[25] His recollection matched that of a couple who saw the gang without masks a day later. "The man who seemed to be the leader," they reported, had "light hair, blue eyes, heavy sandy whiskers, broad shoulders and a straight, tolerably short nose, a little turned up; a tolerably high, broad forehead, intelligent looking, looked like a tolerably well educated man and did not look like a working man." This was as precise a description of Jesse James as anyone could ever hope for. They went on to identify Frank James, who "looked like a man well educated, and very polite, not inclined to talk much," as well as Cole Younger, "large and portly, but not very fleshy; broad shoulders, form straight, is intelligent looking, with large Roman nose, and . . . made quite a pleasant appearance."[26]

It was Jesse who jumped up into the express car, jerked off his mask with careless bravado, and aimed a revolver at Burgess's head. "If you don't open the safe or give me the key," he snarled, "I'll blow your brains out." Burgess gave him the key. After Jesse swung open the heavy iron door, he found $1,672.57, along with another bag for Wells, Fargo & Co., the express firm. The total take would prove to be $2,337, far less than what he had expected. He picked up a U.S. Mail bag and sliced it open, looked inside, then tossed it away. Again he turned on the express messenger. Where's the rest? he demanded. Burgess could only shake his head. That was all there was, he replied—except for that; he indicated numerous bags jumbled on the floor.[27] It was three and a half tons of precious-metal bullion, on its way from Western mines to the gold market in New York.*

---

*Gold and silver remained legal tender, and could be taken in refined bullion form to a U.S. mint, where it would be turned into coin (though the federal government stopped minting silver in 1873). Large shipments of

Back in the cars, two other bandits walked down the aisle through a cacophony of screaming women and children. "My God! We shall be killed!" they wailed. "We shall be killed!" The men sat quietly, dazed from the collision that had thrown them all to the floor. Only conductor William Smith thought of resistance. He darted ahead of the robbers, trying frantically to borrow a revolver.

In the rear he met the fireman Dennis Foley, who had been shoved back onto the train. "Billy," Foley said sadly, "Jack is dead." Engineer John Rafferty's quick reflexes, he explained, had saved everyone—he had reversed power and closed the brakes as soon as he saw the rail move. But after the locomotive toppled over, Foley found Rafferty lying on top of him, dead. His neck had snapped in the crash.[28]

Perhaps the calmest group that night, apart from the gunmen, was in the last sleeper car. Twenty-eight aristocratic Chinese students rode together at the end of the train, accompanied by two guardians, on their way to New England colleges. Passenger Randolph Knight noticed that they seemed undisturbed by the mayhem, in contrast to the panicked Americans. One of the guardians, Wong Shung, later gave an interview with such aplomb, an Iowa newspaper wryly noted, that "it appears that their general impression was that this is a pretty hilly country."[29]

The robbery took only ten minutes. Having plundered the express safe, the bandits saddled up and galloped off to the south. They left the bullion behind; the enormously heavy bars would only be a hindrance to carry and a labor to unload without attracting attention. They later learned through the press that the large express shipment of currency they had anticipated had gone out the night before.

They rode hard toward Missouri, stopping at farmhouses for meals as they had when they were guerrillas. Behind them, Iowa erupted into a frenzy, as special trains carrying detectives and posses rolled back and forth across their path, urged on by a $5,000 reward offered by the management of the railroad.[30]

The Rock Island robbery reflected the Missouri raiders' rising ambitions, which were quickly rewarded with headlines nationwide. They were not the first to attack a railroad; just three days earlier, the *Kansas City Times* had noted that the derailing of trains for the purposes of theft had become alarmingly frequent, a complaint echoed in the *Railroad Gazette*.[31] The difference was that most such incidents led to pilfering during the

bullion were regularly made from the West to New York, where it was sold for greenbacks in the gold market. The Rock Island shipped 8,138,879 pounds of bullion east in the year ending March 31, 1874; *Annual Report to the President, Directors, and Stockholders of the Chicago, Rock Island, and Pacific Railroad Company*, April 1, 1874 (New York: Clarence Levey & Co., 1874), 25; Richard Franklin Bensel, *Yankee Leviathan: The Origins of Central State Authority in America, 1859–1877* (New York: Cambridge University Press, 1990), 255–60.

chaos of a wreck; the armed occupation of an entire train was a crime on a much larger scale, and it startled the country. Amid all the outrage and breathless excitement, however, most observers missed the most striking thing about this attack: it was a sign that the bandits had embraced the symbolism created by Edwards and Jesse James after the Kansas City fair robbery. Back then, they had tagged on a political message after the fact; this time, word and deed came together.

During the robbery in Iowa, one of the two outlaws in the passenger cars began to quote from the "Jack Shepherd" letter to the *Kansas City Times.* "We're none of your petty thieves; we're bold robbers," he announced, a pistol in each hand. "We're robbing the rich for the poor. We are Grangers. We don't want to hurt you; we're going through the express car."[32] Could anything be more clear? In the rising anger at the railroads, they openly embraced the Robin Hood image, declaring themselves avengers of the working man against the monstrous corporations.

There was one complication, however. The newly symbol-conscious bandits sent another signal that evening in Iowa, one that echoed even more loudly than their words. It was their choice of disguise. When the passengers and crew scrambled off the floor after the crash, they looked up at the doors and saw that their attackers were "masked in full Ku-Klux style."[33]

PLUNDER REMAINED the bandits' prime motivation, but they now displayed a growing determination to make statements with their crimes. After all, this is a large part of why posterity remembers these men out of history's many forgotten gangsters. But the James brothers and their confederates did not yet have a completely coherent political program when they struck the Rock Island Railroad in 1873. Just as individuals often work through their thoughts in the act of speaking, the bandits shaped their message in the very effort of expressing it. Their symbolism was jumbled, their statements confusing.

Still, it is possible to locate their still-emerging place in the political landscape. Consider, for example, the arguments of historian David Thelen. He examined the bandits' Robin Hood language in light of Missouri's railroad agitation, and came to the conclusion that they were defenders of traditional society against outside forces of industrialization. The state's tightly knit fabric of self-sufficient farmers had been slashed by interfering Radicals, he writes, who introduced the market economy where it was not wanted. Modernizing Republicans "tried to convert farming from a traditional way of life into a profitable business." Radical promoters, he argues, forced railroads and full-fledged capitalism onto an unwilling populace, which endorsed Jesse James and his comrades in their armed resistance. "At the center of popular support for the bandits," Thelen claims, "was the belief that they sought to reunite the community and reassert tradition."[34]

Thelen's thesis offers a useful place to start, but it requires serious correction. Missourians were not self-sufficient frontier farmers who resisted the market economy. Perhaps some remote areas existed in relative isolation, but the Missouri River valley—the home of the James-Younger group and virtually all of their supporters—had long been a center of profit-oriented commercial farming. Robert James had grown hemp for distant markets in the South as early as the 1840s. Cole Younger's father, Henry, had been a wealthy rural entrepreneur. Like most of the wartime guerrillas from western Missouri, their families had owned a larger-than-average number of slaves, whom they rented out or put to work in raising cash crops. The bandits' families and supporters were among the most market-minded farmers in the state. If anything, the Union victory drove them unwillingly back toward self-sufficiency when their commercial operations were disrupted by emancipation.[35]

Missouri farmers could not be mistaken for bumpkins living in idyllic isolation. Country newspapers reported market prices in St. Louis and New York; backroads merchants kept up with the current gold premium on greenbacks; women engaged in sewing and hatmaking for profit.[36] The Grangers wanted easier and cheaper access to the market, not an abolition of the capitalist system. When the Cass County Patrons of Husbandry met on July 16, 1873, for example, they demanded "the abolition of every restriction upon the commerce of the country."[37]

Thelen makes an important point by connecting the train-robbing bandits with the bond-resistance movement, but he misreads that movement's real meaning. Missourians of all stripes had taken part in the railroad mania of 1867–1872. Several counties had lifted the Oath banning ex-rebels from referendums on bond issues, and secessionists had offered enthusiastic support. In all but one of the cases where county courts issued bonds without a vote, they were acting on citizens' petitions. Even the *Lexington Caucasian* had supported a railroad for Lafayette County. "When we say *all* are interested in such a proposition," it had declared, "we mean precisely that." No less a representative of the old order than Jo Shelby had been a partner in the construction firm that was implicated in the Cass County swindle. He had been on the very train that was stopped in the infamous Gunn City massacre. And when John Edwards attacked the railroads for discriminating against Missouri, his answer was *more* railroads—albeit locally controlled.[38]

All of this raises serious questions about the bandits' significance as economic avengers. They struck banks, which seems to fit with the traditional

Democratic loathing of powerful money monopolies that dated back to Andrew Jackson. But the banks they robbed were relatively small institutions dependent on local capital; all their Missouri targets were in their own communities (with the exception of Ste. Genevieve, which was in another strongly secessionist section). Such banks were not the target of popular financial discontent in the 1860s and '70s, which was largely focused on the structure of the national bank system and the volume of currency in the cash-strapped West and South. If anything, farmers wanted more banks, more loans, and allocations of more national banknotes. It is telling that the James-Younger outlaws robbed their last bank in Missouri at the very moment when they began to portray themselves as public heroes.[39]

Once the bandits decided to appeal for public sympathy, it was inevitable that they would declare, "We're robbing the rich for the poor." As armed robbers, they could claim nothing else—though there is no evidence that they did anything with their loot except spend it on themselves. The difficulty lies in going beyond those simple words, to decipher both their deeper opinions and their popularity. Clearly they were not defenders of self-sufficiency in the face of an invading market economy. Equally clearly, they recognized the public rage against the railroads in 1873, and even claimed to be Grangers. But in embittered Missouri, economic protest inevitably mingled with the politics of war and Reconstruction. Even more important than the bandits' words, when they walked the aisle of the Rock Island train, was the fact that they spoke them through Ku Klux Klan masks.

Missouri's rage against the railroads, in large part, reflected the Confederate reaction against the Radical legacy and rejection of the trend toward centralization that had begun in the Civil War. When tax rates spiked and local lines began to go bankrupt, secessionists blamed the Republicans. They claimed that the Radicals had used the Oath in the 1860s to ram bond issues down the throats of nonvoting former rebel slaveholders, who were the wealthiest members of their communities. (They conveniently forgot that they had largely supported the new rail lines at the time.) Across the state, the railroad bond protests were closely interwoven with secessionist politics, not agrarian populism. The movement to stop paying interest on the bonds began only after rebels regained the right to vote, and it was concentrated in counties where Confederates were particularly numerous.[40]

In the bitter debate over Reconstruction, the railways became an axis of political protest by former rebels who attacked the railroad corporations as the private partners of the Republican Party and the national government it controlled. From Cass County to South Carolina, ex-Confederates turned the railways into symbols of Radical corruption, extravagance, and misrule. In southeastern states, the Ku Klux Klan staged attacks on black railway employees amid ferocious speeches against the corporations by white-supremacist leaders. John Edwards depicted the Republican grip on the country as a comprehensive process of "imperialism and centralization." In political terms, he wrote, this had put the South under the heel of the tyrannical Ku Klux Klan Act and "all manner of desperate and characterless adventurers." In economic terms, it had led to "nothing more or less than a centralization of moneyed wealth in certain financial and commercial centres, and a corresponding spoilation of the general community." By robbing the railroad in KKK costumes, the former bushwhackers made a declaration about the South's continued defiance, especially since several highly publicized Klan cases were under way at that very moment. When the *Kansas City Times* described their holdup as a "Kuklux raid," they must have been proud.[41]

The rebels of Missouri were and always would be Jesse James's constituency.[42] That fact remains paramount despite the tangled messages and symbols that the bandits began to weave in 1873. In the tense weeks following the Rock Island robbery, for example, Jesse, his brother, and some of their colleagues took refuge in Dover, Lafayette County, an old bushwhacker stronghold. They went to town occasionally, one standing guard while the other ran errands. On Sunday evening, August 24, the brothers and a comrade rode into Lexington, where one attended services at the Methodist church, another visited "a house of ill-fame," and the third remained outside as a sentry. The next day, Jesse and Frank appeared in town. They were spotted by an old friend and former guerrilla chieftain, most likely Dave Pool. Word leaked out, and a posse gathered to chase them. "But these bold fellows laugh at the authorities," reported the *Lexington Caucasian*, "and seemingly invite their sleepy enterprise, by bearding the legal lion in his lazy lair."

In telling the story of the James brothers' visit, the fiercely secessionist, white-supremacist *Caucasian* paid them a glowing tribute. "It will not be a prideless reflection to the few who may sympathize with the high-handed actors, to know that Missouri leads [the country] . . . in the heroic splendor and perfect *sangfroid* of her gallant highwaymen," the paper declared. "We reassert, when it comes to a comparison of what Western Missouri can do in the way of furnishing blood-stirring incidents, the whole country and the world sink into insignificance. These old bushwhackers never fail, and then their coolness and indifference 'between drinks' wins our admiration."[43] The bandits' popularity clearly extended beyond Edwards's columns, permeating the ex-Confederate ranks.

Word of the outlaws' further escapades in Clay and Lafayette Counties infuriated Governor Silas Woodson, the first Democrat to be elected chief executive of the state since the war. As a member of the Unionist wing of

the party, he took a grim view of the bushwhackers' continuing depredations. On September 12, 1873, the *Liberty Tribune* printed a dispatch from
Jefferson City that reflected the governor's reaction to their apparent
immunity from capture. "The information received yesterday and today
indicates that the Iowa robbers are being shielded in Clay, Lafayette, and
Jackson counties," the report said. "They flit from one county to another,
as pursuit comes close, and are evidently kept well informed of the movements of the authorities. They are now in Clay and threaten to burn out
certain parties active in efforts to arrest them." Woodson warned that he
would send in an armed force unless the local officials tried harder to capture the bandits, said the anonymous journalist, and he did indeed order
Clay County sheriff George E. Patton to organize a platoon of militia.
Soon after, the governor issued a reward proclamation for the two James
boys, citing their indictment for the murder of John W. Sheets. He offered
an almost unprecedented $1,000 for each of them, far more than the stan-
dard $300 reward.[44]

Clay County's reaction to the uproar reflected its own deep fissures.
Local officials naturally expressed indignation. "The impression is abroad
that notorious law-breaking men find harbor in this, the garden spot of the
State," Sheriff Patton huffed. "I suggest that a meeting of our citizens be
held in the Court House in Liberty on *Saturday, September 20th, 1873*, for
the purpose of organizing a company of men to assist the executive of the
State in promoting peace and order." Not everyone in the local establishment, however, was so outspoken. Editor Miller of the *Liberty Tribune*
exhibited his always keen sense of the county's divided mind. Despite
being an old Unionist, he parsed his own response for his many Confederate readers. The people of Clay "are opposed to all kinds of lawlessness,
and mobocracy in particular," he wrote, conjuring up the image of the
armed Radical groups of the 1860s as a greater threat than the bandits.
More troubling, he mused, was the governor's threat of state intervention,
which "smacks of the war times when [MSM colonel William] Penick ruled
this section. He used to indulge in just such orders as the above, but in the
end accomplished nothing." Besides, he added, simple farmers could do
nothing against "armed desperadoes."[45]

The truth, as Miller knew, was that many of the locals who had fed,
sheltered, and supplied the James brothers when they were bushwhackers
now did the same for them as bandits, believing that the boys were still
fighting the good fight.

MYTHOLOGY REQUIRES EFFORT. Achilles and King Arthur may have
begun as men of flesh and blood, but Homer and Sir Thomas Malory

labored hard to make them the figures we remember. By 1873, John Edwards had already done much the same for Jesse James in his Kansas City newspaper, and on November 23, he put the myth in near-final form for a statewide audience.

On that day, the *St. Louis Dispatch* published "A Terrible Quintet," a special supplement written by Edwards that ran to twenty densely packed pages. (He had joined the St. Louis newspaper a few months before.) This remarkable paean to the bandits offers compelling evidence of Edwards's influence both at the paper and in Missouri's popular culture. The stories that he now told would define Jesse James in the public imagination.[46]

He began by saying that he was writing the piece at the request of his editors, who wanted "the truth concerning Jesse and Frank James, John and Coleman Younger, and A. C. McCoy," the men implicated as the core of the bandit crew. He wrote first and foremost of Jesse, devoting eleven of his twenty pages to the outlaw and his older brother. In the article, as in life, Jesse did all the talking, speaking for Frank as well as himself. Edwards had obviously questioned the pair closely, for many of the stories he presented as coming from Jesse's mouth can be independently verified. As for the half-truths and outright lies, who knows? But the end result was clear: with this extended profile in a major metropolitan newspaper, Jesse James emerged as a heroic figure of statewide stature.

Not all the high points of his later myth appeared in these pages. The tale of his being shot while attempting to surrender, for example, was presented here as a wound received in a standard gunfight. But Edwards told a fanciful version of how the militia had tortured Reuben Samuel, and added a few more stories that bear no resemblance to reality. Jesse, he wrote, was crippled by his lung wound for three full years, until a visit to his uncle's mineral spa, in Paso Robles, California, miraculously healed him. In the interim, he supposedly staved off constant attacks by Radical militiamen. Edwards had Jesse claiming that five of the state's troopers came to arrest him on the night of February 18, 1867, but that he managed to chase them away in a wild gunfight, despite his agonizing injury. It was pure nonsense, of course; no militia units were active then, nor was any gunfight reported in the press. But the event described was close enough in time to Bacon Montgomery's occupation of Lexington to awaken the memories of former secessionists, indirectly associating Jesse with the tragic fate of Archie Clement.[47]

The entire thrust of "A Terrible Quintet" was to glorify the Confederate guerrilla war in Missouri, and hail these five men as fearless, skillful heroes. It said nothing about railroads or corporations. Instead, it offered up tale after gory tale of payback for Unionist atrocities, of ambushes, battles, and revenge. "The five men you desire a history of are eminently creatures of the war," Edwards wrote. "There are memories of the struggle, too, in the hearts of some of them that are terrible even yet." At one point, Jesse's quotations commented darkly on Reconstruction. He had befriended a U.S. Army major on his journey to California in 1868, he said, an "old-time American army officer—of that time when they had gentlemen in the army, and not shysters, negroes, and Yankee dead-beats."*

Edwards also persisted in proclaiming them guiltless while simultaneously praising their daring and glorifying their crimes. Readers came away with the contradictory impression that these were innocent men who would never be taken alive. Edwards began, for example, by hailing Missouri's gunmen as the finest of all Western desperadoes. He went on to quote Jesse's explanation that John W. Sheets had been murdered by the Brotherhood of Death, a group of fifty survivors of Bill Anderson's band who had pledged to kill Samuel P. Cox, the guerrilla's slayer. "I am satisfied Sheets was killed through a mistake," he said. "I am almost convinced that one of the Brotherhood did it, and that he thought he was killing Cox." This was an enormous wink at his supporters, who admired him because they believed he *was* guilty of the charges against him. The essay as a whole was a (barely) encoded plea for rebel sympathy. As Edwards quoted Arthur McCoy, "A true Confederate soldier never betrays a true Confederate."

As in 1872, Jesse swiftly followed Edwards's tribute with a letter to his newspaper, asserting his innocence. He also spoke of himself and his brother as "two of Quantrill's and Anderson's best men," directly echoing the language of Edwards's essay. "We have many enemies in Missouri because of the war," he wrote. Curiously, he became very specific about his great distance from his home state. "Neither Frank nor myself have been in Missouri since the 3rd day of October, 1873," he wrote, "nor nearer Missouri than Denver City." He dated the letter December 20, 1873, from Deer Lodge, Montana, and asked that any return correspondence be directed to the same place.[48]

The year before, Edwards and James had launched a publicity campaign to simultaneously glorify and exonerate the bandits after the Kansas City fair robbery. Now they had improved upon that model, launching a campaign *before* a raid, or, rather, a series of raids. After establishing that Jesse was in Montana, the bandits began an unprecedented rampage, possibly as early as January 8, 1874, when a group of gunmen robbed the Monroe-Shreveport stage in Bienville Parish, Louisiana. One week later, on Janu-

---

*The Regular Army had six black regiments after 1866 (reduced to four in 1869), while Northern men made up more than 90 percent of the postwar officer corps. See T. J. Stiles, "Buffalo Soldiers," *Smithsonian* 29, no. 9 (December 1998): 82–94; Richard Franklin Bensel, *Yankee Leviathan: The Origins of Central State Authority in America, 1859–1877* (New York: Cambridge University Press, 1990), 411–13.

ary 15, the Missourians stopped another stagecoach, this time between Malvern and Hot Springs, Arkansas. In keeping with their theme, they asked if any passengers had fought for the Confederacy. A man from Memphis raised his hand, and they immediately returned his watch and the money they had taken from him. They didn't want to rob Southern veterans, they explained, but "Northern men had driven them to outlawry and they intended to make them pay for it." They menaced another passenger with a New England accent, whom they mistakenly suspected of being a reporter for the Radical *St. Louis Democrat*—"the vilest paper in the West," one of them snarled. A second bandit aimed a shotgun at his skull, saying, "I'll bet I can shoot his hat off without touching a hair of his head."[49]

For more than two weeks after the Hot Springs stage robbery, Jesse guided his horse steadily north.[50] The names of the four men who rode beside him, according to press accounts, were Frank James, Arthur McCoy—the Confederate cavalryman mentioned in "A Terrible Quintet"—Cole Younger, and one of Cole's brothers.[51] By January 27, they had reached Missouri's southern border. They continued north, following the Iron Mountain Railroad through the southeastern section of the state. On January 30, they stopped to eat in Mill Spring, then they continued on, passing through Piedmont, six miles farther north.

That night, they asked for shelter at the home of the widow Gilbreath, three miles north of Piedmont. Three of them set down double-barreled shotguns, she noticed, and when they took off their overcoats, she saw that each of the five carried a pair of large revolvers.[52] They had maps, a compass, and a spare horse; they also came with a fair knowledge of the countryside and the Iron Mountain's schedule.[53]

At perhaps three in the afternoon the next day, they trotted their horses into the hamlet of Gads Hill, just north of where they had spent the night. Founded by George W. Creath just three years earlier, this cluster of two or three houses, a general store, an abandoned sawmill, and a bare railroad platform depended on the Iron Mountain Railroad for its existence. Creath had named his village, deep in rugged, heavily wooded wilderness, after the rural retreat of Charles Dickens. But at least one of the gunmen knew it as the place where Prince Hal robbed Falstaff after Falstaff had robbed the pilgrims, in Shakespeare's *Henry IV, Part I*. Robbing the robbers—as they saw it—would be their work that day.[54]

Jesse and his comrades visited the town merchant, McMillan, and secured his rifle and perhaps $800 of his money (though the flinty store owner slipped $450 more into the lining of his coat). Then they ushered him through the cold winter air to the railroad platform, where they also brought the handful of men, women, and children who lived in the nearby houses. There was no shelter for them by the tracks, as trains rarely both-ered to stop at this remote flag station. But the James brothers and their crew knew a little about railroad procedures. As their prisoners shivered around an open fire, they scrounged up a red signal flag, used to warn of danger ahead. They planned to wave down the Number 7 train, the express from St. Louis to Little Rock, due in at 4:06 p.m. It would probably carry a large shipment of cash, for this was the time of year when money was sent south in great quantities to pay for cotton purchases. Long before the appointed hour, they were ready, red flag in hand, shotguns cradled in their arms, pistols loaded, and a sheet of paper prepared for this occasion.[55]

Four o'clock came and went as they waited in the January chill. Finally, about an hour late, the Number 7 steamed into view. One of the gunmen waved the red flag. The great iron mass of the engine slowed, then clanked through the switch that the bandits had thrown and onto the siding adjacent to the platform. Immediately after the last car passed, one of the bandits threw the switch again, trapping the train.

As the locomotive eased up to the platform, conductor C. A. Alford went to investigate the red flag. "I jumped off the train, thinking that the track was torn up," he reported a few days later. "A man advanced and caught me by the collar and stuck a pistol in my face." For a moment, Alford was utterly confused as he looked at the small crowd huddled around an open fire, and the men with guns. The fellow who held him wore a mask of white cloth that completely covered his head, with holes cut out for his eyes and nose. "I was a little surprised," the conductor reported, "and understood his object only when he shouted, on thrusting his pistol in my face: 'Stand still or I'll blow the top of your head off.' " Then he turned toward the train and bellowed, "If a shot is fired out of the car I will kill the conductor."[56]

The gunmen proceeded quickly and efficiently, following the model they had developed in Iowa the year before. One man stood guard over the prisoners while two walked outside of the train, one on each side. When one of the passengers poked his head out a window, the nearest bandit swung his shotgun toward his skull and warned, "Take your heads in, and not move out of the car!"[57] The last two outlaws collected the engineer and the fireman and put them with the conductor and the other prisoners. Then they stepped up into the baggage car.

Inside, Adams Express messenger William N. Wilson waited nervously by the safe, revolver in hand. As soon as a masked face appeared in the doorway he aimed his weapon—then froze. A second bandit had also appeared, shotgun directed squarely at Wilson's chest. "Give me your pis-tol you son of a bitch," the bandit snarled. The express messenger quickly complied, handing over the safe key as well. The robbers unlocked the iron box and rummaged through its contents. They found a package containing some $1,080. They tore open another marked "watch," but when they saw it was silver, not gold, they tossed it on the floor. "You've got more money than all that comes to!" one of them snapped at Wilson. "Shell out or I'll blow your brains out!" There was no more, however. They ripped open registered mail packages containing various sums of money, and even broke into the conductor's satchel.

They seemed to relax as they rifled the mail. When they were finished, the lead bandit—most likely Jesse—opened the messenger's waybill registration book and scribbled, "Robbed at Gads Hill." He cheerfully added that he had signed such a book before.[58] Then they prodded Wilson and the baggage master to where the other prisoners stood, and went back to rob the passengers.

The work went quickly. There were only two passenger cars—one smoker, one ladies' car—and a Pullman sleeper, carrying just twelve men, five women, and eight children in all. As they passed through, brandishing their revolvers, they ordered the men to show them their hands. "They stated that they did not want to rob workingmen or ladies," the *St. Louis Republican* reported, "but the money and valuables of the plug-hat gentlemen were what they sought."

The two bandits became positively buoyant as they strolled down the aisle, collecting hundreds of dollars in cash and jewelry. One of them playfully exchanged hats with a passenger, while the other recited Shakespeare. When one man introduced himself as a minister, they returned his money and asked him to pray for them. They demanded to know if anyone was named "Pinkerton." Finally they picked out a man, declared that he was a detective, ordered him into a sleeper-car compartment, and ordered him to strip. Every employee of the famous Pinkerton's detective agency, they said, had a secret mark on his body. Satisfied—or simply amused—they soon let the humiliated passenger go.[59]

Once all the passengers had been looted, the gunmen rejoined the group of prisoners on the platform. They finished their work by taking fifty dollars from conductor Alford, along with his gold watch, which prompted an impulsive outburst from the baggage master. "For God's sake, you won't take it," he protested, "for it is a present." The outlaws promptly returned it, and told the railroad men that they were free to go. "When we got ready to start," Alford reported, "the robbers shook hands with the engineer, Wm. Wetton, and told him whenever he saw a red flag he ought to stop. They then strolled off to their horses, tied up about a hundred yards distant, and rode out of sight before we got under way."[60]

As the train chugged off, the crew discovered the bandits' final touch: they had left behind a prepared press release, with instructions that it be telegraphed to the *St. Louis Dispatch.* "The most daring robbery on record," it began. "The south bound train on the Iron Mountain railroad was robbed here this morning by five heavily armed men, and robbed of _____ dollars." The rest of the brief release described the crime with great accuracy, showing that everything had indeed gone according to plan. "The robbers arrived at the station a few minutes before the arrival of the train, and arrested the agent, put him under guard, and then threw the train on the switch. . . . There is a hell of excitement in this part of the country."[61]

Jesse and his comrades escaped west into the forest, carrying at least $2,000. They rode two abreast, each pair almost one hundred yards apart, with the fifth man leading the spare horse in the rear—a formation that would keep them from being trapped together in an ambush. The next night, February 1, they stayed with a widow named Cook on the Current River, where they cleaned and reloaded their arms. They left early the next morning. From there they continued west across southern Missouri. "All along the route they are reported to have conducted themselves as gentlemen, paying for everything they got," the *St. Louis Republican* announced. "They had a map and compass to direct their route, avoiding roads and keeping to the hills as much as possible." A large posse followed behind, gradually disintegrating as its members tired of the fruitless chase.[62]

As the outlaws disappeared into the woods, John Edwards went to work. In a *St. Louis Dispatch* editorial titled "Gads Hill," he rounded out the circle of argument begun with "A Terrible Quintet," or even "The Chivalry of Crime," more than a year earlier.[63] The bandits, he wrote, were the inevitable result of a deeper evil in the United States, an evil that had led to an epidemic of crime. "We believe that the war had a great deal to do with this disease solely because the war made the Radical party a triumphant one. Radicalism has no principle. . . . Everything that was venerable and sacred in the country, it has taught the people to despise. As far as it could it has defamed and derided the constitution. It has declared, because of its uses and manipulations of them, that the courts were marketable things. . . . States have been treated as conquered provinces, abject criminals protected in the exercise of outrageous powers."

But in Missouri, he wrote, the iron hand of Radicalism had raised its own destroyer, a kind of criminal who was entirely admirable. "Is it hard to discriminate between the men of Gads Hill, and the men of the iron clad oath and registration law? Is the line difficult to draw between Rodman* on the one hand, and these daring highwaymen on the other? No, indeed." Here Edwards began the central thrust of his argument: The evils of Radi-

---

*Francis Rodman had invalidated several elections as Republican secretary of state in 1866 and 1868.

cal rule had not yet ended. "But is the curse lifted from Missouri with the passing away of the old *regime?* It were well if it could or would be so. It were well if no knowledge had ever been had of . . . tyranny and oppression, of a disfranchisement that offered a premium to rascality, and of such a destruction of the old order of things as taught to the rising generation only those lessons that have borne fruit at Ste. Genevieve, at Gads Hill, up in Iowa, and at various other places where desperate men have struck and been successful."

Now at full stride, the crusty Confederate wrapped up all the outlaws' disparate messages and symbolism into one comprehensive condemnation of the Republican order. Before the Civil War, he wrote, banditry would have been crime, pure and simple, and would have been snuffed out.

> By and by, however, when the militia came, and when men were shot down in their houses or in their fields, it was because of their disloyalty. . . . And when rich and prosperous counties were made beggars in a night . . . because ten per cent of their population voted debts upon them impossible to pay, it was no longer called robbery. . . . The trees thus planted are bearing wholesome and legitimate fruit. Since 1862, the government has been robbing, so has its officers of high and low degree, so has every administration in every Southern State, so did the administration of Missouri, so have the national banks, the tariff, the custom house, the Indian agents, the railroads, the cabinet officers, Grant himself. . . . To stop it—to break up private as well as official robbery of all kinds—it is only necessary to break up the Radical party. For this Augean stable there must be another Euphrates.

By the time this editorial appeared, on February 10, 1874, Edwards's personal ties to the outlaws were well known; already a rumor circulated that he had been given a gold watch from their plunder.[64] It would be too much to say that he was considered their mouthpiece, for that was too passive a role for the opinionated and increasingly influential editor. Perhaps "official interpreter" would have been the best way to describe him. Few doubted that Edwards's essay cast the bandits as they wished to be seen, as Confederate avengers against an imagined Radical monolith—the invisible empire that extended its corrupt tyranny into every crevice of life. He depicted them as men of the old order who boldly stood against the abominations of Union victory and Radical rule. In this highly political—and secessionist—view, they appeared as part of the great wave of "Redeemers" working to overthrow Reconstruction with their own invisible empire, a systematic application of violence and intimidation.

Edwards and his twenty-six-year-old friend Jesse James had many reasons to put the banditry in this light: a desire to shift the Democratic Party in an explicitly Confederate direction; outrage at the social and political revolution of Reconstruction; and a simple hunger for glory. But neither of them could have predicted how successful their efforts would be in the year that followed. Help was on the way from an unexpected source, a new enemy who would make all of Edwards's arguments about the Radical empire tangible and real, and tear apart the Democratic Party in the process. The bushwhackers were going back to war.

CHAPTER FOURTEEN

Allies and Enemies

W ILLIAM B. DINSMORE'S business was nothing if not predictable. A colorless former bookkeeper, he had joined the Adams Express Company shortly after its founding, in 1840. Through hard work and shrewd management, he had risen to the presidency of this, the country's largest express corporation. He competed with other express firms, such as the United States or the American; he cooperated with railroads, which he paid handsomely to carry his messengers, packages, and safes; and he dealt with clients and colleagues who were much like himself, gray men in gaslit offices in the narrow streets of lower Manhattan. But in 1874 Dinsmore's world went into convulsions, causing him the most unexpected problems.[1]

The first signs of trouble came in 1872, when the steadily chugging economy began to hiccup and cough. The Treasury Department's contractionist monetary policies and the deflationary structure of the national bank system had begun to slow things down even as the first hints appeared that the railways had overexpanded. Europe lost its voracious appetite for American railroad bonds, which starved the aggressive corporations of their primary source of financing. Then, in September 1873, the unthinkable happened: the firm of Jay Cooke—the financial wizard who had helped keep the Union fiscally healthy during the Civil War—found itself unable to finance the Northern Pacific, and went bankrupt. The result was a panic of titanic proportions.[2]

"I now entered the most anxious period of my business life," recalled Andrew Carnegie, soon to be the largest steel manufacturer in the country. Carnegie could hardly help panicking in the Panic of 1873. "All was going well when one morning . . . a telegram came announcing the failure of Jay Cooke & Co. Almost every hour brought news of some fresh disaster. House after house failed. The question every morning was which would go next. Every failure depleted the resources of other concerns. Loss after loss ensued, until a total paralysis of business set in. . . . It was impossible to borrow money, even upon the best collaterals. . . . I could scarcely control myself."[3]

Banks failed; mills closed; prices plunged as the already diminishing stock of money shrank further. Prices for farm products fell so low it was hardly worth the freight charges to send them to market. And the full burden of every sector's losses fell on the railway corporations. "While it has been a season of great general depression of business," declared the *Railroad Gazette* at the end of 1874, "railroad business has suffered especially—more perhaps than any other great industry except iron." The editors likened the impact of the Panic to a war.[4]

With freight traffic, government aid, and foreign investment all evaporating, the railway corporations began to look for new sources of income, and the express business seemed just the thing. As handlers of priority deliveries, Dinsmore's industry was cushioned against the full impact of the depression. It also operated with a high profit margin, since it lacked the enormous overhead sustained by the railroads. In 1875, with the economy still plunging downward, the Adams Express Company enjoyed a stock capitalization of $12 million, even though it could boast of only a small fraction of the physical assets of the average railway. That same year, *Harper's* magazine estimated that the express business had created fifty millionaires (at a time when the president of the United States earned the astronomical salary of $20,000 a year). These lucrative companies depended on the railroads for their survival, making them vulnerable to the owners of the tracks and rolling stock. Jay Gould, for example, canceled Union Pacific's contract with Wells, Fargo & Co. and instituted his own express service. Other lines looked to follow his example.[5]

The Adams Express faced not only changing corporate threats, but new criminal ones as well. From the days of Dinsmore's youth, the express business had always been a target of burglars, sneak thieves, and confidence men. The Adams had suffered armed robberies before, including the Reno brothers' raid on a train in Seymour, Indiana, in 1866, but they had been infrequent, nothing to prepare its president for the ex-Confederate bushwhackers who emptied the company's safe at Gads Hill.

The railroad corporations did almost nothing to catch them. After the Iowa raid in 1873, the Rock Island had posted a reward, put rifle-carrying guards on its trains, and let it go at that. The Iron Mountain line did even less after Gads Hill. But Dinsmore was a hardheaded businessman. He would have seen that robbers had, in fact, cost the railroad companies almost nothing. The Rock Island had repaired its tracks and restored its derailed locomotive—one of 108 it operated in Iowa—the night of the robbery; it didn't even mention the incident in its annual report. The Iron Mountain had suffered even less annoyance, certainly nothing to compare with the $156,700 it earned that month. The *American Railroad Journal* and other industry publications never even bothered to discuss the robberies. Nor did the U.S. Post Office make any effort to pursue the outlaws, despite the rifling of registered mail at Gads Hill (and press reports to the contrary). Dinsmore, however, saw clearly that the Missouri bandits did not rob railroads—they robbed express companies. If anyone was going to put up the money to catch them, it would have to be the Adams Express.[6]

Dinsmore took his problem to Allan Pinkerton, the bearded, squinteyed, fifty-two-year-old Scotsman who was the founder and principal of Pinkerton's National Detective Agency, a private company with its headquarters in Chicago and branch offices in New York and Philadelphia.[7] The patriotic, fiercely abolitionist investigator had risen to fame during the Civil War, sheltering John Brown after his last raid on Missouri, providing security for Lincoln's inaugural journey to Washington, and serving as personal intelligence chief for General George B. McClellan.[8] Like Dinsmore, Pinkerton represented the growing nationalization of American commerce, as trade and industry broke out of local markets and made long-distance connections. Where money went, criminals followed, and traditional law enforcement was ill-equipped to capture outlaws who increasingly operated across county and state boundaries.

When Pinkerton made his start in crime fighting in the 1840s (breaking up a counterfeiting ring in Chicago), the detective was a new figure on the American scene. Old-fashioned town constables had emphasized crime prevention, but the detective promised retribution, by finding the thief and his plunder. Private agencies formed in St. Louis, Baltimore, and Philadelphia between 1846 and 1848. Boston formed a municipal force in 1846, but other major cities did not follow its example until 1857, when New York launched its own squad. Most of these detectives, however, were vulnerable to political control and suffered rampant corruption. (Some officers coordinated their activities with professional burglars, sharing either the loot or the reward.) And all were limited to their localities. Pinkerton's was the first truly national agency, free from the political pressures or graft that influenced county sheriffs, urban detectives, and even U.S. marshals. His advertisements ran, "This agency does not operate for contingent rewards, is independent of Government or Municipal control, and prepared to do all legitimate detective business intrusted to it by Express, Railroad and Insurance Companies, Banks or individuals."[9]

The Scotsman excelled at his work. From the founding of his agency in 1850 through the 1870s, he and his men engaged in an intricate game of domestic espionage and counterespionage with the professional thieves and burglars who stalked the major cities. He built up a "rogue's gallery" of photographs of known pickpockets, confidence men, and safecrackers, and successfully infiltrated their organizations. He had even defeated the original train robbers, the Reno gang. He was, above all else, a man of determination. He had struggled back after a severe stroke in 1869, for example, returning to work within a year; he had survived the great Chicago fire, which destroyed his offices; and he had kept his business open through a drastic cash-flow crisis in 1872. The Missouri bandits could be no worse.[10]

Pinkerton made an art of reconnaissance and infiltration, and he put both tactics to work immediately after Dinsmore gave him the Gads Hill case.[11] The posse that initially chased the bandits, he learned, had tracked them through Texas County toward western Missouri. In February he dispatched an agent who confirmed the report. He also discovered that the gang had dispersed. The Younger brothers had retreated to sparsely settled Monegaw Springs, St. Clair County, and the James boys had gone back to their mother's farm, near Kearney.[12] With the reconnaissance complete, it was time to infiltrate.

"I was in Europe at the time, but the case was in progress on my return," William Pinkerton, the son of the agency's founder, recalled seven years later. William worked as an informal second-in-command in the Chicago headquarters, and he swiftly caught up on the investigation. After the initial probe, "operatives were detailed to go into the respective vicinities to obtain evidence of the guilt or innocence of the parties charged with the robbery. Capt. Louis J. Lull and John Boyle were sent to St. Clair county, and J. W. Whicher was dispatched to Clay county. . . . The detectives were not expected to make arrests, their duty merely being to look over the ground and report what they could learn."[13]

"The detective following the James boys was Joseph W. Whicher," the *New York World* later reported. "He was a young man of twenty-six, stood almost six feet, had blue eyes and light hair, and a smooth, boyish face with but a shadow of a mustache." Whicher had wandered far from his native Des Moines, Iowa, in search of adventure. He had spent his first adult years as a seaman in the Mediterranean, until a broken ankle drove him ashore in 1871. He then entered the Pinkerton ranks, earning a reputation for iron nerve and soft discretion.[14]

At the end of the first week of March 1874, Whicher stepped off the train in Kansas City. There, in that bustling town of stockyards, meatpacking plants, and crisscrossing railway tracks, he prepared for his new role, changing into the worn clothing of a farm laborer.[15] On March 10, he arrived in Liberty. The town had changed since the days when its dirt streets were clogged with Oregon-bound migrants and slave-driven wagons piled with hemp and tobacco. It had a modern feel now, with telegraph wires and locomotive smoke filling the sky, and paved roads and neat stone sidewalks underfoot.[16]

Whicher went to the Arthur House hotel, where he registered as "J. W. Whicher, Mississippi." As he set down the pen, he asked the clerk how he might find the sheriff. Confident, even eager, he walked the short distance to the courthouse, where he wandered into the office of the recorder of deeds, Sidney G. Sandusky.[17] Again he asked for the sheriff. Sandusky returned a few moments later with a vigorous-looking man with one empty sleeve, whom he introduced as Sheriff George E. Patton.

Whicher identified himself as a Pinkerton agent and explained his mission. He opened a valise and produced a set of descriptions, which he read aloud for the sheriff. Did any of them match the James boys? he asked. Patton shook his head. They were imperfect as far as he could tell, Patton informed the detective, but he had not seen Frank since they served together on the Confederate side in the first year of the war, and he had not laid eyes on Jesse since he was outlawed in 1869.

Whicher pressed on, asking for—and receiving—precise directions to Zerelda Samuel's farm. Was it a big operation? he asked. Did they often hire laborers? As he spoke, he extended his hands and examined them; they were too soft, he mused aloud, and might give him away. Patton said the farm was "of the first class and of good size," but he warned the detective to keep clear of it at all costs—the James brothers would never be off their guard. Did that mean they were at home? persisted Whicher. Patton didn't think so; usually one or two of the neighbors let him know when they spotted Frank or Jesse near their mother's place. Whicher thanked Patton and mentioned that he might ask for assistance in the days to come. Then he left his valise in the recorder's care and confidently walked out the door.[18]

His next stop was the Commercial Bank of Liberty, on the southwestern corner of the public square. There he met D. J. Adkins, president of the seven-year-old institution, and introduced himself as a Pinkerton agent.[19] He planned to infiltrate the Samuel household by posing as a laborer, he explained, and had to deposit the fifty dollars he carried, since it was far more than a farmhand would normally carry. Adkins, like Sheriff Patton, was stunned by Whicher's idiocy. He brought the young man into the back room of the bank, then went to get O. P. Moss, the former sheriff. Moss's contempt for Whicher's arrogance must have been profound. Having endured thirteen years of conflict with the county's secessionist bushwhackers, Moss knew that time had only made the James brothers more dangerous. When Whicher protested that Patton had told him that Frank and Jesse were not home, Moss cut him off. It didn't matter, he told him. "The old woman would kill you if the boys don't."[20]

Whicher thought he knew his business best. At 5:15 in the afternoon, he caught a slow-rolling freight train that clacked north out of Liberty, lumbering into Kearney shortly before dusk. He stopped at the telegraph office and sent a report to agency headquarters, then struck out on foot, covering the last couple of miles under the deepening shadows of twilight. Finally he reached that slouching white farmhouse that had been described to him, and knocked on the door.[21]

AT THREE O'CLOCK in the morning on the darkened banks of the Missouri River, the March air would have seized a man like an ice-water bath. J. W. Whicher, however, could do nothing to adjust his clothing—his hands were bound tightly, his ankles looped and tied together under the belly of the horse he rode. His three fellow riders, on the other hand, were warm enough; they had woolen scarves wrapped around their mouths and noses, and hats pulled down over their eyes.

The detective watched and listened as one of them bellowed for the ferryman. He was deputy sheriff Jim Baxter of Clay County, he shouted. They had captured a horse thief and needed to cross over to Jackson County to catch another.[22] As the boat pilot dawdled, the spokesman ordered him to be "damned quick,"[23] adding, "if he did not come out and row them across they would cut his damned boat loose."[24] The ferry master duly appeared and set about his work with perfect equanimity, as if he was roused every night by angry armed men.

As the boat glided across the night water, Whicher could say nothing. A gag kept him from telling the ferryman about what had happened in the hours since he had knocked on the Samuel farmhouse door. He could not say if he had been tackled, tortured, and interrogated, as William Pinkerton later claimed. He could not identify the third man who rode that night with the James brothers—perhaps it was Clell Miller, as Pinkerton thought, or Arthur McCoy or Jim Anderson, as John S. Thomason argued. Whether beaten into submission or simply iron-nerved, the detective remained calm and quiet when the boat slid ashore on the southern bank and his horse was led by the three gunmen onto Jackson County soil. Had they lied to him, promising to let him go, or did he know what to expect when, at a crossroads not far from the ferry, the first of three revolver blasts erupted in his ear?[25]

· · ·

SOME TIME LATER, someone in the headquarters of Pinkerton's National Detective Agency noticed a small item in the *Chicago Times*, "telling of a mysterious murder that had occurred near Independence," recalled William Pinkerton. As the headquarters staff pursued the story, they learned that the victim was indeed their man Whicher. Immediately Allan Pinkerton ordered agent L. E. Angell to the scene to find out what happened and bring the body home.[26]

Whicher was not the only detective in the field. Louis J. Lull, formerly a Chicago police captain, and John Boyle, a veteran of the St. Louis force, had been dispatched to St. Clair County to gather information about the Younger brothers. Lull took the alias W. J. Allen and Boyle that of J. W. Wright, pretending to be buyers for land. "Word was immediately sent to Capt. Lull to be on his guard" after Whicher's death, William Pinkerton reported. But it was already too late.[27]

In midafternoon on March 17, 1874, Lull and Boyle guided their horses through the landscape near Monegaw Springs, St. Clair County—"a hilly, wooded, and sparsely settled country," a reporter later remarked, "just such a locality that a band of outlaws would select for their rendezvous."[28] Beside them rode former deputy sheriff Edwin B. Daniels, who knew their true identities and had promised to help them. They briefly stopped at the farmhouse of Theodrick Snuffer to ask for directions, then cantered their horses away. By coincidence, two of Cole Younger's brothers, Jim and John, happened to be seated at Snuffer's dinner table at the time. The appearance of three heavily armed strangers in this remote part of the country immediately made them suspicious. "After eating their dinner," Snuffer recalled a day or two later, "John Younger remarked to his brother James that they would follow those men and see who they were, stating at the same time that he supposed they were detectives."[29]

As the detectives and Daniels rode slowly down the road through a sparse stand of trees, they heard galloping hoofbeats behind them. Turning in their saddles, they saw Jim and John Younger spurring their horses toward them at a rapid pace. The hard-edged John—who had earlier killed a deputy sheriff in Texas—leveled a double-barreled shotgun, cocked the hammers, and ordered the trio to halt.[30] Boyle, who was a short distance ahead of his companions, immediately kicked his horse into a gallop. The Youngers fired, blasting Boyle's hat off his head, but he rode off unharmed. The Youngers then instructed Lull and Daniels to unbuckle their pistol belts, which they did, letting their holstered revolvers fall to the ground.

John raised the twin muzzles of his shotgun as Jim dismounted and picked up their fallen revolvers. He examined the weapons admiringly. "Damned fine pistols," he remarked. It only fed John's suspicions. You're detectives, he snapped; you were up at Monegaw Springs yesterday asking about us. "I am no detective," Daniels replied, "I can show you who I am and where I belong."

One of the brothers said that he recognized him, and addressed Lull. "What in the hell are you riding around here with all them pistols on for?"

"Good God!" Lull said. "Is not every man wearing them that is traveling, and have I not as much right to wear them as any one else?"

"Hold on, young man," John replied sarcastically. "We don't want any of that." As he spoke, he leveled his shotgun.

Daniels began to speak to the Youngers, trying to save their lives, but all Lull could think about was the shotgun that John held. He will shoot no matter what I say, Lull thought. Reaching behind his back, he grasped his backup weapon, a small Smith & Wesson No. 2 pistol, and quietly cocked the hammer with his thumb. Then he snapped his arm out in front of him and fired at John Younger.

The bullet tore straight through Younger's throat. In the split second before he died, he pulled the trigger of his shotgun, firing the remaining charge. The heavy load of buckshot shattered Lull's right arm. Jim reacted a moment later, blasting a bullet into Lull's side, then snapping off a shot at Daniels, hitting him in the throat. The multiple gunshots sent the detective's horse careering away in a panicked gallop, until Lull struck a branch and fell to the ground.[31]

After killing Daniels, Jim cradled his fallen brother. "Can you see me?" he asked. John made no reply. Jim set him back down, went through his clothing for money and papers, and took his firearms. Then he called to G. W. McDonald, a black farm laborer who had watched the entire affair from a field nearby. Go tell "Snuffer's folks," he said, and tossed the farmhand a Remington revolver that had belonged to either Daniels or Lull.[32]

As Jim disappeared into the countryside, the bleeding, battered Lull staggered from the woods. McDonald went to his assistance and cared for him until he could be moved to the town of Roscoe. Despite his severe wounds, Lull gave a sworn account of the event for a coroner's inquest shortly after the gunfight. Three days later, he died.[33]

The murder of Whicher and the St. Clair County gun battle reverberated in the Pinkerton headquarters in the same way that news of a terrible Union defeat had during the Civil War. The agency was completely demoralized. "I have no soldiers but all officers in my regiment," Allan Pinkerton complained, "all capital men to give orders, [but] few will go forward except somebody goes ahead. . . . Mr. Warner and William refuse to go with the men to Mo.," he said, referring to the superintendent in the Chicago office and his own son, "both declared that they are not to be made a notch to be shot at."

The unprecedented defeat left Pinkerton bitter. "I know that the James' and the Youngers are desperate men, and that when we meet it must be the death of one or both of us," he wrote to George H. Bangs, superintendent of the New York office, on April 17. "My blood was spilt, and they must repay. There is no use talking, they must die."

Pinkerton had planned to launch a major operation to capture the bandits, but called it off when an agent telegraphed him that the James and Younger brothers had left Missouri. He instructed Bangs to tell both Dinsmore and John Hoey, the managing director of the Adams Express Company, that he would send them a full account of his plans. "If I am allowed by Mr. Dinsmore to hunt them up, then of course I will send my men forward," he wrote. "But when the time comes when we find the men can be arrested, then recollect, I shall be with my own men in charge." Bangs had warned against Pinkerton's personal involvement, given his fragile physical condition, but he was undeterred. With even his son backing off, "I make no talk but simply say I am going myself," he wrote, "and will carry my own musket."[34]

A month before Pinkerton's letter, in the days immediately following the Younger gun battle, detective L. E. Angell completed his task in Missouri. On March 19, 1874, he arrived in St. Louis with a coffin containing Whicher's body. During his stopover, he gave a series of angry interviews with the city's reporters. "How do you suppose it was that he was found out?" one of them asked.

"He was roughly dressed, but when he got there they must have noticed that he was a sharp, penetrating-looking fellow, and they probably took notice of his soft hands," Angell replied. "When they searched him and only found a revolver, with no papers or anything else about him to show who he was, they must have tumbled to him, or, if they didn't, that sharp old mother of theirs did."

"Do you suppose anybody gave him away to the James boys?" the journalist asked.

"It is the common talk down there, around and about Liberty, that that was done by the Sheriff," the detective answered, referring to Patton, the one-armed Confederate veteran who had grown up with the James brothers. But the problem went deeper than that, Angell thought. "The people there are of the kind that admire men who ride through town flourishing revolvers, and the James boys have established a sort of terrorism throughout the county," he continued. "But they have a great many friends. They have established the reputation of robbing the rich to give to the poor, and when they have money they fling it around generously."

Friendship and fear worked hand in hand to protect Jesse and his brother. "The people there are so afraid they would not tell where they were if they knew," Angell said. "They would hide themselves, and when they talk about them they assume a mysterious air, talk in low whispers, and you will have to get them into a back room before they will say anything, then they don't dare tell half they know."[35]

Angell himself was ill-equipped to understand the evidence he had uncovered. Clay, like St. Clair, Lafayette, Jackson, and other counties the bandits frequented, was indeed divided between the fearful and the outlaws' friends. However, it was no impermanent boundary of temperament or criminal disposition that split this society in two, but rather the tectonic fault of wartime enmities that dated back to the years of Radical rule, back to the days when the MSM and EMM and bushwhacker bands patrolled the countryside, back to the distant era of border ruffians and proslavery mobs. Though innocent of any collusion with Jesse James, Patton was a natural target, as a former Confederate, for the suspicions of local Unionists. And they would have been twice as suspicious had they known that his new wife, now pregnant with their first child, was the former Bettie Scruggs—the girl whom Jesse had once sweetly asked to visit, and had begged to believe him innocent.[36]

NOTHING ENRAGED Jesse James like being hunted. Ever since the Rock Island robbery, he had been seized by a grinding suspicion that the Pinkertons were after him, a suspicion that had prompted his search for detectives on the Iron Mountain train. He was wrong, of course, since it was only after Gads Hill that the Chicago agency took up the case. Whicher's appearance at his mother's door, however, confirmed his fears, and kindled his anger.

Immediately following the murder of Whicher in the predawn hours of March 11, 1874, Jesse remained calm. He, Frank, and their unnamed companion rode slowly through Independence, leading the horse that had carried their victim. Not long after daybreak, they crossed the Kansas City bridge over the Missouri River and made their way home. But before the day was out, Jesse had worked himself up into a cold fury. In a replay of his behavior after the gunfight with Thomason in 1869, he galloped into Kearney "and threatened two or three citizens to stop their talking about their (the James boys) doing the robbery," according to L. E. Angell. Then he reined his horse back in the direction of his mother's farm, where he made rapid preparations to take to the brush. Sheriff Patton soon arrived with five men, and "saw about the house the tracks of several freshly shod horses," a local newspaper reported, "and other indications that the gang had been at the place very recently." But they were gone.[37]

They did not go far. After his rage subsided, Jesse decided to end his long-running courtship of his first cousin Zee Mimms with a wedding. The families were already interlinked by marriage: Zee's brother Robert, the oldest of twelve children, had wed Zerelda's half-sister, the daughter of Zerelda's mother and Robert Thomason.[38] More to the point, however, was the steady constriction of Jesse's social sphere. First had come the death of his father, and his mother's increasingly bitter struggle to regain her farm and family; then came the war, when neighbors turned into foes; then his initiation into the tight-knit and brutal brotherhood of bushwhackers; then the years underground. Whom could he trust—whom could he even speak to openly—other than a member of his own family?[39]

Unlike Zerelda, Zee was not the towering sort, either physically or emotionally. Diminutive, dark-haired, and a devout Methodist, she asked Rev. William James, uncle of both Jesse and herself, to preside. He balked, but Zee persisted. After all, she had waited nine years for this day. She was almost twenty-nine now, two years older than her fiancé. "She said Jesse had been lied about and persecuted," the minister recalled, "and that he was not half so bad as pictured." Finally he agreed, but only after Jesse himself pleaded his innocence. The minister performed the ceremony at the house of Zee's sister Lucy Browder in Kearney on April 24, 1874. Only a few family members attended. The rites were briefly interrupted in a panic when someone reported the approach of two detectives. After a madcap dash for the doors, the party sheepishly returned to finish the wedding after the report proved to be a false alarm. The couple left to visit Jesse's sister Susie, who was now married to former guerrilla Allen Parmer and taught at a high school in the old bushwhacker winter quarters in Sherman, Texas.[40]

As might be expected, John Edwards wrote up the story of the romance and marriage of Missouri's most famous fugitive. He ran an account on the front page of the *St. Louis Dispatch*. "CAPTURED," shouted the headline on June 9, 1874; "The Celebrated Jesse W. James Taken at Last. His Captor a Woman, Young, Accomplished, and Beautiful." It was a light piece, riddled with intentional errors; the wedding date was one day off, for example, and great stress was placed on the couple's plans to settle in Mexico. "She is a true and consistent Christian, and a member of the M. E. Church, South," he wrote (using the pseudonym "Ranger"). "The whole courtship, engagement, and final marriage has been a most romantic series of events." Edwards quoted Jesse as saying, "Her devotion to me has never wavered for a moment," despite his reputation. "You can say that both of us married for love, and that there cannot be any sort of doubt about our marriage being a happy one."[41]

Edwards's article was far more than a tribute to his friend and a bit of misdirection for the detectives. It was, in fact, another shot fired between

the Democratic Party's feuding factions. "In 1874 came turmoil," wrote
Walter B. Stevens. As city editor of the *St. Louis Dispatch* and a friend and
colleague of Edwards, he viewed the Democrats' intramural skirmishing
from a privileged position. Of all the divisions within the party—by business interests, by section, by city or countryside—only one, the divide of
war, threatened to rip it in half. "Ex-Confederates, disciplined and united
by their years of adventuring in secession, were to be reckoned with," he
wrote. "Union and neutral Democrats were not happy over the dominant
way in which their erring brethren were coming to the front."[42]

The two sides started to load their muskets as early as February 1874.
With an eye on the statewide election in the fall, the influential Unionist-
Democratic *St. Louis Republican* ran an editorial that castigated Kentucky's
Democratic Party for falling into the hands of former rebels. "There is no
room in American politics for a Confederate party," the editors opined.
That provoked "a resentful reply," as the *Republican* itself reported, from
two secessionist standard-bearers, the *St. Joseph Gazette* and the *Kansas
City Times*. Their angry reaction generated more suspicion in turn from
the *Republican*. "Is there, then," it asked, "a scheme to make the party in
this state, too, a Confederate party?"[43]

Into this tensely divided camp galloped the James and Younger brothers—figuratively speaking—waving their Gads Hill loot, dragging the
bodies of dead Pinkertons, and escaping safely between the tents of the old
Confederates. "For ten years past the JAMES brothers and YOUNGER
brothers have robbed and murdered in this and adjacent states with
absolute impunity," the *Republican* stormed.

> They are known to hundreds of persons, and make no effort to conceal
> their identity. After each marauding expedition, they quietly return to their
> farms, there to rest and divide the spoils, relying for protection upon the
> faithfulness of friends and the fears of foes. Judges, sheriffs, constables and
> the whole machinery of law are either set at defiance by a gang of villains,
> or bought or frightened into neutrality. If such a condition of affairs existed
> in central Africa, it might not provoke much surprise, but that it exists in
> Missouri is a fact as remarkable as it is outrageous.[44]

In any other state, this editorial would have passed as conventional wisdom, the kind murmured among like-minded friends. But in war-wounded
Missouri, it represented an angry jab in the chest, a virtual challenge to a
fight. After two years of editorials by Edwards, friendly stories by his successors at the *Kansas City Times*, and praise from Peter Donan of the *Lexington Caucasian*, Jesse James and his companions had emerged as symbols
of Confederate pride. Republicans saw this clearly. "They had been for
years the heroes of an admiring circle of friends, and are admired by them

now," noted the Radical *Kansas City Journal of Commerce*. As the newspaper's editor, former congressman Robert T. Van Horn, observed, the bandits had cultivated this status themselves. "They are not ignorant men, who follow the lawless life they do from want of intelligence to rise above it," Van Horn said. As he saw it, the outlaws clearly understood their political status. "They cannot fail to appreciate the situation which the public understand—that their immunity comes from friendship, present and of the past, of those who sympathize with them."[45] Respect for the bandits had become virtual dogma among many old rebels. So when the *St. Louis Republican* criticized the local community for protecting them, it was consciously attacking the Confederate wing of its own party.

Even as Whicher's casket was being shipped back to Chicago, Republican state legislators gathered in Jefferson City to plan their strategy for the coming election. The ex-Confederates' support for the bandits represented an opening, a chance to split off Unionist Democrats—especially the Grangers, who showed an interest in forming an explicitly political movement in February 1874.[46] The Republicans passed a resolution that defined their campaign theme: it condemned the Democrats' "incompetency and misrule which has already depreciated property in the state to one-half its former value, and now threatens, through disorder and lawlessness, to drive away a large part of our best and peaceable citizens."

The Republicans had found the Democrats' weak spot, the *St. Louis Republican* argued. "There is a good deal of unquestionable truth in that part of the resolution which refers to disorder and lawlessness, at least, and if this charge is pressed home on the Democracy in the canvass, their leaders will have no easy task in replying to it." If the party was to win the election, the paper wrote, it had to address the bandit problem, even if that meant asking for help from Washington. "Anything is better than this tame submission to systematic brigandage."[47]

Governor Woodson heeded the newspaper's advice. He had already offered an enormous $2,000 reward* "for the bodies of each one of the robbers" of the Iron Mountain train. Now, two days after the *Republican*'s stern editorials, he sent an emergency message to both houses of the General Assembly, demanding the authority and the funding for "a secret police force" to catch the famous bandits. Even if the state had "a military force subject to my orders (which we have not)," he complained, there was not "one dollar in the military chest . . . that can be legitimately used in the suppression of a rebellion or enforcement of obedience to law by force! I suppose that there is not another State in the Union of which the same can be truthfully said." What the governor did not say, but which every legis-

---

*The standard governor's reward for fugitives was still $300, often much less.

lator understood, was that the Democrats themselves had brought about this sad state of affairs. Still angry over the Radicals' use of the militia in 1866, they had subjected the force to malign neglect—at best—after they returned to power.[48]

The dominant Unionist faction acted quickly on Woodson's request. The "extraordinary condition of affairs existing in the state," argued one state senator, referring to the bandits' popular support, "would require the use of extraordinary means to suppress the criminal outrages." In a few days, the General Assembly passed a law establishing a secret service, limited to twenty-five men, with a budget of $10,000, for the purpose of capturing the notorious outlaws. Confederate legislators did manage to block another measure to grant pensions to the families of Daniels and Lull, and to offer thanks to the Pinkertons, voting it down because it explicitly named the James and Younger brothers as outlaws.[49]

Woodson's appeal represented a damaging admission of failure, and the Democrats tried to keep it secret. When Republicans moved to have it printed, state senator Charles H. Hardin protested, saying "it was doubtful whether the message should be made public at all." But the Unionist *St. Louis Republican* published a copy under the headline "OUR BANDITTI. A Powerless Governor's Appeal for Assistance." It had caused a "sensation," the newspaper reported; "the reading of the message was listened to with rapt attention." The editors clearly hoped to back former Confederates into a corner with their coverage. "These depredations have become so frequent," the article declared, "that they may no longer be hidden for fear the great Democratic party may suffer."[50]

Woodson put the secret-service fund to work almost immediately, hiring his first agent, J. W. Ragsdale, on April 9, 1874.[51] But the struggle between Unionist and ex-Confederate Democrats intensified as the party convention approached. Edwards fired off ferocious editorials to rally the rebel faithful, prompting an angry response from William F. Switzler, a Unionist Democratic elder. "There can be no question," Switzler wrote in his newspaper, the *Columbia Missouri Statesman*, "we think that the *Dispatch* and some other Democratic organs desire to conduct the next election chiefly if not wholly—just as far as they dare—in the interest of the confederate Democracy, and upon the hypothesis that Union Democrats are orthodox enough to vote but too heterodox to be voted for." Tying former rebels directly to the outlaws, Switzler derided Confederates as Democrats of the "Gads Hill type," who would "divide . . . defeat and destroy the Democratic party." Another newspaper accused Edwards of keeping alive "the bitter passions" of the Civil War, "simply to gratify an unreasoning and morbid desire for revenge."[52]

It was amid this shouting match that Edwards unfurled his article about the wedding of Jesse James. Even so simple a story as this was intricately interlaced with Confederate themes. Zee Mimms, he wrote, "had been of immense service to the Southern guerrillas." He mentioned Jesse's wounding at the end of the war, and announced that the bandit "declared it to be his full intention to return and take trial when he thought he could get a trial other than at the hands of a mob." It seemed to be a part of his effort to rally the "Gads Hill type" of Democrats for the party convention; only the day before he had reminded his readers of "when to be a Democrat in Missouri was to be in danger of the shot-gun or the halter [noose]." Despite this "purifying process," he wrote, the party "needs a little weeding out, and the first day that comes the process should begin."[53]

When the Democratic convention nominated a gubernatorial candidate in August, it turned aside former Confederate general Francis Cockrell in favor of state senator Hardin, a Unionist. (Hardin had attended Governor Jackson's rump legislature in Neosho in 1861, but had cast the only vote in that meeting against secession.) Old rebels gritted their teeth. "Though ten years have elapsed since the war, no Confederate has been nominated by the Democratic party for Governor, Lieutenant Governor, or United States Senator," the *Kansas City Times* observed. Secessionists, wrote Walter B. Stevens, "resented the dictation: 'No ex-Confederates need apply.' It was about this time that John N. Edwards wrote for the *St. Louis Dispatch* an editorial which became historic: 'The boys are crawling out of the brush.' "[54]

Edwards meant his words as a metaphor for the gathering strength of Confederate voters, but they applied quite literally to Jesse and Frank James. Jesse soon returned from his honeymoon in Texas—where, some have suggested, he held up a series of stagecoaches—and reunited with his older brother, now married to Anna Ralston, as the political debate over their banditry raged. Undoubtedly Jesse appreciated the efforts of secessionist newspapers to defend him, but he must have been amused to read a story in the *Kansas City Times* on August 19, 1874, that claimed to prove his innocence. A badly wounded robber in Texas named James H. Reed wanted "to let the public know that McCoy and the James and Younger brothers have been persecuted in Missouri," the paper reported. Just before he died, Reed had confessed to all the crimes laid at their door.[55]

The story would have been doubly amusing because Jesse was already planning his next strike, in the very heart of his old hunting grounds. He and Frank had learned that a Parson Jennings of Mayview, Lafayette County, had gone to St. Louis to sell an extremely large lot of hogs, worth some $5,000. Jennings was expected to return through Lexington the evening of August 30. He would step off the train on the northern side of the Missouri River, they believed, then catch an omnibus, a stagecoach, to the ferry to reach Lexington. That was where they would catch him.[56]

On the afternoon of the appointed day, Jesse, Frank, and one of the Younger brothers rode into the thick belt of timber that lined much of the northern shore of the Missouri. The road from the railroad depot ran westward alongside the trees. The outlaws stationed themselves inside the woods just where the path turned south, before continuing across a bare sandbar to the ferry dock. At about six o'clock, they heard the rattle of harness, wheels, and hoofbeats as the stage approached. They spurred their horses into the open. Frank James, it appears, cut off the team of horses; Jesse and the representative of the Younger clan galloped up and thrust the muzzles of their revolvers through the windows.

"Damn it," one of them said, "he isn't here." Jennings, it turned out, had come home a day early. Making the best of it, the bandits ordered the male passengers and the driver, eight men in all, out onto the road as Jesse dismounted and handed his reins to Frank. The victims waited in a line, hands held high, as Jesse went through their pockets. The brothers' companion, however, noticed a few Sunday strollers walking nearby; he rode his horse over to them and ordered them to join the prisoners outside the stage.

"I know you," one of the pedestrians replied, "in spite of that dirty old veil over your face." She was a young woman from Lexington named Mattie Hamlett, and she had known the James and Younger brothers during the war. Her keen eye for faces, however, was not matched by a memory for names: she referred to the man in front of her as "Will Younger," but there was no brother by that name.[57] When she walked over to the omnibus, she recognized the sharp blue eyes and upturned nose—albeit masked—of the young James boy who had come into Lexington at the end of the war, badly wounded, but she called him Frank instead of Jesse.[58]

"Why, Frank James," she said, putting a hand on Jesse's arm, "I'm astonished to see you have come down to such small work. I thought you never did anything except on a big scale." He warmly shook hands with her, and made no effort to correct her mistaken identification. "Well, I am a little ashamed of it myself," he cheerfully replied. "It's the first time we've ever stooped to such small game. But you needn't call names quite so loud here." As he pulled money and watches from the men's pockets, Hamlett interceded on behalf of some of the victims. Jesse handed back the driver's gold watch at her request, but kept the chain. "No," she huffed, "give back the chain too; I won't have part, if I can't get all." He reluctantly complied.

From Lexington, perched high on a bluff across the river, the robbery could be seen in every detail. Word spread through the streets, and a large crowd gathered to watch the unfolding drama. It did not take long. As the outlaw rifled the passengers' pockets and bags, he pulled the largest sum from William Brown, a prosperous black man, who carried fifty-two dollars and a revolver. When Jesse arrived in front of J. L. Allen, an educator from Kentucky who had come to Lexington to set up a private school for boys, he admired the man's fine coat and vest—a sharp contrast to his own worn-out linen duster. Take them off, he ordered. "Don't take that man's clothes," Hamlett objected, to no effect. But at her request, he passed over a woman who remained in the coach, and the three bandits took their leave. There is no point in chasing us, Jesse said as he mounted. We're riding the finest horses in Missouri, and will be seventy-five miles away by morning. "Good-bye, Miss Mattie," he shouted as they rode away, "you'll never see us again."[59]

The omnibus robbery—taking place in front of hundreds of witnesses—caught the thoroughly embarrassed Governor Woodson on the campaign trail. In a speech in the town of Wellington, he could only sputter that he had not ordered the James boys arrested because he lacked the proper affidavits. The editors of the Radical *Lexington Register* sarcastically offered to send him a copy of their newspaper.[60]

In Jefferson City, Lieutenant Governor Charles P. Johnson hoped to staunch the political bleeding by capturing the famous bandits. Acting in Governor Woodson's absence, he sent a letter on September 1 to C. C. Rainwater, vice president of the St. Louis police board, urgently requesting help. (As noted earlier, the St. Louis police remained under the governor's control.) Two days later, Officer Flourney Yancey walked into Johnson's office, bearing a letter of introduction. "He is an excellent officer," Rainwater wrote, "an experienced soldier, and a brave and determined man." As the *St. Louis Globe* observed, he "was an expert scout during the war"—a background that would prove useful in the coming days.[61]

Johnson immediately sent Yancey to Lexington to meet with Thomas H. Bayliss and other citizens, who were to provide him with details of the omnibus robbery, and gave him authorization to requisition support from local authorities. He also sent orders to St. Louis chief of police L. Harrigan to prepare a half-dozen men to aid Yancey. And then he waited. After a week, he began to telegraph inquiries to Harrigan and Bayliss. "I have not heard from Yancy [sic] except through you," Harrigan replied on September 11. "I don't know anything about him," Bayliss telegraphed on the same day. "Went down the Pacific road when he left here."[62]

Johnson need not have worried: Yancey had found the outlaws' trail. From Lexington he traced them through Lafayette County, some eighteen miles south of Waverly. A U.S. deputy marshal reported that on September 6, the bandits ran into the Lexington brass band on the road, "but the members of the band being well armed presented a bold front, and were allowed to pass on unmolested." From there they circled back north and crossed the Missouri River. Yancey rode alone, asking discreet questions along the way, and learned that the two James brothers and Jim Younger were about twenty hours ahead of him. Near the railroad depot of Norborne in Carroll County, the bandits spent a night at a house belonging to the Pool clan, then trotted west, moving through the rugged Crooked River country north of Richmond on their way back to Zerelda's farm.[63]

Their old home proved to be no safe haven. As Yancey trailed them, Sheriff Patton relentlessly hunted them in Clay County, riding his prize racehorse, Dixie. "She [Dixie] has had a pretty hard time now for some time, running after the James boys and Jim Cummins," Bettie Patton wrote on September 4, 1874. (Cummins, a fellow veteran of Bill Anderson's band, was a friend of the outlaw brothers.) "George has nearly worn himself and horse both out."[64]

Yancey, meanwhile, lost the bandits' trail. He crossed back and forth over the Missouri River until he finally learned that Frank James had gone into Jackson County, and that Jesse and Jim Younger were headed east. He immediately telegraphed the Ray County sheriff, asking him to pull a posse together for service the next day. Then he rode toward Richmond, spending the night at a farmhouse near the boundary of Clay and Ray Counties.

The next morning, Jesse and Jim Younger prepared for their coming encounter with the St. Louis detective. They had been informed by the brother of one of their old bushwhacker comrades that Yancey had been spotted following them. They continued on their ride east through Ray County, but more carefully now, keeping an eye on their trail.

Just east of the village of Fredericksburg, not far from where Bill Anderson had fallen ten years before, they spotted a suspicious fellow following perhaps three hundred yards behind. They continued to a place where the road dipped down and rose up sharply, then stationed themselves some forty yards past this blind spot. The man soon appeared, his horse cantering up out of the dip in the lane. He had a pistol slung on his hip.

"Halt!" Jesse shouted, and he and Younger opened fire. But Yancey kept his nerve, drew his revolver, and shot Jesse, sending him crashing to the dirt. Jesse got to his feet and remounted as Yancey and Younger continued to shoot, pulled his other revolver, and began to fire again. Seconds later, the brief, intense skirmish suddenly ended. Yancey's horse, already dancing skittishly from the noise, went wild as the firing intensified and galloped away uncontrollably, carrying Yancey with it. "The fright of his horse," the *St. Louis Globe* reported, "probably saved his life."[65]

. . .

AS JESSE RETREATED with Younger to the shelter of a friend's farm, he confronted a more serious problem than the slight injury he had suffered. For long months, he and John Edwards had pursued the carefully crafted strategy of glorifying Jesse, glorifying his deeds, but protesting his innocence on any specific count. They had successfully created a fog of cognitive dissonance, allowing old Confederates to salute the outlaws' bravado and defiance and still see them as persecuted men. The Lexington stage robbery, however, had worked Peter Donan, editor of the *Lexington Caucasian,* into such a fit of enthusiasm that he had abandoned the program entirely and praised the James brothers by name.

"In all the history of medieval knight-errantry and modern brigandage, there is nothing that equals the wild romance of the past few years' career of Arthur McCoy, Frank and Jesse James, and the Younger brothers," Donan's story began. He went on to salute their war record under Quantrill and Anderson. "But even this weird, flashing record, combining the endurance and fleetness of the Bedouin Arab, with the savagery of the Cossack and the gallantry of true knighthood," he continued, "has been eclipsed by their exploits of later years. They have become pet institutions of Missouri. Their fame has become national, aye, world-wide. . . . These four or five men have absolutely defied the whole power of Missouri." After continuing in this vein for some time, the story led into the details of the robbery itself with the exclamation, "Lexington has just had the honor of one of their Robin-Hood-like, rattling visits." Donan went on to hail the three robbers by name. "The whole proceeding was conducted in the coolest and most gentlemanly manner possible," he wrote in conclusion. "Prof. Allen doubtless expresses the sentiments of the victims when he tells us that he is exceedingly glad, as he had to be robbed, that it was done by first class artists, by men of national reputation."[66]

Perhaps Donan wanted to stick his thumb in the eye of Unionists who relentlessly attacked the former guerrillas during the political campaign; perhaps he had tired of following the awkward strategy of praise-and-deny; perhaps he simply got carried away. Whatever the reason, Donan invalidated Jesse's alibi that he and his new wife had moved to Mexico. Fortunately for the Clay County outlaws, they had a cunning and determined ally to help control the damage: their mother.

No sooner had Zerelda read the *Kansas City Times*'s reprint of the *Caucasian*'s story than she mailed a letter to Mattie Hamlett, demanding a retraction. The missive arrived in Lexington the next day, and it left Hamlett badly shaken. "After a hasty consideration of its contents," she wrote back, "I have the privilege of replying as follows." Yes, she had identified the bandits, she admitted. "It was repeated, on my authority, that the James brothers were the perpetrators of the deed. After a mature reflection on the subject, I am prepared to doubt the accuracy of my recognition sufficiently to warrant me in refusing to make formal affidavit to the fact." She joined a growing list of witnesses who retracted statements after hearing from Jesse or his family. Zerelda forwarded a copy of the letter to the *Kansas City Times*. The James brothers were now famous enough for the *New York Times* to reprint it as well. Meanwhile, an anonymous note arrived at the *St. Louis Republican*, mocking the press for conjuring up the imaginary "Will" Younger, testifying to Jesse's absence in Mexico, and claiming that Frank was laid up with an old war wound.[67]

After Jesse returned home from his gunfight with Yancey, his mother acted once more to seal the breach in the public relations wall. With Dave Pool and Edwards as intermediaries, she made an appointment for an interview with Donan at the *Lexington Caucasian*'s offices. When she arrived in town with her fifteen-year-old daughter, Sarah, "all Lexington was buzzing with the news," Donan reported.

At three in the afternoon, Pool escorted her to the *Caucasian*'s offices and introduced her to the highly impressed editor. "Mrs. Samuel is a tall, dignified lady," he wrote, "graceful in carriage and gesture; calm and quiet in demeanor; with a ripple of fire now and then breaking through the placid surface; and of far more than ordinary intelligence and culture."

Zerelda repeated the well-established tale of how her boys had been persecuted in war and peace. She described how Jesse had been "seized in the field where he was at work" by Union militiamen, "a rope put around his neck, and instant death threatened," on the day that his stepfather was hanged. "When they went home after the surrender," she said, "they were driven to the brush by Fletcher's loyalists." Over and over she repeated, "No mother ever had better sons; more affectionate, obedient, and dutiful." On the subject of their innocence, she began to flare. "Say what the world may, my sons are gentlemen!" she exclaimed. "But I wish you, sir, to know, that *they are not in this country, haven't been for months, and may never be again.*" Dave Pool interrupted to say that he had received letters sent from Mexico by the boys, and editor Donan noted that Edwards had also assured him of their current exile in Mexico.[68]

Zerelda's interview, among other things, gave the Democratic Party political cover. At a major rally in Jefferson City, journalist Joseph Pulitzer took the stage to defend the record of Democratic rule over the last two years, particularly in regard to the banditry problem. "The Youngers and Jameses," he declared, "have not been arrested simply because they had long since fled the State."[69]

As the *St. Louis Republican* had predicted, however, the James-Younger gang proved to be the opposition's most potent weapon. By now, the Liberal Republican Party had collapsed, leaving the old Radical organization intact, though badly weakened. In an attempt to duplicate the Democrats' "possum policy" of 1870, the Republicans endorsed the new People's Party, a Granger-based set of populists who were concerned primarily with the depression, an expansion in the money supply, and control of the railroad corporations. This farmers' party hardly saw the bandits as Robin Hoods. "We want lawlessness put down in the state of Missouri," declared gubernatorial candidate William Gentry in his convention address. "How can we expect, with this staring us in the face, to get people from other states to come and bring their capital among us?"[70]

On September 24, 1874, Senator Carl Schurz picked up the theme in a major address in St. Louis. As an original Liberal Republican, the German immigrant had linked arms with the Democrats in 1870. After seeing his party disappear beneath his feet, however, he now sternly criticized his old allies. "I have been accused of having called Missouri the 'robber state,' " he declared. "I have to pronounce that utterly false." But the outlaw problem was real, he said. His fellow senators often came to him with newspaper stories of Gads Hill and other raids and asked, "Have you no laws and no government in Missouri?" The bandits, Schurz argued, were tolerated by the Democrats. "Has every party in the state pronounced itself emphatically for a relentless suppression of these outrages and a vigorous enforcement of the laws? . . . The Democratic party in state convention forgot all about it." Even worse, he complained, many Democrats actively supported the outlaws. Taking direct aim at Edwards and the *St. Louis Dispatch*, he observed that "a leading organ of that party [declares the bandits] . . . rather a nice and desirable set of fellows, [and] almost the whole Democratic press lustily chimes in." Please, he begged old secessionists, "Sink the Confederate in the citizen." Wartime hatreds and the toleration of banditry, he claimed—in a persistent Republican refrain—were stifling immigration and driving away investors.[71]

Schurz was on to something. The James and Younger brothers may indeed have helped clog the inflow of settlers and capital, which fell off sharply after 1872, and they were happy to have done it.[72] In Missouri, the quintessential border state, old Confederates had initially welcomed the immigration and railroad expansion of the immediate postwar years. But as the revolt against Reconstruction gained steam, as the depression that began in 1873 fed agrarian populism, some former rebels came to see them as the poisoned fruit of Radical rule, factors that threatened to transform Missouri into a Northern state.

The James-Younger gang had emerged out of the chaos of the Confederate defeat, out of a general defiance of authorities they did not recognize.

As they became more political under Edwards's influence, however, they added deeper meaning to past crimes. The railroads, for example, recruited immigrants from the North and Europe; banks lent money to new settlers. By robbing them, by creating a general sense of insecurity, Jesse and his companions could see themselves as taking direct action to preserve Missouri's Southern character.

"I know people called Missouri the state of bushwhackers and outlaws," Frank James later said. "They said it was the home of the James boys, and life and property were not safe. So the Republican emigrants went through Missouri without stopping. . . . The result is that Missouri is Democratic, her people have been forced to depend on her own resources."[73] Of course, it is impossible to establish that they had this in mind in planning any specific robbery. But as the Republicans expressed outrage in 1874, they congratulated themselves on their achievement.

For a time, it looked as if the People's Party might split off enough Union Democrats to carry the election. At the end of September a fracas erupted over statements by James O. Broadhead, an old ally of Frank Blair. "Rebelism" saturated the party, he complained, infuriating ex-Confederates; the war waged on Radicals "is a war also upon Union men."[74] The Democrats struck back—as the *New York Times* observed— by telling farmers that all their problems were "the fruits of Republican policy. Railroads are oppressive because of Republican ascendency. Monopolies are oppressive because Republicans foster them." Every question was tied to race and Reconstruction. Money, for example, was a key Granger issue: most farmers favored preserving and expanding a paper currency, but eastern financial figures had pushed Congress toward restricting the volume of greenbacks to more closely match the supply of gold. (A target date of 1879 had been set to make the paper notes redeemable at Treasury offices for gold coin.) Even this, the Democrats argued, should be seen in terms of the evils of Reconstruction. "The Republicans of the East look hopefully to a threatened war of the races," asserted the *Kansas City Times*, "as a means of withdrawing the thoughts of their Western brethren from dangerous leanings on the currency question."[75]

In reality, the reverse was true. The Democrats were divided on economic issues, but united behind white supremacy. As the election approached, the party press peppered readers with racist reports of "Radical negro attacks" in Louisiana and Mississippi, of a "war of the races" in Georgia, of Republican plans for "mixing negroes and whites in the public schools," of Senator Charles Sumner's Civil Rights Bill, which would largely ban segregation and discrimination. Partisan newspapers warned wavering followers that the "cloven foot of Radicalism" had left its hoofprints in the People's Party. Even Schurz's complaint about banditry, claimed the *Kansas City Times,* "is the same old Radical cry that has been used in all the Southern States as a pretext for keeping Democratic majorities out of power by fair means or foul." The *Liberty Tribune* responded to Republican complaints about the James boys by conjuring up "the Bacon Montgomery War in Lafayette County."[76]

The strategy worked. Democrats held their coalition together and trounced the People's Party in November. The sweep was nationwide. Battered by the depression, tired of continually suppressing white-supremacist violence in the South, Northern voters handed the House of Representatives to the Democrats for the first time since the war.[77]

It had been a good year so far for Jesse James. Just twenty-seven years old, he had achieved a national reputation. He had carried out two high-profile robberies, defeated the Pinkertons and the state authorities, out-lasted another sheriff—Democrat John S. Groom now replaced Patton—and married his sweetheart cousin. The hard work he and Edwards had put in over the last two years to transform his bandit crew into Confederate heroes had paid off handsomely, as secessionist newspapers rushed to apologize for—even glorify—them in the political campaign. And everything he loathed—Reconstruction, the Republican Party, even the Democrats' Unionist faction—showed signs of crumbling. He may have felt invulnerable.

But in the countryside around his mother's farm, his enemies were gathering, preparing to strike back. No one he had harassed, bullied, or fought in the decade since he first took to the brush had forgotten him: not his Unionist neighbors, not the former militia commanders, not John Groom. And definitely not Allan Pinkerton.

CHAPTER FIFTEEN

The Persistence of Civil War

O N DECEMBER 2, 1874, a man who knew the James brothers spotted Jesse and one of the Youngers near the Hannibal and St. Joseph Railroad terminal in Kansas City. As Jesse so often did, he rode a bay mare renowned throughout western Missouri for its speed; he was frequently identified by his striking and well-known horses. On this occasion, it appears that he and Younger were preparing to end the year as it had begun, with a train robbery.[1]

On the afternoon of December 8, the gang rode west into Kansas. They were headed to Muncie, a remote flag station on the Kansas Pacific Railroad perhaps a dozen miles west of Kansas City, a place that resembled, in some ways, the village of Gads Hill: a mere blink of a railroad stop sitting beneath a high hill, with little more to it than a general store that doubled as the post office, a blacksmith shop, and a few small houses. A dense growth of trees, a newspaper reported, "almost hide it from the eye of man."[2] When the bandits arrived, a few section men—railroad maintenance workers—toiled nearby; otherwise the area was nearly deserted.

The five men divided up. Three rounded up the Kansas Pacific laborers and ordered them to pile spare railroad ties on the tracks. The other two walked into the store and took its occupants prisoner. "When they heard the train coming," reported the store's owner, John Purtee, "they made me go out and flag it, one man covering me with a revolver."[3] The locomotive slowed sharply. As it drew close, the masked men fired a shot or two in the air and ran up to it. They pulled the engineer and the fireman to the ground, and ordered them to uncouple the baggage car. The railroad men dutifully unhitched it from the coal tender. The bandits pondered this rather pointless act, then realized that they had made a mistake. One hastily ordered the railroad workers to uncouple the baggage car from the passenger coaches, and then get back in the engine and pull it to where the ties were piled, about one hundred yards up the tracks.[4]

Inside the baggage car, messenger Frank D. Webster of Wells Fargo Express soon found himself under the control of two well-armed men. "Once inside, one placed a revolver to my head while the other levelled a Henry [Winchester] rifle on the other side, and I was told to unlock the safe," Webster recalled.

> I readily obeyed, and at their order handed out the contents. One of them took a mail-bag, and as I handed out the packages the other threw them into the bag. I took out $18,000 in currency, $5,000 in gold and all the packages of money in the safe. They said they did not want a silver brick that was there, and also gave me back my watch, saying they did not want my personal property. After having got all there was in the safe without touching anything else they ordered me to get out on the ground. While one guarded me the other took the money and got on his horse. The other left me and the others rode away to the north, going over a hill.[5]

Before departing, the bandits forced a passerby to exchange his fresh horse for one of their own worn-out mounts. Then they waved to the train crew. "Good-bye, boys, no hard feelings," they shouted. "We have taken nothing from you." After passing over the high hill to the north, they circled back to the south. Shortly after dark, they made camp for the night near the Kaw River. Sitting around the fire, they slit open the express packages and pulled out cash and jewelry, littering the ground with papers, envelopes, an empty pocketbook, small bills, a $20 Confederate note, and one of their masks. The loot came to almost $30,000—finally, the sort of haul they had expected in their previous express robberies. After dividing it up, they slept a few hours, then escaped undetected.[6]

News of the robbery reached Kansas City that same evening. "In ten minutes after the first rumor," the *Kansas City Times* reported, "the multitudes which just before had been pressing the thoroughfares, many on their return home from business, others just starting out for amusement, were bunched together upon the corners, under the gaslight, hearing and relating news and indulging in many curious speculations, and then turning to other assemblages hoping to learn something additional."[7]

The governor of Kansas offered $2,500 for each of the robbers, which was matched by $5,000 from the Kansas Pacific Railroad. But it was the express company, as always, that had suffered the actual loss and took the strongest interest in capturing the gang. Wells, Fargo & Co. posted a $5,000 reward for the return of the stolen property, and $1,000 for each outlaw. In the coming weeks, it would cooperate closely with the state of Missouri in tracking the outlaws. While railway journals ignored the attack, *Our Expressman* devoted a heartfelt column to it. "Messengers all, be on your guard," it cried. "Some day you will get the chance to distinguish yourselves, and be assured your courage and vigor and fidelity will not go unnoticed nor unrewarded."[8]

The long-suffering Governor Woodson immediately telegraphed the sheriff's office in Independence. "Let them have no shelter in Jackson county or any other county in this state," he ordered.[9] How Woodson must have pitied himself. To his very last days in office, Missouri's invincible bandits plagued him. On January 6, 1875, he used his last message to the General Assembly to address the problem. "The law hangs upon the will of the people," he pleaded, and he cited English law from the reign of Elizabeth—including the mass punishment of the residents near that medieval highwaymen's haunt of Gad's Hill—to make his point. Six days later, Governor Hardin picked up the same theme in his inaugural address. "The character of our State and people has been most violently assailed as being wanting in sentiment and efficiency for the maintenance of law and order," he grieved. To restore Missouri's battered reputation, he appealed to "the better sentiments of the community in active support of the law."[10]

The underlying problem, as the new governor understood, was the way the outlaws catalyzed the resentments of Confederate Democrats. The feud between the two wings of the party had never ceased, nor had secessionist anger toward the Republicans diminished. The increasingly influential John Edwards did his best to stoke the bitterness. On December 15, 1874, the *St. Louis Dispatch* printed a letter from "Justitia"—apparently Edwards—complaining of how Radical newspapers "relentlessly cudgel" the James and Younger brothers, who were powerless to defend themselves against "an incessant tirade of abuse." The letter recited a long list of the persecutions they had suffered in the war; afterward, the writer declared, "these ill-starred men [were] . . . driven into the bush to avoid the cowardly punishment threatened them by a crazed and clamorous mob." The writer ended with the claim that "these outraged citizens appeal for amnesty. Governor Hardin cannot more grandly celebrate his inauguration day than by granting their request."[11]

The shrewder Republicans grasped the outlaws' place in the politics of Confederate memory. It was the rebel-Democratic press, argued Robert T. Van Horn in the Radical *Kansas City Journal of Commerce*, "that gives them a political character." Along with a symbolic role came practical political connections. "That they had powerful friends everybody knew . . . and it was a matter of notoriety that [Arthur] McCoy [of the James-Younger gang] spent several days in Jefferson City during the sitting of the legislature, appearing in the lobby, and known to members on the floor—passing under an *alias*." The ex-Confederates maintained a double standard toward violence, Van Horn claimed, applauding attacks by their own kind, particularly against Republicans.[12]

He had a point. The *Lexington Caucasian* declared that the bandits' Muncie loot was "just as honestly earned as the riches of many a highly distinguished political leader or railroad job manipulator." But the newspaper applied a different standard to Mississippi, a state with a relatively honest government, acclaimed Union general Adelbert Ames as chief executive, and hundreds of earnest black officeholders. The *Caucasian* denounced Ames as "Grant's bayonet governor," and referred to its black legislators and public officials as "a dirty brood of nigger barbers, boot-blacks, and plantation chattels."[13] As long as any kind of racial equity held sway in the South, former Confederates such as the *Caucasian*'s staff and audience refused to believe the Civil War was over, and they refused to condemn the former Confederate guerrillas in the James-Younger band.

Then a strange thing happened: the police caught one of the outlaws. A Kansas City officer named Collopy arrested William "Bud" McDaniel, son of a Kansas City saloon owner and a comrade of the Jameses, shortly after the raid. When the officer patted down the inexperienced bandit, he found four revolvers, six dozen cartridges, $1,035.25, and some jewelry that had been taken from the Wells Fargo safe. McDaniel was soon sent to Kansas to stand trial.[14]

The capture of McDaniel should have been good news for the new Missouri governor. It wasn't. As Jackson County judge T. H. Brougham explained during a meeting in Jefferson City, the arrest by Officer Collopy was a freak accident. The Kansas City chief of police was reputedly a friend of the James boys, and had been seen drinking with McDaniel on the day the robber was caught. Even worse was the terror the James brothers inflicted on the community. Shortly after returning home, Brougham sent Hardin a clipping from the *Kansas City Evening News* reporting that a gunman had been spotted on the streets, late at night, apparently hunting for Collopy. "They will kill him if they get half a chance," Brougham wrote, "as they will have revenge in every particular. . . . It is a fact that any person who becomes obnoxious to the desperadoes is not safe in this part of the state."[15]

IT TOOK TEN years of peace to reveal the true scale of the Civil War. Not the grand scale—that was obvious, perhaps too obvious. The massive clash of armies had created the misleading impression that this was a conventional war between two sovereign governments. The immensity of it masked the smallness of the scale on which the war was truly fought. Only the political struggles that came after revealed how intimate a conflict it had been all along.

In the Reconstruction South—particularly in the black majority states of Louisiana, Mississippi, and South Carolina—the enfranchisement of African Americans drove this point home. As blacks joined the Republican Party en masse, whites had to face the fact that they not only lived side by side with people who had worked to defeat them during the war, but that these people opposed their political plans as well. The conflict was no longer one of distant battles, but of grassroots struggles over town councils and county courthouses. White-supremacist violence became increasingly systematic as the 1870s progressed, coinciding with the rising assertiveness and self-confidence of black voters and officeholders. In Louisiana in early 1873, white paramilitaries attacked the tiny village of Colfax after a disputed election; a force of black men held the town for three weeks before they were forced to surrender. The attackers rounded them up and executed at least fifty of them. In Warren County, Mississippi, the white minority tried to oust the black sheriff in 1874; on December 7, a well-armed force of whites ambushed the sheriff and his supporters, killing as many as three hundred African Americans in the days that followed.[16]

In Missouri, the Civil War had been a personal matter from the beginning. Confederate support had been concentrated in certain regions, of course, particularly along the Missouri and Mississippi Rivers, but even there, communities had divided among themselves, household by household.* After a full decade of peace, people still remembered what their neighbors had done.

These memories burned with new life as Jesse James and his comrades seized headlines. In November 1874, for example, a man approached the circuit clerk of Daviess County, offering to identify the James brothers in the still-open murder case of John W. Sheets. The would-be witness was Frank Cooley, the old Radical Unionist from Lexington who had been a central figure in the 1866 affair that led to the death of Archie Clement. His offer was a hint that Jesse James had been present on that occasion, still bitterly remembered by partisans on both sides.[17]

In Clay County, fear intensified after the murder of Joseph W. Whicher. "You cannot get a word of information," wrote Van Horn after a visit to Clay in early 1875, "save upon the condition that you religiously keep the name of your informer a secret—this being the prerequisite confidence to any conversation." The terror stemmed not from the James brothers alone, but from the continuing division of society along wartime lines. "The

---

*The low number of black Missourians, combined with the deep division of the white population, kept the politics of wartime allegiance in the state from taking on the primarily racial character seen in the old Confederacy.

'James boys' have a very large acquaintance in the county, many of whom became their associates and partisans during the guerrilla and bushwhacking times of the war," Van Horn explained. "They are 'just as good friends of the boys' now as before."[18]

"The business in Clay Co., Mo., is troubling me badly," Allan Pinkerton wrote shortly after the assassination of Whicher. But no one was more discouraged by the deaths of Pinkerton's agents than William B. Dinsmore, president of the Adams Express Company, and he knew when to cut his losses. "Concluding that the robbers had been frightened enough to make them behave," as William Pinkerton sarcastically put it, Dinsmore "withdrew from the prosecution of the case. Allan Pinkerton then took up the matter and expended $10,000 of his own money trying to bring the marauders to justice." For the elder Pinkerton, detective work was always a matter of passion as much as profits; he was, after all, an old abolitionist, a man who had risked much to help the underground railroad and John Brown. He took the murders of Whicher and Lull personally, and he wanted revenge.[19]

As Allan Pinkerton pursued the case—more quietly now, with greater respect for his opponents—he discovered that Clay County's wartime enmities could work in his favor. As the months progressed, he made contact with a succession of old Unionists who were eager to wipe out Jesse and Frank James. First he encountered Samuel Hardwicke, a forty-year-old native of Clay and a leading attorney in Liberty. One contemporary called Hardwicke "a man of unusually quiet manners . . . more given to the study of his books and to reflection than to the enjoyment of society." Though he carried no arms during the Civil War, he had belonged to the Unionist establishment and had helped organize a loyalist mass meeting to honor Lincoln after his assassination.[20] Inconspicuous, well connected, and, above all, a staunch Union man, Hardwicke would be the perfect local coordinator for the detective's plans.

Hardwicke agreed to work for Pinkerton in April or early May 1874. Shortly afterward, he recruited another local Union man, Daniel H. Askew, a former militiaman and—unlike Hardwicke—a staunch Radical Republican. Askew brought to Pinkerton's burgeoning network an absolutely essential ingredient: a base. He owned a 210-acre farm directly adjacent to Zerelda's homestead.[21]

Through the end of the year, Hardwicke sent telegrams to Chicago, coded in a simple word-substitution cipher, keeping Pinkerton informed of the James brothers' movements. Meanwhile, Pinkerton slowly infiltrated men into Clay County. Jack Ladd, for example, showed up on Askew's farm halfway through the year, posing as a laborer. In light of Whicher's murder, Pinkerton intended to hide the budding conspiracy from then-sheriff George E. Patton. He failed. Hardwicke, Patton later explained to his brother-in-law, "had but one confidant here [in Liberty], and that man was my confidant. . . . I have known his operations for the last four months [i.e., since October 1874], but never breathed a word to any living being. They knew nothing of my being posted to their movements, and they never shall, on either side." Indeed, neither Pinkerton nor Jesse James ever did.[22]

To further his efforts, Pinkerton sent letters to Postmaster General Marshall Jewell and Chief Special Agent Patrick H. Woodward, head of the office of mail depredations, asking for a contact in the Kearney post office. Even this delved into the deep division between Unionists and secessionists in Clay County. The man recommended to Pinkerton was the Kearney postmaster, Anthony Harsel. A native of Clay, and a former slaveowner, Harsel had led one of the first EMM companies in the county; his wartime experiences (secessionists torched his house, among other things) had radicalized him, with a capital R. He became a leader of the local Republican Party, supervisor of voter registration, and later the first justice of the peace in Kearney township (organized in 1872). Even after the Democrats' sweeping return to power in Missouri, Harsel remained a political force. Local postmasters were influential figures in post–Civil War America; the president himself used appointments to the post to reward political followers. The old Radical Unionist eagerly joined Pinkerton's crusade. "Harsel the postmaster has appointed a deputy [to help watch the James brothers]," Pinkerton reported to Woodward, "and has himself gone into the country." Whether Harsel also opened mail addressed to the Samuel farm remains unknown.[23]

The cooperation of the post office did not mean, as the press later suggested, that Pinkerton operated on the federal payroll. He approached the department as a supplicant asking a favor. A review of the letters sent from the offices of both the chief special agent and the postmaster general reveals no official correspondence with Pinkerton; indeed, no case file exists for any of the James brothers' robberies. The aid Jewell and Woodward offered was strictly off the record.[24]

After the Muncie train robbery in December, Pinkerton prepared for the final strike. "I am expecting every day to bring this thing to a climax," he wrote to Woodward on December 15. "At least two or three parties are there, but they are well armed, and have all the advantages men could ask. We must be cautious, and make our movements secure, and then I hope every tick of the wire will tell us we have got our men."[25]

With evidence mounting that the James brothers were at home, Hardwicke hastened ahead with the preparations. Sheriff Patton—tipped off by his informer—was surprised to learn that the quiet, bookish lawyer had emerged as "the prime mover of the whole affair, and the getter-up of the plan of operations."[26] Hardwicke met secretly with L. W. Towne, the general superintendent of the Hannibal and St. Joseph Railroad, to arrange for a special train to carry Pinkerton's raiding party. He established a stockpile of guns, so the detectives would not have to carry weapons with them en route. And he recruited one or more guides to lead them to Zerelda's farmhouse. On Christmas Day, Hardwicke was able to send Pinkerton a critical telegram containing his final ideas on how the capture should be carried out.

"I have given it serious thought," Pinkerton replied, "have had Robert with me all the time, and we both accord you great credit in taking care of everything you had to do." He was referring to Robert J. Linden, a senior agent designated to lead the Missouri operation. "Now for the battle," he continued. "It makes us feel like laughing at the great preparations we are making to tackle 2 or 3 men. Still, they have many friends. We may set them down as legion."

Pinkerton then ticked through the remaining work to be done. First, he was going to arrange with the Burlington Railroad to pass through his men and the ammunition, just as the Hannibal and St. Joseph had agreed to do. Second, Linden would visit the U.S. arsenal at Rock Island, Illinois, carrying with him a letter of introduction from General Sheridan, commander of the Military Division of the Missouri, and he would carry away a special device. Third, Pinkerton asked Hardwicke to have Addie Askew, Daniel's wife, prepare food for the detectives; there would be seven men, he noted, including Linden. "It could be left somewhere for Jack [Ladd] to pick it up," he added, "but great care must be taken to excite no suspicion and leave no clue behind." Fourth, a surgeon would accompany the party, at least as far as the Cameron junction in Clinton County. Fifth, Hardwicke's guide had to pick out the shortest route from the railroad tracks to the Samuel farm, for "the men are not woodsmen." Ladd would lead them back. Hardwicke was to hold the special train after the raid until Linden was certain that everyone had returned safely. And Pinkerton was most concerned that they "know positively" when the James brothers were at home. "It won't do for us to take chances," he observed.

He had one final comment. "Above all else destroy the house, wipe it from the face of the earth," he wrote. "How the logs will burn. . . . Burn the house down." Nothing could have better demonstrated how personal the matter had become.[27]

At five o'clock in the afternoon on January 25, 1875, the Pinkerton agency learned—probably through a telegram from Hardwicke—that the

James brothers were at their mother's home. In short order Linden had his
men ready to go, almost certainly waiting at a depot on the Hannibal and
St. Joseph Railroad. The railroad provided them with a light train, consisting of a locomotive and a caboose. The Pinkerton men loaded it with a
large quantity of weapons and equipment—including that special device
from the Rock Island arsenal—and then set out down the line. At 7:30
p.m., they arrived just outside of Kearney. Hardwicke's guide or one of the
Pinkertons on the scene flagged down the train, helped them unload their
supplies, then led them through the woods. What they did for the next four
hours is uncertain; most likely they waited in the woods, eating the food
Addie Askew had prepared for them, then went to a nearby road to collect
the horses that had been tied up for them.[28]

"After getting things ready we advanced on the house," Allan Pinkerton explained to Woodward on January 27. Always prone to self-
aggrandizement, he wrote as if he had been present; he was not, though he
had personal knowledge of what transpired. "Not a word was spoken, and
about half past twelve midnight, we commenced firing the building." The
raiding party—perhaps eight or nine men in all—divided up. Most
remained mounted and stood guard near the barn and the icehouse; two or
three walked up to the farmhouse, pulled loose the weatherboarding that
encased the structure, and inserted "hollow tubes, shaped like a roman can-
dle, and filled with combustible and inflammable material," as a reporter
described them. "These were put between the siding and log walls, and
then ignited."

Having started the fire on the outside, the detectives now produced the
special device from the Rock Island arsenal: an iron ball, seven and a half
inches in diameter, filled with an inflammable liquid that drained slowly out
through a small hole onto a cotton covering. They set it on fire and tried to
throw it inside. "But judge our dismay," Pinkerton wrote, "when we found
every window fastened on the inside with wooden boards, although so
concealed by a curtain that they could not be seen from the outside. . . .
Such is the manner in which the house is kept. It is a perfect citadel, however my men were equal to the occasion, and soon battered in the windows,
then flung the fire balls into the house."[29]

IN THE CHRISTMAS cold of 1874, Jesse James kept close to home. He
and Frank moved in and around Independence, where they were spotted
dining with friends and attending church services.[30] Midway through the
month, Jesse sent his wife back to his mother's farm—perhaps, as the press
surmised, because the newly pregnant Zee was not feeling well.[31] On Janu-

ary 16, she stepped off the train from Kansas City onto the Kearney platform, where Reuben Samuel met her with his wagon and drove her home.
Jesse followed a week later. On January 23, he was spotted on his well-
known horse in Ray County.[32]

The little Samuel house bustled with activity on the night of January 25.
As usual, the black residents of the farm—fifty-four-year-old Charlotte,
eighteen-year-old Ambrose, and six-year-old Perry—busied themselves
with chores and dinner preparations. Though called "servants," they were
living out a practical continuation of slavery, into which Charlotte and
Ambrose had been born; even little Perry would be given no options for
another life. Meanwhile, Zerelda was preparing thirteen-year-old John and
ten-year-old Fannie to go to a party given by a nearby family. (Her oldest
daughter by Reuben now lived in Sherman, Texas, where she attended the
high school taught by Susan James Parmer.) As they went out the door,
they told eight-year-old Archie that he couldn't come with them. "Archie
came to me in the evening after they had gone," Zerelda said two days later,
"and looking into my face, said, 'Ma, I am so hungry, and brother and sister have gone to a party. They wouldn't let me go. . . . You'll go to Kearney
tomorrow, won't you and buy me something?' I dressed him up in his new
suit, as he asked me to do, and he sat upon my knee. I thought he never
looked so beautiful and confiding."[33]

Even with the older children gone, the family dinner table was more
crowded than usual. Informed sources insisted that Jesse, Frank, and Clell
Miller spent that evening in Zerelda's house. A neighbor's farmhand spotted William Fox—known to be a lookout for the James brothers—leading
three horses out into a pasture after nightfall. As Fox tied up the animals,
the watching laborer recognized one of them as Jesse's famous mare. After
darkness fell, Jesse and his companions took their leave, sneaked through
the woods to their horses, and rode away.[34]

With the boys gone, the Samuel household settled in for the night. The
home consisted of three rooms: a parlor at the east end, a family room in
the middle, and the kitchen on the west side.[35] After the children returned
from the party, Zerelda and Reuben made their beds in the family room.
Charlotte, Ambrose, and little Perry retired to the kitchen, bolting the door
to the adjoining room before crawling under quilts on the floor. After a
busy day, silence descended on the farm.

About half past midnight, Ambrose jolted awake. "I heard noise at the
northwest corner of the kitchen, and men talking," he said the next
evening. "I then raised up in my bed and saw a light glimmering through a
crack in the panel of the door. I then got up . . . looking toward the north
window, and saw two men, either one or the other or both with a light in

their hands; they then raised a ball or something that was red and threw it at the window, which knocked me down. It then fell on the floor, and an oily substance ran out over the floor."

In the family room, the hubbub startled Reuben out of a heavy sleep. "Hearing the noise, as though something was falling on the floor, I supposed that the house was falling in from the fire on the negroes," he recalled. "I ran to the door; it being fastened, I went [outside] around to the west end of the house and saw the west end of the kitchen on fire."

As Reuben tore off the flaming weatherboarding, Zerelda also awoke and went to investigate. Finding the kitchen door "barred on the inside by the negroes as usual," she stepped out into the cold night air "and went on round to the north door and went into the kitchen, and on entering I saw something like a bowl on fire in the middle of the floor. I tried to kick it over. Then Reuben took hold of the shovel and threw the said bowl into the fireplace." Seeing that one of the quilts in the kitchen had caught fire, she seized it and went to throw it outside. "I then opened the south door leading onto the porch and went out on the porch, and then immediately turned round [after tossing the quilt aside] and went back into the kitchen and there was some time that I do not know what transpired."[36]

At that moment, the Samuel family and its attendants were clustered around the large, open fireplace where the strange object burned. Standing closest to it were Reuben, Ambrose, John, Zerelda, and little Archie. They did not know—nor would they ever find out—that this was the special device provided to Pinkerton agent Robert Linden by the Rock Island arsenal. It was certainly meant to light up the interior of the house, so the inhabitants could be seen through the windows; it was probably meant to help set the building on fire as well; but it was definitely not intended to do what it did next. When Reuben rolled it into the hearth, it nestled in a roaring fire, far hotter than the flickering of the cotton wick that covered the device. The inflammable material inside superheated. Then the sphere exploded.[37]

The erupting liquid inside shattered the casing, sending heavy chunks of cast iron blasting in every direction. Reuben staggered back when a small piece struck him on the side of the head, and Ambrose fell through the front door when another scrap hit his skull. A larger fragment smashed Zerelda's right arm just above the wrist. One last piece tore through Archie's third rib on his left side and seared through his bowels. The two men regained their feet and carried the wounded boy outside. They returned to help Zerelda, who was moaning that she had been shot. "The first thing that came to my recollection as I gradually grew to myself," she said several hours later, "my arm was hanging loose by my side, it being my right arm, it being broken just above my wrist."[38]

After Reuben got his injured wife into bed, he went outside and bellowed into the night sky for help. Then he heard noises in the woods just beyond the icehouse and other outbuildings—the noisy tramp of horses moving rapidly through the underbrush, followed by a quick patter of gunfire. Unfortunately, the neighbors heard gunfire as well; at least one man who responded to Reuben's call turned around and went home when he heard the shots. Not everyone, however, was deterred. The first person to reach the Samuel house was the family's closest neighbor—Daniel Askew.

With the help of Askew and other fresh arrivals, messages went to nearby doctors; in short order, Dr. James V. Scruggs arrived from Kearney, followed by Dr. William G. Yates from the same town, Dr. Sheets from the village of Greenville, and Dr. Allen from Liberty. As the physicians clustered around Zerelda and her son, someone stole Scruggs's horse from the yard; it turned up about three miles away, thoroughly exhausted, having been ridden at a gallop the entire way. "Everybody has their own opinion about it," wrote Scruggs's daughter. "Pa's is, he [the horse] carried a messenger somewhere." William Fox was soon charged with stealing the animal.[39]

From the first moments after the blast, it was clear that Archie would not live until morning. As the wounded Zerelda waited for medical attention, Reuben brought the dying boy to her side for a last moment together, then carried him to another bed. "After a while Dr. Sheets came in and told me he couldn't live much longer," Zerelda stated the next day. "I said to him, 'Oh God, receive the soul of my child.' Archie heard me and replied, 'Tell my mama I'm better.' They were the last words he spoke." Zerelda, an iron-willed woman who had withstood the death of two husbands, militia raids, military prison, and exile, now quivered with emotion. "I had often thought of what might happen to Jesse and Frank, and was prepared to hear most anything; but I never expected to see this. I never thought I should live to see my pet child stricken down at my side," she said. "I used to be a woman of fortitude and resolution; it is all gone now. I could stand anything but this."[40]

There is no reason to doubt that she spoke honestly, but by the next nightfall she had already begun to recover her inner strength. In the early hours of January 26, Dr. Allen severed her shattered limb. "The Dr. says he don't think he ever saw a human being with more nerve in all his life than Mrs. Samuel has—he'd amputated her right arm just below the elbow," wrote Bettie Patton to her brother. Zerelda endured the excruciating operation in her own home—without anesthesia, needless to say—and remained alert enough to take part in the coroner's inquest that convened in her house that evening. Justice of the Peace Joel T. Albright gathered a jury of five men, including Zerelda's brother, Jesse R. Cole, and Daniel Askew.

"Mrs. Samuels sat by the bedside," wrote a reporter who attended the proceedings, "a portly, dignified woman suffering intense pain, however." She and Reuben gave their testimony, then signed their names to their statements. Ambrose spoke as well; but he had been allowed no education other than that of the fields, so he could only scrawl an X—"his mark."[41]

The next day, the family worked on the damaged house, tended the wounded Zerelda, and prepared Archie's body for burial; a reporter saw the dead boy the next day, "dressed in a suit of Confederate gray." On Thursday they had more visitors: a posse led by Sheriff John S. Groom. A forty-six-year-old native of Clay County, Groom had served under O. P. Moss during the Mexican War, then fought for the Confederacy. He had barely survived the Civil War. Shot through the shoulder at the battle of Lone Jack, he had recuperated for a time before raising a new company, which he led straight into a Union ambush outside of Liberty. He had hid in the brush for nine days as his scattered men were hunted down, then he fled Missouri for the duration of the war. With the coming of peace he had established a store in the new village of Kearney, where he had maintained quiet but uneasy relations with his fellow rebel Jesse James, facing his wrath after the murder of John W. Sheets on one hand, and providing him with an alibi on the other. In the Democratic primary of 1874, he had defeated Sheriff Patton. Now he had the responsibility for catching the James brothers. "I am mighty glad I was not sheriff" when the Samuel farm was attacked, Patton wrote a few weeks later.[42]

Embarrassed into action by the Pinkertons' involvement, Groom gathered forty-six men after the raid. He sent half on a sweep through the countryside, and half he led to the famous farmhouse. There he divided his men into three parties—two to guard the outside, lest anyone try to flee, and the other, led by Liberty township constable W. J. Courtney and James-fighting-veteran Oscar Thomason, to search the house itself. They had heard rumors of subterranean passages leading out of the building, but they found nothing except numerous gun ports cut into the walls. They arrested four young men: William Fox; Edward Samuel, Reuben's nephew; Ed Miller, brother of Clell; and George James, cousin to Jesse and Frank. Before the prisoners departed with the posse, Zerelda called them over to her sickbed. "They're just taking you down there to pump you," she told them. "Keep your mouths shut, and don't tell anything you don't know."

Both the arrests and the fruitless search afterward threatened to turn the entire affair into a farce. George James, for example, was a mere boy, and not a terribly bright one at that. Bettie Patton called his incarceration "the gayest thing of the season." She sent a copy of the press report to her brother and sister, writing, "I think you both would appreciate it knowing

Geo. so well. The idea of his not knowing he was *arrested* until he was nearly to Kearney, was the part that amused me so much." George Patton sarcastically observed that Groom and Courtney had "immortalized themselves." As proprietor of the new *Liberty Advance,* "I could make a big thing out of this," he added. "Many of my friends have begged me to do it, but it won't never do. . . . I am dependent on some of the very parties whom I would delight so much to ventilate before the eyes of the world." But Groom did find Jesse's famous mare in the barn, suggesting that he had come close to capturing the outlaw.[43]

Word of the attack spread across the western Missouri landscape within hours of the explosion. In Kansas City the next afternoon, one reporter learned of it from a breathless stranger on the street. "Have you heard the news?" he asked. "There has been a fight over in Clay county at the home of the James boys; they have been captured and their mother killed in her efforts to defend their lives, and a little boy aged eight years also killed." The journalist caught the next train to Kearney. "On his way to the depot he met numerous persons who stopped and repeated the news," he reported, writing in the third person. "Once at the depot, he was again surrounded by an eager throng, who questioned him as to the truth of the rumor."[44]

Across the river in Clay, people could speak of little else. "The county," scribbled Bettie Patton, "is in perfect commotion over this James affair." Neighbors wrote of the "shocking affair" and the "tragedy." George Patton could not conceal his disgust. "The grand move," as he called it, "has made hundreds of friends for the James boys, when they had but few."[45]

The sensation rapidly spread to the entire state—indeed, the nation at large—as the press poured out dozens of often contradictory stories. Reporters scoured the countryside looking for details, particularly information about the special train that had carried the attackers. They learned that it had proceeded to Kansas City after dropping off the raiders, then had returned to pick them up in the early hours of the morning. "Now as to the 'mysterious car' which conveyed the attacking party," offered the *Kansas City Journal of Commerce,*

> it has been followed carefully, and is found in Brookfield [the Linn County depot where the raiders likely started their journey]. Arriving there, the mysterious men, who conducted and shaped the course of this mysterious car, caused it to be switched off and taken from the main track. It was visited by a citizen of Brookfield, who was seen to take from it a very considerable number of guns and pistols. . . . The inmates, while at Brookfield, preserved the greatest reticence, and all their conversation was carried on in slang peculiar to detectives.

According to the *St. Louis Republican*, one fellow asked the returning men, "What success?" The reply was grim: "Don't ask us; don't say anything about it." At Brookfield, they packed up their firearms and shipped them east by express; then, the press reported, they departed for Illinois.[46]

No one seems to have doubted the identity of the mysterious attackers. "Universal report charges this deed of hell upon Pinkerton's Chicago Detectives," declared the *Lexington Caucasian*, "in revenge for the supposed killing of two or three of their number by Frank and Jesse James." Indeed, virtually every report blamed Allan Pinkerton and his agency. When a loaded revolver was found near the barn, with the initials "P. G. G." filed into the barrel, the press seized on this as direct evidence. First the letters were said to stand for "Pinkerton's Grand Guard," then "Pinkerton's Government Guard." The newspapers overlooked the fact that the agency had apparently *never* been known by either name, even during the Civil War. The letters were probably the owner's initials.[47]

Similar overenthusiastic reporting surrounded the raid itself. Initially it was said—incorrectly—that a wild gunfight had broken out, and that the Pinkertons had succeeded in capturing the outlaws. "But anybody that knows anything about Jesse," wrote Bettie Patton, "knows that whenever he's captured, a black box will suit him better than chains." Another neighbor thought it "useless to conjecture who are the perpetrators of so horrible a crime, but I have no doubt but the 'James brothers' will make a desperate attempt to find out." When they did, Patton added, "Jesse & Frank would make it pretty warm for those men."[48]

WHEN JOHN EDWARDS learned of the attack, while the fate of the James brothers was still unclear, he penned perhaps the most ferocious editorial of his fire-eating career to date. "Men of Missouri, you who fought under Anderson, Quantrell, Todd, Poole . . . recall your woodcraft and give up these scoundrels to the Henry rifle and the Colt's revolver," he wrote in the *St. Louis Dispatch*. He wasted no ink on railroad corporations, government corruption, or the market economy—instead, he appealed purely to wartime loyalties. "It is not for the robberies they are accused of that Pinkerton hates the James brothers. It is because like you they were at Lawrence, and Centralia . . . and wherever else the black flag floated and men neither knew nor wanted quarter."

"The language of the *Dispatch* is remarkable," responded Robert Van Horn, in the *Kansas City Journal of Commerce*. "It does not invoke the proper authority of the state to defend its honor . . . but invokes a lawlessness worse than anything alleged against" the James boys. "It were sickening in any case," he wrote, "but more especially as coming from the official organ of the dominant party, as the sentiment of that party." Van Horn's trenchant editorial zeroed in on the latter point—the most explosive feature of Edwards's editorial, and of the situation in general. "The most unfortunate fact connected with this affair is the political aspect the treatment of the Democratic press attaches to it," he wrote. His fellow Republicans had "somewhat flippantly" accused the Democrats of fostering the James brothers' banditry, he argued, but "the treatment of the affair by the papers which represent the controlling elements of that party fully warrant that charge. . . . The *Dispatch*, it is sad to say, is owned by the master spirit of the Missouri Democracy, and for some time has been regarded as containing the official utterances of the party."[49]

The faction Van Horn spoke of was the ex-Confederate wing, which was indeed represented by the *St. Louis Dispatch*, owned by state legislator Stilson Hutchins. But Van Horn went too far in declaring the former rebels the "ruling element" and Edwards's shoot-them-dead essay the party's official opinion. "The editorial in the *St. Louis Dispatch* has excited considerable unfavorable comment" among Democratic legislators, a journalist reported from the floor of the General Assembly, "and the general expression is that it is a very indiscreet article." In reply, the *St. Louis Republican* offered the opinion of the Unionist faction of Democrats. "The amount of damage the James boys and their gang have done directly," the paper argued, "is nothing compared to the mischief they do in keeping up the impression abroad that lawlessness is . . . encouraged by people who are members of society in the South and Southwest. In other words, the political mischief of which they are the cause is vastly more insufferable than the crimes themselves which they commit."[50]

In fact, Hutchins and Edwards were seizing this very moment to lift the former Confederates to supremacy within the party. The public was outraged by the attack; Edwards and his employer were sincerely outraged as well, but they knew how to turn the situation to their advantage. On January 30, 1875, Hutchins offered a resolution in the state House of Representatives, demanding that the governor look into the affair. In both the document itself and his comments on the floor, Hutchins picked up the language of the anti-Reconstruction Redeemers of the Deep South. "This State has been invaded without authority of law," he thundered. "The peace and dignity of the State have been violated, its sovereignty offensively encroached upon." The resolution silenced Unionist Democrats; given the general outrage, they could scarcely disagree with it in public. When it went to the state senate, "the most peculiar feature of the discussion," the *St. Louis Republican* reported, was that the Democrats made "several uncomplimentary allusions" to their Unionist governor and his predecessor, while only Republicans defended them.

There was a political purpose behind this entire exercise: "to excite the public mind," as one Republican senator put it, for the benefit of ex-Confederate Democrats. "It seemed that after these highwaymen had committed crimes that stamped them outlaws and murderers," he said, "there yet existed a sympathy for them, and that sympathy was now to be excused by the legislature." Shortly afterward, the Republicans offered their own resolution, "requesting the Governor to inquire into the depredations of the James brothers," and asking for advice on special legislation to catch them. The attempt failed under the bitter attacks of Hutchins and his ally Jefferson F. Jones of firmly secessionist Callaway County.[51]

All this was pure political posturing. The day before Hutchins offered his resolution—which easily passed in both houses—Governor Hardin had already asked Adjutant General (and noted artist) George Caleb Bingham to go to the scene of the attack and report back. Hardin presented Bingham's report to the General Assembly on February 4, prefaced by a message that confirmed that men from another state had carried out the raid and that promised to requisition their return to Missouri for trial once they were properly identified. But when Bingham's thorough findings finally appeared in print, all references to the Pinkertons were carefully deleted.[52]

Confederate Democrats were unsatisfied. The attack on the Samuel farm appeared at a propitious moment for them. Across the South, Reconstruction was trembling toward collapse, as Grant and his cabinet lost their will to intervene with federal troops to protect the rights of black citizens. And in Missouri itself, the final assault had begun on the last vestige of the Radical legacy: the constitution of 1865. In the 1874 election, voters had narrowly approved a convention to draw up a new governing document; delegates had been elected in January 1875 and would meet in May. The resentments of former rebels drove this movement: they wished to delegitimize the suppression of their insurrection, to sanctify their cause, and to retroactively humiliate their opponents. At times, it seemed as if they were still fighting the war itself. On February 12, 1875, with the ink on Bingham's report barely dry, the General Assembly demanded that Governor Hardin report on "the military relation . . . between this State and the general government."[53]

John Edwards, meanwhile, used the public outrage to build sympathy for the James and Younger brothers—which he used, in turn, to give added force to the politics of the Lost Cause. The focus for this two-headed campaign was a demand that the bandits receive amnesty. In late February, an article by an anonymous Missouri correspondent appeared in the Democratic *Chicago Times*—an article that matches Edwards's florid style—and was reprinted by the *St. Louis Dispatch*. "There is a growing sentiment here on the part of the legislature in favor of extending amnesty to the James boys and the Younger brothers," the piece began. "Your correspondent has the news on good authority that a bill to this effect will within a day or two be introduced." The lengthy article focused exclusively on the Civil War, depicting Missouri as a Southern state invaded by the outside forces of abolitionist Kansas jayhawkers and Radical Republicans. The James and Younger families suffered terrible abuses, the writer claimed, and the boys had no choice but to fight back. For that, they were persecuted by Radicals even after the peace. "They are outlaws through no fault or crime other than participating in a civil war that was not successful," the writer argued, and were "now so wantonly and unjustly hunted and denounced by all who have partisan passions to gratify."[54]

Edwards continued the campaign throughout March. First he penned an editorial that presented the case for amnesty and discussed the constitutional issues involved. (A governor could only issue a pardon after a conviction.) Then he went to Jefferson City in person at the end of the month to help coordinate the effort. By now, he had emerged as one of the most influential newspaper editors in the state. "For his fame and real worth," wrote a *Lexington Caucasian* correspondent who spotted him on the General Assembly floor, "I must not fail to mention John Edwards. . . . He is one of the oddest and best of men. . . . Noble, generous, childlike in simplicity, but great in mind, a journalist, historian, and altogether one of Missouri's most illustrious sons."[55]

Edwards himself, it appears, crafted an amnesty bill that Representative Jefferson Jones submitted, only to have it declared unconstitutional by the attorney general. Together Edwards and Jones worked up a new version that would pass muster, which Jones offered as a joint and concurrent resolution on March 17. Given the restrictions of the constitution, it would do little in practical terms to protect the James and Younger brothers; it would simply pardon them for wartime offenses and guarantee them a fair trial for crimes committed since. But as a political document it was astounding. In a lengthy preamble that—as contemporaries noted—bore all the marks of Edwards's pen, the bill would have the legislature express frank admiration for the outlaws and endorse an explicitly Confederate version of the state's history. An excerpt:

> WHEREAS, under the outlawry pronounced against Jesse W. James, Frank James, Coleman Younger, Robert Younger, and others, who gallantly periled their lives and their all in the defence of their principles, they are of necessity made desperate, driven as they are from the fields of honest industry, from their friends, their families, their homes, and their country, they can know no law but the law of self-preservation, can have no respect for and feel no allegiance to a government which forces them to the very

acts it professes to deprecate, and then offer a bounty for their apprehension and arms foreign mercenaries with power to capture and kill; and

WHEREAS, believing these men too brave to be mean, too generous to be revengeful, and too gallant and honorable to betray a friend or break a promise; and believing further that most, if not all the offences with which they are charged have been committed by others . . . ; that the return of these men to their homes and friends would have the effect of greatly lessening crime in our State by turning public attention to the real criminals, and that common justice, sound policy, and true statesmanship alike demand that amnesty should be extended to all alike of both parties for all acts done or charged to have been done during the war . . .

In Kansas City, the *Journal of Commerce* published the resolution under the headline "An Excellent Campaign Document for Republicans." Editor Van Horn dissected the proceeding in a lengthy essay. "The whole premise is false," he argued. The Radical constitution had not outlawed the James and Younger brothers, or any former rebels. "Hundreds of those confederated and associated with them during the war returned to their homes at its close and have never been molested," he wrote. "Such is the barbarous depth to which this legislature has descended, that brigands, whose bloody deeds have shocked humanity and made them a terror to this and neighboring states, are to be made the special objects of its protection. . . . It is, we believe, the first instance in all history where a government proposed by a solemn act, to take the side of brigands against society." Van Horn saw the amnesty bill as a part of the reaction against Reconstruction. It was "coupled with" the legislature's cuts in funding for public schools and charitable institutions, attempts to repudiate railroad bonds, and the leasing of convicts as laborers,* which led him to dub the General Assembly "the brigand conclave."[56]

The Unionists in the legislature managed—just barely—to sink the amnesty bill. On March 20, Representative James Shields, a former Federal general, substituted a quieter version that sheared off the jaw-dropping preamble. Then enough Democrats voted with the Republicans to prevent it from passing with the two-thirds majority required for a concurrent resolution. (The House vote was fifty-eight to thirty-nine, with fifty-six Democrats and two Republicans in favor, and twenty Democrats and nineteen Republicans against.) Half of the bolting Democrats hailed from the fiercely Unionist southwestern section of the state.[57]

The failure of the resolution, however, was almost beside the point.

---

*Christopher R. Adamson notes that convict leasing spread throughout the post-Redemption South, with white prisoners generally exempt, making it "a functional replacement for slavery." See "Punishment After Slavery: Southern State Penal Systems, 1865–1890," in *The South:* Part 1, ed. Eric H. Monkkonen (Munich: K. G. Saur, 1992), 3–17.

Edwards and his allies had finally succeeded in sanctifying Jesse James and his comrades as Confederate martyrs. Even the *Jefferson City People's Tribune,* which considered itself the official Democratic organ, wrote that "recent occurrences have had the effect, in a large measure, to change public sentiment in regard to these men." The rebel faction had cunningly exploited this feeling to reshape Missouri's historical memory and lift itself to dominance within the Democratic Party. "This matter ought not to be made a political question," grumbled the *Kansas City Journal of Commerce,* "but the [Confederate Democrats'] manifestation of sympathy forces it into that attitude, and it will have to be so considered and treated."[58]

As the legislature refought the Civil War with words, Samuel Hardwicke feared a reenactment with live ammunition. Almost immediately after the raid, word of his role leaked to the press, with both the *Kansas City Times* and the *St. Louis Republican* identifying him by name. Fearful, he took quarters directly on the town square, reported Susie James Parmer. "So anxious was he," she added, "that he paid a month's rent for a man in order to get him to move out."[59]

In Chicago, Allan Pinkerton returned to his office from various engagements to find two letters from the jittery Hardwicke. Pinkerton must have sighed heavily at the sight of them. "I must say, I am considerably disheartened," he had confessed two days after the botched raid. "It's rather heavy on me spending money continually and not finding them. It's too much for me, and I may probably withdraw." His failure had human consequences, however, which Pinkerton acknowledged to himself as he read Hardwicke's letters. "Your two letters are duly received," he wrote back. "I will meet you wherever you please, say at Quincy, Springfield, Joliet, or Chicago, whichever one you think is best."

The disaster at the Samuel farm, he hinted, had shaken the agency deeply. "I have just received a telegram from Robert J. [Linden]," Pinkerton wrote. "He has taken some money, is badly scared, and says he will borrow himself, as he won't be seen for a long time." Pinkerton himself was the primary suspect for a grand jury in Clay County that was investigating the raid. He voiced nonchalance. "The evidence is plain and clear where I was all the time," he wrote. He had many witnesses to offer him an alibi, including Governor John L. Beveridge of Illinois, who may have promised to refuse requests for extradition of the detectives. "I rather think," Pinkerton added, "it would be troublesome for them to get any of the men from Illinois."[60]

Pinkerton may have been distressed, but it was Hardwicke and Askew who remained on the battlefield, isolated and vulnerable. In Liberty, a grand jury interrogated both men, along with Askew's wife, Adeline. Other witnesses included Reuben and Zerelda—helped by Zee Mimms James, who was "constant in her attention on the old lady," according to the press—former governor Woodson, and officials of the Hannibal and St. Joseph Railroad. Hardwicke's work for the detectives came to light, as did the role of Askew's farm as the base for agent Jack Ladd. In the end, the jury indicted Ladd, along with Pinkerton, Robert J. King (apparently Linden's pseudonym), and five unnamed men. Hardwicke and Askew were not charged.[61]

The law was one thing; the James brothers were another. Their impending retribution shadowed the county during February and March.[62] Many Unionist farmers received threats from the brothers or their sympathizers. "I wish to say that my brother-in-law resides about two miles from the James' place," wrote Daniel Geary to Governor Hardin, "and has been repeatedly warned by these desperadoes or their friends to leave the county. He has paid no attention to these threats, but since the attack on the house of the mother of these boys all Northern men especially, as well as those who have . . . denounced the acts of these bandits, will live in constant fear of assassination."[63] In an interview with the *Kansas City Times,* Susie James Parmer spelled out her family's suspicions of Hardwicke and Askew; Hardwicke was particularly terrified, she noted gleefully, and had written a note to Zerelda begging to see her. "I believe that every man engaged in it will be punished," Parmer stated, "if not in this world certainly in the next."[64]

Askew was made of sterner stuff, and continued to live on his farm. He never even bothered to purchase a firearm—not that it would have done him any good in the end.[65] Shortly before eight o'clock in the evening on April 12, Askew left his house to draw a pail of water from the well in the rear of his property. He picked his way through deep darkness, the moon shrouded in clouds. As he returned, lugging a full bucket in one hand, a figure stepped out from behind a woodpile. The two apparently spoke quietly for five to ten minutes.

Inside the house, Addie Askew heard the dull bark of a revolver echo three times. "[I] came to the front door," she told a coroner's jury, "which being difficult to open I went around and called my husband; [I] received no answer." What she did not tell the jury was what she did next. Assuming the worst, she immediately ordered her children to hide, then gathered up all the letters from Allan Pinkerton and threw them in the fire. As far as she knew, the gunman could be coming for her next; her life might depend on destroying the incriminating evidence. With the correspondence in ashes, she ran outside. "I do not think it was over two minutes between the hearing of the shots and my arrival to where my husband lay," she reported. "[I] looked closely, but could not tell how he was shot, but thought from feeling that his face was mashed in." Three bullets had punctured his head: one had pierced his face below the eye, another had torn off a portion of his skull, and a third had gone through his brain.

Just a few minutes after the shooting, neighbor Henry Sears heard someone shouting "Hallo!" repeatedly in his front yard. He opened the door and peered out into the darkness. "Hello yourself!" he answered. As he strained his eyes, he made out one man on horseback, and had the vague impression there might be more. The mounted figure spoke. "We have killed Dan Askew tonight, and if any one wishes to know who did it say that detectives did it," he declared. "Tell his friends to go and bury the damned son of a bitch tomorrow. Will you do it?" Sears only stared back, dumbfounded. The next morning, he and a friend named Charles D. Poe searched the ground. They found the tracks of a single horse, which matched those found at the Askew farm. The tracks showed that the killer had ridden to another farm that night—that of another man rumored to have aided the Pinkerton agents—only to turn away for some unknown reason.[66]

Survivors of the Civil War would have recognized the technique used in the murder: Catch a Unionist farmer out in his yard, gun him down, then boast of it to a neighbor—as Fletch Taylor's bushwhacker crew had done to Alvis Dagley in 1864. The similarity of method appeared to be no coincidence. At the time of the shooting, a party of three men had been spotted at or near the Samuel farm; they departed on the morning of April 14, two of them riding to Richmond and the third taking the Blue Mills ferry to Jackson County. This last man, the press reported, "was recognized by his fine mare." It was Jesse James, almost certainly the man who shot Askew.[67]

"The victim has been suspected of harboring the detectives who recently visited the Samuels' house, in fact, has been accused of so doing," wrote Van Horn in the *Kansas City Journal of Commerce.* "He denied it, and there was no proof to show that he had done so. He was a Radical, however, and for this was selected as a victim upon whom the vengeful wrath of the James boys should be wreaked. . . . To kill a Radical is no crime in the eyes of certain Democrats. . . . A family has been robbed of a father and husband, and the friends of the Jameses are in ecstacy." Van Horn was quite right. A few weeks after the murder, Zerelda predictably denied that her boys had had anything to do with it, but she spilled no tears for Askew. "He had made enemies during the war," she observed darkly.[68]

That was the echo that sounded again and again in the days after the killing: the war, the war, the war. Even Allan Pinkerton finally understood the historical resentments that had ground up his men in Clay County. "Daniel Askew, when he learned to know me, opened his door widely for shielding my men, who concealed there nearly 3 months," he wrote to Governor Beveridge on April 16, 1875. "Askew was a Union soldier during the late war. . . . There came also those accursed rebels . . . viz. the Jameses, Cole Younger, Major Edwards, Genl. Shelby, and most others, in whose track followed robbery, rapine, and murder and there it is at the present time." The same day, he sent a letter to a contact near the Samuel farm—Dr. J. C. Bernard of Haynesville, Clinton County—asking him to give his best to Askew's widow. "I would like to speak to his wife, but I cannot," Pinkerton wrote. "A reign of terror prevails all through Clay County at the present time."[69]

"The citizens," wrote Sheriff Groom to Governor Hardin, "are as terror stricken as at any time during the war. . . . There are many good men here who expect to meet and share the same fate. There is no doubt about the threats against them by the James brothers and their associates."[70] Even the *Kansas City Times* noted the fear in Clay County. "One of the farmers whose life has been threatened was in Liberty yesterday for the purpose of purchasing arms with which to defend himself," the paper reported on April 18. "He is one of ten or twelve, and he proposes to fight." The next day, Groom sent another letter, this one to Adjutant General Bingham. He pleaded for a supply of breech-loading, ten-gauge shotguns, "the style of arms these murderers carry," saying he would provide the men. "I tell you General the people are terror stricken," he reiterated. Even L. W. Towne, the superintendent of the Hannibal and St. Joseph Railroad who had cooperated in the raid, handed in his resignation and moved to safer parts.[71]

On May 11, Pinkerton finally sent a note to Addie Askew herself. "I have not seen you," he wrote, "but yet I cannot help calling you a friend, and one of those dear friends whom one can never have but once in this life. . . . I thank you, and wish only that I was able to see you."

They were some of the last words that he would ever write related to the outlaws. As he had declared immediately after the disastrous raid, he resolved to give up the hunt, to abandon the vendetta. Addie Askew now passed through the process of estate inventories and probate auctions that Zerelda James had once endured; Samuel Hardwicke fled to St. Paul, Minnesota, in fear for his life; and Pinkerton silently accepted that Jesse James had won.[72]

CHAPTER SIXTEEN

Ambition

I N THE WEEKS following the raid on the Samuel farm, all of the out-law's enemies suffered defeat and disarray. "I am of the opinion," wrote the Daviess County prosecutor, "that all the sheriffs in that section (except Groom of Clay) are afraid of Jesse James." Governor Hardin tried to keep the hunt going, but fear and confusion prevailed. He discovered, for example, that the Iron Mountain Railroad—widely thought to be a prime mover behind the Pinkerton activities—had not concerned itself in the slightest in the chase for the Gads Hill bandits. On February 27, 1875, the governor had written to corporation president Thomas Allen to ask for his aid in extraditing William McDaniel, should he be acquitted in his trial in Kansas for the Muncie robbery. Allen did not bother to reply until May 19; when he did, he promised help, but vaguely added that "we have always supposed" that the James-Younger group had not been involved in the Gads Hill raid.[1]

Stymied by the railroad, the governor found an eager ally in Wells Fargo, which had been robbed at Muncie. In late March 1875, the firm's superintendent in Kansas City, E. M. Cooper, received information that Clell Miller was hiding in Carroll County. Cooper dispatched four men to take him—"which resulted, as usual, in failure," he wrote to Hardin on April 5. The Wells Fargo agents went to the sheriff with their requisition— an extradition order—from the governor of Kansas. The officer accompanied them to the farm of Sharpe Whitsett, Miller's uncle. As the four men waited outside, the sheriff went into the house to talk to the bandit—and was taken hostage. Miller kept a cocked revolver on the hapless official until he himself mounted his horse; then he shouted "Good-bye, gentlemen," and escaped.[2]

Inevitably, the press attributed the bungled arrest to the Pinkerton agency, unaware that it had abandoned the hunt for the Missouri outlaws.

And soon Wells Fargo had to drop the matter as well. In the summer of 1875, Jay Gould took control of the Kansas Pacific and replaced the express company with his own service (which he had begun earlier on the Union Pacific). That left Wells Fargo cut off from any connection with the East. Cooper's position became superfluous, and he abandoned his hunt for the James gang.[3]

The governor had one last ally, who proved to be the most persistent of all: Sheriff Groom of Clay County. At the beginning of May, Groom obtained the shotguns he had requested from the adjutant general, hauling fifty of them from Kansas City. "He had been secretly but busily engaged in organizing a posse [of] 150 men to hunt the James boys," reported the *Liberty Tribune*. He also organized a watch on the Missouri River ferries; through the middle of July, if not even later, he kept four men on duty twenty-four hours a day, paying them with state funds. But the James brothers were already safely across.[4]

At 7:30 p.m. on May 13, four men robbed an isolated store/post office in Henry County, about twelve miles north of Clinton. The bandits "were well-dressed, genteel-looking men, and mounted on splendid horses," according to the press. "We suppose them to be the *Younger* or *James Boys* from the way they proceeded," reported two of the victims, Mrs. D. A. Lambert, wife of the merchant, and Miss Bessie H. Sharp. "They were professional hands at the business. . . . [They stole] every cent we had in the world."

Lambert and Sharp may have been right about the bandits' identities. For one thing, two of the Younger brothers had been spotted nearby two days earlier; for another, the raid was carried out with quiet precision, leaving a blacksmith only fifty yards away unaware of the entire affair. Most telling of all, the robbers fiercely interrogated a Yankee teacher whom they suspected of being a detective, relenting only when he produced his "school certificate." They raided the small store in the belief that the owner had thousands of dollars in gold, but had to content themselves with far less.

Even if the James and Younger brothers were not involved, the incident revealed once again Missouri's sense of helplessness. Lambert and Sharp took it upon themselves to write to Governor Hardin, they explained, because the men "all say it is no use to write anything about it, as they have been committing just such depredations for some time in this State, but *we* thought if the men would not appeal to you we would. We do not fancy being ordered around under the muzzle of a revolver and threatened with death if we offer the least resistance."[5]

All this amused Jesse James immensely. On May 24, just eleven days after the Henry County robbery, he wrote a letter to an unnamed individual, identified by the press seven years later as "an official who was at that time earnestly engaged in hunting the outlaws"—probably Groom. The outlaw masked his whereabouts by mailing the letter to his cousin and sister-in-law Nannie Mimms McBride in Kansas City, who forwarded it on May 26 in a new envelope.

"My Dear Friend," he wrote, "Your welcome letter of date the 21st reached Mrs. ———— yesterday morning, and was forwarded to me immediately. . . . You say you was greatly surprised, you supposed I was in Texas or Mexico. I am generally where people least expect me to be. You asked me if I was innocent why I did not give myself up," he continued. "Don't you know that I have been lied on and persecuted so long that the public prejudice is so great against me that it would take one hundred thousand dollars to defend me. . . . And besides that a requisition would be found for me from Iowa and how long do you suppose I would be spared from a MOB in that radical State."

The note—which the *Journal of Commerce* believed was genuine—bears all the marks of Jesse's writing: the cocky self-assurance, the sense of persecution, the belief that Radicals would never let him live in peace. The political tone was reinforced by a further reference to a newspaper editor, whose name was deleted by the press when the letter was later published, "the dirty dog [who] is writing all those lying newspaper reports about Clay County and the James boys. He fears us and he is telling all the lies he can to get me killed but he will get his just due in time." This was almost certainly the *Journal*'s editor, Robert T. Van Horn. The newspaper may have possessed the letter because it was given to him as a helpful warning.

But there was a surprise buried in the missive. Jesse claimed that the Muncie and Henry County robbers were Clell Miller, Tom McDaniel (brother of the incarcerated William), Jack Keen, and Sol Reed—all known to be followers of the James and Younger brothers.[6] The outlaw heartily encouraged his correspondent to capture them. Perhaps he imagined that they would never be apprehended, or that they would keep their mouths shut if they were (as William McDaniel did). No matter what he thought, the passage betrayed a callous disregard for the welfare of his fellows. Cole Younger had complained of this tendency in an 1874 letter to the *Pleasant Hill Review*. "My name would never have been used in connection with" the Kansas City fair robbery, he had written, "had not Jesse W. James, for some cause best known to himself, published in the *Kansas City Times* a letter stating that John, myself, and he were accused of the robbery. Where he got his authority, I don't know, but one thing I do know, he had none from me."[7]

Younger had tried to stretch the point to argue that he and Jesse "were not on good terms"—a claim he clearly crafted for public consumption.

But intimates of the bandits would later agree that there was something increasingly reckless, something dangerously unpredictable, about Jesse. One official who hunted these men later asserted that Cole "was the only one of the whole number who could control Jesse James, and I am convinced that those who knew both men well told me the truth when they had said that in a number of instances Cole Younger at his own peril prevented Jesse James from taking life."[8]

For Jesse, a few issues were resolved beginning in the summer of 1875. On the night of June 29, William McDaniel was shot to death by a farmer, having escaped from his Kansas jail. He died without ever speaking a word about his fellow robbers at Muncie. In Clay County, Jesse's mother had developed a serious infection in her amputated arm, but the infection healed. And Jesse and Zee moved. At some point following the Pinkerton raid, in part to protect Zerelda from further attacks, they settled in a small house at 606 Boscobel Street in Edgefield, Tennessee (across the Cumberland River from Nashville), just forty miles south of his uncle George Hite's farm near Adairville, Kentucky. They passed themselves off as Josie and John Davis Howard. He claimed to be a wheat speculator, and often disappeared for weeks at a time.

In his role as J. D. Howard, Jesse often asked John Vertrees, the son of a neighboring physician, to stay at his house when he was away. The young man observed many strange things when he was at the Howard home. Zee—Josie—once showed him thousands of dollars in diamonds, claiming that her uncle in Illinois "had bought them for a mere song at an auction sale." Whenever Jesse returned, Vertrees recalled, he handed his wife "rolls of money and other valuables." Perhaps he was carrying out robberies that went unreported, or fetching money he had hidden earlier. But, as a Nashville newspaper later reported, "Mrs. James was always well provided with money, very frequently having as much as $1,500 in her possession."

To the neighbors, J. D. Howard appeared to be a silent, distrusting figure. He frequented the faro games in and around the city, playing with an almost wrathful intensity. Whenever he returned from his extended trips, he immediately fired his house servant and hired a new one. And he kept two exceptionally fine horses, a rather unusual custom for a grain buyer. All this aroused some murmuring in the community—not enough to arouse any official attention, but sufficient to drive the couple deeper into isolation.[9]

Even with Jesse gone, Missouri continued to suffer. First came a raging flood on the Missouri River. "Acre upon acre of the most fertile and well improved farms are melting away like frost under a noonday sun," wrote the *Richmond Conservator* in late April. Then came locusts. "Now is undoubtedly the darkest hour in the history of Western Missouri," mourned another newspaper. "The grasshopper plague is upon us, and as it is generally believed that they will devastate and make desolate the whole country." On May 25, fifteen barrels of grasshoppers—each barrel weighing two hundred pounds—were hauled away from the base of the courthouse in Independence. Residents wrote of vast clouds passing overhead for days at a time. Next door to the Samuel farm, Waltus Watkins lost almost three hundred acres of various crops to the swarming insects. "They sometimes take large fields in a few hours," he grieved. "This is the darkest time that I have ever seen." Governor Hardin proclaimed a day of fasting and prayer. Within a month, the plague lifted.[10]

ISOLATION CAN CHANGE a man. Sometimes it leads to insight, a new understanding of himself; sometimes it warps his perspective. By moving to distant Edgefield, Jesse had separated himself from all the things that had shaped his life: his mother, his mentor John Edwards, his friends and enemies, the familiar trails through the paw-paw bushes of the creekbeds and river bottoms. It got his restless mind moving again. It tempted him to pick up his neglected pen. And it seems to have stoked the deeper, darker fires of his personality—his recklessness, his sense of persecution, and, most of all, his desire for revenge.

After moving to Tennessee, he often visited his uncle's farm in Kentucky, where the naturally loquacious outlaw was able to speak freely with his young cousin, George Hite, Jr. "He wanted to quit the business," Hite recalled, "but he said he had to make a living, and as the whole world seemed to be pitted against him, and he couldn't do anything else, he kept on with it." He quoted Jesse as saying, "They wouldn't let me stay at home, and what else can I do?"

Along with a belief in his own martyrdom came a burning rage for retribution. Hite recalled that his famous cousin went to Chicago for a few months in order to kill Allan Pinkerton. "I want him to know who did it," Jesse told him. "It would do me no good if I couldn't tell him about it before he died. I had a dozen chances to shoot him when he didn't know it. I wanted to give him a fair chance, but the opportunity never came." Whether a fantasy, an excuse, or a true story, the idea of killing Pinkerton clearly ate away at him. Hite said Jesse often repeated the refrain, "I know God will some day deliver Allan Pinkerton into my hands."[11]

And yet, moving to Tennessee ended one kind of isolation: his life underground, with its midnight travels between friendly farms and the constant lookout for pursuers. As J. D. Howard, he once again lived in daily contact with the community. And not just any community—this was the heart of his cherished South, a Confederate state that had long since rolled back Reconstruction and reinstated white supremacy. Here, his perspective changed, his horizons broadened, and with it all came a distressing realization. As he devoured the local newspapers, he discovered that he was seen merely as a curiosity, not a subject of serious discussion. For a man who had dominated the headlines and politics of Missouri for at least two years, this was unbearable.

On July 11, 1875, the *Nashville Republican Banner* (a Democratic publication, despite the name) printed a letter from Jesse, purporting to come from Missouri. Not since December 29, 1873, had he written to a newspaper, but he had not needed to. After more than a year of deliberate symbolism and mythmaking—from the Kansas City fair robbery, in 1872, to the Gads Hill raid, in January 1874—his place in Missouri's politics and popular culture had been firmly established. Now, he desperately wanted the same status in the rest of the South.

The ostensible occasion for his (error-riddled) correspondence was the publication of reports that he, Frank, and the Younger brothers had been spotted in Kentucky. "I have never been out of Missouri since the Amnesty bill was introduced in the Mo. Legislatur last March, asking for pardon for the James and Younger Boys," he wrote, helpfully bringing his new neighbors up to date on his political career. He blamed detective D. T. "Yankee" Bligh of Louisville for the rumors—and here he began to make the real point of his missive. First he dismissed Bligh as a "Sherman bummer";* then he explained that he was a political martyr and a Confederate hero. "For 10 years the Radical papers in Missouri and other states have charged nearly every darring robbery in America to the James and Youngers. It is enough persecution in Northern papers to persecute us without the papers in the South, persecuting us, the land we fought for for four years to save from northern tyranny, to be persecuted by papers claiming to be Democratic, is against reason. The people of the south have heard only one side of the report."[12]

The letter appeared to be genuine, containing much of Jesse's established rhetoric. (He accused his accusers of carrying out the robberies, for example.) The spelling and grammar attracted some skepticism, but, judging from archives of contemporary correspondence, it was no worse than the typical letter of the day, and those who had seen other examples of his unpolished prose agreed that it was authentic. "His spelling was imperfect," Jesse's brother-in-law noted later. "He would dash off a letter without pausing once, and would never read it over." The outlaw concluded the

---

*During General William T. Sherman's march to the sea during the Civil War, the destructive foragers on the edges of his force were called "bummers."

note by describing the bombing of his mother's house (by more "bum-mers") and expressing his thanks to Dr. Paul Eve, a Nashville doctor who, he claimed, had treated his lung wound in 1867.[13]

Jesse blamed Allan Pinkerton's son William for leading the bombing raid, and William made the mistake of responding. On July 28, the *Nashville Republican Banner* published his angry reply, stating that he was in court in Chicago on the day in question. It was exactly what Jesse must have hoped for: a public controversy, a platform where he could stand and beat the Confederate war drum. On August 4, 1875, he drafted his response to Pinkerton's reply, and mailed it to the *Banner* with a cover letter. The newspaper printed both items.

"They is no doubt about Pinkerton's force committing the crime & it is the duty of the press to denounce him," he wrote in his introductory note.

> The St. Louis *Times & Dispatch*. and many other Democrat papers in Mo. have stood up faithfully for us (the James & Youngers) and last winter when the Amnesty bill was before the Legislature every Ex-confederate in the Legislature voted for our pardon. among the number were Gen. Shields, Gen Jones who forwarded the bill & Col. Stichan Hutchens Editor of the St. Louis *Times*.* . . . It is only a question of time about us being granted a full amnesty our friends will forward the Amnesty bill again this winter in the 29th assembly of the Mo Legislature. . . . Major Jno N Edwards of the St. Louis *Dispatch* is at the present time writing the history of Quantrell and his men, which gives the history of the lives of the James & Youngers.

Clearly Jesse remained in contact with his old mentor, who was indeed writing a book about the guerrillas. He concluded with a poke in his old enemy's eye, and a partisan appeal. "Pinkerton has gained great notariety as a Detective, but we have so easily baffled him. & he has got his best men killed by him sending them after us . . . & he wants to poison the minds of all Democrats against us."

All this was simply the cover letter. In the item intended for publication, he offered a detailed alibi for many of his robberies, and went to great lengths to depict his battle with the Pinkertons as a struggle between North and South. "As to Pinkertons proveing he was in Chicago at the time he committed the outrage at mothers I do not doubt," he wrote.

> Pinkerton can prove in Chicago that Black is white and white is Blac so can Gen Wm T Sherman prove in Chicago that Jeff Davisse had Lincoln assas-sinated & that the brave and gallant [Confederate] Gen Wade Hampton

*In 1875, Stilson Hutchins started the *St. Louis Times*, and Edwards joined him.

burnt Columbia, S.C. all this can be proven in Chicago, if people in the South didn't know that Chicago was the home of Phil Sheridan and filled with Shermans Bummers it might have some effect for Pinkerton to say what he can prove in Chicago.

The outlaw continued with increasing fury, swelling with his sense of righteousness and divinely ordained importance. "Providence saved the house from being burnt," he wrote. Pinkerton, he added,

> better never dare to show his Scottish face again in Western Mo. and let him know he is here, or he will meet the fate his comrades, Capt. Lull & Witcher, meet. . . . Justice is slow but sure, and they is a just God that will bring all to justice. Pinkerton, I hope and pray that our Heavenly Father may deliver you into my hands, & I believe he will, for his merciful and protecting arm has ever been with me, and Shielded me, and during all my persecution he has watched over me & protected me from workers of blood money who are trying to seeak my life, and I have hope and faith in him & believe he will ever protect me as long as I serve him.

These letters dripped with an odd mixture of an unhindered, expanding, almost maniacal ego and an astute understanding of politics and the press. Jesse had worked hard to make himself a public figure. An intense partisan and a voracious reader of the newspapers, he crafted his correspondence for deliberate effect. He went out of his way, for example, to praise the current and former sheriffs of Clay County as fellow rebels. "George E. Patton," he wrote, "is a relative of Gen Frank Cheatham, of Tennessee, and a one-armed Confederate, and one of the noblest and bravest officers that ever was in Missouri." Of Groom he wrote, "a more conscientius, braver and honorable officer never lived." Thus he positioned himself carefully on the political landscape: his enemies were not other Confederates, even those in power, but rather vindictive Yankees and Radicals.[14]

All this correspondence conjures up an image of an intense and obsessive Jesse James—and a lonely one. The miserable spelling and grammar demonstrate his isolation from both Edwards and his much-better-educated brother, the probable editors of his previous letters. The family's dispersion affected Frank as well. In the summer of 1875, the *Richmond Conservator* reported, he was recognized near Zerelda's farm, "careworn, haggard, and faded in appearance generally, and seemed only to desire that he should learn the whereabouts and condition of many friends, and be let alone."[15] Still, life went on. On August 31, Zee gave birth to a boy, her first child, who was christened Jesse Edwards James. Jesse wanted to honor John N. Edwards—and, of course, himself.[16]

. . .

A MYSTERY SURROUNDS Jesse James in the fall of 1875. On September 6, four men robbed the Bank of Huntington in the West Virginia town of the same name, not far from the eastern border of Kentucky. They carried out the raid with quiet, even polite professionalism. One matched the descriptions of Cole Younger. Another, wounded and captured on September 14, was Tom McDaniel, brother of the late William and a friend of the James brothers. On September 27, another man believed to have links to them, Thomas J. Webb, was arrested in Fentress County, Tennessee, while carrying $4,000. But no one ever identified the fourth Huntington bandit.[17]

Was Jesse involved, or was he with his wife and newborn son outside of Nashville? Zee later claimed that the family suddenly moved to Baltimore for a short period after the Huntington raid. Though unconfirmed by other sources, the story raises the possibility that Webb's capture in Tennessee prompted them to flee. And then there was a letter from Jesse, published in the *Nashville Daily American* a few days before Webb's arrest. Over his career, his public denials correlated strongly with his actual crimes, though he had good reason to mock the detective fraternity. Before Tom McDaniel's name was finally confirmed, Tom had been identified with great certainty as Cole Younger, then as Jesse James. "Instead of my being shot and captured," Jesse wrote, "I am in St. Louis with friends, well, and feeling better than I have for years." He derided Detective Bligh, who led the hunt, as "the incompetent detective of Louisville," and claimed that he was glad one of the Huntington bandits had been captured. "The world can now see that neither one of the Jameses and Youngers are the men shot and captured." He added, repeating the alibi Younger had previously offered, "I and Cole Younger are not friends, but I know he is innocent of the Huntington robbery, and I feel it my duty to defend him and his innocent and persecuted brothers from the false and slanderous reports circulated about them." Given the highly specific dishonesty of his previous letters, this one suggests that he and Cole were closer than ever, and that the two of them had jointly led the raid.[18]

The open question of Jesse's involvement in the Huntington robbery is significant because it brings us tantalizingly close to understanding a shift in his personality. The long-distance strike into West Virginia had been the most daring operation, geographically speaking, ever attempted by the bandits. If we knew for a fact that it was his doing, it would complete the emerging picture of the outlaw's expanding ambition.

In all of Jesse's writings, in his attention-getting crimes, in his alliance with John Edwards, he had shown himself to be both a believer and an actor in the Confederate project for Missouri. He reveled in his fame and influence, which he closely followed in the press (as seen by his analysis of the vote on the amnesty bill). But by the time he turned twenty-eight, on September 5, 1875, most of his dreams for his home state had been fulfilled. All summer long, the constitutional convention had labored on a new basic law to replace the constitution of 1865. The body itself signaled the triumph of the old rebels: fully half of the delegates were former Confederates or secessionist sympathizers, while only 28 percent were clearly identified Unionists—despite the fact that two-thirds of the state's population had taken the Federal side during the war. And the document they drew up represented a profound rejection of the Radical legacy: it segregated the schools, banned interracial marriages, strictly limited taxation, and mandated regulation of the railroads. More remarkably, the delegates decided to bar serving soldiers and sailors, who had formed a bastion of Radical support during the war, from voting in state elections. They also included something for the outlaws: a provision granting amnesty for all wartime actions taken under Union *or Confederate* authority. Astonishingly, they set the end date for this immunity at August 20, 1866. This covered many of the depredations of the bushwhackers under Archie Clement during that tumultuous year, but not the occupation of Lexington by Bacon Montgomery's militia unit.[19]

The legislature followed suit with its own present for the James brothers: it limited the governor's reward offers to $300. Only four times since 1865 had the governor offered more than that; and during the entire period since the Radicals lost control of the governorship, the James brothers had been the only individuals singled out for rewards larger than $300. The statutory limitation, then, specifically protected them.[20]

Jesse's long struggle had clearly succeeded. Thanks in part to his status as a rebel martyr and avenger, deftly elaborated by Edwards and others, Missouri had begun to acquire a Confederate identity that it had never had during the conflict itself. But by this time, as Jesse's cousin George Hite testified, Jesse truly believed that he was unjustly persecuted, that his enemies would never let him rest, that he carried his life in his own hands. The myth that he had labored so hard to create had finally taken control of him: he truly believed he was doomed to a life of crime.

Self-obsessed, craving attention, certain that he was seized by fate, Jesse probably would have developed wider horizons even if he had not moved away. With Missouri thoroughly redeemed—to use the term coined by white-supremacist Democrats—it would have been natural for him to turn his attention toward the rest of the South, "the land we fought for for four years to save from northern tyranny," as he put it. His 1875 press campaign offers evidence of that. And if he did indeed take part in the Huntington raid, it would suggest that this expanding ambition infected his banditry as well.

Such enthusiasm was understandable. For former Confederates, this was a momentous time. As the year ended, almost every Southern state had been redeemed. With the Grant administration weakened by revelations of corruption and influence peddling among tax collectors in St. Louis—a group known as the "Whiskey Ring"—and with the House of Representatives out of Republican hands, Southern Democrats became bolder in their plans to recapture the last states where African Americans still voted and held public office. In 1875, they focused on Mississippi, where the black majority faced a wave of violence that overshadowed anything seen in the heyday of the Ku Klux Klan. "Nearly all the Democratic clubs in the state were converted into armed military companies," wrote Congressman John R. Lynch, a former slave who had become one of the most important politicians in the state. "Funds with which to purchase arms were believed to have been contributed by the national Democratic organization. Nearly every Republican meeting was attended by one or more of these clubs or companies." An insurrection broke out, turning the entire state, as one sheriff reported, into "one vast camp of armed white leaguers." As the November election approached, the killing began in earnest.[21]

This was revolution—a brutal assault on the ideals that had emerged out of the Civil War and the years that followed. It was a revolution that captured the imagination of Jesse James, who wrote and spoke of little but the war, politics, and his own persecution. In the presidential election year of 1876, this revolution would rise to the national level, carrying with it the inflating ambition of the guerrilla-turned-outlaw, which would soar toward a fatal climax.

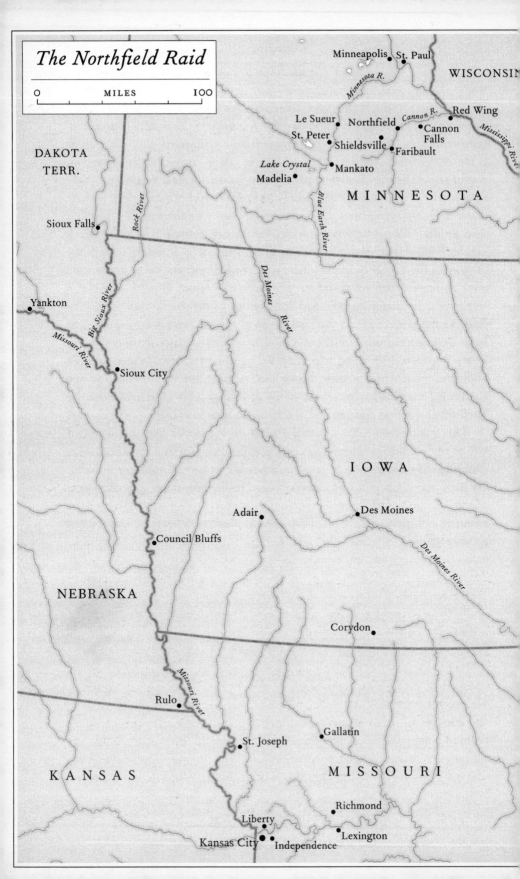

The Northfield Raid

MILES
0   100

Minneapolis   St. Paul

WISCONSIN

Minnesota R.

DAKOTA
TERR.

Le Sueur   Northfield   Cannon R.   Red Wing

St. Peter   Shieldsville   Cannon Falls

Mississippi River

Faribault

Lake Crystal   Mankato

Madelia

MINNESOTA

Blue Earth River

Rock River

Sioux Falls

Des Moines River

Big Sioux River

Yankton

Missouri River

Sioux City

IOWA

Adair   Des Moines

Council Bluffs

Des Moines River

NEBRASKA

Corydon

Missouri River

Rulo

Gallatin

St. Joseph

MISSOURI

KANSAS

Richmond

Liberty

Lexington

Kansas City   Independence

CHAPTER SEVENTEEN

Anabasis

THE YEAR OF CRISIS had arrived. In 1876, Americans could see
the central issues in the life of the republic swelling into towering
conflicts, like a storm front boiling in the distance. In February, the
question of political reform crystallized in the St. Louis trial of Orville
Babcock, President Grant's private secretary, who was accused of profiting
from the illicit Whiskey Ring. In March, the nation's westward expansion
hung in the balance as the army marched out against the last Indians who
still possessed unceded territory. And a tempestuous presidential campaign
loomed—the election in November promised to be a national referendum
on Republican control of the White House, on the staggering economic
depression, and on the continued enforcement of Reconstruction in the
South.

As if propelled by some dramatic force, each struggle was destined to
end in a personal confrontation. Before the year was out, Grant would sit
down with his reforming enemies to give a deposition for the Babcock trial,
Lieutenant Colonel George A. Custer would meet Crazy Horse by the Little Bighorn River, and the political parties would select two champions for
the presidential election. And the battle over Reconstruction would lead
Jesse James into the unlikeliest confrontation of all.

Jesse would strike out at Adelbert Ames, a man who represented the
opposite of everything Jesse stood for. He was a New England Yankee, a
Union war hero, the intellectual product of Eastern cosmopolitan culture,
and a leader of the Radical effort to remake the South. Like the opposing
poles of a magnet, James and Ames would be pulled together by their very
differences, traveling down paths that revealed the two sides of the badly
divided nation. And when they met, one of them would be left shattered
beyond recovery.

In early May 1876, Ames launched himself toward that rendezvous by boarding a train in Washington, D.C., on the first leg of a long journey to Minnesota. He carried himself with the dignified air of the West Point graduate he was, with a rifle-straight posture and a direct, forthright manner. His features have been described as aristocratic: the high dome of his head crested in a swath of thinning brown hair; his lips were concealed under the great drooping horseshoe of a mustache that pointed to either side of his chin; his somewhat sunken eyes stared thoughtfully from under his overhanging brow.[1]

During the trip, Ames had much to think about. The journey to Minnesota was spiritual as much as physical: a passage from agony into relief, from hope into regret, from a daylight-clear sense of purpose into dim uncertainty. His time in the South, the region that had consumed the last fifteen years of his life, was coming to a close.

He had been in Washington as a witness called to testify before a Senate committee. There, he had described the path that took him South, and the crimes that drove him out again.[2] His appearance reminded the senators—and many knew him well—that he, as much as any man, embodied the best America had to offer. Son of a sea captain from Rockland, Maine, he had spent much of his boyhood wandering the ocean on the deck of a sailing ship. Yet he had found time to excel in the sciences and the arts, mastering mathematics and painting alike, graduating near the top of his West Point class in 1861.

From the first day of the Civil War until the last, he had served under fire, rising from leader of a single artillery battery at the first battle of Bull Run through a battlefield promotion at Gettysburg to head of a division, to further division commands in South Carolina, at Petersburg, and the final assault on Fort Fisher.[3] Lee's surrender had brought him new labors. "I am still at my duties," he wrote from South Carolina, more than a year after Appomattox, "which consist in little more than aiding the agents of the Treasury Department and the Freedmen's Bureau in trying white men for killing negroes, of which work we have more than we can well do."

As the nation struggled with the question of how to deal with the defeated South, Ames found few answers, for the country or himself. On August 2, 1866, he took an extended leave and departed for a tour of Europe. There he watched Gladstone and Disraeli debate in Parliament; attended a reading by Charles Dickens; met the Prince of Wales and Emperor Napoleon III. Once he might have been thrilled by such company; now, after four years of war, all he saw was its "hollowness." One day he encountered an old friend, a happy but obscure painter. "I, on the other hand, have accomplished much—but to what end?" Ames mused. "Instead of having that which gives peace and contentment, I am adrift, seeking for what God only knows. I do not. Thus far my life has been with me one severe struggle and now that a time of rest is upon me, I am lost to find my position."[4]

In April 1867, he reported for duty in Vicksburg, Mississippi. There he joined the military administration that would govern the state under the Reconstruction Act, until the voters ratified a new constitution that enfranchised black men. In one of his first tasks, he presided over the trial of white men accused of murdering a group of African Americans and burning their homes. No one was willing to testify. "Thus I was taught," he observed bitterly, "in the equal rights of a free people."[5]

His metamorphosis from soldier to statesman had begun. In 1868, he fell in love with Blanche Butler, a much-admired darling of Washington and daughter of Benjamin F. Butler. Her father had a reputation in the capital as one of the Union army's worst generals and one of the Republican Party's most powerful congressmen. Portly, bug-eyed, balding, Butler stood second only to Thaddeus Stevens in influence with the Radical faction in the House of Representatives—and in devotion to racial equality. He already knew Ames well, having served as his commander during the war. As Ames courted Butler's daughter, the congressman increasingly influenced Ames's thinking. He soon showed how far he had traveled in both passion and politics by sitting with Blanche at the impeachment trial of President Andrew Johnson. But it would be the couple's last meeting for nearly two years.[6]

On June 15, 1868, Ames received orders to take over as provisional military governor of Mississippi. His political vision was now growing clearer by the day, but his task was nearly impossible. To set the state on its new path, he had to face the Ku Klux Klan, led in most places by prominent local planters; subordinates who openly sympathized with white supremacists; and the obstructionism of President Johnson, who continued to hamstring the civil rights acts. More and more, Ames found himself driven to the Radical position by the suffering and determination of African Americans. The New Englander moved forcefully, appointing new public officials at every level, including Mississippi's first black officeholders. "General Ames's knife cut deep," wrote one white Republican, "but . . . Ames's surgery was courageous and skilled."[7]

He had settled on his purpose, and, along with it, a new path, one that led straight into a political jungle. "I found, when I was military governor there," he later told a Senate committee, "that the negroes had no rights whatever." After two years in Mississippi, he strongly identified with their struggle. "I believed that I could render them great service. I felt that I had a mission to perform in their interest, and I hesitatingly consented to represent them, and unite my fortune with theirs."[8] When he next saw Blanche, it was as a U.S. senator, newly elected by the Republican, multiracial legislature of Mississippi.* Soon he traded quiet vows with her in marriage, but he shouted on Capitol Hill for federal action against the Ku Klux Klan. When a conservative faction threatened to tear apart the party in Mississippi, he returned in 1873 to run for governor, taking his place as leader of the Radical wing. With nearly universal black support, he swept the election.

Ames was honest, courageous, and intelligent, his administration notable for its frugality and fairness. But the Republican Party's national troubles, beginning with the depression of 1873, darkened Ames's future. The year after he won the gubernatorial election in Mississippi, white Democrats struck in Alabama, securing a victory at the polls by terrorizing black electors. Racial terror erupted in Louisiana as well, and in the countryside around Vicksburg. It filled him with despair, he wrote, but also the desire "to buckle on my armor anew that I may better fight the battle of the poor and oppressed colored man."[9]

In 1875, he learned that unarmed nobility was no match for brutality. In what became known as the Mississippi Plan, the Democratic Party reorganized its county chapters into paramilitary squads. Heavily armed columns of the party faithful wound through the state, storming Republican rallies and assassinating black activists. In some towns, the Democratic Party formed a virtual army of occupation, complete with patrols, checkpoints, and military encampments in the streets.[10] As Ames stood in the governor's mansion, receiving hourly telegrams of murders and military maneuvers, and as he watched the streets of Jackson fill with refugees from the countryside, he carefully thought through the consequences of his actions. He knew he could not trust his white militiamen, but he feared the outbreak of even greater racial violence if he relied only on black units. He needed an outside force, one that Southerners respected: he needed the U.S. Army.[11]

The governor requested federal troops—and was stunned by the response. "The whole public are tired out with these annual autumnal outbreaks in the South," wrote Attorney General Edwards Pierrepont, "and the great majority are ready to condemn any further interference on the part of the government." With the black vote almost completely suppressed, and with whites unified through racism or terror, the Democrats won control of the new legislature. In early 1876 they immediately began impeachment proceedings against Ames on concocted charges. In the end, Blanche thought up a face-saving compromise: he would resign, and the legislature would dismiss the trumped-up impeachment. But no sooner had he stepped down than the Democrats published the charges, implying that guilt drove him away.[12]

*Direct elections of senators would not occur until the ratification of the Seventeenth Amendment to the Constitution, in 1916.

And so Ames, on the morning of May 11, 1876, found himself at the end of his journey from Washington, stepping off the train in Northfield, a small community in the farmland of southern Minnesota, where his father, Jesse, waited for him. The aging captain had long since given up the sea; now he lived in this landlocked village, where the only water was the calm Cannon River. Jesse, together with his other son, John, owned a flour mill on the Cannon's banks. The business prospered, he told Adelbert, but he complained of getting old. At the house, the whole family turned out for a grand welcome. The gathering made Ames think of his own wife, Blanche, and his two children, whom he had left in Massachusetts with her parents.

"My folks are very kind and considerate," he wrote, "only as loving relatives can be." But running through the reunion was an undercurrent of the tragedy that had left his future in ruins. So his parents now spoke of his joining the family business. "I see that Father expects me to buy," he added, "and that all expect me to settle here. I have said neither yes nor no."

Despite his qualms, he threw himself into work at the mill. "I was running to and fro all day," he observed to his wife, "and when night came I was quite tired and glad enough to go to bed. . . . Thus our life line begins. I hardly realize that I am here to *make money*. I have not yet become impregnated with that thought. . . . Speaking more accurately, I should have said I have not grown to a business frame of mind—an occupation."[13] With no real alternative, his resistance to making a permanent commitment to his father's business slackened. "As yet I have not talked about buying," he wrote to Blanche, "although Father has no doubt I will." His astute wife wrote back promptly: "I think it better, Del, that your Father does wish you to buy the mill. There is nothing here in which you could invest your money so well." Adelbert accepted her judgment. In May, he busied himself with the arrangements. Almost immediately, he began to make modest reforms. "I believe I shall be a better business man," he told Blanche, "than I was a sailor, soldier, or politician."

But politics continued to haunt him. When a chest of documents arrived from his house in the South, he stayed up late poring through the papers, looking for items to send to the Senate committee that was investigating the Mississippi rebellion. At the end of May, he accompanied his brother, John, to St. Paul, where John served as a delegate to the state Republican convention. The presidential election was approaching, and everyone knew it would be the most bitterly contested, and the most momentous, since Lincoln squeaked into the White House in 1860. Even here, in prosperous, remote Northfield, far from the bloody fields of Mississippi, Ames must have suspected that he could not escape the knife edge of partisan hate.[14]

.   .   .

AT THE BEGINNING of July 1876, Jesse James stood beside his horse along a road in western Missouri. In just a day or two, every city and village in the country would celebrate the nation's centennial; Jesse, however, had anything but patriotism on his mind. He and Frank were arguing with Cole and Bob Younger. A short distance away, a young man named Hobbs Kerry strained to hear their words. After listening for some time, he heard the hulking Cole shrug off the debate. "You fellows suggested this," he said to the James brothers, "and I am just going with you."[15]

Kerry was a new recruit, as were two other men who also stood to the side. Actually, they were less recruits than volunteers, for Kerry and his friends had eagerly sought out the famous bandits over the previous weeks. A friend of the Youngers' uncle Bruce, Kerry had cooked up a scheme during the preceding winter to rob the Granby Mining and Smelting Company.[16] In May, he had met two acquaintances of the James and Younger brothers—Kansan Samuel Wells, known as Charlie Pitts, and William Stiles,* a native of Monticello, Minnesota, who went by the name of Bill Chadwell—and they had agreed to ask the James and Younger brothers to help them carry out Kerry's plan.[17]

"They [the bandits] think that it may be that we are fixing some trap to grab them, as it has been tried so often," Kerry wrote on June 9. "They are afraid of everybody. Charlie says he will fix that all right when they get to see me and talk to them, and it will be all right. . . . Bill says they are red hot to do something, and you bet when I get to see them that I will convince them that Granby is the best place." Subsequent attempts to contact the outlaws led to a tense confrontation with a suspicious Frank James, but Pitts and Chadwell put his mind at ease, and soon Jesse and the Youngers allowed the trio to join them. But not for the Granby robbery. Jesse was indeed "red hot to do something," but that something was far bigger than anything contemplated by Kerry. He envisioned a complex, far-reaching operation, the topic of his discussion with Cole and Bob Younger.

After Cole's abrupt gesture of resignation, they all mounted again—the two James and two Younger brothers, Kerry, Pitts, and Chadwell, plus Clell Miller, making eight in all—and rode east across central Missouri in two parties. On Independence Day they reunited at a sympathizer's house just north of California, Missouri. A pelting rain began that night. They spent the next day indoors, watching the water pound the earth outside into mud. On July 6, they broke up into two groups again, meeting once more at around 2 p.m. the next day. The location was an isolated stretch of the Missouri Pacific Railroad about two miles east of the Lamine River, in an excavation known as the Rocky Cut. It was much like the scene of their

*The author is not related to William Stiles.

previous railway robberies: remote, contained by natural obstacles, well suited to the capture and control of a crowded train.[18]

As the sun began to disappear behind the heavy timber that bracketed the tracks, the eight men mounted and rode toward the Lamine bridge, where a water tank stood. In short order, they took the watchman at the pump house prisoner, threw a few railroad ties across the tracks, and placed the blindfolded watchman between the rails, facing west. At about 10 p.m., the distinctive groaning chug of an approaching locomotive rolled through the woods. Wave your lantern, they told their prisoner. The train's air brakes hissed loudly as the Number 4 Express responded to the signal, the cow catcher just plowing up onto the obstructing ties as the engine eased to a halt in the clear moonlight. Chadwell sprinted behind the last car and tossed a few rails across the tracks to block a retreat. The others ran to the engine and express car. Behind them, the watchman pulled his blindfold up over one eye, saw that no one was looking, and raced for the woods.[19]

The man the bandits wanted to see was J. B. Bushnell, a veteran messenger for the United States Express Company. At his post in the baggage and express car, he stood guard over not only his own firm's safe (for which he had a key), but also one belonging to the Adams Express that had been brought aboard, already locked, when the train had stopped at Sedalia to take on passengers and another baggage car from the Missouri, Kansas, and Texas Railroad. Despite Bushnell's long service, the robbery caught him by surprise. "I was standing in the doorway when the train stopped suddenly," he recalled. Peering into the darkness, he heard someone shout, "Shoot the son of a gun!" A bullet smacked into the door frame. Immediately he darted back through all three coaches and the two sleepers until he found the brakeman, who agreed to hide the key to the safe. The railroad man slipped it in his shoe and took a seat, pretending to be a passenger, as Bushnell started forward again.

Back in the baggage and express car, three men hauled themselves up through the side door, each with a mask over his face—except for the leader. One witness described him in terms that matched Jesse James: a tall, sunburnt man with a striped linen coat, dark pants, and hat, "with light, straw-colored hair." Baggage master Peter Conkling, who was in the car at the time, noticed that he had "blue eyes, and blinky eyes," the kind often attributed to Jesse. Indeed, Conkling would always be convinced that Jesse was the very man who now shoved a revolver in his face and demanded the safe key. Conkling did not have it, of course, so the outlaw spun him around and prodded him ahead with his pistol. Point out the messenger, he said.[20]

Down the length of the coaches they marched, as terrified passengers shoveled their money and jewelry out of sight. When one woman began to sob, a man nearby spoke up bravely. "Madam, I'll protect you at the risk of my life." Another passenger smirked. "Why, then, don't you go and fight those fellows in front?" he asked, "to which no reply was vouchsafed," the press reported. In another seat, Rev. J. S. Holmes of Bedford, New York, began a round of hymn singing, followed by loud prayers for their safety and the robbers' repentence.

Jesse found the messenger. "Come forward now and unlock that safe without any nonsense." Bushnell denied having the key. "You want to find it damned quick, or I will kill you," Jesse snapped. Then he marched Conkling and Bushnell back through the train until they found the brakeman, who handed over the key. Back in the baggage car, it took them only a moment to empty the United States Express safe. "They evidently expected no greater difficulty with the other safe," Bushnell recalled, "and were considerably surprised and excited when they found that no one of the keys surrendered would fit its lock. They cursed—indeed, the whole affair was redolent of profanity—and were extremely unwilling to believe that the key was not to be had, until the brakeman explained that the Adams Express had no route over the Missouri Pacific, but only a contract with the United States Company for the transportation of a sealed safe from Sedalia to St. Louis." They managed to smash a hole in the second safe with a heavy iron pick (used to break up coal for the engine), and pulled out papers and envelopes. A quick review of the other baggage car satisfied them they had what they wanted.

Outside, the remaining bandits kept up a steady rattle of gunfire to intimidate the passengers. The only resistance came from the newsboy: he squeaked off a round from a tiny pepperbox pistol, sparking hearty laughter from the gunmen. "Hear that little son of a bitch bark!" one quipped.

"Better go through the passengers," someone suggested. Jesse shook his head. "We've been an hour here already, and can't waste any more time, as trains are coming up. Must get away." As the others jumped out the door, Jesse turned to Bushnell. "Tell Allan Pinkerton and all his detectives to look for us in hell." He nodded to Captain Tibbets, the conductor. "Now, Cap," he said, "you can take your damned old machine and go ahead." Then he hopped down to the ground.[21]

"I expect probably it was an hour before they started off [the train] and came down where we was," Hobbs Kerry recalled. "We all got our horses and started off. We went about twenty miles. . . . Miller carried the bag with the money in it part of the time, Cole Younger and Jesse James also took turns." At one point they rode into a stream to mask their trail. Shortly before dawn, Kerry reported, "we all stopped and divided the money. They tore all the envelopes open and put the money in a pile. Frank

James counted the money and gave each one his share. . . . They gave me about $1,200. Then we all scattered." The loot totaled some $18,300.[22]

As soon as the train arrived at the next station, word of the attack was telegraphed across the state. Governor Hardin posted the largest reward allowed by law, a pitiful $300 for each robber. Cincinnati detective Larry Hazen arrived in St. Louis at the request of the Adams Express to help with the search. And posses formed in the towns nearest the raid: Sedalia, Tipton, and, closest of all, Otterville. The five-man Sedalia party was the smallest, but it proved to be the most determined. It stayed on the bandits' trail through the Lamine River underbrush for days before admitting that the robbers had escaped. The party's persistence surprised no one, for it was led by a man renowned for his grit, and famous for bringing down the notorious Archie Clement—Bacon Montgomery.[23]

Far ahead of Montgomery and his men, Jesse rode to his mother's farm. He must have felt satisfaction. If the other new men received the same share as Hobbs Kerry, then Jesse must have collected almost $3,000. Just how princely was this sum? In 1876, the combined total of all greenbacks, national banknotes, fractional currency, and gold and silver coin in circulation amounted to $948,201,690—just $20.82 for each of the estimated 45,550,000 men, women, and children in the country. (This figure does not include bank deposits, but those were concentrated in New York and New England.)[24] In terms of purchasing power, $10 could buy a good saddle, $100 a respectable horse, and $3,000 a large, improved farm. By any measure, it was a lot of money.

He felt satisfaction, then, but not contentment. A bitter edge marked his behavior during the robbery. Paranoia seeped through his words and actions, along with a continuing obsession with his enemies. About to drink a glass of water from a cooler on the train, he accused baggage master Conkling of poisoning it. "Here, you son of a bitch, take a drink out of that," he said. "I don't propose to take any chances in any of this water business."[25] And he displayed none of the lighthearted joviality seen in previous train raids.

He may have been preoccupied. This robbery was only the first phase of an ambitious operation. Ordinarily the bandits dispersed for months after a big robbery. But this time the Youngers reunited with the James brothers in Clay County as early as August 2. Other signs point to a long-standing plan for a follow-up raid. Chadwell fled to Texas immediately after the Missouri Pacific strike. There, far from direct contact with the James or Younger brothers, he wrote to his sister in Minnesota. He had made some money, he told her; soon he would be coming to Minnesota to make even more.[26]

On the surface, a second robbery made no sense. Nothing could be more dangerous than collecting together so soon after a big raid. And money would not have been their motivation, as the Missouri Pacific operation had been unusually lucrative. What would prompt this departure from well-established—and highly successful—procedure? The answer, it appears, was all around them.

When the July 7 robbery hit the headlines, it had to shoulder its way between stories of the presidential campaign, the public obsession of the entire nation. As the bandits rode to their Lamine River rendezvous, they navigated around town squares teeming with delegates assembled for county conventions, around courthouses, taverns, and churches packed with political meetings. Men, women, and children attended day-long picnics, where brass bands played and orators railed. Even in an ordinary year, notes historian Keith Ian Polakoff, "Electoral activity was an important part of the very social fabric of the nation." And this was no ordinary year. As Polakoff writes, 1876 "was universally expected to be the most closely contested presidential election in more than a generation, even before the candidates were chosen."[27]

Just one week before the Missouri Pacific robbery, the Democratic National Convention in St. Louis had nominated Samuel J. Tilden for president in an atmosphere of hope and expectation not felt in the party since before the Civil War. The sixty-two-year-old New York governor seemed the perfect candidate to end the scandal-ridden Republican era, having smashed the corrupt Tammany Hall organization led by William "Boss" Tweed. Even as the gang waited along the tracks, Democrats were chanting the party mantra, "Tilden and Reform."[28]

All this struck Jesse James in a most particular way. The outlaw was intensely partisan, but not blindly so. If his mother's opinions reflected his own—as she herself claimed—the Unionism of the leading Democratic candidates squelched his enthusiasm. Connecticut-born John S. Phelps, who had served as a Federal officer and military governor of Arkansas, had defeated former Confederate congressman George G. Vest for the gubernatorial nomination in a state convention marked by wartime divisions. "I don't think much of Phelps," Zerelda told a reporter for the *Kansas City Journal of Commerce*. "He was no better than a Radical during the war," she explained, adding that her sons "would never vote for him." She was "equally severe" on Tilden, who was an old abolitionist. She "thought he was a great fraud, but still the worst fraud was better than the best Radical." At one point she squinted at the reporter angrily, demonstrating her knowledge of his paper's Republican politics. "I don't like newspapermen," she snapped, "and I don't like Radicals. I named my youngest girl

Fanny Quantrell, just to have a Quantrell in the family. And I am proud of my boys."[29]

Tilden's slogans about civil service reform and the gold standard meant less than nothing to Jesse. If his politics had been shaped by such questions, he would have switched to the new Greenback Party, which attacked the "oligarchy" of corporate monopolists. But Jesse and his mother were Democrats, ex-Confederate Democrats. For them the decisive question was the end of Reconstruction, as it was for all the white South.[30]

By the summer of 1876, the front lines in the war over Reconstruction had long since moved beyond Missouri. And, in a very real sense, Jesse himself had too. But after his Tennessee letter-writing campaign failed to awaken the old Confederacy to his status as a rebel hero, he decided to act more aggressively.

Jesse James, of course, was always a man in the shadows. His intentions can only be deduced from his actions and the handful of statements he made for the newspapers. But in both word and deed, he now began to hint that he had in mind a stroke with distinctly political overtones. It would not be a grand strategic blow, of course; as befitting a bushwhacker and bandit, it would be tactical, personal—and lucrative. With the climactic election debate raging, he would do as Quantrill had in going after Jim Lane in Lawrence: he would hit the enemy in his own home.

But before the bandits could act, disaster struck: Kerry was arrested. As they later learned, the capture was organized by James McDonough, chief of the St. Louis police, under the state's special outlawry act. Early in the year, McDonough had heard rumors of Kerry's planned Granby robbery and dispatched a team of officers to investigate. Once the Missouri Pacific raid hit the news, McDonough quickly sent his men back to that corner of the state to wait for Kerry's return. The inexperienced bandit reappeared on July 26, throwing money around with reckless abandon. Five days later he was arrested.[31]

Other followers of the James and Younger brothers had been caught, but none had ever said a word about their leaders. Kerry would be different. As early as August 6 the press began to hint that he had broken, publishing an accurate list of the men who had robbed the Missouri Pacific. Three days later came confirmation, followed on August 13 by full details of the arrest and confession. By then the first fruit of his betrayal had fallen. A party of twelve men, apparently hired and led by J. M. Thatcher, officer of the Adams Express, took a special train late on August 10 to a spot near the farm of Samuel Ralston, Frank's father-in-law, which they raided the next morning. They did not find Jesse—but they soon heard from him.[32]

"Last evening," the *Kansas City Times* reported on August 18, 1876, "a friend of his rode up to one of the reporters of the *Times* and handed him the following letter. He was not either Jesse or Frank James, but was much younger than them." As might be expected, Jesse proclaimed his innocence in the message thus delivered, condemning Kerry's "so-called confession" as a "well-built pack of lies." Then he added a rather odd explanation. "Kerry knows that the James and Youngers can't be taken alive," he boasted, "and that is why he has put it on us."[33]

A second missive appeared in the *Kansas City Times* on August 23. Again Jesse attacked Kerry; again he asserted his innocence. Then he turned to his obsessions: politics, his enemies, and himself. Writing with both honest anger and a keen grasp of Confederate resentments, he focused on a man he had hated for the last nine years. "My opinion is that Bacon Montgomery, the scoundrel who murdered Capt. A. J. Clement, Dec. 13, 1866, is the instigator of all this Missouri Pacific affair," he wrote. "But one thing I know he did do when he was in command of Tom Fletcher's cut-throat militia. He had Arch. Clement, one of the noblest boys and the most promising military boy of his age murdered in cold blood, and if poor Clement was living to-day he would be worth more to his country than old Tom Fletcher and all the militia that ever were in Missouri." He declared that Montgomery "had no equal" as a villain, urging that a reporter be sent to Lexington to inquire about the events of 1866. He also alluded to the recent raid at the Ralstons' and the attack on his mother's farm the year before. "I am of the opinion he had a hand in that dirty, cowardly work. Montgomery, roll in your special trains, and break down doors and arrest quiet citizens and put them in irons. Ever where you turn makes friends for me."

He hesitated, he said, to blame the Democratic governor for the raids made on his family and friends. "Gov. Hardin is a man of too much brains to act in a manner that would kill him in the eyes of the majority of the people who have elected him," he wrote, "and think he is the best governor Missouri has had since the war. But I can't vouch for Mr. Bingham's [the adjutant general] innocence." Was this a threat? A boast of his political clout? He seemed to be warning Hardin that the Confederate Democrats who sympathized with the bandits would withdraw their support for him if he tried too hard to catch the James brothers. On the other hand, Jesse despised Bingham as an active Unionist, unlike Hardin, who had sat out the war. Jesse went on to bemoan the failure of the amnesty resolution the previous year. Then he lifted his eyes to a higher level. "If we have a wise Congress this winter, which I believe we will have, I am sure they will grant us a full pardon. I will not say pardon," he added, "for we have done nothing to be pardoned for." He went on to mock President Grant, scorn

Allan Pinkerton, and suggest that the express companies give money to the poor rather than waste it on detectives.[34]

This letter is especially significant because it contains Jesse's unedited opinions. John Edwards was out of circulation, and had no part in it. On September 4, 1875, he had fought a duel with Emory S. Foster, another editor and a former Union officer. Though neither man had suffered injury in the exchange of shots, Edwards had promptly resigned from the *St. Louis Times*. He had retired to his father-in-law's farm in Lafayette County, where he was now completing *Noted Guerrillas*, his history of the Missouri bushwhackers. Had he reviewed Jesse's note, he would never have allowed such condemnation of Montgomery, who was a close friend despite his Radicalism. Indeed, Edwards pointedly defended him in a passage on Clement's death in the book he was now writing.[35]

This bit of correspondence, then, reflected Jesse's personal mixture of emotion and calculation. The appearance of Montgomery at this critical juncture struck him as more than a coincidence; few enemies were more significant in his personal mythology of persecution and revenge. Jesse's fury at Clement's death was as vivid and real as his love for his mother or his pity for himself. For Clement's killer to show up now, leading the chase after Jesse himself, made perfect sense in his mind: it sealed the connection between his bushwhacking and his banditry, between the political turmoil of 1866 and that of 1876.

Jesse shrewdly seized on Montgomery, the old militia officer, as a spark to rekindle the sympathies of his friends and supporters. It offered him a chance to highlight the history of Missouri's bitterest conflicts, to fan the partisan fires while he pleaded his innocence. And his discussion of Hardin, Bingham, and Congress was striking. He asserted to the world that he was a political actor, one to be reckoned with, one who deserved the attention of the Democratic Congress he confidently expected after the election. He placed himself firmly in the context of the great political revolution that everyone saw coming in November: like the white South, he would only be free when the Republicans were crushed.

And as he lifted his rhetoric to the national level, he and his gang set out to act on the national stage. Jesse was determined to take his place as a warrior against Reconstruction, as a hero of all the South, and he would do so by taking personal vengeance on an unsuspecting target in the fastness of his final refuge. When a reply from Montgomery appeared in the *Kansas City Times* on August 24, 1876, Jesse was already well on his way to the quiet Minnesota town of Northfield.

. . .

I WILL NOT attempt to tell you what a revolution I have seen and been through," Adelbert Ames wrote to his wife in June. "The certain monotony of a money-getting existence cannot be wholly analyzed and realized much less intelligibly expressed."[36] But for all his thoughtful self-reflection, he once again applied himself with the iron sense of duty that had always driven him. "I make progress whenever I comprehend what is to be done and how to do it," he added. "As I become interested the difficulties of the change disappears."

As he became interested, he became active. As he pored through the mill's books, he found some $4,000 in fat to be slashed from the annual payroll. He insisted on sending samples of their flour to the Centennial Exposition in Philadelphia. There, at that grand party the nation was throwing for itself, America's newest products were going on display, from the seven-hundred-ton, forty-foot-high Corliss steam engine, to the telephone and the electric light, to packaged yeast and linoleum. Agricultural goods would compete for special awards. A prize won there would go far toward securing future business; indeed, more than ten million people would attend the exposition. But Ames's father and brother were slow to see the possibilities. "The fact is," he told Blanche, "this firm has been doing an honest plodding business and are far behind others in the details which often amount to so much in a year. Surely I have much work before me."[37]

With each day he became better acquainted with Northfield. From the western side of town, where the mill stood and the railroad tracks ran, Ames could make a short walk across the Cannon River bridge to reach the central square. On its eastern side, it opened onto the main avenue, Division Street, which ran north and south beneath a low plateau. Carleton College stood on those modest heights farther up, and the usual small-town businesses lined Division: the Dampier Hotel; a drugstore run by a man named Wheeler; two hardware stores, one owned by J. S. Allen and the other, on the southern side of the square, by Anselm Manning; and various dry-goods stores. On most days, Division rattled with carriages and wagons driven in from the countryside, as farmers, tradesmen, artisans, and professionals clogged the streets.

Ames also grew familiar with the First National Bank, where the mill kept its accounts. The firm owned about a quarter of the bank, in fact; his father was the vice president and his brother a director, as they had been since it opened on January 1, 1873. It was typical of national banks in southern Minnesota, with a bare-minimum stock capitalization of $50,000, loans of around $100,000, and a vault reserve of some $10,000 in greenbacks— prosperous, in other words, but unremarkable. Adelbert often stepped through its Division Street entrance—it occupied the rear of the Scriver block, a building on the southeastern corner of the square—and chatted with the employees: cashier George M. Phillips; teller Alonzo E. Bunker; assistant bookkeeper Frank J. Wilcox; and bookkeeper Joseph L. Heywood.[38] Heywood, who served as treasurer of both the town and Carleton College, was a particularly serious man. Once, Ames learned, he had been happily married, but some time back his wife had grown gravely ill. If she died, she told her husband, she wanted him to marry an old friend and schoolmate of hers, to give their daughter a mother. When she passed away, Heywood carried out his wife's wishes. Ames, ever appreciative of a sense of duty, remembered the story well.[39]

Nothing pleased Ames more than his reunion with his brother. "John and I are closer than ever," he told Blanche—but John's wife grew cold. "If I am not mistaken, Nellie and I are further apart than ever. I do not think John observes it at all." It mystified Adelbert. "Nothing has passed between us, Nellie and me, which differs in the least from what our relations have always been." Far more troubling was his isolation from Blanche. "Our present separation seems to me somewhat different from any previous one and disproportionally long," he wrote on June 8. "We, both, are taking upon ourselves new parts which, not being fully learned, fit less comfortably than our occupation of old." The distance inflamed the couple's barely suppressed quarrel about where they should settle. "All my people are anxious that we should come here and live," he wrote. Blanche responded immediately. "Still, Sweetheart, in my own mind, I desire very much that we remain here for many reasons," she wrote from Lowell, Massachusetts. "I am sure I can make you happy here—but I will say nothing about the matter at present."

Adelbert, too, saw the need to say little about it, but for a very different purpose. "For political reasons, I still hold my residence in Miss., and so can frankly say I am not taking up my residence here at this time, but am here only on a visit."[40] It was a remarkable statement. Here he stood in distant Northfield, with no future before him except the mundane one of business, but he still felt the pull of the war he had left behind. On June 9, he traveled to Cincinnati for the Republican National Convention, where the party's leading men waged a fierce struggle to succeed Grant. "Yet, to be wholly frank about the subject," he wrote sadly to his wife, "I would confess that I care but little at best about the political contest we are now in." The real battle for the soul of the republic—the battle over Reconstruction—had been lost. Ames belonged to a political age that had already passed. Despite the surprise nomination of Ohio's governor, Rutherford B. Hayes, Ames's main sensation at the end of the convention was relief. On June 16, he caught the first train east. He visited the Centennial Exposition, spent two weeks by the sea with Blanche, and returned alone to Northfield.[41]

As Ames enjoyed a summer of calm, dramatic events erupted with volcanic fury across the national landscape. With Independence Day celebrations well under way, the press announced that Custer—Ames's West Point classmate—and more than two hundred cavalrymen had been annihilated by Lakota and Northern Cheyenne warriors; days earlier the same warriors had thrashed another column of one thousand troops under General George Crook. The nation's tiny army, already largely withdrawn from the South, marched west to avenge the defeats.[42]

On July 8, the bloodiest outrage of the political campaign staggered the state of South Carolina. A prominent Democrat, Matthew C. Butler, stormed the largely black town of Hamburg with a white paramilitary company. With cannons and hundreds of reinforcements, Butler smashed a black militia unit that gathered to resist his forces. After killing untold numbers of African Americans, the Democrats captured twenty-five; Butler personally picked out five for an on-the-spot execution. "If you can find words to characterize [this] atrocity and barbarism," wrote Daniel Chamberlain, the Republican governor, "your power of language exceeds mine."[43]

It was merely one atrocity of many. The election in Louisiana's rural parishes, Senator John Sherman later reported, "seems more like a history of hell than of civilized and Christian communities. The means adopted are almost incredible." In South Carolina, Democratic gubernatorial candidate Wade Hampton—the former cavalry commander for the Confederate Army of Northern Virginia—toured the state at the head of hundreds of paramilitary soldiers known as Red Shirts. They no longer feared federal intervention. As one white landlord said to a black tenant, the Democrats would win the election "if we have to wade in blood knee-deep."[44]

Hayes struggled to respond to these events. In his nomination acceptance message, he said that the Republicans would promote "the blessings of honest and capable self government," knowing that the phrase implied an end to federal enforcement of civil rights.[45] Tilden, however, advanced swiftly in the North, swinging the twin swords of reform and depression. Hayes and his team began to panic. Despite their decided lack of enthusiasm for civil rights laws, they quickly seized on fears of a newly assertive South. Hayes himself jotted down such slogans as, "Are you for the Rebel South, or are you for the loyal North?" Local chapters of the Grand Army of the Republic turned out in full uniform for party rallies. Speaker Robert G. Ingersoll repeatedly delivered a highly popular, highly bellicose speech. "Every man that shot Union soldiers was a Democrat," he bellowed. "Every man that loved slavery better than liberty was a Democrat."[46] In many respects, this "waving the bloody shirt" was the mirror image of the Democratic campaign in the South. Both sides wished to reenact the Civil War, only Dixie's Democrats planned a very different ending.

This lithograph shows the officials of the Radical administration that triumphed in Missouri in 1864 and emancipated the state's slaves. The Radicals also drafted and enforced a state constitution that extended new civil rights to African Americans, and barred former Confederates from the ballot box, juries, many professions, and the pulpit. (Library of Congress)

Below: *After the war, President Andrew Johnson accepted white supremacy in the South and extended pardons to all former rebels, helping to trigger a Northern blacklash. This 1866 cartoon by Thomas Nast illustrates Northern revulsion by casting the conservative president as Iago, linking him to white-supremacist violence in the South.* (Library of Congress)

Above: *The Reconstruction Acts (passed over President Johnson's vetoes) extended new political rights to African Americans. Former Confederate soldiers responded with paramilitary organizations that terrorized black activists and their white allies. Many adopted the garb and rituals of the Ku Klux Klan, which first appeared in Tennessee in 1866. The disguises of the James-Younger outlaws in their first train robbery, in 1873, were described by witnesses as Klan masks.* (Library of Congress)

Left: *Union general Ulysses S. Grant served as president from 1869 to 1877. He supported congressional Reconstruction policies and pushed prosecutions of the Klan in the South. In his letters to the press, Jesse James repeatedly attacked Grant as a tyrant.* (Library of Congress)

Below: *This 1870 photograph shows a locomotive, a coal tender, and a baggage car of the Burlington and Missouri River Railroad. The James-Younger bandits concerned themselves almost exclusively with this section of the trains they stopped; they held up passengers only twice in eight years of railway robberies. Their target was the cash and valuables in the express safe in the baggage car.* (Denver Public Library)

Left: *Union general and Republican Thomas C. Fletcher was governor of Missouri from 1865 to 1869. Jesse James and his mother frequently singled out Fletcher and the militia he deployed aggressively against the ex-Confederate guerrillas as the direct cause of Jesse's fugitive status.*
(State Historical Society of Missouri, Columbia)

Right: *Missouri governor Silas Woodson, who served from 1873 to 1875, had no sympathy for the outlaws, seeing them as a political liability and an obstruction to the inflow of immigrants and investment. In 1874 he pushed the legislature to pass a secret-service act to fund the hunt for the bandits.* (State Historical Society of Missouri, Columbia)

Left: *Charles H. Hardin, governor from 1875 to 1877, made the hunt for the outlaws a centerpiece of his administration—only to see them emerge as statewide heroes after a bloody raid by Pinkerton operatives on the Samuel farm in 1875.* (Missouri State Archives)

Allan Pinkerton, shown here in 1862, led the foremost private detective agency in the country. He was hired by the Adams Express Company in 1874 to hunt for the James and Younger brothers; after the murder of two of his agents, he carried on at his own expense. The struggle proved to be the most serious defeat of his career. (Library of Congress)

Jesse James around the time of his thirtieth birthday. Here again his striking blue eyes can be seen, along with his somewhat unusual upturned nose.
(Library of Congress)

Jesse and his first cousin Zerelda "Zee" Mimms, named for his mother, married in 1874. They had two children: Jesse Edwards (named after John N. Edwards) and Mary. (State Historical Society of Missouri, Columbia)

A graduate of West Point, Adelbert Ames received the Medal of Honor for his wartime heroics in the Union army. A champion of civil rights, he was elected U.S. senator, then governor, of Mississippi. In the spring of 1876 he moved to Northfield, Minnesota, where his family shared an interest in the First National Bank, which is why the James-Younger gang targeted it in September 1876. (Library of Congress)

Left: *This photograph shows the Northfield, Minnesota, town square, viewed from the outlaws' perspective as they approached the First National Bank. In the foreground is the bridge over the Cannon River. The large building straight across the square is the Dampier Hotel; the Scriver block (with the bank in the rear) faces onto the square at the right.* (Northfield Historical Society)

Right: *Here the Scriver block is seen from the perspective of the ground floor of the Dampier Hotel. The bank is in the rear of the building, facing onto Division Street; the square is to the right. The Younger brothers fought the last part of the brief gun battle during the robbery with their backs to the wall, under the exterior staircase.* (Northfield Historical Society)

The interior of the bank, essentially as it appeared in 1876. Joseph L. Heywood sat behind a desk to the right, facing inward; Alonzo E. Bunker sat behind the counter to the left, closest to the teller window, with Frank Wilcox toward the rear. The safe is just visible within the vault. (Northfield Historical Society)

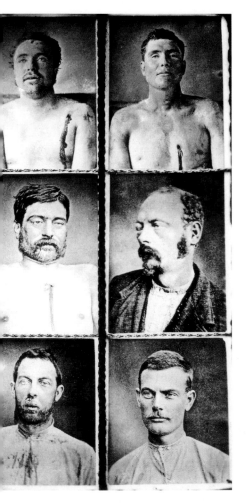

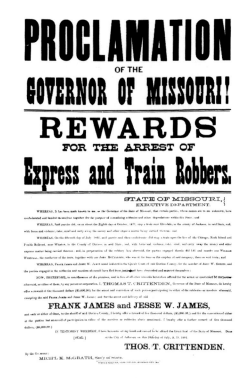

Above: *This poster announces a reward, funded by the railroad corporations. The offer has often been misrepresented as "dead or alive"—though that was how it was applied.* (State Historical Society of Missouri, Columbia)

Above, clockwise from top left: *Clell Miller, killed at Northfield; William Stiles, alias Bill Chadwell, killed at Northfield; Cole Younger, captured near Madelia during the escape; Bob Younger, captured near Madelia; Jim Younger, captured near Madelia; Samuel Wells, alias Charlie Pitts, killed near Madelia.* (Northfield Historical Society)

Right: *Thomas T. Crittenden, a former militia officer, was Missouri governor from 1881 to 1885. He devoted much of his first two years to coordinating the effort to destroy Jesse James's resurrected gang. He convened a meeting of railroad and express executives to raise money for a large reward, and met with Bob Ford shortly before Ford assassinated Jesse.* (Missouri State Archives)

The house where Jesse James was killed in St. Joseph, Missouri (the building was later relocated). The "bullet hole" noted on the sign was unrelated to the shooting; testimony at the coroner's inquest indicated that the lethal bullet (the only one fired) lodged just under the skin above Jesse's left eye. This modest building was typical of the houses Jesse and Zee rented after their marriage. (Library of Congress)

The two bullet wounds Jesse James suffered in the Civil War are visible on the right side of his chest. As seen here, he grew his beard and dyed it black toward the end of his life.
(Library of Congress)

To Ames in his Northfield refuge, the rising crescendo of partisan hatred was nothing more than the distant thunder of a storm that had already struck and passed on. Like Conrad's Baron Heyst, Ames had retreated from the world, mystified by its undeserved calumnies, his dignity unbroken. He spent his days bent over the mill's accounts and pondering the mysteries of wheat. In the evening he galloped his horse, or went shooting with his happily retired father, or penned another letter to his beloved Blanche. On September 7, another day in a chain of days no different from the others, Ames went home for lunch and wrote a quick note to his wife. Afterward he returned to the mill to mail the letter and pore through the books once more. Then he heard gunfire.

ON AUGUST 23, 1876, two hard-looking men strolled into the lobby of the Nicollet Hotel in Minneapolis and requested a room for themselves and a sick friend. The clerk snapped open a registration book, and they signed the names J. C. Horton and H. L. West of Nashville, Tennessee. The manager did not like the look of Horton and West; they claimed to be Grangers, yet they handled the pen with soft, pale hands. He liked it still less when they were joined by three friends the next day: W. G. Huddleson of Maryland, J. C. King of Virginia, and John Wood (or Ward), also of Virginia. The men would storm into the dining room with their hats still on, with an exaggerated bumpkin rudeness, and they spent an hour on the second-floor balcony, amusing themselves by dropping dollars to a poor organ grinder.[47]

The manager had good reason to be suspicious. The men who checked into his hotel on the twenty-third were almost certainly the James brothers, and perhaps Bill Chadwell or Bob Younger. That night they took a hack to "a notorious house kept by Mollie Ellsworth," according to press reports. There the madam and Jesse James recognized each other from the days when she kept a bordello in St. Louis. "I used to know him well," the woman said. She asked Jesse what he was doing "up here," prompting the bandit to smile. "Oh, nothing," he replied. "I am going out into the country for a few days, and will be back soon, then you and I will go to the Centennial." The hack driver confirmed the story, and the madam was most insistent. "I know that it was Jesse James," she said.[48]

No doubt exists about the three men who registered on August 24. The man who signed as King would soon be identified as Cole Younger, the fellow named Wood (or Ward) as Charlie Pitts, and Jim Younger would admit that he was Huddleson, and had stayed at the Nicollet.[49] The trio had spent the previous night at the Merchant's Hotel in St. Paul, where Clell Miller and the eighth man remained.

The outlaws' interest in St. Paul would have been understandable to Minnesotans of the day. Though a smaller city than Minneapolis, it had earned a reputation as a fast town, with some 240 saloons—70 more than in its larger neighbor. The city had chosen to regulate rather than stamp out its gambling dens and brothels; every month, each of St. Paul's madams would appear in police court, plead guilty to keeping a house of ill fame, and pay a small fine—obtaining, in essence, a license to stay open another thirty days, provided she ran her businesses in an orderly manner. Thirteen bordellos operated at the time, and hundreds of freelance women engaged in "plain sewing," to use the local euphemism, walking the streets or operating out of cigar stores. When the Youngers left, Miller and the other man stayed behind to enjoy themselves. The pair spent the night in a gambling saloon, blowing a staggering $200 in the course of play. At one point they caused a small stir by taking off their coats, each man revealing a pair of revolvers suspended from cartridge belts.[50]

Even as Miller and his companion tossed away their money and frightened their fellow gamblers, Jesse was huddled in his hotel room, finalizing his plans with Frank and the Younger brothers. In many ways, the operation they now discussed was the most significant of their outlaw careers. Not because of the money involved—no unusually large haul awaited them at their chosen destination—nor because of the great distance from their Missouri birthplaces—Huntington, West Virginia, had been just as far. It was because of *who* they were coming to rob, here in the far North, a target of truly national significance: former general, senator, and governor Adelbert Ames.

Just one month after this final planning session in the Nicollet Hotel, Bob Younger would explain the bandits' purpose in coming to Minnesota. They had learned, he would say, that "ex-Governor Ames, of Mississippi, had money in the Northfield bank; one of the boys had a spite against him, and so the robbery was planned."[51] Bob would speak these words to a crowd of Yankees, many of them Republicans and Union veterans, so his statement could hardly be considered an attempt to win sympathy. He would be isolated from Cole at the time of his comments, but Cole would repeat the same claim in three successive written accounts. "We had been informed that ex-Governor Ames of Mississippi and General Benjamin Butler of Massachusetts had deposited $75,000 in the National Bank," Cole would write in 1897, "and it was the above information that caused us to select the bank of Northfield." He would make this declaration in a statement written for a prison warden in Minnesota; so it, too, could hardly be considered a calculated excuse.[52]

Jesse was most likely both the plotter and the harborer of spite. Cole had hinted that one of the James brothers was the moving force when he said,

"You fellows suggested this, and I am just going with you." By that time, the bandits already planned a mission to Minnesota.[53] Jesse had always been the intense partisan who craved the political spotlight. In his letters to the Nashville press in 1875 and to the *Kansas City Times* in August 1876, he infused almost every sentence with his fury at the Radicals, his fascination with the political situation, and his hunger for heroic stature throughout the South.[54]

Ames offered a natural focus for his rising anger and ambition. Since taking office as Mississippi governor in 1874, Ames had been doused with a torrent of abuse by the Democratic newspapers of Missouri—abuse that connected him with his better-known father-in-law. (Butler had been given the nickname "Beast" by the rebels for his stern administration of Union-occupied New Orleans.) "When Beast Butler's son-in-law, Ames, a resident of Massachusetts, was 'elected' by Grant bayonets governor of Mississippi," wrote the *Lexington Caucasian*, "a dirty brood of nigger barbers, boot blacks and plantation chattels were put in office all over the state." The Democratic press twisted episodes of white-supremacist violence in Mississippi into examples of Radical oppression, and when the insurrection of 1875 finally crushed black political freedom, the newspapers cheered. Mississippi, stated the *St. Louis Republican*, "was cursed by the meanest and most despicable tyranny that ever disgraced the soil of the republic. . . . The Ames dynasty has been literally a stench in the national nostrils."[55]

Ames had moved to Northfield in May 1876, just a month before the bandits began to plan their raid. In Minnesota, he had attracted virtually no attention. But a student of the national and Southern press—especially one with "a spite against him"—could have discovered much about this fighter for racial equality. On May 2, for example, the *New York Times* printed a lengthy interview with Ames. Dixie's newspapers closely followed the Senate committee that was investigating the Mississippi insurrection, as well as the uproar over the chamber's refusal to seat the newly elected L. Q. C. Lamar, the revolt's mastermind. For Jesse, Ames remained an object of hate, an inviting target for an attention-getting robbery, for a very personal political blow amid this climactic campaign.[56]

In the cloistered privacy of that room in the Nicollet Hotel, the James and Younger brothers firmed up their plans, drawing on Chadwell's knowledge of his native state, and on a map they had purchased at a nearby bookstore. They decided to split into two groups and approach Northfield in a pincer movement, one party coming from the west and the other from the east. This would allow them to better reconnoiter their escape route, and avoid the suspicions that eight men traveling together might raise. On August 26, they checked out, flashing thick rolls of currency as they settled their bill. Four of them took the train to Red Wing, east of Northfield on the Mississippi River; the other two returned to St. Paul, collected Miller and the eighth man, and then took a train southwest to St. Peter.[57]

The bandits carried some vital pieces of equipment: revolvers—two apiece, most of them new-model Smith & Wessons—along with cartridge belts and abundant ammunition. Minnesotans lacked the habit of carrying firearms, however, so the Missourians and their two new recruits concealed theirs under long linen dusters. They purchased their horses—all particularly fine ones, each worth at least $150—in St. Paul, St. Peter, and Red Wing.[58]

A story would later circulate that the gang started to rob a bank in Mankato, only to be frightened away; the tale originated when a man named Charley Robinson claimed, some weeks later, to have recognized Jesse on the street. Cole Younger, however, would explicitly deny these claims, asserting that the bandits remained in two parties until they met at Northfield on the morning of September 7. Contemporary press reports confirm Younger's account; indeed, no newspaper stories placed all eight men together until that fateful day. It appears that Cole headed the Mankato team, while Jesse led the squad that went to Red Wing. Four men checked into the National Hotel in that Mississippi River town on the night of August 26, signing as Horton and West of Nashville and Charles Wetherby of Indiana. (Again, one man did not register.)[59]

For almost two weeks they scouted the terrain in and around Northfield, inadvertently attracting attention along the way. In Faribault, "they were noted for their fine physique," the press reported, with their "pants tucked in boots, long spurs, and peculiar swagger." They often asked about the roads in their distinctive Southern accents, explaining that they were cattle buyers—a story that was generally accepted, especially since they were considered "jovial and pleasant" everywhere they went. Around the first of September, two of them opened negotiations to buy the farm of John Mulligan, who plowed the dirt two and a half miles from Northfield. They questioned him closely about the town. They seemed particularly concerned about whether it was "a peace-loving, law-abiding" community. "Why," one of them said, "according to your statement of the Northfield people a very few men so inclined could capture the town, couldn't they?" Mulligan readily agreed.[60]

On the morning of September 7, the eight men reunited south of Northfield for one last reconnaissance. Around ten o'clock, four of them cantered through town, drawing stares with their smart clothes and excellent horses. George E. Bates, who owned a store across from the bank, remarked to a visiting salesman that he had never seen "four nobler looking fellows." But, he added, "there was a reckless, bold swagger about them that seemed to indicate that they would be rough and dangerous fellows to handle."[61] Elias Hobbs, the town marshal, reassured another merchant that they were cattle buyers who had visited the town previously, but he started to pay close attention when two of them made an oddly brief visit to the bank. As the strangers poked around the stores and streets, they asked where they might purchase rifles. They were directed to the hardware store of Anselm Manning, who told them he had only shotguns for sale. The outlaws begged off politely, saying they were only interested in rifles.[62]

When the clock ticked past eleven, five of the bandits stopped for lunch at J. G. Jeft's restaurant on the western side of the Cannon River, near the railway depot; the others ate elsewhere in town. Jeft had yet to prepare his dinner menu, so the outlaws ordered hearty portions of ham and four eggs each. The men appeared relaxed; they had politics on their minds, and discussed the subject loudly. At one point they offered to bet the restaurant owner $1,000 that Minnesota would go Democratic in the coming election. Meanwhile, Northfield resident John Archer admired their horses tied up outside. "They were all first-class horses," he said, "and would attract attention anywhere."[63]

After the meal, the men gathered for one last consultation. "Early in the afternoon," Cole Younger later explained, "we rode back on the Janesville road two or three miles to consult and arrange our plans. We agreed, by a majority vote, to rob the bank. . . . Three were to ride ahead and enter the bank as soon as Clell Miller and myself had crossed the bridge leading into the square. . . . Another quarter of a mile behind us the remaining three, including Jim Younger, were to take up their stand near the bridge. . . . If the alarm was given, I was to signal those at the bridge and they were to give the rebel yell and fire their pistols in the air to scare the people off the street." Though he wrote this account twenty-one years later, he accurately described the bandits' plan of operations. Indeed, the scheme was almost an exact replica of the Columbia robbery in 1872, when Jesse had led the charge into the bank and Cole had kept the streets clear. But Younger's story left out one item the gang must have discussed: an article that Clell Miller had cut from the *Rice County Journal*, hailing the new Yale Chronometer time lock on the bank's safe.[64]

As 2 p.m. approached, the outlaws rode past the Ames mill in their assigned divisions, their horses clopping onto the bridge that led into the square. It seems most likely that the last unit consisted of Bob and Jim Younger, along with Chadwell; that the middle pair comprised Miller and Cole Younger, as Cole later claimed; and that the first three were Charlie Pitts, Frank, and Jesse.[65]

Jesse and the two others cantered over the dirt square to the Scriver block, past Lee & Hitchcock's dry-goods store on the ground floor of the building, then down to the bank entrance on Division Street. Again they attracted attention. George Bates watched from across the way as they "dismounted and tied their horses to the hitching posts . . . and two went down to the staircase leading up into the upper stories of Lee & Hitchcock's."[66] Elias Hobbs observed as they "held [a] short conversation on [a] dry goods box" in front of Lee & Hitchcock's. Dentist D. J. Whiting, whose office was at the top of the staircase, peered down to see one of them "apparently describing something to the other and illustrating the same with marks upon the box on which they sat."[67]

The two men looked toward the bridge; Cole Younger and Miller were riding slowly across, right on time. Rising from the box, they walked back to their companion in front of the bank, their long spurs dragging, linen dusters flapping. As Younger and Miller halted in front of the door, the three men stepped inside.

Jesse and his companions walked into a narrow space shaped like a capital L, as viewed from the door, partitioned by a counter that formed a smaller L within it. Innermost of all was the vault, opening toward Division Street. Three men sat behind the glass-paneled counter: F. J. Wilcox, farthest from the door; A. E. Bunker, closest to the corner where there was an opening in the glass panels; and J. L. Heywood, to the right behind the cashier's desk, facing in with his back to the wall. In the back, another open door, obstructed only by a hanging blind, led out into an alley that ran down to Water Street alongside the river. The setting was quiet, peaceful, industrious—the perfect target for a man with a gun.[68]

The three intruders drew their revolvers from under their coats, strode straight for the counter, jumped up, and scrambled over. "Throw up your hands, for we intend to rob the bank," one of them shouted, "and if you hallo we will blow your God-damned brains out." Waving their pistols, they ordered the startled bank employees onto their knees. Which one of you is the cashier? they demanded. "He is not in," Heywood responded, though he himself was the acting cashier. (George M. Phillips was at the Centennial in Philadelphia.)[69]

Heywood, a bearded, thirty-nine-year-old bookkeeper who had fought at Vicksburg and Arkansas Post in the 127th Illinois Infantry Regiment during the war, clearly realized that, as the acting cashier, the weight of events rested on his shoulders alone. Only a week earlier, he had contemplated his actions in just such a crisis. President Strong of Carleton College had come by to see the new time lock on the bank's safe. Bringing up the wartime robbery of the bank in St. Albans, Vermont, by Confederate raiders, Strong had asked Heywood if he would have handed over the money under such circumstances. "I do not think I should," Heywood had said, according to Strong, "with his characteristically quiet manner."[70]

Now his "quiet manner" faced its final test. The stress he felt must have been the most intense of his life. The man who held the gun had learned to cope with the emotional burden of life-and-death situations by constant repetition. As for Heywood, apart from his brief military service, his traumas had been at the bedside of his dying wife; his burdens had been his employers' expectations, his family's needs. In this moment, a thirst for revenge confronted an unarmed sense of duty. Today duty would win, but at a price.

Flummoxed by Heywood's response, the outlaws turned to Bunker. "You are the cashier," they said; he denied it, as did Wilcox. Then they looked again at Heywood—not only the oldest, but the only one who had been seated behind a desk. "You are the cashier," one of the bandits said angrily. "Now open the safe you God-damned son of a bitch."

"It is a time lock," Heywood said, "and cannot be opened now." One of the robbers saw that the vault was open and darted inside. Heywood jumped from his chair and heaved the heavy door shut. Immediately another bandit seized him by the collar, dragged him back, and released his trapped colleague. One man—described by Wilcox as the bandit in charge—drew a glittering bowie knife and held it to Heywood's throat. "Damn you!" he seethed, and shallowly sliced across his esophagus, drawing blood. "Open that door or we'll cut your throat from ear to ear."

Heywood pushed himself free. "Murder!" he shouted. The gunman smashed his revolver against Heywood's skull. The bookkeeper collapsed in a daze as his attacker crouched over him, threatening and demanding.[71]

All this time another bandit loomed over Bunker and Wilcox, who waited obediently on their knees. The twenty-six-year-old Bunker thought quickly: with the gunmen devoting most of their attention to Heywood, he might be able to reach a small Smith & Wesson revolver he kept under the counter. He began to edge gradually over to it, sliding his knees inch by inch across the floor. But one of the outlaws snatched it up and shoved it in his pocket.

When the robber turned toward the vault again, Bunker raised himself up slightly to see if he could catch someone's attention outside. Whoever was guarding him saw this and became furious. Bunker later claimed that the gunman crowded Bunker's head to the floor with the muzzle of his revolver. If you rise up again, he snarled, I will kill you. Where's the teller's cash? he demanded. The teller gestured to a tray containing some rolled-up nickels, but the outlaw seemed to know that there was more money than that outside the vault. He continued to search, jerking open one drawer that contained the bank's stationery, but he passed over another that held some two thousand dollars.

A shot cracked in the room. Bunker's guard turned toward the vault entrance, where another bandit held a smoking revolver at the head of the semiconscious Heywood. In his attempts at intimidation, he had fired a round next to Heywood's skull, leaving him uninjured but no more cooperative. With all of the outlaws focused on the crumpled bookkeeper, Bunker leaped up and sprinted for the back door, crashing through the hanging blind and darting into the alley. Pitts immediately followed and shot Bunker in the back. The bullet passed through his upper chest, missing any organs or arteries, and he was able to stagger to safety.

Until that moment, the bandits had been fixed on the events inside the bank. After Bunker's escape, they realized that gunfire was cracking furiously outside.[72]

WHEN COLE YOUNGER and Miller rode their horses across the bridge at two o'clock, they carefully watched their two comrades sitting on the dry-goods box in front of Lee & Hitchcock's. "They are going in," Miller breathed, as the other outlaws rose and strode back to the bank. The mounted men turned onto Division, then stopped and swung out of their saddles. Trying to be inconspicuous, Cole bent his two-hundred-pound body to tighten his saddle girth while Miller pulled the bank door shut.[73]

Merchant J. S. Allen, meanwhile, watched these proceedings with rising suspicion. "Who are those men?" he asked John Archer, as the first three bandits rode up from the bridge. "I don't like the looks of them." His worries heightened as they waited on the dry-goods box, then rose to meet the two other men who rode across the square. "I believe they are here to rob the bank," he said. Allen decided to investigate. Striding purposefully to the bank, he just glimpsed the face of Heywood through the closing door. The man who was pulling it shut "took me by my collar," Allen reported, and said, "You son of a bitch, don't you holler." In Allen's words, "I broke and run. Then they began to fire."[74]

W. H. Riddel was watching these events from his store directly across from the bank. He, too, was concerned about the strangers' intentions, and when he saw Allen so roughly handled—when he caught the words "son of a bitch"—he realized what was transpiring. "Robbers at the bank!" he shouted. Immediately the bigger of the two strangers vaulted into his saddle, drew a revolver, and squeezed off a few rounds, roaring at Riddel, "Get in there, you God-damn son of a bitch!"[75]

Chaos erupted on Division Street, as the two men in front of the bank began to fire in the air and order everyone inside. Three more bandits came galloping up from the bridge, thundering up and down the dirt lane, shooting and cursing. Some of the citizens looked around in confusion, then scrambled for cover; others, who had noticed the strangers earlier, grasped what was happening. At the first shot, George Bates looked at the salesman visiting his store and exclaimed, "Them men are going for the town—they mean to rob the bank." Looking out the door, they saw the riders shooting and shouting, "Clear the street!" Bates ran for a shotgun. On the same side of the street, a young medical student named Henry Wheeler saw these events from his father's drugstore. Seizing an old breech-loading carbine, he sprinted into the Dampier Hotel, shouting to clerk Charlie Dampier to bring him cartridges. Running upstairs to a second-floor window, Wheeler took two rounds, hastily loaded his gun, and snapped off a quick shot at the riders below.[76]

For Cole, the situation grew worse by the minute. He had hoped to get a start out of town before the alarm could be raised, as they had done at Huntington. That was now impossible, so they would have to follow the Columbia model: terrorize the citizens and keep the streets clear. Swinging a stout leg over his saddle, he drew a revolver and fired the shots that brought Jim and Bob Younger, along with Bill Chadwell, up from the bridge. Swearing and shooting, he and the others galloped up and down Division Street, driving everyone indoors.

Then things started to go wrong. Cole caught a glimpse of weapons held by men who peeked out from windows and storefronts. Already the first crack of return fire had burst from the second floor of the hotel looming across the street. Then he saw Miller crawling back into his saddle, his face bleeding from a dozen tiny wounds. Though Cole could not know it at the time, his comrade had been injured by Elias Stacey, who had fired a shotgun loaded with lightweight birdshot. Another round cracked from that window in the Dampier Hotel; Miller's horse suddenly stopped short as the outlaw tumbled face first to the ground.[77]

"I jumped from my horse," Cole recalled, "ran to Miller to see how badly he was hurt, and, while turning him over, was shot in the left hip." Younger spoke to his friend, but he could see that he was dying. He unbuckled Miller's cartridge belt and pulled it loose, knowing that he would soon need the extra pistols. Then he remounted and spurred his horse. Directly above, dentist Whiting observed from the head of the staircase. "The fight was becoming hot," he recalled, "not so many shots were being fired, but there was a more evident purpose to shoot to kill." He had no difficulty identifying the man in charge: it was the hulking Cole Younger, still thundering up and down the street as the others collected in front of the bank.[78]

At one point during the gun battle, Nellie Ames drove her light, four-wheeled carriage up a side street from Water toward Division. She saw

Bunker staggering along, holding one hand to his shoulder. "What's the matter, Mr. Bunker?" she asked. "I'm shot," he replied, and continued on his way. Another man ran toward her. "Mrs. Ames," he said in alarm, "get out of that carriage quick. You'll be killed."

As she stepped to the ground, she looked up and saw men on horseback, firing rapidly. The noise seemed to be attracting a stream of men that poured out of a basement saloon between her position and Division Street, men who quickly scattered as they realized what was going on. One of the horsemen reined in and looked straight at her. "Lady," he said, "get off the street or you will be killed." Then he turned to the last man coming out of the saloon, who was obviously drunk, and shot him. "His command, accompanied by the shot fired, fixed my attention upon him," she stated later, "and as soon as their photographs appeared, I at once confidently recognized Coleman Younger." At least two others would also identify him as the man who shot the bystander. The victim was Nicolaus Gustavson, a Swedish immigrant who spoke no English; badly wounded by a bullet to the head, he would die not many days later. Mrs. Ames went into a panic, shouting, "Oh John! John! Where's John! Oh, I want John!"[79]

Back on Division Street, the citizens of the town were acting with increasing focus and determination. Bates, discovering that his shotgun would not fire, seized a pistol and ran back to his store entrance. The weapon was unloaded, but he aimed it anyway to draw the bandits' fire, shouting, "Now I've got you!" Each time he did so a bullet would crash through the plate glass or rip into the door frame; one of them grazed his face. A man named J. B. Hyde blasted away with a double-barreled shotgun. Elias Hobbs, the town marshal, found himself unarmed—so he began to throw rocks. And across the street, on the square down toward the river, A. R. Manning seized a Remington rifle and ran across the front of Lee & Hitchcock's. With the crack of gunshots echoing, with smoke drifting across Division Street, he poked his head around the staircase.[80]

At that moment, Adelbert Ames was marching swiftly across the bridge. A few minutes earlier, a messenger had appeared at the mill, speaking breathlessly of the raid. Ames had stepped to the door and heard the rising swell of gunfire across the river. Then the old soldier acted as he had at Fredericksburg and Fort Fisher—he went straight toward the sound of the guns. For a man who had spent countless hours in battle, it seemed the most natural thing in the world.

Weaponless but curious, the man whom Jesse James had come to rob strode across the square to Lee & Hitchcock's. He saw people hiding behind buildings all along the street, either cowering for safety or firing down Division. He saw a man at the corner with a rifle, crouched down at the foot of the staircase, and recognized him as Manning, the hardware-store owner. Ames walked up behind him, and the two men peered around the corner.[81]

When Ames and Manning looked down Division toward the bank, the gunmen outside were still mounted, galloping up and down the street, shooting and shouting. Then Miller fell from his horse, and Cole jumped down and ran over to him. Manning raised his rifle to his shoulder and fired. Ames noticed that the merchant's hands were trembling. The former general spoke to him confidently and reassuringly, as he had to his artillery battery at Malvern Hill and his infantrymen at Gettysburg. With gunshots echoing and smoke drifting over the street, Manning aimed down the block at a bandit who clung to his horse's neck, using the animal for cover in the style favored by Indian warriors. He fired, and Bill Chadwell—or William Stiles, as he was known here in his native state—fell to the ground, dead.[82]

With Miller and Chadwell down, the three Younger brothers consolidated their position in front of the bank. They clicked through their revolvers' cylinders, firing at the plate-glass windows that lined the far side of the street as incoming bullets and buckshot smacked into the dirt and masonry around them. Bob and Jim dismounted and crouched behind one of their horses, using it for cover.* The animal suddenly staggered and fell. The two Youngers turned and saw Manning holding a smoking rifle. They immediately fired, forcing him—and Ames—to pull back behind the staircase. Then a dance began: the merchant would slip out, squeeze off a round, then jump back to safety to avoid the brothers' bullets.

The duel infuriated the wounded Cole. "Charge up on him!" he ordered as he returned fire at the windows and storefronts across the street. His brothers, however, continued the game of duck-and-shoot. "Shoot through the stairs!" he shouted. Finally Bob responded. He raised the pistol in his right hand and began to blast holes in the wooden steps and slats that shielded Manning and Ames.[83]

At the very moment when Bob began to fire, Henry Wheeler returned to his position at the second-story window of the Dampier Hotel. After firing his only two bullets, he had run to find more ammunition. Now he rejoined the battle just at the moment when he was needed most. As he angled his carbine toward the street below, he heard a cry of warning rise from the ground. In response, Manning and Ames pulled back behind the corner of the Scriver building, just escaping the rounds that splintered through the stairs. Wheeler squinted down the barrel of his rifle at the gunman and pulled the trigger—a little too low, he thought, believing he had

---

*Cole later claimed that Bob was one of the three who entered the bank, and emerged before the others to join the street fight. No witnesses inside or outside of the bank testified to anyone exiting separately, however. Bob was clearly identified outside the bank during the affair, which only took a few minutes; he could not have been in both places.

hit the man in the leg. In fact, the bullet shattered Bob Younger's right elbow. Bob switched his revolver to his left hand, letting his wounded limb hang uselessly at his side.[84]

Only a few minutes had passed, yet Cole already realized that the outlaws had been defeated. In later years, he would come up with excuses for the catastrophe that he now faced on Division Street: the men who went into the bank were drunk, he would say, or they violated the plan by going in despite the large crowd on the street.[85] At this moment, however, he would have seen the truth. The bandits' main advantages were surprise and intimidation. Over the years, however, their very success had prepared the public for the possibility of a bank robbery. When this one began, the citizens jumped to the correct conclusion. And by driving everyone inside, the outlaws simply forced their foes to take cover, allowing them to fire from protected positions. Now they found themselves in a tactical trap. Exposed along a bare masonry wall, they were caught in Manning's crossfire and dominated by Wheeler's second-story perch. Cole knew what had to be done. He galloped furiously up to the bank door and kicked it in. "The game is up," he shouted inside. "We are beaten."[86]

FOR THE THREE men inside the bank, Cole's anguished voice punctuated an emerging awareness of their own failure. Pitts jumped over the counter, followed by the man who had guarded Wilcox and Bunker. The last outlaw, the leader, paused on his way out. Wilcox watched as he turned toward Heywood, who had risen unsteadily to his feet and now groped toward his desk. In all likelihood, the man who glared at the dazed banker, who extended a pistol toward his head, was the same outlaw who had shot John Sheets at Gallatin and R. A. C. Martin at Columbia—who had composed the famous letter to the *Kansas City Times* after the Kansas City fair robbery. "A man who is a d———d enough fool to refuse to open a safe or a vault when he is covered with a pistol ought to die," he had written. "If he gives the alarm, or resists, or refuses to unlock, he gets killed." In all likelihood, the gunman was Jesse James.

It was all over. Their biggest, most carefully planned operation was ending in disaster. As the others raced out the door, this last man held a revolver to the head of the quiet bookkeeper who had destroyed his plans. He squeezed the trigger and killed Joseph Heywood. The gunman leaped over the counter and disappeared out the door. In the vault he left behind, the safe sat unmolested—and unlocked.[87]

Out on the street, the bandits scrambled into their saddles through the acrid clouds of gunsmoke. The storm of bullets continued, one of them catching Jim Younger in the shoulder. "For God's sake don't leave me boys," Bob wailed behind them, staggering along with a shattered arm. "I'm shot." Cole swung around and reached down with a meaty hand, hauling his little brother up onto his own horse. Digging in their spurs, they set off at hard gallop, heading south.[88]

Within two weeks, Pitts would be dead, the Youngers captured, and the James brothers clinging to freedom on the most desperate ride of their lives.

IN NORTHFIELD, THE citizens slowly emerged from their hiding places, some still gripping rifles and shotguns. They bent down to examine the corpses in the street; they filed into the bank to find the bloody remains of Heywood; and John Ames ran to the telegraph office to wire an alert that would spark a statewide manhunt.[89] They had won, but at a bitter cost. And in the days and years to come, they would wonder why this band of Missourians had come here, hundreds of miles from their hunting grounds, to rob a modest bank in a modest town. It was a question they could never properly answer for themselves. The next morning, the one man who could put that question in its proper context was at the bank, standing where Jesse James had so recently stood, counting the money with the other shareholders. Adelbert Ames soon discovered that the robbers had taken virtually nothing. As the manhunt progressed, however, the bank would deplete its capital by a quarter as it paid rewards and supported Heywood's widow. The foiled robbery would cost Ames personally almost a thousand dollars.

But it wasn't the money that came to Ames's mind, as he pondered the events of September 7. "The time yesterday," he wrote, "reminded me of an election in Mississippi." The context seemed to him inescapable, even if it escaped the Minnesotans around him. "Is it not strange," he wrote to Blanche in his next letter, "that Mississippi should come to visit me? The killing of Republicans by a set of Mississippi K.K. [Ku Klux Klansmen] produces a similar state of sensation as the murdering of a number of men by Missouri cut-throats who are after plunder."[90]

Ames had hit upon precisely the right comparison, the one the bandits themselves had intended. Instead, an obstinate bookkeeper had saved Ames's money, a sharpshooting young doctor had saved his life, and the Northfield robbery would be forever remembered not as a bold blow against a leading Radical, but as the day Jesse James reached beyond his grasp.[91]

PART FOUR

Fate

1876–1882

They continued the war after the war ended; such, at first, was their declared purpose, and, in a measure, so executed. But as time passed on the war, even to them, was a thing of the past, but having imbued their natures in crime, they . . . became the outlaws they now are.

—*Kansas City Times*
July 27, 1881

We called him outlaw, and he was; but fate made him so.

—John N. Edwards,
Sedalia Democrat
April 13, 1882

Anybody that knows anything about Jesse, knows that whenever he's captured, a black box will suit him better than chains.

—Bettie Scruggs Patton
January 29, 1875

CHAPTER EIGHTEEN

Resurrection

I N 1879, as John Davis Howard wandered his rented farm near Box Station in Humphreys County, Tennessee, where he lived with his wife, Mary, and his young son, Tim, and looked back over the previous thirty-odd months, they seemed packed with meaningful events. In the election of 1878, for example, the Greenback Party had made a surprisingly strong showing, with its calls for strict control of corporations and a larger money supply to cope with the depression. More than a million people had cast their ballots for Greenback candidates, sending fourteen congressmen to Washington. Before that, in the summer of 1877, there had been a stunning wave of national strikes, beginning on July 16 and ending on July 29. For thirteen days, railroad employees and other workers had shut the country down in protest against repeated wage cuts. In the end, President Rutherford B. Hayes had sent troops into the major cities to put the strike down by force.

Hayes's presidency itself was the result of another great event: the election of 1876. Democrat Samuel Tilden had apparently won, but the Republicans had cried foul, claiming that black voters had been suppressed in Louisiana, South Carolina, and Florida. Indeed, threats and outright force had prevented African Americans from going to the polls throughout the South; if they had been able to vote freely, there is little question that Hayes would have won easily. After months of angry disputes, investigations, and secret negotiations, Southern Democrats had agreed to allow Hayes to take office. They had made a number of demands (including federal support for the Texas Pacific Railroad and other infrastructure in Dixie), but had set two absolute conditions: the appointment of a Democrat as postmaster general—the most important dispenser of patronage in Washington—and an end to federal intervention in Southern elections—that is, an end to federal protection for African Americans. In the Compromise of 1877—sealed, ironically, at a hotel owned by a black man named James Wormley— Reconstruction had finally met its tragic end.[1]

So it had been an eventful period, even for a typical farmer, though Howard's neighbors knew that he was not exactly typical. He could be boastful and flashy, such as the time he bragged that he would corner the corn market by buying the county's entire harvest. He could also be resentful and sullen, as he was with merchant W. K. Jackson, who broke the corner. He could be combative, as he was in dealing with a lawsuit brought against him by one Steve Johnson in early 1878. And he could suffer hardship like anyone—in February 1878 his wife had given birth to twins, only to see them die soon afterward.

He also seemed to be, in the parlance of the times, a sporting man. A patron of the racetrack, he loved fine horses. He kept a particulary remarkable animal saddled at all times, claiming that constant exercise kept it in shape. His more respectable "brother-in-law," B. J. Woodson, shared his passion for horses and often accompanied him to the track. Howard also frequented the faro "banks"—or parlors—in and around Nashville, and he would sometimes return home with thick rolls of cash, explaining that he had been trading livestock. He was just as likely to return penniless, however; at one point or another, it seemed that he owed money to most of the county, and he even swindled a local farmer out of $900 in cattle when he was particularly short of cash.

Given the often-conflicting stories he told about himself, the revolvers he always carried, and his guarded air, he "was generally regarded as a desperado," in Jackson's words. Once, for example, he was playing cards in Nashville, and began to suspect that the dealer was using a stacked deck. Silently he drew his revolver, placed it in his lap, and said, "Nothing like that goes."[2]

Restless, suspicious, and edgy, Howard appeared to be half farmer, half hustler—in any case, not a man given to reflection. But the people of Humphreys County didn't know that he was the famous outlaw Jesse James, or that "B. J. Woodson" was Frank James. They had no reason to think that this was a man who was accustomed to commanding headlines, to seeing his own writings splashed across the front pages, to being the topic of legislative debates and statewide elections. As drawn out as the last three years had been for everyone, they must have been torturous for the newly pacified James, struggling to lead a new life in Tennessee. For him, the autumn of 1876 would have been another epoch. No one he now nodded to at the post office or bantered with about horses could have grasped what he had been through in those harrowing days. By all rights, he should not have survived them, and as he scraped by on cards, corn, and horse racing, he may have felt that he had outlived his allotted time.

IT HAD ALL changed in fewer than fifteen minutes. At 2 p.m. on September 7, 1876, the James and Younger brothers had been an invincible force, slayers of detectives and heroes of Confederates; by quarter past two, they had become fugitives, wounded and wanted men who galloped south from Northfield as fast as their horses could run. Cole Younger, wincing from the bullet that had torn his hip, carried with him his badly injured brother Bob. Jim Younger reeled in the saddle from a shoulder wound. Charlie Pitts and the Jameses had escaped unharmed, but they left behind the corpses of Clell Miller and Bill Chadwell, the Minnesotan who could have guided them on their escape.[3]

Before the riders had gone very far, they stopped to bandage Bob's bleeding arm. Then they galloped on, stopping just past the village of Dundas to pour a bucket of water over the wound and rewrap it. They halted a farmer on the road and took a draft horse from his wagon for Bob to ride; one of the other Youngers led the horse, as Bob cradled his arm in his lap, blood dripping from the fingertips.[4]

Back in Northfield, Henry Wheeler leaped into a saddle to lead the chase. He and the small party he led soon returned, however, their less-than-prime horses having given out after a few minutes of hard riding. But in towns across the southern half of the state, telegraphs clicked out the news of the robbery, thanks to John Ames's hasty report. Parties of police from Minneapolis and St. Paul quickly gathered at the train stations for the journey south, and posses formed in villages all around the outlaws. "The past two days have been those of unusual excitement," wrote John E. Risedorph of Le Sueur, Minnesota, on September 9, "although the cause of the excitement was many miles away. . . . The whole country are on their track and report says have them surrounded." As A. W. Henkle wrote several days later, "most every man who was not a coward" joined in the manhunt.[5]

The six men they were after knew the search would begin immediately. Riding three abreast, they spurred their horses into exhaustion as they galloped southwest. Two hours after the robbery, they entered the village of Shieldsville, where they found a wagonload of guns; the owners, members of a posse, were inside a saloon drinking beer. They debated breaking the weapons, but decided to ride on. Then their troubles began to multiply. A party from Faribault caught sight of them and opened a long-range firefight, but no one was injured. Bob's horse stumbled and fell. They took another from a passing farmer, but it, too, was a draft animal, unused to saddle and spurs, and they let it go after failing to bring it under control. Exhausted, they turned into a stretch of woods for the night.[6]

The next day, they pushed south across a bend in the Cannon River, fending off a handful of guards. They found two boys named Rosenhall plowing a field nearby. They took their animals and forced one of the brothers to guide them. After riding for a while into some woods, they ordered the boy to remain and continued on to another campsite. That night a storm struck. The six outlaws had rubber coats, but they were soon cold and wet to the bone, and increasingly hungry. The next morning they abandoned their horses and moved west through the brush on foot, slowly and cautiously, eating corn and potatoes they took from the fields. They often caught sight of their pursuers through the trees, and could even hear their voices. But the old bushwhackers put their vast experience to work: they waded through streams to mask their trail, or hopped from rock to rock, or walked directly in each other's footsteps. Hampered by wounds and the increasingly systematic pursuit, they made slow progress. And all the while it rained, day after day, turning the ground into mud, saturating their clothes, and filling their boots with water.[7]

Early on the morning of September 13, the six men reached the outskirts of Mankato, at the southern bend of the Minnesota River. They were hiking across a field belonging to farmer Henry Shaubert when they encountered one of his hired hands, a fellow named Dunning. Immediately they drew their pistols, ordering him to keep still as they tied his arms. As he marched with them, the bandits heatedly debated his fate. "Let's shoot the son of a bitch," one of them argued, "then he will be sure not to tell." The others demurred, and simply forced him to take a solemn vow to not tell anyone of this encounter. And they had one other exchange with their prisoner. "The Captain, he is so called by the gang," Dunning told reporters, "said if the cashier had opened the vault he would not have shot him, and said the next time they thought the cashier would open up." Only Jesse would ever be called "our captain" by fellow gang members.[8]

They released Dunning as promised, but they placed little faith in his vow. They immediately doubled back, circled to the south, then went into a stretch of dense timber near Mankato as search parties crisscrossed the area. To the west, their hunters formed a picket line "in regular army style," according to the *Minneapolis Tribune,* with small groups moving along the railroads with handcars and deploying at evenly spaced intervals. Faced with this tightening net, the robbers decided to do the last thing anyone expected: that night, near midnight, they walked straight through Mankato itself, stopping to steal a cabbage, some melons, and a couple of chickens along the way. After clearing the western edge of town, they confronted one last obstacle: the Blue Earth River, which blocked their west-ward march. In pitch darkness, rain still pouring down, the six bandits scut-tled across a railroad trestle bridge on hands and knees, slipping past unwary guards on the other side.[9]

In the woods on the western bank of the Blue Earth, the six weary, sod-den men made camp. Under the cover of hanging raincoats, they made a fire to roast their chickens, and looked forward to their first meal in days. But yet another party of pursuers forced them to flee, leaving the food and some of their coats behind.

On September 14, 1876, Jesse and Frank James discussed their situation with Pitts and the Youngers as they crouched in the brush, listening for their hunters. For a week now they had been creeping west, moving mostly on foot, in the midst of a constant downpour. Their horses were gone, the Youngers were wounded, and they were all, as Bob Younger put it, "fear-fully hungry." They suffered from exposure as well, especially now that some had lost their coats. The temperature had dropped markedly; as one of their pursuers wrote, "I never suffered more from cold than I did that night." It was time, the James brothers said, to split up. Their old comrades could only nod their heads. Pitts elected to remain with the Youngers as Frank and Jesse departed in the midnight darkness, "with the knowledge and consent of the others," as Cole explained a few days later.[10]

Jesse and Frank clearly grasped how desperate their position was. In the days to come, they would ruthlessly drive their own suffering bodies as they pushed relentlessly toward the Dakota Territory. Immediately after they left the others, they stole a horse from a nearby barn. They rode together on the same animal through the wet night, trying to slip though the picket line that guarded the passages between a chain of lakes to the west. They bent forward, closely hugging the horse as they walked it slowly down a sandy road that ran through the forested shore of Lake Crystal. Suddenly a shotgun erupted. The spray of pellets caught Frank in the right foot and Jesse in the right knee, struck one of them in the side, and blew off one of their hats. With cool aplomb they slipped to the ground and crept away as their frightened horse galloped off, decoying their pursuers down the lane.[11]

Now wounded for the first time, they continued on foot. Perhaps two hours later, at three o'clock in the morning, they approached a barn to look for horses. One of the brothers stepped inside its open door and saw a man standing guard with a musket. The outlaw jumped forward, swept the rifle out of the man's hand, and smashed the butt of a revolver against his head. As the man fell senseless to the floor, the brothers saw a pair of large gray horses behind him. They found no saddles in the barn, however, so they each stuffed a pair of grain bags with hay and tied them together with a rope to make a set of improvised stirrups; then they bridled the horses, mounted, and set out for the western horizon.[12]

Finally they began to make rapid progress. They covered another twenty miles by seven o'clock in the morning, when they stopped at a farmhouse to buy a loaf of bread and a new hat. As they kicked their horses ahead, the morning sun lit the vast, rippling, almost treeless plain of southwestern Minnesota. With little cover to hide in, speed was their only protection. At dusk they stopped at the home of a German immigrant, who agreed to put them up for the night. After they came inside, the man's wife helped dress Jesse's wounded knee. They were injured when their wagon broke down, they explained—accounting for their lack of saddles as well as their wounds. They pored over a map, asking detailed questions about the roads. Then they went to sleep in their clothes, their first night of rest in at least two days.

The next morning, September 16, they set out at seven o'clock, changing direction sharply once they were out of their hosts' sight. At two in the afternoon, they forded the Des Moines River and asked for lunch at a house belonging to a man named Swan. Rather than waste any time, they had the farmer bring them bread, milk, and meat as they sat on their horses. As they ate, they peppered Swan with polite questions about the distances to various railroads. Then they turned southwest and rode all afternoon, all through the night, into the early hours of the next day.

At half past seven on Sunday morning, Jesse and Frank reined in on the western bank of the Rock River and got their breakfast at a nearby house. They radiated physical agony as they shuffled into the kitchen, barely able to lift their feet. They had spent the last twenty-four hours on horseback, in the same clothes they had worn for ten days through pounding rain. In addition to exhaustion and muscle pain, they must have suffered from chafed and peeling skin inside their thighs. Their wounds affected them as well. Though they refused to unbutton their raincoats—reaching up under them to get money to pay for their meal—one of them was obviously injured in the right side, his garment being torn there, and he could barely sit up to eat. But the iron will they had inherited from their mother drove them on. They returned to their horses once more, though they had to climb a fence slowly in order to mount.[13]

As the brothers pushed themselves ahead, they benefited from the timidity of their pursuers. When the Rock County sheriff caught sight of them some two hundred yards away, he decided not to risk a confrontation. That evening, close to sunset, the brothers finally reached the Dakota Territory. Shortly after crossing the line, they stopped at a barn and swapped their horses for a black pair, only to find that one had a blind eye and the other was entirely sightless. Ten miles on they switched again, stealing two gray geldings, then trotted through Sioux Falls in the predawn hours of September 18. Just south of town they overtook the stage to Yankton. They asked the driver where he was going, then turned and rode northwest. As they expected, the driver went back and warned the townspeople, who organized a posse that gave chase in that direction, as the brothers resumed their ride south.[14]

"In every way," one of the James brothers' pursuers remarked, "they were masters of the situation. Their bravery at Mankato, Lake Crystal, and at Seymour's farm [where they stole the first pair of gray horses], and their endurance on horseback for days and nights, wounded and almost starving, and without sleep, are without parallel in the history of crime." But they were not out of danger yet, even here in the Dakota Territory, some two hundred miles from Northfield. That night they went to sleep at a farm near the Iowa border. At six the next morning they bolted awake as a posse approached. Sprinting for their horses, they mounted and galloped toward the Sioux River, then splashed through its waters into Iowa, riding up a bluff on the far side. At the top they stopped and fired several rounds, hitting one of their foes' horses. The hunters jumped out of their saddles to take cover. When they looked up to return fire, the James brothers had already escaped into a stretch of timber.[15]

Jesse and Frank now rode straight toward Sioux City, where the Missouri River bent south and flowed toward home. Late in the afternoon of September 20, they saw a lone horseman ride up to them. His name was Dr. Mosher, he explained, and he needed directions to the home of a patient near James Station. The brothers chatted with him briefly, bringing up the subject of the Northfield robbery. Had he heard of it? Were the robbers thought to be close by? As Mosher replied, they drew their pistols. "We are two of the Northfield boys," they told him. "You are the man we want. You've been following us, and we have a description of you." Then they patted down the startled doctor before finally accepting his stuttered denial.

A friend of Mosher's explained what happened next. "He was made to undress and change clothing with the larger of the two men, and the doctor put his legs into a pair of pants six inches too long." The dirty, worn-out trousers had a large hole near the right knee; clearly Jesse, who was distinctly bigger than Frank, had been the worst hit in that shotgun blast on the night they left the Youngers. "The rubber coat torn by the charge of shot at Lake Crystal was exchanged for the new one the doctor wore," Mosher's friend added. They also took his horse, leaving him with one of their exhausted mounts. The doctor noticed that "they seemed to be pretty well worn down, especially the wounded man."[16]

Worn down—but free. After forcing Mosher to rebandage Jesse's wounded knee, the brothers let the doctor go, then rode south into the darkness.[17] Their trail was never found again. Ruthless, relentless, and utterly iron-willed, they had outrun, outfought, and outsmarted perhaps a thousand pursuers, crossing hundreds of miles of hostile territory. And they had survived.

Their comrades could not say the same. The next day, September 21, the three Younger brothers and Charlie Pitts were discovered near Madelia, Minnesota. They had remained on foot, and were moving slowly west when they approached a farmhouse belonging to Ole Sorbel. "We were very imprudent this morning in going to the house for food," Bob Younger explained later that day, "but we were so fearfully hungry." Sorbel's teenage son Oscar mounted a horse and galloped eight miles to Vaught's Hotel in Madelia, where he breathlessly described the men to Sheriff James Glispin of Watonwan County. Glispin immediately organized a large party that cornered the bandits in five acres of brush along the Watonwan River. A vicious firefight ensued, with several members of the posse very narrowly escaping serious injury.

A few minutes into the battle, Bob shouted, "I give up; the rest of the boys are all shot to pieces!" Glispin and his men moved in and found Pitts dead and all the Youngers badly wounded—Bob in the right side, Cole in the face, and Jim in the right thigh and upper jaw. The sheriff transported the brothers back to Faribault, the seat of Rice County, where people poured in to see them. After only the briefest resistance, the bandits freely admitted their identities. But they refused to name the two men who had escaped—until a reporter played a small—perhaps inadvertent—trick on them. The James boys had been caught, he said; one was dead, the other dying. "This seemed to affect them," the journalist wrote. Cole asked who had been killed, the larger or smaller one? "Mind, I don't say they are the James brothers," he added. Then he asked if they had said anything about himself and his brothers. No, the reporter replied. Cole nodded. "Good boys to the last."[18]

"They . . . tell many affecting incidents in their cases," John E. Risedorph noted cynically in his diary. "When they speak of their sister they break into tears." But after a few days of their weepy storytelling for the crowds that visited the jail, even Risedorph, a Union veteran and die-hard Republican, began to feel some sympathy. "One has to pity the bandits," he wrote three days later, "when we look back and imagine only a few short years ago they were promising children growing up under the care of a loving mother and intelligent, cultured father."[19]

One visitor refused to soften. He understood what sort of men the outlaws were, having dealt with their kind in Mississippi. When Adelbert Ames stood outside the bars of the Rice County jail, he pointedly interrogated Cole about his role in the robbery. You're the man who shot the Swede, he said. You were the best horseman in the group. "One rider is as good as another," Younger replied warily. What about the killing of Heywood? Ames asked; that was a cowardly act. The bandit waved him off, saying piously that they never had intended to kill anyone. Ames scoffed. You certainly tried to kill Manning, he said (as he well knew, having stood behind Manning during the fight). Younger grew angry. It is "no use to talk to illiterate people," he fumed. "They could not appreciate a sublime life!"[20]

The three Youngers were soon sentenced to spend the rest of their sublime lives in prison. On December 11, they pleaded guilty to robbery and being accessories to murder, thereby evading the hangman's noose, and were admitted to the Minnesota penitentiary at Stillwater. Meanwhile, long before that day in court, the authorities confirmed the identities of the three dead bandits with the help of St. Louis police chief James McDonough, who took the train to Minnesota on September 22, carrying Hobbs Kerry's detailed description. And in Northfield, the townspeople heard from Bill Chadwell's father, Elias Stiles, who was living in Grand Forks, Dakota Territory. "I thought he was in Texas," he said of his dead son. "I suppose he got in with a lot of them damned pirates."[21]

Only two of those "damned pirates" remained free. But where had they gone?

JAMES MCDONOUGH was an obstinate man. In January 1873, for example, he had made dozens of important enemies—including Stilson Hutchins, the state legislator and founder of the *St. Louis Dispatch*—by accusing commissioner Julius Hunicke of corruption. But McDonough had remained undeterred: once he reached a conclusion, he rarely gave way.[22]

It was a trait that would haunt him in the summer of 1876, as he assumed responsibility for the hunt after Frank and Jesse James. On August 18, after the capture of Kerry, Governor Hardin ordered McDonough to organize another special force under the terms of the outlawry act signed by Governor Woodson. Funding for the elite unit began to flow on August 24. Within five days, the police chief had dispatched a squad of nine men to the state's western border.

By that time, the outlaws were already well on their way to their epic battle in Minnesota, but McDonough convinced himself that they were hiding out with a mysterious Cal Carter near Dennison, Texas. Even after the Northfield robbery made the headlines, he refused to believe that the famous bandits had carried it out. All throughout the James brothers' desperate ride for home, he had his men—led by Morgan Boland, who had arrested Kerry—prowling through Texas and the Indian Territory. Not until he saw the bandits who had died in Minnesota did his men rush into Clay County and take up positions along the railroads in northwestern Missouri. By then the James brothers had already found refuge.[23]

Despite this grave mistake, McDonough kept Boland and his men in the field, searching for signs of the wounded fugitives. At the end of September, they heard reports that Frank and Jesse had not gone directly to their mother's farm, but had circled through the Indian Territory into southern Missouri, and then to the homes of sympathizers in Jackson County. About the same time, Annie Ralston James appeared on her father's farm, suggesting that the brothers had indeed returned to their old haunts. On October 13, Boland led a raid on the home of a Dr. Noland, near Independence. He hauled away a man with a suspicious wound to the knee, whom he believed to be Frank James.

McDonough soon learned that it was yet another error. "I must frankly admit that my faith in associating him with the Northfield robbery remained unshaken until yesterday, when a competent surgeon pronounced the wound of long standing," he wrote to the governor on October 19. But this arrest of an innocent man "reflects no discredit on the State, or the Police Department," he said. "I may add that a few of our citizens here of the old Confederate element seem to differ with me, and are disposed to characterize the affair as an outrage, &c., &c., . . . and may prejudice the public to an injurious extent." The special anti-bandit police unit was soon disbanded, however, never to be resurrected again. It was the last of a succession of detectives and ad hoc squads funded under the outlawry act. Their only success had been the capture of Kerry, an outsider and raw recruit.[24]

"The old Confederate element," meanwhile, was indeed enraged, and not only in St. Louis. "Jackson county is angry, and well it might be," wrote the *Kansas City Times*. "The old folks are mad and the boys are brightening up their shooting irons for work; and when Jackson county boys settle down to business, they mean it. There is no foolishness about this thing this time as the Chicago and St. Louis policemen will find out the next time they venture to invade Jackson county and kidnap and carry away, without due process of law, peaceable and innocent citizens of this county."[25]

Across town, Robert Van Horn heaved a heavy editorial sigh in the Republican *Kansas City Journal of Commerce*. "Never have we felt so humiliated as we do to-day, to find the spirit of opposition to authority so rampant as it is," he wrote in response to the *Times*. Two days later, he once again bemoaned the Civil War allegiances that turned the James brothers into heroes. "Now, there is not a man of average intelligence in this county who does not know that these outlaws have been harbored and befriended, and are so to-day, by men who harbored and befriended them during the war, and by nobody else, and for no other reason."[26]

Even as Van Horn typeset his words for publication, Zerelda Samuel lacerated him in the *Kansas City Times.* "Her idea of the devil is 'Old Van Horn,' " a reporter wrote after an impromptu interview. She turned every question into an attack on Van Horn. "The old villain is pursuing me and mine to the death," she said. "Go you and ask him. He appears to know more about Frank and Jesse than I do."[27]

A week later, she squelched her anger to give a cultivated performance in another interview with the *Times.* She was moving to Texas to escape her troubles, she announced. "I hope I shall at last find peace and rest in the new home I hope to find," she said, wiping away a few tears. "I am very old now, and not the woman I was thirteen years ago, when trouble came upon me and mine with the war. My husband was hung by the Federals, and Jesse, then only a boy of 15 years old, was whipped by the same gang until speechless because he could not tell where his brother Frank was." She wailed about her poverty and her burdens—including Charlotte, whom she called an "old darkey. . . . She will never leave us; she is too old to do for herself, and will not take her freedom." She also listed Perry, referring to him as "a little negro child adopted by me," and an old paralyzed black man "belonging to the family." And this in an attempt to win sympathy.[28]

How familiar it all seemed: the personal involvement of the governor; the bumbling raid by detectives; the outrage of Confederate Democrats and the tut-tutting of Republicans; Zerelda's calculated appeals for sympathy; and, of course, the invulnerability of the James brothers themselves. Probably no one realized how rapidly it would all disappear.

The political landscape was undergoing a drastic change, eroding the partisan conflicts that Jesse had addressed so directly. One element would remain the same, of course: the Republicans still lambasted the Democrats. "The popular sentiment of the ruling party in our State is in favor of the brigands," wrote the *St. Louis Globe-Democrat.* "We assert that the Youngers and the James boys have been upheld in their robberies and in their bloodshed by the low state of Democratic opinion in Missouri."[29] Within the Democratic Party, however, the chasm between the Confederate and Unionist factions began to narrow. Thanks in part to the battles over the outlaws, which had rallied and united the old rebels, the Confederates now wielded virtually equal power within the party. Though the Democrats nominated a string of Unionists for governor through the 1870s, they chose two die-hard rebels for the U.S. Senate: in 1875, Francis

Marion Cockrell, a brigadier general in the Southern army, followed four years later by George Graham Vest, who had represented Missouri in the Confederate congress.[30]

Jesse and his comrades had symbolized secessionist resentments, but when the dust settled after the election of 1876, there was nothing left to resent. The nation had repudiated Reconstruction, along with all the egalitarian ideals of the Radical Republicans. Missouri had tossed aside the constitution of 1865, and the leaders of the rebellion now held power as legislators on Capitol Hill and in Jefferson City. A new Confederate consciousness had emerged within Missouri, reshaping the memory of the war from a struggle between neighbors—the great majority of them Unionists—into an uprising by the people against rampaging Kansans bent on destroying the state. The change was sealed by the publication, in 1877, of John Edwards's *Noted Guerrillas,* a romantic history of Missouri's war.

In a very real sense, the Civil War had been refought in the years since Appomattox—and the Confederates had won. In the heat of victory, the politics of wartime allegiance evaporated, leaving gritty economic issues. The main problem for Democrats in Missouri would not be the Republicans, or even internal struggles, but the rising appeal of the Greenback Party. Senator Cockrell, for example, would jump onto the populist platform by championing bimetallism—the idea that the government should expand the money supply by minting silver as well as gold. (Silver had been essentially demonetized in 1873.) And state railroad commissioner John Sappington Marmaduke, a major general in the rebel army, gained widespread popularity by pushing for strict regulation of railway corporations.[31]

One factor, however, remained constant: the James brothers' invulnerability. It would be demonstrated yet again in the immediate aftermath of the disputed election, as Sheriff Groom carried on the hunt after the St. Louis police returned home. On November 22, 1876, Groom learned that the boys had returned to see their mother, who had come back after her monthlong visit to Texas. He quickly gathered four men and armed them with shotguns, then rode to the outskirts of the Samuel farm. There the posse dismounted and crept through the darkness on a cold, rainy evening. The sheriff waved his men into hiding places around the main building—knowing, perhaps, that the James brothers often slept in the woods, rather than risk spending a night in the house.[32]

As Groom and his men peered through the darkness, they heard someone tramping through the mud and dripping leaves. It was one of the James brothers. The sheriff shouted a command to halt. The outlaw immediately drew his revolver and fired in the air. Groom and a nearby colleague each squeezed off a shotgun blast, then ducked behind a tree for cover. A bullet splintered the trunk that protected the sheriff as the bandit returned fire.

Then the fugitive turned and sprinted through the brush to his brother and their waiting horses. "Come on, you cowardly sons of bitches," the brothers yelled, then they galloped off through the woods.[33]

Groom searched frantically for the outlaws in the days following the brief exchange of gunfire. He also telegraphed the sheriff of Ray County and asked him to post a guard on the Missouri River across from Sibley, where the old bushwhackers liked to cross. Nothing came of it. The James brothers had, once again, simply vanished.[34]

THAT WAS ALMOST three years before. To the man who passed himself off as J. D. Howard in Tennessee in 1879, it must have seemed like far longer. Almost everything he knew had come to an end. His cause had ebbed away, and all his old comrades had been killed or captured or had taken peaceful paths. Only he and Frank remained, and they, too, had set out in a new direction. In 1877, Jesse had moved his family to Humphreys County; in August, by Frank's account, he and Annie had settled nearby, eventually renting a farm on Hyde's Ferry Hill near White's Creek, close to Nashville. Their careers as bandits were over.

The brothers remained close. Dr. W. A. Hamilton, who treated Jesse on March 17, 1879, later noted that "both Howard and Woodson had a strong love for horses, had plenty of money, and seemed to be very liberal in spending it." Frank, for example, entered two of his horses in races at the state fair and elsewhere. "Howard and Woodson frequently appeared at the various faro banks in Nashville and always together," Hamilton added. "Woodson rarely ever had anything to say, while Howard spoke occasionally, and even then only when a question was asked. Howard at all times seemed to have control of Woodson."[35]

And yet, their lives had increasingly diverged as their crimes receded into the past. Perhaps it was due to Frank's age, or to his new son, Robert Franklin (who was born on February 6, 1878), or perhaps he had simply discovered the pleasures of a legitimate life. Whatever it was, it had sprouted and blossomed in Tennessee. "I worked regularly every day on the farm, seldom failing to put in my full ten hours per day in the field," Frank said later. "At the end of the year I engaged to team for one year on Jeff Hyde's place, for the Indiana Lumber Company, and I carried out my agreement to the letter, driving a four-mule team every day, taking my meals in the woods with the darkies, and never doing less than a full hand's work." His neighbors would agree. He had undergone a noticeable change soon after his arrival, they observed. He had stopped cursing, had taken to the Methodist church, and often shared his love of Shakespeare with friends, including the clerk of the county court, Charles H. Eastman, who lived across the road. And he made a point of befriending Nashville police-men, including Detective Fletcher W. Horn.[36]

All had changed, changed utterly—and Frank was glad of it. For Jesse, on the other hand, a terrible boredom was born. In his restless card playing, track going, and grain speculating, he seemed unable to adapt to the exchange of steady labor for a steady income. He wanted more, faster, and for less. Nor was there any thrill in driving a mule team or wrestling with a plow. His early immersion in the business of killing had wrought perma-nent changes in his personality.[37] At age sixteen, he had gone almost directly from the schoolhouse to murdering his neighbors, and had risked his life in every year that followed, until shortly before his thirtieth birth-day. By contrast, Frank had already passed through adolescence when the war swept over him, and was far more capable of finding his footing again once the waters receded.

In early 1879, Jesse moved his family into Frank's house on Hyde's Ferry Hill, perhaps for the safety of his wife and child as he began to wan-der again. According to one highly questionable report, he visited Las Vegas, New Mexico, in July 1879, where he made friends with Henry Antrim, alias Billy Bonney, alias Billy the Kid. More likely he was at home when Zee gave birth to a baby girl, Mary, on July 17.[38] But he did not remain home for long.

In August or September of 1879, Jesse made his way to the Lafayette County home of Jo Shelby, his friend and patron. Using Shelby's farm as a base, he visited relatives and sympathizers, speaking to a number of young men who seemed well suited to his purposes. He knew them from years past or his recent travels. They included his cousin Wood Hite; Ed Miller—Clell's younger brother—who had been arrested at the Samuel farm the night of the Pinkerton raid; Bill Ryan, an Irish-born ruffian who lived in Jackson County; and Tucker Bassham, a Jackson boy whom Ryan had contacted in April. None was a former guerrilla.

Rounding out the squad was James Andrew Liddil, better known as "Dick," a Jackson County farmhand who had met Jesse in 1872 or '73, before serving almost four years in prison for horse theft. His recruitment was probably typical of the others. One day in September 1879 an old bush-whacker named Ben Morrow ran into Liddil and told him that Jesse James wanted to see him. "About 2 o'clock in the afternoon I went to Ben's, and I found Jesse in the yard getting some water out of a barrel," he recalled. "We had a little chat and went out to where his horse was tied in the woods. He said he was broke and wanted to make a raise, and he wanted me to help him. I agreed." Liddil went to a Kansas City pawnshop and purchased a pair of Smith & Wesson revolvers. Jesse continued to organize his squad, moving between the farms of such sympathizers and former guerrillas as

Jim Hulse and Thomas Eddington. It was widely reported that he visited the Kansas City fair as well.[39]

Shortly after six in the evening of October 8, 1879, Jesse and his five followers rode to a schoolhouse near Glendale, an isolated stop on the Chicago and Alton Railroad just east of Independence, Missouri. Jesse kept his newer recruits ignorant of the others' identities, calling his cousin Wood Hite "Bob" or "Father Grimes," the unschooled Bassham, "Arkansas," and Dick Liddil, "Underwood." Bassham had no weapons, so the others lent him a pistol and a shotgun. Jesse himself carried a pair of Colt's .45 caliber revolvers. They guided their horses through the heavily timbered countryside to Glendale itself. The hamlet was virtually identical to the scene of so many of Jesse's previous train raids: a house or two, a single store/post office—run by Joe Matts, "an old settler," according to the *Kansas City Journal*—and a two-story depot, where telegraph operator John McIntyre lived with his mother. All except Jesse and Hite pulled on masks. Then they split into two groups, Bassham, Ryan, and Liddil going to the store, Jesse, Miller, and Hite taking the depot.

The operation began smoothly. The first squad quickly rounded up Matts and a dozen or so Glendale residents, then marched them over to the depot, where they were told to "sit down, act clever, and keep still." As Matts shuffled to a seat, he recognized the leader of the bandits as a tall fellow with light whiskers who had stopped several times at his store over the previous week. Jesse, meanwhile, briskly carried out his self-assigned task. First he hauled McIntyre and his mother, along with F. B. Bridges, the railroad's traveling auditor, down from their dinner table on the second floor. Then he, Miller, and Hite went through their pockets. As the other bandits arrived with their prisoners, Jesse demanded that McIntyre put out a red light to stop the train. I don't have a red light, the man responded. "At this," Bridges reported, "he attempted to telegraph a word of warning, but was pulled back, and several of the gang who were then in the office began tearing the telegraph instruments from the table." The ignorant Bassham, thinking it was a sewing machine, tried to stop Jesse from wrecking it, much to Liddil's disgust.

Now furious, Jesse told McIntyre to put out a green light instead—a signal to halt for passengers or new orders. "But the train will stop if I do that," McIntyre protested. Jesse cocked one of his revolvers and shoved the barrel into McIntyre's mouth. "That is just what we want," he said, "and the sooner you obey my orders the better. I will give you a minute to lower the light." McIntyre quickly provided the sought-after lantern. While this was going on, one of the bandits cheerfully told Bridges "that the robbers knew there was $380,000 in bullion on the train; that they had watched it all the way from Denver and were going to have it." A large shipment of gold and silver was indeed coming from Leadville, Colorado. Unlike the previous time Jesse had stopped a train full of bullion—on the Rock Island, in Iowa—this one would be passing through his home territory; the heavy precious metal could easily be hidden nearby for later retrieval.

Having secured the depot and all the residents of the village, the robbery proceeded with little incident. At eight o'clock, the eastbound train duly slowed to a halt at the station. Liddil covered the engineer and fireman as Jesse and Miller went to the express car. Inside, United States Express messenger William R. Grimes locked the doors, stuffed the contents of the safe into his satchel, and tried to escape out the back. Miller seized a coal hammer and smashed open the forward door. Jesse rushed in and swung the butt of his revolver down on Grimes's head. He seized the money, but found no bullion; after coming off the Kansas Pacific at Kansas City, the shipment had rolled onto another line. Their work done, the bandits mounted and galloped away, howling as they went.[40]

In every detail, the Glendale raid echoed Jesse's previous train robberies, right down to the fruitless pursuit by Jackson County marshal James Liggett, as the bandits dispersed through the rugged "Six-Mile country," where Confederate guerrillas had once roamed. The Chicago and Alton and the U.S. Express offered the usual rewards, even though, as always, the railway itself had suffered no losses. These rewards came to $1,000 per man from the railroad, up to a total of $15,000, and $250 per man from the express company, or $25,000 for the entire gang. And Jesse clearly intended to grab the headlines, just as he had back at the peak of his career. Before he mounted his horse and rode off into the night, he handed the telegraph operator a press release he had composed for the *Kansas City Journal*.

But times had changed, making this strike a whisper compared with the great chorus of raids silenced some three years earlier. The loot, for example: Grimes told Jesse and Ed Miller that the safe contained tens of thousands of dollars, bringing them a fleeting moment of joy. They soon discovered that only $6,000 of it was in cash; the rest was in checks and financial instruments that were worthless to them.[41] What foiled them was the growing integration of the nation's financial structure. The spread of checking to country banks and the emergence of the express companies as financial intermediaries were gradually making the economy less dependent on cross-country shipments of cash, and less vulnerable to robberies.[42]

Even the land itself turned away from Missouri's increasingly archaic outlaw. Of the three counties where most of Jesse James's supporters lived, Jackson had always been perhaps the most important, home to the largest number of former Quantrill and Anderson bushwhackers. But the rapid expansion of Kansas City was turning this former stronghold of slave-labor agriculture into an urban and industrial center. In 1865, Kansas City had been home to 3,500 people; in 1870, it had grown to more than 32,000; and in 1880, the census takers would count 55,785 residents, making it the thirtieth largest city in the country. The metropolis voraciously consumed neighboring farmland, adding thirteen new subdivisions in 1879, to be followed by twenty-seven more in 1880.[43] In a very tangible, physical sense, there was less and less space for the outlaw to operate safely.

Most important, the *meaning* was gone. Jesse hungered for publicity as much as he ever had, but his purpose had disappeared. His press release, for example, offered none of the potent symbolism of his former pronouncements, back when he had worked hand in hand with John Edwards to advance the politics of the Lost Cause. "To the Kansas City Journal," he began, addressing the city's Republican newspaper. "We are the boys that are hard to handle and will make it hot for the party that ever tries to take us." He signed it, "James Brothers, Jim Connors, Underwood, Jackson, Flinn, Jack Bishop." On the other side he wrote the cryptic message, "Adams Express Co. has no charter, therefore cannot convict guilty men," with the signatures, "Cal Worner, Frank Jackson."[44] So much bravado, so much defiance—yet hollow, unfocused, and empty for all that.

Jesse was grasping at the past. It was a fact easily missed in the furor over the Glendale robbery, but he himself dropped hints of his sense of lost purpose and diminished stature. The week of the Kansas City fair, he had sought out John C. Moore, the cofounder, with John Edwards, of the *Kansas City Times* and now editor of the *Independence Democrat*. He had come back to Missouri "for the purpose of killing detective Pinkerton," Jesse told Moore, "who, he understood, was to be in attendance upon the Kansas City Exposition." Recalling the raid on his mother's farm, Jesse "swore to kill him before he (James) went under." He mentioned sadly that he had sent a note to John Edwards, now editor of the *Sedalia Democrat*, asking to meet him, but had heard nothing back. "Jesse," Moore wrote, "seemed to feel much aggrieved thereat."[45] Perhaps Edwards thought it was the safest course for both of them. But his silence was telling. All their battles had been fought and won. The great political partnership between the gunman and the journalist and power broker had come to an end.

There would be one more news story about Jesse in 1879, a tale that was part farce, part prophecy. In early November, the one-eyed former bushwhacker and bandit George Shepherd—the man arrested by D. T. Bligh in Chaplin, Kentucky, after the Russellville robbery in 1868—announced that he had killed Jesse James. Marshal Liggett soon confirmed the story, admitting that he had recruited Shepherd to infiltrate the gang. The claim, then, had credibility. Edwards caught the first train for Short Creek, site of the reputed slaying, and even Zerelda—having "broken visibly" in recent

years, according to the press—seemed worried. But she refused to answer
any "military questions," and declared that it "had better be a two-eyed
man" who would dare ride up to Jesse and shoot him.[46]

When the corpse failed to reveal itself to searchers at the designated
killing ground, the public began to question the story. The doubts were
best summarized by Robert Pinkerton. "No one should know more about
Jesse James than I do, for our men have chased him from one end of the
country to the other," he said. "His gang killed two of our detectives, who
tracked them down, and I consider Jesse James the worst man, without any
exception, in America. He is utterly devoid of fear, and has no more compunction about cold-blooded murder than he has about eating his breakfast. I don't believe that Shepherd would dare to shoot at him."[47]

The dead man was alive and well, of course, having returned to Tennessee. "Jesse was down at Nashville at the time," Frank recalled, "and my
wife read him a telegraphic account of it from the newspapers the morning
after it occurred. We laughed a good deal over it but never learned what it
all meant."[48] In fact, Shepherd's fraudulent claim marked a turning point.
The former guerrillas had always been loyal to each other. Only Hobbs
Kerry had ever turned on his comrades, but he had not belonged to the
bushwhacker fraternity. For Shepherd even to pretend to betray Jesse was
an omen.

CHAPTER NINETEEN

Assassins

J ESSE JAMES DID NOT behave as if he were afraid of death. Like an addict unable to restrain himself, he indulged as never before in the vices of his brigand life. He gambled so frequently and so recklessly that even the quiet Zee, who had stood so much over the years, began to complain. In the spring of 1880, he returned to Missouri to cavort with his followers and hangers-on, including Jim Cummins, an old guerrilla comrade. Ed Miller introduced him to two young brothers who lived in Ray County, Bob and Charley Ford, whom he quickly befriended (especially Charley, the older of the two). Thanks to this emerging circle of friendships, the center of Jesse's social life shifted to the home of the Fords' sister, a youthful widow named Martha Bolton, who lived in Ray just east of Richmond. She was an attractive woman, and Dick Liddil in particular became fond of her. Bolton's home soon emerged as the regular rendezvous for the outlaws and their associates. Jesse visited his mother, then took Liddil with him back to Tennessee.[1]

In Nashville, the outlaw and his disciple caroused while Frank continued to put in long days hauling logs with his mule team. Frank would soon claim that he had been thinking of abandoning crime "ever since [Joseph] McClurg was governor"—that is, since the murder of John W. Sheets. Perhaps. But he was certainly devoting himself to a legitimate existence now. These years "of quiet, upright life," Frank said, were "the happiest I have spent since my boyhood, notwithstanding the hard labor attending them. My old life grew more detestable the further I got away from it."[2]

Jesse, on the other hand, could not endure the world that Frank so cherished. For three years he had fitfully tried to live at peace. Then, at Glendale, he had turned back for good. Empty as it now was, it was still the only life he had ever known, and the only one he had ever wanted. In a sense, it truly was his fate.

Starting in August 1880, he plunged into a succession of robberies unprecedented in their rapidity. After just two weeks at home, he and Liddil went to George Hite's farm in Kentucky to collect Ryan for a new operation: Jesse planned to stop the tourist stagecoach at Mammoth Cave. A rainstorm induced him to put it off for a few days, however, and Liddil went to Tennessee. Perhaps ten days later, Jesse and Ryan returned to Nashville with a load of cash and valuables. On September 3, they explained, they had held up a coach full of passengers outside the cave. They laughed about the incident, describing how they had forced a black preacher to drink whiskey. Jesse sorted through the plunder and pulled out a fine diamond ring, which he had resized for Zee's finger. Then he took his small crew back out again, this time to rob a store belonging to John Dovey in the mining town of Mercer, Kentucky. On October 15, they raided the establishment—just missing a delivery of the miners' payroll that was to have been lodged in Dovey's safe.[3]

Jesse moved compulsively from crime to crime. After he and his men returned to the Hite farm from Dovey's store, Ryan departed for Nashville in a buggy with Clarence Hite, Wood's younger brother. But Jesse wanted to test his luck again. He took Liddil into the country to hold up a stagecoach. Along the way, they encountered two mounted men on a country lane, and Jesse decided to rob them. The intended victims, however, immediately drew their own revolvers, and both sides opened fire. A brief, indecisive skirmish ensued. The resistance discouraged the bandits, who gave up their plans and returned home.[4]

The robberies and plans for robberies continued, interspersed with revelry. In Nashville, Jesse and Liddil attended the horse races. Then they traveled to Atlanta in late October for more of the same. Jesse may have been running his own colt, which he owned in partnership with Jonas Taylor; the horse won nine of twenty-one races during this period, earning a handsome $5,350. But Jesse soon returned home and sold the animal to merchant Jim Greener, then boarded a train for Missouri in November. There he tried to organize another strike as he moved between the homes of his mother and such sympathizers as Martha Bolton, in Ray County, and Bob Hudspeth, in Jackson. After idling with the Ford brothers, Ryan, and Cummins, Jesse abandoned his plans. He took Ryan, Cummins, and Liddil on the return trip, riding stolen horses, and arrived in Nashville about December 1, 1880.

Amid this wandering and restless life, a forbidding aspect of Jesse's personality asserted itself: he became increasingly suspicious. Before departing for Missouri, he had shifted his family to a boardinghouse in Nashville. As soon as he returned, he moved again, renting a house in suburban Edgefield, where he had once lived. Over the next several weeks, as he made forays into the countryside to scout fresh targets, Jesse began to doubt Cummins's loyalty. Frank, who considered this would-be bandit "an apprehensive, nervous sort of chap," said that "his fidgetting and restlessness attracted Jesse's attention, and he became suspicious that Jim was nerving himself up to betray us." Convinced of his duplicity, Jesse decided to act first. "While living at Edgefield," Liddil recalled, "Jesse tried to get us to agree to have Cummins killed, but I would not agree to it." Soon afterward, in early 1881, Cummins disappeared. Convinced that he had gone to the authorities, the outlaws quickly relocated within the city.[5]

It turned out that Jesse was wrong, though he never admitted it to himself. Indeed, outright paranoia had begun to sink its roots into him. Sometime in 1880, he had focused his worries on Ed Miller. The two argued, "and they bravely agreed to settle it by fighting it out," wrote a journalist who interviewed George Hite, Jr. According to Clarence Hite, the duel took place in Jackson or Lafayette County, Missouri. "They were in a fuss about stopping to get some tobacco," he said, "and after riding some distance, Ed shot at Jesse and shot a hole through his hat and then Jesse turned and shot him off his horse."[6]

Having disposed of these distractions, Jesse resumed his relentless cascade of holdups. In early 1881, he set out with Ryan and another man, probably Wood Hite. He had discovered a particularly inviting target: a remote army engineering crew working on the Muscle Shoals canal in northern Alabama. At ten o'clock on March 11, 1881, Jesse led his two followers to Thomas H. Peden's saloon, just one hundred yards from the canal. The innkeeper's recollections were riddled with inaccuracies, but he did notice that one man had something wrong with a finger. This fellow was "very correct & intelligent in conversation, quick spoken, and to all appearances the leader of the crowd," Peden said. "He talked politics most of the time, remarking he was well acquainted with Secretaries Windom & Lincoln." (This was a reference to William Windom and Robert Todd Lincoln, the newly designated heads of the Treasury and War Departments, respectively.) Jesse seemed particularly interested in the incoming president, James A. Garfield. He also inquired in detail about whether "the negroes in slavery" had been harder to "manage" than they were now.[7]

Jesse seemed to have regained his old form, chatting about race and politics before a potentially lethal confrontation—just like the lunch at Northfield—and mischievously claiming to know Abraham Lincoln's son. Indeed, everything ran smoothly that day. Combining excellent intelligence with good luck, the three bandits caught Alexander G. Smith, the receiver of materials for the Bluewater division of the canal project, as he returned from the bank in the town of Florence with a month's payroll. They stole $5,240.18—some in gold and silver coin, some in greenbacks and national banknotes—but hesitated at a small sum in Smith's vest pocket. "The robber inquired if the money was government money or my own money," Smith recalled. "I told them it was mine, meaning that it would form a part of my salary. The robber told me, he did not want it, neither did they take my watch. They said, they only wanted government money."[8]

The outlaws ordered Smith to follow them as they rode north. Shortly before nightfall, Jesse halted the group as they emerged from the woods onto a road and asked directions from a farmer. The fellow he spoke to, E. N. Hartsfield, proved to be that rarest kind of man—an accurate witness. Hartsfield described Jesse as having "light complexion, sandy hair, full face, *keen* blue eyes and riding a fine bay horse." Jesse peppered Hartsfield with questions about the distance to Tennessee and other points, and asked if any "still houses" were nearby. The local man said No to the last question. Jesse smiled and rode off, heading toward a spot where an illicit distillery had recently stood. That night he let Smith go. The army engineers dispatched an agent named Daniel Comer to hunt the bandits down, but they escaped safely.[9]

Muscle Shoals was a perfect robbery—but its aftermath was a disaster. On March 25, 1881, Ryan, passing under the name of Thomas Hill, departed for the Hite farm in Kentucky. A few miles north of Nashville, he decided to stop for a drink at a store on the White's Creek turnpike. Before long he was drunk. Turning to W. L. Earthman, he roared in his distinctive Irish accent that "he was an outlaw against State, county and the Federal Government, and was now acting as a government detective." Unfortunately for Ryan, Earthman was *Justice* Earthman, of Davidson County. In short order Earthman had Ryan under arrest. On patting him down, he found two revolvers and some $1,400. Five days later, Smith walked into the Nashville jail to see the prisoner, and immediately recognized him as one of the three Muscle Shoals bandits.[10]

The day after Ryan's arrest was a Saturday. Liddil was at Jesse James's house that afternoon. Since Jesse thought it best to stay inside so soon after a robbery, Liddil went into Nashville for him to collect money from the sale of some of Jesse's furniture. "I got an evening paper," Liddil recalled, "and saw from the description [of the arrested man] that it was Ryan. I went over and told Jesse and Frank." For the increasingly edgy Jesse, the capture must have conjured up the ghost of Hobbs Kerry. Ryan, too, was a non-bushwhacker recruit who had been caught because of his reckless behavior. In this case, however, the danger stemmed not only from the imprisoned bandit, but from the man who made the arrest. The two James brothers knew W. L. Earthman personally, having met him at a racetrack in

1879. It would not take him long to connect Ryan to the man he knew as J. D. Howard.[11]

Both brothers decided to flee Nashville immediately. That same day they set out for the Hite farm with Liddil. Jesse sent Zee and the children on to Donny Pence's home, in Nelson County, Kentucky, and Frank hurried Annie and little Robert on to Kansas City by train. While they were resting at the Hite house, Clarence—a tall, stoop-shouldered young man—ran in with the news that three heavily armed men were riding up the road. Startled, they snatched up their rifles and shotguns and took defensive positions—Frank at the parlor window, Jesse at the front door, Liddil in the hallway behind him. They watched as the suspicious party approached the house, then slowly rode past without firing a shot.

After the tension lifted, Liddil, Frank, and Jesse joined Zee at Pence's home. She and the children went to Louisville with Clarence to catch the train back to Kearney. Just before she "took the cars," in the expression of the time, she reportedly raised some $70 by renting a horse and buggy, then selling both to a pair of unsuspecting gentlemen. A week later, Liddil and Jesse took the same route. The two men rode stolen horses all the way to the depot; indeed, Jesse was a chronic and indiscriminate horse thief.[12]

Frank lingered in Kentucky another week before reluctantly departing for Missouri. His life had been upended overnight, and it left him depressed. "Try as we might to break off from our Bohemian life, something would always occur to drive us back," he reflected sadly a year and a half after the escape from Nashville. "It was with a sense of despair that I drove away from our little home . . . and again became a wanderer."[13] He blamed the reckless Ryan for his troubles, but he must have seen that the real cause was closer at hand. No matter how hard he worked, no matter what choices he made, his fate was lashed tight to his younger brother's impulsive decisions. What he could not know was how soon that would end.

AS THE DRAMA of the James brothers played out in their secret strongholds, another story unfolded among their enemies—a story of will and a lack of will. In the wake of the Muscle Shoals robbery and Ryan's capture, U.S. deputy marshal W. S. Overton tracked the James brothers and Liddil on their flight from Tennessee. With two hired guns, James B. Murphy and A. J. Sullivan, Overton followed their trail into Kentucky, to the Hite house; it was Overton and his men who rode past while Frank and Jesse waited at the windows, weapons ready. But Overton was well out of his northern Alabama jurisdiction, so he applied to the local sheriff to make the actual arrest. The sheriff declined, according to Overton and Sullivan, "saying it would be unsafe for him, for the James boys' friends would kill him, that they had large connections in that county, that he knew that they had been making Hite's their headquarters for the last three or four years." Sullivan suggested that he be appointed a deputy, but the sheriff refused to have anything to do with the matter.*

Overton turned to the federal commissioner, a low-ranking judicial officer, in Russellville. "He refused to issue a warrant," Overton complained, "[explaining] that he would have to read the warrant to the parties, and then they would find out who issued it, and their friends would kill him." Thoroughly stymied, Overton went back to Major W. R. King of the army engineers; King promptly applied to Washington for troops to make the arrest. The matter landed on the desk of President Garfield himself, who referred it to the attorney general—who said that no soldiers would be forthcoming. He cited the Posse Comitatus Act of June 18, 1878 (actually a rider attached to an army appropriations bill). Passed at the insistence of resurgent, anti-Reconstruction Democrats, the act prohibited the use of the military in law enforcement, except in cases of insurrection. The law largely stripped the federal government of its police powers.[14]

As the officials in Kentucky and Washington, D.C., took refuge in legalities and outright fear, a more courageous set stepped forward in Missouri. In Clay County, former bushwhacker James Timberlake succeeded John Groom as sheriff. "The people of that section speak of him as a man utterly devoid of fear, strictly upright and conscientious," one reporter noted. Despite his former affiliation with the James brothers, Timberlake was determined to stop them; indeed, he offered proof that, though all their sympathizers were former rebels, not all former rebels were sympathizers.[15]

More evidence of this came in 1880 with William H. Wallace's campaign for the post of Jackson County prosecutor. The son of a slaveowning family, Wallace had been forced to flee under General Order No. 11 during the war, but he detested the James gang, and he loudly pledged to wipe it out. The Democratic Party saw this as an attack on Confederates in general and denied him the nomination, so Wallace ran as an independent. "I made my campaign alone on horseback throughout the country part of the county," he recalled, "speaking in storerooms or country churches or school houses, usually at night. I charged specifically and by name that Jesse James, Frank James, Ed Miller, Dick Liddil, William Ryan . . . were committing the train robberies, bank robberies, and murders throughout the State. . . . My foolhardiness—for such, indeed, it was—occasioned

---

*This reluctance on the part of law enforcement in Kentucky was not unique to the case of Jesse James; the state was notorious for its toleration of crime. See Robert M. Ireland, "Law and Disorder in Nineteenth-Century Kentucky," in *The South*, part 1, ed. Eric H. Monkkonen (Munich: K. G. Saur, 1992), 230–48.

astonishment, and intense excitement." Despite death threats and Democratic ridicule, Wallace won.[16]

And then there was the new governor, Thomas T. Crittenden, the man who would emerge as Jesse James's most prominent foe in the days to come. Like his three predecessors, he was a Unionist Democrat. As a lieutenant colonel in the Missouri State Militia, he had personally battled guerrillas during the war. But his nomination, in 1880, reflected in part the growing harmony within the statewide party; he had been the law partner of Francis M. Cockrell, the former Confederate general who now served as a U.S. senator. (Crittenden himself served two terms in the House in the 1870s.) Indeed, former rebels were now so powerful within the party that Republicans could plausibly attack the Democrats "for their abject servile submission to the dictates of the confederate wing of their party."[17]

In light of the coming conflict between Crittenden and the outlaws, the new governor would later be called "the candidate of the railroad companies and their political friends."[18] This is a mistake. He favored immigration and economic development, true, but in that he was identical to every other governor in the country. As the press observed, Crittenden was a liberal in the classical sense—a believer in laissez faire, intending to protect the railways from excessive regulation while denying them government aid. He would actually prove far less of an ally of corporate interests than the Democratic regimes of the post-Reconstruction South. The second most important battle he would wage as governor would be *against* the Hannibal and St. Joseph Railroad, which still owed interest on an antebellum loan from the state.[19]

His most important battle would be against Jesse James. On January 10, 1881, Crittenden devoted much of his inaugural address to a virtual declaration of war on the outlaws. "Missouri cannot be the home and abiding place of lawlessness of any character. No political affiliations shall ever be evoked as the means of concealment of any class of law-breakers," he announced. The most startling aspect of this speech was its stern recognition of the political nature of the bandits' support. "I confess there was a large element of my own party who had more sympathy with such outlaws than with my undertaking to suppress them," he later mused. "If not in full sympathy with them, giving the glad hand of welcome day and night, they acquiesced in their acts with suppressed joy, with eyes half closed on their crimes as those of a medieval saint upon the sins of the devotees."[20] And yet, the very fact that he confronted such sympathy so openly showed how it had weakened since the fall of Reconstruction.[21]

Even with forceful officials and a newly favorable political environment, the war against the outlaws required luck—and luck soon came. William Wallace had been in office barely three months when the Kansas

City police received a telegram from Nashville describing a desperado arrested on the outskirts of the city on March 25, 1881. Some thought it might be Ryan, known to be an associate of Jesse James. "I had known Ryan well at Independence before he became an outlaw," Wallace recalled, "and I went at once to police headquarters to see the description. I was sure it was Ryan." Wallace asked Crittenden to request extradition, which was promptly done. Then he went to the state penitentiary to see Tucker Bassham. The novice at crime had been captured in July 1880, charged with the Glendale robbery, and imprisoned after pleading guilty. Wallace convinced him to testify against Ryan in return for a pardon, which Crittenden happily agreed to provide.[22]

On the evening of July 15, 1881, the governor's burgeoning war on banditry seemed to be progressing smoothly. Wallace was deep in his preparations for the Ryan trial, and Jesse James had not struck in Missouri for almost two years. Before the clock ticked past midnight, however, the wires carried the news that a Rock Island train had been robbed that very night near the village of Winston.

Upon returning to Missouri in April, Jesse had boldly settled his family right in Kansas City. Then he had gathered his recruits for yet another train robbery. Frank had agreed to help—reluctantly, perhaps, after his years of peaceful labor—joining his cousins Wood and Clarence Hite, along with Dick Liddil. But Jesse had developed an infected tooth, abruptly terminating their plans. During his recovery, he had heard the news that the president had been shot. Jesse, now sporting a full beard, dyed black, had spent July 4 in a Kansas City newspaper office, fascinated by the fast-arriving bulletins on the attempted assassination. Only recently inaugurated, the mortally wounded Garfield would linger until September 19.[23]

On the night of July 14, the gang gathered again east of Winston. They tied up their horses too far from the railroad tracks, however, and missed the train they intended to rob. The next evening they decided to be more careful. After leaving their mounts in the woods, they walked west into town, then boarded the train. "Jesse was our captain," reported his young cousin, Clarence. The James brothers and Wood took seats in the smoking car; Clarence and Liddil stepped onto the front platform of the express car. The robbery began as Jesse rose from his seat and commenced firing a terrifying fusillade, killing the conductor, William Westfall, and a passenger named Frank McMillan. The bandits emptied the express safe, stopped the train near their horses, then mounted and rode into the Crooked River basin that the James brothers had haunted during the war. "Jesse and Frank said they knew the country," Clarence recalled. "We went down the river five or six miles and stopped on a bluff." The loot came to roughly $600— just $120 each.

"Jesse said he was sorry he had killed the conductor," Clarence said. Even witnesses believed that the homicide had been an accident. Most of Jesse's shots—fired for the sake of intimidation—went into the roof of the car; Westfall had just been straightening up after taking a ticket when the bullet struck him. But the press soon reported that Westfall had been in charge of the special train that had carried the Pinkertons on the famous raid on Zerelda's farm, and speculated that it had been a revenge killing. "We got the papers regularly," Hite noted. When Jesse learned that he had killed a man involved in the raid, "he said he was glad of it." Then, as always, the gang dispersed.[24]

James Timberlake immediately went to the scene, then returned to Clay County and assembled a posse. "Sheriff Timberlake believes that Jesse James is alive, and he entertains the belief that the full whiskered man who murdered Conductor Westfall was Jesse," reported the *Kansas City Times*. "His height answers to his, and the whiskers were an easy disguise." As an old guerrilla himself, Timberlake knew whom to suspect and whom to avoid as he led the chase through the backcountry. "Many farm houses were passed but no stop made, owing to the fact, as the sheriff afterwards told the newspaper men, that he 'would not trust the occupants,'" a journalist observed. Perhaps the most notable member of the posse was W. H. Wymore, the Liberty marshal. "He is inclined to think the James boys had a hand in the affair," the reporter continued, "and has by no means forgotten the wanton brutal murder of his brother on the streets of Liberty [in 1866]."[25]

As the search continued—aided by Jackson County officials, among others—politics once again bubbled to the surface. "If it shall turn out that the James boys or any of their old gang had a hand in it, then the Democratic party of this state is responsible," argued the *Kansas City Journal*, "for had it not been for sympathizing friends, all of whom are Democrats, the whole gang would long since have been caught." Such crimes did happen in other states, "but unfortunately for the good name of this commonwealth, the perpetrators were all Missouri Democrats."[26]

Halfway across the state, John Edwards disingenuously complained in the *Sedalia Democrat* about "the political twists and turnings given to each train robbery" by the Republicans. "Eliminate politics altogether from each transaction," he demanded. Unfortunately for Edwards, it was the Democrats who did just that. The *Kansas City Times* denounced the Winston raid as "the most atrocious of the many desperate robberies of this class that have disgraced our State of late years," and actually called for special legislation to fight banditry! Even Jesse James's supporters grumbled about him, albeit anonymously. "How can I help myself?" one complained to the press. When Jesse called, the farmer had to give him what he wanted or face dark consequences. "I simply say, 'Glad to see you Jesse. Come in and make yourself at home. How are the children and the old lady?' "

Observers could see the bandits' grassroots support was fading away. Four days after the robbery, the *Kansas City Evening Star* published a mocking account of an old "unreconstructed rebel" in Liberty. "This county possesses not a few of these people," it noted, "although it is gratifying to know that they are fast disappearing." Even in Kearney, people began to speak openly against the James brothers. "The writer overheard a conversation between Mrs. Samuels, the mother of Frank and Jesse James, and a prominent merchant of Kearney," wrote a reporter. "In substance, Mrs. Samuels indignantly inquired if he had been out after the boys. He replied that he had, and with all deference to her feelings, he said he had hoped to catch and hang them."[27]

And yet, none of this was sufficient to bring Jesse down. Earlier officials had fought valiantly against the bandits, as had angry neighbors. Indeed, between militia action and lynch mobs, the former bushwhackers had been nearly wiped out during Governor Fletcher's administration. Certainly the changes in society weakened the outlaws, made them less popular and more vulnerable, but the critical transformation was within their own ranks. They were not the same group they once were. None of the bandits Jesse had recruited since Northfield were former guerrillas. They lacked that intense bond of loyalty, forged out of ideology and wartime experience.

And that was where Governor Crittenden hoped to strike. "As money *was their object* in the first place in their lawless pursuit," he later explained, "I believed an offer of a large sum as a reward by the law officers of the state would eventually reach those who had become tired of the life, and more tired of being led on in blood and crime by a desperate leader." But he lacked the means to proclaim a large reward, thanks to the statutory three-hundred-dollar limit. In a sense, the governor was a victim of a problem of his party's own making. As elsewhere across the South, once the Democrats had taken control back from the Republicans, they had immediately set about dismantling the power of government. "The state, once Redeemed," notes historian Scott Reynolds Nelson, "was worth less than the Redeemers expected." With few resources available, Crittenden had to turn to the same forces he was currently confronting over their debts to the state: the railroads.[28]

On the evening of July 25, exactly ten days after the Winston robbery, the governor boarded a train for St. Louis. The next morning, he walked into the gentlemen's parlor of the Southern Hotel. The luxuriously appointed room hummed with the conversation of more than a dozen men, all called together at Crittenden's urgent request. They were vice presidents, superintendents, managers, and attorneys—representing all the major railroads in Missouri, including the Wabash, the Missouri Pacific, the Rock Island, the Chicago and Alton, and the Iron Mountain—along with S. H. Laflin, head of a gunpowder firm, and an agent from the United States Express Company. The doors were closed, and the meeting began.

To all appearances, the conference was a curious balance between public and private interests. On one hand, the issue of banditry simply did not much affect the railroads. Train robberies remained quite rare—only the Rock Island had been hit twice by the James gang—and it was the express companies, of course, that suffered the losses. It was much more of a political question for a governor who wished to attract immigrants and investment to Missouri. The railroads, however, had begun to worry that the state's poor reputation might be affecting their business over the long run. A representative of the Chicago and Alton mentioned that he had heard a man at a hotel in New York discussing reports of a Missouri train robbery, saying, "He'd be d———d if he'd pass through the state of Missouri. He'd go 500 miles around the state in case he had occasion to reach the other side of it." And the murder of conductor Westfall particularly sparked the railway executives' interest. "These companies have been thoroughly aroused by this cold-blooded butchery," a reporter wrote, "and they have made up their minds to protect their men, cost what it may."

At one point, the gunpowder magnate, Laflin, rose and delivered an emotional speech. "You are the governor," he declared, "and these robbers must be taken at all hazards, if we have to watch all day and night, and noon and Sundays; and to do this I will agree to furnish gratis all the powder that may be necessary." The railway officials loudly applauded his words; then they began to make demands. "Several of the railroad men insisted that a special clause be inserted in the proclamation offering a $10,000 reward for the arrest of each of the James boys, without considering whether they were connected with the Winston robbery or not," the press reported. "This was acceded to." On July 28, 1881, Governor Crittenden proclaimed a $10,000 reward for each of the James brothers—half on capture, half on conviction—along with $5,000 for each of the other Winston and Glendale bandits, funded by the railroads.[29]

WHEN THE NEWS of Crittenden's conference with the railroads and of his reward proclamation came, the thought of being hunted aroused Jesse's wrath, as always. "Jesse said . . . that if he only knew on what train Gov. Crittenden was he would take him off and hold him for a ransom," Clarence Hite recalled. "Thought he could get about $25,000."[30]

Ultimately, Jesse decided to rob another train as soon as possible. As had so often happened lately, however, the first attempt failed. The gang dispersed for a few weeks. Liddil and Charley Ford robbed a stagecoach near Excelsior Springs, then Liddil, Wood Hite, and both Charley and Bob Ford held up another stage in Ray County. In early September, Jesse once again gathered the crew to seize a train south of the Missouri River—on the Chicago and Alton line, east of Independence, in an excavation known as the Blue Cut. Wood and Clarence, Liddil, and Frank took part, along with Charley.

On the night of September 7, 1881, the bandits piled rocks between the tracks at a spot where the trains had to slow for a curve. With a red cloth wrapped around a lantern, they flagged down an eastbound locomotive, then quickly ran through the well-established motions—down to the routine pistol-whipping of the express messenger when the safe turned out to be nearly empty. For only the second time in all of Jesse's train raids, he decided to rob the passengers. The bandits slowly marched through the cars, Charley waving a revolver in the terrified passengers' faces as they shoveled their valuables into a meal sack held by Wood. Jesse, however, knew what to expect. He ordered a porter to point out where everyone had hidden their money. You've gotten it all, the railroad employee replied. "Jesse then went to the first seat," Clarence reported, "turned it up and got about $60 and a gold watch."

But the outlaw's demeanor was more lighthearted than cruel. "He then went to the brakeman and told him the same thing," Clarence continued. "The brakeman said: 'I gave you 50 cents—all I had.' Jesse then gave him $1 or $1.50, saying, 'This is the principal and interest on your money.' " When one woman fainted from fright, a passenger observed, "the leader seemed to be very solicitous about her. He went and wet a handkerchief and bathed her face, and then gave her back a dollar that they had taken from her."

Jesse actually seemed energized by the railroad conference and the governor's reward proclamation. Once again, he found himself in the place he liked best: alone in the spotlight, at center stage. Perhaps this was what he had missed most during his three years in exile—not so much plunder or thrills, but a grand enemy, whose very enmity inflated him into the mythic figure he imagined himself to be. "He kept talking all the while," one passenger reported. Speaking in "a decided Southern accent," Jesse declaimed at length to his literally captive audience. "If you are getting tired of holding up your hands so straight, why, slip them around behind your head and rest them. I suppose most of you put your hands up two or three times a day. . . . I suppose the detectives will all be here in a day or two. They will all come on free passes, but they won't find us here. They can't stop us from robbing trains; it's our business. We could do it just the same if the baggage car was full of soldiers." Another passenger quoted him saying, "We expect to keep this up all our lives; if they put soldiers on the train we will wreck everything and gather up the spoils, and if these [rail]roads offer more rewards we will cut the sleeper off and burn the damn cars next time." He quoted the Bible repeatedly, saying that it was as evil to lie as to steal. "If we are going to be wicked," he added, "we might as well make a good job of it." After going through the Pullman sleeper car, he turned and gave a deep bow. "Good-bye," he said. "This is the last time you will ever see Jesse James."

This remarkable performance had not yet ended. "When the thing was all over the robbers came back to the front of the train," the engineer reported. "The leader was a tall, rather good looking fellow, with dark, heavy beard . . . and wore a broad slouch hat. He came up, shook hands, and said his name was Jesse James." The outlaw's oration in the cars had left him feeling buoyant. He handed two dollars to the engineer, saying, "You're a good one; take this and spend it with the boys. You'd better quit running on the road. We're going to make it so hot for this damned Alton road they can't run." Then he disappeared over the bank.[31]

The Blue Cut raid would be the last train robbery ever carried out by Jesse James. Tellingly, it was also the *first* in which he publicly denounced the railroad corporations. Though his speech making reveals his taste for highly publicized battles with outsized enemies, it also demonstrates why his significance was declining. The struggles that had made him a hero at the zenith of his career had revolved around the politics of Civil War loyalties and Reconstruction, and they were long since over. Only now, at the very end of Jesse's outlaw life, did he condemn the railways—not as enemies of the small farmer or as economic oppressors, but as his personal foes. His words merely voiced his own spite against them for funding the governor's efforts. As he stormed and gestured up and down the aisles of the Chicago and Alton cars, he had never been more defiant, never more famous, and never more hollow.

THE NEXT SEVEN months belonged to his enemies, and to the making of enemies. Governor Crittenden immediately issued an outraged address. "We are again shocked by the intelligence of another express and train robbery," he fumed. "It is said—and I fear with truth—that these outlaws are secreted and protected by a class of citizens who reside in the Western counties of Missouri. . . . The people of the state must rise en masse and apprehend not only the criminals themselves, but every known ally. Those who furnish asylum to the robbers must be taught that the law recognizes but one treatment for crime—swift punishment." He boarded the first train to Kansas City, where he met with the division superintendent of the Chicago and Alton. He also spoke with Frank Tutt, the district coal oil inspector, ordering him to Lafayette County to lead a search party of twenty-five men. As the meeting broke up, reporters observed Tutt strapping on a revolver. "If I get the drop on them," he told the governor, "I shall bring them in dead or alive."[32]

Crittenden may have suspected that simple pursuit would never be enough. Jackson County teemed with posses in the hours after the robbery. One of them was led by Kansas City police commissioner Henry H. Craig, who—in a gesture that perfectly symbolized the futility of the endeavor—accidentally shot off his own toe. Then came heartening news: Some of the searchers had made arrests, rounding up a set of suspicious young men near the scene of the crime. The more experienced bandit hunters raised their eyebrows at the prisoners' utterly obscure names. But one of them, John Land, strangely made a confession, and all were charged in the holdup.[33]

Then the trial of Bill Ryan finally began. Prosecutor Wallace had devoted months to his preparations. "After fifteen years of unchecked robbery and bloodshed it was the test case between the law and the bandit," he recalled. "Many of my friends advised me to dismiss the case and let it go. They said it was not worth a man's life to conduct the prosecution, and in the end would only result in an acquittal." Wallace's words barely begin to convey the tension that surrounded the Jackson County courthouse in Independence as the case went forward in the last week of September 1881. There was still a great deal of support for the outlaws in nearby Cracker Neck, a rural district thick with former bushwhackers.

The governor came to observe, accompanied by eight marshals. "It is presumed that in the event of Ryan's conviction an attempt would be made to rescue him," the press reported. "The streets are lined with people from the neighborhood of Cracker's Neck [sic], and every motion of the marshal is watched. The prevailing thought is that the attempt will be made at the time of Ryan's departure for jail from the court house. Quite a number of Craig Rifles [a local militia unit] are present as also Captain Craig, police commissioner, and should a rescue be attempted much bloodshed will be the result." The terrified officials of the Chicago and Alton refused to testify. When Tucker Bassham took the stand, a mob stormed his house and set it on fire. But the jury took only five minutes on September 28 to find Ryan guilty.[34]

"It begins to look as if the day of reckoning with these villains had come at last," said the *St. Louis Republican*. "The conviction of Ryan at Independence, in spite of the threats of his confederates, shows that the law-and-order element in Jackson county is uppermost and means business." Few missed the significance of this event—the first time that a Missouri jury had convicted one of Jesse James's comrades. It followed close behind another telling moment, when a reunion of former Confederate soldiers in Moberly, Missouri, had voted to condemn the Blue Cut robbery. In a ringing resolution, the old rebels said that they "will be content with nothing less than the extermination of this class of enemies of society."[35]

Those enemies of society began to exterminate each other. Tensions within the gang were fed by Jesse himself, who had turned against Jim Cummins and murdered Ed Miller. Bassham's betrayal intensified his already intense suspicions. Charley Ford said that Jesse "watched every move we made. He thought we were true, but he watched everybody, even his own brother." Meanwhile, Liddil and Wood grew increasingly edgy around each other. Wood accused Liddil of stealing from the Blue Cut loot, but the real problem apparently grew out of their shared interest in Martha Bolton. After Ryan's conviction, Jesse sent word that he wanted everyone to meet at the Hite farm in order to rob a train in Kentucky. Only five days after Liddil arrived, his dispute with Wood flared. The two marched into the yard and pulled their pistols, firing with such wild inaccuracy that neither man was hurt. Liddil promptly departed for Missouri.[36]

Wood Hite, furious and frustrated, fumed for two or three weeks more. Then a black farm laborer named John Tabor made the mistake of calling him a horse thief within earshot. Hite shot Tabor dead. "About ten days afterwards [he] was arrested," his brother Clarence recalled, "made his escape, and left, saying we would never see him again."[37] His destination was the home of Martha Bolton.

And that was where Liddil had spent most of his time since returning to Missouri after the gunfight. (But not all of his time: he had a wife in Jackson County.)[38] On the morning of December 4, 1881, Liddil came down for breakfast in Bolton's home and found Wood. "Liddil refused to shake hands," Bolton observed, "and said he had no use for him." The two men began to argue. Liddil said that Hite had once claimed that he could prove his theft charges, and now he wanted that proof. Hite denied it. Liddil snapped back. Then they both drew their pistols.

They stood at either end of the small dining room, cocking and firing their revolvers as fast as their fingers could work. A bullet tore through Liddil's right thigh, but Hite was fatally wounded, perhaps by twenty-one-year-old Bob Ford, who had walked into the room after the fight erupted and opened fire.[39]

Ford and Liddil had just crossed a terrible line. Their victim was a blood relative of Jesse James, the most dangerous man they had ever met. The implications filled Liddil with dread. He could not forget the fate of Ed Miller, whose ties to Jesse had been far closer than his own. "On the night of Thursday, 29th of December," Liddil recalled, "Jesse and Charley Ford came down to Mrs. Bolton's, where I had been since being wounded, and tried to get me to go with them. I declined to go. I mistrusted that Jesse wanted to kill me, and so [they] left."[40]

Liddil was caught between the law and Jesse James. The law struck first. On or about the night of January 6, 1882, Sheriff Timberlake stormed Bolton's house with a posse. The wounded outlaw crept out a back door and hid in a nearby field, remaining there all the next day. Clearly he could evade neither side for long, so he decided to take his chances with the authorities, sending his mistress to Jefferson City to make a deal.

"There was a mysterious individual that came to me," Governor Crittenden later told the press. "She was dressed in black and heavily veiled, and desired to negotiate for the surrender of Dick Liddil. She was, I think, a widow named Bolton." She soon returned to her boyfriend's hiding place at her uncle's farm in Ray County and presented the governor's terms: Liddil was to surrender to Sheriff Timberlake; if he testified against the James brothers, he would not be prosecuted. He agreed. He arranged to meet Timberlake in a nearby pasture, and on January 24 he gave himself up.[41]

Liddil felt himself to be a victim of circumstances. Bob Ford, on the other hand, had been diligently manipulating the situation to his own advantage for some time. Ever since Crittenden issued the enormous reward proclamation in July, he later said, he had been trying to think of ways to bring down Jesse. Of course, the twenty-one-year-old had not yet joined the gang, but his older brother Charley had. "I talked with him a good deal about killing Jesse for the large reward," Bob said a few months later. "He agreed to assist me."[42]

To murder the famous outlaw was in itself a daunting mission, but Bob also faced an entire retinue of followers. So when Liddil and Hite suddenly began to blast away at each other in Bob's sister's dining room, he saw an opportunity to do away with two foes with a single shot—by killing one and turning the other against Jesse.

When Bolton whispered through her veil into Crittenden's ear, she spoke not only for her frightened lover, but also for her greedy brother, Bob. He had information to relay, she said, and a plot to carry out, provided the governor offered assurances. He replied with encouraging words, and agreed to meet the young man. On January 13, 1882, Crittenden came to Kansas City for the annual ball hosted by the Craig Rifles at the St. James Hotel. At some point during the evening, the governor retired from the festivities to a room where Ford waited. The agreement was made: a pardon and the reward money in return for Jesse James.

The first fruits of Liddil's surrender and Ford's pact with the governor came with a midnight raid on the Hite farm in Kentucky, led by Timberlake and Commissioner Craig, on February 11. Unlike previous searches in the state in late 1881, this one resulted in the capture of Clarence Hite. Having learned the lesson of Deputy Marshal Overton's problems the year before, the Missourians struck without the knowledge of local officials. Hite was quickly hustled back to Missouri. Faced with Liddil's detailed confession, he pleaded guilty to participation in the Winston robbery.[43]

Between Jesse's own vengeance, bad luck, personal enmities, and Ford's scheming, the entire gang had been wiped out, leaving only Charley Ford. (Frank had since departed for the East.) On March 22 or so, Bob heard from Jesse himself. He needed help, he said, and he invited the young man to move with Charley into his new house in St. Joseph. Bob readily agreed.[44] Jesse James had only two followers remaining, and both were plotting to killing him.

NOVEMBER 8, 1881, was moving day. Zee James never publicly complained about the family's frequent relocations, but they must have exhausted her; this would be the fourth move since they came to Missouri seven months earlier, passing under the name of Jackson. Now Jesse had decided it was best to load their possessions into a wagon and cart themselves from Kansas City to St. Joseph. There they unloaded their furniture and clothing at the corner of Lafayette and Twenty-first Streets, where Jesse rented a house under the name of Thomas Howard.[45]

Charley moved in with them, at Jesse's request. "He loved Charley," Frank declared. Jesse trusted the twenty-four-year-old recruit as much as he trusted anyone, and he took comfort in his companionship. He was increasingly lonely as his comrades disappeared. Frank was gone, Bill Ryan had been convicted, Clarence Hite was in Kentucky, and Wood had vanished. Sometime in November he scribbled a letter to Clarence. "It stated, in substance," his cousin said, "that he was getting lonesome and he wanted me to come out and live with him."[46]

On Christmas Eve, Jesse moved his family for the last time. "He said he had just the place he wanted—on a high hill," Charley Ford said. "He could see everybody and no one could see him, and he said he would not be afraid of a hundred men if he knew they were coming." The house was literally around the corner, on 1318 Lafayette Street. Five days later, after Jesse settled his wife and children into their new home, he took Ford to Ray County to get Liddil. He discovered to his alarm that this former stalwart had turned sullen and disagreeable; he may have noticed Liddil's leg wound as well. He made no connection between Liddil and Hite's disappearance, however, and he left Liddil in peace. But he continued to mull over his strange behavior. Shortly after returning home, he wrote another letter to his cousin. "He said . . . that I had better leave home," Clarence recalled. "Dick was in with the detectives and they would soon take me away." (Hite was soon captured. He would die a year later from tuberculosis.)[47]

Despite the grim omens and his own mounting suspicions, Jesse remained outwardly calm, even cheerful. He regularly stopped to buy cigars at a drugstore on Sixth Street in St. Joseph, where he would sit for half an hour or more and tell funny stories, winning the warm friendship of the owner. He reportedly applied for a job at the new train depot, claiming— with his characteristic sense of humor—to have extensive experience in the express and railroad business.

He also plunged ahead with his profession. "Jesse went to Nebraska . . . to find a place to live where he could go farming," Zee claimed. He did, in fact, open negotiations to purchase a farm there. But it appears to have been a ploy to learn more about the local banks, much like the feigned farm purchase before the Northfield robbery. In mid-March, he took Charley on a tour of eastern Kansas, moving from town to town in search of a ripe bank. "He wanted to know if I knew anybody who would help us," Charley recalled. It was exactly the opportunity Ford had been waiting for. "I told him I thought I could get my brother to help us if I could go down and see him." They went to Zerelda's farm to see Jesse's half-brother John, who had been shot after getting drunk at a party and was not expected to live. Then they rounded up Bob Ford, who moved in with them on March 23.[48]

"Jesse told me to be very particular about what I said to Bob, as he might not be true," Charley said. Charley promised that his brother could be trusted. "Well," Jesse replied, "it is better for us to know our own business. My wife don't know anything about my exploits, and I never want her to." He tried to keep both brothers in sight at all times, Charley claimed, and "watched every move we made."

For the Fords, the last week of March was a time of unrelenting stress. "My brother and I had made it up to kill him," Charley said. "I knew he was quicker than I, and I would not try it when he had his arms on. He was so watchful no man could get the drop on him." Bob agreed. "We waited a long time to catch Jesse without his revolvers," he noted, "knowing that unless he put them off we could not fetch him." The tension rose still higher when the story of Liddil's surrender broke on the last day of March. The betrayal infuriated Jesse, but the thought of defying his enemies filled him with pleasure. On April 2, he lay back on his bed and listened to Bob Ford read a press account of the gang's activities, culminating in the prediction that Jesse would soon be captured. Jesse laughed, Bob reported, "and remarked that he might have to go under eventually, but before he did he would shake up the country once or twice more."[49]

He had a specific exploit in mind: to rob the bank in Platte City (Platts-burg, by some accounts), while a dramatic murder trial diverted the town's attention. "We intended to start for Platte City Monday night [April 3] and rob the bank Tuesday morning," Charley said. "Jesse said on Monday morning . . . that it would be a fine scheme and would be published all over the United States as a daring robbery."[50]

After breakfast that morning, Jesse and Charley went out to the stable to feed and curry the horses. By the time they returned, Jesse had become uncomfortable in his customary finery. "It's an awfully hot day," he complained. He took off his coat and unbuttoned his vest and threw both on his bed. "I guess I'll take off my pistols," he mused aloud, "for fear somebody will see them if I walk in the yard." He unbuckled his belt and tossed aside his holstered revolvers.[51]

As Zee and the children busied themselves in the kitchen, Jesse glanced up at the pictures on the walls of the main room. He picked up a brush, pushed a chair forward, stepped up, and began fastidiously to sweep away the dust. Then he heard a sound more familiar to him than any other: the metallic clack of cocking pistols. He turned his head toward the noise just as an enormous roar erupted, accompanied by the brief sensation of his skull disintegrating just behind his ear.[52]

CHAPTER TWENTY

Apotheosis

EATH REDEEMED THE TRUTH. For twelve years, ever since Jesse James's name had come to public attention with the murder of Captain Sheets, his comings and goings had remained a matter of conjecture and deliberate misinformation; even his death had been reported falsely in late 1879. On April 3, 1882, however, there could be no mistake about the identity of the dead man on the floor of that small house in St. Joseph, or about the manner of his demise. The single bullet that killed him started a cascade of names and places and details in the days that followed, pouring into public view so much of what had been hidden.

Before the smell of burning gunpowder could dissipate over the corpse, the Ford brothers darted out of the house as Zee ran in from the kitchen. Charley paused long enough to tell her that the pistol had gone off by accident. "Yes," she replied in grief and fury, "I guess it went off on purpose." They ran to the telegraph office to wire the news to Sheriff Timberlake in Clay County, Police Commissioner Craig in Kansas City, and Governor Crittenden in Jefferson City. Then they went to the office of the town marshal, Enos Craig, only to learn that he had already gone to the scene of the crime. So they returned, identified themselves, and narrated their deed with cold-blooded candor. After Jesse had climbed on a chair to dust the pictures, Charley had winked at Bob. Silently they had drawn their revolvers. Bob, a bit quicker, fired the fatal shot. The distraught Zee confirmed her husband's identity for the startled marshal and fast-arriving reporters.

The Fords, Timberlake, Zee, and Zerelda all testified at a coroner's inquest immediately following the murder, relating details of the bandit's private life and criminal activities over the last few years. Zerelda in particular captivated the gathering. "Is that the body of your son?" the coroner asked her. "It is," she replied. Then she burst into tears, sobbing, "Would to God it was not." Despite the later claims of a large corps of pretenders, there was never any doubt about the identity of the corpse. (And it was confirmed more than a century later by a DNA test on the remains.) After Zerelda concluded her testimony, she moved to the door, where she spotted Liddil. "Traitor, traitor, traitor!" she raged. "God will send vengeance on you for this. You are the cause of all this—oh, you villain! I would rather be in the cooler as my poor boy is than in your place."[1]

Throughout April, the Missouri press seemed to carry little else but coverage of the killing. Relatives came forward with their stories; neighbors spoke up; old wartime comrades gave interviews. More details about Liddil's revelations appeared, and even Governor Crittenden responded to questions. With the names of all the recent gang members verified, charges were dropped against the young men arrested after the Blue Cut raid, now standing trial in Jackson County, and a man convicted in the Mammoth Cave robbery was pardoned by the governor of Kentucky. And the personality of Jesse James emerged more distinctly. Brother-in-law T. W. Mimms, for example, dismissed George Shepherd's claim that Frank was the real thinker and had written the famous missives to the newspapers. While Jesse had had his schooling cut short, Mimms said, "he read the newspapers constantly, and frequently wrote letters. He would dash off a letter without pausing once, and would never read it over." He added, "Jesse was of a roving disposition, restless and daring. He liked some reckless expedition, and was a wonderful horseman. He could ride 100 miles a day without any trouble."[2]

On April 6, two thousand people came to Kearney for the funeral of the famous outlaw, hoping to get a glimpse of his corpse. As the service progressed at the Baptist church, followed by a burial in the yard outside the house where Jesse had been born, Zerelda played to the crowd. "She is a woman of great dramatic power," the *Kansas City Times* observed. "The James family are nothing unless dramatic or tragic."[3]

"I have no excuses to make," declared Crittenden, "no apologies to render to any living man for the part I played in this bloody drama, nor has Craig nor has Timberlake. The life of one honest law-abiding man however humble is worth more to society and a state than a legion of Jesse Jameses." Many who had actually lived side by side with the outlaw and his family agreed; to them, it seemed as if a demon had been exorcised from the community. "I shall ask $500 more for my property," declared W. J. Courtney, the former Liberty marshal. "It is a great relief and a great blessing to Kearney to have Jesse James dead. I don't mind saying so much." In Liberty, a mass meeting gathered on May 1 to offer wholehearted approval of the governor's actions; it selected six men to draft a statement to that effect, including Samuel Hardwicke, long since returned from exile.[4]

Others were not so quick to reconcile the ends with the means. "It is revolting in the extreme," Rabbi Elias Eppstein of Kansas City wrote in his diary, "to contemplate upon the fact, that a mere boy lures himself into the friendship of a man to abide his time and opportunity to assassinate him for blood-money. . . . The death of J. J. is a happy event in the annals of Missouri—but the manner of his going is a stroke into the face of morality and civilization." The governor claimed that he had never sanctioned plans to kill the outlaw, but he promptly pardoned the Ford brothers when they were convicted of murder in St. Joseph. (Bob was later acquitted in Ray County of Wood Hite's murder.) Crittenden also prompted the railroad companies to turn in the reward money, which, according to press reports, he distributed to Timberlake, Craig, Liddil, and the Fords.[5]

In all the sputterings of disapproval in the press over Crittenden's methods, one voice of outrage sounded above them all. On April 13, John Edwards published a roaring obituary in the *Sedalia Democrat*, heralding his friend of many years and railing against his murder. "We called him outlaw, and he was; but fate made him so," he wrote. "When the war closed Jesse James had no home. Proscribed, hunted, shot, driven away from among his people, a price put upon his head—what else could the man do, with such a nature, except what he did do? . . . He refused to be banished from his birthright, and when he was hunted he turned savagely about and hunted his hunters. Would to God he were alive to-day to make a righteous butchery of a few more of them." Edwards lacerated the killing as "cowardly and unnecessary," saying "this so-called law is an outlaw." Nine days later he insulted the governor in the sternest way he knew, by comparing the assassination plot to the thinking behind Radical Reconstruction.[6]

Edwards, however, pursued a pragmatic course amid the bluster. He quickly began a fund to raise money for Jesse's widow and children. (The dead man had left surprisingly little cash behind, and all the stolen valuables that could be identified were soon returned to their rightful owners.) He also began secret negotiations with the governor for the safe return of Frank James. As early as May 29, 1882, word of the talks leaked to the press, but they dragged on through the summer months. "Be perfectly quiet," Edwards wrote to Frank on July 17. "There is nobody particularly anxious to find you, although the sooner we can settle this thing the better." Progress was slowed by the editor's drinking binges. "I have just returned home from the Indian Territory," he wrote on August 1, using his personal euphemism for an extended drunk. "I have been to the Governor myself, and things are working. Lie quiet and make no stir."[7]

On October 5, after a formal exchange of letters with the governor, Frank and Edwards arrived in Jefferson City for the surrender ceremony. Crittenden waited in his office in the capitol building with a party of journalists, representatives of the express companies, and state officials, including the treasurer, auditor, adjutant general, and a supreme court justice. "The hands of the clock on the south wall of the office were close upon the hour of 5," a reporter wrote, "when the expectant ears of those present heard the sound of footsteps entering the rotunda of the building. A moment later the well-known form of Maj. John N. Edwards appeared in the open doorway." Behind him came the erect figure of Frank James, whom Edwards formally presented. "This brief introduction," the writer continued, "brought face to face the Executive of Missouri and the noted outlaw, whose name has been a terror in this State and is familiar throughout our land, if not the whole world. It was a scene without precedent in the annals of the State, and to all present was intensely interesting and dramatic. To all appearances, Frank James was the coolest and least moved man in the room."

James deftly unbuckled his belt and held out his holstered revolvers. "Governor, I am Frank James," he said quietly. "I surrender my arms to you. I have removed the loads from them; they are not loaded. They have not been out of my possession since 1864. No other man has ever had them since then. I now give them to you personally. I deliver myself to you and the law." As Frank explained later that day, Crittenden's comments to the press in the wake of Jesse's death had impressed him. "I told my wife then that I believed that Governor Crittenden would deal fair and square with me," he remarked, "and would do what McClurg and Woodson had refused to do. I had a conviction then that Governor Crittenden would be fair and impartial if I surrendered."[8]

Frank's calm and cultivated appearance captivated the press and public alike, leading to some grumbling by Republicans. "There was a surrender at Jefferson City the other day," commented the *St. Louis Globe-Democrat*, "but whether it was Frank James to the State of Missouri or the State of Missouri to Frank James, is not entirely clear." Indeed, the nature of Jesse's death, Frank's admirable conduct, and the passage of time had made the surviving James brother positively respectable. After William Wallace and other prosecutors sorted through the various charges and decided to put him on trial for the Winston train robbery, Edwards managed to arrange a phalanx of defense attorneys that included some of the leading men in the state, including former congressman John F. Philips and former lieutenant governor Charles P. Johnson. (Johnson had ordered Detective Flourney Yancey to pursue the James brothers after the Lexington stage robbery in 1874.)[9]

The Republican press, long attuned to the place of the bandits in Democratic politics, saw Johnson's participation in Frank's defense as an electoral maneuver. "This being interpreted," opined the *Globe-Democrat*, "means that . . . he will stand forth as the candidate of the Edwards-James wing of the Democratic party for Governor of Missouri." In reality, Frank's trial would further the ongoing erosion of wartime enmities that had long divided the party. When the case went to trial in Gallatin on August 21, 1883, Crittenden actually testified for the defense (as did Jo Shelby, who appeared in court visibly drunk); his fairly friendly role in all these transactions earned him Edwards's lasting gratitude. He later suffered at the hands of his enemies within the Democratic ranks, but this stemmed from the issue of railroad regulation far more than for his part in the death of Jesse James. Edwards, too, was declining in political influence. At the time that Frank surrendered, Edwards started a new daily newspaper, only to have it fold within six months; he did not return to the editorial ranks for most of the next year.

After a dramatic sixteen-day trial, Frank was acquitted. The prosecution had been forced to rely primarily on the testimony of Dick Liddil, thanks to the death of Clarence Hite, and the defense had deftly created reasonable doubt. The verdict undercut the outstanding charges, including the murders of Westfall and Sheets. Then the state supreme court issued a ruling that called into question the right of Liddil, as a convicted felon, to testify. On February 11, 1884, Wallace dropped the prosecution of Frank in connection with the Blue Cut robbery. In April he stood federal trial for the Muscle Shoals raid; in this case, however, he was in fact innocent, and he easily won acquittal. In February 1885, he was to have been tried for the 1876 Missouri Pacific robbery, but the key witness died, and the prosecution dropped the case.

On March 18, 1885, Edwards sent Frank a triumphant letter. He had just been to see Crittenden's successor as governor, former Confederate general John S. Marmaduke. "Tell Frank James from me to go on a farm and go immediately to work," he quoted the governor as saying. "Tell him to keep out of the newspapers. Keep away from the fairs and fast horses, and to keep strictly out of sight for a year." Then he explained the promise that came with this stern request. "I am here to say to you *that under no circumstances in life will Gov. Marmaduke ever surrender you to the Minnesota authorities, even should they demand you, which I am equally well satisfied, will never be done.*"[10]

In the end, Jesse's death redeemed his brother's life. Both symbolically and, to a great extent, in reality, the two had existed as a mythic pair of opposites, their fates inextricably linked. Jesse had been impetuous, Frank quiet and studious; Jesse had fumed about politics and thrust himself into the headlines, while Frank had sought Shakespeare and solitude; Jesse had been unable to relinquish a life in crime, while Frank had grown weary of his refugee existence. Jesse's assassination severed the bond, and generated enough sympathy to free his older brother to live his life in peace.

As it was for Frank James, so it was for his beleaguered home state. "I think the days of lawlessness & train robbing in Missouri are about over," one man wrote to his brother in the East, almost a year after Jesse's death, "and if any peaceably disposed persons from the hillsides of New England desire to occupy the rich fertile prairies of that great state it will be perfectly safe for them to do so. And for my part I hope many may choose to do so, for . . . they will also be the means by which Missouri will be able to take first place in the great sisterhood of states."[11] So long an outcast in the Union, seen as a place of vicious guerrillas and untouchable bandits, Missouri finally emerged as a state that was simply, refreshingly normal.

IF THE DEATH of Jesse James unveiled the small truths—his identity, his crimes, the names of late associates—it shrouded the larger truths about his life and significance. In a sense, this was because he died too late. He had outlived the issues that had brought him to public attention, so that his personal fame now eclipsed the causes he represented. He seemed archaic and out of place, like a fossil of a strange sea creature found in the middle of the continent—the ocean that once sustained him unknown to observers, having long since disappeared. The farther from his birthplace, the less the real reasons for his notoriety were seen or understood.

For example, *The Nation*—a respectable voice of mainstream opinion, published in New York by cosmopolitan Republicans—thought Jesse James was merely an accomplished criminal whose career illustrated the "curiously medieval flavor" of life in the primitive West. "In fact, the James territory," *The Nation* added, "which includes the adjacent corners of four States, is a region which seems closely to resemble in its religious and moral condition a Frankish kingdom in Gaul in the sixth century. . . . He served as a guerrilla in the war, and when peace was concluded became a common bandit of the Greek or Italian type," the editors noted. "His operations, however, extended over an area, and conducted with a boldness, which make the most famous of the Greeks or Italians seem a petty knave." To *The Nation*, the outlaw's fame simply grew out of his success. "In fact, when we consider the extent of country over which his jurisdiction extended, the character of his crimes, the long period during which he enjoyed impunity, and the smallness of the force with which his blows were struck," they concluded, "we must admit him to be the greatest robber of either ancient or modern times."[12]

Some historians, too, have taken essentially the same view. In 1959,

British historian Eric Hobsbawm took up the question: When is a criminal more than a criminal? In response, he created a concept that has dominated the scholarly debate over Jesse James: the social bandit. He elaborated his ideas in *Bandits*, in which he placed Jesse in precisely the same context used by the editors of *The Nation* in 1882, that of European brigands. Social bandits, he writes, are "a special type of peasant protest and rebellion. . . . They are peasant outlaws whom the lord and state regard as criminals, but who remain within peasant society, and are considered by their people as heroes, as champions, avengers, fighters for justice, perhaps even leaders of liberation, and in any case as men to be admired, helped, and supported."

Hobsbawm specifically names Jesse James as an example of the noble robber, the basic category of social bandit. The noble robber's image defines his relationship with the peasantry, he argues, listing nine characteristic traits that seem to have been drawn, in part, from the James myth. The noble robber begins his career as a victim of injustice; he rights wrongs; he steals from the rich and gives to the poor; he kills only in self-defense or for just revenge; he remains in the community; he is helped and admired by the people; he dies by treason; he is "invisible and invulnerable"; and he is not an enemy of the ruler, but only of the local gentry.[13]

The social bandit thesis has come under fierce attack.[14] Like all big, provocative ideas, this one tends to break down when specific cases are examined in detail. In the American context, the most important critique comes from Western historian Richard White. "The shortcomings of a literal reading of Hobsbawm are obvious," he writes. "Jesse James could not be a peasant champion because there were no American peasants to champion." Nor can the social bandit concept be saved by claiming that Jesse was a defender of a traditional society of self-sufficient homesteaders. White notes, "Both the outlaws and their supporters came from modern, market-oriented groups and not from poor, traditional groups."[15]

And yet, White accepts the fact that Jesse was a popular figure, best described as a social bandit, and he struggles to explain it. Perhaps, White muses, Jesse can be explained "as an exotic appendage of the agrarian revolt of post–Civil War America." This happens to be Hobsbawm's position. "U.S. rural society did not share the city enthusiasm for railroads, partly because it wanted to keep out government and strangers, partly because it regarded railroad companies as exploiters," Hobsbawm argues. He calls banks the "quintessential public villains," saying that bank robbery "marks the adaptation of social banditry to capitalism." White counters by observing that Missouri farmers were highly organized by the 1870s in such bodies as the Grange and the People's Party, which specifically denounced banditry. Instead, he weakly posits that Jesse and others reflected "masculine virtue," attracting respect as "strong men who could protect and revenge themselves."[16]

Despite the great strengths of White's argument, this is not a satisfactory explanation. There are unspoken assumptions behind the social bandit concept that must be addressed. When Hobsbawm insists that social bandits are products of the peasantry, he is not simply being descriptive; he speaks from a theoretical model of how societies work, and what makes a peasant a peasant. To be specific, it is a Marxist model. In "The Eighteenth Brumaire of Louis Bonaparte," Karl Marx argues that self-sufficiency is the defining characteristic of the peasantry. "Their mode of production isolates them from one another, instead of bringing them into mutual intercourse. . . . Each individual peasant family . . . produces the major part of its consumption and thus acquires its means of life more through exchange with nature than in intercourse with society." Though the peasants are alike, their extremely limited economic relations mean that they have no sense of themselves as a class; they are merely piled up next to each other "as potatoes in a sack form a sackful of potatoes." This has grave political consequences. "They are consequently incapable of enforcing their class interests in their own name. . . . They cannot represent themselves, they must be represented."[17]

This thinking is the stuff that holds together Hobsbawm's concept of the social bandit. Marx stresses the primary importance of economic relations, and economic interests. From these, all politics springs. And since peasants have such limited economic lives, he argues, they must be primitive or backward politically. These two points are indispensible to any understanding of the social bandit, and whether the concept applies to Jesse James. "Bandits belong to the peasantry," Hobsbawm writes. "They cannot be understood except in the context of . . . peasant society."

If social bandits can only emerge from a self-sufficient agrarian society, then the primitive nature of the people necessarily limits the political sophistication of the outlaw. Hobsbawm makes this point again and again. He calls the archtypical noble robber—including Jesse James—"an extremely primitive form of social protest, perhaps the most primitive there is. He is an individual who refuses to bend his back, that is all." The Robin Hood type of outlaws "are very far from modern guerrillas . . . partly because they are organizationally and ideologically too archaic." He writes that "traditional primitive rebels are united by a common and inherited set of values and beliefs about society so strong as hardly to need, or to be capable of, formal articulation." This limited outlook prevents them from thinking politically; they—and their supporters—can only picture the injustices of the world, and their resistance to it, in extremely personal terms.[18]

White tries to junk the outward trappings of Hobsbawm's argument—his use of the word "peasantry"—but he retains the hidden assumptions behind it, depicting Jesse James and his colleagues as politically unsophisticated individuals. White says they suffered from a "stubborn refusal to envision the social problems enmeshing them in anything but personal terms," guaranteeing that their social impact would be small. Michael Fellman, a historian of Missouri's guerrilla conflict, makes much the same argument. He notes that the Confederate bushwhackers, including those who turned bandit, described their actions in terms of individual retribution against wrongs. "Almost no ex-guerrillas generalized politically beyond this personal [vision]," he writes. "These men were limited to the intellectual discourse to which they had access." On this point, White and Fellman virtually paraphrase Hobsbawm, who writes, "Bandits, except for their willingness or capacity to refuse individual submission, have no ideas other than those of the peasantry . . . of which they form a part."[19]

Having drained the outlaws of all powers of higher reasoning, all three historians attribute their importance to the eye of the beholder. "I would stress," writes Fellman, "that it was not the actual bandit but the *emblematic* nature of the guerrilla-outlaw figure that gave him such force in popular culture." Hobsbawm has made precisely the same point repeatedly in his work.[20]

There are important insights throughout these arguments, but the reality of rural Missouri was far different from the simple, apolitical society imagined by Hobsbawm (let alone Marx), and the real outlaw was far from an inarticulate symbol created by others. When the unspoken assumptions are cleared away, a truly substantial Jesse James emerges, strikingly more significant—and purposeful—than historians have imagined.

First the society: the Civil War created the most politically active population in perhaps all of American history, and nowhere more than in badly divided Missouri. Levels of participation reached remarkable heights; electoral activity permeated daily life, inflated by intense partisanship; virtually all newspapers aligned themselves with political parties—even factions within parties—and covered politics at length and in detail. Nor were these humble farmers incapable of expressing their class interests. Such groups as the Grange and the People's Party articulated clear and plausible responses to rural economic difficulties, and the Greenback Party, far from being a bunch of backward inflationists, advanced sophisticated solutions to a very real shortage of currency in the countryside, such as the interconvertible bond conceived by Alexander Campbell.[21]

It was in this highly political rural world that Jesse James won widespread sympathy. Significantly, popular support for him and his confederates was at its lowest when the connection between banditry and politics was weakest (1867 through 1869, and 1879 through 1882) and reached its height when the connection was strongest (in 1866 and 1870 through 1876, with a peak in 1874 and 1875).

But what exactly was the connection to politics? Here we have to wave away another Marxist assumption—that all politics is ultimately economics. Hobsbawm and David Thelen, for example, think that the outlaws were popular because they struck at businesses that oppressed the traditional farmer, forcing him to give up self-sufficiency. But, as argued earlier, this was not so. The bandits' families and their supporters farmed for profit; they belonged to an agricultural sector long integrated into national markets. One searches in vain through Missouri of the 1870s for defenders of traditional self-sufficiency. The Grangers opposed monopolies as barriers to market access; they did not complain about the intrusion of capitalism itself. Greenbackers and other populists did not attack banks; they attacked the structure of the national bank system, the maldistribution of national banknotes, the deflationary return to the gold standard. No one saw brigandage as a way to counter these problems. In 1872, for example, a letter to the *Liberty Tribune* groaned that it was actually "the good farmer" who was "the scape-goat of . . . bank robbers." It is significant that the bandits stopped raiding Missouri banks as they reached the zenith of their popularity, opting for railroads instead.[22]

But, significantly, Jesse James did not rob *railroads*. He robbed express companies, which oppressed no one; few farmers ever had contact with them, since they handled small, expensive, high-priority shipments, not freight. The railway corporations generally ignored the bandits, only acting in 1881 at the urging of Governor Crittenden, and after the rare murder of one of their employees. It was the express companies that funded the Pinkerton detectives, and it was the state governors who obsessed over the outlaws, whom they correctly saw as a political problem.

In the near-endless newspaper columns devoted to the famous outlaws, only a few lines related their public impact to economic questions. Neither their opponents nor their supporters condemned or praised them for attacking controversial businesses. This is not to say that their choice of targets played no role in their popularity, but it was much more complicated than the crowd cheering them on for striking a villain. By (usually) robbing impersonal institutions, they were not seen as victimizing the average man or woman. And there was the heroic aura they generated by going after outsized foes. Both factors could be heard in the comments of Mattie Hamlett to the outlaws when they held up the Lexington stage in 1874. "I'm astonished to see you have come down to such small work," she said. "I thought you never did anything except on a big scale." Their selection of targets thus created a strong favorable impression, but that does not mean

that this stemmed from public resentment of those they robbed. As Scott
Reynolds Nelson has shown, Ku Klux Klansmen in the Southeast made the
railways the focus of political fury that had little to do with anger at railroads as such; these business institutions became the *axis* of political violence, rather than the specific target.[23]

Of course, the public did grumble about the powerful railway corporations, and took some satisfaction at the embarrassment they suffered when
their trains were stopped with impunity. The *Kansas City Times* expressed
this in a backhanded way in arguing that Jesse James should give himself
up. "The bold highwayman who does not molest the poor or the ordinary
traveler, but levies tribute on banks and railroad corporations and express
monopolies," the editors wrote, "is not generally such an object of popular
detestation that he cannot secure a fair trial in our courts. It is the horse
thief, the ravisher, the stealthy murderer of the innocent and helpless that
fall victims to mob law."[24] So the bandits' choice of institutions as their primary targets was essential to maintaining their popularity—but it was not
the driving force, the engine that propelled them into political debate.

In this intense, sophisticated political environment, what made Jesse
James and his colleagues heroes was simply a matter of war. The debate
that raged over them revolved monotonously around their roles as Confederate heroes, as undefeated champions of the Lost Cause, as galvanizers
of rebel resentments. Wartime allegiance alone can account for their
importance. At the moment when they were most central to Missouri politics, when newspapers and politicians took public stands in favor of them,
they were the central issue in a struggle between the Union and Confederate wings of the Democratic Party, factions that were ideologically identical in every respect except the sides they took during the Civil War. Of
course, many Confederates frowned on Jesse James—he was a criminal,
after all—but virtually every one of his grassroots supporters was a former
rebel. As the hostile *Kansas City Journal of Commerce* noted, "There is not a
man of average intelligence in this county who does not know that these
outlaws have been harbored and befriended . . . by men who harbored
and befriended them during the war, and by nobody else, and for no other
reason." And all of the newspapers that sympathized with him were
secessionist-aligned—the *Lexington Caucasian,* for example, along with
John Edwards's publications—framing their favorable commentary strictly
in terms of Confederate political aspirations.[25]

Of course, the politics of the Lost Cause were far from simple. The sentiments that animated ex-Confederate Democrats included deep-seated
racism in the face of emancipation and civil rights laws; a fierce resentment
of the political restrictions imposed by the constitution of 1865; anger at
Congress's treatment of the South and Radical Reconstruction generally; a

longing for the conditions of the antebellum era; and a conservative vision of both government and private life. But the impact of the Civil War as a searing social and political event cannot be overstated. In Missouri, more than anywhere else, neighbor literally fought neighbor, invading homes, looting, burning, and murdering unarmed partisans of the other side. It would be remarkable indeed if wartime allegiance had not become a defining element in postwar politics. Could the average farmer or merchant honestly be expected to forget the fact that his neighbor stole his horses, killed his son or brother, or burned his house? With peace, the rebels saw their cause delegitimated and their service cited as a reason to bar them from politics. Small wonder that, however bad their cause might have been, they sought to overturn the Radical legacy, win power as a group within the Democratic Party, and find for themselves a place of glory.

Indeed, Confederates waged their struggle on a broad front, fighting to win respect in politics, to achieve social standing, and to realign Missouri's sense of itself as a Southern state in popular culture. This is part of the reason why Jesse James's main advocate, Edwards, framed his praise for the outlaw in such personal terms. He positioned Jesse within the Southern tradition of honor, of the right to defend both self and home with deadly force. "It was his country," he wrote in Jesse's obituary. "The graves of his kindred were there. He refused to be banished from his birthright, and when he was hunted he turned savagely about and hunted his hunters." This was not just a defense of Jesse—it was an argument in favor of the entire Confederate endeavor in Missouri, and an assertion that the state was an inheritor of Southern cultural traditions. It was the culmination of a long fight for the identity of a badly splintered border community, stretching beyond the war to the campaign of border ruffians against dissenters, back to the debate between slaveholders and abolitionists in Robert James's own church.[26]

All this turns scholarly assumptions about the bandits upside down. "At the center of popular support for the bandits," David Thelen argues, "was the belief that they sought to reunite the community and reassert tradition." In fact, the reverse was true: the outlaws were popular because they *divided* the community, asserting the pride and power of a group created by the Civil War itself. Jesse James was not seen to be standing against corporations so much as against fellow Missourians, those who had taken up arms for the Union and possessed a northward-looking vision. This remained true to the very end of his life. "Would to God he were alive to-day to make a righteous butchery of a few more of them," Edwards wrote in his obituary. On the streets of St. Joseph, Jesse's supporters expressed their feelings after his assassination by repeatedly shouting, "Hurrah for Jeff Davis!"[27]

Those cheers for the Confederate president, in far northwestern Missouri, remind us that Jesse James's career also played out in a national context. Too often his actions have been seen in light of frontier criminals, men such as Billy the Kid or Butch Cassidy. But Jesse James himself looked South, not West; he, his brother, and his bandit colleagues were proud products of the Confederate war effort. Moreover, this was the period of the greatest outbreak of political violence in all of American history. Confederate veterans returned home to find a social and political revolution breaking out. Like German and Italian veterans after World War I, they banded together to suppress it. Their efforts included assassination of officeholders and political leaders; raids on black homes to intimidate assertive African Americans; and, finally, outright insurrection. Organized mass violence played a primary role in overthrowing state governments from Louisiana to South Carolina, while Ku Klux Klan raids occurred in outlying states such as Texas, Kentucky, and Missouri itself. In Missouri, however, Unionism had such a broad base of support in the white population—and the black population was so small—that anti-Reconstruction violence was necessarily fractured, and waged on a far smaller scale than in the Deep South.[28]

"It is easy to forget," writes George C. Rable in his important study of this era, "that political violence was accompanied by ordinary crime."[29] This was true of the Missouri bushwhackers during and after the Civil War. In 1866, Archie Clement led the former Bill Anderson gang into a year-long confrontation with the state government by robbing a distinctly Radical bank in Liberty—in essence, the business headquarters of the Republican Party in Clay County. The struggle that ensued resembled low-intensity warfare at times; indeed, citizens across the political spectrum feared that a second civil war would erupt. It culminated in the bushwhackers' armed occupation of the town of Lexington on election day, followed by Clement's death at the hands of Bacon Montgomery's militia detachment. During this tumultuous year, no one saw the robberies carried out by Clement's men as simple crime. They placed them in the context of guerrilla warfare and political violence. They had no context of daylight bank robbery, as exists today. In this setting, bushwhacker violence could only be seen as political in nature.

"They continued the war after the war ended," observed the Democratic *Kansas City Times*, "such, at first, was their declared purpose, and, in a measure, so executed." The Republican *Kansas City Journal of Commerce* agreed. "Their exploits all partook of a semi-military character, and could only have resulted from experience." These contemporaries grasped the Reconstruction context in which the outlaws operated. Richard White asked the wrong question when he pondered whether the outlaws were "an

exotic appendage of the agrarian revolt of post–Civil War America."
Rather, Missouri's outlawry was an appendage of the Southern-separatist,
white-supremacist revolt of the former Confederacy. The *Journal of Commerce* expressed this crudely but effectively. "If some man from abroad was
to meet Jesse James and shoot him down in the road, he would not fare half
so well before a jury as the man who 'killed a nigger in self defense,' while
he was armed with a revolver and the 'nigger' with his bare hands, only," it
fumed. "There is not a dispassionate, honest man of forty years of age in
Jackson county, who has lived here ten years, who does not know it is but
the fact."[30]

After Clement's death, however, his followers degenerated into simple
robbers. Their confrontation with the state had failed; the Radicals had
emerged stronger than ever, and former Confederates found themselves
frozen out of politics. Only after Jesse James's emergence in 1870 as the
leading bushwhacker-bandit personality—occurring simultaneously with
his befriending of Edwards and the return of the rebels' right to vote—did
the outlaws once again become a political force. And this raises a critical
question: To what extent was Jesse James a conscious agent in the making
of his public image? Did he win fame by virtue of simply being there? Or
was he a self-aware actor on the political stage? Hobsbawm, White, and
Fellman say he was a creation of others, a dream given form by the frustrated hopes of the mob. But the outlaw himself tells us otherwise.

The extent to which Jesse James was operational leader of the bandits
may never be determined for certain. Though he was much more of an
extrovert than his brother and clearly held sway in later years, the gang
probably operated largely by consensus before it was decimated in 1876.
But there can be no question about Jesse's centrality to the bandits' political role. His was the name that appeared on the famous letters to the press;
he was the bandit specifically cited by newspaper editors and politicians; he
was the one singled out by Edwards for special coverage and special praise.

Jesse's relationship with Edwards has clouded the question of whether
he was his own man, at least as far as he was a public figure. After all, the
newspaperman was absolutely essential to the outlaw's prominence.
Edwards's florid storytelling and exaggerated praise created a mythic aura
that Jesse's exploits alone would not have sustained. Equally important
were his lengthy editorials that explicitly tied the bandit to politics, and
made them central symbols in the Confederate campaign to recapture Missouri both politically and culturally in the 1870s. Other editors followed his
lead. And Edwards operated as the gang's inside man in the Democratic
Party, lobbying legislators in Jefferson City and even, it was rumored,
writing the original amnesty bill in 1875.

The bond between Edwards and James, however, was a partnership, not puppetry.[31] Jesse James was a highly political man who was intensely aware of his effect on Missouri politics. This should not be surprising. Even if he were merely the typical product of his society, he would have had strong opinions about politics. He came, as well, from an intensely partisan family, as seen by his mother's oft-expressed opinions—she, who criticized a Democratic gubernatorial candidate for his Union war record, and attacked Republican newspaper editor Robert T. Van Horn by name. Jesse not only fought in the war, he belonged to a group that continued to confront the Radical government after it was over. He read the newspapers continually, as both gang members and relatives attested. And Jesse's famous letters returned again and again to politics, hammering away at Radicals, President Grant, and the North in general. Edwards undoubtedly polished some of them. But during their robberies, the bandits repeated the same phrases seen in those letters.

There is little doubt Jesse himself was responsible for his famous statements to the press. As his brother-in-law noted, he was a compulsive correspondent. His missives to newspapers with no connection to Edwards echoed the same political themes. When he wrote to the *Nashville Republican Banner* in 1875, for example, he attacked "the Radical papers in Missouri" for persecuting him and pleaded for sympathy from Democratic newspapers in the South, "the land we fought for for four years to save from northern tyranny." He even analyzed the legislature's vote on the amnesty resolution, noting that all the Confederates in the Missouri House had endorsed it. When he wrote to the *Kansas City Times* in 1876, in a letter that was clearly untouched by Edwards, he dwelt at length on state and national politics, arguing that a Democratic Congress would vindicate him.[32] Again and again, he looked beyond his personal circumstances to generalize politically. He was, after all, a bandit who tried to wager on Minnesota's presidential vote just prior to the Northfield robbery and bantered intelligently about Garfield's new cabinet before the Muscle Shoals holdup.

This was why Edwards formed an alliance with Jesse specifically. Edwards did not simply pick out one bandit to glorify—Jesse thrust himself forward. As he revealed in comments to Bob and Charley Ford just before they killed him, he temperamentally craved publicity, planning his robberies with at least one eye on their effect on the public. Even the hostile *Kansas City Journal of Commerce* noted that Jesse and his companions "were no common thieves or vulgar robbers, but had an ambition to make themselves famous."[33] Of course, he was also extraordinarily good at what he did, as were his brother and the Youngers. Though they were often unlucky in the amount of their plunder, they carried out complex operations with cold-blooded skill—even playing to the crowd as they did so. But if Jesse James had simply been a successful criminal, he would have remained a footnote to history; indeed, he would probably not have survived for long, since he would have had no grassroots support. He was, first and foremost, a distinctly political hero who actively pursued a role in public life.

It was also a role he played to great effect. The repercussions of banditry in Missouri can be seen in two ways: in economic terms, and in its effect on politics. Did property values and immigration in western Missouri drop because of the outlaws? It is impossible to say, since the outlaws began to receive widespread publicity just as an economic depression swept over the country. A substantial number of residents, however, firmly believed that banditry hurt the state economically. The Republican Party made this claim a virtual joist in its campaign platforms throughout the 1870s, and the Democratic ex-marshal of Liberty gleefully announced that his property was worth $500 more once Jesse was assassinated. Frank James himself publicly took satisfaction in later years that he and his brother had frightened Yankee Republicans away from Missouri. But there can be no question that the outlaws helped realign politics in Reconstruction Missouri. Between Edwards's opinion making, Jesse's letters, the dramatic effect of their supposedly victimless holdups, and the blundering Pinkerton raid of 1875, the bandits galvanized the pride and political assertiveness of former rebels. They helped create a Confederate consciousness in what had been a mainly Unionist state, as reflected in the growing clout of the rebel caucus of the Democratic Party, the rising number of former Confederate officeholders (eventually including both U.S. senators), the amnesty resolution of 1875, and the new constitution of the same year. More broadly, the social and political revolution of Radical Reconstruction was arrested in Missouri. Jesse was far from the sole cause of all this, but he played a highly visible part, as he well knew.[34]

Instead of an unreflective champion of apolitical small farmers, Jesse James was an intensely partisan and articulate hero of one specific segment of a politically sophisticated population. Certainly he took credit for some of the mythic qualities of the noble robber: a career supposedly born of injustice, an avowed determination to rob the rich rather than the poor, and invulnerability to the law (or private detectives). But in his political consciousness and close alliance with a propagandist and power broker, in his efforts to win media attention with his crimes and his denunciations of his enemies, he resembles a character well known to our times. In many respects, Jesse James was a forerunner of the modern terrorist.

Hobsbawm actually has a name for this kind of romantic political killer, who belongs to the modern world yet adopts the myth and methods of Robin Hood: the expropriator.[35] Here, perhaps, is where we should place Jesse James: a transitional figure, standing between the agrarian slaveholding past and the industrial, violent, media-savvy future, representing the worst aspects of both.

SO MUCH CAN be said for Jesse James; but what does Jesse James say about us? Numerous accounts have been written of the imagined outlaw, the folklore, fiction, and dramatizations that have sprung up about Jesse James.[36] But what does his actual career reveal about American history and society? If he is a window on our past, what do we see when we peer into him deeply?

The motto of the United States is "E pluribus unum": One out of many. But James's life illustrates how bitterly divided Americans have been in the course of their history. His story reveals the Civil War not as a clash between sections, a collision of armies and sovereign governments, but as a savage neighbor-against-neighbor struggle, waged between people of the same race, religion, ethnicity, and regional background. Here was the Civil War as truly a civil war, with lasting repercussions. Throughout Jesse's later career, we see the anger and enmities resulting from the conflict, both in high politics and in personal decisions to offer shelter to the outlaws or provide aid to the Pinkertons. Historians rightly look for deeper causes for surface events, but the James story shows how the legacy of the Civil War was a powerful force in and of itself for decades after it ended. The story challenges the great myth of American progress, the idea that we have made a steady march toward ever-greater freedom and equality, peacefully resolving our differences and quickly reconciling after Appomattox.[37] It demonstrates the intense bitterness of our past political disputes, and a startling willingness to resort to bloodshed that both led to the Civil War and was fed by it.

Paradoxically, however, this tale also reveals the integration of the nation's past. The life of Jesse James is, in many ways, an African-American story. His entire existence was tightly wrapped around the struggle for—or, rather, against—black freedom. Raised in large part by an African-American woman in a mostly black household, he had a father who battled abolitionists in the Baptist church, a mother who kept two black children in virtual slavery after the war, a guerrilla unit that casually murdered African Americans, and a bandit career that pitted him openly against Radical Republicans. Missouri's white population was too badly divided to make race alone the starkest aspect of Jesse's public image, yet it formed a patina that covered it all. At the beginning of his life, the secessionist movement in Missouri emerged from an especially intolerant faction that had mobilized to defend slavery in the 1850s; toward the end of his life, he selected as his target Adelbert Ames, one of the nation's leading spokesmen for racial equality.

His strange, tangential part in the struggle over race and freedom also illuminates the rise of violence in American life. His career emerged from the conjunction of two grim forces: a new, more lethal, more affordable firearms technology, and a complete disruption of political and social codes of conduct. Before the Civil War, most firearms were handmade by local gunsmiths. Rapid-firing handguns, designed to kill people, were relatively uncommon. There was so little demand for Samuel Colt's revolutionary revolver that his Patent Arms Manufacturing Company went bankrupt in 1843. The Civil War changed all that by putting firearms in the hands of millions of men, fostering mass production of revolvers, and launching a new marketing offensive by weapons makers. On May 5, 1865, with scattered skirmishes still flaring in Missouri, Secretary of War Edwin M. Stanton wired a striking message to the military commander there. "Gun manufacturers are applying for leave to sell guns and ammunition to the loyal people of Missouri," he wrote. "Is there any objections to opening the trade to the sale of fire-arms and ammunition, and under what restrictions, if any?" There were neither objections nor limitations, and weapons sales soon began. Before long, there set in the habit of mass revolver-carrying that startled observers in 1866.[38]

Citizens began to carry firearms, however, because the war had destroyed the social conventions and political institutions that had contained private disputes. Violence had always been present in American life, of course, especially in the Southern backcountry, but it had been limited both by society and technology; black-white disputes, for example, were largely channeled through the person of the slaveholder. The Civil War unleashed new means of killing along with new battle lines of race and politics, creating a pandemic of murder. This was obvious to everyone in the case of the Ku Klux Klan or armed squads of Redeemers; it was less obvious in the case of Jesse James, yet his blood-soaked career belonged to this same continuum. Historian Richard Maxwell Brown has found that even late-nineteenth-century gunfights in the far West regularly pitted partisans of the Union against those of the Confederacy, showing how widespread the impact of the Civil War was on American ways of violence.[39]

Jesse James remains, in many ways, a hidden figure whose life will always be half-known at best. We can only wonder how he was affected by the domineering presence of his mother, or the early death of his father, or his poor treatment at the hands of his first stepfather. By any measure, however, he was a complex individual. He was a loving husband, father, and son; he had a ready smile, an outgoing manner, and a mischievous sense of humor; and he was deeply imbued with the Baptist religion, leading him to voice regrets more than once about his chosen path. He was also a foul-mouthed killer who hated as fiercely as anyone on the planet. He was polit-ical, well read on current events, skillful in manipulating the press; he was also a compulsive thrill seeker who could not bear to abandon the criminal life. It is true that he was daring, brave, and capable of astonishing feats of endurance; but it is also true that most of his homicide victims after the Civil War were unarmed and helpless, as were many of the men he mur-dered as a teenage guerrilla. So why do so many still worship him as a hero?

Cultural critics and social commentators have often explored what later generations of Americans have chosen to see in Jesse James. The unan-swered question, however, is what they have chosen *not* to see. In the decade after the Civil War, more than half of the population rejected the causes represented by the Missouri outlaw. Slavery, Southern separatism, even racism had been discredited to some extent after the Union victory. But time erodes all virtues. Even before the final restoration of white supremacy in 1877, faith in Radical ideals had begun to fade in the North, sandpapered away by the economic depression and Democratic intransi-gence. "By the turn of the century," Eric Foner writes, "Reconstruction was widely viewed as little more than a regrettable detour on the road to reunion."

Early-twentieth-century historians, led by Columbia University's John W. Burgess and William A. Dunning, wrote openly racist accounts of the period. In a book on Mississippi, for example, a Dunning student named John W. Garner systematically attacked the career of Adelbert Ames. He was forced to admit that even Ames's "political opponents testify to his personal integrity," but he had a ready response. Ames, Garner wrote, suf-fered from "over-confidence in the mental and moral ability of the black race, so far as their ability to govern themselves was concerned. He did not know that a superior race will not submit to the government of an inferior one."[40] Slightly later, historians such as Howard Beale concentrated on the material interests that lurk behind politics; the focus on Missouri, for instance, shifted to such topics as the origins of the Populist Party. In this interpretive environment, Jesse James easily lost his status as a divisive fig-ure. In death, the public's memory of him was reshaped along with its memory of all of Reconstruction, emerging as a comforting tale of a proto-Progressive Robin Hood who—in one famous story—held up a banker to return a mortgage to a poor widow.[41]

It was a process helped along by the sheer banality of the lives and deaths of his family and friends in the decades after his assassination. Edwards died in 1889 in Jefferson City, widely heralded but past his prime.

Zee died in 1900, after struggling against poverty for eighteen years. Frank spent twenty years in relative obscurity, working as a horse-race starter, livestock trader, and doorman at a St. Louis burlesque house; then he began to make stage appearances. Cole Younger was paroled in 1901, then pardoned in 1903 and allowed to leave Minnesota. He and Frank then formed a traveling show, "The Great Cole Younger and Frank James Historical Wild West." Neither man starred in the actual productions, and the venture lasted less than a year. Zerelda died in 1911, after years of charging tourists to see the farm, and Frank moved in. He died there in 1915. Younger passed on at Lee's Summit a year later. The two old outlaws had outlasted almost everyone they had ever known. Bob Younger had died of tuberculosis in prison in 1889, and Jim killed himself in 1902. The Ford brothers had disappeared from view after touring in their own show, "How I Killed Jesse James." Charley Ford shot himself in 1884, and Bob was murdered in Colorado in 1892. Dick Liddil died of a heart attack in 1901. Jesse's children, Jesse Edwards James and Mary James Barr, appeared in the 1920 movie *Jesse James Under the Black Flag*. Jesse, Jr., became a lawyer in Los Angeles, while Mary settled across the road from the Samuel farm.[42]

All that remained was the apotheosis of Jesse James. In his time, he had been a polarizing symbol, a figure hated and loved but never viewed with indifference. To the extent that American society today is admirable—and less than admirable—it largely owes to the battles that defined his life. In death, however, he became bland and empty, drained of his true significance by a people who no longer wished to dwell on their divisions. Jesse James never apologized for what he was, and that alone should give us pause as we consider who we, as Americans, have been.

Acknowledgments

There is an old saying that you can never go home again. I'm not sure why it has such currency; in my experience, you can't avoid it. Home, in my case, is Northfield, Minnesota, where I attended Carleton College. The building that housed the First National Bank in 1876 is still there, as is the Ames mill. Every September, the town celebrates the annihilation of the James-Younger gang. I never gave it much thought when I was there; indeed, I had no particular interest in Jesse James at the time, or for many years afterward. But life so often moves in unexpected circles.

As with locations, so with my chosen discipline. I learned to love history at an early age because of its dramatic power, its abundant stories of great events and the individuals who shaped them. Later, in my professional studies, I learned to love its explanatory power. "History from the ground up" was the cry, fostered by a sense that the real past could be found at the grass roots. I departed academia, however; my absence may have spared me the pressures of the profession—the rush to find ever narrower and more specialized fields of study, so that one might make a mark. So when I returned to writing history, it was with the sensibility of a synthesizer: I still appreciated academic insights, but I also had that love of a good tale that first attracted me to the discipline, and I wanted to bring the two together. Jesse James gripped my imagination because he offered a remarkable way of combining story and study; his eventful life is a classic American drama, one that illuminates many of the central themes and conflicts of U.S. history.

I should address one aspect of this subject that is beyond the scope of the text, but inescapable nonetheless. Unlike almost any other figure in American history (except for a few presidents, generals, and entertainers), Jesse James has a fervent popular following. Collectors, researchers, and outright fans have devoted decades to the study and even veneration of this man. In some cases, such as the work of Robert J. Wybrow, Milton F. Perry, and Ted P. Yeatman, they have turned up invaluable facts and sources; this book would be incomplete without their efforts. I do not belong to this fraternity, however, and its members may have mixed emotions about the biography I have written. I hope that they welcome it. I think they will agree that Jesse James is worthy of far more attention by professional historians than he has hitherto received. For my part, I have tried to provide an honest assessment derived from a broad understanding of his times. Many will find their preconceptions challenged by my findings. So be it. But I have taken Jesse James very seriously; rather than debunking him, I have found him to be more significant than perhaps even his admirers realize.

Of all the people I want to thank for their help, support, and enthusiasm for this project, the first is Nadine Spence. Her clearheaded assessments, scrupulous reading and rereading, and sacrifices have meant more to me than I can ever say. I want to thank my agent, Jill Grinberg, who saw the potential of my approach and represented me so well. I owe much to my editor, Jonathan Segal; this is a far better book for his truly fine editing.

Like all historians, I owe an unpayable debt of gratitude to the volunteers and employees who staff the many archives and libraries where I conducted my research. I once heard an archivist say that it is the historian's job to find the diamond in the dung heap, and it is the archivist's job to catalog dung. Poorly paid, unrecognized, yet tirelessly professional, they deserve far better than the obscurity in which they work. I would like to thank the staffs of the Chicago Historical Society, the William R. Perkins Library at Duke University, the Missouri Historical Society, the Missouri State Archives, the National Archives in Washington, D.C., the Library of Congress, the Southern History Collection at the University of North Carolina, the Western History Department at the Denver Public Library, the Minnesota Historical Society, the New York Public Library, and the libraries of Columbia University. I want to single out Shirley Fansher, a volunteer researcher at the Clay County Archives; Tim Peterson and Beth Beckett of the Clay County Department of Parks and Recreation; David F. Moore and William T. Stoltz of the Western Historical Manuscripts Collection at the State Historical Society of Missouri; Christine Montgomery, also of the State Historical Society of Missouri; Timothy Rives of the National Archives, Kansas City; Lori Swingle of the Western History Department of the Denver Public Library; and Anneliese Detwiler of the Northfield Historical Society. I particularly appreciate the help offered by the staff of the Watkins Woolen Mill State Historical Site and Park; this facility is no archive, yet it houses a priceless, little-known collection of copies of letters written by the neighbors of the James and Samuel family. I warmly remember their forebearance as I worked in their midst. In addition, Brice Hammack and Nora Wertz aided my research for the maps. Philip and Kathleen Brady housed me during my research trips to Washington, despite the chaos of remodeling and the demands of a new baby. Will Goldstein put a roof over my head in St. Louis. And my sister Karen and her husband, Ted Patton, put me up in North Carolina. Thanks to all.

I also offer my gratitude to the scholars who reviewed the manuscript and otherwise supported my work. The fine Missouri historians William E. Parrish and Christopher Phillips detected errors, offered perceptive comments, and made helpful suggestions for further reading as I completed this book, as did Carl Weiner of Carleton College, an old mentor. I want to specially thank Robert Bonner, my old college adviser and the recently retired head of the American Studies program at Carleton College. He read the manuscript carefully and shared his insights; he also taught me more about the craft of history than anyone before or since. More important, he and his wife, Barbara, imparted lessons about dignity and humanity that I bear in mind every day. I would also like to thank Richard Maxwell Brown for his support from start to finish. Without his groundbreaking work on violence in American history, which takes seriously those figures better known through folklore and Westerns, this book would not exist. Few historians have had such an opportunity to shape the study of a neglected aspect of the past, and he has made the most of it. Yet he approached my project without any hint of a proprietary air. He read and reread these chapters with great generosity, offering suggestions and warm encouragement throughout. He, too, has been a model of decency as well as good scholarship, and it has been an honor to benefit from his help.

T.J.S.

Abbreviations Used in the Notes

CWH: *Civil War History*

Duke: William R. Perkins Library, Duke University, Durham, North Carolina

Fellman: Michael Fellman, *Inside War: The Guerrilla Conflict in Missouri During the American Civil War* (New York: Oxford University Press, 1989)

History III: William E. Parrish, *A History of Missouri*, vol. 3, *1860 to 1875* (Columbia: University of Missouri Press, 1973)

History of Clay: *History of Clay and Platte Counties, Missouri* (St. Louis: National Historic Company, 1885)

MHR: *Missouri Historical Review*

MHS: Missouri Historical Society, St. Louis, Missouri

Militia Report: *Report of the Committee of the House of Representatives of the Twenty-Second General Assembly of the State of Missouri, Appointed to Investigate the Conduct and Management of the Militia* (Jefferson City: W. M. Curry, 1864; reprinted 1999 by the State Historical Society of Missouri, Columbia)

MnHS: Minnesota Historical Society, St. Paul, Minnesota

MSA: Missouri State Archives, Jefferson City, Missouri

NA: National Archives, Washington, D.C.

O.R.:   *The War of the Rebellion: A Compilation of the Official Records of the Union and Confederate Armies* (Washington, D.C.: Government Printing Office, 1880–1901). Citations as follows: series (arabic): volume (roman), part (arabic): page number (arabic).

Pinkerton Papers: Papers of Pinkerton's National Detective Agency, Library of Congress, Washington, D.C.

Provost-1:   One-Name Citizen File, Union Provost Marshal Papers, Record Group 109, Microfilm Publication M–345, National Archives, Washington, D.C.

Provost-2:   Two or More Name Citizen File, Union Provost Marshal Papers, Record Group 109, Microfilm Publication M–416, National Archives, Washington, D.C.

Settle: William A. Settle, Jr., *Jesse James Was His Name, or, Fact and Fiction Concerning the Careers of the Notorious James Brothers of Missouri* (Lincoln: University of Nebraska Press, 1977)

Shoemaker: Floyd C. Shoemaker and Grace Gilmore Avery, eds., *The Messages and Proclamations of the Governors of the State of Missouri* (Columbia: State Historical Society of Missouri, 1924)

UNC: Southern History Collection, University of North Carolina, Chapel Hill, North Carolina

Watkins Mill: Collated typescript Blythe, Culbertson, Frass, and William Jewell letter collections, Watkins Woolen Mill State Historic Site and Park, Lawson, Missouri

WHMC: Western Historical Manuscripts Collection, State Historical Society of Missouri, Columbia, Missouri

WHMC-KC: Western Historical Manuscripts Collection, State Historical Society of Missouri, Kansas City, Missouri

Yeatman: Ted P. Yeatman, *Frank and Jesse James: The Story Behind the Legend* (Nashville: Cumberland House, 2001)

Notes

Prologue

1. *Kansas City Times*, April 4, 1882; see also Stella F. James, *In the Shadow of Jesse James* (Thousand Oaks, Calif.: Dragon Books, 1990), 7.

2. Statistics compiled from Shoemaker, vols. 4–6. Newspaper reports indicate that some reward offers were issued that were not included in this work.

3. Popularizations of Jesse James's life started before his death, with James William Buel's *The Border Bandits*, and fictional dime novels published by Frank Tousey; see Michael Denning, *Mechanic Accents: Dime Novels and Working-Class Culture in America*, rev. ed. (London: Verso, 1998), 160–6. Later popular literature on the outlaws includes such classics as *The Rise and Fall of Jesse James*, by Robertus Love (Lincoln: University of Nebraska Press, 1990, orig. pub. 1925), and Homer Croy's *Jesse James Was My Neighbor* (Lincoln: University of Nebraska Press, 1997, orig. pub. 1949). Recent examples include descendant James R. Ross's *I, Jesse James* (Thousand Oaks, Calif.: Dragon Publishing, 1988) and Marley Brant, *Jesse James: The Man and the Myth* (New York: Berkley, 1998). One recent popular account stands out: Ted P. Yeatman's *Frank and Jesse James: The Story Behind the Legend* (Nashville: Cumberland House, 2001). A diligent researcher, Yeatman helpfully offers extended primary-source quotes and lengthy appendices. Though a valuable resource, it is more an extended research report than a scholarly historical work, in that it does not critically engage its (sometimes problematic) sources, contextual issues, or the historiography on the period. The first serious full-length biography of the James brothers was the groundbreaking *Jesse James Was His Name, or, Fact and Fiction Concerning the Careers of the Notorious James Brothers of Missouri*, by the late William A. Settle, Jr. (Lincoln: University of Nebraska Press, 1977, orig. pub. 1966).

4. Edwards's close connection to the guerrillas and the James gang in particular has long been known. For useful discussions of Edwards's polishing of the myth of the "noble guerrilla," see Fellman, 247–66, and Richard Slotkin, *Gunfighter Nation: The Myth of the Frontier in Twentieth-Century America* (New York: Atheneum, 1992), 129–36.

5. Christopher Phillips, *Missouri's Confederate: Claiborne Fox Jackson and the Creation of a Southern Identity in the Border West* (Columbia: University of Missouri Press, 2000), 285–92. The importance of Phillips's work exceeds the limited scope suggested by the title. It includes an excellent analysis of Missouri's postwar politics that neatly fits the argument made in this book, which was being written when *Missouri's Confederate* was published. On banditry as a historical problem, see Eric J. Hobsbawm, *Bandits*, rev. ed. (New York: Pantheon, 1981, orig. pub. 1969). Hobsbawm's concept of the "social bandit" is discussed in chapter 20, as are analyses by both Fellman and Richard White, "Outlaw Gangs of the Middle Border: American Social Bandits," *Western Historical Quarterly* 12, no. 4 (October 1981): 387–408.

6. Jesse James's purposeful role in creating his own public image is developed throughout this book; see especially the summary in chapter 20. It should be noted that this book was written before September 11, 2001. The interpretation presented here, including the use of the word "terrorist," was not influenced by the events of that day, nor by subsequent developments.

PART ONE: ZION

CHAPTER ONE: The Preacher

1. Francis Parkman, *The Oregon Trail* (New York: Penguin, 1969), 37–45; see introduction by David Levin, 7–26, and editorial note, 29–30; see also Herman Melville's review in *The Literary World*, March 31, 1849.

2. R. Douglas Hurt, *Agriculture and Slavery in Missouri's Little Dixie* (Columbia: University of Missouri Press, 1992), 170–1.

3. E. Carter to My Ever Dear Mother and Sisters, November 25, 1847, Watkins Mill.

4. Perry McCandless, *A History of Missouri*, vol. 2, *1820–1860* (Columbia: University of Missouri Press, 1972), 137; Parkman, 37–8.

5. Mark Twain, *Life on the Mississippi* (New York: Penguin, 1984), 67, 81; McCandless, 139; William E. Lass, "The Fate of the Steamboats: A Case Study of the 1848 St. Louis Fleet," *MHR* 96, no. 1 (October 2001): 2–15.

6. McCandless, 138; Lass, 5; Elizabeth Carter to My Ever Dear Mother and Sisters, November 25, 1847, Watkins Mill. The Kanzas or Kansas nation is now known as the Kaw. Erratic punctuation and spelling were common in nineteenth-century letters; all have been standardized in this book, except where the original is pertinent (e.g., all letters by Jesse James).

7. Parkman, 39.

8. Alphonso Wetmore, *Gazetteer of the State of Missouri* (St. Louis: C. Keemle, 1837), 57; Joseph Trego quoted in Thomas Goodrich, *War to the Knife: Bleeding Kansas, 1854–1861* (Mechanicsburg, Pa.: Stackpole Books, 1998), 19 (a badly flawed work cited here merely for its quotations).

9. For a discussion of Indian removal and the permanent Indian frontier, see Robert M. Utley, *The Indian Frontier and the American West, 1846–1890* (Albuquerque: University of New Mexico Press, 1984), 37. McCandless writes that an annual average of $100,000 to $200,000 in silver flowed into the state via the Santa Fe trade, 130; Hurt, 73–4, 96, 104, 133.

10. Parkman, 97; Elizabeth Carter to My Ever Dear Mother and Sisters, November 25, 1847, Watkins Mill; James M. McPherson, *Battle Cry of Freedom: The Civil War Era* (New York: Oxford University Press, 1988), 31; Fellman, 1–7.

11. Ross A. Webb, "Kentucky: 'Pariah Among the Elect,' " in *Radicalism, Racism, and Party Realignment: The Border States During Reconstruction*, ed. Richard O. Curry (Baltimore: The Johns Hopkins University Press, 1969), 107; David Hackett Fischer, *Albion's Seed: Four British Folkways in America* (New York: Oxford University Press, 1989), 605, 767; see also Richard Maxwell Brown's important study of the Regulator movement in *Strain of Violence: Historical Studies of American Violence and Vigilantism* (New York: Oxford University Press, 1975).

12. Jane W. Gill to My Dear Mother & Sisters, March 29, 1846, and Jane W. Gill to Beloved Mother & Sisters, June 15, 1846, Watkins Mill; Joan M. Beamis and William E. Pullen, *Background of a Bandit: The Ancestry of Jesse James* (n.p.: 1970), 16–9; Louis W. Potts, "Waves of Revivalism in Clay County, 1840–1918," *MHR* 88, no. 3 (April 1994): 262–9.

13. For an example of hiring a wagon, see Elizabeth Carter to My Ever Dear Mother and Sisters, November 25, 1847, Watkins Mill; description of the farm—admittedly, decades later—in the *St. Louis Republican*, February 4, 1875. The farmhouse still exists, though it has been altered over the years, and is a county park in Kearney, Missouri. On roads, see Hurt, 155, 170–1.

14. Jane W. Gill to My Dear Mother & Sisters, March 29, 1846, Watkins Mill; Hurt, 97–100, 109. Robert James Probate Records, 1851–1854, Clay County Archives, Liberty, Missouri, show that he was a commercial hemp farmer.

15. Jane W. Gill to Beloved Mother & Sisters, June 15, 1846, Watkins Mill; Beamis and Pullen, 16–19.

16. See letters from Robert to Zerelda James cited in Settle, 8; Beamis and Pullen, 8, 16–9, 58–9. Newspaper accounts frequently said Zerelda was six feet tall; e.g., *Kansas City Times*, April 4, 1882.

17. Settle, 6–7; *Liberty Tribune*, April 14, 1882. Robert James and a friend posted a marriage bond with a penalty of fifty pounds of tobacco. The use of tobacco as money in regions that depended on the leaf economically dated back to the early seventeenth century, when the colony of Virginia made it legal tender; see Paul Einzig, *Primitive Money: In Its Ethnological, Historical, and Economic Aspects* (Oxford: Pergamon Press, 1949), 278–86; and Leslie V. Brock, *The Currency of the American Colonies 1700–1764: A Study in Colonial Finance and Imperial Relations* (New York: Arno Press, 1975), 2–37.

18. *Liberty Tribune*, April 14, 1882; Potts, 263–5.

19. *Liberty Tribune*, April 14, 1882; Potts, 263–5; Anne C. Loveland, *Southern Evangelicals and the Social Order, 1800–1860* (Baton Rouge: Louisiana State University Press, 1980), 27; Christine Leigh Heyrman, *Southern Cross: The Beginnings of the Bible Belt* (New York: Alfred A. Knopf, 1997), 103–13. Preachers were usually men, but not always; Catherine A. Brekus has uncovered a rich tradition of female preaching in *Strangers and Pilgrims: Female Preaching in America, 1740–1845* (Chapel Hill: University of North Carolina Press, 1998).

20. Loveland, 68–9, 82; Wayne Flint, *Alabama Baptists: Southern Baptists in the Heart of Dixie* (Tuscaloosa: University of Alabama Press, 1998), 80, 161; Ellen Eslinger, *Citizens of Zion: The Social Origins of Camp Meeting Revivalism* (Knoxville: University of Tennessee Press, 1999), xxi, 225–6; *Liberty Tribune*, April 14, 1882. Frances Lea McCurdy emphasizes the stress placed on individual liberty and agency in rural oratory in *Stump, Bar, and Pulpit: Speechmaking on the Missouri Frontier* (Columbia: University of Missouri Press, 1969).

21. Settle, 6–7; Potts, 264–5; Tabitha Gill to ?, May 17, 1846, Watkins Mill. Heyrman, 94–113, discusses the itinerant preaching tradition.

22. Hurt, x–xiii; Potts, 263–4; Heyrman, 113. The term "Little Dixie" originated shortly after the Civil War, but it offers a useful term for this region, defined by Hurt as those counties with at least a 24 percent slave population: Clay, Lafayette, Saline, Boone, Callaway, Howard, and Cooper Counties. See also Robert M. Crisler, "Missouri's 'Little Dixie,' " *MHR* 42, no. 2 (January 1948): 130–9.

23. Dorothy B. Dorsey, "The Panic and Depression of 1837 to 1843 in Missouri," *MHR* 30, no. 1 (October 1935): 132–61; McCandless, 229; Hurt, 58, 62; Harry S. Gleick, "Banking in Early Missouri," part 1, *MHR* 61, no. 4 (July 1967): 427–43, and "Banking in Early Missouri," part 2, *MHR* 62, no. 1 (October 1967): 30–44; Bray Hammond, *Banks and Politics in America from the Revolution to the Civil War* (Princeton: Princeton University Press, 1957), 460–86; Timothy W. Hubbard and Lewis E. Davids, *Banking in Mid-America: A History of Missouri's Banks* (Washington, D.C.: Public Affairs Press, 1969), 97.

24. McCandless, 229; Hurt, 58, 62, 109; Settle, 7; Marley Brant, *Jesse James: The Man and the Myth* (New York: Berkley, 1998), 8, 270; Hurt, 63; Robert James Probate Records; Yeatman, 26.

25. Dorsey, 160–1; for a description and first-person account of the Great Migration, see T. J. Stiles, ed., *Warriors and Pioneers* (New York: Berkley, 1996), 5–8, 21–7; Hurt, 82–97, 243; McCandless, 257; Miles W. Eaton, "The Development and Later Decline of the Hemp Industry in Missouri," *MHR* 43, no. 4 (July 1949): 344–59; Robert James Probate Records.

26. Hurt, 65, 225, 233–6; Harrison A. Trexler, "The Value and Sale of the Missouri Slave," *MHR* 8, no. 1 (January 1914): 69–85; *Seventh Census of the United States: Slave Schedules*, Clay County, Missouri, September 16, 1850 (to be cited as U.S. Census, 1850). Robert James Probate Records list six slaves in Robert James's possession in 1850; see also Settle, 7. Christopher Phillips, *Missouri's Confederate: Claiborne Fox Jackson and the Creation of a Southern Identity in the Border West* (Columbia: University of Missouri Press, 2000), argues forcefully and well that Missourians saw themselves as part of a distinct region, the border West, and that they refused to choose between North and South until after the outbreak of the Civil War (see 181–6, 240–1). This is an important argument, though it understates regional variations within the state, the strength of family ties to the South, and early challenges to this border identity.

27. Hurt, 99, 102, 108–9. The total number of slaves is often erroneously given as seven, following an error by Settle. A careful review of probate and census records shows that six was the correct number in 1850.

28. Potts, 265–6; Tabitha Gill to ?, May 17, 1846, Jane W. Gill to My Dear Mother & Sisters, March 29, 1846, and Jane W. Gill to Beloved Mother & Sisters, June 15, 1846, Watkins Mill. See William W. Freehling, *The Road to Disunion: Secessionists at Bay, 1776–1854* (New York: Oxford University Press, 1990), for a discussion of the tense ambivalence over slavery in the border South in the 1840s.

29. Loveland, 186–218; Heyrman, 92, 138; McCandless, 215; Tabitha Gill to ?, May 17, 1846, Jane W. Gill to My Dear Mother & Sisters, March 29, 1846, Watkins Mill. Controversies such as this one show that challenges to a border-state identity occurred earlier than allowed for by Phillips.

30. Jane W. Gill to Beloved Mother & Sisters, June 15, 1846, Watkins Mill; see Loveland, 187–8. For an influential perspective on the complex response of Southern churchmen to slavery, see Eugene D. Genovese's collection of lectures, *A Consuming Fire: The Fall of the Confederacy in the Mind of the White Christian South* (Athens: University of Georgia Press, 1998).

31. Freehling, 353–452; quote from Adams appears on 413.

32. Joseph G. Dawson, III, *Doniphan's Epic March: The 1st Missouri Volunteers in the Mexican War* (Lawrence: University Press of Kansas, 1999), 28–30; William E. Parrish, *David Rice Atchison of Missouri: Border Politician* (Columbia: University of Missouri Press, 1961), 38–64; Freehling, 353–456; McPherson, 47–9; McCandless, 232–45; Hurt, 270–6; Jane W. Gill to Beloved Mother & Sister, June 15, 1846, Watkins Mill.

33. Beamis and Pullen, 58–59.

34. Nadine Hodges and Mrs. Howard W. Woodruff, eds., *Genealogical Notes from the Liberty Tribune* (Liberty, Mo.: n.p., 1975), 15, 28–9; Beamis and Pullen, 58, put the wedding date at December 23, 1846; M. L. Lawson, "Founding and Location of William Jewell College," *Missouri Historical Society Collections* 4, no. 3 (1914): 275–89. Hurt, 196–7; New Hope Congregation pledge, April 19, 1851, written on the back of J. C. Minter to Dear Cousin, September 9, 1847, Watkins Mill; Settle, 7.

35. Yeatman, 26, claims Robert James owned 275 acres, but the careful inventory of the estate in the Robert James Probate Records indicates otherwise (though it is possible that James himself rented the eighty acres indicated); Settle, 6–7; Jane W. Gill to Beloved Mother & Sisters, June 15, 1846, Watkins Mill; *Seventh Census of the United States* (September 16, 1850). Settle, 7–8, discusses folklore that Robert might not have been the father of Jesse; as he notes, however, there is no evidence for this.

36. *Liberty Tribune*, October 25, 1850; Carter to Dear Mother and Sisters, August 7, 1849, Watkins Mill; Potts, 263–6; see also *History of Clay*, 504–5, and Loveland, 67–83. Zerelda claimed to her granddaughter-in-law that she had been present with Jesse; see Stella James, *In the Shadow of Jesse James* (Thousand Oaks, Calif.: Dragon Books, 1990), 38.

37. Kate L. Gregg, "Missourians in the Gold Rush," *MHR* 39, no. 1 (October 1944): 137–54; Hurt, 96–9, 127–8; Gregg, 150–3.

38. Jane W. Gill to My Dear Sisters, April 14, 1850, Watkins Mill; Settle, 7. See Hurt, 79.

39. *Kansas City Times*, April 14, 1882; *Kansas City Journal*, April 6, 1882.

40. *History of Clay*, 152–53; Robert James Probate Records indicate he advanced at least $32.45 for his travel partnership.

41. Clay County Probate Records; Settle, 7–8. Zerelda often repeated the story to reporters in later years.

CHAPTER TWO: The Widow

1. Wright submitted a detailed invoice to the administrator of James's estate in an attempt to collect the remaining $26.30 he was owed; see Robert James Probate Records, Clay County Archives, Liberty, Missouri. Usually James's death is placed in August 1850; this may be true, but Wright's bill for Dr. Newman's services suggests that he died in the first two weeks of September.

2. *Liberty Tribune*, February 2, 1851, and October 25, 1850.

3. Jane W. Gill to My Dear Sisters, April 14, 1850, Watkins Mill; Robert James Probate Records.

4. *Kansas City Times,* April 4, 1882; *St. Louis Republican,* April 7, 1882; Stella F. James, *In the Shadow of Jesse James* (Thousand Oaks, Calif.: Dragon Books, 1990), 58–62; Moss quoted in Settle, 60.

5. Robert James Probate Records. The idea that Zerelda was not always so fierce is bolstered by Catherine Clinton's argument that women who did not display a culturally acceptable feminine softness lost respectability; see *The Other Civil War: American Women in the Nineteenth Century* (New York: Hill and Wang, 1984), 147–8.

6. George C. Rable, *Civil Wars: Women and the Crisis of Southern Nationalism* (Urbana: University of Illinois Press, 1989), 23–4. All information presented here regarding the administration of the estate can be found in the sixty-page Robert James Probate Records. This file is exceptionally detailed, including invoices, receipts, inventories, and bills of sale.

7. Robert James Probate Records; New Hope church subscription, April 19, 1851, written on the back of J. C. Minter to Dear Cousin, September 9, 1847, Watkins Mill.

8. Robert James Probate Records.

9. Rable, 25–30, has found that few widows in the South owned property, and what they had tended to dissipate; Settle, 6–7; Perry McCandless, *A History of Missouri,* vol. 2, *1820–1860* (Columbia: University of Missouri Press, 1972), 191–2; R. Douglas Hurt, *Agriculture and Slavery in Missouri's Little Dixie* (Columbia: University of Missouri Press, 1992), 102, 203, 207; Jane W. Gill to My Dear Mother and Sisters, March 29, 1846, Jane W. Gill to Beloved Mother and Sisters, June 15, 1846, and Jane W. Gill to My Dear Sisters, April 14, 1850, Watkins Mill. The 1850 census noted that Frank had attended school during the previous year; by 1860, both boys were in school, apparently a typical makeshift country school; see the *Seventh* and *Eighth Census of the United States,* 1850 and 1860, and *History of Clay,* 266–7.

10. E. Carter to Dear Mother and Sister, August 7, 1849, E. A. Carter to My Dear Sisters, August 30, 1850, and E. A. Carter to Dear Brother and Sister, July 31, 1851, Watkins Mill; McCandless, 219–20; Hurt, 75.

11. Robert James Probate Records. See George F. Lemmer, "Farm Machinery in Ante-Bellum Missouri," *MHR* 40, no. 4 (July 1946): 467–80, for a discussion of the slowness of Missouri farmers in adopting labor-saving devices and new farm equipment; Hurt, 109, however, points out that hemp farming, unlike corn or wheat cultivation, did not lend itself to mechanization. Clinton, 166–7, demonstrates the importance of female social networks in women's lives, clearly seen in Zerelda's dependence on the Wests.

12. See Milton F. Perry's appendix to Stella James, 127–8; also Jane W. Gill to Beloved Mother & Sister, June 15, 1846, Watkins Mill; Nanon Lucile Carr, ed., *Marriage Records of Clay County, Missouri, 1822–1852* (privately printed: 1957); Katherine Gentry Bushman, ed., *Index of the First Plat Book of Clay County, Missouri, 1819–1875* (n.p., n.d.), 82.

13. *Kansas City Times,* April 4, 1882; *History of Clay,* 266; Milton Perry in Stella James, 127–8.

14. *History of Clay,* 266; Elizabeth Carter to Martha James and Mother, June 12, 1853, Watkins Mill.

15. Robert James Probate Records; Clay County Court Book, vol. 12, 21, and vol. 13, 116–17, Clay County Archives, Liberty, Missouri; *Liberty Tribune,* October 5, 1855.

16. Stella James, 129, 59; E. M. Samuel to General Samuel Bassett, August 9, 1864, Provost-1. Clinton, 40–53, 147–8, discusses the "cult of domesticity" that circumscribed women's lives; at the same time, being a wedded wife gave Zerelda social standing and expansive responsibilities she would have lacked as a widowed mother.

17. County Court Book, vol. 13, 116–17, Clay County Archives; Yeatman, 27–8. See Clarence Hite's confession in *St. Louis Republican,* November 12, 1883; *Kansas City Times,* April 4, 1882. On prenuptial agreements (and their limitations), see Rable, 22–3; see also Clinton, 40–53, 147–8.

18. McCandless, 215–18; Barbara Oliver Korner and Carla Waal, eds., *Hardship and Hope: Missouri Women Writing About Their Lives, 1820–1920* (Columbia: University of Missouri Press, 1997), 150; Hurt, 208, 211–12; see also Robert C. Fuller, *Alternative Medicine and American Religious Life* (New York: Oxford University Press, 1989).

19. Joan M. Beamis and William E. Pullen, *Background of a Bandit: The Ancestry of Jesse James* (n.p.: 1970), 60.

20. See Zerelda's comments about Jesse and Frank's youth, *Kansas City Times,* April 4, 1882.

21. *Westport Border Star* quoted on 426 in Janet Bruce, "Of Sugar and Salt and Things in the Cellar and Sun: Food Preservation in Jackson County in the 1850s," *MHR* 75, no. 4 (July 1981): 417–47. On July 11, 1870, Reuben Samuel spoke of assisting his brother-in-law Jesse Cole in slaughtering hogs in the month of December; *Liberty Tribune,* July 22, 1870. For a broader discussion, see Glenda Riley, *The Female Frontier: A Comparative View of Women on the Prairie and the Plains* (Lawrence: University Press of Kansas, 1988), 42–75.

22. Quoted in Bruce, 430.

23. An icehouse is mentioned in the *St. Louis Republican,* February 4, 1875; it was standard in the 1850s.

24. Contemporary references to "six weeks' want" in Bruce, 423; see also Hurt, 157–8.

25. Quoted in Bruce, 438.

26. *Eighth Census of the United States, 1860,* Clay County, Missouri.

27. See, for example, Margaret Kelso's story in Korner and Waal, 149–50.

28. Hurt, xiii, 243, persuasively argues that commercial farming dominated Little Dixie. Quote from R. Douglas Hurt, "Planters and Slavery in Little Dixie," *MHR* 88, no. 4 (July 1994): 397–415.

29. This discussion of hemp markets is based largely on Hurt's excellent overview, *Agriculture and Slavery,* 103–30, and Miles W. Eaton, "The Development and Later Decline of the Hemp Industry in Missouri," *MHR* 43, no. 4 (July 1949): 344–59.

30. *Liberty Tribune,* October 22, 1858.

31. Michael A. Bellesiles, "The Origins of Gun Culture in the United States, 1760–1865," *Journal of American History* 83, no. 2 (September 1996): 425–55, and his *Arming America: The Origins of a National Gun Culture* (New York: Alfred A. Knopf, 2000); Kate L. Gregg, "Missourians in the Gold Rush," *MHR* 39, no. 2 (October 1944): 137–54. Bellesiles's work has come under harsh criticism, mainly for his assertions regarding the colonial era. His writings on the antebellum period, however, generally reflect my own findings. At the start of the Civil War, both sides suffered a severe shortage of firearms.

32. *History of Clay,* 451, 504; Robert James Probate Records; Hurt, 210–11, 220; McCandless, 151, 188, 197; Korner and Waal, 86; Elbert R. Bowen, "The Circus in Early Rural Missouri," and "Negro Minstrels in Early Rural Missouri," *MHR* 47, no. 1 (October 1952); 1–17 and 103–9; see also Lewis A. Atherton, *The Frontier Merchant in Mid-America* (Columbia: University of Missouri Press, 1971), 9–58.

33. *Kansas City Times,* January 28, 1875; *St. Louis Republican,* February 5, 1875; W. B. Kemper, Assistant Provost Marshal, to Col. Joseph Dann, Acting Provost Marshal General, December 2, 1864, file 13681, Provost-2.

CHAPTER THREE: The Slaves

1. *Seventh Census of the United States, 1850: Slave Schedules,* Clay County, Missouri (to be cited as U.S. Census, 1850); *Eighth Census of the United States, 1860: Slave Schedules,* Clay County, Missouri, 1860 (to be cited as U.S. Census, 1860); the slave codes were amended in 1847 to forbid the education of slaves in reading and writing, Perry McCandless, *A History of Missouri,* vol. 2, *1820–1860* (Columbia: University of Missouri Press, 1972), 58; Fellman, 7; R. Douglas Hurt, *Agriculture and Slavery in Missouri's Little Dixie* (Columbia: University of Missouri Press, 1992), 219. William W. Freehling, *The Road to Disunion,* vol. 1, *Secessionists at Bay, 1776–1854* (New York: Oxford University Press, 1990), 540, makes the colonial New York comparison.

2. Fellman, 8; McCandless, 39–41, 135; Eric Foner, *Free Soil, Free Labor, Free Men: The Ideology of the Republican Party Before the Civil War* (New York: Oxford University Press, 1995), 121; Hurt, x–xii; Freehling, 538–41. Note that Freehling's map, 539, showing slave population percentages in Missouri, is inaccurate; compare to Hurt, 218–22.

3. For an excellent discussion of the divisions within Missouri, see Jonas Viles, "Sections and Sectionalism in a Border State," *Mississippi Valley Historical Review* 21, no. 1 (June 1934): 3–22. Viles, like most historians of his era, mistakenly assumes that large-scale plantation agriculture was a necessary component for the survival of slavery and a Southern identity.

4. Hurt, 218–23; the percentage of slaves in Clay County's population in 1850 and 1860 was 27 percent. The case for slavery's minimal importance is made by Fellman, 7, and Freehling, 541, though I have adapted Hurt's numbers. R. Douglas Hurt, "Planters and Slavery in Little Dixie," *MHR* 88, no. 4 (July 1994): 397–415.

5. McCandless, 48, 200–4; Robert E. Shalhope, "Eugene Genovese, the Missouri Elite, and Civil War Historiography," part 1, *Missouri Historical Society Bulletin* 26, no. 4 (July 1970): 217–82. Only 17 of 113 counties had farmland worth $4,000,000 or more; most abutted the Missouri River.

6. The antebellum belief in slave labor as efficient, indeed necessary, is stressed by every recent study of Little Dixie. See especially James William McGettigan, Jr., "Boone County Slaves: Sales, Estate Divisions, and Families, 1820–1855," part 1, *MHR* 72, no. 2 (January 1978): 176–97, and part 2, *MHR* 72, no. 3 (April 1978): 271–95; Philip V. Scarpino, "Slavery in Callaway County, Missouri: 1845–1855," part 1, *MHR* 71, no. 1 (October 1976): 22–43, and part 2, *MHR* 71, no. 3 (April 1977): 266–83; Hurt, *Agriculture and Slavery,* 123, believes that slavery was necessary for hemp cultivation especially, and, 181, records that the labor price in the 1850s was "unprecedented"; see also Hurt, "Planters and Slavery"; Frank Blair, Jr., made his comments in 1855, quoted by Harrison A. Trexler, *Slavery in Missouri, 1804–1865* (Baltimore: The Johns Hopkins University Press, 1914), 55. Slave traders were active in every important Little Dixie town, but there were no signs of a large-scale sell-off to the Deep South. Trexler relies on politically stilted newspaper commentary to claim that a major sell-off began around 1860, but contradicts himself with harder evidence that slave prices remained high right up to the outbreak of the Civil War; see Harrison A. Trexler, "The Value and the Sale of the Missouri Slave," *MHR* 8, no. 1 (January 1914): 69–85. McGettigan, part 1, and Hurt, *Agriculture and Slavery,* 223, show that slave traders experienced great difficulty buying slaves for the Deep South market, and that the demand for slaves within Missouri actually grew through 1860.

7. Hurt, "Planters and Slavery," 412–14; McGettigan, part 1, 176–97, part 2, 271–95; Scarpino, part 1, 22–43, part 2, 266–83. It should be noted that a skilled slave would more likely be sold privately, rather than in auction.

8. Robert James Probate Records, Clay County Archives, Liberty, Missouri.

9. Stella F. James, *In the Shadow of Jesse James* (Thousand Oaks, Calif.: Dragon Books, 1990), 59; U.S. Census, 1850; U.S. Census, 1860; Leeann Whites, "The Civil War as a Crisis in Gender," in *Divided Houses: Gender and the Civil War,* ed. Catherine Clinton and Nina Silber (New York: Oxford University Press, 1992), 3–21; see also Jane W. Gill to Beloved Mother and Sisters, June 15, 1846, Watkins Mill. An informative if irritatingly written overview of slave-master relations is in Freehling, 59–97; Eugene Genovese discusses the language of family, and some of the problems carried within it, in *Roll, Jordan, Roll: The World the Slaves Made* (New York: Vintage, 1976), 74–5.

10. Elizabeth Carter to My Dear Sisters, August 30, 1850, Watkins Mill. McCandless finds that slaves were usually allowed some social life and local freedom of movement, 63–4, but McGettigan's study of Boone County (part 2), cautions that slaves were not allowed to travel great distances, 284.

11. Brenda E. Stevenson, *Life in Black and White: Family and Community in the Slave South* (New York: Oxford University Press, 1996), 206–44; Hurt, "Planters and Slavery," 409–11. For a discussion about the debate over whether matriarchal households predominated in slave families, see Deborah Gray White, "Female Slaves: Sex Roles and Status in the Antebellum South," in *Half Sisters of History: Southern Women and the American Past,* ed. Catherine Clinton (Durham, N.C.: Duke University Press, 1994), 56–75. As Stevenson shows, the small number of slaves per household in the border states appears to have led to greater instability in bond servant families, as compared to large plantations in the Deep South.

12. McGettigan, "Boone," part 2, 285. The precariousness of slave marriages is underscored by every study cited so far. But Lorenzo J. Greene, Gary R. Kremer, and Antonio F. Holland argue, "The slave family, although often separated by sale and death, was the stabilizing unit of the slave community"; *Missouri's Black Heritage,* rev. ed. (Columbia: University of Missouri Press, 1993), 35–6.

13. U.S. Census, 1850; Robert James Probate Records. The census, taken only three months before the probate inventory, mistakenly records the youngest child as male; the more thorough inventory lists not only the girl's sex, but her name as well. Stevenson's study of the ratio of women

to children in Virginia suggests that adult female slaves averaged two children each, under fourteen, at any given time; see 248.

14. Hurt, *Agriculture and Slavery*, 225–36, 262–4; McGettigan conducted a careful survey that bolsters these points, "Boone," part 1, 193–7; Trexler in 1914 wrote of "quite a local negro exchange" in Little Dixie, saying a "golden age of slave values" began in the 1850s, *MHR*, 69–78.

15. Hurt, *Agriculture and Slavery*, 233; Hurt, "Planters and Slavery," 409.

16. George Rawick, ed., *The American Slave: A Composite Autobiography* (Westport, Conn.: Greenwood, 1979), 11: 342; Greene, 29–32. After the Civil War, the black "servants" on the farm slept in the kitchen during the winter; *Kansas City Times*, January 28, 1875.

17. Rawick, 258; Greene, 32; McGettigan, part 2, 276.

18. Trexler, 37; Scarpino, part 2, 268; Hurt, *Agriculture and Slavery*, 265; Greene, 33; Rawick, 157, 330–2.

19. Hurt, *Agriculture and Slavery*, 103–30; Miles W. Eaton, "The Development and Later Decline of the Hemp Industry in Missouri," *MHR* 43, no. 4 (July 1949): 344–59; Greene, 25–9; Robert James Probate Records.

20. Robert James Probate Records.

21. Hurt, "Planters and Slavery," 411; U.S. Census, 1860.

22. Rawick, 140, 324; Jane W. Gill to Beloved Mother and Sister, June 15, 1846, and E. Carter to My Ever Dear Mother and Sisters, November 25, 1847, Watkins Mill; Scarpino, parts 1 and 2, comments effectively on the contradictory mind-set of slaveowners in Little Dixie; later evidence shows that Charlotte never left the Samuel farm, even after emancipation.

23. Frederick Douglass, *Narrative of the Life of Frederick Douglass, an American Slave, Written by Himself* (New York: Penguin, 1968), 103; "Address to the British People," May 12, 1846, reprinted in T. J. Stiles, ed., *The Citizen's Handbook* (New York: Berkley, 1993), 97.

24. Rawick, 281.

25. Rawick, 146, 176, 322–3. Slaveholders' latent fear of their servants is generally accepted; see David Brion Davis, *The Slave Power Conspiracy and the Paranoid Style* (Baton Rouge: Louisiana State University Press, 1969), 32; quote from *History of Clay*, 179.

26. Benjamin G. Merkel, "The Underground Railroad and the Missouri Borders, 1840–1860," *MHR* 37, no. 4 (July 1943): 271–85. McGettigan, part 2, 277.

27. McCandless, 57–8; Hurt, 247, 259; Greene, 39; Rawick, 96, 281. Genovese provides the general context of Southern laws controlling slaves, 25–49; John Hope Franklin and Loren Schweninger, *Runaway Slaves: Rebels on the Plantation* (New York: Oxford University Press, 1999), argue that patrols were ineffective in actual practice, 150–6.

28. Hurt, *Agriculture and Slavery*, 247–59; Greene, 46.

29. Hurt, *Agriculture and Slavery*, 258–9. Merkel claims that outsiders were essential to escape attempts, 285.

30. Trexler, "Value and Sale," 68–72; McGettigan, part 2, 285; Greene, 28, 47–9; Hurt, *Agriculture and Slavery*, 254.

31. Hurt, *Agriculture and Slavery*, 254; Trexler, *Slavery in Missouri*, 180–5. The specific political context, and repercussions, of this growing paranoia is discussed below; for a general discussion, see Davis, 32–61. For a thorough discussion of antebellum mob action throughout the South, see David Grimsted, *American Mobbing, 1828–1861: Toward Civil War* (New York: Oxford University Press, 1998), 100–34. Grimsted shows that the suppression of dissent was widespread in the region, and increased in the late 1850s.

32. *Liberty Tribune*, October 5, 1855; *History of Clay*, 174.

33. James M. McPherson, *Battle Cry of Freedom: The Civil War Era* (New York: Oxford University Press, 1988), 54; Hurt, *Agriculture and Slavery*, 273–5; Freehling, 432–3; William E. Parrish, *David Rice Atchison of Missouri: Border Politician* (Columbia: University of Missouri Press, 1961), 86–9, 98, 112–16; Christopher Phillips, *Missouri's Confederate: Claiborne Fox Jackson and the Creation of a Southern Identity in the Border West* (Columbia: University of Missouri Press, 2000), 170; Shalhope, 217–82; Benjamin G. Merkel, "The Slavery Issue and the Political Decline of Thomas Hart Benton, 1846–1856," *MHR* 38, no. 4 (July 1944): 388–407; McCandless, 241–55; James C. Malin,

"The Proslavery Background of the Kansas Struggle," *Mississippi Valley Historical Review* 10, no. 3 (December 1923): 285–305. Little Dixie politicians dominated the legislature, due in part to constitutional inequities in representation, enhanced by the legislative reapportionment of 1849.

34. Parrish, 98, 112–16; Merkel, "Benton," 388–407; Hurt, 273–5; McCandless, 241–55; Malin, 286; McPherson, 78–86.

35. Parrish, vii–16, 92, 115–16, 151; McPherson, 81; Malin, 286.

36. Parrish, 121–4, 149; Floyd C. Shoemaker, "Missouri's Pro-Slavery Fight for Kansas, 1854–1855," part 1, *MHR* 48, no. 2 (January 1954): 221–36; Hurt, *Agriculture and Slavery*, 275; Malin, 290–1.

37. Parrish, 139–151; McPherson, 121–3; Malin, 290.

38. Davis, 38–41.

39. Foner, 90–3. Foner's classic study is the basis for this review of Northern views of the South.

40. Foner, 42–3; Davis, 53, 56; Freehling, 558–60; McPherson, 54–5.

41. Foner, 57; McPherson, 55.

42. Foner, 94, 116; McPherson, 123–6.

43. Shoemaker, 226–7; Stephen B. Oates, *To Purge This Land With Blood: A Biography of John Brown* (Amherst: University of Massachusetts Press, 1970), 82–4.

44. Parrish, 162–3; Atchison quoted in James A. Rawley, *Race and Politics: "Bleeding Kansas" and the Coming of the Civil War* (Philadelphia: J. B. Lippincott, 1969), 81.

45. Parrish, 162–3; *History of Clay*, 168; Milton E. Bierbaum, "Frederick Starr: A Missouri Border Abolitionist: The Making of a Martyr," *MHR* 58, no. 3 (April 1964): 309–25; Lester B. Baltimore, "Benjamin F. Stringfellow: The Fight for Slavery on the Missouri Border," *MHR* 62, no. 1 (October 1967): 14–29. Parrish gives the date as July 29; I am following Bierbaum.

46. Parrish, 162; *History of Clay*, 170; Thomas Goodrich, *War to the Knife: Bleeding Kansas 1854–1861* (Mechanicsburg, Pa.: Stackpole Books, 1998), 27–8.

47. David Rice Atchison to Jefferson Davis, September 24, 1854, David Rice Atchison Papers, WHMC. Ironically, Atchison had helped quiet attacks on the Mormons during the crisis of the 1830s.

48. Oates, 84–9; quote in Thomas Goodrich, *War to the Knife: Bleeding Kansas 1854–1861*, (Mechanicsburg, Pa.: Stackpole Books, 1998), 49.

49. Fellman, 291–3; Baltimore, 22; Jay Monaghan, *The Civil War on the Western Border* (Boston: Little, Brown, 1958), 18–9; Floyd C. Shoemaker, "Missouri's Pro-Slavery Fight for Kansas, 1854–1855," part 2, *MHR* 48, no. 3 (April 1954): 325–40.

50. Parrish, 175–80; Monaghan, 24–33.

51. *History of Clay*, 174–7; Hurt, 289.

52. Parrish, 200–1; McPherson, 148–9.

53. McPherson, 149–52, 155–7; Rawley, 160–1.

54. Parrish, 203–7; McPherson, 161; Rawley, 159–60.

55. Phillips, 181–205, in his argument that Missourians considered themselves part of the border West, not South, underplays the internal conflict created by proslavery extremism, which was a central element of the secessionist struggle in Missouri. Michael Fellman has painted a vivid portrait of how the Kansas conflict shaped Northern views of proslavery Missourians, but he, too, overlooks Missouri's internal battle; see Michael Fellman, "Rehearsal for the Civil War: Antislavery and Proslavery at the Fighting Point in Kansas, 1854–1856," in *Antislavery Reconsidered: New Perspectives on the Abolitionists*, ed. Michael Fellman and Lewis Perry (Baton Rouge: Louisiana State University Press, 1979), 287–307. Grimsted, 246–65, offers a fine summary of the fighting in Kansas, but he also misses the role of the border ruffians inside Missouri.

56. Parrish, 162; Bierbaum, 318–25; Baltimore, 22; Shoemaker, part 2, 325–40; Roy G. Magers, "The Raid on the *Parkville Industrial Luminary*," *MHR* 30, no. 1 (October 1935): 39–46; *History of Clay*, 171–2.

57. *Liberty Tribune*, February 21, 1855, and November 11, 1854; Hurt, *Agriculture and Slavery*, 276–8.

58. Hurt, *Agriculture and Slavery*, 290–1. This is a modification (but an essential one) of Phillips's argument (see, for example, 185).

59. *History of Clay*, 160–3.

60. Hurt, *Agriculture and Slavery*, 279–84; Magers, 39–46; Bierbaum, 324.

61. *History of Clay*, 171–2, 177; Hurt, *Agriculture and Slavery*, 279–84.

62. Hurt, *Agriculture and Slavery*, 284–9; Shalhope, 217–82.

63. Rawley, x–xi; Merkel, "Underground Railroad," 278–80; Hurt, *Agriculture and Slavery*, 273–4. George C. Rable, *Civil Wars: Women and the Crisis of Southern Nationalism* (Urbana: University of Illinois Press, 1989), 31–49, shows how Southern women emerged as "defenders of the faith" regarding slavery.

PART TWO: FIRE

CHAPTER FOUR: Rebels

1. *Liberty Tribune*, May 10, 1861; Yeatman, 30; James M. McPherson, *Battle Cry of Freedom: The Civil War Era* (New York: Oxford University Press, 1988), 273–4, 317; *History of Clay*, 190–202. The anonymous author of the *History of Clay* discusses the unprecedented role of women in the secession debate (lending credence to the notion that Zerelda may have attended this meeting). Christopher Phillips, *Missouri's Confederate: Claiborne Fox Jackson and the Creation of a Southern Identity in the Border West* (Columbia: University of Missouri Press, 2000), 240–1, argues that Missouri neutralism was sincere, a product of the border mentality of the state. He has an excellent point, but this was one of the most strongly secessionist sections of the state. War had already erupted, animating pro-Southern partisans, who clearly influenced the document's language.

2. McPherson, 198; Robert V. Bruce, "The Shadow of the Coming War," in *Lincoln the War President*, ed. Gabor S. Borrit (New York: Oxford University Press, 1992), 3–28; see also Henry Adams, *The Education of Henry Adams* (New York: Penguin, 1995), 99.

3. William E. Parrish, *David Rice Atchison: Border Politician* (Columbia: University of Missouri Press, 1961), 208–10; Kenneth M. Stampp, *America in 1857: A Nation on the Brink* (New York: Oxford University Press, 1990), 270–1, 288–93; McPherson, 149, 162–9.

4. Benjamin G. Merkel, "The Underground Railroad and the Missouri Borders, 1840–1860," *MHR* 37, no. 4 (July 1943): 271–85; Stephen B. Oates, *To Purge This Land With Blood: A Biography of John Brown* (Amherst: University of Massachusetts Press, 1970), 254, 261–5; Floyd C. Shoemaker, "Missouriana: John Brown's Missouri Raid," *MHR* 26, no. 1 (October 1931): 78–83; McPherson, 202–13; Philip T. Tucker, "'Ho, for Kansas': The Southwest Expedition of 1860," *MHR* 86, no. 1 (October 1991): 22–36.

5. McPherson, 213–21.

6. T. M. Scruggs to M. B. R. Williams, August 1860, Watkins Mill; John N. Edwards, "A Terrible Quintet," special supplement to the *St. Louis Dispatch*, November 23, 1873, Walter B. Stevens Scrapbook, vol. 34, coll. 1424, WHMC; *History of Clay*, 184–6.

7. McPherson, 212, 224–5, 229.

8. *History III*, 1–5; Christopher Phillips, "Calculated Confederate: Claiborne Fox Jackson and the Strategy for Secession in Missouri," *MHR* 94, no. 4 (July 2000): 389–414; T. M. Scruggs to M. B. R. Williams, August 1860, Watkins Mill; McPherson, 232–5.

9. R. Douglas Hurt, *Agriculture and Slavery in Missouri's Little Dixie*, (Columbia: University of Missouri Press, 1992), 298–300; *History of Clay*, 187–8; *History III*, 8. Attempts to gauge Missouri's bias toward disunion have usually rested on election results (see, for example, William Boed, "Secessionist Strength in Missouri," *MHR* 72, no. 4 [July 1978]: 412–23), but the state did not yet use the secret ballot, making voters susceptible to public pressure.

10. *History of Clay*, 191–2; *History III*, 5, 79–80; John W. Luke to Mary W. Handy, February 11, 1861, Watkins Mill.

11. *History III*, 1–6; Phillips, *Missouri's Confederate*, 235–8; Christopher Phillips, *Damned Yankee: The Life of General Nathaniel Lyon* (Columbia: University of Missouri Press, 1990), 133; Thomas L. Snead, "The First Year of the War in Missouri," in *Battles and Leaders of the Civil War*, ed. Clarence Clough Buel and Robert Underwood Johnson (New York: Century Co., 1887), 1: 262; William E. Parrish, *Frank Blair: Lincoln's Conservative* (Columbia: University of Missouri Press,

1998), 90–2; William E. Parrish, *Turbulent Partnership: Missouri and the Union, 1861–1865* (Columbia: University of Missouri Press, 1963), 4–8; Robert E. Miller, " 'One of the Ruling Class,' Thomas Caute Reynolds: Second Confederate Governor of Missouri," *MHR* 80, no. 4 (July 1986): 442–8.

12. *History III*, 1–9; Parrish, *Frank Blair*, 90–5; Parrish, *Turbulent Partnership*, 7–17; Phillips, *Damned Yankee*, 129–30, 135–49; Phillips, *Missouri's Confederate*, 238–40; *History of Clay*, 192–3.

13. Phillips, *Missouri's Confederate*, 245–9; Phillips, *Damned Yankee*, 156–7; *History III*, 10–2; Parrish, *Frank Blair*, 95–6; Parrish, *Turbulent Partnership*, 17, 20–1; *O.R.*, 1: I: 684, 690; *History of Clay*, 195–7.

14. Phillips, *Damned Yankee*, 163–5, 177–82; Phillips, *Missouri's Confederate*, 251; Miller, 427–9; *History of Clay*, 197–8. The people of Missouri, like most Americans, were unprepared for war; see Michael A. Bellesiles, "The Origins of Gun Culture in the United States, 1760–1865," *Journal of American History* 83, no. 2 (September 1996): 425–55, and *Arming America: The Origins of a National Gun Culture* (New York: Alfred A. Knopf, 2000), 406–23; John Glendower Westover discusses the near abandonment of the militia after the Mexican War in "The Evolution of the Missouri Militia, 1804–1919" (Ph.D. diss., University of Missouri, 1948), chaps. 2 and 3; he notes, 119, that only 1,464 men were in the militia in 1861, most of them in St. Louis. See also the testimony of O. P. Moss, *Militia Report*, 388, who referred to his service in the "cornstalk militia," a common phrase across America that alluded to the lack of military arms. This characterization of Clay County is drawn from *History of Clay*, 200–3, and the testimony of E. M. Samuel, F. R. Long, James M. Jones, J. H. Moss, and O. P. Moss, *Militia Report*, 381–404.

15. Phillips, *Damned Yankee*, 180–93; *Memoirs of General William T. Sherman* (New York: Da Capo Press, 1984), 172–74; Albert Castel, *General Sterling Price and the Civil War in the West* (Baton Rouge: Louisiana State University Press, 1968), 12–3; Parrish, *Turbulent Partnership*, 23–4.

16. Phillips, *Damned Yankee*, 157, 190–3; Phillips, *Missouri's Confederate*, 252–3; *History of Clay*, 199–203; Castel, 14–5; for an earlier view of these events, see Jonas Viles, "Sections and Sectionalism in a Border State," *Mississippi Valley Historical Review* 21, no. 1 (June 1934): 3–22. Phillips is quite critical of Lyon, as is Mark Grimsley, *The Hard Hand of War: Union Military Policy Toward Southern Civilians, 1861–1865* (New York: Cambridge University Press, 1995), 36–7.

17. Phillips, *Damned Yankee*, 204–14; Castel, 18–9; Parrish, *Turbulent Partnership*, 25–31; *History of Clay*, 203.

18. Phillips, *Missouri's Confederate*, 256–7; Castel, 16–21; Parrish, *Frank Blair*, 108; see also Snead, in Buel and Johnson, 267; Thomas L. Snead, *The Fight for Missouri* (New York: Scribner's, 1886), 196–7; *History III*, 17–23. Kansas had been accepted as a free state in 1861. This version of Lyon's quote appeared in the press only a few weeks after the conference; Snead's book offers a much-cited later variant.

19. Castel, 35, 28–9; Snead, in Buel and Johnson, 270.

20. *History of Clay*, 203–5; Castel, 25–30; Snead, in Buel and Johnson, 267–73; *O.R.* 1: III: 734–6, VII: 496–7, LIII: 696. The difficulties in communication with Price's army are amply demonstrated in the 1861 letters of T. M. Scruggs, Watkins Mill.

21. Phillips, *Damned Yankee*, 215–57; McPherson, 350–2; Castel, 31–49.

22. McPherson, 317–24; *Militia Report*, 408.

23. Chase spoke on August 7, 1863, quoted in Fellman, 56–7, second quote dated July 1864, 47.

24. *Militia Report*, 368; Stephen Z. Starr, *Jennison's Jayhawkers: A Civil War Cavalry Regiment and Its Commander* (Baton Rouge: Louisiana State University Press, 1973), 41–2, 60, 99–102; Parrish, *Turbulent Partnership*, 30.

25. Edward Samuel denied any relationship with Reuben Samuel; see E. M. Samuel to General Samuel Bassett, August 9, 1864, Provost-1.

26. *History of Clay*, 205–7, 220; Parrish, *Turbulent Partnership*, 66–7; *Militia Report*, 381–3, 386–9, 395–404.

27. Richard S. Brownlee, *Gray Ghosts of the Confederacy: Guerrilla Warfare in the West, 1861–1865* (Baton Rouge: Louisiana State University Press, 1958), 31; Parrish, *Turbulent Partnership*, 54; *History III*, 60; Albert Castel, "Quantrill's Bushwhackers: A Case Study in Partisan Warfare," in *Winning and Losing the Civil War: Essays and Stories*, ed. Albert Castel (Columbia: University of

South Carolina Press, 1996), 135. Fellman also blames the Kansans (see, for example, 35), but he also writes that "communities were usually divided and fought among themselves," 38, which he amply illustrates. Don R. Bowen argues that "the uprising, from the microcosm of Jackson County, was a defensive war against an intruding external world"; Don R. Bowen, "Counterrevolutionary Guerrilla War: Missouri, 1861–1865," *Conflict* 8, no. 1 (1988): 69–78. Bowen's analysis of the social status of Jackson County insurrectionists is most useful, though his conclusions about the rebellion's source are incorrect.

28. *History of Clay*, 203–21; Phillips, *Damned Yankee*, 263; Phillips, *Missouri's Confederate*, 256; Grimsley, 35–52. Starr's excellent study of Jennison's regiment illustrates the cooperation between Kansas forces and local Unionists, demonstrating that Jennison did not think all Missourians were rebels. In 1864, James M. Jones, a Clay County court judge, reported that only three raids from Kansas had penetrated the county since the war began, *Militia Report*, 396.

29. *Militia Report*, 409, 448.

30. The importance of prewar mobilization over Kansas lies in three areas: the foundations it built for paramilitary organization; the internal divisions it fostered in an otherwise relatively politically homogenous region; and the ideological basis it established for secessionism, with regard to the threat seen against slavery-based society. The 1850s, then, provided the "incubation period" for guerrilla warfare identified by Walter Laqueur, *Guerrilla Warfare: A Historical and Critical Study* (New Brunswick, N.J.: Transaction, 1998), 392–3.

31. See chap. 3; *Kansas City Times*, December 3, 1872; *History III*, 88–9; Don R. Bowen, "Guerrilla War in Western Missouri, 1862–1865: Historical Extensions of the Relative Deprivation Hypothesis," *Comparative Studies in Society and History* 19, no. 1 (January 1977): 30–51; Bowen, "Counterrevolutionary Guerrilla War"; see also David Brion Davis, *The Slave Power Conspiracy and the Paranoid Style* (Baton Rouge: Louisiana State University Press, 1969). I am arguing directly against the idea expressed by Brownlee, that the state had "good prospects for peace" until Union troops destroyed them, 52. The slavery struggle has been mistakenly slighted as a cause for rebellion; see, for example, Bowen, "Counterrevolutionary Guerrilla War"; Castel, "Quantrill's Bushwhackers," 137, and Edward E. Leslie, *The Devil Knows How to Ride: The True Story of William Clarke Quantrill and His Confederate Raiders* (New York: Da Capo Press, 1998), 85–6n.

32. A. J. McRoberts quoted in Fellman, 45. Many militia officers in Clay and elsewhere testified to being slaveowners; see *Militia Report*, 380, 392, 398.

33. In *Missouri's Confederate*, Christopher Phillips argues that Missourians did not have a sense of themselves as Southerners, even at the outbreak of the war. I argue, however, that his thesis does not apply equally to all areas of the state; a Southern identity had definitely taken hold in Clay County by 1861. See also Fellman, 44–52.

34. *History of Clay*, 266; James A. Mulligan, "The Siege of Lexington, Mo.," *Battles and Leaders*, 1: 307–13; John C. Frémont, "In Command in Missouri," in Buel and Johnson, 1: 278–88; Parrish, *Turbulent Partnership*, 49–67; Castel, 49–57.

35. *O.R.* 1: III: 193–4; *History of Clay*, 207–19; McPherson, 325.

36. Snead, in Buel and Johnson, 274; Mulligan, in Buel and Johnson, 311; Castel, 49–60; *History III*, 34–46; Parrish, *Turbulent Partnership*, 66–8; *O.R.* 1: III: 639, 719, 722; *History of Clay*, 220; Phillips, *Missouri's Confederate*, 268–9. McPherson, 353, astutely notes, "Since capturing Lexington, Price had learned the difference between an invasion and a raid. He lacked the manpower and logistical capacity to turn his raid into a successful occupation of captured territory."

37. *History of Clay*, 266–7; Hurt, 301; Miles W. Eaton, "The Development and Later Decline of the Hemp Industry in Missouri," *MHR* 43, no. 4 (July 1949): 344–59; Harrison A. Trexler, "The Value and Sale of the Missouri Slave," *MHR* 8, no. 1 (January 1914): 69–85.

38. Parrish, *Turbulent Partnership*, 49–50. The two-thirds figure given here is admittedly impressionistic, but reflects the proportion of men who joined Union versus Confederate forces.

39. Parrish, *Turbulent Partnership*, 57; Mexico citizens' quote in Fellman, 44; see also 44–7.

40. Parrish, *Turbulent Partnership*, 49–75; *O.R.* 1: III: 466–7; Brownlee, 26–7. My discussion of martial law, trials of civilians, and Lincoln's policies relies heavily on Mark E. Neely's important study, *The Fate of Liberty: Abraham Lincoln and Civil Liberties* (New York: Oxford University Press,

1991), 34–5. Many writers mistakenly claim that Frémont declared all slaves free; those of loyal slaveholders were not.

41. Parrish, *Turbulent Partnership*, 63, 67–8, 108; Brownlee, 149–51; Neely, 40–2, 129, 168; *History III*, 65–6; *O.R.* 1: VIII: 405–6; the existing provost marshal network was formalized by General Order No. 4, on June 27, 1862, *O.R.* 1: XIII: 453.

42. Brownlee, 160–3; Neely, 44–6.

43. Parrish, *Turbulent Partnership*, 54–5, 75–84; Neely, 36–9; Westover, 140–9; James A. Hamilton, "The Enrolled Missouri Militia: Its Creation and Controversial History," *MHR* 69, no. 4 (July 1975): 415. *O.R.* 1: VIII, 476–8, 834; 1: XIII: 7–21; and 1: XXII, part 2: 43–5, 48. A regiment consisted of ten to twelve companies (usually ten for infantry, twelve for cavalry); a full-strength company had eighty-three men. Initially 13,800 men enrolled; Congress soon limited the force to 10,000. The various militia organizations have often been lumped together, a rather serious error; see, for example, Leslie, 154, 180; Brownlee, 51, 104; Castel, "Quantrill's Bushwhackers," 137, 141; Albert Castel, *William Clarke Quantrill: His Life and Times* (New York: Frederick Fell, 1962), 114, 173.

44. Parrish, *Turbulent Partnership*, 88–9; *O.R.* 1: VIII: 557, 832; Brownlee, 145–51.

45. *History III*, 65–7, 77; Ulysses S. Grant, *Personal Memoirs of U.S. Grant* (Cleveland: 1885; reprinted by Da Capo Press, New York, 1982), 132.

46. *O.R.* 1: VIII: 381.

47. *O.R.* 1: VIII: 426, 462–3, 818; Parrish, *Turbulent Partnership*, 53; Brownlee, 24–7; *History of Clay*, 221, puts the incursion on Sunday, December 8, 1861; E. M. Samuel testified that twenty-five hundred men marched in and stayed for three or four days, *Militia Report*, 382.

48. *History of Clay*, 222–3; Grimsley, 38–9.

49. Fellman, 67, 251, demonstrates beyond doubt how guerrilla warfare pervaded the state, despite the special attention given (by this book, among others) to the western border. See also Mark J. Crawford, "An Eye for an Eye," *Columbiad* 2, no. 3 (fall 1998): 118–36. The best place to begin any investigation of this subject is Daniel E. Sutherland, "Sideshow No Longer: A Historiographical Review of the Guerrilla War," *CWH* 46, no. 1 (March 2000): 5–23.

50. Starr, 82–107; quote on 86; see also 111–13.

51. Quote in Fellman, 76–7; see also 35, 66–8; Mary to Dear Friend, January 5, 1862, Watkins Mill; Albert Castel, "Kansas Jayhawking Raids into Western Missouri in 1861," *MHR* 54, no. 1 (October 1959): 1–11; Starr, 88–90, 110–17; Parrish, *Turbulent Partnership*, 85–6.

52. Starr, 23, 96–7, Lane quote on 48; *O.R.* 1: VIII: 507.

53. Snead, in Buel and Johnson, 274; Mulligan, in Buel and Johnson, 311; Castel, *Price*, 49–60; *History III*, 34–46; Parrish, *Turbulent Partnership*, 66–8; *O.R.* 1: III: 639, 719, 722; *History of Clay*, 220; Phillips, *Missouri's Confederate*, 268–9.

54. *History III*, 46–8; Castel, *Price*, 65–8; Westover, 135–7; *History of Clay*, 266.

CHAPTER FIVE: Neighbors

1. James M. McPherson, *Battle Cry of Freedom: The Civil War Era* (New York: Oxford University Press, 1988), 392–405; for a description of Clay County, see Kate Watkins to Uncle and Aunt, June 9, 1862, Watkins Mill.

2. Kate Watkins to Uncle and Aunt, June 9, 1862, Watkins Mill; *Militia Report*, 378–82; *History of Clay*, 223–5. Union commanders banned Kansan forays into Missouri in January 1862; by April, three companies of troops patrolled the border; William E. Parrish, *Turbulent Partnership: Missouri and the Union, 1861–1865* (Columbia: University of Missouri Press, 1963), 85–6.

3. Anna Slayback to M. Blythe, May 9, 1862, Anna Slayback to M. Blythe, April 8, 1862, Watkins Mill.

4. Kate Watkins to Uncle and Aunt, June 9, 1862, Watkins Mill.

5. Edward E. Leslie, *The Devil Knows How to Ride: The True Story of William Clarke Quantrill and His Confederate Raiders* (New York: Da Capo Press, 1998), 95–7, 185; *O.R.* 1: VIII: 57–8. The spelling of Quantrill's name (often rendered "Quantrell") is corrected in most quotations.

6. Leslie, 97–119; Richard S. Brownlee, *Gray Ghosts of the Confederacy: Guerilla Warfare in the West, 1861–1865* (Baton Rouge: Louisiana State University Press, 1958), 58–69; *Kansas City Journal*

of Commerce, April 18, 1862. The abilities of Quantrill and his guerrillas have often been overstated; see, for example, Albert Castel, "Quantrill's Bushwhackers: A Case Study in Partisan Warfare," *Winning and Losing the Civil War: Essays and Stories* (Columbia: University of South Carolina Press, 1996), 133–4, and Fellman, 251. Castel praises the guerrillas' prowess, but fails to note that they suffered a critical failing: They lacked any strategic plan. Quantrill claimed to be from Maryland, and lied to his followers that free-state Kansans had killed his brother; see John McCorkle to W. W. Scott, May 6, 1881, W. W. Scott Papers, Duke.

7. Yeatman, 33; Settle, 20; *History III,* 65–7; *O.R.* 1: XIII: 361; *Liberty Tribune,* May 2, 1862; *Kansas City Times,* April 7, 1882.

8. *O.R.* 1: XIII: 234, 793 (the Masonic superior was Major General Samuel L. Curtis); *Militia Report,* 382, 385, 386, 389.

9. *O.R.* 1: XIII: 7–11, 506; John Glendower Westover, "The Evolution of the Missouri Militia, 1804–1919" (Ph.D. diss., University of Missouri, 1948), 151–61; James A. Hamilton, "The Enrolled Missouri Militia: Its Creation and Controversial History," *MHR* 69, no. 4 (July 1975): 416–32; Brownlee, 71–91. Halleck organized the Military District of Missouri with Schofield as commander on June 5, 1862.

10. *O.R.* 1: XIII: 11, 522–3, 534–5; Parrish, *Turbulent Partnership,* 92; *History III,* 51–5; *Liberty Tribune,* September 12, 1862. For an example of the panic about the order, see Dorothy Brown Thompson, "A Young Girl in the Missouri Border War," *MHR* 58, no. 1 (October 1963): 63; W. Wayne Smith, "An Experiment in Counterinsurgency: The Assessment of Confederate Sympathizers in Missouri," *Journal of Southern History* 35, no. 3 (August 1969): 362–80. Frank was not asked to fight against his friends, as sometimes suggested (e.g., Yeatman, 34–5).

11. *History of Clay,* 228; *Militia Report,* 364, 367, 378.

12. *Militia Report* 392, 398, 400.

13. *Militia Report* 382, 391, 393, 402; see excerpts from Elvira Scott's diary, July 9, 1862, in *Hardship and Hope: Missouri Women Writing About Their Lives, 1820–1920,* ed. Barbara Oliver and Carla Waal (Columbia: University of Missouri Press, 1997), 92–3.

14. *Militia Report,* 379; Westover, 154–6 (the federal government did not issue food, forage, and equipment to the EMM until June 1863); Sue Carter to Margaret Blythe, November 14, 1862, Watkins Mill. Hamilton, 423–6, notes that the EMM was not under federal control, unlike the MSM, and that zero funding was the price for such a state force.

15. *O.R.* 1: XIII: 7–11, 506; Westover, 151–61; Hamilton, 416–32; Brownlee, 71–91.

16. William E. Parrish, "Reconstruction Politics in Missouri, 1865–1870," in *Radicalism, Racism, and Party Realignment: The Border States During Reconstruction,* ed. Richard O. Curry (Baltimore: The Johns Hopkins University Press, 1969), 1–35. The role of militiamen in creating the Radical Party in Clay County will be discussed later; for a roll of the founding members, see Republican Central Committee Meeting, Clay County, January 1, 1866, coll. 970, fold. 161, Clarence W. Alvord and Idress Head Collection, WHMC; and Republican Central Committee of Clay County to Governor Thomas C. Fletcher, January 3, 1866, Thomas C. Fletcher Papers, MSA. For this critique of Jesse James's claim to Confederate loyalties, see William H. Wallace, *Speeches and Writings of Wm. H. Wallace, with Autobiography* (Kansas City, Mo.: Western Baptist Publishing Co., 1914), 269.

17. Sue Carter to Cousins Kate and Mat, March 22, 1863, Watkins Mill; *History of Clay,* 228; *Militia Report,* 115, 364, 367, 378–9; Westover, 151–3. The role of Colonel Moss in catching slaves was a matter of intense controversy, and fills many pages of the *Militia Report.* A full study of the death of slavery in Missouri has yet to be written. Michael Fellman's writing ("Emancipation in Missouri," *MHR* 83, no. 1 [October 1988]: 36–56, and *Inside War,* 65–73) includes important observations, but has no chronological framework. For primary sources and historical insights, see Ira Berlin, Steven F. Miller, Joseph P. Reidy, and Leslie S. Rowland, eds., *Freedom: A Documentary History of Emancipation: 1861–1867* (New York: Cambridge University Press, 1993), ser. 1, vol. 1, chap. 7. For an excellent brief discussion of the conflicting Union attitudes, authorities, and policies regarding slaveholding in the state, see vol. 2, chap. 5, especially 553–6.

18. William E. Parrish, *Missouri Under Radical Rule, 1865–1870* (Columbia: University of Missouri Press, 1965), 1–5; Kate Watkins to Uncle & Aunt, June 9, 1862, Watkins Mill.

19. A total of nine Provisional regiments went on duty in early 1863; the Forty-eighth EMM had already dwindled to less than half its size, as its members paid the exemption fee or joined full-time units; Westover, 162–3; *Militia Report*, 364, 367, 373, 382, and especially 216–33.

20. *Militia Report*, 386; for a description of the bitterness of the Unionists in Andrew County, and the reasons for it, see John R. Carter's testimony, 409, and Walter Williams, ed., *A History of Northwest Missouri* (Chicago: Lewis Publishing Company, 1915), 1: 319–21. For examples of the multiplying slave escapes, see Mary and M. Blythe to Son, May 9, 1863, and Kate Watkins to Miss Josephine Hollingsworth, September 1, 1863, Watkins Mill. Note that, since the Provisionals were selected from the standard EMM, they were often (confusingly) identified by their old EMM units, which were still subject to call-up for active duty.

21. *History of Clay*, 266; Yeatman, 35.

22. This town is cited as "Richfield" in the *O.R.* and other reports; in 1859, Richfield had been incorporated into Missouri City, along with the village of St. Bernard; Nathan H. Parker, *Missouri as it is in 1867* (Philadelphia: J. B. Lippincott, 1867), 230.

23. *O.R.* 1: XXII, part 1: 335–6; *Liberty Tribune*, May 22, 1863. Yeatman, 36, claims that Frank had been jailed with Moses McCoy, another member of the squad, and that both had been freed by McCoy's wife; Albert Castel, *William Clarke Quantrill: His Life and Times* (New York: Frederick Fell, 1962), misdates this skirmish, 109. Gravenstein's name was spelled differently everywhere it appeared, from "Gravenstein" in the *Liberty Tribune* to "Grafenstein" in the *O.R.* A fanciful version of these events can be read in John N. Edwards, *Noted Guerrillas, or the Warfare of the Border* (St. Louis: H. W. Brand & Co., 1879), 168–72.

24. Frank later disparaged Wilson's Creek, *Columbia Herald*, September 24, 1897.

25. *Liberty Tribune*, May 29, 1863; affidavits of David M. Bivens, July 1, 1863, and James W. Griffith, August 18, 1863, record 21428, Provost-1. Bivens incorrectly dated the incident on May 25; both his statement and the *Tribune* place it on a Sunday, which was the twenty-fourth.

26. *Liberty Tribune*, May 22, 1863, June 5, 1863; *O.R.* 1: XXII, part 1: 335–6; *Militia Report*, 228.

27. *History of Clay*, 267; Yeatman, 41. Edwards provides elaborate details of spying by Jesse and his mother, which probably reflect some truth, 168–72. Castel, *Quantrill*, 113, and Leslie, 179–80, offer useful discussions of revolvers. See also Robert M. Utley, *Billy the Kid: A Short and Violent Life* (Lincoln: University of Nebraska Press, 1989), 196–7; as Utley notes, Colt handguns were referred to as "Colt's" in the nineteenth century. The Navy earned its name from an engraving on the original model; it was supplemented by the 1860 Army model, a popular .44 caliber weapon. The revolver did not catch on after it was patented in 1835; Samuel Colt's company actually went bankrupt in 1841, only to revive as the Civil War approached; see Bill Barol, "American Made: The Army Colt," *American Heritage Civil War Chronicles* (New York: Forbes, Inc., 1992), 56; Michael A. Bellesiles, *Arming America: The Origins of the National Gun Culture* (New York: Alfred A. Knopf, 2000), 377–81; and Castel, "Quantrill's Bushwhackers," 141. Numerous stories have circulated about how Jesse lost his fingertip; the one given here follows Yeatman's account. For an early report that Jesse was turned away for being too young, see *Kansas City Times*, April 4, 1882.

28. Yeatman, 41; R. Douglas Hurt, *Agriculture and Slavery in Missouri's Little Dixie* (Columbia: University of Missouri Press, 1992), 100.

29. Yeatman, 39–41, has done pioneering work in uncovering new sources on this incident; *St. Joseph Morning Herald*, May 29, 1863; *Kansas City Journal*, April 6, 1882; *History of Clay*, 267; *Militia Report*, 228. I place this raid on Monday, May 25, because the *Liberty Tribune* of May 29, 1863, reported that the militia had attacked and scattered the bushwhackers on that day. The men of the deactivated Forty-eighth EMM were ordered to report for service in Liberty on the morning of the twenty-fifth, which freed the Provisionals for this large operation (*Liberty Tribune*, May 22, 1863); on June 5, the *Tribune* reported that three companies of the Twenty-fifth Missouri were on duty in the county, and that O. P. Moss's company remained in arms. As Yeatman illustrates, this incident was later embellished, most often by Zerelda herself, but none of these retellings admitted that Reuben Samuel had given information; see, for example, Edwards, 167, and John N. Edwards, "A Terrible Quintet," special supplement to the *St. Louis Dispatch*, November 23, 1873, Walter B. Stevens Scrapbook, vol. 34, coll. 1424, WHMC. Rogers described Samuel as old, but he was only thirty-five.

30. *Liberty Tribune*, June 5, 1863.

31. Mrs. Z. Samuel, Parole and Oath of Allegiance, June 5, 1863; Reuben Samuel, Parole, June 24, 1863; A. C. Courtney, L. J. Larkin, and Alvah Maret to Maj. J. M. Bassett, July 6, 1863, Provost-1. Edward M. Samuel attached an endorsement of their appeal.

32. *Kansas City Journal of Commerce*, August 13, 1876; Settle, 9; W. B. Kemper, Assistant Provost Marshal, to Col. Joseph Dann, Acting Provost Marshal General, December 2, 1864, Record 13681, Provost-2.

CHAPTER SIX: Terror

1. Gorgas quoted in James M. McPherson, *Battle Cry of Freedom: The Civil War Era* (New York: Oxford University Press, 1988), 665; see also 626–65.

2. Smith quoted in Fellman, 73; *History of Clay*, 236–7; *Liberty Tribune*, July 24, 1863.

3. *Militia Report*, 373, 382, 383.

4. *Militia Report*, 383; Richard S. Brownlee, *Gray Ghosts of the Confederacy: Guerilla Warfare in the West, 1861–1865* (Baton Rouge: Louisiana State University Press, 1958), 113–15; Edward E. Leslie, *The Devil Knows How to Ride: The True Story of William Clarke Quantrill and His Confederate Raiders* (New York: Da Capo Press, 1998), 173–8; *O.R.* 1: XXII, part 1: 574–5, and 1: XXII, part 2: 315, 428–9, 450; Albert Castel, *A Frontier State at War: Kansas, 1861–1865* (Lawrence: Kansas Heritage Press, 1958), 25–6; Albert Castel, "Order No. 11 and the Civil War on the Border," *MHR* 57, no. 4 (October 1962): 357–68. Ewing complained that he had insufficient troops to put down the guerrillas, and he seems to have been right. A military rule of thumb, developed by the British in Malaysia in the 1950s, is that ten soldiers are required to defeat each partisan insurgent; in August 1863, Ewing reported 3,187 officers and men present for duty, probably less than the necessary ten-to-one ratio; *O.R.* 1: XXII, part 2: 503–5, 579–85. The Union army, of course, lacked such advantages as air support and radio communication, making the ten-to-one figure conservative indeed for the Civil War.

5. Archer Jones, *The Art of War in the Western World* (New York: Oxford University Press, 1987), 418–19. In the controversy around Ewing's actions, his military logic has largely been forgotten; see Castel, "Order No. 11," 365. As harsh as Ewing's orders were, they were not as ferocious as the depopulation carried out by the guerrillas, who employed murder rather than legal measures.

6. Charles F. Harris, "Catalyst for Terror: The Collapse of the Women's Prison in Kansas City," *MHR* 89, no. 3 (April 1995): 290–306; Brownlee, 115–20; Leslie, 196–9; Castel, "Order No. 11," 357–68; *O.R.* 1: XXII, part 2: 460–1. Harris corrects the often-mistaken address of the building, and Leslie offers solid evidence that it had been inadvertently undermined by Union soldiers who secretly visited another set of prisoners, women "of bad character and diseased." Yeatman, 43, incorrectly states that the parole given to Zerelda and Reuben Samuel protected them from these orders; they simply lived outside of Ewing's jurisdiction.

7. On August 7, 1863, the *Liberty Tribune* reported that Frank and two companions had robbed a man west of Liberty; most likely, this was on his return from Clay to Jackson County; *Louisville Courier-Journal*, September 29, 1901; William Gregg, "A Little Dab of History Without Embellishment" (unpub. man., written in 1906), coll. 1113, fold. 1, 127, WHMC. Yeatman, 35, suggests rather incredibly that Frank James rowed across the Missouri in May 1863, joined Quantrill, then rowed back to join Scott. The confusion may result from the mistaken idea that Quantrill was somehow Scott's superior officer. Quantrill was perhaps five feet nine or ten inches, though most remembered him being tall; see Leslie, 185.

8. Gregg manuscript, 128; John McCorkle, as told to O. S. Barton, *Three Years with Quantrell: A True Story* (Armstrong, Mo.: Armstrong Herald Print, n.d.), 65–9; Albert Castel and Thomas Goodrich, *Bloody Bill Anderson: The Short, Savage Life of a Civil War Guerrilla* (Mechanicsburg, Pa.: Stackpole Books, 1998), 23; for Cole Younger's exploits, see *O.R.* 1: XXII, part 2: 72–82. The spelling of David Pool's surname, like so many in the mid-nineteenth century, had variant spellings. This book uses "Pool" consistently. David Pool's close relative, James M. Pool, spelled his name without a final "e" in a letter to Governor Charles H. Hardin, March 28, 1876, Charles H. Hardin Papers, MSA.

9. *Liberty Tribune*, August 7, 1863.

10. Christopher Phillips, *Missouri's Confederate: Claiborne Fox Jackson and the Creation of a Southern Identity in the Border West* (Columbia: University of Missouri Press, 2000), 283.

11. Albert Castel, *William Clarke Quantrill: His Life and Times* (New York: Frederick Fell, 1962), 122–43; Leslie, 193–237; see also Ann Davis Niepman, "General Orders No. 11 and Border Warfare During the Civil War," *MHR* 66, no. 2 (January 1972): 185–210. Leslie, 237n, summarizes the case for a minimum death count of about 200. The customary count of 450 guerrillas is probably far too high; see McCorkle, 79, and Frank James's comment that no more than "350 or 400 from one end of the war to the other" rode with Quantrill or his successors, *Columbia Herald*, September 24, 1897. General Ewing, who had good reason to exaggerate the enemy's numbers, put the tally at 300, *O.R.* 1: XXII, part 1: 579–85. The higher count of 450 has been used as a device for lessening the raiders' moral culpability; see especially Yeatman, 44. John N. Edwards, *Noted Guerrillas, or the Warfare of the Border* (St. Louis: H. W. Brand, 1879), 194, incorrectly claimed that Jesse James was at Lawrence, leading astray many later writers.

12. Quote from Leslie, 209.

13. *O.R.* 1: XXII, part 2: 472–3, 1: XXII, part 1: 574–5. The best analysis of General Order No. 11 is by Albert Castel, "Order No. 11." A common version of these events attributes the order to pressure from Jim Lane (see, for example, Castel, *Quantrill*, 144), but the quote from Schofield shows that no such pressure was necessary. Mark E. Neely, Jr., has shown that Lincoln conveyed to Schofield, through the medium of Frank Blair, that he would tacitly accept judicious depopulation measures; Mark E. Neely, Jr., " 'Unbeknownst' to Lincoln: A Note on Radical Pacification in Missouri During the Civil War," *CWH* 44, no. 3 (September 1998): 212–16.

14. Bazel F. Lazear to Dear Wife, September 10, 1863, coll. 1014, Bazel F. Lazear Papers, WHMC.

15. Niepman, 185–210; *History of Clay*, 238; Thomas Goodrich, *Black Flag: Guerrilla Warfare on the Western Border, 1861–1865* (Bloomington: Indiana University Press, 1995), 100 (this book fails as a work of history, and is cited here purely for the primary sources it quotes). The effectiveness of General Order No. 11 was swiftly undermined by successive resettlement orders, first issued by Ewing himself on November 20, 1863, then by the new commander for the region, Brigadier General Egbert B. Brown, on January 14; see Castel, "Order No. 11," 367.

16. Bazel F. Lazear to Dear Wife, September 10, 1863, and Bazel F. Lazear to Dear Wife, September 24, 1863, coll. 1014, Bazel F. Lazear Papers, WHMC. As in all quotes from primary sources, I have corrected the spelling except where mistakes seem pertinent. See also *O.R.* 1: XXII, part 1: 579–85.

17. Quotations from Goodrich, *Black Flag*, 102–5. The original diary is in the collection of the Kansas State Historical Society, Topeka, Kansas.

18. Kate Watkins to Miss Josephine Hollingsworth, September 1, 1863, Watkins Mill. For reports of armed black patrols, see James H. Moss to Col. A. W. Doniphan, October 3, 1863, Hamilton R. Gamble Papers, MHS, and testimony of Colonel John F. Williams, January 27, 1864, *Militia Report*, 373.

19. James H. Moss to Col. A. W. Doniphan, October 3, 1863, Hamilton R. Gamble Papers, MHS; *Militia Report*, 364–8, 381, 388, 391; Loyalty oaths of John S. Thomason and George S. Story, coll. 970, fold. 305, Clarence W. Alvord and Idress Head Collection, WHMC.

20. *Militia Report*, 382, 388–9, 395

21. *O.R.* 1: XXII, part 2: 584, 587, 591, 1143, and 1: XXXIV, part 2: 382–4; Todd North Gentry, "General Odon Guitar," *MHR* 22, no. 4 (July 1928): 419–45; Stephen B. Oates, *Confederate Cavalry West of the River* (Austin: University of Texas Press, 1961), 131–40; *Militia Report*, 383, 391–2; Howard V. Canan, "The Missouri Paw-Paw Militia of 1863–1864," *MHR* 62, no. 4 (July 1968): 431–48. Jon W. Blassingame, "The Recruitment of Negro Troops in Missouri During the Civil War," *MHR* 57, no. 3 (April 1964): 326–38, notes that conservative militia officers hampered recruiting across the state, which furnished only 8,344 black troops directly (though many enlisted after escaping to neighboring states). Only 40 were recruited in Clay County. See Lorenzo J. Greene, Gary R. Kremer, and Antonio F. Holland, *Missouri's Black Heritage*, rev. ed. (Columbia: University

of Missouri Press, 1993), 80–1. For a discussion of Clay County's polarization, see *History of Clay*, 246–7. Confusion reigns in historical works about the Paw Paws. Castel, *Quantrill*, 173, mistakenly says "most" Union troops in Missouri in early 1864 consisted of Paw Paws; Castel and Goodrich, 53, write in error of secessionists being "pressed" into the Paw Paws, and of them fighting Bill Anderson in July 1864. In fact, only the Eighty-first and Eighty-second EMM Regiments—voluntarily enlisted and stationed strictly in Clay and Platte Counties—qualified as Paw Paws, and neither served after July 10, 1864.

22. Wife to My own dear Husband, January 27, 1864, Phineas Messenger Savery Papers, Duke.

23. *History of Clay*, 245, states eighteen citizens of Clay had been murdered as of January 1, 1864—four by bushwhackers, fourteen by Union Volunteers and militia.

24. Quote cited by George S. Park, March 28, 1864; *O.R.* 1: XXXIV, part 2: 759–61. Canan, 442; *O.R.* 1: XLI, part 1: 56–9, and part 2: 216, 293. Price had sent Winston and Thornton to determine if such an invasion was feasible; see Fellman, 108–9. The Union command took the notion of a conspiracy quite seriously; *O.R.* 2: VII: 228–39. As winter ended, Unionists grew nervous; on March 4, 1864, Edward M. Samuel wrote to the commander in St. Louis that the "Unconditional Union men" in Clay were "relying upon *you* to *sustain* and *stand by us* if we are *wrongfully treated*"; E. M. Samuel to Major General William Rosecrans, March 4, 1864, Provost-1.

25. Leslie, 268–301; Castel, *Quantrill*, 149–71; Frank James's presence in Sherman in the winter of 1863–64 is confirmed by a comment he made about riding back from Texas with a comrade who died in September 1864, *Columbia Herald*, September 24, 1897. See also William B. Geise, "Missouri's Confederate Capital in Marshall, Texas," *MHR* 58, no. 1 (October 1963): 37–54.

26. Leslie, 190, 192, 289, 296–7; Castel, *Quantrill*, 123, 158–72, 178; Brownlee, 138–41. Clement is best known as Bill Anderson's lieutenant, but two sources put him in Clay County with Fletcher: the very reliable *History of Clay*, 247, and the far less dependable Edwards, *Noted Guerrillas*, 237. Extensive circumstantial evidence suggests a close friendship between Jesse and Clement; see, for example, Jesse's letter to the *Kansas City Times*, August 23, 1876, Frank James's comments in the *Columbia Herald*, September 24, 1897, and a photo that may show the two posing together, Phillip W. Steele and George Warfel, *The Many Faces of Jesse James* (Gretna, La.: Pelican Publishing, 1995), 10.

27. Bodwell quoted in Fellman, 191; Frank James quoted in the *Columbia Herald*, September 24, 1897; Sergeant Colby quoted by Philip Caputo, *A Rumor of War* (New York: Ballantine, 1977), 137.

28. A photograph taken in Platte City in July 1864 shows Jesse James in a guerrilla shirt with three revolvers; see plate 10.

29. Leslie, 178–9; Michael A. Bellesiles, *Arming America: The Origins of a National Gun Culture* (New York: Alfred A. Knopf, 2000), 406–35, and "The Origins of Gun Culture in the United States, 1760–1865," *Journal of American History* 83, no. 2 (September 1996): 425–55. The Union command struggled to confiscate private arms and limit weapons sales in Missouri, while simultaneously confronting the inadequate weaponry of many EMM companies, which had to equip themselves.

30. *O.R.* 1: XXXIV, part 3: 351; McPherson, 671–6, 744.

31. James E. Kirby, Jr., "How to Become a Union General Without Military Experience," *MHR* 66, no. 3 (April 1972): 360–76.

32. *O.R.* 1: XXXIV, part 3: 366, 613, and part 4: 34; Canan, 431–48.

33. *History of Clay*, 247–8; Edwards, 364–5; Yeatman, 50–1; Castel, *Quantrill*, 135; *O.R.* 1: XLI, part 2: 252; F. Y. Hedley, "Clay County," in *Encyclopedia of the History of Missouri*, ed. Howard L. Conard (St. Louis: Southern History Company, 1901), 2: 22. Yeatman gives Bond's name as "Brantley," but both Hedley and the *History of Clay* call him "Bradley." The estate of a Brantley Bond was still being administered in October 1869, a rather late date for a man who died in 1864; see the *Liberty Tribune*, October 1, 1869. It is not clear that Jesse took part in those first two killings. Significantly, Captain Kemper believed that he had been in the brush as early as March 1864, which is possible if he first joined Colonel Thornton; see W. B. Kemper to Col. Joseph Dann, December 2, 1864, record 13681, Provost-2, and the undependable memoirs of a fellow bushwhacker, Jim Cummins, *Jim Cummins the Guerrilla* (Excelsior Springs, Mo.: Daily Journal, 1908), 49; see also Jim

Cummins, *Jim Cummins' Book Written by Himself* (Denver: Reed Publishing, 1903), 60, and his claim that he and Jesse James were among the first to join Fletch Taylor, 86.

34. Lonnie Athens, *The Creation of Dangerous Violent Criminals* (London: Routledge, 1989). For the applicability of Athens's work to a military setting, see Richard Rhodes, *Why They Kill: The Discoveries of a Maverick Criminologist* (New York: Alfred A. Knopf, 1999), 286–312. Athens's emphasis on social interactions does not preclude a biological explanation of violent behavior. Recent research has revealed how traumatic experience can permanently change brain chemistry; see, for example, Debra Niehoff, *The Biology of Violence: How Understanding the Brain, Behavior, and Environment Can Break the Vicious Circle of Aggression* (New York: Free Press, 1999), 115–49, especially 121. Scientists William R. Clark and Michael Grunstein argue that genetics contribute about 50 percent of behavior, though the exact contribution to particular behaviors is difficult to identify; see *Are We Hardwired? The Role of Genetics in Human Behavior* (New York: Oxford University Press, 2000). An important essay on atrocities in the guerrilla war in Missouri is Michael Fellman's "At the Nihilist Edge: Reflections on Guerrilla Warfare During the American Civil War," in *On the Road to Total War: The American Civil War and the German Wars of Unification, 1861–1871,* ed. Stig Forster and Jorg Nagler (New York: Cambridge University Press, 1997), 519–40.

35. The quote was supposedly from William "Bloody Bill" Anderson; see Settle, 27, 32. Zerelda commended guerrilla atrocities; see W. B. Kemper, Assistant Provost Marshal, to Col. Joseph Dann, Acting Provost Marshal General, December 2, 1864, record 13681, Provost-2, discussed below. Violentization describes Jesse James's evolving behavior far better than post-traumatic stress disorder. Though it is impossible to diagnose a mental disorder given the distance in time and scarcity of evidence, nothing indicates that Jesse suffered the symptoms associated with PTSD, such as flashbacks, nightmares, panic, or depression. See Eric T. Dean, Jr., " 'We Will All Be Lost and Destroyed': Post-Traumatic Stress Disorder and the Civil War," *CWH* 37, no. 2 (June 1991): 138–53.

36. Yeatman, 50–1, insists that Bond and Dagley hanged Reuben Samuel, which agrees with Edwards's account, 364–5 (Edwards was later close to the James brothers, so his account, though factually unreliable, may reflect their views); see also Edwards's "A Terrible Quintet," special supplement to the *St. Louis Dispatch,* November 23, 1873, vol. 34, coll. 1424, Walter B. Stevens Scrapbook, WHMC.

37. James M. McPherson, *For Cause and Comrades: Why Men Fought in the Civil War* (New York: Oxford University Press, 1997), shows how social pressure and small-unit bonding can coexist with ideological motivations. Jesse James's many letters to the newspapers in later years reflect his self-justification.

38. George Orwell, "Shooting an Elephant," *The Orwell Reader* (San Francisco: Harcourt Brace Jovanovich, 1956), 3–9.

39. Anna Slayback to M. Blythe, April 8, 1862, Watkins Mill.

40. *O.R.* 1: XXXIV, part 4: 93–5, 301–2, 320, 399–400, 434, 523; *History of Clay,* 250–1; Canan, 436.

41. *O.R.* 1: XXXIV, part 4: 399–400, and 1: XLI, part 2: 62–3.

42. Statement of Captain W. B. Kemper, file 21428, Provost-2. Kemper gave no date, but placed the event in June. Edwards, 339, describes a similar incident.

43. *History of Clay,* 230, 248–50; Edwards, 338; *O.R.* 1: XLI, part 2: 42–5, 62–3; *Liberty Tribune,* July 8, 1864. Both the unreliable Edwards and the dependable *History of Clay* describe Jesse as wounded in this fight (the *History* placing the loss of his fingertip in this incident, not in 1863).

44. *O.R.* 1: XLI, part 2: 42–5, 62–3; *History of Clay,* 250.

45. *Liberty Tribune,* July 8, 1864; *History of Clay,* 249; Fellman, 138, draws a few lines out of context to mistakenly suggest that Taylor was offering to duel with Kemper, like medieval champions. As Fellman tellingly notes, however, guerrillas concocted ranks for political legitimacy, 136.

46. *O.R.* 1: XLI, part 2: 163–4; *History of Clay,* 248, 251. Yeatman, 53, writes that the mass meeting was a protest against the Union troops; in fact, it was called at the urging of Colonel James H. Ford, the Union commander. See *O.R.* 1: XLI, part 2: 246.

47. *History of Clay,* 41; W. M. Paxton, *Annals of Platte County, Missouri* (Kansas City: Hudson-Kimberly Publishing, 1897), 367; Steele and Warfel, 25; see also plate 10, photo insert 1.

48. Canan, 440–8; Paxton, 367–9; Castel, *Quantrill,* 178; *O.R.* 1: XLI, part 1, 52–5, XLI, part 2: 152–3, 158–9, 179.

49. Edwards, 238; *O.R.* 1: XLI, part 2: 163–4. Clement is commonly thought to have been with Bill Anderson on July 11, 1864; see, for example, Castel and Goodrich, 44.

50. Mailiss to My Dear Kate, July 24, 1864, Watkins Mill. Colonel Ford had nearly five hundred Colorado and MSM cavalrymen, though the Kansas troops withdrew on July 18; *O.R.* 1: XLI, part 2: 246, 249–50.

51. *O.R.* 1: XLI, part 1, 52–5, and part 2: 252.

52. *Militia Report,* 386–7; W. B. Kemper, Assistant Provost Marshal, to Col. Joseph Dann, Acting Provost Marshal General, December 2, 1864, file 14504, Provost-2. See also Fellman, 23–65. He notes that "terror was both a method and goal"; however, his achronological, cultural approach, though rich in examples, lacks a systematic analysis of the guerrilla program of depopulation, and may overemphasize the centrality of personal revenge.

CHAPTER SEVEN: Horror

1. Albert Castel and Thomas Goodrich, *Bloody Bill Anderson: The Short, Savage Life of a Civil War Guerrilla* (Mechanicsburg, Pa.: Stackpole Books, 1998), 12, 26–44; *O.R.* 1: XLI, part 2: 75–7.

2. Castel and Goodrich, 44–7; Edward E. Leslie, *The Devil Knows How to Ride: The True Story of William Clarke Quantrill and His Confederate Raiders* (New York: Da Capo, 1998), 308–12, writes that Anderson rendezvoused with Fletch Taylor's band in Carroll County in late July. "Most of rebels have left Platte and Clay Counties," Ford reported on July 18, "and, from best information I can get, have gone into Ray"; *O.R.* 1: XLI, part 2: 246. Anderson did hit one military target, burning down a bridge on the Hannibal and St. Joseph Railroad at Shelbina; see *O.R.* 1: XLI, part 2: 421–3.

3. *Liberty Tribune,* August 12, 1864; Richard S. Brownlee, *Gray Ghosts of the Confederacy: Guerrilla Warfare in the West, 1861–1865* (Baton Rouge: Louisiana State University Press, 1958), 209; *O.R.* 1: XLI, part 1: 60–2, 177–9, and part 2: 443; Castel and Goodrich, 50–4; Yeatman, 54; Albert Castel, *William Clarke Quantrill: His Life and Times* (New York: Frederick Fell, 1962), 181; *History of Clay,* 252; John N. Edwards, *Noted Guerrillas, or the Warfare of the Border* (St. Louis: H. W. Brand, 1879), 240. On August 8, General Fisk reported that "various sources" described a large force of guerrillas concentrating in Clay County; *O.R.* 1: XLI, part 2: 608.

4. *Liberty Tribune,* June 19, 1863; E. M. Samuel to Genl. Wm. Bassett, August 9, 1864, Provost-1.

5. E. C. Catherwood to General, August 16, 1864; Clinton B. Fisk endorsement, August 23, 1864; J. M. Burnett to Genl. Fisk, August 30, 1864; file 11277, Provost-2.

6. Jim Cummins, *Jim Cummins, the Guerrilla* (Excelsior Springs, Mo.: Daily Journal, 1908), 32; Thomas M. Goodman, *A Thrilling Record* (Des Moines: Mills & Co., 1868), 30.

7. *Liberty Tribune,* August 12 and 26, 1864; *O.R.* 1: XLI, part 1: 249–50, and part 2: 622–3; Leslie, 314; Castel and Goodrich, 54.

8. Amanda Savery to Dear Mother, August 28, 1864, Phineas Messenger Savery Papers, Duke.

9. *History of Clay,* 252–3; *Columbia Herald,* September 24, 1897.

10. *Liberty Tribune,* August 12 and 19, 1864; *O.R.* 1: XLI, part 1: 249–51, and part 2: 622–3, 640, 748, 762; *History of Clay,* 253; Leslie, 314.

11. Report of Brigadier General J. B. Douglass, December 15, 1864, Missouri Militia Papers, Duke. Catherwood kept up a steady pursuit, but suffered from worn-out horses; *O.R.* 1: XLI, part 1: 249–51; Edwards, 240.

12. Thomas Riley Shouse, "My Father and Jesse James," vol. 17, coll. 995, no. 464, 1939, WHMC. Thomas Shouse's account is based on the writings of his father, John W. Shouse, who was a Confederate soldier and a neighbor and friend of Jesse James. Jesse reportedly claimed that this event occurred in the southern portion of Ray County, near the Carroll County line, which meant it must have taken place on the afternoon of August 13, according to reports on Anderson's movements; see Settle, 27, and *O.R.* 1: XLI, part 1: 249–51. Jim Cummins later claimed that he helped carry him away from "Highsinger's house"; Cummins, *Jim Cummins, the Guerrilla,* 49.

13. *Kansas City Star,* June 30, 1902. Ridge recalled that he saw Jesse at John Mimms's inn, across the river from Kansas City; it seems he conflated a later incident at the end of the war with this one (his account includes a few other inaccuracies), since it was highly unlikely that the suffering Jesse would have been shifted all the way across Ray and Clay Counties, with Union forces on the alert.

14. For Clay County (and the weather) during this period, see Kate Watkins to A. C. Smith, August 16, 1864, Watkins Mill; Charles C. Curtiss Diary, Chicago Historical Society, Chicago, Illinois, entries for August 25 and 26.

15. *O.R.* 1: XLI, part 1: 415–17, and part 3: 8; S. S. Eaton to Father, September 26, 1864, Civil War Collection, fold. 386, MHS; quote in Castel and Goodrich, 58–9.

16. For the location of his wound, see photo insert 2, plate 36. Castel and Goodrich, 153n, and Thomas Fyfer, *History of Boone County, Missouri* (St. Louis: Western Historical Company, 1882), 462, doubt his presence with the guerrillas in September. An array of sources, however, convincingly place Jesse with them at this time. See especially Frank James's emphatic insistence in the *Columbia Herald,* September 24, 1897; Dr. I. M. Ridge in *Kansas City Star,* June 30, 1902; Thomas Riley Shouse, "My Father and Jesse James," vol. 17, coll. 995, no. 464, 1939, WHMC; Cummins, *Jim Cummins, the Guerrilla,* 49; Edwards, 297; and W. B. Kemper to Col. Joseph Dann, Acting Provost Marshal General, December 2, 1864, record 13681, Provost-2.

17. Castel and Goodrich, 59–60, seem to confuse the circumstances of the killing of the tax collectors with those of the six men on September 23; my account follows S. S. Eaton to Father, September 26, 1864, fold. 386, Civil War Collection, MHS. For Anderson's horse, see testimony of Paris Bass, quoted in Fellman, 71.

18. Castel and Goodrich, 60; Leslie, 315–17.

19. Cummins, *Jim Cummins, the Guerrilla,* 49, states, "He [Jesse] and I, with Arch Clemmens [sic], were in advance of Anderson's command when we went into Fayette"—a plausible statement from an unreliable source.

20. *O.R.* 1: XLI, part 1: 415–17; S. S. Eaton to Father, September 26, 1864, fold. 386, Civil War Collection, MHS; *Columbia Herald,* September 24, 1897; Castel and Goodrich, 1–5, 60–1; Hemp B. Watts quoted in Leslie, 317–8; Yeatman, 54; John McCorkle, as told to O. S. Barton, *Three Years with Quantrell: A True Story* (Armstrong, Mo.: Armstrong Herald Print, n.d.), 111–12.

21. McPherson, *Battle Cry,* 653, 664, 724, 744, 777. For a discussion of the guerrillas' numbers, see Fyfer, 440, and Castel and Goodrich, 70.

22. Robert W. Duffner, "Guerrilla Victory at Centralia, September 27, 1864," *Bulletin of the Missouri Historical Society* 29, no. 3 (April 1973): 312–44; Brownlee, 216; Cummins, *Jim Cummins, the Guerrilla,* 6.

23. Fyfer, 440–1; Castel and Goodrich, 70. Castel and Goodrich's account of the ensuing events is very good, though it suffers from an overuse of ellipses.

24. The quotations given here appear in primary sources. Most cannot be considered literally accurate, but various sources affirm their general tone and content.

25. Quotes from Fyfer, 441–4. The account that follows is based in particular on Castel and Goodrich, 73–86; Fyfer, 445–52; Goodman, 21–8; and the *St. Louis Democrat,* October 4, 1864.

26. Fyfer, 446.

27. Goodman, 22.

28. Ibid.

29. Fyfer, 447; *Columbia Herald,* September 24, 1897.

30. Fyfer, 447.

31. Goodman, 23.

32. *St. Louis Missouri Democrat,* October 4, 1864.

33. Fyfer, 449.

34. *St. Louis Missouri Democrat,* October 4, 1864.

35. Fyfer, 449; Goodman, 24. They also wrecked a construction train afterward.

36. Sister Kate to My Dear Brother, September 25, 1864, Watkins Mill.

37. *Liberty Tribune,* September 23, 1864; W. B. Kemper, Assistant Provost Marshal, to Col. Joseph Dann, Acting Provost Marshal General, December 2, 1864, file 13681, Provost-2. Kemper's

conclusions were endorsed by the ubiquitous Edward M. Samuel. Kemper's assessment was grave indeed, considering Union soldiers' wariness of secessionist women in general; see Michael Fellman, "Women and Guerrilla Warfare," in *Divided Houses: Gender and the Civil War*, ed. Catherine Clinton and Nina Silber (New York: Oxford University Press, 1992), 147–65.

38. Goodman, 26–30.

39. Goodman, 31–2; Castel and Goodrich, 87–90.

40. Castel and Goodrich, 70–2, 88–9; *O.R.* 1: XLI, part 1: 432–3. Johnston discussed the situation with leading citizens, who urged him to stay put (Fyfer, 545); Castel and Goodrich argue that the major had little choice but to pursue the guerrillas.

41. Castel and Goodrich, 90–5; Fyfer, 454–65; see also Goodman, 31–2, McCorkle, 114–5, and Duffner, "Guerrilla Victory," 131–44. Frank James was most emphatic about Jesse's presence, *Columbia Herald*, September 24, 1897.

42. McPherson, 471–7. They were also commonly called Springfield or Enfield rifles, after their manufacturing sites.

43. Quote from *Columbia Herald*, September 24, 1897; Robert L. O'Connell, *Of Arms and Men: A History of War, Weapons, and Aggression* (New York: Oxford University Press, 1989), 199–200.

44. Fyfer, 457–8.

45. Johnston's revolver was found with three empty chambers; Fyfer, 460–2; Goodman, 33–4.

46. McCorkle, 115. Frank James insisted that his brother killed Johnston (*Columbia Herald*, September 24, 1897), a claim made earlier by John N. Edwards, *Noted Guerrillas*, 300. As Castel and Goodrich correctly argue, no one could be sure who shot him; but the James brothers clearly believed that Jesse did, indicating at the very least that Jesse was near the center of the line and aimed for Johnston. Fyfer, 461, describes Shepherd as nearly seven feet tall, which helps account for why he got hit (in the head) when the Federals fired high.

47. *Columbia Herald*, September 24, 1897; *O.R.* 1: LXI, part 1: 440–1; Goodman, 33; Castel and Goodrich, 95; Fyfer, 462. In 1882, Frank James would display a belt he "captured" at Centralia, saying "it's as good yet as the day I got it"; *Nashville American*, October 9, 1882.

48. "Sadistic fiends" is from Castel, *Quantrill*, 192; see Fellman, 213–14; Eugene B. Sledge, *With the Old Breed* (New York: Oxford University Press, 1992), an excellent memoir of the Marines in World War II. Both Fellman and Mark Grimsley argue that the ethnic, religious, and racial similarity of most combatants helped limit the severity of the war in general; see Grimsley, *The Hard Hand of War: Union Military Policy Toward Southern Civilians, 1861–1865* (New York: Cambridge University Press, 1995), 224; and Michael Fellman, "At the Nihilist Edge: Reflections on Guerrilla Warfare During the American Civil War," in *On the Road to Total War: The American Civil War and the German Wars of Unification, 1861–1871*, ed. Stig Forster and Jorg Nagler (New York: Cambridge University Press, 1997), 519–40. This makes such incidents as Centralia all the more remarkable.

49. Goodman, 36.

CHAPTER EIGHT: Exile

1. Stephen B. Oates, *Confederate Cavalry West of the River* (Austin: University of Texas Press, 1961), 140–4; Joseph Conan Thompson, "The Great-Little Battle of Pilot Knob," part 1, *MHR* 83, no. 2 (January 1989): 139–60; Albert Castel, *General Sterling Price and the Civil War in the West* (Baton Rouge: Louisiana State University Press, 1968), 190–207; *O.R.* 1: XXXIV, part 2: 1029, and 1: XLI, part 2: 1023–4, 1040–1.

2. *O.R.* 1: XLI, part 2: 1040.

3. James M. McPherson, *Battle Cry of Freedom: The Civil War Era* (New York: Oxford University Press, 1988), 756–61, 774, 786–8. It should be noted that Price's campaign only became possible after Major General Richard Taylor defeated a Union force on the Red River in Louisiana in April; Alvin M. Josephy, Jr., *The Civil War in the American West* (New York: Alfred A. Knopf, 1991), 191–224.

4. Josephy, 375.

5. John N. Edwards, *Shelby and His Men: or, The War in the West* (Cincinnati: Miami Printing and Publishing, 1867), 11.

6. Major J. F. Stonestreet, quoted in Rev. George Plattenburg, "John Newman Edwards: Biographical Sketch," in *John N. Edwards: Biography, Memoirs, Reminiscences, and Recollections*, ed. Jennie Edwards (Kansas City: Jennie Edwards, 1889), 15, also 9–11; Castel, *Price*, 205; *O.R.* 1: XLI, part 1: 718; F. Y. Hedley, "John Newman Edwards," in *Encyclopedia of the History of Missouri*, ed. Howard L. Conard (St. Louis: Southern History Company, 1901), 2: 354–6; Dan Saults, "Let Us Discuss a Man: A Study of John Newman Edwards," *Bulletin of the Missouri Historical Society* 19, no. 2 (January 1963): 150–60.

7. Oates, 144; Thompson, 141–3.

8. Thompson, 147; *O.R.* 1: XLI, part 2: 967.

9. Thompson, 148–60.

10. Joseph Conan Thompson, "The Great-Little Battle of Pilot Knob," part 2, *MHR* 83, no. 2 (January 1989): 169–94; Castel, *Price*, 208–21; *O.R.* 1: XLI, part 1: 307–9.

11. Albert Castel, *William Clarke Quantrill: His Life and Times* (New York: Frederick Fell, 1962), 196.

12. *O.R.* 1: XLI, part 1: 415–18; *St. Joseph Herald & Tribune*, October 14, 1864; Thomas M. Goodman, *A Thrilling Record* (Des Moines: Mills & Co., 1868), 36–53; John McCorkle, as told to O. S. Barton, *Three Years with Quantrell: A True Story* (Armstrong, Mo.: Armstrong Herald, n.d.), 116.

13. Fellman, 111; Castel, *Quantrill*, 196; Albert Castel and Thomas Goodrich, *Bloody Bill Anderson: The Short, Savage Life of a Civil War Guerrilla* (Mechanicsburg, Pa.: Stackpole Books, 1998), 113–14.

14. Edwards, *Shelby*, 398. This passage does not seem much of a defense, of course, but its acceptance of "murder" underscores Missouri's bitter divisions.

15. Castel, *Price*, 222–8; Edwards, *Shelby*, 471; *O.R.* 1: XLI, part 1: 419. See also John N. Edwards and R. I. Laurence to Thomas C. Reynolds, May 17, 1866, typescript copy, Reynolds Collection, MHS.

16. Oates, 142, 146; *O.R.* 1: XLI, part 2: 1040; Robert E. Miller, " 'One of the Ruling Class': Thomas Caute Reynolds, Second Confederate Governor of Missouri," *MHR* 80, no. 4 (July 1986): 422–48.

17. *O.R.* 1: XLI, part 4: 354.

18. *O.R.* 1: XLI, part 1: 432, 659–62, and part 3: 893; Richard S. Brownlee, *Gray Ghosts of the Confederacy: Guerrilla Warfare in the West, 1861–1865* (Baton Rouge: Louisiana State University Press, 1958), 225; Castel and Goodrich, 114–22; *Richmond Missourian*, June 6, 1938.

19. *O.R.* 1: XLI, part 1: 423–4; Castel and Goodrich, 120; Brownlee, 225–8.

20. Diary of Thomas Hankins, excerpted in *Richmond Missourian*, June 6 and 13, 1938.

21. S. Harlan to Mother and Father, November 1, 1864, Bond-Fentriss Family Papers, UNC.

22. Brownlee, 227–8.

23. Ibid.; diary of Thomas Hankins, *Richmond Missourian*, June 20, 1938.

24. *O.R.* 1: XLI, part 1: 52–5; *Kansas City Star*, August 13, 1913; Castel and Goodrich, 124.

25. *O.R.* 1: XLI, Part 1: 442; Yeatman, 57–8; diary of Thomas Hankins, *Richmond Missourian*, June 20 and 27, 1938.

26. Castel and Goodrich, 125–30; *Kansas City Star*, August 13, 1913; Brownlee, 227–30; Yeatman, 57–8.

27. Oates, 148–52; Castel, *Price*, 229–49; McPherson, 787–8.

28. Edward E. Leslie, *The Devil Knows How to Ride: The True Story of William Clarke Quantrill and His Confederate Raiders* (New York: Da Capo Press, 1998), 334; Castel, *Quantrill*, 197–8; Robert W. Frizzell, " 'Killed by Rebels': A Civil War Massacre and its Aftermath," *MHR* 71, no. 4 (July 1977): 369–95.

29. S. Harlan to Mother and Father, November 1, 1864, Bond-Fentriss Family Papers, UNC; Fellman, 28–9, cites this same letter, but mistakenly places these events in Chariton County. See also *History of Clay*, 254, 256; and E. M. Samuel to Col. Jos. Dann, Jr., Acting Provost Marshal General, November 29, 1864, record 1209, and E. M. Samuel to Col. Joseph Dann, Jr., December 10, 1864, Provost-1.

30. It is generally believed that the brothers parted ways after both met Quantrill in December, an idea contradicted somewhat by Faucett's account; Statement of Ralph Faucett, January 20, 1865, file 21428, Provost-2; McCorkle, 128–35; Leslie, 341–4; Castel, *Quantrill*, 201–7; Yeatman, 59–61.

31. W. B. Kemper, Assistant Provost Marshal, to Col. Joseph Dann, Acting Provost Marshal General, December 2, 1864, E. M. Samuel and James M. Jones to Col. Jos. Dann, Jr., December 2, 1864, File 13681, J. W. Barnes to Brig. Genl. C. B. Fisk, January 9, 1865, and General Order No. 9, file 14504, Provost-2.

32. *Liberty Tribune*, February 5, 1865; Settle, 30; Yeatman, 63.

33. William Lamb, "The Defense of Fort Fisher," in *Battles and Leaders of the Civil War*, ed. Clarence Clough Buel and Robert Underwood Johnson (New York: Century Co., 1887), 4: 642–54; McPherson, 820. The most comprehensive work on the battle for Fort Fisher is Rod Gragg, *Confederate Goliath: The Battle of Fort Fisher* (Baton Rouge: Louisiana State University Press, 1991). Unfortunately, Gragg unquestioningly accepts the criticisms of Colonel Newton Curtis, Ames's subordinate and personal rival, who was knocked unconscious an hour into the battle yet claimed credit for crafting the final victory. See also Adelbert Ames, "The Capture of Fort Fisher," in *Civil War Papers* (Boston: The Commandery, 1890), and *O.R.* 1: XLVI, part I: 393–425.

34. Letter dated February 9, 1865, quoted in Blanche Ames Ames, *Adelbert Ames, 1835–1933: General, Senator, Governor* (London: MacDonald, 1964), 68–88, 201.

35. Stephen W. Sears, *To the Gates of Richmond: The Peninsula Campaign* (Boston: Houghton Mifflin, 1992), 325; John J. Pullen, *The Twentieth Maine: A Volunteer Regiment in the Civil War* (Philadelphia: J. B. Lippincott, 1957), 3–4, 18–9, 37–8, 131, 170; *Chronicles from the Nineteenth Century: Family Letters of Blanche Butler and Adelbert Ames*, comp. Blanche Butler Ames (Clinton, Mass.: n.p., 1957), 1: 10–20; Harry W. Pfanz, *Gettysburg: Culp's Hill and Cemetery Hill* (Chapel Hill: University of North Carolina Press, 1993), 248–9, 252–62, 268–75; Charles P. Hamblen, *Connecticut Yankees at Gettysburg* (Kent, Ohio: Kent State University Press, 1993), 18; A. Wilson Greene, "From Chancellorsville to Cemetery Hill: O. O. Howard and Eleventh Corps Leadership," in *The First Day at Gettysburg: Essays on Confederate and Union Leadership*, ed. Gary W. Gallagher (Kent, Ohio: Kent State University Press, 1992), 77–81; Allan Nevins, ed., *A Diary of Battle: The Personal Journals of Colonel Charles S. Wainwright, 1861–1865* (New York: Da Capo, 1998), 242; *New York Herald*, February 6, 1897. The assault on Fort Wagner was memorialized in the movie *Glory*.

36. Merlin E. Sumner, ed., *The Diary of Cyrus B. Comstock* (Dayton, Ohio: Morningside, 1987), 303; Adelbert Ames, "The Capture of Fort Fisher," 283; quote in Ames, 191–2; Lamb, 650.

37. Sumner, 304; *O.R.*, 1: XLIV, part 2: 410–11, 414–15.

38. Ames Ames, 200; George Rawick, ed., *The American Slave: A Composite Autobiography* (Westport, Conn.: Greenwood, 1979), 11: 379–82; Becky Carlson, " 'Manumitted and Forever Set Free': The Children of Charles Lee Younger and Elizabeth, a Woman of Color," *MHR* 96, no. 1 (October 2001): 16–31. It should be noted that emancipation had just been declared in Missouri; see chap. 9.

39. McPherson, 810–5, 825–30, 844–9.

40. Andrew Rolle, *The Lost Cause: The Confederate Exodus to Mexico* (Norman: University of Oklahoma Press, 1965), 15–20.

PART THREE: DEFIANCE
CHAPTER NINE: A Year of Bitterness

1. James M. McPherson, *Battle Cry of Freedom: The Civil War Era* (New York: Oxford University Press, 1988), 852–3.

2. S. P. Harlan to Brother, April 12, 1865, Bond-Fentriss Family Papers, UNC.

3. Sarah P. Harlan to Sister, April 19, 1865, Bond-Fentriss Family Papers, UNC.

4. *O.R.* 1: XLVIII, part 2: 215.

5. *O.R.* 1: XLVIII, part 2: 323–5.

6. John N. Edwards, *Noted Guerrillas, or the Warfare of the Border* (St. Louis: H. W. Brand & Co., 1879), 332; Albert Castel and Thomas Goodrich, *Bloody Bill Anderson: The Short, Savage Life*

of a Civil War Guerrilla (Mechanicsburg, Pa.: Stackpole Books, 1998), 133; Albert Castel, *William Clarke Quantrill: His Life and Times* (New York: Frederick Fell, 1962), 217; Yeatman, 72–3.

7. *St. Louis Globe-Democrat,* August 24, 1876.

8. *Kansas City Daily Journal of Commerce,* May 12, 1865; *O.R.* 1: XLVIII, part 2: 410–1; Castel, *Quantrill,* 217; Yeatman, 74; *Kansas City Daily Journal of Commerce,* May 13, 1865; Nathan H. Parker, *Missouri as it is in 1867* (Philadelphia: J. B. Lippincott, 1867), 63.

9. *Kansas City Daily Journal of Commerce,* May 10–12, 1865; *O.R.* 1: XLVIII, part 2: 323–5; Castel and Goodrich, 133–4; Yeatman, 73–4; Edwards, 332–3.

10. *O.R.* 1: XLVIII, part 2: 323–5, 404–5, 410–1, 420–2.

11. The military offered full amnesty, but this did not extend to any civil charges that might be filed. Edwards, 333, describes an intense debate in the guerrilla camp; though his narrative is often questionable, this particular claim rings true.

12. *O.R.* 1: XLVIII, part 2: 420–2, 470.

13. Thomas Riley Shouse, "My Father and Jesse James," manuscript dated 1939, vol. 17, coll. 995, no. 464, WHMC; *St. Louis Republican,* April 27, 1882; Yeatman, 75–6; Settle, 30. Yeatman, 76, presents evidence that the man who shot Jesse James was Private John J. Jones, a twenty-one-year-old Welsh immigrant in Company I.

14. The bullet was found in Jesse James's remains when his body was exhumed, July to September 1995; see Yeatman, 371–6; *Kearney Courier,* special edition (n.d.); quote from Shouse manuscript.

15. John N. Edwards, "A Terrible Quintet," special supplement to the *St. Louis Dispatch,* November 23, 1873, vol. 34, coll. 1424, Walter B. Stevens Scrapbook, WHMC; *St. Louis Republican,* April 27, 1882; Yeatman, 77.

16. Edwards, "A Terrible Quintet"; Yeatman, 77, 83–4; *History of Clay,* 268; Edwards, *Noted Guerrillas,* 449; Settle, 31.

17. Ante Petricevic, Nenad Ilic, Zeljko Mimica, Mirko Petricevic, and Jozo Ivancevic, "War Wounds of the Lungs Treated in Rama, Bosnia and Herzegovina," *Croatian Medical Journal* 38, no. 1 (1997); see *History of Clay,* 268, and the account of Zerelda Mimms's brother, T. W. Mimms, in the *Kansas City Daily Journal of Commerce,* April 5, 1882.

18. See, for example, accounts by John Groom, *Liberty Tribune,* July 22, 1870, and W. H. Ridge and W. J. Courtney, *St. Louis Republican,* April 7, 1882.

19. McPherson, 839, 854; Eric Foner, *Reconstruction, 1863–1877: America's Unfinished Revolution* (New York: Harper & Row, 1988), 11–8, 66.

20. Fellman, 242; Foner, 19; for Northern wartime expansion in general, see McPherson, 816–9. The state census of 1864 calculated a loss of 262,146, a number that certainly grew in the aftermath of Price's invasion and subsequent Union countermeasures; James Fernando Ellis, *The Influence of Environment on the Settlement of Missouri* (St. Louis: Webster Publishing, 1929), 144–5.

21. *History of Clay,* 255, 265; A. G. Savery to Husband, June 18, 1865, A. G. Savery to Husband, July 1, 1865, Phineas Messenger Savery Papers, Duke; see also P. M. Savery to My Dear Wife, June 10, 1865 (same collection), and Sarah P. Harlan to Brother, April 12, 1865, Bond-Fentriss Family Papers, UNC.

22. This discussion of Missouri's late-war and early-postwar politics relies on several sources. Most important is William E. Parrish, *Missouri Under Radical Rule, 1865–1870* (Columbia: University of Missouri Press, 1965), 1–12, 45–6. See also Foner, 41–2; Christopher Phillips, *Missouri's Confederate: Claiborne Fox Jackson and the Creation of Southern Identity in the Border West* (Columbia: University of Missouri Press, 2000), 285–92; William E. Parrish, *Frank Blair: Lincoln's Conservative* (Columbia: University of Missouri Press, 1998), 230–40; Michael Fellman, "Emancipation in Missouri," *MHR* 83, no. 1 (October 1988): 36–56; John Starrett Hughes, "Lafayette County and the Aftermath of Slavery, 1861–1870," *MHR* 75, no. 1 (October 1980): 51–63; and Robert M. Crisler, "Republican Areas of Missouri," *MHR* 42, no. 4 (July 1948): 299–309. In an important study, Mark Grimsley overlooks the unusual role of civilian politics in shaping Union military policies in Missouri, a result of the large local role in military affairs in the state; see Mark Grimsley, *The Hard Hand of War: Union Military Policy Toward Southern Civilians, 1861–1865* (New York: Cambridge University Press, 1995), 36–52.

23. William E. Parrish, "Reconstruction Politics in Missouri, 1865–1870," in *Radicalism, Racism, and Party Realignment: The Border States During Reconstruction*, ed. Richard O. Curry (Baltimore: Johns Hopkins University Press, 1969), 1–35; John H. Reppy, "Thomas Clement Fletcher," in Shoemaker, 4: 43–52.

24. Parrish, *Radical*, 13–8; David D. March, "Charles D. Drake and the Constitutional Convention of 1865," *MHR* 47, no. 2 (January 1953): 110–23; Lorenzo J. Greene, Gary R. Kremer, and Antonio F. Holland, *Missouri's Black Heritage*, rev. ed. (Columbia: University of Missouri Press, 1993), 88; Sarah McDonald to Dear Children, January 18, 1865, coll. 1012, fold. 1, Charles B. France Papers, WHMC. With tens of thousands of black Missourians still enslaved (a large percentage of them women and children), it is clear that four years of war had badly damaged, but not "virtually destroyed," slavery in the state, as argued in Ira Berlin, Steven F. Miller, Joseph P. Reidy, and Leslie S. Rowland, eds., *Freedom: A Documentary History of Emancipation: 1861–1867* (New York: Cambridge University Press, 1993), ser. 1, 2: 551.

25. Parrish, *Radical*, 20–33; March, 110–23; Foner, 41–2. Traditionally, Radical Reconstruction in Missouri has been castigated by historians, a local reflection of the scholarly reaction against Reconstruction that followed the late-nineteenth-century triumph of white supremacy. A more balanced view of Missouri's case began to emerge in the 1960s in Parrish's work and Fred DeArmond's "Reconstruction in Missouri," *MHR* 61, no. 3 (April 1967): 364–77—still a valuable reappraisal.

26. Foner, *Reconstruction*, 32; Parrish, *Radical*, 18.

27. Parrish, *Radical*, 25, 33–6; D. Peterson to Brother, August 7, 1866, Jane Peterson Papers, Duke; Martha Kohl, "Enforcing a Vision of Community: The Role of the Test Oath in Missouri's Reconstruction," *CWH* 40, no. 4 (December 1994): 292–307.

28. David D. March, "The Campaign for the Ratification of the Constitution of 1865," *MHR* 47, no. 3 (April 1953): 223–32; Kohl, 294–301. For a discussion of the free-labor critique of slavery, see chap. 3, and, especially, Eric Foner, *Free Soil, Free Labor, Free Men: The Ideology of the Republican Party Before the Civil War* (New York: Oxford University Press, 1995, orig. pub. 1970).

29. Foner, *Reconstruction*, 60–1; John Glendower Westover, "The Evolution of the Missouri Militia, 1804–1919" (Ph.D. diss., University of Missouri, 1948), 171–2; *Kansas City Daily Journal of Commerce*, May 11, 1865; Kohl asserts, quite correctly, "The popularity of the test oath in 1865 among Unionists—especially in rural Missouri where the fighting had been fiercest—cannot be overestimated," 294.

30. Joseph Dixon to Hon. Thomas C. Fletcher, March 17, 1865, Thomas C. Fletcher Papers, MSA; Parrish, *Radical*, 29–33, 45–6; March, "Campaign," 223–32.

31. A. G. Savery to Husband, June 18, 1865, Phineas Messenger Savery Papers, Duke.

32. *Lexington Caucasian*, May 2, 1866, and October 17, 1866. See also Thomas S. Barclay, *The Liberal Republican Movement in Missouri, 1865–1871* (Columbia: State Historical Society of Missouri, 1926), 48–9.

33. The starting point of the discussion that follows is Michael Fellman's excellent analysis of postwar violence and enmities in *Inside War*, 231–47.

34. S. P. Harlan to Mother and Father, June 9, 1865, Bond-Fentriss Family Papers, UNC; *History of Clay*, 257.

35. A. G. Savery to Husband, June 18, 1865, A. G. Savery to Husband, July 1, 1865, Phineas Messenger Savery Papers, Duke.

36. Fellman, 237; Richard Maxwell Brown, *No Duty to Retreat: Violence and Values in American Society* (New York: Oxford University Press, 1991), 59–62; Joseph G. Rosa, *They Called Him Wild Bill: The Life and Adventures of James Butler Hickok* (Norman: University of Oklahoma Press, 1974), 72–9.

37. George Miller, *Missouri's Memorable Decade, 1860–1870* (Columbia, Mo.: E. W. Stephens, 1898); S. P. Harlan to Sister, June 16, 1866, Bond-Fentriss Family Papers, UNC.

38. Edith Abbott, "The Civil War and the Crime Wave of 1865–1870," *Social Service Review* 1, no. 2 (June 1927): 212–34; Ted Robert Gurr, "On the History of Violent Crime in Europe and America," in *Violence in America: Historical and Comparative Perspectives*, ed. Hugh Davis Graham and Ted Robert Gurr (Beverly Hills: Sage, 1979); Lonnie Athens, *The Creation of Dangerous Violent*

Criminals (London: Routledge, 1989). Richard Rhodes applies Athens's work to the military setting in *Why They Kill: The Discoveries of a Maverick Criminologist* (New York: Alfred A. Knopf, 1999), 286–312. Many veterans may have suffered post-traumatic stress disorder, though this concept does not fit Jesse James and his fellow guerrillas; see Eric T. Dean, Jr., " 'We Will All Be Lost and Destroyed': Post-Traumatic Stress Disorder and the Civil War," *CWH* 37, no. 2 (June 1991): 138–53.

39. Bertram Wyatt-Brown, *Southern Honor: Ethics and Behavior in the Old South* (New York: Oxford University Press, 1982), 350–61; Bertram Wyatt-Brown, "Dueling," and Andrew Kevin Frank, "South," in *Violence in America: An Encyclopedia,* ed. Ronald Gottesman (New York: Charles Scribner's Sons, 1999), 1: 445–7, 3: 183–9; Elliot J. Gorn, " 'Gouge and Bite, Pull Hair and Scratch': The Social Significance of Fighting in the Southern Backcountry," *American Historical Review* 90, no. 1 (February 1985): 18–43; David Hackett Fischer, *Albion's Seed: Four British Folkways in America* (New York: Oxford University Press, 1989), 765–71. In *Duels and the Roots of Violence in Missouri* (Columbia, Mo.: University of Missouri Press, 2000), Dick Steward shows how dueling was a means of social advancement in antebellum Missouri and influenced other forms of violence, which were widespread.

40. Michael A. Bellesiles, "The Origins of Gun Culture in the United States, 1760–1865," *Journal of American History* 83, no. 2 (September 1996): 425–55, and *Arming America: The Origins of the National Gun Culture* (New York: Alfred A. Knopf, 2000), 377–81 (the strongest part of Bellesiles's controversial work is his treatment of the Civil War and its aftermath, which has not received the same criticism as his conclusions about the colonial period); T. J. Stiles, ed., *Robber Barons and Radicals: Reconstruction and the Origin of Civil Rights* (New York: Berkley, 1997), 26; *St. Louis Republican,* November 10, 1866. As late as 1875, Charles Nordhoff would be startled by the prevalence of arms wearing in the South; Otis A. Stingletary, *Negro Militia and Reconstruction* (New York: McGraw-Hill/University of Texas Press, 1971), 3.

41. 2nd Lieutenant James B. Burbank to General, October 25, 1866, B 232, Department of the Missouri, Letters Received 1861–1867, entry 2395, RG 393, part 1, NA; Dan to Brother, May 17, 1866, Jane Peterson Papers, Duke. Elliot J. Gorn, " 'Gouge,' " correctly attributes the decline of rough-and-tumble fighting to the spread of firearms, but incorrectly dates this well before the Civil War. Gun manufacturers began to petition for permission to sell weapons and ammunition in Missouri less than a month after Appomattox (which was granted), *O.R.* 1: XLVIII, part 2: 322.

42. Parrish, *Radical,* 29–33, 45–6; Radical Union Men of Ray County to His Excellency, Thomas C. Fletcher, February 24, 1865, Joseph E. Black and D. P. Whitmer to Col. A. J. Barr, March 18, 1865, and A. J. Barr to His Excellency Governor Thomas C. Fletcher, March 19, 1865, Thomas C. Fletcher Papers, MSA.

43. *History of Clay,* 259; Parrish, *Radical,* 58–61.

44. Parrish, *Radical,* 29–33, 45–6, 61–5.

45. Kohl, 297; Fellman, 233, 237–8; *Kansas City Daily Journal of Commerce,* July 2, 1865; *Lexington Caucasian,* April 28, 1866.

46. Foner, *Reconstruction,* 9, 119–23; see also *Report of the Joint Committee on Reconstruction at the First Session, Thirty-Ninth Congress* (Westport, Conn.: Negro Universities Press, 1969, orig. pub. 1866); Barry Crouch, "A Spirit of Lawlessness: White Violence, Texas Blacks, 1865–1868," in *Black Freedom/White Violence, 1865–1900,* ed. Donald G. Nieman (New York: Garland, 1994), 51–65. George C. Rable, *But There Was No Peace: The Role of Violence in the Politics of Reconstruction* (Athens: University of Georgia Press, 1984), xi, writes that whites "found an outlet for their frustration by attacking those deemed responsible for their suffering: white Republicans and blacks." Gaines M. Foster, in *Ghosts of the Confederacy: Defeat, the Lost Cause, and the Emergence of the New South, 1865 to 1913* (New York: Oxford University Press, 1987), 22–35, argues that the South suffered deep shame and a sense of a loss of manhood, an argument that actually bolsters Rable's point. For a classic study of the grassroots fight between Fascists and socialists in post–World War I Italy, see Paul Corner, *Fascism in Ferrara, 1915–1925* (Oxford: Oxford University Press, 1975). For an important study in the German context, see Eve Rosenhaft, *Beating the Fascists? The German Communists and Political Violence, 1929–1933* (Cambridge: Cambridge University Press, 1983).

47. Parrish, *Radical,* 106–7; *History III,* 152–3; Greene, Kremer, and Holland, 81; Fellman,

"Emancipation," 50; Phillips, *Missouri's Confederate*, 285–8. For an excellent brief discussion of the outbreak of violence against freed people in Missouri, see Berlin et al., 562–3.

48. Rogers quoted in Fellman, 236; *O.R.* 1: XLVIII, part 1: 239; part 2: 669, 738; Castel and Goodrich, 136; Andrew M. Hamilton to Andrew Johnson, March 1, 1866, in *The Papers of Andrew Johnson*, ed. Paul H. Bergeron (Knoxville: University of Tennessee Press, 1992), 10: 202–3. See also Hughes, 51–63.

49. Edwards, "A Terrible Quintet"; Yeatman, 77, 83–4; *History of Clay*, 268; Settle, 31. The presence of a young woman is suggested by both the list of slaves on the farm in 1860 (see chap. 3), and the fact that someone on the farm gave birth to a biracial boy in 1868, at a time when Charlotte was possibly too old to bear a child; see the U.S. Census for Clay County, 1870, 1880, and 1890.

50. Edwards, "A Terrible Quintet"; in their two-year study, Petricevic et al. found pneumothorax in only 7.8 percent of war wounds of the lung; Yeatman, 71, 80.

51. *St. Louis Republican*, April 7, 1882; *Liberty Tribune*, July 22, 1870.

52. *St. Joseph Gazette*, December 17, 1869.

53. Edwards, *Noted Guerrillas*, 449; S. P. Harlan to Mother and Father, November 1, 1864, Bond-Fentriss Family Papers, UNC; Proverbs 28:1.

54. William A. Pinkerton, *Train Robberies, Train Robbers, and the "Holdup" Men* (New York: Arno Press, 1974, orig. pub. 1907), 11–16. The *History of Clay*, 268, notes that the James brothers reunited with their old comrades. James Pool became a candidate for sheriff of Lafayette County in 1866; see next chapter for a full discussion.

55. Republican Central Committee Meeting, Clay County, January 1, 1866, coll. 970, fold. 161, Clarence W. Alvord and Idress Head Collection, WHMC; Republican Central Committee of Clay County to Governor Thomas C. Fletcher, January 3, 1866, Thomas C. Fletcher Papers, MSA; *Liberty Tribune*, June 2, 1865; for rebel grumbling, see M. Scruggs to Son, January 30, 1866, Watkins Mill.

CHAPTER TEN: The Guerrillas Return

1. On the concentration of Radical Unionists in towns during the war, see Joseph Dixon to Hon. Thomas C. Fletcher, March 17, 1865, Thomas C. Fletcher Papers, MSA, and *History of Clay*, 252–60.

2. In addition to Love, Sheriff James M. Jones and county clerk William Brining served as directors. *Liberty Tribune*, June 18, 1863, June 2, 1865, February 16, 1866, September 24 and October 1, 1869, August 5, 1870; advertisement of E. M. Samuel, commission and forwarding merchant, 106 North 2nd Street, St. Louis, April 24, 1866, coll. 970, fold. 107, Clarence W. Alvord and Idress Head Collection, WHMC; E. M. Samuel to Col. Jos. Dann, Jr., Acting Provost Marshal General, November 29, 1864, record 1209, and E. M. Samuel to Col. Joseph Dann, Jr., December 10, 1864, Provost-1. A list of depositors and borrowers includes many leading Republicans, strongly reinforcing the notion that the bank was a distinctly Radical institution; it also seems to have lent E. M. Samuel $81.72 to establish his business in St. Louis; Greenup Bird, "Clay County Savings Association Robbery Description, 1866," typed copy, coll. 693, WHMC. The Farmer's Bank of Missouri was based in Lexington, where it originated as a branch of the State Bank of Missouri; William Young, *Young's History of Lafayette County, Missouri* (Indianapolis: B. F. Bowen, 1910), 302–3.

3. Lewis E. Davids and Timothy W. Hubbard, *Banking in Mid-America: A History of Missouri's Banks* (Washington, D.C.: Public Affairs Press, 1969), 97; Irwin Unger, *The Greenback Era: A Social and Political History of American Finance, 1865–1879* (Princeton: Princeton University Press, 1964), 17. See also Esther Rogoff Taus, *Central Banking Functions of the United States Treasury, 1789–1941* (New York: Columbia University Press, 1943), 26–7, for a discussion of discounting. Harry S. Gleick, "Banking in Early Missouri," parts 1 and 2, *MHR* 61, no. 4 (July 1967): 427–43, and 62, no. 1 (October 1967): 30–44, discusses antebellum Missouri. The quote from the *St. Louis Democrat* was in the *Kansas City Daily Journal of Commerce*, April 14, 1873. For a concise, general overview of the changes in American money, see the author's "As Good as Gold?," *Smithsonian* 31, no. 6 (September 2000): 106–17. Note that silver was officially a legal-tender precious metal, but the effects of Gresh-

am's Law drove it out of circulation.

4. Herman E. Kroos, ed., *Documentary History of Banking and Currency in the United States* (New York: Chelsea House Publishers, 1965), 1315–6. The extent of the government's role in the suspension of gold payments is disputed by historians, but certainly it played a role; Robert P. Sharkey, *Money, Class, and Party: An Economic Study of Civil War and Reconstruction* (Baltimore: The Johns Hopkins University Press, 1959), 15–28; James K. Kindahl, "Economic Factors in Specie Resumption, 1865–1879," in *The Reinterpretation of American Economic History*, ed. Stanley L. Engerman and Robert W. Fogel (New York: Harper & Row, 1971), 468–79; also Unger, 13–14. See also Milton Friedman and Anna Jacobson Schwartz, *A Monetary History of the United States, 1867–1960* (Princeton: Princeton University Press, 1963), 3–14.

5. Sharkey, 28–50; James M. McPherson, *Battle Cry of Freedom: The Civil War Era* (New York: Oxford University Press, 1988), 442–50; John Jay Knox, *A History of Banking in the United States* (New York: Augustus M. Kelley, 1969, orig. pub. 1903), 91–104. In addition to federal restrictions, the new Missouri constitution of 1865 denied state banks the right to issue notes, and required laws to enable them to reorganize as national banks; see Isidor Loeb, "Constitutions and Constitutional Conventions in Missouri," *MHR* 16, no. 2 (January 1922): 189–238.

6. Davids and Hubbard, 110–12; Richard Sylla, "Federal Policy, Banking Market Structure, and Capital Mobilization in the United States, 1863–1913," *Journal of Economic History* 29, no. 4 (December 1969): 657–86; see also H. Peers Brewer, "Eastern Money and Western Mortgages in the 1870s," *Business History Review* 50, no. 3 (autumn 1976): 356–80; Allan G. Bogue, "Financing the Prairie Farmer," in Engerman and Fogel, 301–10; Lance E. Davis, "Capital Mobility and American Growth," in Engerman and Fogel, 285–300. As of October 1, 1865, only twelve national banks had been organized in Missouri, seven of them in St. Louis; one of them (in Columbia) had already been liquidated; *Report of the Comptroller of the Currency, 1865* (Washington, D.C.: Government Printing Office, 1865), 4–5, 110. Even if the capital requirements could be met, it was thought such a sum could be more profitably invested in something other than a rural national bank.

7. *Report of the Comptroller, 1865*, 4–5; Richard Franklin Bensel, *Yankee Leviathan: The Origins of Central State Authority in America, 1859–1877* (New York: Cambridge University Press, 1990), 268–74, offers an important review of this disparity in currency circulation, noting that the per capita circulation of national banknotes in the South and border states ran roughly at one-tenth that of the eastern seaboard (see especially map on 270). Taus, 63–4, notes that checking only began to spread widely in the 1880s. The first clearinghouse in St. Louis was not organized until 1868; Howard L. Conard, ed., *Encyclopedia of the History of Missouri* (New York: Southern History Company, 1901), 2: 23–5.

8. Jules Tygiel, *Past Time: Baseball as History* (New York: Oxford University Press, 2000), 38; William A. Berkey, *The Money Question: The Legal Tender Paper Money System of the United States* (New York: Greenwood Press, 1969, orig. pub. 1876), 16–17, 164–73, discusses the use of bonds as currency. The selling of U.S. bonds to private individuals was a wartime innovation; see McPherson, 442–3.

9. Bogue, 304–5; Clay County Savings Association advertisement, *Liberty Tribune*, June 2, 1865. Lists of country banks, with correspondent banks in New York, can be found in the issues of the *Bankers' Magazine and Statistical Register* for the late 1860s; see, for example, the January 1866 issue, 584–7. This assessment of small-bank lending is based partly on a study of the discount book, 1859–1881, of Hughes & Wasson, a bank in Richmond, Ray County, Missouri; J. S. Hughes & Co., vol. 3, coll. 277, WHMC. Bogue notes one possible reason that loans were for such short periods is that interest rates trended downward, a disincentive to long-term borrowing.

10. For the Paw Paw controversy and Bird's minor part in it, see chap. 6, and *O.R.* 1: XXII, part 2: 584, 587, 591, 1143; see also a receipt for payment to Greenup Bird, county clerk, out of the estate of Robert James, Robert James Probate Records, Clay County Archives. Judging by an advertisement for the Clay County Savings Association in the *Liberty Tribune*, June 2, 1865, Bird became cashier in late 1865, at a time when the Radical identity of the bank was becoming firmer. James Love, for example, became president of the bank, replacing A. J. Calhoun, at about the same time

that he replaced Calhoun as circuit clerk under the Ouster Ordinance; Calhoun appears nowhere in documents recording the names of Clay County Republicans, in newspapers, the Missouri State Archives, or anywhere else.

11. Bird gave the amounts as $5,008.46 in coin (mostly gold) from special deposits, $8,668.18 in greenbacks and national banknotes, $3,096 in state military bonds, $300 in old Farmer's Bank notes, and $40,000 in U.S. 7.30 bonds; Greenup Bird, "Clay County Savings Association Robbery Description, 1866," typed copy, coll. 693, WHMC; Bird's tally varies slightly from the one published in the *Liberty Tribune*, February 16, 1866; *Kansas City Journal of Commerce*, February 16, 1866; Robert J. Wybrow, " 'Ravenous Monsters of Society': The Early Exploits of the James Gang," *Brand Book* 27, no. 2 (summer 1990), published by the English Westerners' Society, 1–24; Republican Central Committee Meeting, Clay County, January 1, 1866, coll. 970, fold. 161, Clarence W. Alvord and Idress Head Collection, WHMC; Yeatman, 85–6. The detail of the rearing horse was repeated by Wymore's father, William H. Wymore, Sr.; see *Portrait and Biographical Record of Clay, Ray, Carroll, Chariton, and Linn Counties, Missouri* (Chicago: Chapman Brothers, 1893), 146; for Mount Gilead Church, see W. H. Woodson, *History of Clay County, Missouri* (Topeka: Historical Publishing Company, 1920), 202.

12. Settle, 34; *Liberty Tribune*, February 16, 1866. For an insightful look at the prominent place of professional thieves in American crime, see Larry K. Hartsfield, *The American Response to Professional Crime, 1870–1914* (Westport, Conn.: Greenwood, 1985), 11–37. Hartsfield's notion that burglary was the primary problem for police detectives reflects the author's findings in an extensive review of crime reports in newspapers and professional journals such as the *Bankers' Magazine*. (Of the sixteen crimes it reported in the March 1866 issue, for example, the Liberty raid was the only holdup.) The relative—perhaps total—absence of antebellum bank holdups is partially explained by the lack of revolvers; see chap. 9 for a discussion of the postwar arming of the population. As late as 1876, a prominent detective argued that violent crime was foreign to the American criminal (Hartsfield, 51). See also David R. Johnson, *Policing the Underworld: The Impact of Crime on the Development of the American Police, 1800–1887* (Philadelphia: Temple University Press, 1979), esp. 41–67. As late as 1897, two Boston police officials cast the armed robber as a relatively marginal kind of criminal; in *Our Rival the Rascal* (Boston: Pemberton, 1897), Superintendent of Police Benjamin F. Eldridge and Chief Inspector of the Detective Bureau William B. Watts devoted ten of thirteen chapters on the various types of criminal to nonviolent burglars, safecrackers, forgers, and confidence men; one to arsonists, one to "highwaymen," and one to train robbers, with much emphasis placed on pilferers and sneak thieves.

13. *Liberty Tribune*, February 16, 1866; *Portrait and Biographical Record of Clay*, 184, 196–7; 2nd Lieutenant James B. Burbank to General, October 25, 1866, B 232, Department of the Missouri, Letters Received 1861–1867, box 20, A-C 1866, entry 2395, RG 393, part 1, NA.

14. *Kansas City Daily Journal of Commerce*, February 13, 1866.

15. Richard S. Brownlee, *Gray Ghosts of the Confederacy: Guerrilla Warfare in the West, 1861–1865* (Baton Rouge: Louisiana State University Press, 1958), 253–61.

16. *Liberty Tribune*, February 16, 1866; the evidence regarding the names of the robbers is catalogued by Wybrow, "Ravenous Monsters," 6–7. Frank Triplett claimed that former guerrillas told him that Arch Clement planned and led the robbery, *The Life, Times, and Treacherous Death of Jesse James* (New York: Konecky & Konecky, 1970, orig. pub. 1882), 330; Jim Cummins confirmed this in *Jim Cummins' Book Written by Himself* (Denver: Reed Publishing, 1903), 97. James D. Horan, *Desperate Men: The James Gang and the Wild Bunch* (Lincoln: University of Nebraska Press, 1997, orig. pub. 1949), 53, claims to have seen an account by Jackson County farmhand R. I. Stepp relating the Minter identification in the papers of Pinkerton's National Detective Agency. Unlike myself, Yeatman, 85–6, accepts the long-standing alibi regarding Jesse James's May 1865 lung wound. For more on Munkers, see Woodson, 202. Dick Liddil later claimed that Jesse James told him he did not take part, though Frank did; the reliability of this secondhand account, however, is highly questionable, as other lists of robbers Liddil provided in the same statement proved flatly wrong; *St. Louis Republican*, September 9, 1883.

17. H. H. Williams to Thos. C. Fletcher, March 10, 1866, coll. 970, fold. 376, Clarence W.

Alvord and Idress Head Collection, WHMC.

18. Thomas C. Fletcher to the Adjutant General, March 10, 1866, and H. H. Williams to Thos. C. Fletcher, March 10, 1866, coll. 970, fold. 376, Clarence W. Alvord and Idress Head Collection, WHMC; Shoemaker, 4: 222–3, 280–1; John Glendower Westover, "The Evolution of the Missouri Militia, 1804–1919" (Ph.D. diss., University of Missouri, 1948), 169–70.

19. Tho. C. Fletcher to Col., March 19, 1866, coll. KC 200, WHMC-KC.

20. *Liberty Tribune*, March 30, 1866; Wybrow, "Ravenous Monsters," 7; Albert Castel and Thomas Goodrich, *Bloody Bill Anderson: The Short, Savage Life of a Civil War Guerrilla* (Mechanicsburg, Pa.: Stackpole Books, 1998), 136–7.

21. *Lexington Caucasian*, May 2, 1866; Castel and Goodrich, 137.

22. Yeatman, 87.

23. Shelby M. Cullom, *Fifty Years of Public Service: Personal Recollections of Shelby M. Cullom* (Chicago: A. C. McClurg & Co., 1911), excerpted in T. J. Stiles, ed., *Robber Barons and Radicals: Reconstruction and the Origins of Civil Rights* (New York: Berkley, 1997), 33. For a full discussion of the differences between moderate Republicans and the Radicals in Congress, see Eric Foner, *Reconstruction, 1863–1877: America's Unfinished Revolution* (New York: Harper & Row, 1988), 228–39.

24. Foner, 177, 44; for Johnson's attempt to reconstruct the South, see 176–227, the primary basis of the discussion that follows.

25. Stiles, *Robber Barons*, 34. For the text of Johnson's proclamations, see Edward McPherson, *The Political History of the United States During the Period of Reconstruction*, 2nd ed. (New York: Negro Universities Press, 1969, orig. pub. 1875), 7–18.

26. Quoted in Patrick W. Riddleberger, *1866: The Critical Year Revisited* (Carbondale: Southern Illinois University Press, 1979), 179; McPherson, *Political History*, 29–44.

27. Joseph B. James, *The Framing of the Fourteenth Amendment* (Urbana: University of Illinois Press, 1965), 3–20.

28. Foner, 239–51; quotes from 250–1; McPherson, *Political History*, 68–81.

29. Riddleberger, 180–97; Foner, 261–3.

30. Riddleberger, 202, 228–9; Foner discusses the impact of the riots, 263–5. Even before the riots, Congress's Joint Committee on Reconstruction began to hear graphic testimony on the atrocities and injustices inflicted on the freed people, which was reprinted and distributed by Republicans in the 1866 electoral campaign; Benjamin B. Kendrick, *The Journal of the Joint Committee of Fifteen on Reconstruction* (New York: Negro Universities Press, 1969, orig. pub. 1914), 264–5.

31. Edward Bates to Andrew Johnson, July 12, 1866, in Paul H. Bergeron, ed., *The Papers of Andrew Johnson* (Knoxville: University of Tennessee Press, 1992), 10: 538–9; Putnam County quote from Parrish, *Radical*, 79–81; Vernon County quote from M. C. Anderson and Robert W. McNeil to Andrew Johnson, June 7, 1866, in *Johnson Papers*, 10: 568–9.

32. Blair's relationship with Johnson, his intense racism, and his role in building the Conservative Party is discussed in William E. Parrish, *Frank Blair: Lincoln's Conservative* (Columbia: University of Missouri Press, 1998), 230–40; Frank Blair to Andrew Johnson, March 1866, *Johnson Papers*, 10: 270.

33. Parrish, *Radical*, 64–71; Parrish, *Blair*, 241–50.

34. Abner L. Gilstrap to Andrew Johnson, May 26, 1866, *Johnson Papers*, 10: 538–9; George N. Early to Samuel P. Simpson, Adjutant General, May 4, 1866, coll. 970, fold. 376, Clarence W. Alvord and Idress Head Collection, WHMC; Thomas J. Gantt to John Hogan, August 10, 1866, Department of the Missouri, Letters Received 1861–1867, entry 2395, RG 393, part 1, NA; Shoemaker, 4: 186; see especially Parrish, *Radical*, 89–96.

35. Thomas C. Ready to Andrew Johnson, July 24, 1866, *Johnson Papers*, 10: 727–9; Brigadier General F. Cooley to Sam P. Simpson, Adjutant General, May 5, 1866, coll. 970, fold. 376, Clarence W. Alvord and Idress Head Collection, WHMC.

36. Montgomery Blair to Andrew Johnson, August 1866, and William T. Sherman to Andrew Johnson, August 9, 1866, *Johnson Papers*, 11: 3, 51–3; see also 10: 727–9; Thomas J. Gantt to John Hogan, August 10, 1866, Department of the Missouri, Letters Received 1861–1867, entry 2395, RG 393, part 1, NA; Parrish, *Radical*, 92–5. Fletcher, of course, was being pilloried for necessary steps he

had taken to fight the guerrillas; see, for example, the *Kansas City Daily Journal of Commerce,* September 6, 1866; Parrish, *Radical,* 92–5.

37. John W. Sheets to Col. J. McFerran, August 14, 1866, John W. Sheets to Col. McFerran, August 21, 1866, Department of the Missouri, Letters Received 1861–1867, entry 2395, RG 393, part 1, NA.

38. James N. Primm, "The G.A.R. in Missouri, 1866–1870," *Journal of Southern History* 20, no. 3 (August 1954): 356–75; Robert B. Beath, *History of the Grand Army of the Republic* (New York: Bryan, Taylor, & Co., 1889), 546–8; Riddleberger, 203; *History III,* 138–40; Parrish, *Radical,* 82–92; F. R. Sieg to James, August 26, 1866, Sieg Papers, Duke.

39. George to Cousins Mat and Kate, August 4, 1866, Watkins Mill. A "dutchman" was a German. (Germans were nicknamed "Dutch" after the German word for "German," *Deutsch.*) Secessionists despised Germans as Radicals and abolitionists.

40. Affidavit of Samuel Crawford, September 1, 1866, file 19433, Provost-2; McClair Wilson to Major General Hancock, September 1, 1866, Allan P. Richardson to Maj. Genl. Hancock, September 12, 1866, Affidavit of T. W. McAuthor, September 2, 1866, Department of the Missouri, Letters Received 1861–1867, entry 2395, RG 393, part 1, NA. These are only a few of many letters in this file. Probably the best part of Fellman's work is its discussion of 1866, 238–41, though he omits the role of the national controversy and conflates Unionist Conservatives with secessionists.

41. *Johnson Papers,* 11: 91–2, 359–60; Austin A. King to General Hancock, October 22, 1866, A. H. Buchanan to A. A. King, October 22, 1866, Department of the Missouri, Letters Received 1861–1867, entry 2395, RG 393, part 1, NA; Fellman, 240. Many letters to the army in 1866 relate to arms that each party said the other was ordering.

42. *Kansas City Daily Journal of Commerce,* September 5, 1866; D. Peterson to Brother, September 6, 1866, Jane Peterson Papers, Duke.

43. John Cawgill to My Dear Friend, September 3, 1866, Department of the Missouri, Letters Received 1861–1867, entry 2395, RG 393, part 1, NA.

44. L. M. Matz to My Dear Cousin, April 2, 1866, L. M. Matz to My Dear Cousin, October 29, 1866, William Dunlap Simpson Papers, Duke; see also *Lexington Caucasian,* May 2, 1866.

45. Andrew Rolle, *The Lost Cause: The Confederate Exodus to Mexico* (Norman: University of Oklahoma Press, 1965); Daniel O'Flaherty, *General Jo Shelby: Undefeated Rebel* (Chapel Hill: University of North Carolina Press, 2000, orig. pub. 1954), 226–326; Thomas B. Alexander, "Political Reconstruction in Tennessee, 1865–1870," and Ross A. Webb, "Kentucky: 'Pariah Among the Elect,'" in *Radicalism, Racism, and Party Realignment: The Border States During Reconstruction,* ed. Richard O. Curry (Baltimore: The Johns Hopkins University Press, 1969), 37–145; for typical press coverage of "the Southern exiles," see the *St. Louis Republican,* November 3, 1866.

46. Tho. C. Fletcher to Maj. Genl. W. S. Hancock, September 15, 1866, H. D. Branch to Maj. Genl. Wm. S. Hancock, August 24, 1866, Department of the Missouri, Letters Received 1861–1867, entry 2395, RG 393, part 1, NA; L. M. Matz to My Dear Cousin, October 29, 1866, William Dunlap Simpson Papers, Duke.

47. *Missouri Valley Register,* December 27, 1866, also October 25, 1866, and January 24, 1867; Wybrow, "Ravenous Monsters," 9; Brownlee, 241. The *Missouri Valley Register,* which pointedly observed Pool's behavior that day, was a Radical paper, owned by the Republican leader in Lexington, Frank Cooley; see Young, 295.

48. *Lexington Caucasian,* October 31, 1866; *Missouri Valley Register,* December 27, 1866; Wybrow, "Ravenous Monsters," 9. For an advertisement describing the bank's business, see *Lexington Caucasian,* October 17, 1866. George N. Moses blamed the robbery on Arch Clement; George N. Moses to William Connelly, box 1, fold. 37, William Connelly Collection, Denver Public Library. Mitchell made no effort to catch the bandits; see *St. Louis Republican,* November 3, 1866. He was called "a prominent Union citizen" in the *Lexington Caucasian,* October 31, 1866, January 8, 1867, but did not appear in the lengthy roster of Lexington Radicals in a Petition to Appoint Dr. F. Cooley as Supervisor of Registration, December 18, 1865, Thomas C. Fletcher Papers, MSA. A company of federal troops stationed nearby was out of town on the day of the robbery.

49. F. M. Fulkerson to His Excellency Gov. Fletcher, Oct. 9, 1866, Petition to His Excellency T.

C. Fletcher, October 1, 1866, Department of the Missouri, Letters Received 1861–1867, entry 2395, RG 393, part 1, NA.

50. Woodson, 202; Sheriff James M. Jones to Bvt. Maj. Genl. Wm. Hoffman, November 7, 1866, Department of the Missouri, Letters Received 1861–1867, entry 2395, part 1, RG 393, NA (Sheriff James M. Jones, Deputy J. H. Rickards, county clerk William Brining, and registrar Harsel signed their names to the appeal); *Kansas City Journal of Commerce*, November 24, 1866; W. M. Paxton, *Annals of Platte County, Missouri* (Kansas City, Mo.: Hudson-Kimberly Publishing, 1897), 426; Shoemaker, 4: 315–16.

51. *Kansas City Daily Journal of Commerce*, November 24, 1866.

52. Ibid., December 7, 1866.

53. *Lexington Caucasian*, October 21, October 31, November 14, 1866; John Starrett Hughes, "Lafayette County and the Aftermath of Slavery, 1861–1870," *MHR* 75, no. 1 (October 1980): 51–63. The heavily German composition of the Radical Party in Lexington is seen in the names on a petition asking that Cooley be named supervisor of registration, December 18, 1865, Thomas C. Fletcher Papers, MSA.

54. *Lexington Caucasian*, October 21, 1866.

55. James J. Emerson, Capt. 14th U.S. Infantry, November 6, 1866, and Thos. Adamson, Sheriff, Lafayette County, to Governor T. C. Fletcher, November 8, 1866, Department of the Missouri, Letters Received 1861–1867, entry 2395, RG 393, part 1, NA. The James brothers' connection to Lexington and Dave Pool continued for many years; see *Lexington Caucasian*, August 30, 1873, and October 17, 1874.

56. W. S. Hancock, Maj. Genl., to Genl. Simpson, November 10, 1866, and W. P. Wilson to Major General Hancock, December 3, 1866, Department of the Missouri, Letters Received 1861–1867, entry 2395, RG 393, part 1, NA. Hancock, a future Democratic presidential candidate, had received his Missouri command at the urging of the state's Conservatives.

57. Enlistment in the three regiments was voluntary, under the terms of General Order No. 7, issued October 10, 1866; *Kansas City Daily Journal of Commerce*, December 14, 1866; clipping from *St. Louis Dispatch*, December 11, 1866, and W. P. Wilson to Major General Hancock, December 3, 1866, Department of the Missouri, Letters Received 1861–1867, entry 2395, RG 393, part 1, NA.

58. *O.R.* 1: XVII, part 1: 725–7; 1: XXIV, part 1: 349–52, 490–4; 1: XXIV, part 2: 578–9; 1: XXIV, part 3: 21; 1: XXVI, part 1: 369–70, 376, 710, 828; 1: XXXIV, part 1: 175; 1: XLI, part 1: 277–8, 882; 1: XLI, part 4: 362; 1: XLVIII, part 1: 1020. Montgomery was also a supervisor of registration in Saline County. Fellman, 241, offers a partial account of these events in Lexington.

59. Austin A. King to General Hancock, December 4, 1866, Richard C. Vaughan to Maj. Genl. Hancock, December 5, 13, and 23, 1866, Robert Nugent to General, December 20, 1866, and First Lieutenant James R. Kelly to Bvt. Brig. General C. McKeever, December 12, 1866, Department of the Missouri, Letters Received 1861–1867, entry 2395, RG 393, part 1, NA. The investigating officer's report was tainted by the prevailing racism and conservatism of the postwar officer corps; see, for example, *Report of the Joint Committee on Reconstruction at the First Session, Thirty-Ninth Congress*, part 2 (Westport, Conn.: Negro Universities Press, 1969, orig. pub. 1866), 60, 234, and Edward M. Coffman, *The Old Army: A Portrait of the American Army in Peacetime, 1784–1898* (New York: Oxford University Press, 1986), 234–46. See also George N. Moses to William Connelley, box 1, fold. 37, William Connelly Collection, Denver Public Library; *Lexington Caucasian*, January 9 and February 23, 1867. For Montgomery's own reflections, see *St. Louis Globe-Democrat*, August 24, 1876.

60. Brownlee, 242; *Missouri Valley Register*, December 20, 1866; Statement of J. M. Turley, box 1, fold. 37, William Connelly Collection, Denver Public Library; First Lieutenant James R. Kelly to Bvt. Brig. General C. McKeever, December 12, 1866, Department of the Missouri, Letters Received 1861–1867, entry 2395, RG 393, part 1, NA; *Lexington Caucasian*, February 23, 1867. Some writers (e.g., Brownlee) mistakenly state that enlistment at this time was mandatory. Under General Order No. 7, it was voluntary; see *Kansas City Daily Journal of Commerce*, December 14, 1866.

61. Brownlee, 242–3; *Missouri Valley Register*, December 20, 1866; *St. Louis Globe-Democrat*, August 24, 1876. Most details from the fight in the City Hotel and the chase up the street are taken from mutually supporting statements from Moses and Turley in the Connelly Collection, cited pre-

viously.

62. Richd. C. Vaughan to Major General Hancock, December 13, 1866, Robert Nugent to General, December 20, 1866, and Richard C. Vaughan to Major General Hancock, December 23, 1866, Department of the Missouri, Letters Received 1861–1867, entry 2395, RG 393, part 1, NA; *Lexington Caucasian*, January 9 and February 23, 1867. Moses identified Turley as the leader of the raid on the newspaper. Montgomery's trial was heavily covered in the *Lexington Caucasian*, but through the assistance of Timothy Rives of the National Archives facility in Kansas City, I have been unable to find any evidence that he was indicted on criminal charges. Since criminal trial outcomes in the federal district court for central Missouri were all recorded, this almost certainly indicates that Montgomery faced a civil lawsuit.

63. *Lexington Caucasian*, January 9 and 16, February 2, 9, 16, and 23, 1867; *St. Louis Republican*, March 27, 1867. Adjutant General Samuel Simpson ordered the militia force that occupied Lexington mustered out of service on February 6, 1867; Samuel Simpson to Brig. General Bacon Montgomery, February 6, 1867, Letterbook, Dec. 17, 1866 to Jan. 22, 1869, Office of the Adjutant General, MSA.

64. *Kansas City Times*, August 23, 1876. To grasp his sincerity, contrast these words with John N. Edwards, *Noted Guerrillas, or the Warfare of the Border* (St. Louis: H. W. Brand & Co., 1879), 365–6.

CHAPTER ELEVEN: The Death of Captain Sheets

1. Fears of a renewed outbreak of fighting were not limited to Missouri; see William A. Ross, Jr., "Was There Danger of a Second Civil War During Reconstruction?," *Mississippi Valley Historical Review* 25, no. 1 (June 1938): 39–58.

2. It is important to note that the leading Conservatives of Lexington were Unionists (though they had family ties to rebels, as in the case of James M. Pool). In fact, one of U.S. assessor Richard C. Vaughan's complaints about the militia, in his suit against Bacon Montgomery, was that he had enlisted Confederate bushwhackers. This Unionism must be kept in mind when reading the Conservatives' strident anti-Radical rhetoric. (Frank Blair, for example, declared that Governor Fletcher had "declared war" on the people of Lafayette and Jackson Counties.) See the *Lexington Caucasian*, January 9, 1867. On March 4, 1867, Governor Fletcher wrote to inform Major Reeves Leonard that there were no more militiamen on duty in the state; coll. 1013, fold. 494, Abiel Leonard Papers, WHMC.

3. L. M. Matz to Cousin, February 13, 1867, William Dunlap Simpson Papers, Duke.

4. Captain W. E. Chester to Thomas C. Fletcher, December 27, 1866, coll. 970, fold. 376, Clarence W. Alvord and Idress Head Collection, WHMC; Chester remained with his company near Warrensburg as late as February 12, 1867; Adjutant General to Bacon Montgomery, February 12, 1867, Letterbook, Dec. 17, 1866 to Jan. 22, 1869, Office of the Adjutant General, MSA.

5. Settle, 31–2, notes that the guerrillas themselves provoked a hostile reaction from postwar society, but he largely misses the political frenzy of 1865–67 that framed their emergence as bandits. Albert Castel, *William Clarke Quantrill: His Life and Times* (New York: Frederick Fell, 1962), 221–2, comes closer, though he misses the complexities of postwar violence. It appears incorrect, or at least insufficient, to say that the bushwhackers suffered from post-traumatic stress disorder, as their postwar violence was organized and purposeful, not merely compulsive; see Eric T. Dean, Jr., " 'We Will All Be Lost and Destroyed': Post-Traumatic Stress Disorder and the Civil War," *CWH* 37, no. 2 (June 1991): 138–53.

6. For a study of the social background of the guerrilla gangs centered in Jackson County, see Don R. Bowen, "Guerrilla War in Western Missouri, 1862–1865: Historical Extensions of the Relative Deprivation Hypothesis," *Comparative Studies in Society and History* 19, no. 1 (January 1977): 30–51.

7. William E. Parrish, *Missouri Under Radical Rule, 1865–1870* (Columbia: University of Missouri Press, 1965), 100–1; Eric Foner, *Reconstruction, 1863–1877: America's Unfinished Revolution* (New York: Harper & Row, 1988), 261–71; *Kansas City Journal of Commerce*, November 16, 1866.

8. In an important study, Walter Laqueur repeatedly notes, "There is in fact no clear dividing

line between guerrilla warfare, terror and brigandage"; Laqueur, *Guerrilla Warfare: A Historical and Critical Study* (New Brunswick, N.J.: Transaction, 1998), 93–8, 384–7. Part of what divides banditry from guerrilla warfare, he writes, is the "political incentive" of the guerrilla; as this book shows, that ingredient was present in the postwar bushwhackers, making the distinction between their crimes and irregular warfare or terrorism even more indistinct.

9. *St. Louis Republican*, May 23, 28, and 29, 1867; *Liberty Tribune*, May 15 and 31, 1867; *Richmond Conservator*, June 1, 1867; *History III*, 233.

10. A link between the Savannah robbers and the bushwhackers associated with the James brothers has been disputed. Contemporary newspaper reports do not identify any known guerrillas (*St. Louis Republican*, March 3, 1867; *Liberty Tribune*, November 23, 1866, March 8 and 29, 1867), and Robert J. Wybrow's careful review casts doubt on any connection; see his " 'Ravenous Monsters of Society': The Early Exploits of the James Gang," *Brand Book* 27, no. 2 (summer 1990), published by the English Westerners' Society, 1–24. However, Governor Fletcher issued a reward offer on March 15, 1867, for Jim White, a bushwhacker who would also be a suspect in the events described below; Shoemaker, 4: 306–9. The *Banker's Magazine and Statistical Register*, May 1867, attributed the Savannah robbery to "a band of desperadoes, under notorious bushwhackers." The evidence is at best inconclusive. For the Titus brothers, see Shoemaker, 4: 315–16, and W. M. Paxton, *Annals of Platte County, Missouri* (Kansas City: Hudson-Kimberly Publishing, 1897), 426.

11. *Richmond Conservator*, May 24, 1867; for references to the "exceedingly rough weather" of March, see the *St. Louis Republican*, March 28, 1867.

12. *Portrait and Biographical Record of Clay, Ray, Carroll, Chariton, and Linn Counties, Missouri* (Chicago: Chapman Brothers, 1893), 428, 708–9.

13. *Richmond Conservator*, May 25, 1867; *Biographical Record*, 191; Wybrow, "Ravenous Monsters," 11–12. Deputy Sheriff Tom Reyburn was probably a relative of Sheriff Adam K. Reyburn, a leading Radical; see Ray County Petition to His Excellency Thomas C. Fletcher, February 24, 1865, Thomas C. Fletcher Papers, MSA. The gunfight was also reported in the *Liberty Tribune*, May 31, 1867.

14. *Liberty Tribune*, May 31, 1867; *St. Louis Republican*, May 30, 1867. Wasson informed the *Tribune* that $4,000 had been stolen, a figure later amended to $3,500. The smaller take, relative to Liberty, may be due to the fact that Richmond had a less active economy, and that Hughes & Wasson engaged primarily in small, short-term loans, and may not have kept much cash on hand; see the discount book, 1859–1881, J. S. Hughes & Co., vol. 3, coll. 277, WHMC.

15. Richard S. Brownlee, *Gray Ghosts of the Confederacy: Guerrilla Warfare in the West, 1861–1865* (Baton Rouge: Louisiana State University Press, 1958), 253–61.

16. *Kansas City Journal of Commerce*, May 28, 1867.

17. *Liberty Tribune*, May 24 and 31, 1867; *St. Louis Republican*, May 31, 1867. The killing of one of the Hulse clan by the militia in 1866 had prompted President Johnson to dispatch General William T. Sherman to confer with Governor Fletcher; Thomas C. Ready to Andrew Johnson, July 24, 1866, Paul H. Bergeron, ed., *The Papers of Andrew Johnson* (Knoxville: University of Tennessee Press, 1992), 10: 727–9. The rumors about Bradley's involvement were alluded to in the *St. Louis Republican*, May 28, 1867; Wybrow, "Ravenous Monsters," 12–3. Reyburn personally offered a $500 reward for the capture of the bandits; *Richmond Conservator*, June 1, 1867. For a political spin on the robbery, see *St. Louis Republican*, May 31, 1867.

18. *St. Louis Republican*, May 30, 1867; Wybrow, "Ravenous Monsters," 13; Yeatman, 92. The *Liberty Tribune*, May 31, 1867, reported the governor's reward proclamation, though apparently no copy was still in existence when Shoemaker and Avery compiled their authoritative *Messages and Proclamations*. It should be noted that the state constitution of 1865 preserved the governor's control over the St. Louis police, as established during the secession crisis of 1861; *History III*, 202–3.

19. The rumors were reported by merchant Daniel Conway in the *St. Joseph Gazette*, December 17, 1869; the anonymous neighbor was interviewed in the *St. Louis Dispatch*, February 10, 1874.

20. Wybrow, "Ravenous Monsters," 13; Settle, 36; Edward E. Leslie, *The Devil Knows How to*

Ride: The True Story of William Clarke Quantrill and His Confederate Raiders (New York: Da Capo, 1998), 288.

21. *Richmond Conservator,* November 30, 1867; Wybrow, "Ravenous Monsters," 13. The bank can be identified by the names of the officers, Preston Roberts and William McCoy, cited in the letter to the *Conservator;* see *Report of the Comptroller of the Currency, December 2, 1867* (Washington, D.C.: Government Printing Office, 1867), 551.

22. *Richmond Conservator,* March 22, 1868; *St. Louis Republican,* March 27, 1868; *Liberty Tribune,* July 24, 1868; Leslie, 394; Settle, 37; Wybrow, "Ravenous Monsters," 13.

23. The identity of the bandits and their rendezvous in Chaplin was uncovered by Louisville detective D. T. Bligh (see below). Bligh presented his findings in a letter to the governor of Missouri dated March 3, 1875. This letter has long been cited as an important source on the James brothers' activities, but I was unable to locate it in the Missouri State Archives. See Wybrow, "Ravenous Monsters," 15–18; Robert J. Wybrow, "The James Gang in Kentucky: A Tale of Murder and Robbery in the Blue Grass State," *Brand Book* 15, no. 2 (January 1973), published by the English Westerners' Society, 22–34; Settle, 37–8; Yeatman, 93–5.

24. *St. Louis Dispatch,* February 10, 1874.

25. Settle, 96–7; William N. Gregg to George M. Bennett, April 9, 1898, and E. G. Bower to George M. Bennett, April 25, 1898, Younger Brothers Pardon Application Files, fold. 2: Petitions and Letters in Support of Parole, nos. 555 and 556, 1889–1901, in "Northfield (Minnesota) Bank Robbery of 1876: Selected Manuscripts Collection and Government Records" (microfilm publication), MnHS; Marley Brant, *The Outlaw Youngers: A Confederate Brotherhood* (Lanham, Md.: Madison Books, 1993), 49–56, 82–5. In *The Story of Cole Younger by Himself* (Lee's Summit, Mo.: n.p., 1903), 50–8, Younger claims that although he had fought alongside Frank James, he did not meet Jesse during the war. Detective Bligh placed Jesse and Frank James at Chaplin, the raiders' starting point, on the day of the robbery itself; Settle, 37–8. Years later, Dick Liddil claimed that Jesse told him that he, Frank, George Shepherd, John Jarrette, Cole Younger, and one other person carried out the robbery; *St. Louis Republican,* September 9, 1883. Though this is a plausible account, it is secondhand information, and questionable; other lists of robbers Liddil provided in the same statement proved flatly wrong.

26. Norton had been the proprietor of the Southern Bank, which continued on after he and Long opened their firm in 1863, and his brother Elijah had served as a Unionist delegate to the Missouri convention on secession, as a wartime congressman, and later as a state supreme court justice; Paxton, 543–4; *Banker's Magazine and Statistical Register,* January 1866. Yeatman, 92–5, says that Long had financed Robert James's college education, which the bandits were unlikely to know.

27. Wybrow, "Kentucky," 22–5; Wybrow, "Ravenous Monsters," 15–18; Settle, 37–8; *St. Louis Republican,* March 23 and 26, 1868; Settle, 37–8; Yeatman accepts Jesse James's later alibis at face value, 92–5. Counterfeit notes were a serious problem; see *Banker's Magazine and Statistical Register,* March 1866, and David R. Johnson, *Illegal Tender: Counterfeiting and the Secret Service in Nineteenth-Century America* (Washington, D.C.: Smithsonian Institution Press, 1995).

28. *Jefferson City People's Tribune,* April 15, 1868; Wybrow, "Kentucky," 24; Yeatman, 94–5.

29. Yeatman, 92; Settle, 37; Ross A. Webb, "Kentucky: 'Pariah Among the Elect,' " in *Radicalism, Racism, and Party Realignment: The Border States During Reconstruction,* ed. Richard O. Curry (Baltimore: The Johns Hopkins University Press, 1969), 105–45; *St. Louis Republican,* July 13, 1868; *Liberty Tribune,* July 24, 1868; *Jefferson City People's Tribune,* April 15, 1868; *Jefferson City People's Tribune,* April 15, 1868.

30. *U.S. Census,* Clay County, 1870, 1880, and 1900; *History of Clay,* 269. The 1870 census lists two children, Sarah and Mary, who do not appear in Settle, 9. See also Stella F. James, *In the Shadow of Jesse James* (Thousand Oaks, Calif.: Dragon Books, 1990), 59. Contemporary accounts describe freed slaves sometimes returning to their former masters in search of employment; see, for example, L. M. Matz to Cousin, February 13, 1867, William Dunlap Simpson Papers, Duke. In 1875, the eighteen-year-old Ambrose signed an affidavit with the illiterate's "X—his mark"; a press report also claimed that Charlotte "refused to accept her freedom"; *Kansas City Times,* January 28, 1875. Certainly Zerelda felt victimized herself, a common reaction by white Southern women; see Cather-

ine Clinton, *The Other Civil War: American Women in the Nineteenth Century* (New York: Hill and Wang, 1984), 89. Elsewhere Clinton demonstrates the ways in which freed women suffered violence in the domestic setting; see "Bloody Terrain: Freedwomen, Sexuality, and Violence During Reconstruction," in *Half Sisters of History: Southern Women and the American Past*, ed. Catherine Clinton (Durham, N.C.: Duke University Press, 1994), 136–53. Many studies emphasize black families' struggle for domestic autonomy after emancipation, making Charlotte's situation a notable exception that strongly suggests the perpetuation of her antebellum status. See Laura F. Edwards, *Gendered Strife and Confusion: The Political Culture of Reconstruction* (Urbana: University of Illinois Press, 1997), 24–65; Ira Berlin, Steven F. Miller, and Leslie S. Rowland, "Afro-American Families in Transition from Slavery to Freedom," and Rebecca Scott, "The Battle Over the Child: Child Apprenticeship and the Freedman's Bureau in North Carolina," in *The African American Family in the South, 1861–1900*, ed. Donald G. Nieman (New York: Garland, 1994), 1–33, 215–27.

31. Paul W. Gates, "The Railroads of Missouri, 1850–1870," *MHR* 26, no. 2 (January 1932): 126–41; Irene D. Neu and George Rogers Taylor, *The American Railroad Network, 1861–1890* (Cambridge, Mass.: Harvard University Press, 1956), 67–79; Edwin L. Lopata, *Local Aid to Railroads in Missouri* (New York: Columbia University Press, 1937), 6, 36–8, 42, 61–100; *Lexington Caucasian*, July 25, 1866. The county bond-issuing frenzy was a departure from antebellum practice; all the local governments in Illinois, for example, issued only $4 million in bonds (less than 5 percent of costs) through 1860; Albert Fishlow, "The Dynamics of Railroad Extension into the West," in *The Reinterpretation of American Economic History*, ed. Stanley L. Engerman and Robert W. Fogel (New York: Harper & Row, 1971), 402–16.

32. Gates, 126–41; S. P. Harlan to Sister, October 2, 1867 (for reference to Irish workers, see S. P. Harlan to Sister, August 7, 1867), Bond-Fentriss Family Papers, UNC; *History of Clay*, 262–3; W. H. Woodson, *History of Clay County, Missouri* (Topeka: Historical Publishing Company, 1920), 205; *History III*, 222–3.

33. James W. Goodrich and Donald B. Oster, eds., " 'Few Men But Many Widows': The Daniel Fogle Letters, August 8–September 4, 1867," *MHR* 80, no. 3 (April 1986): 273–303; *Portrait and Biographical Record*, 216–17; *History III*, 198–201; A. J. Spease to Brother & Sister, April 19, 1868, James C. Zimmerman Papers, Duke; Lopata, 70.

34. Goodrich and Oster, 273–303; James Fernando Ellis, *The Influence of Environment on the Settlement of Missouri* (St. Louis: Webster Publishing, 1929), 142–50; Norman L. Crocket, "A Study in Confusion: Missouri's Immigration Program, 1865–1916," *MHR* 57, no. 2 (January 1963): 248–60; Fellman, 242–44; Parrish, *Radical Rule*, 177–210.

35. Goodrich and Oster, 273–303; see also Dan to Brother, April 26, 1867, Jane Peterson Papers, Duke; see also *History III*, 170.

36. Foner, quote on 235, 251–61, 271–7.

37. Foner, 277–8, 333–6; for firsthand accounts, see T. J. Stiles, ed., *Robber Barons and Radicals: Reconstruction and the Origins of Civil Rights* (New York: Berkley, 1997), 64–79, 151–66. On this constitutional revolution, and how it reflected the African-American vision of the federal government's role, see Eric Foner, "Rights and the Constitution in Black Life During the Civil War and Reconstruction," *Journal of American History* 74, no. 3 (December 1987): 863–83.

38. Foner, *Reconstruction*, 281–91, quote on 283; Stiles, 80–104, 167–80, 195–214, 276–300; Richard Nelson Current, *Those Terrible Carpetbaggers: A Reinterpretation* (New York: Oxford University Press, 1988), 78–84. See also Edward Magdol, "Local Black Leaders in the South, 1867–1875: An Essay Toward the Reconstruction of Reconstruction History," in *The Politics of Freedom: African Americans and the Political Process During Reconstruction*, ed. Donald G. Nieman (New York: Garland, 1994), 223–52.

39. Allen W. Trelease, *White Terror: The Ku Klux Klan Conspiracy and Southern Reconstruction* (Baton Rouge: Louisiana State University Press, 1971), xlii–xlviii, 3–21, 26–35, 49–54, 62–4, 89–91; Foner, *Reconstruction*, 342–3, 425–36; Rable, 59–80; see also *Report of the Joint Committee on Reconstruction at the First Session, Thirty-Ninth Congress* (Westport: Negro Universities Press, 1969, orig. pub. 1866). Many local studies reveal the depth and breadth of racial and political violence in the South; see, for example, Randolph B. Campbell, *Grass-Roots Reconstruction in Texas, 1865–1880*

(Baton Rouge: Louisiana State University Press, 1997), 80–3, and Michael W. Fitzgerald, "Extralegal Violence and the Planter Class: The Ku Klux Klan in the Alabama Black Belt During Reconstruction," in *Local Matters: Race, Crime, and Justice in the Nineteenth-Century South*, ed. Donald G. Nieman and Christopher Waldrep (Athens: University of Georgia Press, 2001), 155–71. See also the articles in Donald G. Nieman, ed., *Black Freedom/White Violence, 1865–1900* (New York: Garland, 1994).

40. *Lexington Caucasian*, November 30, 1867, May 2 and 16, 1868; John Starrett Hughes, "Lafayette County and the Aftermath of Slavery, 1861–1870," *MHR* 70, no. 1 (October 1980): 51–63; Lewis O. Saum, "Donan and the *Caucasian*," *MHR* 63, no. 4 (July 1969): 419–50; see also Parrish, *Radical Rule*, 106–38.

41. *Lexington Caucasian*, August 1, 1868; Hughes, "Lafayette," 51–63.

42. *St. Joseph Gazette*, December 17, 1869.

43. William E. Parrish, *Frank Blair: Lincoln's Conservative* (Columbia: University of Missouri Press, 1998), 248–60, quote, 254; Foner, *Reconstruction*, 340.

44. Parrish, *Blair*, 252; Cousin Will to Cousin Kate, October 25, 1868, Watkins Mill.

45. *Richmond Conservator*, December 18, 1869; Yeatman, 95. The horse's name was given in the *Liberty Tribune*, July 22, 1870, and its reputed price in the *St. Joseph Gazette*, December 17, 1869. Yeatman accepts at face value a story that Jesse James went to California for most of 1868, to his uncle Drury Woodson James's mineral springs at Paso Robles—a possibility, but more likely a fiction.

46. *Kansas City Daily Journal of Commerce*, December 9, 1869; *St. Joseph Gazette*, December 9, 10, and 15, 1869; see also Gallatin Bank Postcard, coll. 801, WHMC. (A warrant was a promise to pay, often issued by local governments. They would circulate at a discount, much like antebellum banknotes.) The killer was identified by witnesses as Jesse James, based on his relative youth and the bay mare, an animal of some note around Kearney; see *St. Joseph Gazette*, December 17, 1869, and *Richmond Conservator*, December 18, 1869. When the family offered alibis for Jesse (see chap. 12) in the *Liberty Tribune*, July 22, 1870, they could not deny the existence of the horse (whose name was given as Kate), though they claimed that it was owned by Susan James. See also Yeatman, 96, and the *St. Louis Globe-Democrat*, October 17, 1942, which offers the recollections of Edward Clingan seventy-three years after the fact. Settle, 38, misidentifies McDowell as a clerk, and Wybrow, "Ravenous Monsters," 18, mistakenly states that $700 was taken, based on an early press report that was later corrected. It is impossible to know for certain who robbed the Gallatin bank, of course, but the evidence clearly points to the two brothers, with Jesse as the shooter. Settle, 40, notes a press report that bandits claimed to have killed "Sheets and Cox," suggesting the bandits recognized the cashier; the version given here is based on my firm belief that the "Sheets and Cox" reference garbled the accounts of witnesses, and the shooter did not actually say "Sheets." For example, the *St. Joseph Gazette*, December 10, 1869, states, "They said they had killed Maj. S. P. Cox, if they had not made a mistake in the man." Years later, Dick Liddil claimed that Jesse James told him that he and Jim White carried out the crime; *St. Louis Republican*, September 9, 1883. Though a possibility, it is secondhand information, and questionable; other lists of robbers Liddil provided proved wrong.

47. Jesse James himself later made the mistaken-identity explanation, though he did not admit to pulling the trigger; see John N. Edwards, "A Terrible Quintet," special supplement to the *St. Louis Dispatch*, November 23, 1873, vol. 34, coll. 1424, Walter B. Stevens Scrapbook, WHMC.

48. *St. Joseph Gazette*, December 10 and 15, 1869; *Militia Report*, 55–9; John W. Sheets to Col. J. McFerran, August 14, 1866, John W. Sheets to Col. McFerran, August 21, 1866, Department of the Missouri, Letters Received 1861–1867, entry 2395, RG 393, part 1, NA. See also list of Clay County sheriffs, Woodson, 333; and Yeatman, 97.

49. *St. Joseph Gazette*, December 9, 1869.

50. *Militia Report*, 383, 387–9, 394, quote on 389. Moss had been thirty-three at the outbreak of the Mexican War, in 1846; Joseph G. Dawson, III, *Doniphan's Epic March: The 1st Missouri Volunteers in the Mexican War* (Lawrence: University Press of Kansas, 1999), 28–30.

51. This account is based on that of Liberty mayor F. R. Long, *Richmond Conservator*, Decem-

ber 18, 1869.

52. *St. Joseph Gazette,* December 17, 1869; *Liberty Tribune,* December 17, 1869.

53. *Kansas City Times* in *Richmond Conservator,* December 18, 1869; *Liberty Tribune,* December 17, 1869; *Platte City Reveille* in *Liberty Tribune,* January 14, 1870; Paxton, 485; J. W. McClurg to Sheriff, December 24, 1869, coll. 1746, WHMC. This assessment represents a flat disagreement with Settle, 40, who uses the same evidence to argue that the brothers were somehow not considered criminals.

CHAPTER TWELVE: The Chivalry of Crime

1. Andrew Rolle, *The Lost Cause: The Confederate Exodus to Mexico* (Norman: University of Oklahoma Press, 1965), 3–19; Edwards quoted in Dan Saults, "Let Us Discuss a Man: A Study of John Newman Edwards," *Bulletin of the Missouri Historical Society* 19, no. 2 (January 1963): 150–60; see also F. Y. Hedley, "John Newman Edwards," in *Encyclopedia of the History of Missouri,* ed. Howard L. Conard (St. Louis: Southern History Company, 1901), 2: 354–6.

2. Rolle, 21–64.

3. Rolle, 65–77, 96–9, 159–71; Daniel O'Flaherty, *General Jo Shelby: Undefeated Rebel* (Chapel Hill: University of North Carolina Press, 1954), 282–326; John N. Edwards to Darling Sisters, April 6, 1866, coll. 1973, John N. Edwards Letters, 1865–1866, WHMC.

4. Quoted in Rolle, 99.

5. J. N. Edwards to Darling Sister Fanny, September 18, 1866, coll. 1973, John N. Edwards Letters, 1865–1866, WHMC.

6. Rolle, 96–9, 151–3, 180–2.

7. John N. Edwards, *Shelby and His Men, or, The War in the West* (Cincinnati: Miami Printing and Publishing, 1867), 448; Saults, 150–60; Hedley, 354–6.

8. *History III,* 142–50, 236–59.

9. See, for example, Edwards, 398. O'Flaherty, 133, claimed that the James brothers had served with Shelby in the fall and winter of 1862, which is demonstrably untrue.

10. William Hyde, "Newspapers and Newspaper Men of Three Decades," *Collections of the Missouri Historical Society* 12 (1896): 5–24, notes that Edwards's direct connection to the James brothers was widely rumored among newspapermen; John N. Edwards, "A Terrible Quintet," special supplement to the *St. Louis Dispatch,* November 23, 1873, vol. 34, coll. 1424, Walter B. Stevens Scrapbook, WHMC. On the James brothers' connection to Shelby, see, for example, O'Flaherty, 332.

11. *Kansas City Times* in the *Liberty Tribune,* June 24, 1870.

12. Robert J. Wybrow argues the case for Edwards's authorship (with no actual evidence) in "From the Pen of a Noble Robber: The Letters of Jesse Woodson James, 1847–1882," *Brand Book* 24, no. 2 (summer 1987), published by the English Westerners' Society, 1–22; see also Yeatman, 97.

13. *U.S. Census,* Washington Township, Clay County, Missouri, 1860, 1870. For testimony on Frank James's literary tastes, see *Columbia Herald,* September 24, 1897. Jesse James was described by acquaintances as an eager newspaper reader; see, for example, Clarence Hite's testimony in George Miller, Jr., *The Trial of Frank James for Murder* (St. Louis: n.p., 1898), 309, 313.

14. See Edwards, *Shelby,* 448. The expression seems to have been unknown during the war.

15. *Kansas City Times* in the *Liberty Tribune,* July 15, 1870.

16. Ibid., July 22, 1870.

17. *Liberty Tribune,* August 5, 1870, September 24 and October 1, 1869; Settle, 42; W. H. Woodson, *History of Clay County, Missouri* (Topeka: Historical Publishing Company, 1920), 328–35.

18. *St. Louis Republican,* April 7, 1882; Edwards, "Quintet"; Settle, 61; Marley Brant, *The Outlaw Youngers: A Confederate Brotherhood* (Lanham, Md.: Madison Books, 1993), 97–103; *Kansas City Star,* August 2, 1925; Yeatman, 99. Younger claimed that he and his brothers spent most of 1868 to 1871 in Texas; Thomas Coleman Younger, *The Story of Cole Younger by Himself* (Lee's Summit, Mo.: n.p., 1903), 62–3. The story was later confirmed by a former district attorney and judge in Texas, E. G. Bower to George M. Bennett, April 25, 1898, "Northfield (Minnesota) Bank Robbery of 1876: Selected Manuscripts Collection and Government Records" (microfilm publication), MnHS; Hed-

ley, 354–6; Saults, 150–60; Yeatman, 119–20.

19. Coll. 3507, Harry C. Hoffman Papers, WHMC; *Kansas City Times*, September 11, 1881, and August 16, 1876; Yeatman, 120–1; Settle, 31, 69–70, 91–2. On the James brothers' love of racing, see the *Nashville Daily American*, October 9 and 12, 1882.

20. *Hamilton News* in *Richmond Conservator*, June 17, 1871; *Cameron Observer* in *Liberty Tribune*, June 16, 1871; Settle, 43; Yeatman, 99–100. Dick Liddil later claimed that Jesse James told him that he, Frank, Clell Miller, Cole Younger, and John Younger went to Corydon; though this particular list sounds plausible, the reliability of this secondhand account is questionable, as other lists of robbers he provided in the same statement proved wrong; *St. Louis Republican*, September 9, 1883.

21. S. A. Moore, "Hostile Raid into Davis County, Iowa," *Annals of Iowa* 13, no. 5 (July 1922): 362–74; Edgar White, "Henry Clay Dean, 'The Orator of Rebel Cove,' " *MHR* 22, no. 4 (July 1928): 450–5; Mark Twain, *Life on the Mississippi* (New York: Penguin, 1984), 393–4.

22. *Hamilton News* in *Richmond Conservator*, June 17, 1871.

23. William Pinkerton in *Kansas City Evening Star*, July 21, 1881.

24. *Hamilton News* in *Richmond Conservator*, June 17, 1871; *Cameron Observer* in *Liberty Tribune*, June 16, 1871.

25. William A. Pinkerton, *Train Robberies, Train Robbers, and the "Holdup" Men* (New York: Arno Press, 1974, orig. pub. 1907), 22; William Pinkerton quoted in *Kansas City Evening Star*, July 21, 1881. The *Cameron Observer* (in *Liberty Tribune*, June 16, 1871) reported only twenty shots were expended in the Civil Bend fight, which tends to confirm Pinkerton's claim that only two men pursued into Missouri.

26. Quotes from *Hamilton News* in *Richmond Conservator*, June 17, 1871.

27. William Young, *Young's History of Lafayette County, Missouri* (Indianapolis: B. F. Bowen, 1910), 295; *Kansas City Times* in *Richmond Conservator*, July 8, 1871.

28. *Kansas City Times* in *Richmond Conservator*, July 8, 1871; compare with his letter in *Kansas City Times*, August 23, 1876, attacking Bacon Montgomery, a personal friend at that time of John Edwards.

29. *History III*, 253–67; Thomas S. Barclay, *The Liberal Republican Movement in Missouri, 1865–1871* (Columbia: State Historical Society of Missouri, 1926), 208–9, 249–82; Norma L. Peterson, *Freedom and Franchise: The Political Career of B. Gratz Brown* (Columbia: University of Missouri Press, 1965), 168–90.

30. Christopher Phillips, *Missouri's Confederate: Claiborne Fox Jackson and the Creation of Southern Identity in the Border West* (Columbia: University of Missouri Press, 2000), 288–9; for a discussion of the factionalization of the Democratic Party, see Homer Clevenger, "Railroads in Missouri Politics, 1875–1887," *MHR* 43, no. 2 (January 1949): 220–36.

31. For an example of Edwards's ongoing glorification, see the poem in the *Kansas City Times*, February 9, 1872, and his serialization of "Shelby's Expedition to Mexico" (e.g., September 22, 1872). Ross A. Webb, "Kentucky: 'Pariah Among the Elect,' " in *Radicalism, Racism, and Party Realignment: The Border States During Reconstruction*, ed. Richard O. Curry (Baltimore: The Johns Hopkins University Press, 1969), 105–45. For the Unionist reaction in Missouri, see the *St. Louis Republican*, March 13, 1874.

32. *Kansas City Times* in *Liberty Tribune*, June 24, 1870.

33. See, for example, John Hatfield to Governor, January 11, 1870, John Hatfield to His Excellency B. Gratz Brown, February 7, 1871, John Hamlin to His Excellency B. Gratz Brown, May 21, 1871, B. Gratz Brown Papers, MSA.

34. Foner, 454–9; *Richmond Conservator*, July 8, 1871. These trials gained great publicity, but unfortunately they proved ineffective in the long run; see Lou Falkner Williams, "The South Carolina Ku Klux Klan Trials and Enforcement of Federal Rights, 1871–1872," *CWH* 39, no. 1 (March 1993): 47–66.

35. Testifying in 1882, under the influence of alcohol, Shelby placed the incident in 1872; Miller, 109.

36. Brother to Darling Sister, March 8, 1872, Watkins Mill.

37. *Liberty Tribune*, March 8, 1872; Settle, 44; Yeatman, 100–1, suggests Miller was actually

innocent.

38. *Louisville Courier-Journal*, May 2 and 5, 1872. In *St. Louis Republican*, October 12, 1882, and Settle, 44, the *Pilgrim's Progress* detail later became an elaborate story of how Frank—not Jesse— befriended an old woman in order to borrow her copy, and nearly finished it before he left for Columbia.

39. *Louisville Courier-Journal*, May 1–5, 1872, *Columbia Spectator*, May 2, 1872 in the *Louisville Courier-Journal*, May 4, 1872. Also of interest is the tribute to Martin in the *Banker's Magazine and Statistical Register*, October 1876.

40. Foner, 488–500; Adams quote on 497.

41. Alan Trachtenberg, *The Incorporation of America: Culture and Society in the Gilded Age* (New York: Hill and Wang, 1982), 165; Mark Wahlgren Summers, *The Era of Good Stealings* (New York: Oxford University Press, 1993), 89–96; Foner, 467–8.

42. The best account of the gold speculation of 1869 is in Maury Klein, *The Life and Legend of Jay Gould* (Baltimore: The Johns Hopkins University Press, 1986), 99–115. See also T. J. Stiles, "As Good as Gold?," *Smithsonian* 31, no. 6 (September 2000): 106–17; William S. McFeely, *Grant: A Biography* (New York: Norton, 1982), 319–31; Edward Chancellor, *Devil Take the Hindmost: A History of Financial Speculation* (New York: Farrar Straus Giroux, 1999), 182–3; and T. J. Stiles, *Robber Barons and Radicals: Reconstruction and the Origin of Civil Rights* (New York: Berkley, 1997), 217–29.

43. Summers, 95–6.

44. Foner, 488–507, quote on 499; see also McFeely, 380–1. For a Missouri-focused account that explicitly adopts the Liberal Republican critique of Reconstruction, see Peterson, 198–227.

45. Lewis O. Saum, "Donan and the *Caucasian*," *MHR* 63, no. 4 (July 1969): 419–50; *Kansas City Times*, September 24, 1872.

46. *History III*, 193; *Kansas City Times*, September 24–26, 1872.

47. *Kansas City Times*, September 27, 1872. Had the bandits struck one day later, they might have encountered Wild Bill Hickok, who performed at the fair on Friday; Joseph G. Rosa, *They Called Him Wild Bill: The Life and Adventures of James Butler Hickok* (Norman: University of Oklahoma Press, 1974), 220.

48. *Kansas City Times*, September 25 and 27, 1872.

49. See, for example, *St. Louis Republican*, May 28, 1873.

50. David R. Johnson, *Policing the Underworld: The Impact of Crime on the Development of the American Police, 1800–1887* (Philadelphia: Temple University Press, 1979), 41–67; Larry K. Hartsfield, *The American Response to Professional Crime, 1870–1914* (Westport, Conn.: Greenwood, 1985), 11–37, 51. Hartsfield's notion that burglary was the primary problem for police detectives has been verified by this author's findings in an extensive review of crime reports in newspapers and professional journals. For a typical news report on urban crime, see *Chicago Tribune*, April 2, 1875. As late as 1897, two senior Boston police officials depicted the armed robber as a marginal sort of criminal: in *Our Rival the Rascal* (Boston: Pemberton, 1897), Benjamin P. Eldridge and William B. Watts devoted most of their discussion to burglars, safecrackers, forgers, con men, pilferers, and other nonviolent types; they even argued that killing in the course of robbery was rare.

51. *Kansas City Times*, September 29, 1872.

52. See, for example, a circular of the Missouri Southern Relief Association, 1866, coll. 970, fold. 167, Clarence W. Alvord and Idress Head Collection, WHMC.

53. *Kansas City Times*, October 16, 1872.

54. Ibid., October 15, 1872.

55. *Kansas City Journal*, April 5, 1882; see also Charley Ford's comments in *St. Louis Republican*, April 6, 1882, and Bob Ford's in *St. Louis Republican*, April 7, 1882. Settle, 41–2, discusses the link between Jesse's letters and Edwards.

56. *Kansas City Times*, October 20 and 25, 1872. Dick Liddil later claimed that Jesse James told him that he, Frank, Jim Cummins, Ol Shepherd, and Arthur McCoy carried out the robbery; *St. Louis Republican*, September 9, 1883. This secondhand account is more than questionable: not only is the number of men wrong, but Ol Shepherd was already dead.

CHAPTER THIRTEEN: Invisible Empires

1. Bettie A. Scruggs to M. D. Scruggs, April 3, 1873, Watkins Mill.

2. *Kansas City Times*, September 19, 1872.

3. Ibid., November 1, 1872.

4. Ibid., November 5, 1872.

5. Ibid., December 3 and 11, 1872.

6. *St. Louis Republican*, August 24, 1872, and May 28, 1873; W. Lawson to B. Gratz Brown, March 14, 1872, Parson E. K. Cooper to Mr. Brown, April 3, 1872, B. Gratz Brown Papers, MSA; *Kansas City Journal of Commerce*, May 30, 1873; Settle, 47.

7. Fellman, 205–6, 252–4; Shoemaker, 4: 261–2; Silas Woodson to T. C. Fletcher, September 27, 1873, Silas Woodson Papers, MSA; M. C. Eden, "Missouri's First Train Robbery," *Brand Book* 16, no. 2 (January 1974), published by the English Westerners' Society, 13–24.

8. *Sioux City Journal*, July 26, 1873.

9. *St. Louis Republican*, May 28, 1873; *Kansas City Journal of Commerce*, Friday, May 30, 1873, and Settle, 47.

10. Quoted by Robert Ford, *St. Louis Republican*, April 7, 1882.

11. Esther Rogoff Taus, *Central Banking Functions of the United States Treasury, 1789–1941* (New York: Columbia University Press, 1943), 79, 85–6, 102, 112; Richard Franklin Bensel, *Yankee Leviathan: The Origins of Central State Authority in America, 1865–1877* (New York: Cambridge University Press, 1990), 262–74, 287–8; Richard Sylla, "Federal Policy, Banking Market Structure, and Capital Mobilization in the United States, 1863–1913," *Journal of Economic History* 29, no. 4 (December 1969): 657–86; H. Peers Brewer, "Eastern Money and Western Mortgages in the 1870s," *Business History Review* 50, no. 3 (autumn 1976): 356–80; T. J. Stiles, "As Good as Gold?," *Smithsonian* 31, no. 6 (September 2000): 106–17.

12. A. L. Stimson, *History of the Express Business* (New York: Baker & Godwin, 1881), 51–99, 108–13, 209–10, 303–22, 369–70; *Our Expressman*, May 1874; Alvin F. Harlow, *Old Waybills: The Romance of the Express Companies* (New York: D. Appleton-Century Co., 1934), 48–50, 300, 342; see also Scott Reynolds Nelson, *Iron Confederacies: Southern Railways, Klan Violence, and Reconstruction* (Chapel Hill: University of North Carolina Press, 1999), 58–62. Express companies must be distinguished from fast-freight lines, which were administrative arrangements for moving freight cars across several rail companies without interruption; see Irene D. Neu and George Rogers Taylor, *The American Railroad Network, 1861–1890* (Cambridge, Mass.: Harvard University Press, 1956), 67–79. Each railroad corporation publicly listed its express companies and fast-freight affiliations; see Edward Vernon, ed., *American Railroad Manual for the United States and the Dominion* (Philadelphia: J. B. Lippincott, 1873).

13. Edwin L. Lopata, *Local Aid to Railroads in Missouri* (New York: Columbia University Press, 1937), 6–12, 22–37, 62–81, 132–3; Paul W. Gates, "The Railroads of Missouri, 1850–1870," *MHR* 26, no. 2 (January 1932): 126–41. The primary dissenting view is that of David Thelen, *Paths of Resistance: Tradition and Dignity in Industrializing Missouri* (New York: Oxford University Press, 1986), 29–65. He argues that "popular prejudice and conservative fiscal traditions" formed an obstacle to railroad development (for which I find little evidence).

14. Lopata, 81–105; Virginia Rust Frazier, "Dallas County Railroad Bonds," *MHR* 61, no. 4 (July 1967): 444–62; E. M. Violette, "The Missouri and Mississippi Railroad Debt," *MHR* 15, no. 3 (April 1921): 467–518, and no. 4 (July 1921): 617–47; Thelen, 63–4.

15. Lopata, 105–7; *St. Louis Republican*, April 26 and May 1, 1872; Albert Sigel to B. Gratz Brown, telegram dated May 3, 1872, and Jonathon F. Phillips and F. M. Cockrell to B. Gratz Brown, May 1, 1872, B. Gratz Brown Papers, MSA.

16. Lopata, 107; Vernon, 501–4; Julius Grodinsky, *The Iowa Pool: A Study in Railroad Competition, 1870–1884* (Chicago: University of Chicago Press, 1950), 1–4, 59–61, 89; see also George H. Miller, *Railroads and the Granger Laws* (Madison: University of Wisconsin Press, 1971), 3–22.

17. Charles F. Adams, Jr., "A Chapter of Erie," *North American Review* (July 1869), 30–106, quote on 104; see also Alan Trachtenberg, *The Incorporation of America: Culture & Society in the Gilded Age* (New York: Hill and Wang, 1982), 57–60.

18. *Annual Report to the President, Directors, and Stockholders of the Chicago, Rock Island, and Pacific Railroad Corporation, April 1, 1874* (New York: Clarence Levey, 1874), 6–9; *Annual Report of the Comptroller of the Currency, December 1, 1873* (Washington, D.C.: Government Printing Office, 1873), 7–8, 31.

19. James A. Ward, *Railroads and the Character of America, 1820–1851* (Knoxville: University of Tennessee Press, 1986), 151.

20. Grodinsky, 6–38, 108–9; *Kansas City Times*, November 27, 1872. See also Wyatt W. Belcher, *The Economic Rivalry Between St. Louis and Chicago, 1850–1880* (New York: Columbia University Press, 1947).

21. *Kansas City Times*, February 19 and July 23, 1873; Homer Clevenger, "Railroads in Missouri Politics, 1875–1887," *MHR* 43, no. 2 (January 1949): 222; *History III*, 284–6. Local histories and newspapers abound with stories of Grange lodges forming in early 1873; see, for example, William Young, *Young's History of Lafayette County, Missouri* (Indianapolis: B. F. Bowen, 1910), 232.

22. See, for example, Robert M. Utley's discussion in *Billy the Kid: A Short and Violent Life* (Lincoln: University of Nebraska, 1989), photo insert, 196–7.

23. The account that follows is based on the following sources: *Kansas City Times*, July 23, 1873; *New York Times*, July 23, 24, and 26, 1873; and the *Sioux City Journal*, July 23–26, 1873. Further notes indicate the source of quotes or specific information when necessary.

24. *Kansas City Times*, July 23, 1873; *Sioux City Journal*, July 23, 1873.

25. *Sioux City Journal*, July 24, 1873. For descriptions of Jesse James by those who knew him best, see George Miller, Jr., *The Trial of Frank James for Murder* (St. Louis: n.p., 1898), 40, 113.

26. *Sioux City Journal*, July 25, 1873.

27. Ibid., July 24, 1873.

28. *New York Times*, July 23, 1873.

29. *Sioux City Journal*, July 24, 1873.

30. The night after the robbery, they had dinner with a Mr. and Mrs. Stuckeye in Ringgold County, who provided the fine description above; *Sioux City Journal*, July 24 and 25, 1873. See also the *Kansas City Times*, July 23, 1873.

31. *Kansas City Times*, July 18, 1873; *Railroad Gazette*, August 2, 1873. As is often noted, the Reno gang seems to have originated train robbery; see Settle, 47, and James Mackay, *Allan Pinkerton: The Eye Who Never Slept* (Edinburgh: Mainstream Publishing, 1996), 188.

32. *Des Moines Republican* in the *Sioux City Journal*, July 24, 1873. This language is all the more striking for appearing in an Iowa newspaper with no connection to John Edwards or other bandit glorifiers.

33. *Kansas City Times*, July 23, 1873; *Sioux City Journal*, July 23, 1873.

34. Thelen, 13–17, 29–35, 59–65, 70–7.

35. See chaps. 1–3 for the antebellum James-Samuel family; Marley Brant, *The Outlaw Youngers: A Confederate Brotherhood* (Lanham, Md.: Madison Books, 1993), 8–15; see especially Richard White, "Outlaw Gangs of the Middle Border: American Social Bandits," *Western Historical Quarterly* 12, no. 4 (October 1981): 387–408, which shares many points of this analysis. Dick Liddil testified that during his entire acquaintance with Jesse James, from the 1870s through 1881, former bushwhackers provided hiding places and material support for the outlaws; these guerrillas were identified by Don R. Bowen as members of some of the wealthiest families in Jackson County; see *St. Louis Republican*, September 9, 1883; Don R. Bowen, "Guerrilla War in Western Missouri, 1862–1865: Historical Extensions of the Relative Deprivation Hypothesis," *Comparative Studies in Society and History* 19, no. 1 (January 1977): 30–51; and Don R. Bowen, "Counterrevolutionary Guerrilla War: Missouri, 1861–1865," *Conflict* 8, no. 1 (1988): 69–78.

36. See, for example, *Kansas City Times*, November 1, 1872, and February 6, 1873; on rural millinery, see, for example, the letters of Sarah Harlan, May 3 and June 9, 1865, June 16, 1866, Bond-Fentriss Family Papers, UNC.

37. *Kansas City Times*, July 23, 1873.

38. Lopata, 78–81; *Lexington Caucasian*, July 25, 1866; *St. Louis Republican*, April 26, 1872;

Kansas City Times, November 27, 1872; Daniel O'Flaherty, *General Jo Shelby: Undefeated Rebel* (Chapel Hill: University of North Carolina Press, 2000, orig. pub. 1954), 334–41.

39. George L. Anderson, "Western Attitude Toward National Banks," *Mississippi Valley Historical Review* 23, no. 2 (September 1936): 205–16; Sylla, 657–86; Brewer, 356–80; Allan G. Bogue, "Financing the Prairie Farmer," in *The Reinterpretation of American Economic History,* ed. Stanley L. Engerman and Robert W. Fogel (New York: Harper & Row, 1971), 301–10; Bensel, 262–93. Brewer and Bogue both note that eastern insurance companies provided much of the mortgage lending in the region.

40. Lopata, 78–81; Thelen, 35–65; Clevenger, 222–4, notes that former Confederate Democrats Richard P. Bland, Francis M. Cockrell, and George G. Vest emerged as spokesmen for farmers' interests in the 1870s.

41. Nelson, 81–139; *Kansas City Times,* November 5 and 9, December 11, 1872; see also *Kansas City Times,* December 31, 1872, July 23 and 25, 1873; *Liberty Tribune,* September 19, 1873.

42. As noted earlier, Dick Liddil later provided a list of sympathizers, all of whom had been secessionists; *St. Louis Republican,* September 9, 1883; see also the commentary of the *Kansas City Journal of Commerce,* October 20, 1876.

43. *Lexington Caucasian,* August 30, 1873.

44. Shoemaker, 5: 343–4.

45. *Liberty Tribune,* September 12, 1873.

46. John N. Edwards, "A Terrible Quintet," special supplement to the *St. Louis Dispatch,* November 23, 1873, vol. 34, coll. 1424, Walter B. Stevens Scrapbook, WHMC. Settle, 51–6, offers a thorough review and insightful discussion.

47. Governor Thomas Fletcher's orders to call up the militia in December 1866 extended only to the counties south of the Missouri River; a review of the letterbooks of the adjutant general for that period reveals no orders to units to cross to the north side. On March 4, 1867, Governor Fletcher wrote to Major Reeves Leonard that there were no more militiamen on duty in the state; coll. 1013, fold. 494, Abiel Leonard Papers, WHMC.

48. *St. Louis Dispatch,* December 29, 1873; Robert J. Wybrow, "From the Pen of a Noble Robber: The Letters of Jesse Woodson James, 1847–1882," *Brand Book* 24, no. 2 (summer 1987), published by the English Westerners' Society, 1–22; *Liberty Tribune,* January 9, 1874.

49. Eden, 13–14; Yeatman, 109–10.

50. Jesse James's presence would later be confirmed by his wife. *Kansas City Evening Star,* April 20, 1882.

51. Eden, 20; *St. Louis Dispatch,* February 10, 1874; see also Brant, 35.

52. *St. Louis Republican,* February 2, 1874.

53. Ibid., February 11, 1874.

54. Eden, 14; Yeatman, 21; see also Shakespeare's *1 Henry IV,* act 1, scene 2.

55. This account of the Gads Hill robbery draws on the following sources: *New York Times,* February 2 and 3, 1874; *St. Louis Republican,* February 1, 2, 3, and 11, 1874; *Boonville Weekly Advertiser,* February 4, 1874; *Liberty Tribune,* February 6, 1874; *Lexington Caucasian,* February 7, 1874; Yeatman, 19–23; Eden, 13–24; Settle, 49–51. Further citations refer to specific quotations.

56. *St. Louis Republican,* February 2, 1874. Most accounts give Alford's middle initial as "A.," but the *Republican*'s report of the conductor's account gives it as "W."

57. Ibid., February 2, 1874.

58. Ibid., February 1 and 2, 1874.

59. Ibid., February 1 and 2, 1874. Yeatman, 21, doubts the report that the bandits spoke about not robbing working men, saying that conductor Alford never mentioned it. But Alford would not have known either way, since he was held captive on the platform.

60. Ibid., February 2, 1874.

61. *Liberty Tribune,* February 6, 1874.

62. *St. Louis Republican,* February 11, 1874. Eden misquotes the name of the widow Cook as "Cork," an error Yeatman duplicates. Yeatman, 21, suggests a total haul of $6,080.

63. *St. Louis Dispatch*, February 10, 1874.

64. William Hyde, "Newspapers and Newspaper Men of Three Decades," *Collections of the Missouri Historical Society* 12 (1896): 5–24; *Our Expressman*, May 1874.

CHAPTER FOURTEEN: Allies and Enemies

1. A. L. Stimson, *History of the Express Business* (New York: Baker & Godwin, 1881), 53–6, 108–12, 117–24, 128. In the fiscal year ending April 1, 1874, the Rock Island alone received $107,098.22 in fees from express companies; *Annual Report to the President, Directors, and Stockholders of the Chicago, Rock Island, and Pacific Railroad Company, April 1, 1874* (New York: Clarence Levey & Co., 1874), 8.

2. Richard Franklin Bensel, *Yankee Leviathan: The Origins of Central State Authority in America, 1859–1877* (New York: Cambridge University Press, 1990), 268–93; Eric Foner, *Reconstruction: America's Unfinished Revolution, 1863–1877* (New York: Harper & Row, 1988), 512; James K. Kindahl, "Economic Factors in Specie Resumption, 1865–1879," in *The Reinterpretation of American Economic History*, ed. Stanley L. Engerman and Robert W. Fogel (New York: Harper & Row, 1971), 468–79. Edwin L. Lopata, *Local Aid to Railroads in Missouri* (New York: Columbia University Press, 1937), 73–4, notes that European dissatisfaction with American railroad bonds began before the Panic.

3. *Autobiography of Andrew Carnegie* (Boston: Houghton Mifflin, 1920), excerpted in T. J. Stiles, ed., *Robber Barons and Radicals: Reconstruction and the Origins of Civil Rights* (New York: Berkley Books, 1997), 315–16.

4. Foner, 512–16; *Railroad Gazette*, December 26, 1874; see also Irwin Unger, *The Greenback Era: A Social and Political History of American Finance, 1865–1879* (Princeton: Princeton University Press, 1964), 220–31.

5. Stimson, 369; Alvin F. Harlow, *Old Waybills: The Romance of the Express Companies* (New York: D. Appleton-Century Co., 1934), 315–17; *Our Expressman*, August 1875.

6. Stimson, 331, 341; James Mackay, *Allan Pinkerton: The Eye Who Never Slept* (Edinburgh: Mainstream Publishing, 1996), 188; *Our Expressman*, August 1874, June and August 1875; *Sioux City Journal*, July 23–26, 1873; *Railroad Gazette*, August 9, 1873, February 21 and March 31, 1874; Rock Island *Annual Report*, 1874. Governor Charles H. Hardin's correspondence with Thomas Allen, president of the Iron Mountain Railroad, strongly indicates that the company never employed private detectives to pursue the bandits, as Hardin had to beg for Allen to make a complaint against one of the gang after he was captured in Iowa; see C. H. Hardin to Thomas Allen, February 27, 1875, and Thomas Allen to C. H. Hardin, May 19, 1875, Charles H. Hardin Papers, MSA. Yeatman, 113, cites the *New York World*, March 28, 1874, as evidence that the U.S. Post Office hired the Pinkertons. But the *World* appears to have been reporting rumors. No direct evidence implicates the post office. The U.S. Secret Service frequently handled cases of mail robbery, and sometimes hired the Pinkertons, but it had no role in the investigations of the James-Younger gang. See Record of Arrests and Convictions, 1869–1930, entry 33, and Register of Letters Received at New York, April 1, 1870–September 1874, entry 12, Records of the U.S. Secret Service, RG 87, National Archives, College Park, Maryland.

7. All sources from the Pinkerton agency itself identify only the Adams Express as the hiring party. See, for example, an interview with Pinkerton agent L. E. Angell, *Columbia Missouri Statesman*, April 10, 1874; an interview with William Pinkerton, *Kansas City Evening Star*, July 21, 1881; and Allan Pinkerton's comment that he planned to report to Adams president Dinsmore, in his letter to George H. Bangs, April 17, 1874, Pinkerton Papers. The Adams had hired Pinkerton before; see R. B. Macy, "Detective Pinkerton," *Harper's Magazine* (October 1873): 720–7. For a typical Pinkerton advertisement, see *Our Expressman*, August 1875.

8. *Chicago Herald*, July 2, 1884; Stephen B. Oates, *To Purge This Land With Blood: A Biography of John Brown* (Amherst: University of Massachusetts Press, 1970), 254, 261–5; Edwin C. Fishel, *The Secret War for the Union: The Untold Story of Military Intelligence in the Civil War* (Boston: Houghton Mifflin, 1996), 53–5. Fishel, 102, argues that Pinkerton excelled at spy-catching, that

McClellan was the "dominant party" in the famous overestimation of Confederate forces.

9. David R. Johnson, *Policing the Urban Underworld: The Impact of Crime on the Development of the American Police, 1800–1887* (Philadelphia: Temple University Press, 1979), 7–15, 28–65; Larry K. Hartsfield, *The American Response to Professional Crime, 1870–1917* (Westport, Conn.: Greenwood Press, 1985), 40–8; Jacqueline Pope, *Bounty Hunters, Marshals, and Sheriffs: Forward to the Past* (Westport, Conn.: Praeger, 1998), 74–5; *Our Expressman*, August 1875; R. B. Macy, 720. See also David Johnson's *Illegal Tender: Counterfeiting and the Secret Service in Nineteenth-Century America* (Washington, D.C.: Smithsonian Institution Press, 1995), ix–xviii, 63–6.

10. Mackay, 188–208, 214; Hartsfield, 73. Pinkerton wrote of his stroke as a "very severe shock" in a letter dated September 13, 1870; for a typical operation, see Allan Pinkerton to President, Cook County National Bank, June 20, 1872; Allan Pinkerton Papers, Chicago Historical Society.

11. Pinkerton's tactics are illustrated in R. B. Macy, 720–7.

12. The *New York World*, March 28, 1874, reported that the bandits had gone south to Arkansas, "giving out" that they were going to Texas before doubling back to Missouri. This seems to have been a misreading of Missouri news reports that the bandits had passed west through Texas County; compare with the *St. Louis Republican*, February 11, 1874. Seven years later William Pinkerton said, "The gang was traced to St. Clair county by a man who was sent on to make a preliminary report, and there the members scattered"; *Kansas City Evening Star*, July 21, 1881.

13. Interview with William Pinkerton, *Kansas City Evening Star*, July 21, 1881. Whicher's name was misspelled "Witcher" in this article, and has been corrected. Detective L. E. Angell confirmed that Whicher was not supposed to make arrests; *St. Louis Globe*, March 20, 1874. On William Pinkerton's place in the company, see Mackay, 205 (though he exaggerates somewhat the role of Allan's sons William and Robert, giving them credit for actually running the agency, which was not the case).

14. *New York World*, March 28, 1874.

15. Interview with William Pinkerton, *Kansas City Evening Star*, July 21, 1881.

16. *Kansas City Times*, September 18, 1872.

17. This account of Whicher's visit to the courthouse was written by an anonymous county official, though it seems obvious that it was the recorder, Sandusky; *Kansas City Times*, reprinted in the *Liberty Tribune*, March 27, 1874. On Whicher's state of mind, see an interview with L. E. Angell, *St. Louis Globe*, March 20, 1874. For the identity of the recorder, never named in this account, see W. H. Woodson, *History of Clay County, Missouri* (Topeka: Historical Publishing Company, 1920), 335.

18. *Liberty Tribune*, March 27, 1874.

19. Woodson, 352, discusses the Commercial bank and its personnel.

20. Whicher's visit to the bank is better known than his earlier visit to the courthouse, since it was reported by L. E. Angell in newspaper interviews; the most reliable account seems to be in the *St. Louis Globe*, March 20, 1874, but see also *St. Louis Republican*, March 20, 1874, and an independent investigation by the *Hamilton News*, quoted in *St. Louis Republican*, March 23, 1874.

21. *St. Louis Globe*, March 20, 1874; *St. Louis Republican*, March 20, 1874; interview with William Pinkerton, *Kansas City Evening Star*, July 21, 1881.

22. *Columbia Missouri Statesman*, April 10, 1874.

23. *Hamilton News* in the *St. Louis Republican*, March 23, 1874.

24. *St. Louis Globe*, March 20, 1874.

25. The ferryman noticed his calm demeanor; *Hamilton News* in the *St. Louis Republican*, March 23, 1874; *St. Louis Globe*, March 20, 1874; *Columbia Missouri Statesman*, April 10, 1874; the leg ropes were left at the scene of the shooting, *Kansas City Times*, March 14, 1874, reprinted in the *Liberty Tribune*, March 20, 1874. Both Allan and William Pinkerton believed that he had been beaten, interrogated, and bound in the Samuel farmhouse; see the *Kansas City Evening Star*, July 21, 1881, and Allan Pinkerton to P. H. Woodward, January 27, 1875, Pinkerton Papers. Years later, Dick Liddil claimed that Jesse James told him that he, Frank, Tom McDaniels, and Jim Cummins were at the house when Whicher arrived; *St. Louis Republican*, September 9, 1883. Though a distinct possibility, this is secondhand information, and highly questionable.

26. Interview with William Pinkerton, *Kansas City Evening Star,* July 21, 1881.

27. *Kansas City Evening Star,* July 21, 1881. "Allen" was identified as Lull, former Chicago police captain, in the *St. Louis Republican,* March 23, 1874. Allan Pinkerton thought highly of Lull. On January 10, 1874, Pinkerton wrote to Secret Service chief Hiram Whitley to recommend Lull for appointment as an agent; Register of Letters Received at New York, April 1, 1870–September 1874, entry 12, Records of the U.S. Secret Service, RG 87, National Archives, College Park, Md.

28. *St. Louis Times* in the *Columbia Missouri Statesman,* April 10, 1874.

29. Interview with Theodrick Snuffer, *Osceola Democrat* in the *St. Louis Republican,* March 24, 1874.

30. E. G. Bower to George M. Bennett, April 15, 1898, "Northfield (Minnesota) Bank Robbery of 1876: Selected Manuscripts Collection and Government Records," (microfilm publication), MnHS.

31. The account of the gunfight to this point (including all dialogue) is drawn from Lull's testimony to a coroner's inquest under the name W. J. Allen, March 18, 1874, *Osceola Democrat* in the *St. Louis Republican,* March 24, 1874.

32. *St. Louis Republican,* March 21, 1874; McDonald, mentioned in most news reports simply as "a negro," testified at the coroner's inquest, *Osceola Democrat* in the *St. Louis Republican,* March 24, 1874; the revolver was identified in the *St. Louis Times* in the *Columbia Missouri Statesman,* April 10, 1874. See also *St. Louis Republican,* March 20, 1874; *Clinton Democrat Extra* in the *Boonville Missouri Advertiser,* March 27, 1874; *Clinton Democrat Extra,* March 21, in the *Liberty Tribune,* March 27, 1874.

33. *Clinton Democrat Extra,* March 21, in the *Liberty Tribune,* March 27, 1874; *Osceola Democrat* in the *St. Louis Republican,* March 24, 1874; *St. Louis Republican,* March 21 and 23, 1874.

34. Allan Pinkerton to George H. Bangs, April 17, 1874, Pinkerton Papers. For Hoey, see Stimson, 111–2. This letter offers solid evidence that the Adams Express Company was the sole employer of the Pinkertons in the Gads Hill case, and had complete control of the progress of the investigation. It is highly unlikely that Pinkerton actually would have led a raid, given his stroke a few years earlier; see, for example, his letter of September 13, 1870, Allan Pinkerton Papers, Chicago Historical Society.

35. *St. Louis Globe,* March 20, 1874.

36. In the *Liberty Tribune,* March 27, 1874, Patton published an angry reply to the reports that implicated him in tipping off Jesse James, and he threatened a libel lawsuit against the *St. Louis Globe* and the *Republican;* see also Settle, 62. On Bettie Scruggs Patton's marriage and pregnancy, see Bettie A. Patton to M. D. Scruggs, August 14, 1874, Watkins Mill. Richard Slotkin notes in *Gunfighter Nation: The Myth of the Frontier in Twentieth-Century America* (New York: Atheneum, 1992), 130–3, that the *New York World* report of March 28, 1874, on the murders of the Pinkerton detectives was one of the first big stories on the outlaws in the national press; as a conservative Democratic sheet, owned by August Belmont, the paper placed the James-Younger bandits in the context of the reaction against Reconstruction (see also Slotkin's *The Fatal Environment: The Myth of the Frontier in the Age of Industrialization, 1800–1890* [New York: Atheneum, 1985], 334–45, 358–70).

37. On reports that detectives were searching for him as early as August 1873, see Settle, 58. The timing of Jesse James's visit to Kearney was listed differently in almost every news report; Angell was quoted as saying Friday, March 13, in the *St. Louis Globe,* March 20, 1874, and on Thursday, March 12, in the *St. Louis Republican,* March 20, 1874, whereas the *Hamilton News* in the *St. Louis Republican,* March 23, 1874, states that he was seen in Kearney on the day of the murder. An appearance on March 11, before the brothers went underground, makes more sense, and the *Hamilton News* interviewed the sheriff and other locals. The *Liberty Tribune,* March 27, 1874, states that Patton took a posse to the Samuel farm immediately after learning of the murder.

38. *History of Clay,* 502–3.

39. *Kansas City Times,* January 28, 1875; *St. Louis Republican,* February 5, 1875.

40. *Kansas City Journal,* April 6, 1882; *Lexington Caucasian,* October 17, 1874; see Zee Mimms James's account to a coroner's inquiry, *Kansas City Times,* April 4, 1882, and *Kansas City Journal,* April 4, 1882, and a secondhand version in Stella F. James, *In the Shadow of Jesse James* (Thousand

Oaks, Calif.: Dragon Books, 1989), 19, 32–3 (editor Milton F. Perry lists Zee Mimms's birthdate as July 21, 1845); Settle, 69–70; Yeatman, 119. Zee Mimms's father had died in 1869; *History of Clay*, 502–3.

41. *St. Louis Dispatch*, June 9, 1874. An assumption is made here that Edwards wrote this article; it is possible, but unlikely, that it came from an independent source.

42. Walter B. Stevens, "The Political Turmoil of 1874 in Missouri," *MHR* 31, no. 1 (October 1936): 3–9; *History III*, 280–1. Stevens aroused Edwards's wrath at one point by printing a story naming the James and Younger brothers as perpetrators of the Gads Hill robbery; Settle, 50. See also Homer Clevenger, "Railroads in Missouri Politics, 1875–1887," *MHR* 43, no. 2 (January 1949): 220–36.

43. *St. Louis Republican*, March 13, 1874.

44. Ibid., March 21, 1874. The role of the bandits in the Democratic Party's internal split was first discussed in William A. Settle, Jr., "The James Boys and Missouri Politics," *MHR* 36, no. 4 (July 1942): 412–29.

45. *Kansas City Journal of Commerce*, April 16, 1874. Donan led the *Caucasian* until 1875, and often praised the bandits; Lewis O. Saum, "Donan and the *Caucasian*," *MHR* 63, no. 4 (July 1969): 419–50; on Van Horn, see J. M. Greenwood, "Col. Robert T. Van Horn," *MHR* 4, no. 2 (January 1910): 92–105, and 4, no. 3 (April 1910): 167–81, who observes that Van Horn wrote the paper's editorials.

46. *History III*, 287.

47. *St. Louis Republican*, March 21, 1874; Settle, 64–7, discusses the gang as a political issue in 1874.

48. Shoemaker, 5: 350–1, 326–8; John Glendower Westover notes that virtually every unit in the militia had been disbanded by 1874, in "The Evolution of the Missouri Militia, 1804–1919" (Ph.D. diss., University of Missouri, Columbia, 1948), 173–83; for a brief discussion of the bandit issue in politics, see *History III*, 287.

49. *St. Louis Republican*, March 24, 1874; Settle, 62–3.

50. *St. Louis Republican*, March 24, 1874.

51. J. W. Ragsdale to Silas Woodson, December 4, 1874, Silas Woodson Papers, MSA.

52. *Columbia Missouri Statesman*, June 5, 1874 (spelling errors have been corrected); North Todd Gentry, "William F. Switzler," *MHR* 24, no. 2 (January 1930): 161–76; *St. Louis Dispatch*, June 6, 1874.

53. *St. Louis Dispatch*, June 8 and 9, 1874.

54. *Kansas City Times*, September 29, 1874; Stevens, 4; Switzler noted with satisfaction that no "Gads Hill type" candidates had been nominated, *Columbia Missouri Statesman*, September 4, 1874.

55. Settle, 70; Robertus Love, *The Rise and Fall of Jesse James* (Lincoln: University of Nebraska Press, 1990, orig. pub. 1925), 163–5; *Kansas City Times*, August 19, 1874. For the story of Frank's secret wedding, see *Kansas City Times*, August 16, 1876, and September 11, 1881; see also Yeatman, 121.

56. *Kansas City Times*, September 1, 1874. For a map of Missouri railroads, see the *Kansas City Times*, January 1, 1873, and Paul W. Gates, "The Railroads of Missouri, 1850–1870," *MHR* 26, no. 2 (January 1932): 126–41.

57. *St. Louis Globe*, October 4, 1874, reported that the James brothers were spotted with Jim Younger after the robbery.

58. Yeatman, 121–2, offers a solid argument for Hamlett's mistaken identification.

59. The main source for these events was a special edition of the *Lexington Caucasian;* the story ran again in the regular edition, *Lexington Caucasian*, September 5, 1874, and was reprinted in the *St. Louis Republican*, September 2, 1874, and the *Kansas City Times*, September 1, 1874, which added information from the *Lexington Register* (formerly the *Missouri Valley Register*).

60. *Lexington Register* in *Kansas City Times*, September 1, 1874.

61. *St. Louis Globe*, October 4, 1874; C. C. Rainwater to Chas. P. Johnson, September 3, 1874, Silas Woodson Papers, MSA.

62. *St. Louis Globe*, October 4, 1874; L. Harrigan to Chas. P. Johnson, September 4, 1874, Har-

rigan to Chas. P. Johnson, September 11, 1874, T. H. Bayliss to C. P. Johnson, September 11, 1874, Silas Woodson Papers, MSA. I am following Settle, 73, who spells the detective's name "Yancey," rather than "Yancy," as it appears elsewhere; Settle relied on correspondence from Yancey himself that I was not able to locate in the Missouri State Archives.

63. *St. Louis Globe*, October 4, 1874; *St. Louis Republican*, September 8, 1874.

64. Bettie Scruggs Patton to M. D. Scruggs, September 4, 1874, Watkins Mill.

65. *St. Louis Globe*, October 4, 1874; the press report of the tip-off is supported by a telegram from the St. Louis police chief, reporting that Yancey had been given away, L. Harrigan to Chas. P. Johnson, September 13, 1874, Silas Woodson Papers, MSA. The *Globe*'s extremely detailed account of Yancey's pursuit and gunfight seems quite accurate, judging from supporting evidence in the state archives.

66. *Lexington Caucasian*, September 5, 1874.

67. *Kansas City Times*, September 9, 1874; *New York Times*, September 15, 1874.

68. *Lexington Caucasian*, October 17, 1874. Zerelda also mentioned that her daughter Susie James Parmer was teaching high school in Sherman, Texas, and that she was escorting her daughter Sarah to that place to enroll her.

69. *Jefferson City People's Tribune*, September 30, 1874.

70. *Columbia Missouri Statesman*, September 11, 1874. See also Settle, 63–7, and "The James Boys and Missouri Politics," 412–29.

71. *St. Louis Republican*, September 25, 1874; for an example of this complaint in other contexts, see *Jefferson City People's Tribune*, July 15, 1874. See also *History III*, 286–9; Settle, 66–7.

72. James Fernando Ellis, *The Influence of Environment on the Settlement of Missouri* (St. Louis: Webster Publishing Company, 1929), 155–7. Ellis argues that larger factors also slowed immigration, particularly the depression; but he shows that Missourians honestly believed that turmoil in their state discouraged settlers.

73. Lopata, 67–70; *Kansas City Times*, November 2, 1872; *Columbia Herald*, September 24, 1897.

74. *Kansas City Times*, September 25 and 29, 1874. For Democratic attacks on and wooing of the Grangers, see the *Columbia Missouri Statesman*, April 17, 1874; *St. Louis Dispatch*, June 8 and 10, 1874; *Liberty Tribune*, September 18 and 25, 1874.

75. *New York Times*, February 3, 1874; *Kansas City Times*, September 2, 1874. On the greenback issue, see Robert P. Sharkey, *Money, Class, and Party: An Economic Study of Civil War and Reconstruction* (Baltimore: The Johns Hopkins University Press, 1959); Milton Friedman and Anna Jacobson Schwartz, *A Monetary History of the United States, 1867–1960* (Princeton: Princeton University Press, 1963), 3–14; Foner, 335; T. J. Stiles, "As Good as Gold?," *Smithsonian* 31, no. 6 (September 2000): 106–7. The most important book on the currency debate is Irwin Unger, *The Greenback Era: A Social and Political History of American Finance, 1865–1879* (Princeton: Princeton University Press, 1964).

76. *Kansas City Times*, August 11, 12, 18, and 19, September 2, 3, and 29, October 2 and 17, 1874; *Jefferson City People's Tribune*, July 15 and 22, 1874; *Lexington Caucasian*, October 10, 1874; *Liberty Tribune*, October 16 and 30, 1874; *St. Louis Dispatch*, June 10, 1874. On Sumner's Civil Rights Bill, see Foner, 504–5, 532–4.

77. *History III*, 286–9; Foner, 512–63; George E. Patton to M. D. Scruggs, October 23, 1874, Bettie Patton to Mattie Scruggs, November 15, 1874, Bettie Patton to Mattie Scruggs, November 26, 1874, Watkins Mill. Another factor in the Democratic victory was the revelation that Gentry had sold a slave late in the Civil War, when emancipation was impending; Stevens, 3–9. Lawrence O. Christensen and Gary R. Kremer argue in *A History of Missouri*, vol. 4, *1875 to 1919* (Columbia: University of Missouri Press, 1997), 1–9, that electoral triumph stemmed from the Democrats' ability to coopt their opponents' issues; but the emphasis on party loyalty in this Democratic state, against the backdrop of Reconstruction, seems a more central element.

CHAPTER FIFTEEN: The Persistence of Civil War

1. *St. Louis Republican*, December 11 and 12, 1874; Settle, 75; *Kansas City Journal of Commerce*,

December 9, 1874; see also *St. Louis Republican*, December 12, 1874.

2. *Kansas City Journal of Commerce*, December 9, 1874.

3. *St. Louis Republican*, December 12, 1874. The distance to Muncie from Kansas City was reported as both twelve and seven miles; see the *St. Louis Republican*, December 11, 1874.

4. *Kansas City Journal of Commerce*, December 9, 1874; *Kansas City Times*, December 9, 1874, in the *St. Louis Republican*, December 11 and 12, 1874.

5. The gold was being sent to a brokerage house in New York; *St. Louis Republican*, December 11, 1874. The Henry rifle was an early lever-action rifle, a design picked up by Winchester with its popular 1873 model; Harrison Buckland reported that the heavyset bandit who came into the store had a Winchester rifle, in addition to two ivory-handled revolvers; *St. Louis Republican*, December 12, 1874.

6. *Kansas City Journal of Commerce*, December 9, 1874; *St. Louis Republican*, December 12, 1874; see also *St. Louis Republican*, December 9, 10, and 11, 1874. Yeatman, 127, mistakenly reports that $105 in currency was found at the campsite. It was customary to use a space instead of a decimal point, so the "$1 05" reported in the press should be read as "$1.05."

7. *Kansas City Times*, December 9, 1874, in the *St. Louis Republican*, December 11, 1874.

8. *St. Louis Republican*, December 9, 1874; E. M. Cooper [Wells, Fargo superintendent in Kansas City] to C. H. Hardin, March 1, 1875, and E. M. Cooper to C. H. Hardin, April 5, 1875, Charles H. Hardin Papers, MSA; *Our Expressman*, January 1875.

9. *St. Louis Republican*, December 10, 1874.

10. Ibid., December 12, 1874; Shoemaker, 5: 289–92, 391–3.

11. *St. Louis Dispatch*, December 15, 1874. "Justitia" also referred to a widely reprinted letter from Cole Younger which offered alibis for each robbery; Cole claimed that he and Jesse James "were not on good terms at the time [of the Kansas City fair robbery], nor haven't been for several years"; *St. Louis Republican*, November 30, 1874.

12. *Kansas City Journal of Commerce*, December 12, 1874.

13. *Lexington Caucasian*, December 12, 1874. On Ames and Mississippi, see Eric Foner, *Reconstruction: America's Unfinished Revolution, 1863–1877* (New York: Harper & Row, 1988), 296, 349, 353, 442, 538–42, 558–63; Richard Nelson Current, *Those Terrible Carpetbaggers: A Reinterpretation* (New York: Oxford University Press, 1988), 115–9, 172–9, 181–92, 306–24; T. J. Stiles, ed., *Robber Barons and Radicals: Reconstruction and the Origins of Civil Rights* (New York: Berkley Books, 1997), 80–105, 167–80, 195–214, 245–62, 276–300; William S. McFeely, *Grant: A Biography* (New York: W. W. Norton & Co., 1982), 345, 359–64. See also Eric Foner, *Freedom's Lawmakers: A Directory of Black Officeholders During Reconstruction* (New York: Oxford University Press, 1993), 244–6.

14. *St. Louis Republican*, December 11 and 12, 1874; *Kansas City Journal of Commerce*, December 12, 1874; Settle, 75. The James-Younger gang was accused of robbing the Timishingo Savings Bank in Corinth, Mississippi, on December 7, one day before the Muncie raid; it is my opinion that the Missourians had nothing to do with the Mississippi crime; *St. Louis Republican*, December 9, 1874.

15. T. H. Brougham to Gov. Hardin, February 10, 1875 [mistakenly dated "1874" in the original], Charles H. Hardin Papers, MSA.

16. Foner, *Reconstruction*, 437; Current, 315–16; Stiles, *Robber Barons*, 325–47.

17. A. P. McFarland to William B. Smith, February 22, 1875, Charles H. Hardin Papers, MSA.

18. *Kansas City Journal of Commerce*, May 5, 1875.

19. Allan Pinkerton to George H. Bangs, May 12, 1874, Pinkerton Papers; Yeatman, 120; *Kansas City Evening Star*, July 21, 1881. William Pinkerton's claims are substantiated by the sudden disappearance, after the deaths of Whicher and Lull, of any mention of the Adams Express Company or its officials from Allan Pinkerton's correspondence relating to the Missouri bandits; in addition, Pinkerton himself mentioned in his letters the expenditure of his own money in the case.

20. *History of Clay*, 336–9; *Portrait and Biographical Record of Clay, Ray, Carroll, Chariton, and Linn Counties, Missouri* (Chicago: Chapman Bros., 1893), 285–6.

21. *Kansas City Times*, April 14, 1875; *Kansas City Journal of Commerce*, April 15, 1875; Daniel H. Askew Probate Records, Clay County Archives, Liberty, Missouri; Allan Pinkerton to George

H. Bangs, May 12, 1874, Pinkerton Papers.

22. *St. Louis Republican*, February 4, 1875; *Richmond Conservator*, April 3, 1875; Geo. E. Patton to M. D. Scruggs, February 21, 1875, Watkins Mill. For an example of Pinkerton's code, see Allan Pinkerton to P. H. Woodward, December 15, 1874, Pinkerton Papers.

23. Allan Pinkerton to P. H. Woodward, December 15, 1874, Pinkerton Papers; *Militia Report*, 378–9, 383, 386–8, 397–400; *History of Clay*, 448; Republican Central Committee Meeting, Clay County, January 1, 1866, coll. 970, fold. 161, Clarence W. Alvord and Idress Head Collection, WHMC; Republican Central Committee of Clay County to Governor Thomas C. Fletcher, January 3, 1866, Thomas C. Fletcher Papers, MSA; Richard Franklin Bensel, *Yankee Leviathan: The Origins of Central State Authority in America, 1859–1877* (New York: Cambridge University Press, 1990), 351.

24. Yeatman, 128, calls the post office Pinkerton's "federal employer" (see also page 140). This is incorrect. Pinkerton wrote, "It is rather hard on me spending money continually. . . . I may probably withdraw, but I have not yet decided"; Allan Pinkerton to P. H. Woodward, January 27, 1875, Pinkerton Papers. See Letters Sent by the Chief Special Agent, and Case Files, Office of Special Agents and Mail Depredations, 1875–1877, entry 228, and Letters Sent 1789–1952, vol. 84, Office of the Postmaster General; Records of the Post Office Department, RG 28, NA. Not only was there no official correspondence with the Pinkerton Agency, but there was no reference to the bandits in any correspondence with F. W. Schaunte, special agent for the post office department in St. Louis. The post office records indicate that Woodward was chief special agent at the time, contrary to Yeatman's account.

25. Allan Pinkerton to P. H. Woodward, December 15, 1874, Pinkerton Papers.

26. Geo. E. Patton to M. D. Scruggs, February 21, 1875, Watkins Mill.

27. Hardwicke's letters and telegrams have not survived, but his note of the twenty-fifth is referred to specifically in Pinkerton's letter (signed with his old Civil War pseudonym), E. J. Allen to Samuel Hardwicke, December 28, 1874, Pinkerton Papers. The letter of introduction from Sheridan, dated December 30, is preserved in the records of the Rock Island arsenal; Yeatman, 131–2. Regarding L. W. Towne, see the *Liberty Tribune*, April 16, 1875.

28. Allan Pinkerton to P. H. Woodward, January 27, 1875, Pinkerton Papers; *St. Louis Republican*, February 4 and 5, 1875; see also *Kansas City Times*, January 27–30, 1875, and *Kansas City Journal of Commerce*, January 30, 1875. The *Kansas City Times* of January 27 mentions that seven horses had been tied up on the Haynesville road.

29. Allan Pinkerton to P. H. Woodward, January 27, 1875, Pinkerton Papers; *Kansas City Times*, January 28, 1875; *Kansas City Journal of Commerce*, January 29, 1875. Pinkerton's letter suggests that there was more than one iron ball, but evidence on the scene pointed to a single device. He was most likely returning from New York at the time. He had suffered a second stroke, and was not in shape to lead a raid himself. See Allan Pinkerton to John F. Tracy, January 24, 1875, and Geo. McQueen [a Pinkerton pseudonym] to Sam Hardwicke, February 16, 1875, Pinkerton Papers.

30. *Kansas City Times*, January 29, 1875.

31. *St. Louis Republican*, February 4, 1875.

32. Ibid., February 2, 1875; *Kansas City Times*, January 30, 1875; *Kansas City Times*, January 28, 1875.

33. *Kansas City Times*, January 28, 1875; Zerelda said she was taking Sarah to Texas, in an interview with the *Lexington Caucasian*, October 17, 1874.

34. *Kansas City Journal of Commerce*, January 30, 1875; *St. Louis Republican*, February 2, 1875. The *Republican*'s source said the three horses were led out on Tuesday night; this appears to be an error in recollection or reporting. Allan Pinkerton wrote of "being positively assured that the James boys and others were at home in their mother's house" that night, and that they "must have left the house after dark"; Allan Pinkerton to P. H. Woodward, January 27, 1875, Pinkerton Papers.

35. An excellent description of the farm is in the *St. Louis Republican*, February 4, 1875; see also the *Kansas City Times*, January 27, 1875 (which has a diagram with the kitchen and parlor reversed).

36. Quotes are from the coroner's inquest, *Kansas City Times*, January 28, 1875; additional details appear in the same issue, and in the *Kansas City Times*, January 27, 1875.

37. Yeatman, 141, cites the analysis of writer Fred Egloff to argue that the device was meant to explode. Those who examined its remains at the time, however, concluded otherwise; see, especially, the *Kansas City Journal of Commerce*, January 29, 1875; also the *Kansas City Times*, January 28, 1875.

38. The sphere consisted of two halves, one of wrought and the other of cast iron; the wrought-iron portion remained intact; *Kansas City Times*, January 28, 1875.

39. *Kansas City Times*, January 27 and 28, 1875; *St. Louis Republican*, February 2, 1875; Settle, 76–7; Siss Scruggs to M. D. Scruggs, February 26, 1875, Watkins Mill.

40. *Kansas City Times*, January 28, 1875.

41. Bettie A. Patton to M. D. Scruggs, January 29, 1875, Watkins Mill; *Kansas City Times*, January 27 and 28, 1875.

42. *Kansas City Times*, January 28 and 30, 1875; *St. Louis Republican*, January 30 and February 2, 1875; *History of Clay*, 334–6; George E. Patton to M. D. Scruggs, February 21, 1875, Watkins Mill.

43. *St. Louis Republican*, January 30 and February 2, 1875; *Kansas City Times*, January 28–30, 1875; *Kansas City Journal of Commerce*, January 29, 1875; *Liberty Tribune*, January 29, 1875. Bettie Patton to My Dear Sister, February 9, 1875, and George E. Patton to M. D. Scruggs, February 21, 1875, Watkins Mill.

44. *Kansas City Times*, January 27, 1875.

45. Bettie A. Patton to M. D. Scruggs, January 29, 1875; Lizzie to M. D. Scruggs, January 26, 1875; Siss Scruggs to M. D. Scruggs, February 26, 1875; George E. Patton to M. D. Scruggs, February 21, 1875; all Watkins Mill.

46. *Kansas City Journal of Commerce*, January 30, 1875; *St. Louis Republican*, February 2, 1875; *Hannibal Clipper* in *Kansas City Times*, January 29, 1875; see also *Kansas City Times*, January 28 and 30, 1875.

47. *Lexington Caucasian*, January 30, 1875; *St. Louis Republican*, February 4, 1875; see also *Kansas City Times*, January 27 and 29, April 3, 1875; *St. Louis Republican*, January 27, 1875; *Jefferson City People's Tribune*, February 3, 1875. On Pinkerton's wartime work, see Edwin C. Fishel, *The Secret War for the Union: The Untold Story of Military Intelligence in the Civil War* (New York: Houghton Mifflin, 1996). Allan Pinkerton denied that the pistol was agency property, in a private letter; E. J. A. to Dave, February 26, 1875, Pinkerton Papers.

48. Bettie A. Patton to M. D. Scruggs, January 29, 1875, and Lizzie to M. D. Scruggs, January 26, 1875, Watkins Mill; for early press reporting, see, for example, *Kansas City Times*, January 27, 1875, and *St. Louis Dispatch*, February 1, 1875.

49. *Kansas City Journal of Commerce*, January 29, 1875.

50. *Kansas City Times*, January 29, 1875; *St. Louis Republican*, February 2, 1875. Settle's astute analysis of the politics surrounding this affair, 77–84, misses some (but not all) of the Democrats' intraparty feuding; he calls the *St. Louis Republican*, for example, an "opposition" newspaper, when in fact it represented the (once) dominant Unionist faction of the Democratic Party.

51. *Kansas City Times*, January 31, 1875; *St. Louis Republican*, January 31 and February 3, 1875; *Jefferson City People's Tribune*, February 3 and 10, 1875. For signs of the shift among even Unionist Democrats toward sympathy, see the *Richmond Conservator*, January 30, 1875; for an astute editorial on the Confederate politics of these resolutions, see the *Kansas City Journal of Commerce*, February 2, 1875.

52. *St. Louis Republican*, February 5, 1875; *Liberty Tribune*, February 12, 1875; Shoemaker, 5: 443; Yeatman, 140; Settle, 78–9.

53. Lawrence O. Christensen and Gary R. Kremer, *A History of Missouri*, vol. 4, *1875 to 1919* (Columbia: University of Missouri Press, 1997), 1–9; Isidor Loeb, "Constitutions and Constitutional Conventions in Missouri," *MHR* 16, no. 2 (January 1922): 189–238; Shoemaker, 5: 446–7. On the Grant administration's collapsing commitment to protecting the freed people, see McFeely, 400–25.

54. *St. Louis Dispatch*, March 1, 1875.

55. *Richmond Conservator*, April 3, 1875. The praise for Edwards was accompanied by scathing attacks on important Democrats who were Unionist former Whigs, showing the persistence of

political divisions dating back to the 1850s.

56. *Kansas City Times*, March 18, 1875; *Kansas City Journal of Commerce*, March 19, 1875; Settle, 81–3.

57. Settle's analysis of the vote, 82–4, is excellent; see also *Journal of the House of Representatives at the Regular Session of the Twenty-Eighth General Assembly of the State of Missouri* (Jefferson City: Regan & Carter, 1875), 1176; *Jefferson City People's Tribune*, March 24, 1875; *St. Louis Republican*, March 26, 1875; *Kansas City Times*, March 21, 1875.

58. *Jefferson City People's Tribune*, March 24, 1875; *Kansas City Journal of Commerce*, April 25, 1875.

59. *St. Louis Republican*, February 4, 1875; George E. Patton to M. D. Scruggs, February 21, 1875, Watkins Mill; *Kansas City Times*, April 3, 1875.

60. Allan Pinkerton to P. H. Woodward, January 27, 1875, and Geo. McQueen to Sam Hard-wicke, February 16, 1875, Pinkerton Papers. Pinkerton often wrote under pseudonyms; all letters cited, however, were copied into his personal letterbook, and clearly were authored by the detective chief himself. See also E. J. A. to Dave, February 26, 1875, Pinkerton Papers, which reinforces the case that Pinkerton had no paying client for his chase after the James brothers.

61. *Richmond Conservator*, March 27, 1875; *Kansas City Times*, April 3, 1875; *Liberty Tribune*, April 9, 1875; Yeatman, 143.

62. George E. Patton to M. D. Scruggs, February 21, 1875, Watkins Mill.

63. Daniel Geary to Gov. C. H. Hardin, April 17, 1875, Charles H. Hardin Papers, MSA.

64. *Kansas City Times*, April 3, 1875.

65. See the inventory of personal property, Daniel Askew Probate Records, Clay County Archives, Liberty, Missouri. Such inventories, carried out by a third party, were usually quite care-ful, lest heirs hold back possessions from probate auctions.

66. *Kansas City Times*, April 14 and 18, 1875; *Liberty Tribune*, April 16, 1875; *Richmond Conser-vator*, April 24, 1875; Allan Pinkerton to My Dear Friend [Adeline Askew], May 11, 1875, Pinkerton Papers.

67. *Kansas City Times*, April 18, 1874; *Richmond Conservator*, April 24, 1875. Years later, Dick Liddil claimed that Jesse told him he had waited a week for a chance to kill Askew, and that Clell Miller accompanied him; *St. Louis Republican*, September 9, 1883. Though possible, this is second-hand information, and highly questionable.

68. *Kansas City Journal of Commerce*, April 15, 1875; *Liberty Tribune*, May 28, 1875.

69. Allan Pinkerton to His Excellency John L. Beveridge, April 16, 1875, and Allan Pinkerton to Dr. J. C. Bernard, April 16, 1875, Pinkerton Papers.

70. John S. Groom to Charles Hardin, April 16, 1875, Charles H. Hardin Papers, MSA. This letter includes spelling errors which have been corrected in the version given here, notably "wore" instead of "war."

71. *Kansas City Times*, April 18, 1875; John S. Groom to Genl. George Bingham, April 19, 1875, Charles H. Hardin Papers, MSA; *Liberty Tribune*, April 16, 1875.

72. Allan Pinkerton to My Dear Friend [Adeline Askew], May 11, 1875, Pinkerton Papers; Daniel H. Askew Probate Records, Clay County Archives, Liberty, Missouri; *Liberty Tribune*, Sep-tember 22, 1876. Addie Askew was able to administer her husband's estate, unlike Zerelda James a quarter of a century earlier, thanks to modest advances in women's property rights during Recon-struction; see Suzanne D. Lebsock, "Radical Reconstruction and the Property Rights of Southern Women," in *Half Sisters of History: Southern Women and the American Past*, ed. Catherine Clinton (Durham, N.C.: Duke University Press, 1994), 110–35.

CHAPTER SIXTEEN: Ambition

1. W. M. Rush, Jr., to C. H. Hardin, February 14, 1876; C. H. Hardin to Thomas Allen, February 27, 1875; Tho. Allen to C. H. Hardin, May 19, 1875; all Charles H. Hardin Papers, MSA.

2. E. M. Cooper to C. H. Hardin, March 1, 1875, and E. M. Cooper to C. H. Hardin, April 5, 1875, all Charles H. Hardin Papers, MSA; *Carrollton Journal*, April 2, 1875 (quoted in its entirety on

April 3 by the *Kansas City Times* and *St. Louis Republican*).

3. *Our Expressman*, August 1875. The Adams Express expanded in Colorado, Nebraska, and Kansas as a result of opportunities created by Gould's move; see *Our Expressman*, September 1875. Cooper's last letter to Governor Hardin was written on July 3, 1875, Charles H. Hardin Papers, MSA.

4. *Liberty Tribune*, May 7, 1875; L. W. Burris to C. H. Hardin, July 21, 1875, Charles H. Hardin Papers, MSA.

5. Mrs. D. A. Lambert and Miss B. H. Sharp to Governor Hardin, May 15, 1875, and G. C. Bingham to C. H. Hardin, May 25, 1875, Charles H. Hardin Papers, MSA; *Kansas City Times*, May 15, 1875; *St. Louis Republican*, May 16, 17, and 19, 1875.

6. *Sedalia Daily Democrat*, May 20, 1882; see also Robert J. Wybrow's useful article, "From the Pen of a Noble Robber: The Letters of Jesse Woodson James: 1847–1882," *Brand Book* 24, no. 2 (summer 1987), published by the English Westerners' Society, 1–22. This letter also contained various boasts; he claimed, for example, to have "a few good friends on the [Pinkerton] detective force who keep me fully posted," and to be carrying on a secret correspondence with Governor Hardin (for which no evidence exists in the Missouri State Archives).

7. *St. Louis Republican*, November 30, 1874.

8. William H. Wallace to Board of Pardons of Minnesota, July 6, 1897, Younger Brothers Pardon Application Files, nos. 555 and 556, 1889–1901, fold. 2, "Northfield (Minnesota) Bank Robbery of 1876: Selected Government Records" (microfilm publication), MnHS.

9. *Kansas City Journal of Commerce*, July 1, 1875; *St. Louis Republican*, May 19, 1875; *Liberty Tribune*, May 28, 1875; *St. Louis Republican*, April 21, 1882; *Nashville American*, October 9, 1882; Yeatman, 150–1.

10. *Richmond Conservator*, April 24, 1875; *Liberty Tribune*, May 28, 1875; W. L. Watkins to M. D. Scruggs, June 7, 1875, Watkins Mill; W. M. Paxton, *Annals of Platte County, Missouri* (Kansas City: Hudson-Kimberly Publishing, 1897), 585, 604–5; Shoemaker, 5: 483–4.

11. *St. Louis Republican*, April 11, 1882. Jesse claimed to have decided not to kill "the younger one"; this would have been William Pinkerton, who worked in Chicago; the other son, Robert, was superintendent of the New York office. Starting in June 1875, William began an eight-month stint with the U.S. Secret Service in Washington, D.C., mainly to investigate a theft in its office there. See the reports of William Pinkerton, Daily Reports of U.S. Secret Service Agents, 1875–1936, microfilm publication T-915, roll 238, Records of the U.S. Secret Service, RG 87, National Archives, College Park, Md.

12. *Nashville Republican Banner*, July 11, 1875; see also Wybrow, 2–4, and Yeatman, 151–2.

13. *Liberty Tribune*, July 23, 1875; Yeatman, 92–3; *Kansas City Journal*, April 5, 1882.

14. *Nashville Republican Banner*, August 8, 1875, in *Kansas City Times*, August 12, 1875.

15. *Richmond Conservator*, August 27, 1875.

16. Yeatman, 161; *Nashville American*, October 9, 1882; *St. Louis Republican*, April 21, 1882.

17. Yeatman, 154–61; *Louisville Courier-Journal*, September 15–18, 20, 21, and 23, 1875; *St. Louis Republican*, September 16 and 18, 1875; *Liberty Tribune*, September 24, 1875; J. H. Russel to C. H. Hardin, October 6, 1875, and Robert T. Oney to C. H. Hardin, no date (appears to be from October 1875), Charles H. Hardin Papers, MSA. Years later, Dick Liddil claimed that Jesse James had told him that he, Frank, Tom McDaniels, Clell Miller, and Jack Kean carried out the robbery; *St. Louis Republican*, September 9, 1883. As secondhand information, this statement is highly questionable, and appears to conflict with other evidence. See Yeatman, note 10, 422–3, for the speculations of bandit buffs.

18. *Nashville Daily American*, reprinted in the *Louisville Courier-Journal*, September 25, 1875; *Nashville Daily World*, April 22, 1882; Yeatman, 161–2.

19. Lawrence O. Christensen and Gary R. Kremer, *A History of Missouri*, vol. 4, *1875 to 1919* (Columbia: University of Missouri Press, 1997), 1–9; Isidor Loeb and Floyd C. Shoemaker, eds., *Debates of the Missouri Constitutional Convention of 1875* (Columbia: State Historical Society of Missouri, 1930–1944), II: 5; Isidor Loeb, "Constitutions and Constitutional Conventions in Missouri," *MHR* 16, no. 2 (January 1922): 189–238; Christopher Phillips, *Missouri's Confederate:*

Claiborne Fox Jackson and the Creation of a Southern Identity in the Border West (Columbia: University of Missouri Press, 2000), 285–92. In the Missouri state constitution of 1875, see in particular article VIII, section 11; article X, sections 10–12; article XII, section 5; and article XIV, section 2.

20. Compiled reward offers, Shoemaker, vols. 4 and 5. The total number of rewards from 1865 through 1875 approached three hundred (Shoemaker's compilation was incomplete). Settle, 218, footnote 22, states that this was a constitutional limit; a thorough review of the constitution of 1875 shows this to be a mistake, though a legal limit was put in place; see H. H. Crittenden, ed., *The Crittenden Memoirs* (New York: G. P. Putnam's Sons, 1936), 59–60.

21. T. J. Stiles, ed., *Robber Barons and Radicals: Reconstruction and the Origin of Civil Rights* (New York: Berkley, 1997), 347, 365–84; Current, 314–27; James B. Murphy, *L. Q. C. Lamar: Pragmatic Patriot* (Baton Rouge: University of Louisiana Press, 1973), 148–61; George C. Rable, *But There Was No Peace: The Role of Violence in the Politics of Reconstruction* (Athens: University of Georgia Press, 1984), 148–62. For a capsule biography of Lynch, see Eric Foner, *Freedom's Lawmakers: A Directory of Black Officeholders During Reconstruction* (New York: Oxford University Press, 1993), 138–9; for details on the Mississippi insurrection, see *Mississippi in 1875: Report of the Select Committee to Inquire into the Mississippi Election of 1875, with the Testimony and Documentary Evidence* (Washington, D.C.: Government Printing Office, 1876).

CHAPTER SEVENTEEN: Anabasis

1. Richard Nelson Current, *Those Terrible Carpetbaggers: A Reinterpretation* (New York: Oxford University Press, 1988), 112–13; Blanche Butler Ames, ed., *Chronicles from the Nineteenth Century: Family Letters of Blanche Butler and Adelbert Ames* (Clinton, Mass.: n.p., 1957), 2: 368.

2. *New York Times,* May 2, 1875. For Ames's full testimony, see *Mississippi in 1875: Report of the Select Committee to Inquire into the Mississippi Election of 1875, with the Testimony and Documentary Evidence* (Washington, D.C.: Government Printing Office, 1876), 1: 1–16.

3. For a brief review of Ames's wartime record, see chap. 8, pages 141–2.

4. Current, 112–15; Blanche Ames Ames, *Adelbert Ames, 1835–1933: General, Senator, Governor* (London: MacDonald, 1964), 236–7. Many, perhaps most, Regular Army officers had mixed feelings about the military occupation of the South; see Edward M. Coffman, *The Old Army: A Portrait of the American Army in Peacetime, 1784–1898* (New York: Oxford University Press, 1986), 234–46.

5. Ames Ames, 255.

6. Current, 112; Ames Ames, 265.

7. Current, 115–17, 172–5; John R. Lynch, *Reminiscences of an Active Life: The Autobiography of John Roy Lynch* (Chicago: Chicago University Press, 1970), 33, 54–7; T. J. Stiles, ed., *Robber Barons and Radicals: Reconstruction and the Origins of Civil Rights* (New York: Berkley, 1997), 195–200; for details on widespread black political organization, see Eric Foner, *Reconstruction: America's Unfinished Revolution, 1863–1877* (New York: Harper & Row, 1988), 281–91.

8. *The Miscellaneous Documents of the Senate of the United States for the Second Session of the Forty-Fourth Congress* (Washington, D.C.: Government Printing Office, 1877), 6: 17.

9. Current, 172–6, 306–12; Lynch, 166; Stiles, 327.

10. Stiles, 365–81; Current, 314–27; James B. Murphy, *L. Q. C. Lamar: Pragmatic Patriot* (Baton Rouge: University of Louisiana Press, 1973), 148–61; George C. Rable, *But There Was No Peace: The Role of Violence in the Politics of Reconstruction* (Athens: University of Georgia Press, 1984), 148–62. See also *Miscellaneous Documents of the Senate of the United States for the Second Session of the Forty-Fourth Congress,* vol. 6 (Washington, D.C.: Government Printing Office, 1877), and *Mississippi in 1875.*

11. In one town, the rumor of troops caused armed Democrats to flee; Stiles, 376.

12. Stiles, 380; Blanche Butler Ames, 257, 259; Current, 325.

13. Blanch Butler Ames, 368–9.

14. Ibid., 370–3.

15. *St. Louis Republican,* August 13, 1876. On black celebrations of Independence Day, see Eric Foner, "Rights and the Constitution in Black Life During the Civil War and Reconstruction," *Jour-*

nal of American History 74, no. 3 (December 1987): 863–83.

16. This would often be misreported as a plan to rob the Granby bank; see *Kansas City Journal of Commerce*, August 30, 1876.

17. *St. Louis Republican*, August 13, 1876; *Minneapolis Tribune*, September 26, 1876.

18. *St. Louis Republican*, August 13, 1876.

19. Ibid., July 9 and 10 and August 13, 1876; *Sedalia Daily Democrat*, July 8, 1876; *Expressman's Monthly*, August 1876; *Sedalia Daily Democrat*, July 8, 1876; *Kansas City Journal of Commerce*, July 9, 1876.

20. *Boonville Daily Advertiser*, July 11, 1876; *Kansas City Times*, July 9, 1876; *Expressman's Monthly*, August 1876; Robertus Love, *The Rise and Fall of Jesse James* (Lincoln: University of Nebraska Press, 1990), 179–85, quote on 182. Conkling's version, given to Love years later, matches well with contemporary press accounts (except for the spelling of his name, which Love gives as "Conklin").

21. *Boonville Daily Advertiser*, July 8 and 11, 1876; *Expressman's Monthly*, August 1876; *Sedalia Daily Democrat*, July 9, 1876; Love, 179–85; *St. Louis Republican*, July 9, 1876.

22. *St. Louis Republican*, August 13, 1876; *Kansas City Times*, July 11, 1876; *Sedalia Daily Democrat*, July 9, 1876. The United States Express safe yielded $15,000, and the Adams held the rest.

23. *Sedalia Daily Democrat*, July 8 and 11, 1876; *Kansas City Times*, July 11, 1876; *Kansas City Journal of Commerce*, July 9 and 11, 1876; *St. Louis Republican*, July 10 and 18, 1876; Shoemaker, 5: 510–11. Hazen's employment by the Adams Company was confirmed by the *St. Louis Globe-Democrat*, September 25, 1876.

24. *Annual Report of the Comptroller of the Currency: December 4, 1876* (Washington, D.C.: Government Printing Office, 1876), 51–2, 69. The U.S. population has been extrapolated from census data for 1870 and 1880. These figures may understate the scarcity of money in the country, given the regional concentration of banks in the Northeast and tightened lending and reserve practices after the Panic of 1873; see Richard Franklin Bensel, *Yankee Leviathan: The Origins of Central State Authority in America, 1859–1877* (New York: Cambridge University Press, 1990), 268–74. There is a problematic tendency in historical writing to simply translate figures into contemporary amounts. The money supply and markets were lumpy in the nineteenth century; far more than in the modern economy, purchasing power varied dramatically from urban to rural areas.

25. *Boonville Daily Advertiser*, July 8 and 11, 1876; *Expressman's Monthly*, August 1876; *Sedalia Daily Democrat*, July 9, 1876; *St. Louis Republican*, July 9, 1876.

26. *Kansas City Times*, August 9, 1876; *Minneapolis Tribune*, September 26, 1876; Joseph Have Hanson, *The Northfield Tragedy: A History of the Northfield Bank Raid and Murders* (St. Paul: n.p., 1876), 13; A. E. Bunker, "Recollections of the Northfield Raid," August 24, 1894, in "Northfield (Minnesota) Bank Robbery of 1876: Selected Manuscripts Collection and Government Records" (microfilm publication), MnHS (to be cited as "Northfield Robbery"). In June 1876, Frank James made a point of telling Samuel Ralston that Anna was well, suggesting an imminent extended departure; *Kansas City Times*, August 16, 1876. Marley Brant, *Jesse James: The Man and the Myth* (New York: Berkley, 1998), 161–72, claims to have seen letters written by Bob Younger, testifying to Jesse James having planned early on to carry out a bank robbery in Minnesota, with the Missouri Pacific raid as a prelude. The authenticity of these letters, however, has not been confirmed by any authorities. St. Louis police chief James McDonough thought that all the bandits fled to Texas, which proved untrue; James McDonough to C. H. Hardin, September 22, 1876, Charles H. Hardin Papers, MSA.

27. Keith Ian Polakoff, *The Politics of Inertia: The Election of 1876 and the End of Reconstruction* (Baton Rouge: Louisiana State University Press, 1973), 4, 95. References may be made almost at random to newspapers in May through November 1876 for evidence of the political frenzy. See, for example, *St. Louis Republican*, July 9, 1876, and "Democratic Picnic Summary, Buckner, Missouri, September 16, 1876," coll. 1825, WHMC.

28. Foner, *Reconstruction*, 568.

29. Lawrence O. Christensen and Gary R. Kremer, *A History of Missouri*, vol. 4, *1875–1919* (Columbia: University of Missouri Press, 1997), 9–11; *Kansas City Journal of Commerce*, August 13,

1876.

30. Foner, *Reconstruction*, 568. In the first half of the twentieth century, historians began to place great stress on the economic influences behind the reaction against Reconstruction; see especially C. Vann Woodward, *Reunion and Reaction: The Compromise of 1877 and the End of Reconstruction* (Boston: Little, Brown, 1951), and Woodward's introduction to Robert P. Sharkey, *Money, Class, and Party: An Economic Study of Civil War and Reconstruction* (Baltimore: The Johns Hopkins University Press, 1959), vii–ix. More recently, scholars have stressed racism as a primary motivation. Richard Franklin Bensel's massive economic and political study, for example, leads him to conclude that "southern separatism, not the economic and social dislocations of northern industrial expansion," was the primary issue of the age (Bensel, 415). The statements here about the preoccupations of Jesse James are based on his published writings, but fit tightly with this interpretation.

31. *St. Louis Republican*, August 13, 1876.

32. Ibid., August 6, 8, 10, 11, and 13, 1876; *Kansas City Times*, August 9, 12, 13, and 15, 1876; *Sedalia Daily Democrat*, August 16, 1876. The basis for the idea that the Adams Company hired the men is threefold: first, Thatcher helped interrogate Kerry; second, the party was heard to address a "Captain Thatcher"; third, Governor Hardin's papers in the Missouri State Archives make no mention of the raid.

33. *Kansas City Times*, August 18, 1876.

34. *Kansas City Times*, August 23, 1876.

35. F. Y. Hedley, "John Newman Edwards," in *Encyclopedia of the History of Missouri*, ed. Howard L. Conard (St. Louis: Southern History Company, 1901), 2: 354–6; George Plattenburg, "Biographical Sketch," in *John N. Edwards: Biography, Memoirs, Reminiscences, and Recollections*, ed. Jennie Edwards (Kansas City: n.p., 1889), 9–36; Dan Saults, "Now Let us Discuss a Man," *Bulletin of the Missouri Historical Society* 19, no. 2 (January 1963): 150–60; John N. Edwards, *Noted Guerrillas, or the Warfare of the Border* (St. Louis: H. W. Brand & Co., 1879), 365–6.

36. Blanche Butler Ames, 389–90, 412.

37. Foner, *Reconstruction*, 564; Dee Brown, *The Year of the Century: 1876* (New York: Charles Scribner's Sons, 1966), 129–32; Blanche Butler Ames, 389.

38. Franklyn Curtiss-Wedge, ed., *History of Rice and Steele Counties, Minnesota* (Chicago: H. C. Cooper, Jr., 1910), 1: 463; *Annual Report of the Comptroller of the Currency: December 6, 1875* (Washington, D.C.: Government Printing Office, 1875), 698; *Annual Report of the Comptroller of the Currency: December 4, 1876* (Washington, D.C.: Government Printing Office, 1876), 726–35; *Northfield News*, August 9, 1929; D. L. Leonard, *Funeral Discourse of Joseph Lee Heywood* (Minneapolis: Steam Book Printers, 1876), 6–7; *Rice County Journal*, September 14, 1876.

39. Blanche Butler Ames, 412; Leonard, 4.

40. Blanche Butler Ames, 382–3, 392.

41. Foner, *Reconstruction*, 566–7, Polakoff, 12–40, Blanche Butler Ames, 389, 393–5; Stiles, 381–4.

42. James E. Sefton, *The United States Army and Reconstruction, 1865–1877* (Baton Rouge: Louisiana State University Press, 1967), 261–3, shows that troop levels in the South had dropped to 7,701 by October 1874—4,271 in Texas, with its Indian hostilities; Louisiana was the only other state with more than 1,000 troops, at 1,164. See also T. J. Stiles, ed., *Warriors and Pioneers* (New York: Berkley, 1996), 190.

43. Foner, *Reconstruction*, 571–2; see especially Richard Zuczek, "The Last Campaign of the Civil War: South Carolina and the Revolution of 1876," *CWH* 42, no. 1 (March 1996): 18–31. The Democrats later elected Butler to the U.S. Senate.

44. Foner, *Reconstruction*, 572–5; Stiles, *Robber Barons*, 403.

45. Polakoff, 105, notes that Hayes (influenced by Carl Schurz) "was expressing the intense Northern desire to be rid of the troublous issues left over from the Civil War."

46. Polakoff, 135–46.

47. *Minneapolis Tribune*, September 9, 1876. The most influential secondary source for the events that fill the rest of this chapter has been George Huntington, *Robber and Hero: The Story of the Northfield Bank Raid* (St. Paul: Minnesota Historical Society Press, 1986). Originally published in 1895, this book was in large part a work of oral history, drawing on interviews with participants

eighteen or nineteen years after 1876. The narrative given here is based on primary sources, with a strong preference for contemporary accounts, and thus leaves out some details Huntington provided, and contradicts some claims he made. The most recent book-length treatment, Robert Barr Smith, *The Last Hurrah of the James-Younger Gang* (Norman: University of Oklahoma Press, 2001), makes limited use of the available primary sources, relying primarily on popular Western writers.

48. *Kansas City Times*, September 24, 1876. The James brothers had been reported in brothels before; see, for example, *Lexington Caucasian*, August 30, 1873.

49. Hanson, 51–2.

50. *Chicago Times*, September 10, 1876; Hanson, 51; Joel Best, *Controlling Vice: Regulating Brothel Prostitution in St. Paul, 1865–1883* (Columbus: Ohio State University Press, 1998), 3–5, 20–4. Contemporary reports in Hanson and the *Chicago Times* (the saloonkeeper identified Miller from a photograph) generally support Cole Younger's account, *The Story of Cole Younger, by Himself* (Springfield, Mo.: Oak Hills, 1996, orig. pub. 1903), 86, in which he said he went to St. Paul, then to Minneapolis, then back to St. Paul, where the bandits gambled.

51. *Minneapolis Tribune*, September 25, 1876. This quote has been missed by virtually all writers on the subject, who usually refer to Cole Younger's later statements.

52. The statement, written in 1897 at the request of the Stillwater prison warden, was given to the penitentiary surgeon, D. A. E. Hedback, and was published in the *Northfield News*, November 26, 1915; both this published version and an identical typescript of the original appear in "Northfield Robbery." Cole Younger's two other accounts appear in *Story of Cole Younger* and "Real Facts About the Northfield, Minnesota, Bank Robbery," in *Convict Life at the Minnesota State Prison*, ed. W. C. Heilbron (Stillwater, Minn.: n.p, 1911), 125–47. Settle, 95, was unaware of either Bob Younger's early statement or Cole's account for the prison warden, so he (incorrectly) dismissed the Ames connection as a "rationalization" made for Southern readers. I have used the 1897 version (from the *Northfield News*) for most quotes from Younger, as it was his earliest account and not written for publication.

53. *St. Louis Republican*, August 13, 1876; *Minneapolis Tribune*, September 26, 1876; Hanson, 13.

54. It is worth noting that, just a few years later, one man who knew both brothers declared that Jesse "at all times seemed to have control" of Frank; *Nashville American*, October 9, 1882. There is a possibility that the bandits went to St. Paul with the intention of assassinating Samuel Hardwicke. But no evidence exists of any attempt to find and kill Hardwicke; and the gang soon set out for Northfield with apparent forethought, suggesting that it had been their target all along.

55. *Lexington Caucasian*, December 14, 1874; *St. Louis Republican*, December 18, 1875; see also *Liberty Tribune*, November 12, 1875, *Kansas City Times*, October 7 and 8, 1875, and *St. Louis Republican*, September 17, 1875.

56. *New York Times*, May 2, 1876. Adelbert Ames's name appeared only once in the contemporary press reports of the gang's activities in Minnesota, when Bob Younger declared that he was their target.

57. *Minneapolis Tribune*, September 9, 1876; *Rice County Journal*, September 14, 1876; *Chicago Times*, September 10, 1876; see also *Story of Cole Younger*, 86–8, and *Northfield News*, November 26, 1915.

58. *Faribault Democrat*, September 15, 1876; *Rice County Journal*, September 14, 1876; *Chicago Times*, September 10, 1876; *Minneapolis Tribune*, September 8, 9, and 11, 1876. Cole Younger later confirmed that four men had purchased their horses in one place, two in another, two in another, spending a total of $1,250 for the eight; *Liberty Tribune*, October 20, 1876.

59. *Faribault Democrat*, September 15, 1876; *Rice County Journal*, September 14, 1876; *Chicago Times*, September 10, 1876; *Minneapolis Tribune*, September 8, 9, and 11, 1876; *Northfield News*, November 26, 1915; see also Hanson, 4–5. Unfortunately, the Mankato story was perpetuated by Huntington, 1–6. Even Hanson, who relates the Robinson story, mentions only five men in Mankato.

60. *Northfield News*, November 26, 1915; *Minneapolis Tribune*, September 8, 9, 11, and (Extra Edition) 13, 1876; *Faribault Democrat*, September 15, 1876; *Rice County Journal*, September 14, 1876;

St. Paul and Minneapolis Pioneer Press and Tribune, September 14, 1876; *Chicago Times,* September 10, 1876.

61. *Northfield News,* November 26, 1915; *Chicago Times,* August 11, 1876.

62. Statement of J. E. Hobbs, September 8, 1876, "Northfield Robbery"; *Minneapolis Tribune,* September 14, 1876; *Rice County Journal,* September 14, 1876.

63. *Minneapolis Tribune,* September 8, 1876; *Northfield News,* September 26, 1915; Hanson, 6. The party seems to have included Jesse James, as the three men who first crossed the bridge to begin the raid were said by the *Tribune* to have eaten at Jeft's.

64. *Northfield News,* September 26, 1915; *Chicago Times,* September 11, 1876; *Minneapolis Tribune,* September 11, 1876. According to one story, the bandits ran into Adelbert Ames as he crossed the bridge, and called him "Governor," to Ames's alarm; see, for example, Yeatman, 172. This is possible, as Ames later said he "met the James crowd" on the bridge (*Northfield News,* August 2, 1929). However, Ames made no mention of the incident in his letters.

65. The following factors weigh in the distribution of the bandits described here. First, every bandit except the James brothers and Charlie Pitts was clearly identified outside the bank during this brief affair. Second, these three were also the only ones who seem to have been unwounded in Northfield, which strongly suggests they were inside. Third, no Northfield witnesses describe any robber exiting the bank before the others. Fourth, two witnesses identified Charlie Pitts inside the bank, leaving the identity of only the other two open to question. Fifth, a combination of eyewitness accounts and evidence of who was shot outside supports Younger's story that he and Miller formed the second contingent. Huntington, 13–14, relied on an account written for him eighteen years later by A. E. Bunker, but Bunker never offered a description of the men inside; instead, he simply named them as Pitts, Bob Younger, and one of the James brothers, and he may well have been mistaken. Cole Younger's accounts, written twenty years later, agreed with this distribution. Bob Younger, however, was wounded outside the bank, and was not seen leaving it as Cole described. Cole may have been trying to protect Frank James, who was still alive and had not been tried for the events in Northfield. Therefore, the account here does not describe Bob entering, then leaving, the bank, as often claimed.

66. *Chicago Times,* September 11, 1876; see also Blanche Butler Ames, 404.

67. Statement of J. E. Hobbs, September 8, 1876, and Affidavit of D. J. Whiting, July 12, 1897, "Northfield Robbery." The *Minneapolis Tribune,* September 8, 1876, also describes the "making figures," though it incorrectly described the men as sitting on a hay bale, not a box.

68. The identity of the leader (if there was one) was unclear, just as the names of the three bandits in the bank cannot be confirmed. Wilcox and Bunker both identified Pitts as being in the bank. Bunker later identified the second man as Bob Younger, but he may have resembled Frank James at the time, and he was clearly outside the bank during these events; most important, Wilcox never said that Bob was in the bank. See Hanson, 17–20; *Chicago Times,* September 11, 1876; *Rice County Journal,* September 14, 1876; *Minneapolis Tribune,* September 8, 1876; A. E. Bunker, "Recollections of the Northfield Raid," August 24, 1894, "Northfield Robbery"; *Minneapolis Tribune,* September 22, 1876. Apart from identifying Pitts, Wilcox's later descriptions would vary. On Jesse's leadership over Frank, see the *Nashville American,* October 9, 1882.

69. Statement of F. J. Wilcox, September 8, 1876, "Northfield Robbery"; *Rice County Journal,* September 14, 1876; *Chicago Times,* September 11, 1876; *Minneapolis Tribune,* September 8, 1876.

70. Leonard, 6; *Minneapolis Tribune,* September 26, 1876.

71. Wilcox gave at least three slightly contradictory accounts on the day of the robbery and the day that followed; this version of events in the bank is drawn from a combination of them: "Statement of F. J. Wilcox," September 8, 1876, "Northfield Robbery"; *Minneapolis Tribune,* September 8, 1876; *Rice County Journal,* September 14, 1876; see also *Chicago Times,* September 11, 1876. Bunker, who has often been quoted in accounts of the robbery, did not give his first statement until weeks later; the emphasis in this narrative, therefore, is on Wilcox's accounts immediately following the robbery.

72. This version of Bunker's experience comes from a statement he gave to Hanson a few weeks after the robbery (Hanson, 20–1), supplemented slightly by a narrative he wrote for George

Huntington on August 24, 1894, "Recollections of the Northfield Raid," in "Northfield Robbery." Both he and Wilcox identified Charlie Pitts as Bunker's assailant. Bunker, unfortunately, gave no descriptions; he simply named Bob Younger as the man who stood guard over him. For Wilcox's quote, see *Rice County Journal*, September 14, 1876, and *Chicago Times*, September 11, 1876. For more on Bunker, see *Northfield News*, August 9, 1929.

73. *Northfield News*, November 26, 1915. Cole Younger's account included an elaborate description of how he wanted to call off the raid at this point; this was likely an attempt to curry favor with the prison warden, for whom he wrote his narrative. When Younger was taken to Stillwater prison a few weeks later, after fasting much of the time, he weighed 206 pounds; "Northfield Robbery."

74. Statement of J. S. Allen, September 8, 1876, "Northfield Robbery."

75. Affidavit of W. H. Riddel, July 8, 1897, "Northfield Robbery." Riddel claimed to have been the first to raise the alarm; his account, however, was given twenty-one years later, making any such specificity suspect. The quote attributed to the robbers, however, appears in numerous contemporary accounts.

76. *Chicago Times*, September 11, 1876; *Minneapolis Tribune*, September 8, 1876; *Rice County Journal*, September 14, 1876; Statement of J. E. Hobbs, September 8, 1876, "Northfield Robbery."

77. *Chicago Times*, September 11, 1876; *Rice County Journal*, September 14, 1876.

78. *Northfield News*, November 26, 1915; *Chicago Times*, September 11, 1876; see also a slightly incorrect version in the *Minneapolis Tribune*, September 9, 1876; Affidavit of D. J. Whiting, July 12, 1897, "Northfield Robbery."

79. *Rice County Journal*, September 14, 1876; Affidavit of Ellen M. Ames, July 12, 1897, Affidavit of John Morton, July 8, 1897, Affidavit of P. S. Dougherty, July 12, 1897, A. E. Bunker, "Recollections of the Northfield Raid," in "Northfield Robbery." These accounts, though given twenty-one years later, support each other on all the key points. For the correct spelling of Gustavson's name, see John T. Ames to George N. Baxter, November 14, 1876, "Northfield Robbery."

80. *Chicago Times*, September 11, 1876; *Rice County Journal*, September 14, 1876; *Minneapolis Tribune*, September 8, 1876; *Faribault Democrat*, September 15, 1876.

81. Blanche Butler Ames, 403.

82. *Northfield News*, August 2, 1929; *Minneapolis Tribune*, September 8, 1876; *Chicago Times*, September 11, 1876; *Rice County Journal*, September 14, 1876.

83. Affidavit of D. J. Whiting, July 12, 1897, "Northfield Bank Robbery." Though caution must be used in relying on accounts given two decades later (in this case), this is a particularly good description and fits well with contemporary reports. See also *Minneapolis Tribune*, September 8, 1876; *Chicago Times*, September 11, 1876; *Rice County Journal*, September 14, 1876.

84. Blanche Butler Ames, 403; *Rice County Journal*, September 14, 1876.

85. *Northfield News*, November 26, 1915; *The Story of Cole Younger*, 89–95.

86. *Rice County Journal*, September 14, 1876; *Chicago Times*, September 11, 1876.

87. *Kansas City Times*, October 15, 1872; *Minneapolis Tribune*, September 8, 1876; *Rice County Journal*, September 14, 1876; Statement of F. J. Wilcox, September 8, 1876, Affidavit of F. J. Wilcox, June 10, 1897, and A. E. Bunker, "Recollections of the Northfield Raid," in "Northfield Robbery." Smith, 183–92, summarizes the feverish speculation by popular writers about who shot Heywood (along with who cut him, who hit him, who shoved him around), much of it based on attempts to decipher Cole Younger's dying words. But no special information is necessary; the obvious answer is probably right.

88. *Rice County Journal*, September 14, 1876; *Minneapolis Tribune*, September 8, 1876. Cole Younger later claimed that Pitts mounted behind him; contemporary witnesses, however, cited in both the *Rice County Journal* and the *Minneapolis Tribune*, claimed that the "wounded man" with an injured arm rode behind someone else, making it clear that this man was Bob Younger.

89. *Rice County Journal*, September 14, 1876.

90. Blanche Butler Ames, 404–6.

91. Ames soon left Northfield and joined Blanche in Massachusetts. He became a very success-

ful businessman; in addition to the family flour mill, he invested in textile manufacturing and real estate. He became a prolific inventor as well, developing everything from a pencil sharpener to flour-milling machinery. He returned to the army to serve as a brigadier general in Cuba during the Spanish-American War, and retired to Florida, where he became a close friend of John D. Rockefeller. He died in 1933 at the age of ninety-seven, the last surviving Civil War general of either side. See *New York Times*, April 14, 1933; Stiles, *Robber Barons*, 429; Robert Chernow, *Titan: The Life of John D. Rockefeller, Sr.* (New York: Random House, 1998), 611; Blanche Butler Ames, 617, 618, 620; Ames Ames, 495, 516–18.

PART FOUR: FATE

CHAPTER EIGHTEEN: Resurrection

1. Eric Foner, *Reconstruction, 1863–1877: America's Unfinished Revolution* (New York: Harper & Row, 1988), 575–87; for a discussion of this period in Missouri, see Lawrence O. Christensen and Gary R. Kremer, *A History of Missouri*, vol. 4, *1875 to 1919* (Columbia: University of Missouri Press, 1997), 9–13. Richard Zuczek writes that the 1876 electoral canvass in South Carolina "was really a military operation, complete with armies, commanders, and bloodshed"; Richard Zuczek, "The Last Campaign of the Civil War: South Carolina and the Revolution of 1876," *CWH* 42, no. 1 (March 1996): 18–31. C. Vann Woodward's classic *Reunion and Reaction: The Compromise of 1877 and the End of Reconstruction* (New York: Oxford University Press, 1966; orig. pub. 1951) places great stress on the role of Pennsylvania Railroad chief Thomas Scott, who lobbied to make aid for his Texas and Pacific Railroad part of the deal. But, as Richard Franklin Bensel argues in *Yankee Leviathan: The Origins of Central State Authority in America, 1859–1877* (New York: Cambridge University Press, 1990), 368–78, "When northern Republicans and southern Democrats began to bargain in earnest, asking for written commitments and honor-bound promises, the subject of negotiations was not the Texas and Pacific Railroad but withdrawal of federal troops from the Louisiana and South Carolina state houses."

2. *Nashville American*, October 9 and 10, 1882; *St. Louis Republican*, April 22, 1882, and September 9, 1883; *St. Louis Post-Dispatch*, June 24, 1923. See also Yeatman, 197–206, who provides extensive minutiae (though he relies heavily on the questionable oral history of the *Post-Dispatch* article).

3. Much has been made of the gang losing a guide when Chadwell died; however, he had not spent much of his life in southern Minnesota. A native of Monticello (north of Minneapolis), he had lived in the Dakota Territory and Texas for the previous two years; *Minneapolis Tribune*, September 26, 1876. No contemporary source states that Jim Younger was wounded in Northfield, though Cole Younger was firm about it in his 1897 account; *Northfield News*, November 26, 1915. No accounts from the scene in Northfield describe the other three men as wounded, and Younger explicitly stated a few days later that the James brothers had not been injured; *Faribault Democrat*, October 6, 1876.

4. *Minneapolis Tribune*, September 8, 1876; *Faribault Democrat*, September 15, 1876.

5. *Rice County Journal*, September 14, 1876; *Minneapolis Tribune*, September 8, 1876; John E. Risedorph Diary, John E. Risedorph Papers, MnHS; A. W. Henkle to Cousin William, September 29, 1876, "Northfield (Minnesota) Bank Robbery of 1876: Selected Manuscripts Collection and Government Records" (microfilm publication), MnHS (to be cited as "Northfield Robbery").

6. *Minneapolis Tribune*, September 9, 1876; *Faribault Democrat*, September 15, 1876.

7. *Faribault Democrat*, September 15, 1876; *Minneapolis Tribune*, September 11, 1876; see a description of the robbers' trail-masking methods in *Minneapolis Tribune*, September 15, 1876. Cole Younger vividly described the gang's escape in *Faribault Democrat*, October 6, 1876.

8. *Minneapolis Tribune*, September 13, 1876; *Faribault Democrat*, October 6, 1876. For a reference to Jesse James as "our captain," see Clarence Hite's confession in *St. Louis Republican*, November 12, 1883.

9. *Faribault Democrat*, October 6, 1876; *Minneapolis Tribune*, September 11, 13, 14, and 18, 1876; see also Bob Younger's comments, *Kansas City Times*, September 26, 1876. An excellent

account of the pursuit, by one of the hunters, appears in the *St. Louis Globe-Democrat*, December 5, 1876.

10. *Minneapolis Tribune*, September 15, 1876; *Faribault Democrat*, September 29 and October 6, 1876; *Kansas City Times*, September 26, 1876; A. W. Henkle to Cousin William, September 29, 1876, "Northfield Robbery."

11. *Minneapolis Tribune*, September 15, 18, and 19, 1876; *St. Louis Globe-Democrat*, December 5, 1876; *Kansas City Times*, October 13, 1876; A. W. Henkle to Cousin William, September 29, 1876, "Northfield Robbery." There has been some confusion about whether the James brothers were hit by the shotgun blast; Cole Younger, however, explicitly stated a few days later that they were not wounded prior to their departure; *Faribault Democrat*, October 6, 1876. The man wounded in the knee would often be identified as Frank; Dr. Mosher of Sioux City, who saw them a few days later, clearly identified the larger of the two—Jesse—as the man so injured; *Minneapolis Tribune*, September 22 and 26, 1876.

12. *Minneapolis Tribune*, September 15, 1876; *St. Louis Globe-Democrat*, December 5, 1876. The horses' owner was described as a Methodist minister named Rockwell, according to the *Globe-Democrat*, or Rockwood, according to the *Minneapolis Tribune;* he had brought them there to help the resident farmer (named Seymour) with his harvest.

13. *St. Louis Globe-Democrat*, December 5, 1876; *Minneapolis Tribune*, September 19, 1876 (the *Tribune*'s valuable story seems to have been copied in the *St. Louis Republican*, October 22, 1876).

14. *Minneapolis Tribune*, September 19, 1876; *St. Louis Globe-Democrat*, December 5, 1876.

15. *St. Louis Globe-Democrat*, December 5, 1876; *St. Louis Globe-Democrat*, September 25, 1876.

16. *Minneapolis Tribune*, September 22 and 26, 1876. Yeatman, 184, gives the doctor's full name as Dr. Sydney P. Mosher, but he relies heavily on accounts given decades later, erring in the date of this encounter and the identity of the brother who changed clothes with Mosher. For descriptions of Jesse James as a large man, close to six feet, see the testimony of Dick Liddil and John T. Samuel in George Miller, Jr., *The Trial of Frank James for Murder* (St. Louis: n.p., 1898), 40, 113.

17. James McDonough to Governor C. H. Hardin, October 19, 1876, Papers of Charles H. Hardin, MSA. McDonough thought that Frank had the wounded knee.

18. *St. Peter Tribune Extra*, September 22, 1876; *Kansas City Times*, September 26, 1876; *St. Louis Globe-Democrat*, September 25, 1876. Yeatman, 181, notes Sorbel's correct name (given as Suborn in the press).

19. Entries for September 22 and 25, John E. Risedorph Diary, John E. Risedorph Papers, MnHS. See also Settle, 93–4.

20. Joseph Have Hanson, *The Northfield Tragedy: A History of the Northfield Bank Raid and Murders* (St. Paul: n.p., 1876), 67–9. Clearly, the Youngers did not recognize Ames, despite accounts that the bandits identified him in Northfield (Yeatman, 172).

21. Settle, 94; Yeatman, 191; *St. Louis Globe-Democrat*, September 25, 1876; James McDonough to Governor C. H. Hardin, September 22, 1876, Charles H. Hardin Papers, MSA; *Minneapolis Tribune*, September 26, 1876.

22. Stilson Hutchins to Gov. Woodson, telegram, January 31, 1873, Thos. C. Reynolds to Silas Woodson, January 23, 1873, and Julius Hunicke to Silas Woodson, January 27, 1873, Silas Woodson Papers, MSA.

23. McDonough sent the governor a detailed list of expenses, which shows the movements of his men during this period; James McDonough to Governor C. H. Hardin, October 25, 1876, Charles H. Hardin Papers, MSA. See also his letters of August 15 and 19, and September 12 and 22, 1876. The order creating this special force does not appear in Shoemaker.

24. *Kansas City Times*, October 13, 1876; *St. Louis Globe-Democrat*, October 15–19, 1876; James McDonough to Governor C. H. Hardin, September 29, 1876, and October 19, 1876, Charles H. Hardin Papers, MSA. The man arrested was John Goodin of Louisiana.

25. *Kansas City Times*, October 17, 1876.

26. *Kansas City Journal of Commerce*, October 18 and 20, 1876. Van Horn was quite correct; the confession of later gang member Dick Liddil included a lengthy list of former secessionists who reg-

ularly hid the James brothers; *St. Louis Republican*, September 9, 1883.

27. *Kansas City Times*, October 17, 1876.

28. Ibid., October 24, 1876.

29. *St. Louis Globe-Democrat*, October 16, 1876.

30. Lloyd A. Hunter, "Missouri's Confederate Leaders After the War," *MHR* 67, no. 3 (April 1973): 371–96. Bensel, 405–13, details the rising Confederate representation in Washington; in the Forty-seventh Congress (1881–1883) rebel veterans held an actual majority of the Democratic House seats.

31. Hunter, 385–97. For a discussion of the Greenbackers' rising success in Missouri, see Christensen and Kremer, 13–14. Missouri congressman Richard P. Bland was also a forceful champion of silver, having helped push through the Bland-Allison Silver Act of 1878, which required the federal government to purchase and coin at least $2 million in silver each month.

32. Dick Liddil later described Jesse's custom of remaining in the woods, even when hosted by relatives and sympathizers; *St. Louis Republican*, September 9, 1883.

33. *Liberty Advance*, November 30, 1876; *St. Louis Globe-Democrat*, November 26, 1876. The St. Louis newspaper identified the man encountered by the posse as Frank James, though his identity could hardly have been clear on this dark, rainy night, in the midst of a gunfight. A controversy ensued when the county refused to pay members of the posse; see Settle, 100–1.

34. *Richmond Conservator*, November 24, 1876.

35. *Nashville American*, October 9 and 12, 1882; Yeatman, 207–9, 216; Miller, 19–20. In court in 1883, Frank contradicted himself on his arrival date (Miller, 123, 134); his comments to the press seem far more accurate.

36. *Nashville American*, October 9, 1882; Miller, 96–7, 238; Yeatman, 203. Many people testified to Frank James's love of Shakespeare over the years; see, for example, Miller, 61, 78, 88.

37. Recent research has revealed how traumatic experience can permanently change brain chemistry; see, for example, Debra Niehoff, *The Biology of Violence: How Understanding the Brain, Behavior, and Environment Can Break the Vicious Circle of Aggression* (New York: Free Press, 1999), 115–49, especially 121.

38. *Nashville American*, October 9, 1882; *St. Louis Republican*, April 21, 1882; Miller, 35; Robert M. Utley, *Billy the Kid: A Short and Violent Life* (Lincoln: University of Nebraska Press, 1989), 124, 247–8; Yeatman, 209–11. The coincidental meeting of these two utter strangers, in a place Jesse had never frequented, at a time when he zealously guarded his identity, is patently absurd.

39. Liddil's full confession, given in 1882, appears in the *St. Louis Republican*, September 9, 1883; an edited version appears in Miller, 283–305. It is thorough and remarkably accurate. See also the *Kansas City Times*, October 9 and November 5, 1879; *Kansas City Journal*, October 10, 1879; Settle, 113; Yeatman, 211–12. Richard S. Brownlee, *Gray Ghosts of the Confederacy: Guerrilla Warfare in the West, 1861–1865* (Baton Rouge: Louisiana State University Press, 1958), 258, lists Morrow as a follower of Quantrill. One of the Hulse clan was killed by the state militia in July 1866; see p. 179.

40. Grimes may have relented and let them in; *Kansas City Times*, October 9, 1876; *Kansas City Journal*, October 10 and 11; *Expressman's Monthly*, October 1879, 282–6; Settle, 114; see also Dick Liddil's detailed confession, *St. Louis Republican*, September 9, 1883.

41. *Kansas City Times*, October 9, 1876; *Kansas City Journal*, October 10 and 11; *Expressman's Monthly*, October 1879, 282–6; *Liberty Tribune*, October 17, 1879. An even division of the loot gave each man $1,025, Liddil reported; *St. Louis Republican*, September 9, 1883.

42. Esther Rogoff Taus, *Central Banking Functions of the United States Treasury, 1789–1941* (New York: Columbia University Press, 1943), 63–4, 79, 85–6, 102, 112; Milton Friedman and Anna Jacobson Schwartz, *A Monetary History of the United States, 1867–1960* (Princeton: Princeton University Press, 1963), 3–14, 113–22. Industry periodicals often discussed the express companies' role as financial intermediaries; see, for example, *Expressman's Monthly*, February and October 1879.

43. Christensen and Kremer, 44–5; Campbell Gibson, "Population of the 100 Largest Cities and Other Urban Places in the United States: 1790 to 1990," Population Division Working Paper no. 27, June 1998, Population Division, U.S. Bureau of the Census, Washington, D.C.; see also Charles N. Glaab, *Kansas City and the Railroads: Community Policy in the Growth of a Regional Metropolis* (Madi-

son: State Historical Society of Wisconsin, 1962).

44. *Kansas City Journal,* October 10, 1879.

45. *Kansas City Times,* November 5, 1879; Howard L. Conard, ed., *Encyclopedia of the History of Missouri* (St. Louis: Southern History Company, 1901), 2: 355; Settle, 101–3.

46. *Kansas City Times,* November 4–6, 1879; *Liberty Tribune,* November 7, 1879.

47. *Richmond Democrat,* November 20, 1879.

48. *Nashville American,* October 9, 1882.

CHAPTER NINETEEN: Assassins

1. Ryan stopped at the Hite farm in Kentucky, rather than continue on to Nashville with Jesse; *Kansas City Journal,* April 4 and 5, 1882; *St. Louis Republican,* April 22, 1882, and September 9, 1883; *Nashville American,* October 6, 9, and 12, 1882; see also Yeatman, 217–18, though he relies too heavily on Jim Cummins's highly questionable memoirs and reminiscences given decades later.

2. *Nashville American,* October 9 and 12, 1882. Dick Liddil was one of many to testify to Frank's legitimate pursuits at this time, *St. Louis Republican,* September 9, 1883.

3. *St. Louis Republican,* September 9, 1883; George Hite, Jr., described how Ryan and James told of the robbery, *St. Louis Republican,* April 11, 1882. For detailed accounts of these robberies, see Yeatman, 218–22, and R. J. Wybrow, "The James Gang in Kentucky: A Tale of Murder and Robbery in the Blue Grass State," *Brand Book* 15, no. 2 (January 1973), published by the English Westerner's Society, 22–34.

4. *St. Louis Republican,* September 9, 1883; see also Liddil's comments in *Kansas City Times,* April 5, 1882.

5. Liddil's account neatly matches Frank's for this period; *St. Louis Republican,* September 9, 1883; *Nashville American,* October 9 and 12, 1882. The name of the particular horse mentioned is rendered differently in various accounts; see the testimony of Jonas Taylor, *Nashville American,* April 20, 1884. Numerous witnesses later testified to the James brothers' changes of address; see, for example, George Miller, Jr., *The Trial of Frank James for Murder* (St. Louis: n.p., 1898), 19–20, 23–7, 36. In Miller, 20, John Trimble, Jr., said that he rented a house at 814 Fatherland Street in Edgefield to B. J. Woodson on February 5, 1881, which may date Cummins's disappearance. In a curious footnote, John Edwards's *Sedalia Democrat* reported on January 7, 1881, that Jesse James had met one of the newspaper's journalists—apparently Bacon Montgomery—in Denver, Colorado; this inexplicable story conflicts with the accounts of Frank James, Dick Liddil, and others who were with Jesse at the time; Settle, 107.

6. *St. Louis Republican,* April 11, 1882, and September 12, 1883; Miller, 324; see also Dick Liddil's comments in *Kansas City Times,* April 5, 1882.

7. *Nashville American,* April 19, 1884; Major W. R. King, Memorandum Relative to the Muscle Shoals Robbery, December 17, 1881, and Affidavit of Thomas H. Peden, September 1, 1881, Letters Received Bulky Package File 1871–1881, 4521 GR 1881 #348, General Records Division, Special Collections: 1789–1923, Unregistered Letters, Reports, Histories, Regulations, and Other Records, 1817–1984, entry 292A, Record Group 77, Records of the Office of the Chief of Engineers, NA (to be cited as "Bulky Package File"). Frank James was eventually accused of taking part; as Yeatman notes, 237, later trial testimony by reliable witnesses showed that Frank was in Nashville at the time; see *Nashville American,* April 21 and 22, 1884. In Dick Liddil's initial confession, he admitted he knew nothing about the robbery; *St. Louis Republican,* September 9, 1883.

8. Affidavit of Alexander G. Smith, May 7, 1881, Bulky Package File. Smith had $21 in his pocket, the remainder from $50 that he had set aside from the rest to pay two casual laborers who lived in Florence; *Nashville American,* April 1, 1881.

9. Affidavit of Alexander G. Smith, May 7, 1881; Affidavit of E. N. Hartsfield, September 20, 1881; Affidavit of Daniel Comer, June 16, 1881; all in Bulky Package File. For a more detailed account, based largely on the National Archives file, see Yeatman, 231–44.

10. Miller, 19–20, 23; *Nashville American,* April 1, 1881; Affidavit of Alexander G. Smith, May 7, 1881, Bulky Package File.

11. *Nashville American,* April 20, 1884; Miller, 19–20, 23.

12. Miller, 24–6, 37, 49–51; *St. Louis Republican,* April 22, 1882, and September 9 and 12, 1883;

St. Louis Republican, November 5, 1881; Settle, 148, makes a similar observation about the bandits' horse theft.

13. *St. Louis Republican*, September 9, 1883; *Nashville American*, October 9, 1882.

14. *St. Louis Republican*, November 1, 1881, and April 22, 1882; Major W. R. King, Memorandum Relative to the Muscle Shoals Robbery, December 17, 1881, Bulky Package File; King to Chief of Engineers, telegram, April 14, 1881, and Wayne MacVeagh to President, April 16, 1881, letter 2715, microfilm publication M–689, roll 24, Letters Received 1881–1889, Adjutant General's Office, RG 94, NA. For further details on this episode, see Yeatman, 240–3, 246–7; see also Robert M. Utley, *High Noon in Lincoln: Violence on the Western Frontier* (Albuquerque: University of New Mexico Press, 1987), 84. The U.S. marshals operated on a fee-for-service basis, often serving as officers of the federal courts, and hesitated to take a strong role in actual law enforcement in many areas; Frederick S. Calhoun, *The Lawmen: United States Marshals and Their Deputies, 1789–1889* (Washington, D.C.: Smithsonian Institution Press, 1990), 49–63.

15. *Kansas City Evening Star*, July 18, 1881.

16. William H. Wallace, *Speeches and Writings of Wm. H. Wallace, with Autobiography* (Kansas City, Mo.: Western Baptist Publishing Co., 1914), 255–8, 273; Settle, 107; for an example of official Democratic indignation on his candidacy, see *Kansas City Times*, October 31, 1880.

17. Lawrence O. Christensen and Gary R. Kremer, *A History of Missouri*, vol. 4, *1875 to 1919* (Columbia: University of Missouri Press, 1997), 14; for an example of Crittenden's wartime activities, see *O.R.* 1: XXII, part 1: 622.

18. Settle, 106, 123.

19. Homer Clevenger, "Railroads in Missouri Politics, 1875–1887," *MHR* 43, no. 2 (January 1949): 220–36; Christensen and Kremer, 15–16; H. H. Crittenden, ed., *The Crittenden Memoirs* (New York: G. P. Putnam's Sons, 1936), 55–7; for a contemporary reference to Crittenden as a liberal, see *Richmond Conservator*, July 28, 1882; see also his inaugural address, Shoemaker, 6: 275. On the alliance between business interests and Democratic governments in the South, see two pivotal studies: C. Vann Woodward, *Origins of the New South, 1877–1913* (Baton Rouge: Louisiana State University Press, 1971), and Edward L. Ayers, *The Promise of the New South: Life After Reconstruction* (New York: Oxford University Press, 1992).

20. Shoemaker, 6: 175–6; Crittenden, 59.

21. Compare Crittenden's speech with the efforts of then state senator Charles H. Hardin to keep Governor Silas Woodson's anti-bandit address out of the press; *St. Louis Republican*, March 24, 1874.

22. Wallace, 274, 277; Settle, 113.

23. *Kansas City Journal*, July 16–18, 1881; *Kansas City Times*, July 16, 1881; *Kansas City Evening Star*, July 16, 1881; *St. Louis Republican*, September 9 and 12, 1883.

24. *St. Louis Republican*, September 9 and 12, 1883; *Kansas City Journal*, July 16–18, 1881; *Kansas City Times*, July 16, 1881; *Kansas City Evening Star*, July 16, 1881. See also Miller, 41–4, 78, 86, 88.

25. *Kansas City Times*, July 17, 1881; *Kansas City Evening Star*, July 18, 1881.

26. *Kansas City Journal*, July 19, 1881.

27. *Sedalia Democrat*, July 22, 1881; *Kansas City Times*, July 17 and 20, 1881; *Kansas City Evening Star*, July 19, 1881.

28. *St. Louis Republican*, July 26, 1881; Crittenden, 60; Scott Reynolds Nelson, *Iron Confederacies: Southern Railways, Klan Violence, and Reconstruction* (Chapel Hill: University of North Carolina Press, 1999), 178.

29. *St. Louis Republican*, July 27 and 28, 1881; *Kansas City Journal*, July 29, 1881; Shoemaker, 6: 494–6.

30. *St. Louis Republican*, September 12, 1883.

31. According to Dick Liddil, in the first, failed attempt, Jesse and Frank fixed a piece of iron to the rails of the Missouri Pacific, hoping to ditch the engine, only to see the locomotive speed safely past; *St. Louis Republican*, September 8, 1881, September 9 and 12, 1883; passenger and engineer quotes from *Kansas City Journal*, September 8, 1881, and *Kansas City Times*, September 8, 1881. The

engineer, L. "Chappy" Foote, gave somewhat conflicting accounts to various newspapers; it appears that the leader met him after the robbery finished, though he also suggested that he did so at the beginning, in which case another bandit must have introduced himself as Jesse James.

32. *Kansas City Journal*, September 9, 1881.

33. *Kansas City Journal*, September 10, 1881; *St. Louis Republican*, September 11, 1881.

34. *Liberty Tribune*, September 30, 1881; *St. Louis Republican*, September 28 and 29, 1881; Wallace, 275–9. Most militia companies formed since 1868, like the Craig Rifles, were social organizations with colorful names. See John Glendower Westover, "The Evolution of the Missouri Militia, 1804–1919" (Ph.D. diss., University of Missouri, Columbia, 1948), 173–96.

35. *St. Louis Republican*, September 29 and 30, October 10, 1881. The *Kansas City Journal*, September 10, 1881, also noted, somewhat sourly, that the newspapers that once supported the bandits now loudly condemned them.

36. *St. Louis Republican*, April 6 and 11, 1882, September 9 and 12, 1883; *Kansas City Times*, April 7, 1882; Settle, 116. Jesse's brother-in-law T. M. Mimms noticed his rising suspicions; *Kansas City Journal*, April 5, 1882.

37. *St. Louis Republican*, April 11, 1882, and September 12, 1883; Crittenden, 153. According to Wallace, 279, Hite left the body in a hog pen and the animals devoured the corpse.

38. Liddil's wife, Mattie Collins, had earlier been acquitted of murdering her brother-in-law, on grounds of temporary insanity. William Wallace and his partners had served as her defense attorneys; Wallace, 280; *Kansas City Journal*, April 4, 1882.

39. "He exhibited an empty chamber in his revolver," Liddil reported. "Bob claimed that his shot was the fatal one." Ford and his brothers Elias and Wilbur wrapped Hite in a horse blanket and carried him upstairs; by nightfall he was dead. They stripped off his clothes and buried him in a shallow grave nearby. See the *St. Louis Republican*, September 9, 1883. See also *Kansas City Times*, April 7, 1882; *Kansas City Journal*, April 4, 1882; *St. Louis Republican*, April 5, 1882; Miller, 62–8.

40. *Kansas City Times*, April 5, 1882; *St. Louis Republican*, September 9, 1883.

41. Miller, 55, 62; *St. Louis Republican*, April 1, 1882, and September 9, 1883; *Kansas City Journal*, April 4, 1882; *Kansas City Journal*, April 5, 1882. Wallace, 280, claimed that Liddil sent his wife, Mattie Collins, to see him first; this assertion, made decades later, is not confirmed by contemporary accounts, nor is it particularly relevant, as even Wallace admits it led nowhere.

42. *St. Louis Republican*, April 5 and 6, 1882.

43. *Kansas City Journal*, April 4 and 5, 1882; *St. Louis Republican*, November 1 and 4, 1881, April 1, 5, and 11, 1882; *Sedalia Democrat*, February 2, 1882; *Liberty Tribune*, February 24, 1882; Miller, 62; Yeatman, 266–7.

44. *Kansas City Journal*, April 4, 1882; *Nashville American*, October 9, 1882. Charley Ford said that the last time he saw Frank was in September 1881; *St. Louis Republican*, April 6, 1882.

45. *Kansas City Journal*, April 5, 1882.

46. Ibid., April 4 and 5, 1882; *Nashville American*, October 9, 1882; *St. Louis Republican*, September 12, 1883.

47. *Kansas City Journal*, April 4, 1882; *St. Louis Republican*, April 6, 1882, September 9 and 12, 1883; Settle, 137.

48. *St. Louis Republican*, April 7, 1882; *Sedalia Democrat*, April 15, 1882; *Kansas City Journal*, April 4, 1882; Yeatman, 267, details the real estate inquiry.

49. *St. Louis Republican*, April 1, 5–7, 1882; *Kansas City Journal*, April 4 and 5, 1882; Settle, 116.

50. *St. Louis Republican*, April 6, 1882.

51. The quotes, given by the Ford brothers, appear in the *Kansas City Journal*, April 4, 1882. They differ very slightly from Charley Ford's testimony to a coroner's inquest in their reference to Jesse's worries about being seen if he went outside; without this detail, his actions seem inexplicable.

52. *Kansas City Journal*, April 4 and 5, 1882.

CHAPTER TWENTY: Apotheosis

1. *Kansas City Journal*, April 4 and 5, 1882; *Kansas City Times*, April 4 and 6, 1882. On later impostors, see Settle, 167–71. Yeatman, 371–6, provides a transcript of a press conference given by the forensic analysis team on February 23, 1996.

2. *Kansas City Journal*, April 5, 1882; Settle, 129–30; Yeatman, 273–4; for other examples of interviews with relatives, see *Kansas City Journal*, April 6, 1882, and *St. Louis Republican*, April 11, 1882.

3. *Liberty Tribune*, April 14, 1882; *Kansas City Times*, April 7, 1882.

4. *St. Louis Republican*, April 7, 1882; *Kansas City Times*, April 6, 1882; *Liberty Tribune*, May 5, 1882.

5. Entry for April 28, 1882, Diary of Elias Eppstein, 1880–1883, coll. 2733, WHMC; *Richmond Conservator*, April 21, 1882; *St. Louis Republican*, April 6, 1882; *Kansas City Times*, April 8, 1882; Yeatman, 275.

6. *Sedalia Democrat*, April 13 and 22, 1882. For a discussion of the press and political response, see Settle, 120–6.

7. *Sedalia Democrat*, April 16, 1882; *Liberty Tribune*, June 1, 1882; J. N. Edwards to My Dear Frank, July 17, 1882, and August 1, 1882, coll. 1531, John N. Edwards Papers, WHMC; Settle, 118, 130.

8. *St. Louis Globe-Democrat*, October 6, 1882.

9. Ibid., October 10, 1882; George Miller, Jr., *The Trial of Frank James for Murder* (St. Louis: n.p., 1898), 6; Settle, 134–6. Edwards also raised money for Frank's defense from former Confederates, calling on their wartime loyalties to a comrade; see John N. Edwards to Gen. D. M. Frost, April 12, 1883, Fordyce Collection, MHS.

10. *St. Louis Globe-Democrat*, October 8, 1882; Gerard S. Petrone, *Judgment at Gallatin: The Trial of Frank James* (Lubbock: Texas Tech University Press, 1998), 51–168; Settle, 123, 136–43, 149–55, 158; see also Yeatman, 283–4, and Miller, who drafted the closest thing to a trial transcript in existence. Italics are in the original, quoted in Settle.

11. Edward P. Clark to My Dear Brother, March 6, 1883, coll. 83, Charles W. Clark Papers, WHMC.

12. *The Nation*, April 13, 1882.

13. Eric J. Hobsbawm, *Primitive Rebels: Studies in Archaic Forms of Social Movements in the 19th and 20th Centuries* (New York: W. W. Norton, 1965), orig. pub. in 1959 as *Social Bandits and Primitive Rebels*, and Eric J. Hobsbawm, *Bandits*, rev. ed. (New York: Pantheon Books, 1981), 17, 40–56.

14. See, for example, Anton Blok, "The Peasant and the Brigand: Social Banditry Reconsidered," and Eric J. Hobsbawm, "Social Bandits: A Reply," *Comparative Studies in Society and History* 14, no. 4 (September 1972): 494–505; Paul Sant Cassia, "Banditry, Myth, and Terror in Cyprus and Other Mediterranean Societies," *Comparative Studies in Society and History* 15, no. 4 (October 1993): 773–95; Giannes Koliopoulos, *Brigands with a Cause: Brigandage and Irredentism in Modern Greece, 1821–1921* (Oxford, U.K.: Clarendon Press, 1987); and also Hobsbawm's reply to his critics in the revised edition of *Bandits*, 138–64.

15. Richard White, "Outlaw Gangs of the Middle Border: American Social Bandits," *Western Historical Quarterly* 12, no. 4 (October 1981): 387–408.

16. Hobsbawm, *Bandits*, 153; White, 395–7, 402, 406–7.

17. Karl Marx, "The Eighteenth Brumaire of Louis Bonaparte," in *The Marx-Engels Reader*, 2nd ed., ed. Robert C. Tucker (New York: W. W. Norton & Co., 1978), 608. For an example of a thoughtful discussion of political violence based to some extent on the Marxian framework, see Charles Tilly, "Collective Violence in European Perspective," in *Violence in America: Historical and Comparative Perspectives*, ed. Hugh Davis Graham and Ted Robert Gurr (Beverly Hills: Sage, 1979), 83–152.

18. Hobsbawm, *Bandits*, 24, 55, 130, 158;

19. Hobsbawm, *Bandits*, 153; White, 395–7, 402, 406–7; Fellman, 254.

20. Fellman, 263. It should be noted that Fellman addressed Jesse James directly in a biographical entry in Ronald Gottesman, ed., *Violence in America: An Encyclopedia* (New York: Charles Scribner's Sons, 1999), 2: 188–90. This brief essay relies primarily on Thelen's arguments. The

stress on the primacy of the bandit mythology over reality also appears in Richard Slotkin's work, *Gunfighter Nation: The Myth of the Frontier in Twentieth-Century America* (New York: Atheneum, 1992), 125–55, and (more generally) *The Fatal Environment: The Myth of the Frontier in the Age of Industrialization, 1800–1890* (New York: Atheneum, 1985).

21. Keith Ian Polakoff, *The Politics of Inertia: The Election of 1876 and the End of Reconstruction* (Baton Rouge: Louisiana State University Press, 1973), 155–7; for more on the interconvertible bond, see Irwin Unger, *The Greenback Era: A Social and Political History of American Finance, 1865–1879* (Princeton: Princeton University Press, 1964), 96–101. A Marxist, of course, might argue that any accommodation with the capitalist economy would not be a proper expression of the farmers' class interests.

22. *Liberty Tribune,* March 1, 1872. Don R. Bowen has deftly shown the wealth and commercial orientation of the western Missouri guerrillas, who both rode with and provided critical support to the James and Younger brothers after the war; see, for example, Don R. Bowen, "Counterrevolutionary Guerrilla War: Missouri, 1861–1865," *Conflict* 8, no. 1 (1988): 69–78. A keynote speaker at the Greenback convention in 1884 also denounced the bandits; Homer Clevenger, "Railroads in Missouri Politics, 1875–1887," *MHR* 43, no. 2 (January 1949): 220–36. Most of the bandits' grassroots opponents were farmers. Jackson County marshal James L. Liggett, for example, was a Granger; *Kansas City Times,* August 18, 1874. If economic grievances and fear of outsiders had been the driving force behind local support for the outlaws, then much of the public debate would have revolved around eastern insurance and mortgage companies, which began to lend heavily in the region after the Civil War; but they passed unmentioned by the outlaws, their supporters, or their opponents. See H. Peers Brewer, "Eastern Money and Western Mortgages in the 1870s," *Business History Review* 50, no. 3 (autumn 1976): 356–80; Allan G. Bogue, "Financing the Prairie Farmer," in *The Reinterpretation of American Economic History,* ed. Stanley L. Engerman and Robert W. Fogel (New York: Harper & Row, 1971), 301–10; Lance E. Davis, "Capital Mobility and American Growth," in Engerman and Fogel, 285–300. For more on the deflationary gold standard, see Michael D. Bordo and Anna J. Schwartz, eds., *A Retrospective on the Classical Gold Standard* (Chicago: University of Chicago Press, 1984), 11, 613; Milton Friedman and Anna Jacobson Schwartz, *A Monetary History of the United States, 1867–1960* (Princeton: Princeton University Press, 1963), 89–95.

23. *Lexington Caucasian,* September 5, 1874; Scott Reynolds Nelson, *Iron Confederacies: Southern Railways, Klan Violence, and Reconstruction* (Chapel Hill: University of North Carolina Press, 1999); Nelson found that anti-railroad activity ceased once the corporations actively enlisted the support of white-supremacist Democratic leaders. See also C. J. M. Drake, "The Role of Ideology in Terrorists' Target Selection," *Terrorism and Political Violence* 10, no. 2 (summer 1998): 53–85.

24. Quoted in Settle, 90.

25. *Kansas City Journal of Commerce,* October 20, 1876. White, 399, argues the opposite, saying support for the outlaws was "not a simple reflection of Union/Confederate divisions." He is mistaken, though the nature of those divisions were complicated.

26. *Sedalia Democrat,* April 13, 1882. On honor and Southern violence, see Edward L. Ayers, *Vengeance and Justice: Crime and Punishment in the 19th-Century American South* (New York: Oxford University Press, 1984), 9–74. The argument here wholeheartedly echoes that of Christopher Phillips, *Missouri's Confederate: Claiborne Fox Jackson and the Creation of Southern Identity in the Border West* (Columbia: University of Missouri Press, 2000), 274–96.

27. David Thelen, *Paths of Resistance: Tradition and Dignity in Industrializing Missouri* (New York: Oxford University Press, 1986), 75; *Sedalia Democrat,* April 13, 1882; *Kansas City Journal,* April 5, 1882. Slotkin, *Gunfighter Nation,* 127–30, 137–9, and Michael Denning, *Mechanic Accents: Dime Novels and Working-Class Culture in America,* rev. ed. (London: Verso, 1998), 157–66, argue that the dime-novel representations of Jesse James positioned him as a social bandit, striking out against powerful monied interests; but neither writer is particularly interested in the real Jesse James, or the roots of his very real support in Missouri.

28. See especially George C. Rable, *But There Was No Peace: The Role of Violence in the Politics of Reconstruction* (Athens: University of Georgia Press, 1984); Allen W. Trelease's classic *White Terror: The Ku Klux Klan Conspiracy and Southern Reconstruction* (Baton Rouge: Louisiana State Uni-

versity Press, 1971); and the following chapters from Graham and Gurr: Richard Maxwell Brown, "Historical Patterns of American Violence," 19–48, Brown, "The American Vigilante Tradition," 153–85 (which notes the political divisions often expressed in vigilante and anti-vigilante groups), and G. David Garson and Gail O'Brien, "Collective Violence in the Reconstruction South," 243–60. Donald G. Nieman has gathered a useful collection of articles (some of them dated), *Black Freedom/White Violence, 1865–1900* (New York: Garland, 1994). Two instructive studies are William J. Crotty, James F. Kirkham, and Sheldon G. Levy, *Assassination and Political Violence: A Report to the National Commission on the Causes and Prevention of Violence* (New York: Praeger, 1970), 1–59, 212–95, and Ida Waller Pope, "Violence as a Political Force in the Reconstruction South" (Ph.D. diss., University of Southwestern Louisiana, 1982). See also Ayers, 141–84, though I strongly disagree with his suggestion that the violence of this era was "not nearly as novel and as political as it appeared to outsiders" (163). Special note must be made of the work of Richard Maxwell Brown, one of the most insightful interpreters of American violence; see especially three recent works, *No Duty to Retreat: Violence and Values in American History and Society* (New York: Oxford University Press, 1991); "Western Violence: Structure, Values, Myth," *Western Historical Quarterly* 24, no. 1 (February 1993): 5–20; and "Violence," in *The Oxford History of the American West*, ed. Clyde A. Milner, II, Carol A. O'Connor, and Martha A. Sandweiss (New York: Oxford University Press, 1994), 393–425.

29. Rable, 12. Richard Maxwell Brown has made the same point repeatedly and effectively. Walter Laqueur notes, "There is in fact no clear dividing line between guerrilla warfare, terror and brigandage"; Laqueur, *Guerrilla Warfare: A Historical and Critical Study* (New Brunswick, N.J.: Transaction, 1998), 93–8, 384–7. Part of what divides banditry from guerrilla warfare, he writes, is the "political incentive" of the guerrilla; it has been argued here that this incentive was present in the band of former bushwhackers, at fluctuating levels, from the end of the war to the end of Reconstruction.

30. *Kansas City Times*, July 27, 1881; *Kansas City Journal of Commerce*, September 27, 1876, and October 12, 1879; White, 395.

31. This argument runs counter to the claims of Slotkin, *Gunfighter Nation*, 134, that Edwards and other Missouri newspaper editors "fabricated for Jesse" the myth that he was a political figure in the context of continuing Confederate resistance to the Union victory and Reconstruction.

32. *Nashville Republican Banner*, July 11 and 28, 1875; *Kansas City Times*, August 23, 1876.

33. *Kansas City Journal of Commerce*, September 27, 1876.

34. Slotkin, *Gunfighter Nation*, 128, 138, argues that Jesse James's "greatest significance was not developed in the folklore of the provincial community whose resentments and resistance they initially symbolized," but rather in the dime-novel-driven "mass cultural myth of social banditry. . . . As historical social bandits, the James boys had been a distinctly local and partisan phenomenon whose careers ended in failure." I strongly question whether the dime-novel representation of Jesse James can be considered more significant than his often central role in the political and cultural battles of his home region, or that he can be considered a failure (despite his early death). Slotkin's assessment, appearing in a very perceptive and significant work of history, seems to reflect both his concern with mass-culture mythology in general, and his lack of detailed knowledge of James's life.

35. Jesse James's career resembles in some respects (though not in specific political content) Hobsbawm's account of Francisco Sabaté Llopart, a Spanish Republican who battled the Franco regime as a political outlaw; see Hobsbawm, *Bandits*, 114–26.

36. See Slotkin, *Gunfighter Nation*, 125–55, and, for a more general discussion of the frontier myth, *The Fatal Environment;* Denning, 149–66; and Kent L. Steckmesser, *The Western Hero in History and Legend* (Norman: University of Oklahoma Press, 1965). For an inventory of Jesse James folklore, books, and movies, see Settle, 160–201; Yeatman, 223–4, 275–6, 296–7, 368–70; and Frank Richard Prassel, *The Great American Outlaw: A Legacy of Fact and Fiction* (Norman: University of Oklahoma Press, 1993).

37. Eric Foner is particularly eloquent on this point in *The Story of American Freedom* (New York: W. W. Norton, 1998), xiii–xxii, 95–113.

38. Michael A. Bellesiles, *Arming America: The Origins of a National Gun Culture* (New York:

Alfred A. Knopf, 2000), 377, 406–44; *O.R.* 1: XLVIII, part 2: 322. Colt began to prosper in the 1850s, but the Civil War marked a clear departure in revolver production, ownership, and use.

39. Brown, *No Duty to Retreat,* 39–86.

40. Eric Foner, *Reconstruction: America's Unfinished Revolution, 1863–1877* (New York: Harper & Row, 1988), 608–9; James W. Garner, *Reconstruction in Mississippi* (Gloucester, Mass.: Peter Smith, 1964, orig. pub. 1901), 408. The estimate that at least half the public supported the Reconstruction agenda is based on Republican victories in 1868 and 1872, when African Americans were allowed to vote (particularly in 1872). See also an important recent study, David W. Blight, *Race and Reunion: The Civil War in American Memory* (Cambridge: Harvard University Press, 2001).

41. C. Vann Woodward identified Howard Beale's *The Critical Year* as a decisive book in creating a non-Marxist economic interpretation of Reconstruction; see Woodward's introduction to Robert P. Sharkey, *Money, Class, and Party: An Economic Study of Civil War and Reconstruction* (Baltimore: The Johns Hopkins University Press, 1959), vii–ix, itself an influential work in this regard. The work of Charles A. and Mary R. Beard contributed to this trend; see, for example, *The Rise of American Civilization* (New York: Macmillan, 1927), 2: 111–14, which places an economic interpretation on the framing of the Fourteenth Amendment. On the widow story, see Settle, 171–2, 227. As railroad historian Maury Klein notes, there is "a folklore of reform in which the struggle between the railroads and 'the people' occupies a prominent niche"; Maury Klein, *The Life and Legend of Jay Gould* (Baltimore: The Johns Hopkins University Press, 1986), 160–1.

42. Settle, 160–6; Yeatman, 287–321; F. Y. Hedley, "John Newman Edwards," in *Encyclopedia of the History of Missouri,* ed. Howard L. Conard (St. Louis: Southern History Company, 1901), 2: 354–6; Petrone, 189–209. Bob Ford attempted to cash in on his notoriety almost immediately, asking for free passes on the railroads; Bob Ford, Slayer of Jessie James, to President, Wabash, St. Louis & Pacific RR., October 14, 1882, Railroads Collection, MHS. Zee James offered to sell some items to Eugene Field in 1896, writing, "I am not in good circumstances and a little money would greatly assist me"; Mrs. Jesse James to Eugene Field, April 1, 1896, Field Collection, MHS. Zerelda briefly rented out the farm in 1902; during that period, she reinterred Jesse's body in a Baptist cemetery in Kearney when she discovered that the tenants were selling flowers from his grave for twenty-five cents each; *Kansas City Star,* June 30, 1902. Jesse Jr. was tried and acquitted in 1899 for the holdup of a Missouri Pacific train on September 23, 1898. He died in 1951; Settle, 165.

Bibliography

Unpublished Primary Sources

Chicago Historical Society, Chicago, Illinois
  Charles C. Curtiss Diary
  Allan Pinkerton Papers
Clay County Archives, Liberty, Missouri
  Daniel Askew Probate Records
  Robert James Probate Records
William R. Perkins Library, Duke University, Durham, North Carolina
  Missouri Militia Papers
  Phineas Messenger Savery Papers
  Jane Peterson Papers
  W. W. Scott Papers
  William Dunlap Simpson Papers
  James C. Zimmerman Papers
Minnesota Historical Society, St. Paul, Minnesota
  "Northfield (Minnesota) Bank Robbery of 1876: Selected Manuscripts Collection and Govern-
    ment Records" (microfilm publication)
  John E. Risedorph Papers
Missouri Historical Society, St. Louis, Missouri
  Civil War Collection
  Field Collection
  Hamilton R. Gamble Papers
  Railroads Collection
  Reynolds Collection
Missouri State Archives, Jefferson City, Missouri
  Governors' Papers:
    B. Gratz Brown Papers
    Thomas C. Fletcher Papers
    Charles H. Hardin Papers
    Silas Woodson Papers
  Office of the Adjutant General: Letterbook, December 17, 1866 to January 22, 1869
National Archives, College Park, Maryland
  Records of the U.S. Secret Service, Record Group 87:
    Daily reports of U.S. Secret Service Agents, 1875–1936, Microfilm Publication T-915

Record of Arrests and Convictions, 1869–1930

Register of Letters Received at New York, April 1, 1870–1874

National Archives, Washington, D.C.

Office of the Adjutant General, Record Group 94:

Letters Received 1881–1889, Microfilm Publication M–689

Office of the Chief of Engineers, Record Group 77:

Letters Received Bulky Package File 1871–1881, 4521 GR 1881 #348, General Records Division, Special Collections: 1789–1923, Unregistered Letters, Reports, Histories, Regulations, and Other Records, 1817–1984

Department of the Missouri, U.S. Army Continental Commands, 1821–1920, Record Group 393:

Letters Received 1861–1867

Post Office Department, Record Group 28:

Letters Sent by the Chief Special Agent, Office of Special Agents and Mail Depredations, 1875–1877

Case Files, Office of Special Agents and Mail Depredations, 1875–1877

Letters Sent 1789–1952, Office of the Postmaster General

Union Provost Marshal Papers, Record Group 109:

One-Name Citizen File, Union Provost Marshal Papers, Microfilm Publication M-345

Two or More Name Citizen File, Union Provost Marshal Papers, Microfilm Publication M-416

Western Historical Manuscript Collection, State Historical Society of Missouri, Columbia, Missouri

Clarence W. Alvord and Idress Head Collection

David Rice Atchison Papers

"Democratic Picnic Summary, Buckner, Missouri, September 16, 1876"

Greenup Bird, "Clay County Savings Association Robbery Description, 1866"

Charles W. Clark Papers

John N. Edwards Letters, 1865–1866

Elias Eppstein, "Kansas City Diary," 1880–1883

Charles B. France Papers

Gallatin Bank Postcard

William Gregg, "A Little Dab of History Without Embellishment"

J. S. Hughes & Co. Discount Book

Bazel F. Lazear Papers

Abiel Leonard Papers

Thomas Riley Shouse, "My Father and Jesse James"

Walter B. Stevens Scrapbook

Other Archives

Bond-Fentriss Family Papers, Southern History Collection, University of North Carolina, Chapel Hill, North Carolina

Blythe, Culbertson, Frass, and William Jewell collated and typescript letter collections, Watkins Woolen Mill State Historic Site and Park, Lawson, Missouri

William Connelly Collection, Denver Public Library, Denver, Colorado

Tho. C. Fletcher to Col., March 19, 1866, Collection KC 200, Western Historical Manuscript Collection, State Historical Society of Missouri, Kansas City, Missouri

Papers of Pinkerton's National Detective Agency, Library of Congress, Washington, D.C.

Published Primary Sources

Adams, Charles F., Jr., "A Chapter of Erie." *North American Review* (July 1869): 30–106.

Adams, Henry. *The Education of Henry Adams.* New York: Penguin, 1995.

Ames, Adelbert. "The Capture of Fort Fisher." *Civil War Papers.* Boston: The Commandery, 1890.

Ames, Blanche Butler, ed. *Chronicles from the Nineteenth Century: Family Letters of Blanche Butler and Adelbert Ames.* Clinton, Mass.: n.p., 1957.

Annual Report of the Comptroller of the Currency. Washington, D.C.: Government Printing Office, 1865, 1867, 1868, 1869, 1870, 1871, 1872, 1873, 1874, 1875, 1876.

Annual Report to the President, Directors, and Stockholders of the Chicago, Rock Island, and Pacific Railroad Company, April 1, 1874. New York: Clarence Levey & Co., 1874.

Appler, Augustus C. *The Younger Brothers: The Life, Character, and Daring Exploits of the Youngers, the Notorious Bandits Who Rode with Jesse James and William Clarke Quantrill*. New York: Frederick Fell, 1955. Orig. pub. 1876.

Beath, Robert B. *History of the Grand Army of the Republic*. New York: Bryan, Taylor, & Co., 1889.

Bergeron, Paul H., ed. *The Papers of Andrew Johnson*. Knoxville: University of Tennessee Press, 1992.

Berkey, William A. *The Money Question: The Legal Tender Paper Money System of the United States*. New York: Greenwood Press, 1969. Orig. pub. 1876.

Berlin, Ira, Steven F. Miller, Joseph P. Reidy, and Leslie S. Rowland, eds. *Freedom: A Documentary History of Emancipation: 1861–1867*. New York: Cambridge University Press, 1993.

Britton, Wiley. *The Civil War on the Border*. New York: G. P. Putnam's Sons, 1899.

Buel, Clarence Clough, and Robert Underwood Johnson, eds. *Battles and Leaders of the Civil War*. New York: Century Co., 1887.

Bunyan, John. *The Holy War*. New York: New York University Press, 1967. Orig. pub. 1682.

Bushman, Katherine Gentry, ed. *Index of the First Plat Book of Clay County, Missouri, 1819–1875*. N.p., n.d.

Carnegie, Andrew. *Autobiography of Andrew Carnegie*. Boston: Houghton Mifflin, 1920.

Carr, Nanon Lucile, ed. *Marriage Records of Clay County, Missouri, 1822–1852*. Privately printed: 1957.

Crittenden, H. H., ed. *The Crittenden Memoirs*. New York: G. P. Putnam's Sons, 1936.

Cullom, Shelby M. *Fifty Years of Public Service: Personal Recollections of Shelby M. Cullom*. Chicago: A. C. McClurg & Co., 1911.

Cummins, Jim. *Jim Cummins' Book Written by Himself*. Denver: Reed Publishing, 1903.

———. *Jim Cummins, the Guerrilla*. Excelsior Springs, Mo.: Daily Journal, 1908.

Douglass, Frederick. *Narrative of the Life of Frederick Douglass, an American Slave, Written by Himself*. New York: Penguin, 1968.

Edwards, Jennie, ed. *John N. Edwards: Biography, Memoirs, Reminiscences, and Recollections*. Kansas City, Mo.: Jennie Edwards, 1889.

Edwards, John N. *Noted Guerrillas, or the Warfare of the Border*. St. Louis: H. W. Brand & Co., 1879. Orig. pub. 1877.

———. *Shelby and His Men: or, The War in the West*. Cincinnati: Miami Printing and Publishing, 1867.

Eldridge, Benjamin P., and William B. Watts. *Our Rival the Rascal*. Boston: Pemberton, 1897.

Fyfer, Thomas. *History of Boone County, Missouri*. St. Louis: Western Historical Company, 1882.

Goodman, Thomas M. *A Thrilling Record*. Des Moines: Mills & Co., 1868.

Goodrich, James W., and Donald B. Oster, eds. " 'Few Men But Many Widows': The Daniel Fogle Letters, August 8–September 4, 1867." *Missouri Historical Review* 80, no. 3 (April 1986): 273–303.

Grant, Ulysses S. *Personal Memoirs of U. S. Grant*. New York: Da Capo, 1982. Orig. pub. 1885.

Greenwood, J. M. "Col. Robert T. Van Horn." *Missouri Historical Review* 4, no. 2 (January 1910): 92–105, and 4, no. 3 (April 1910): 167–81.

Hanson, Joseph Have. *The Northfield Tragedy: A History of the Northfield Bank Raid and Murders*. St. Paul: n.p., 1876.

Heilbron, W. C., ed. *Convict Life at the Minnesota State Prison*. Stillwater, Minn.: n.p., 1911.

History of Clay and Platte Counties, Missouri. St. Louis: National Historic Company, 1885.

Hodges, Nadine, and Mrs. Howard W. Woodruff, eds. *Genealogical Notes from the Liberty Tribune*. Liberty, Mo.: n.p., 1975.

James, Stella F. *In the Shadow of Jesse James*. Thousand Oaks, Calif.: Dragon Books, 1990.

Journal of the House of Representatives at the Regular Session of the Twenty-Eighth General Assembly of the State of Missouri. Jefferson City: Regan & Carter, 1875.

Korner, Barbara Oliver, and Carla Waal, eds. *Hardship and Hope: Missouri Women Writing About Their Lives, 1820–1920*. Columbia: University of Missouri Press, 1997.

Kroos, Herman E., ed. *Documentary History of Banking and Currency in the United States*. New York: Chelsea House Publishers, 1965.

Leonard, D. L. *Funeral Discourse of Joseph Lee Heywood*. Minneapolis: Steam Book Printers, 1876.

Loeb, Isidor, and Floyd C. Shoemaker, eds. *Debates of the Missouri Constitutional Convention of 1875*. Columbia: State Historical Society of Missouri, 1930–1944.

Lynch, John R. *Reminiscences of an Active Life: The Autobiography of John Roy Lynch*. Chicago: Chicago University Press, 1970.

McCorkle, John, as told to O. S. Barton, *Three Years with Quantrell: A True Story*. Armstrong, Mo.: Armstrong Herald Print, n.d.

McPherson, Edward. *The Political History of the United States During the Period of Reconstruction*. 2nd ed. New York: Negro Universities Press, 1969. Orig. pub. 1875.

Macy, R. B. "Detective Pinkerton." *Harper's Weekly* (October 1873): 720–7.

Miller, George. *Missouri's Memorable Decade, 1860–1870*. Columbia: E. W. Stephens, 1898.

Miller, George, Jr. *The Trial of Frank James for Murder*. St. Louis: n.p., 1898.

The Miscellaneous Documents of the Senate of the United States for the Second Session of the Forty-Fourth Congress. Washington, D.C.: Government Printing Office, 1877.

Mississippi in 1875: Report of the Select Committee to Inquire into the Mississippi Election of 1875, with the Testimony and Documentary Evidence. Washington, D.C.: Government Printing Office, 1876.

Nevins, Allan, ed. *A Diary of Battle: The Personal Journals of Colonel Charles S. Wainwright, 1861–1865*. New York: Da Capo Press, 1998.

Official Express Guide and Rail Road Manual. New York: Bass & Gilbert, 1871.

Parker, Nathan H. *Missouri as it is in 1867*. Philadelphia: J. B. Lippincott, 1867.

Parkman, Francis. *The Oregon Trail*. New York: Penguin, 1969. Orig. pub. 1849.

Paxton, W. M. *Annals of Platte County, Missouri*. Kansas City: Hudson-Kimberly Publishing, 1897.

Pinkerton, William A. *Train Robberies, Train Robbers, and the "Holdup" Men*. New York: Arno Press, 1974. Orig. pub. 1907.

Portrait and Biographical Record of Clay, Ray, Carroll, Chariton, and Linn Counties, Missouri. Chicago: Chapman Brothers, 1893.

Rawick, George, ed. *The American Slave: A Composite Autobiography*. Vol. 11. Westport, Conn.: Greenwood, 1979.

Report of the Committee of the House of Representatives of the Twenty-Second General Assembly of the State of Missouri, Appointed to Investigate the Conduct and Management of the Militia. Jefferson City: W. M. Curry, 1864. Reprinted in 1999 by the State Historical Society of Missouri, Columbia.

Report of the Joint Committee on Reconstruction at the First Session, Thirty-Ninth Congress. Westport, Conn.: Negro Universities Press, 1969. Orig. pub. 1866.

Sherman, William T. *Memoirs of General William T. Sherman*. New York: Da Capo Press, 1984.

Shoemaker, Floyd C., and Grace Gilmore Avery, eds. *The Messages and Proclamations of the Governors of the State of Missouri*. Columbia: State Historical Society of Missouri, 1924.

Snead, Thomas L. *The Fight for Missouri*. New York: Scribner's, 1886.

Stevens, Walter B. "The Political Turmoil of 1874 in Missouri." *Missouri Historical Review* 31, no. 1 (October 1936): 3–9.

Stiles, T. J., ed. *The Citizen's Handbook*. New York: Berkley, 1993.

———. *Robber Barons and Radicals: Reconstruction and the Origin of Civil Rights*. New York: Berkley, 1997.

———. *Warriors and Pioneers*. New York: Berkley, 1996.

Stimson, A. L. *History of the Express Business*. New York: Baker & Godwin, 1881.

Sumner, Merlin E., ed. *The Diary of Cyrus B. Comstock*. Dayton, Ohio: Morningside, 1987.

Thompson, Dorothy Brown. "A Young Girl in the Missouri Border War." *Missouri Historical Review* 58, no. 1 (October 1963): 56–68.

Twain, Mark. *Life on the Mississippi*. New York: Penguin, 1984. Orig. pub. 1883.

United States Census. Washington, D.C.: Government Printing Office. Seventh, Eighth, Ninth, and Tenth: 1850, 1860, 1870, 1880 (including slave schedules for 1850 and 1860).

Vernon, Edward, ed. *American Railroad Manual for the United States and the Dominion*. Philadelphia: J. B. Lippincott, 1873.

Wallace, William H. *Speeches and Writings of Wm. H. Wallace, with Autobiography*. Kansas City, Mo.: Western Baptist Publishing Co., 1914.

The War of the Rebellion: A Compilation of the Official Records of the Union and Confederate Armies. Washington, D.C., Government Printing Office, 1880–1901.

Wetmore, Alphonso. *Gazetteer of the State of Missouri*. St. Louis: C. Keemle, 1837.

Woodward, P. H. *Guarding the Mails; or, The Secret Service of the Post Office Department*. Hartford, Conn.: Dustin, Gilman & Co., 1876.

Younger, Thomas Coleman. *The Story of Cole Younger by Himself*. Lee's Summit, Mo.: n.p., 1903.

Newspapers and Periodicals

American Railroad Journal
Bankers' Magazine and Statistical Register
Boonville Advertiser
Carrollton Journal
Chicago Times
Chicago Tribune
Columbia Herald
Columbia Missouri Statesman
Expressman's Monthly
Faribault Democrat
Harper's Weekly
Jefferson City People's Tribune
Kansas City Evening Star
Kansas City Journal of Commerce (later *Kansas City Journal*)
Kansas City Times
Kearney Courier
Lexington Caucasian
Liberty Advance
Liberty Tribune
Louisville Courier (later *Louisville Courier-Journal*)
Minneapolis Tribune
Missouri Valley Register (later *Lexington Register*)
Nashville American
Nashville Republican Banner
Nashville World
New York Herald
New York Times
New York World
Northfield News
Our Expressman
Railroad Gazette
Rice County Journal
Richmond [Missouri] *Conservator*
Richmond [Missouri] *Missourian*
St. Joseph Gazette
St. Joseph Herald & Tribune
St. Joseph Morning Herald
St. Louis Dispatch (later *St. Louis Post-Dispatch*)

St. Louis Globe (later St. Louis Globe-Democrat)
St. Louis Republican (also St. Louis Missouri Republican)
St. Peter Tribune
Sedalia Daily Democrat
Sioux City Journal

Secondary Sources: Articles and Dissertations

Abbott, Edith. "The Civil War and the Crime Wave of 1865–1870." *Social Service Review* 1, no. 2 (June 1927): 212–34.

Anderson, George L. "Western Attitude Toward National Banks." *Mississippi Valley Historical Review* 23, no. 2 (September 1936): 205–16.

Baltimore, Lester B. "Benjamin F. Stringfellow: The Fight for Slavery on the Missouri Border." *Missouri Historical Review*, 62, no. 1 (October 1967): 14–29.

Barol, Bill. "American Made: The Army Colt." *American Heritage Civil War Chronicles*. New York: Forbes, Inc., 1992.

Bellesiles, Michael A. "The Origins of Gun Culture in the United States, 1760–1865." *Journal of American History* 83, no. 2 (September 1996): 425–55.

Bierbaum, Milton E. "Frederick Starr: A Missouri Border Abolitionist: The Making of a Martyr." *Missouri Historical Review* 58, no. 3 (April 1964): 309–25.

Blassingame, Jon W. "The Recruitment of Negro Troops in Missouri During the Civil War." *Missouri Historical Review* 57, no. 3 (April 1964): 326–38.

Blok, Anton. "The Peasant and the Brigand: Socal Banditry Reconsidered." *Comparative Studies in Society and History* 14, no. 4 (September 1972): 494–505.

Boed, William. "Secessionist Strength in Missouri." *Missouri Historical Review* 72, no. 4 (July 1978): 412–23.

Bowen, Don R. "Counterrevolutionary Guerrilla War: Missouri, 1861–1865." *Conflict* 8, no. 1 (1988): 69–78.

———. "Guerrilla War in Western Missouri, 1862–1865: Historical Extensions of the Relative Deprivation Hypothesis." *Comparative Studies in Society and History* 19, no. 1 (January 1977): 30–51.

Bowen, Elbert R. "The Circus in Early Rural Missouri." *Missouri Historical Review* 47, no. 1 (October 1952): 1–17.

———. "Negro Minstrels in Early Rural Missouri." *Missouri Historical Review*, 47, no. 1 (October 1952): 103–9.

Brewer, H. Peers. "Eastern Money and Western Mortgages in the 1870s." *Business History Review* 50, no. 3 (autumn 1976): 356–80.

Brown, Richard Maxwell. "Western Violence: Structure, Values, Myth." *Western Historical Quarterly* 24, no. 1 (February 1993): 5–20.

Bruce, Janet. "Of Sugar and Salt and Things in the Cellar and Sun: Food Preservation in Jackson County in the 1850s." *Missouri Historical Review* 75, no. 4 (July 1981): 417–47.

Campbell, Randolph B. "The Burden of Local Black Leadership During Reconstruction: A Research Note." *Civil War History* 39, no. 2 (June 1993): 148–53.

Canan, Howard V. "The Missouri Paw-Paw Militia of 1863–1864." *Missouri Historical Review* 62, no. 4 (July 1968): 431–48.

Carlson, Becky. " 'Manumitted and Forever Set Free': The Children of Charles Lee Younger and Elizabeth, a Woman of Color." *Missouri Historical Review* 96, no. 1 (October 2001): 16–31.

Cassia, Paul Sant. "Banditry, Myth, and Terror in Cyprus and Other Mediterranean Societies." *Comparative Studies in Society and History* 15, no. 4 (October 1993): 773–95.

Castel, Albert. "Kansas Jayhawking Raids into Western Missouri in 1861." *Missouri Historical Review* 54, no. 1 (October 1959): 1–11.

———. "Order No. 11 and the Civil War on the Border." *Missouri Historical Review* 57, no. 4 (October 1962): 357–68.

Clevenger, Homer. "Railroads in Missouri Politics, 1875–1887." *Missouri Historical Review* 43, no. 2 (January 1949): 220–36.

Crawford, Mark J. "An Eye for an Eye." *Columbiad* 2, no. 3 (fall 1998): 118–36.

Crisler, Robert M. "Missouri's 'Little Dixie.'" *Missouri Historical Review* 42, no. 2 (January 1948): 130–9.

——. "Republican Areas of Missouri." *Missouri Historical Review* 42, no. 4 (July 1948): 299–309.

Crocket, Norman L. "A Study in Confusion: Missouri's Immigration Program, 1865–1916." *Missouri Historical Review* 57, no. 2 (January 1963): 248–60.

Dean, Eric T., Jr. "'We Will All Be Lost and Destroyed': Post-Traumatic Stress Disorder and the Civil War." *Civil War History* 37, no. 2 (June 1991): 138–53.

DeArmond, Fred. "Reconstruction in Missouri." *Missouri Historical Review* 61, no. 3 (April 1967): 364–77.

Dorsey, Dorothy B. "The Panic and Depression of 1837 to 1843 in Missouri." *Missouri Historical Review* 30, no. 1 (October 1935): 132–61.

Drake, C. J. M. "The Role of Ideology in Terrorists' Target Selection." *Terrorism and Political Violence* 10, no. 2 (summer 1998): 53–85.

Duffner, Robert W. "Guerrilla Victory at Centralia, September 27, 1864." *Bulletin of the Missouri Historical Society* 29, no. 3 (April 1973): 312–44.

Eaton, Miles W. "The Development and Later Decline of the Hemp Industry in Missouri." *Missouri Historical Review* 43, no. 4 (July 1949): 344–59.

Eden, M. C. "Missouri's First Train Robbery." *Brand Book* 16, no. 2 (January 1974), published by the English Westerners' Society, 13–24.

Fellman, Michael. "Emancipation in Missouri." *Missouri Historical Review* 83, no. 1 (October 1988): 36–56.

Foner, Eric. "Rights and the Constitution in Black Life During the Civil War and Reconstruction." *Journal of American History* 74, no. 3 (December 1987): 863–83.

Frazier, Virginia Rust. "Dallas County Railroad Bonds." *Missouri Historical Review* 61, no. 4 (July 1967): 444–62.

Frizzell, Robert W. "'Killed by Rebels': A Civil War Massacre and its Aftermath." *Missouri Historical Review* 71, no. 4 (July 1977): 369–95.

Gates, Paul W. "The Railroads of Missouri, 1850–1870." *Missouri Historical Review* 26, no. 2 (January 1932): 126–41.

Geise, William B. "Missouri's Confederate Capital in Marshall, Texas." *Missouri Historical Review* 58, no. 1 (October 1963): 37–54.

Gentry, Todd North. "General Odon Guitar." *Missouri Historical Review* 22, no. 4 (July 1928): 419–45.

——. "William F. Switzler." *Missouri Historical Review* 24, no. 2 (January 1930): 161–76.

Gibson, Campbell. "Population of the 100 Largest Cities and Other Urban Places in the United States: 1790 to 1990." Population Division Working Paper No. 27, June 1998, Population Division, U.S. Bureau of the Census, Washington, D.C.

Gleick, Harry S. "Banking in Early Missouri." Part 1. *Missouri Historical Review* 61, no. 4 (July 1967): 427–43.

——. "Banking in Early Missouri." Part 2. *Missouri Historical Review* 62, no. 1 (October 1967): 30–44.

Gorn, Elliot J. "'Gouge and Bite, Pull Hair and Scratch': The Social Significance of Fighting in the Southern Backcountry." *American Historical Review* 90, no. 1 (February 1985): 18–43.

Gregg, Kate L. "Missourians in the Gold Rush." *Missouri Historical Review* 39, no. 1 (October 1944): 137–54.

Hamilton, James A. "The Enrolled Missouri Militia: Its Creation and Controversial History." *Missouri Historical Review* 69, no. 4 (July 1975): 410–32.

Harris, Charles F. "Catalyst for Terror: The Collapse of the Women's Prison in Kansas City." *Missouri Historical Review* 89, no. 3 (April 1995): 290–306.

Hobsbawm, Eric J. "Social Bandits: A Reply." *Comparative Studies in Society and History* 14, no. 4 (September 1972): 494–505.

Hughes, John Starrett. "Lafayette County and the Aftermath of Slavery, 1861–1870." *Missouri Historical Review* 75, no. 1 (October 1980): 51–63.

Hunter, Lloyd A. "Missouri's Confederate Leaders After the War." *Missouri Historical Review* 67, no. 3 (April 1973): 371–96.

Hurt, R. Douglas. "Planters and Slavery in Little Dixie." *Missouri Historical Review* 88, no. 4 (July 1994): 397–415.

Hyde, William. "Newspapers and Newspaper Men of Three Decades." *Collections of the Missouri Historical Society* 12 (1896): 5–24.

Ilic, Nenad, Ante Petricevic, Zeljko Mimica, Mirko Petricevic, and Jozo Ivancevic. "War Wounds of the Lungs Treated in Rama, Bosnia and Herzegovina." *Croatian Medical Journal* 38, no. 1 (1997).

Kirby, James E., Jr. "How to Become a Union General Without Military Experience." *Missouri Historical Review* 66, no. 3 (April 1972): 360–76.

Kohl, Martha. "Enforcing a Vision of Community: The Role of the Test Oath in Missouri's Reconstruction." *Civil War History* 40, no. 4 (December 1994): 292–307.

Lass, William E. "The Fate of the Steamboats: A Case Study of the 1848 St. Louis Fleet." *Missouri Historical Review* 96, no. 1 (October 2001): 2–15.

Lawson, M. L. "Founding and Location of William Jewell College." *Missouri Historical Society Collections* 4, no. 3 (1914): 275–89.

Lemmer, George F. "Farm Machinery in Ante-Bellum Missouri." *Missouri Historical Review* 40, no. 4 (July 1946): 467–80.

Loeb, Isidor. "Constitutions and Constitutional Conventions in Missouri." *Missouri Historical Review* 16, no. 2 (January 1922): 189–238.

McGettigan, James William, Jr. "Boone County Slaves: Sales, Estate Divisions, and Families, 1820–1855." Part 1. *Missouri Historical Review* 72, no. 2 (January 1978): 176–97.

———. "Boone County Slaves: Sales, Estate Divisions, and Families, 1820–1855." Part 2. *Missouri Historical Review* 72, no. 3 (April 1978): 271–95.

Magers, Roy G. "The Raid on the *Parkville Industrial Luminary*." *Missouri Historical Review* 30, no. 1 (October 1935): 39–46.

Malin, James C. "The Proslavery Background of the Kansas Struggle." *Mississippi Valley Historical Review* 10, no. 3 (December 1923): 285–305.

March, David D. "The Campaign for the Ratification of the Constitution of 1865." *Missouri Historical Review* 47, no. 3 (April 1953): 223–32.

———. "Charles D. Drake and the Constitutional Convention of 1865." *Missouri Historical Review* 47, no. 2 (January 1953): 110–23.

Merkel, Benjamin G. "The Slavery Issue and the Political Decline of Thomas Hart Benton, 1846–1856." *Missouri Historical Review* 38, no 4 (July 1944): 388–407.

———. "The Underground Railroad and the Missouri Borders, 1840–1860." *Missouri Historical Review* 37, no. 4 (July 1943): 271–85.

Miller, Robert E. " 'One of the Ruling Class,' Thomas Caute Reynolds: Second Confederate Governor of Missouri." *Missouri Historical Review* 80, no. 4 (July 1986): 442–8.

Moore, S. A. "Hostile Raid into Davis County, Iowa." *Annals of Iowa* 13, no. 5 (July 1922): 362–74.

Neely, Mark E., Jr. " 'Unbeknownst' to Lincoln: A Note on Radical Pacification in Missouri During the Civil War." *Civil War History* 44, no. 3 (September 1998): 212–6.

Niepman, Ann Davis. "General Orders No. 11 and Border Warfare During the Civil War." *Missouri Historical Review* 66, no. 2 (January 1972): 185–210.

Phillips, Christopher. "Calculated Confederate: Claiborne Fox Jackson and the Strategy for Secession in Missouri." *Missouri Historical Review* 94, no. 4 (July 2000): 389–414.

Pope, Ida Waller. "Violence as a Political Force in the Reconstruction South." Ph.D. dissertation: University of Southwestern Louisiana, 1982.

Potts, Louis W. "Waves of Revivalism in Clay County, 1840–1918." *Missouri Historical Review* 88, no. 3 (April 1994): 262–78.

Primm, James N. "The G.A.R. in Missouri, 1866–1870." *Journal of Southern History* 20, no. 3 (August 1954): 356–75.

Riegel, Robert E. "Trans-Mississippi Railroads During the Fifties." *Mississippi Valley Historical Review* 10, no. 2 (September 1923): 153–72.

Ross, William A., Jr. "Was There Danger of a Second Civil War During Reconstruction?" *Mississippi Valley Historical Review* 25, no. 1 (June 1938): 39–58.

Saults, Dan. "Let Us Discuss a Man: A Study of John Newman Edwards." *Bulletin of the Missouri Historical Society* 19, no. 2 (January 1963): 150–60.

Saum, Lewis O. "Donan and the *Caucasian*." *Missouri Historical Review* 63, no. 4 (July 1969): 419–50.

Scarpino, Philip V. "Slavery in Callaway County, Missouri: 1845–1855." Part 1. *Missouri Historical Review* 71, no. 1 (October 1976): 22–43.

———. "Slavery in Callaway County, Missouri: 1845–1855." Part 2. *Missouri Historical Review* 71, no. 3 (April 1977): 266–83.

Settle, William A., Jr. "The James Boys and Missouri Politics." *Missouri Historical Review* 36, no. 4 (July 1942): 412–29.

Shalhope, Robert E. "Eugene Genovese, the Missouri Elite, and Civil War Historiography." *Missouri Historical Society Bulletin* 26, no. 4, Part 1 (July 1970): 217–82.

Shoemaker, Floyd C. "Missouriana: John Brown's Missouri Raid." *Missouri Historical Review* 26, no. 1 (October 1931): 78–83.

———. "Missouri's Pro-Slavery Fight for Kansas, 1854–1855." Part 1. *Missouri Historical Review* 48, no. 2 (January 1954): 221–36.

———. "Missouri's Pro-Slavery Fight for Kansas, 1854–1855." Part 2. *Missouri Historical Review* 48, no. 3 (April 1954): 325–40.

Smith, W. Wayne. "An Experiment in Counterinsurgency: The Assessment of Confederate Sympathizers in Missouri." *Journal of Southern History* 35, no. 3 (August 1969): 362–80.

Steckmesser, Kent L. "Robin Hood and the American Outlaw." *Journal of American Folklore* 79 (April–June 1966).

Stiles, T. J. "As Good as Gold?," *Smithsonian* 31, no. 6 (September 2000): 106–17.

———. "Buffalo Soldiers." *Smithsonian* 29, no. 9 (December 1998): 82–94.

Sutherland, Daniel E. "Sideshow No Longer: A Historiographical Review of the Guerrilla War." *Civil War History* 46, no. 1 (March 2000): 5–23.

Sylla, Richard. "Federal Policy, Banking Market Structure, and Capital Mobilization in the United States, 1863–1913." *Journal of Economic History* 29, no. 4 (December 1969): 657–86.

Thompson, Joseph Conan. "The Great-Little Battle of Pilot Knob." Part 1. *Missouri Historical Review* 83, no. 2 (January 1989): 139–60.

———. "The Great-Little Battle of Pilot Knob." Part 2. *Missouri Historical Review* 83, no. 2 (January 1989): 169–94

Trexler, Harrison A. "The Value and Sale of the Missouri Slave." *Missouri Historical Review* 8, no. 1 (January 1914): 69–85.

Tucker, Philip T. " 'Ho, for Kansas': The Southwest Expedition of 1860." *Missouri Historical Review* 86, no. 1 (October 1991): 22–36.

Viles, Jonas. "Sections and Sectionalism in a Border State." *Mississippi Valley Historical Review* 21, no. 1 (June 1934): 3–22.

Violette, E. M. "The Missouri and Mississippi Railroad Debt." Part 1. *Missouri Historical Review* 15, no. 3 (April 1921): 467–518.

———. "The Missouri and Mississippi Railroad Debt." Part 2. *Missouri Historical Review* 15, no. 4 (July 1921): 617–47.

Westover, John Glendower. "The Evolution of the Missouri Militia, 1804–1919." Ph.D. dissertation, University of Missouri, 1948.

White, Edgar. "Henry Clay Dean, 'The Orator of Rebel Cove.' " *Missouri Historical Review* 22, no. 4 (July 1928): 450–5.

White, Richard. "Outlaw Gangs of the Middle Border: American Social Bandits." *Western Historical Quarterly* 12, no. 4 (October 1981): 387–408.

Williams, Lou Falkner. "The South Carolina Ku Klux Klan Trials and Enforcement of Federal Rights, 1871–1872." *Civil War History* 39, no. 1 (March 1993): 47–66.

Wybrow, Robert J. "From the Pen of a Noble Robber: The Letters of Jesse Woodson James, 1847–1882." *Brand Book* 24, no. 2 (summer 1987), published by the English Westerners' Society, 1–22.

———. "The James Gang in Kentucky: A Tale of Murder and Robbery in the Blue Grass State." *Brand Book* 15, no. 2 (January 1973), published by the English Westerners' Society, 22–34.

———. " 'Ravenous Monsters of Society': The Early Exploits of the James Gang." *Brand Book* 27, no. 2 (summer 1990), published by the English Westerners' Society, 1–24.

Zuczek, Richard. "The Last Campaign of the Civil War: South Carolina and the Revolution of 1876." *Civil War History* 42, no. 1 (March 1996): 18–31.

Secondary Sources: Books

Ames, Blanche Ames. *Adelbert Ames, 1835–1933: General, Senator, Governor.* London: MacDonald, 1964.

Athens, Lonnie. *The Creation of Dangerous Violent Criminals.* London: Routledge, 1989.

Atherton, Lewis A. *The Frontier Merchant in Mid-America.* Columbia: University of Missouri Press, 1971.

Ayers, Edward L. *The Promise of the New South: Life After Reconstruction.* New York: Oxford University Press, 1992.

———. *Vengeance and Justice: Crime and Punishment in the 19th-Century American South.* New York: Oxford University Press, 1984.

Barclay, Thomas S. *The Liberal Republican Movement in Missouri, 1865–1871.* Columbia: State Historical Society of Missouri, 1926.

Beamis, Joan M., and William E. Pullen. *Background of a Bandit: The Ancestry of Jesse James.* N.p.: 1970.

Beard, Charles A., and Mary R. Beard. *The Rise of American Civilization.* New York: Macmillan, 1927.

Belcher, Wyatt W. *The Economic Rivalry Between St. Louis and Chicago, 1850–1880.* New York: Columbia University Press, 1947.

Bellesiles, Michael A. *Arming America: The Origins of a National Gun Culture.* New York: Alfred A. Knopf, 2000.

Bensel, Richard Franklin. *Yankee Leviathan: The Origins of Central State Authority in America, 1859–1877.* New York: Cambridge University Press, 1990.

Best, Joel. *Controlling Vice: Regulating Brothel Prostitution in St. Paul, 1865–1883.* Columbus: Ohio State University Press, 1998.

Bordo, Michael D., and Anna J. Schwartz, eds. *A Retrospective on the Classical Gold Standard.* Chicago: University of Chicago Press, 1984.

Borrit, Gabor S., ed. *Lincoln the War President.* New York: Oxford University Press, 1992.

Brant, Marley. *Jesse James: The Man and the Myth.* New York: Berkley, 1998.

———. *The Outlaw Youngers: A Confederate Brotherhood.* Lanham, Md.: Madison Books, 1993.

Brekus, Catherine A. *Strangers and Pilgrims: Female Preaching in America, 1740–1845.* Chapel Hill: University of North Carolina Press, 1998.

Brock, Leslie V. *The Currency of the American Colonies 1700–1764: A Study in Colonial Finance and Imperial Relations.* New York: Arno Press, 1975.

Broehl, Wayne G. *The Molly Maguires.* Cambridge: Harvard University Press, 1964.

Brown, Dee. *The Year of the Century: 1876.* New York: Charles Scribner's Sons, 1966.

Brown, Richard Maxwell. *No Duty to Retreat: Violence and Values in American Society.* New York: Oxford University Press, 1991.

————. *Strain of Violence: Historical Studies of American Violence and Vigilantism*. New York: Oxford University Press, 1975.

Brownlee, Richard S. *Gray Ghosts of the Confederacy: Guerrilla Warfare in the West, 1861–1865*. Baton Rouge: Louisiana State University Press, 1958.

Calhoun, Frederick S. *The Lawmen: United States Marshals and Their Deputies, 1789–1889*. Washington, D.C.: Smithsonian Institution Press, 1990.

Campbell, Randolph B. *Grass-Roots Reconstruction in Texas, 1865–1880*. Baton Rouge: Louisiana State University Press, 1997.

Caputo, Philip. *A Rumor of War*. New York: Ballantine, 1977.

Castel, Albert. *A Frontier State at War: Kansas, 1861–1865*. Lawrence: Kansas Heritage Press, 1958.

————. *General Sterling Price and the Civil War in the West*. Baton Rouge: Louisiana State University Press, 1968.

————. *William Clarke Quantrill: His Life and Times*. New York: Frederick Fell, 1962.

————. *Winning and Losing the Civil War: Essays and Stories*. Columbia: University of South Carolina Press, 1996.

Castel, Albert, and Thomas Goodrich. *Bloody Bill Anderson: The Short, Savage Life of a Civil War Guerrilla*. Mechanicsburg, Pa.: Stackpole Books, 1998.

Chancellor, Edward. *Devil Take the Hindmost: A History of Financial Speculation*. New York: Farrar Straus Giroux, 1999.

Chernow, Robert. *Titan: The Life of John D. Rockefeller, Sr.* New York: Random House, 1998.

Christensen, Lawrence O., and Gary R. Kremer. *A History of Missouri*. Vol. 4. *1875 to 1919*. Columbia: University of Missouri Press, 1997.

Clark, William R., and Michael Grunstein. *Are We Hardwired? The Role of Genetics in Human Behavior*. New York: Oxford University Press, 2000.

Clinton, Catherine. *The Other Civil War: American Women in the Nineteenth Century*. New York: Hill and Wang, 1984.

Clinton, Catherine, ed. *Half Sisters of History: Southern Women and the American Past*. Durham, N.C.: Duke University Press, 1994.

Clinton, Catherine, and Nina Silber, eds. *Divided Houses: Gender and the Civil War*. New York: Oxford University Press, 1992.

Coffman, Edward M. *The Old Army: A Portrait of the American Army in Peacetime, 1784–1898*. New York: Oxford University Press, 1986.

Conard, Howard L., ed. *Encyclopedia of the History of Missouri*. St. Louis: Southern History Company, 1901.

Corner, Paul. *Fascism in Ferrara, 1915–1925*. Oxford: Oxford University Press, 1975.

Crotty, William J., James F. Kirkham, and Sheldon G. Levy. *Assassination and Political Violence: A Report to the National Commission on the Causes and Prevention of Violence*. New York: Praeger, 1970.

Croy, Homer. *Jesse James Was My Neighbor*. Lincoln: University of Nebraska Press, 1997. Orig. pub. 1949.

Current, Richard Nelson. *Those Terrible Carpetbaggers: A Reinterpretation*. New York: Oxford University Press, 1988.

Curry, Richard O., ed. *Radicalism, Racism, and Party Realignment: The Border States During Reconstruction*. Baltimore: The Johns Hopkins University Press, 1969.

Curtiss-Wedge, Franklyn, ed. *History of Rice and Steele Counties, Minnesota*. Chicago: H. C. Cooper, Jr., 1910.

Davids, Lewis E., and Timothy W. Hubbard. *Banking in Mid-America: A History of Missouri's Banks*. Washington, D.C.: Public Affairs Press, 1969.

Davis, David Brion. *The Slave Power Conspiracy and the Paranoid Style*. Baton Rouge: Louisiana State University Press, 1969.

Dawson, Joseph G., III. *Doniphan's Epic March: The 1st Missouri Volunteers in the Mexican War*. Lawrence: University Press of Kansas, 1999.

Denning, Michael. *Mechanic Accents: Dime Novels and Working-Class Culture in America*. Rev. ed. London: Verso, 1998.

Donald, David H. *The Politics of Reconstruction, 1863–1867*. Baton Rouge: Louisiana State University Press, 1965.

Edwards, Laura F. *Gendered Strife and Confusion: The Political Culture of Reconstruction*. Urbana: University of Illinois Press, 1997.

Einzig, Paul. *Primitive Money: In Its Ethnological, Historical, and Economic Aspects*. Oxford, U.K.: Pergamon Press, 1949.

Ellis, James Fernando. *The Influence of Environment on the Settlement of Missouri*. St. Louis: Webster Publishing, 1929.

Engerman, Stanley L., and Robert W. Fogel, eds. *The Reinterpretation of American Economic History*. New York: Harper & Row, 1971.

Eslinger, Ellen. *Citizens of Zion: The Social Origins of Camp Meeting Revivalism*. Knoxville: University of Tennessee Press, 1999.

Fellman, Michael. *Inside War: The Guerrilla Conflict in Missouri During the American Civil War*. New York: Oxford University Press, 1989.

Fellman, Michael, and Lewis Perry, eds. *Antislavery Reconsidered: New Perspectives on the Abolitionists*. Baton Rouge: Louisiana State University Press, 1979.

Fischer, David Hackett. *Albion's Seed: Four British Folkways in America*. New York: Oxford University Press, 1989.

Fishel, Edwin C. *The Secret War for the Union: The Untold Story of Military Intelligence in the Civil War*. Boston: Houghton Mifflin, 1996.

Flint, Wayne. *Alabama Baptists: Southern Baptists in the Heart of Dixie*. Tuscaloosa: University of Alabama Press, 1998.

Foner, Eric. *Free Soil, Free Labor, Free Men: The Ideology of the Republican Party Before the Civil War*. New York: Oxford University Press, 1995. Orig. pub. 1970.

———. *Freedom's Lawmakers: A Directory of Black Officeholders During Reconstruction*. New York: Oxford University Press, 1993.

———. *Reconstruction, 1863–1877: America's Unfinished Revolution*. New York: Harper & Row, 1988.

———. *The Story of American Freedom*. New York: W. W. Norton, 1998.

Foner, Eric, and John A. Garraty, eds. *The Reader's Companion to American History*. Boston: Houghton Mifflin, 1991.

Forster, Stig, and Jorg Nagler, eds. *On the Road to Total War: The American Civil War and the German Wars of Unification, 1861–1871*. New York: Cambridge University Press, 1997.

Foster, Gaines M. *Ghosts of the Confederacy: Defeat, the Lost Cause, and the Emergence of the New South, 1865 to 1913*. New York: Oxford University Press, 1987.

Franklin, John Hope, and Loren Schweninger. *Runaway Slaves: Rebels on the Plantation*. New York: Oxford University Press, 1999.

Freehling, William W. *The Road to Disunion: Secessionists at Bay, 1776–1854*. New York: Oxford University Press, 1990.

Friedman, Lawrence M. *Crime and Punishment in American History*. New York: Basic Books, 1993.

Friedman, Milton, and Anna Jacobson Schwartz. *A Monetary History of the United States, 1867–1960*. Princeton: Princeton University Press, 1963.

Fuller, Robert C. *Alternative Medicine and American Religious Life*. New York: Oxford University Press, 1989.

Gallagher, Gary W., ed. *The First Day at Gettysburg: Essays on Confederate and Union Leadership*. Kent, Ohio: Kent State University Press, 1992.

Garner, James W. *Reconstruction in Mississippi*. Gloucester, Mass.: Peter Smith, 1964. Orig. pub. 1901.

Genovese, Eugene D. *A Consuming Fire: The Fall of the Confederacy in the Mind of the White Christian South*. Athens: University of Georgia Press, 1998.

———. *Roll, Jordan, Roll: The World the Slaves Made*. New York: Vintage, 1976.

Glaab, Charles N. *Kansas City and the Railroads: Community Policy in the Growth of a Regional Metropolis*. Madison: State Historical Society of Wisconsin, 1962.

Goodrich, Thomas. *Black Flag: Guerrilla Warfare on the Western Border, 1861–1865*. Bloomington: Indiana University Press, 1995.

————. *War to the Knife: Bleeding Kansas, 1854–1861*. Mechanicsburg, Pa.: Stackpole Books, 1998.

Gottesman, Ronald, ed. *Violence in America: An Encyclopedia*. New York: Charles Scribner's Sons, 1999.

Gragg, Rod. *Confederate Goliath: The Battle of Fort Fisher*. Baton Rouge: Louisiana State University Press, 1991.

Graham, Hugh Davis, and Ted Robert Gurr, eds. *Violence in America: Historical and Comparative Perspectives*. Beverly Hills: Sage, 1979.

Greene, Lorenzo J., Gary R. Kremer, and Antonio F. Holland. *Missouri's Black Heritage*. Rev. ed. Columbia: University of Missouri Press, 1993.

Grimsley, Mark. *The Hard Hand of War: Union Military Policy Toward Southern Civilians, 1861–1865*. New York: Cambridge University Press, 1995.

Grimsted, David. *American Mobbing, 1828–1861: Toward Civil War*. New York: Oxford University Press, 1998.

Grodinsky, Julius. *The Iowa Pool: A Study in Railroad Competition, 1870–1884*. Chicago: University of Chicago Press, 1950.

————. *Jay Gould: His Business Career, 1867–1892*. Philadelphia: University of Pennsylvania Press, 1957.

————. *Transcontinental Railway Strategy, 1869–1893: A Study of Businessmen*. Philadelphia: University of Pennsylvania Press, 1962.

Hamblen, Charles P. *Connecticut Yankees at Gettysburg*. Kent, Ohio: Kent State University Press, 1993.

Hammond, Bray. *Banks and Politics in America from the Revolution to the Civil War*. Princeton: Princeton University Press, 1957.

————. *Sovereignty and an Empty Purse: Banks and Politics in the Civil War*. Princeton: Princeton University Press, 1970.

Harlow, Alvin F. *Old Waybills: The Romance of the Express Companies*. New York: D. Appleton-Century Co., 1934.

Hartsfield, Larry K. *The American Response to Professional Crime, 1870–1914*. Westport, Conn.: Greenwood, 1985.

Heyrman, Christine Leigh. *Southern Cross: The Beginnings of the Bible Belt*. New York: Alfred A. Knopf, 1997.

Hobsbawm, Eric J. *Bandits*. Rev. ed. New York: Pantheon Books, 1981. Orig. pub. 1969.

————. *Primitive Rebels: Studies in Archaic Forms of Social Movements in the 19th and 20th Centuries*. New York: W. W. Norton, 1965.

Hopkins, James F. *A History of the Hemp Industry in Kentucky*. Lexington: University of Kentucky Press, 1951.

Horan, James D. *Desperate Men: The James Gang and the Wild Bunch*. Lincoln: University of Nebraska Press, 1997. Orig. pub. 1949.

Huntington, George. *Robber and Hero: The Story of the Northfield Bank Raid*. St. Paul: Minnesota Historical Society Press, 1986. Orig. pub. 1895.

Hurt, R. Douglas. *Agriculture and Slavery in Missouri's Little Dixie*. Columbia: University of Missouri Press, 1992.

James, Joseph B. *The Framing of the Fourteenth Amendment*. Urbana: University of Illinois Press, 1965.

Johnson, David R. *Illegal Tender: Counterfeiting and the Secret Service in Nineteenth-Century America*. Washington, D.C.: Smithsonian Institution Press, 1995.

————. *Policing the Underworld: The Impact of Crime on the Development of the American Police, 1800–1887*. Philadelphia: Temple University Press, 1979.

Jones, Archer. *The Art of War in the Western World*. New York: Oxford University Press, 1987.

Josephy, Alvin M., Jr. *The Civil War in the American West*. New York: Alfred A. Knopf, 1991.

Kendrick, Benjamin B. *The Journal of the Joint Committee of Fifteen on Reconstruction*. New York: Negro Universities Press, 1969. Orig. pub. 1914.

Klein, Maury. *The Life and Legend of Jay Gould*. Baltimore: The Johns Hopkins University Press, 1986.

Knox, John Jay. *A History of Banking in the United States*. New York: Augustus M. Kelley, 1969. Orig. pub. 1903.

Koliopoulos, Giannes. *Brigands with a Cause: Brigandage and Irredentism in Modern Greece, 1821–1921*. Oxford, U.K.: Clarendon Press, 1987.

Laqueur, Walter. *Guerrilla Warfare: A Historical and Critical Study*. New Brunswick, N.J.: Transaction, 1998.

Leslie, Edward E. *The Devil Knows How to Ride: The True Story of William Clarke Quantrill and His Confederate Raiders*. New York: Da Capo Press, 1998.

Lopata, Edwin L. *Local Aid to Railroads in Missouri*. New York: Columbia University Press, 1937.

Love, Robertus. *The Rise and Fall of Jesse James*. Lincoln: University of Nebraska Press, 1990. Orig. pub. 1925.

Loveland, Anne C. *Southern Evangelicals and the Social Order, 1800–1860*. Baton Rouge: Louisiana State University Press, 1980.

McCandless, Perry. *A History of Missouri*. Vol. 2. *1820–1860*. Columbia: University of Missouri Press, 1972.

McCurdy, Frances Lea. *Stump, Bar, and Pulpit: Speechmaking on the Missouri Frontier*. Columbia: University of Missouri Press, 1969.

McFeely, William S. *Grant: A Biography*. New York: W. W. Norton & Co., 1982.

McPherson, James M. *Battle Cry of Freedom: The Civil War Era*. New York: Oxford University Press, 1988.

———. *For Cause and Comrades: Why Men Fought in the Civil War*. New York: Oxford University Press, 1997.

Mackay, James. *Allan Pinkerton: The Eye Who Never Slept*. Edinburgh: Mainstream Publishing, 1996.

Miller, George H. *Railroads and the Granger Laws*. Madison: University of Wisconsin Press, 1971.

Milner, Clyde A., II, Carol A. O'Connor, and Martha A. Sandweiss, eds. *The Oxford History of the American West*. New York: Oxford University Press, 1994.

Monaghan, Jay. *The Civil War on the Western Border*. Boston: Little, Brown, 1958.

Monkkonen, Eric H., ed. *The South*. Part 1. Munich: K. G. Saur, 1992.

Murphy, James B. *L. Q. C. Lamar: Pragmatic Patriot*. Baton Rouge: University of Louisiana Press, 1973.

Neely, Mark E. *The Fate of Liberty: Abraham Lincoln and Civil Liberties*. New York: Oxford University Press, 1991.

Nelson, Scott Reynolds. *Iron Confederacies: Southern Railways, Klan Violence, and Reconstruction*. Chapel Hill: University of North Carolina Press, 1999.

Neu, Irene D., and George Rogers Taylor. *The American Railroad Network, 1861–1890*. Cambridge, Mass.: Harvard University Press, 1956.

Niehoff, Debra. *The Biology of Violence: How Understanding the Brain, Behavior, and Environment Can Break the Vicious Circle of Aggression*. New York: Free Press, 1999.

Nieman, Donald G., ed. *The African American Family in the South, 1861–1900*. New York: Garland, 1994.

———. *Black Freedom/White Violence, 1865–1900*. New York: Garland, 1994.

———. *The Politics of Freedom: African Americans and the Political Process During Reconstruction*. New York: Garland, 1994.

Nieman, Donald G., and Christopher Waldrep, eds. *Local Matters: Race, Crime, and Justice in the Nineteenth-Century South*. Athens: University of Georgia Press, 2001.

Oates, Stephen B. *Confederate Cavalry West of the River*. Austin: University of Texas Press, 1961. Repr. 1995.

———. *To Purge This Land With Blood: A Biography of John Brown*. Amherst: University of Massachusetts Press, 1970.

O'Brien, Patrick. *The Economic Effects of the American Civil War*. Atlantic Highlands: Humanities Press International, 1988.

O'Connell, Robert L. *Of Arms and Men: A History of War, Weapons, and Aggression*. New York: Oxford University Press, 1989.

O'Flaherty, Daniel. *General Jo Shelby: Undefeated Rebel*. Chapel Hill: University of North Carolina Press, 2000. Orig. pub. 1954.

Orwell, George. *The Orwell Reader*. San Francisco: Harcourt Brace Jovanovich, 1956.

Parrish, William E. *David Rice Atchison of Missouri: Border Politician*. Columbia: University of Missouri Press, 1961.

———. *Frank Blair: Lincoln's Conservative*. Columbia: University of Missouri Press, 1998.

———. *A History of Missouri*. Vol. 3. *1860 to 1875*. Columbia: University of Missouri Press, 1973.

———. *Missouri Under Radical Rule, 1865–1870*. Columbia: University of Missouri Press, 1965.

———. *Turbulent Partnership: Missouri and the Union, 1861–1865*. Columbia: University of Missouri Press, 1963.

Peterson, Norma L. *Freedom and Franchise: The Political Career of B. Gratz Brown*. Columbia: University of Missouri Press, 1965.

Petrone, Gerard S. *Judgment at Gallatin: The Trial of Frank James*. Lubbock: Texas Tech University Press, 1998.

Pfanz, Harry W. *Gettysburg: Culp's Hill and Cemetery Hill*. Chapel Hill: University of North Carolina Press, 1993.

Phillips, Christopher. *Damned Yankee: The Life of General Nathaniel Lyon*. Columbia: University of Missouri Press, 1990.

———. *Missouri's Confederate: Claiborne Fox Jackson and the Creation of a Southern Identity in the Border West*. Columbia: University of Missouri Press, 2000.

Polakoff, Keith Ian. *The Politics of Inertia: The Election of 1876 and the End of Reconstruction*. Baton Rouge: Louisiana State University Press, 1973.

Pope, Jacqueline. *Bounty Hunters, Marshals, and Sheriffs: Forward to the Past*. Westport, Conn.: Praeger, 1998.

Prassel, Frank Richard. *The Great American Outlaw: A Legacy of Fact and Fiction*. Norman: University of Oklahoma Press, 1993.

Pullen, John J. *The Twentieth Maine: A Volunteer Regiment in the Civil War*. Philadelphia: J. B. Lippincott, 1957.

Rable, George C. *But There Was No Peace: The Role of Violence in the Politics of Reconstruction*. Athens: University of Georgia Press, 1984.

———. *Civil Wars: Women and the Crisis of Southern Nationalism*. Urbana: University of Illinois Press, 1989.

Rawley, James A. *Race and Politics: "Bleeding Kansas" and the Coming of the Civil War*. Philadelphia: J. B. Lippincott, 1969.

Rhodes, Richard. *Why They Kill: The Discoveries of a Maverick Criminologist*. New York: Alfred A. Knopf, 1999.

Riddleberger, Patrick W. *1866: The Critical Year Revisited*. Carbondale: Southern Illinois University Press, 1979.

Riley, Glenda. *The Female Frontier: A Comparative View of Women on the Prairie and the Plains*. Lawrence: University Press of Kansas, 1988.

Rolle, Andrew. *The Lost Cause: The Confederate Exodus to Mexico*. Norman: University of Oklahoma Press, 1965.

Rosa, Joseph G. *They Called Him Wild Bill: The Life and Adventures of James Butler Hickok*. Norman: University of Oklahoma Press, 1974.

Rosenhaft, Eve. *Beating the Fascists? The German Communists and Political Violence, 1929–1933*. Cambridge, U.K.: Cambridge University Press, 1983.

Ross, James R. *I, Jesse James*. Thousand Oaks, Calif.: Dragon Publishing, 1988.

Ryle, Walter F. *Missouri: Union or Secession*. Nashville: George Peabody College for Teachers, 1931.

Sears, Stephen W. *To the Gates of Richmond: The Peninsula Campaign*. Boston: Houghton Mifflin, 1992.

Sefton, James E. *The United States Army and Reconstruction, 1865–1877*. Baton Rouge: Louisiana State University Press, 1967.

Settle, William A., Jr. *Jesse James Was His Name, or, Fact and Fiction Concerning the Careers of the Notorious James Brothers of Missouri*. Lincoln: University of Nebraska Press, 1977. Orig. pub. 1966.

Sharkey, Robert P. *Money, Class, and Party: An Economic Study of Civil War and Reconstruction*. Baltimore: The Johns Hopkins University Press, 1959.

Singletary, Otis A. *Negro Militia and Reconstruction*. New York: McGraw-Hill/University of Texas Press, 1971.

Sledge, Eugene B. *With the Old Breed*. New York: Oxford University Press, 1992.

Slotkin, Richard. *The Fatal Environment: The Myth of the Frontier in the Age of Industrialization, 1800–1890*. New York: Atheneum, 1985.

———. *Gunfighter Nation: The Myth of the Frontier in Twentieth-Century America*. New York: Atheneum, 1992.

Smith, Robert Barr. *The Last Hurrah of the James-Younger Gang*. Norman: University of Oklahoma Press, 2001.

Stampp, Kenneth M. *America in 1857: A Nation on the Brink*. New York: Oxford University Press, 1990.

———. *The Era of Reconstruction*. New York: Alfred A. Knopf, 1965.

Starr, Stephen Z. *Jennison's Jayhawkers: A Civil War Cavalry Regiment and Its Commander*. Baton Rouge: Louisiana State University Press, 1973.

Steckmesser, Kent L. *The Western Hero in History and Legend*. Norman: University of Oklahoma Press, 1965.

Steele, Phillip W., and George Warfel. *The Many Faces of Jesse James*. Gretna, La.: Pelican Publishing, 1995.

Steward, Dick. *Duels and the Roots of Violence in Missouri*. Columbia: University of Missouri Press, 2000.

Summers, Mark Wahlgren. *The Era of Good Stealings*. New York: Oxford University Press, 1993.

Taus, Esther Rogoff. *Central Banking Functions of the United States Treasury, 1789–1941*. New York: Columbia University Press, 1943.

Thelen, David. *Paths of Resistance: Tradition and Dignity in Industrializing Missouri*. New York: Oxford University Press, 1986.

Trachtenberg, Alan. *The Incorporation of America: Culture and Society in the Gilded Age*. New York: Hill and Wang, 1982.

Trelease, Allen W. *White Terror: The Ku Klux Klan Conspiracy and Southern Reconstruction*. Baton Rouge: Louisiana State University Press, 1971.

Trexler, Harrison A. *Slavery in Missouri, 1804–1865*. Baltimore: The Johns Hopkins University Press, 1914.

Triplett, Frank. *The Life, Times, and Treacherous Death of Jesse James*. New York: Konecky & Konecky, 1970. Orig. pub. 1882.

Tucker, Robert C., ed. *The Marx-Engels Reader*. 2nd ed. New York: W. W. Norton & Co., 1978.

Tygiel, Jules. *Past Time: Baseball as History*. New York: Oxford University Press, 2000.

Unger, Irwin. *The Greenback Era: A Social and Political History of American Finance, 1865–1879*. Princeton: Princeton University Press, 1964.

Utley, Robert M. *Billy the Kid: A Short and Violent Life*. Lincoln: University of Nebraska Press, 1989.

———. *High Noon in Lincoln: Violence on the Western Frontier*. Albuquerque: University of New Mexico Press, 1987.

———. *The Indian Frontier and the American West, 1846–1890*. Albuquerque: University of New Mexico Press, 1984.

Ward, James A. *Railroads and the Character of America, 1820–1851.* Knoxville: University of Tennessee Press, 1986.

Williams, Walter, ed. *A History of Northwest Missouri.* Vol. 1. Chicago: Lewis Publishing Company, 1915.

Woodson, W. H. *History of Clay County, Missouri.* Topeka, Kan.: Historical Publishing Company, 1920.

Woodward, C. Vann. *Origins of the New South, 1877–1913.* Baton Rouge: Louisiana State University Press, 1971.

———. *Reunion and Reaction: The Compromise of 1877 and the End of Reconstruction.* Boston: Little, Brown, 1951.

Wyatt-Brown, Bertram. *Southern Honor: Ethics and Behavior in the Old South.* New York: Oxford University Press, 1982.

Yeatman, Ted P. *Frank and Jesse James: The Story Behind the Legend.* Nashville: Cumberland House, 2001.

Young, William. *Young's History of Lafayette County, Missouri.* Indianapolis: B. F. Bowen, 1910.

Index